D0836601

Langenscheidt
Universal Dictionary

Italian

Italian – English
English – Italian

edited by the
Langenscheidt editorial staff

Langenscheidt

Munich · Vienna

Based on Langenscheidt's Pocket Dictionary Italian
compiled by LEXUS

Neither the presence nor the absence of a designation
indicating that any entered word constitutes a trademark
should be regarded as affecting the legal status thereof.

© 2011 Langenscheidt GmbH & Co. KG, Munich
Printed in Germany

Contents
Indice

Abbreviations / Abbreviazioni.................... 4
Pronuncia delle parole inglesi 8
Italian pronunciation............................... 11
Italian – English / Italiano – Inglese 13
English – Italian / Inglese – Italiano 281
Verbi irregolari inglesi 633
Numbers / Numerali 637

Abbreviations / Abbreviazioni

vedi	☞	see
marchio registrato	®	registered trademark
aggettivo	*adj*	adjective
avverbio	*adv*	adverb
aggettivo	*agg*	adjective
agricoltura	AGR	agriculture
inglese americano	*Am*	American English
anatomia	ANAT	anatomy
architettura	ARCHI	architecture
articolo	*art*	article
astronomia	AST	astronomy
astrologia	ASTR	astrology
uso attributivo	*attr*	attributive usage
automobilismo	AUTO	motoring
aviazione	AVIA	civil aviation
avverbio	*avv*	adverb
biologia	BIO	biology
botanica	BOT	botany
inglese britannico	*Br*	British English
chimica	CHEM	chemistry
chimica	CHIM	chemistry
commercio	COM	commerce, business
informatica	COMPUT	computers, IT term
congiunzione	*cong*	conjunction
congiunzione	*conj*	conjunction
diritto	DIR	law
eccetera	*ecc*	et cetera
educazione	EDU	education

elettricità, elettronica	EL	electricity, electronics
elettricità, elettronica	ELEC	electricity, electronics
specialmente	*esp*	especially
eccetera	*etc*	et cetera
eufemismo	*euph*	euphemistic
familiare	F	familiar, colloquial
femminile	*f*	feminine
sostantivo femminile e aggettivo	*f/agg*	feminine noun and adjective
ferrovia	FERR	railways
figurato	*fig*	figurative
finanze	FIN	financial
fisica	FIS	physics
uso formale	*fml*	formal usage
fotografia	FOT	photography
femminile plurale	*fpl*	feminine plural
femminile singolare	*fsg*	feminine singular
gastronomia	GASTR	cooking
generalmente	*gen*	generally
geografia	GEOG	geography
geologia	GEOL	geology
grammatica	GRAM	grammatical
informatica	INFOR	IT term
interiezione	*int*	interjection
invariabile	*inv*	invariable
diritto	LAW	law
maschile	*m*	masculine
sostantivo maschile e aggettivo	*m/agg*	masculine noun and adjective
marineria, navigazione	MAR	nautical

matematica	MAT	mathematics
matematica	MATH	mathematics
medicina	MED	medicine
maschile e femminile	m/f	masculine and feminine
militare	MIL	military
mineralogia	MIN	mineralogy
automobilismo	MOT	motoring
maschile plurale	mpl	masculine plural
maschile singolare	msg	masculine singular
musica	MUS	music
sostantivo	n	noun
marineria, navigazione	NAUT	nautical
sostantivo plurale	npl	plural noun
sostantivo singolare	nsg	singular noun
sé, se stesso	o.s.	oneself
popolare	P	popular, slang
spregiativo	pej	pejorative
fotografia	PHOT	photography
fisica	PHYS	physics
pittura	PITT	painting
plurale	pl	plural
politica	POL	politics
participio passato	pp	past participle
preposizione	prep	preposition
pronome	pron	pronoun
preposizione	prp	preposition
psicologia	PSI	psychology
psicologia	PSYCH	psychology
qualcosa	qc	something

qualcuno	qu	someone
radio	RAD	radio
ferrovia	RAIL	railways
religione	REL	religion
sci	SCI	skiing
singolare	*sg*	singular
qualcuno	s.o.	someone
sport	SP	sports
uso spiritoso	*spir*	humorous
uso spregiativo	*spreg*	pejorative
qualcosa	sth	something
congiuntivo	*subj*	subjunctive
teatro	TEA	theatre
tecnica	TEC	technology
tecnica	TECH	technology
telecomunicazioni	TELEC	telecommunications
teatro	THEA	theatre
tipografia	TIP	typography, typesetting
televisione	TV	television
volgare	V	vulgar
verbo ausiliario	*v/aus*	auxiliary verb
verbo ausiliario	*v/aux*	auxiliary verb
verbo intransitivo	*v/i*	intransitive verb
verbo transitivo	*v/t*	transitive verb
zoologia	ZO	zoology

Pronuncia delle parole inglesi

Vocali e dittonghi

[ɑ:]	*a* molto lunga, più che in *mare*: *far* [fɑ:(r)]
[ʌ]	simile alla seconda *a* in *mamma* non accentata: *mother* ['mʌθə(r)]
[æ]	simile alla prima *a* in *mamma*: *man* [mæn]
[ɛə]	dittongo composto da una *e* molto aperta e lunga e da [ə]: *care* [kɛə(r)]
[aɪ]	dittongo composto da [a] e [ɪ]: *time* [taɪm]
[aʊ]	dittongo composto da [a] e [ʊ]: *cloud* [klaʊd]
[e]	*e* aperta e breve, più che in *bello*: *get* [get]
[eɪ]	dittongo composto da una *e* lunga, seguita da un leggero suono di *i*: *name* [neɪm]
[ə]	suono atono simile alla *e* nell'articolo francese *le*: *about* [ə'baʊt]
[ɜ:]	forma più prolungata del suono anteriore: *bird* [bɜ:d]
[ɪ]	suono molto breve tra la *i* di *fitto* e la *e* di *fetta*: *city* ['sɪtɪ]
[i:]	*i* molto lunga, più che in *vino*: *tea* [ti:]
[ɪə]	dittongo composto da [ɪ] e da [ə]: *here* [hɪə(r)]
[ɒ]	simile alla *o* di *lotta*: *not* [nɒt]
[ɔ:]	*o* aperta e lunga, più che in *noto*: *ball* [bɔ:l]
[ɔɪ]	dittongo composto da [ɔ] e [ɪ]: *boy* [bɔɪ]
[əʊ]	dittongo composto da una *o* lunga, seguita da un leggero suono di *u*: *boat* [bəʊt]
[ʊ]	suono molto breve tra la *u* di *tutto* e la *o* di *rotto*: *book* [bʊk]

[uː] u lunga, più che in *fiume*: *fruit* [fruːt]

[ʊə] dittongo composto da [ʊ] e [ə]: *sure* [ʃʊə(r)]

Consonanti

Le consonanti si pronunciano nella maggior parte dei casi quasi come in italiano. Le doppie si pronunciano come se fossero semplici.

[b] come la *b* in *burro*: *bag* [bæg]

[d] come la *d* in *dare*: *dear* [dɪə(r)]

[f] come la *f* in *forte*: *coffee* ['kɒfɪ]

[g] come la *g* in *gatto*: *give* [gɪv]

[h] suono aspirato simile a quello della *c* di *casa* dei fiorentini: *head* [hed]

[j] come la *i* in *ieri*: *yes* [jes], *use* [juːz]

[k] ome la *c* in *casa*: *come* [kʌm]

[l] come la *l* in *lungo*: *land* [lænd]

[m] come la *m* i *madre*: *summer* ['sʌmə(r)]

[n] come la *n* in *no*: *night* [naɪt]

[p] come la *p* in *pane*: *top* [tɒp]

[r] una *r* gutturale che si pronuncia soltanto quando precede una vocale: *right* [raɪt], *carol* ['kærəl]

[s] *s* aspra come in *sono*: *cycle* ['saɪkl], *sun* [sʌn]

[t] come la *t* in *torre*: *take* [teɪk]

[v] come la *v* in *valore*: *vain* [veɪn]

[w] come la *u* in *uomo*: *wait* [weɪt], *quaint* [kweɪnt]

[z] *s* dolce come in *rosa*: *rose* [rəʊz]

[ŋ] come la *n* in *banca*: *bring* [brɪŋ]

[ʃ]	come *sce* in *scena*: *she* [ʃiː]
[tʃ]	come *ce* in *cento*: *chair* [tʃeə(r)], *rich* [rɪtʃ]
[dʒ]	come *ge* in *gente*: *join* [dʒɔɪn], *range* [reɪndʒ]
[ʒ]	non esiste in italiano, simile alla *j* francese in *je*: *leisure* ['leʒə(r)], *usual* ['juːʒʊəl]
[θ]	lingua tra i denti: *think* [θɪŋk]
[ð]	lingua dietro l'arcata superiore dei denti: *the* [ðə], *lather* ['lɑːðə(r)]
'	il segno dell'accento viene sempre collocato prima della sillaba accentata, es. *ability* [ə'bɪlətɪ]

Italian pronunciation

Vowels

a	mare	as in **fa**ther but shorter
e	bello	as in b**e**d
	neve	like the e sound in th**ey**
i	vino	as in mach**i**ne
o	lotta	as in p**o**t
	nome	like the o sound in bl**ow**
u	fiume	as *oo* in c**oo**l but shorter

Consonants

b, d, f, l, m, n, p, t and **v** are pronounced as in English.
When a word has double consonants, each consonant is
pronounced separately: contat-to.

c	certo	before *e* and *i* as *ch* in **ch**urch
	canto	before *a, o, u* (almost) as in **c**ake
ch	chiamare	before *e* and *i* to make *c* hard as in **c**at
g	gelo	before *e* and *i* as in **g**eneral
	gatto	before *a, o, u* as in **g**ate
gh	laghi	before *e* and *i* to make *g* hard as in **g**ot
gl	biglietto	like English *lli* in mi**lli**on
gn	ogni	like English *ni* in o**ni**on
h	hanno	not pronounced
r	rotto	with the tongue against the upper teeth
s	sole	unvoiced as in **c**ase
	rosa	voiced as in chee**s**e
sc	uscire	before *e* and *i* like *sh* in **sh**ip
z	prezzo	unvoiced as *ts* in ha**ts**
	mezzo	voiced as *ds* in mai**ds**
j, k, w,		these letters do not belong to the
x, y		Italian alphabet and are found only in foreign words

Italian-English
Italiano-Inglese

A

A (= *autostrada*) M (= motorway), *Am* I (= interstate)

a ◇ *stato in luogo* at; **~ Roma** in Rome; **~ casa** at home ◇ *moto a luogo* to; **andare ~ Roma** go to Rome ◇ *tempo*: **alle quattro** at four o'clock; **~ Natale** at Christmas; **~ maggio** in May; **~ vent'anni** at the age of twenty; **~ due a due** two at a time ◇ *modo*: **~ piedi** on foot ◇ *mezzo*: **ricamato ~ mano** embroidered by hand ◇ *prezzo, misura*: **~ che prezzo** at what price; **al metro** by the metre; **100 km all'ora** 100 km an hour

abate *m* abbot

abbacchio *m* GASTR young lamb

abbagliante 1 *agg* dazzling **2** *m gen pl* **-i** AUTO full beam; **abbagliare** dazzle

abbaiare bark

abbandonare abandon; **abbandono** *m* abandon; (*rinuncia*) abandonment

abbassare lower; *radio* turn down; **abbassarsi** (*chinarsi*) bend down; *di prezzo* come down; *fig* **~ a** stoop to; **ab-basso**: **~ la scuola!** down with school!

abbastanza enough; (*alquanto*) quite

abbattere knock down; *casa* demolish; *albero* cut down; *aereo* shoot down; *fig* dishearten; **abbattersi** fall; *fig* become disheartened; **abbattuto** disheartened

abbazia *f* abbey

abbellire embellish

abbi, abbia ☞ **avere**

abbigliamento *m* clothing; **~ sportivo** sportswear

abbinare match; (*combinare*) combine

abboccare *di pesce* bite; *fig* swallow the bait

abbonamento *m a giornale*, TEA subscription; *a treno*, *bus* season ticket; **abbonare** take out a subscription for; (*condonare*) deduct; **abbonarsi** subscribe; **abbonato** *m* subscriber; TELEC **elenco degli -i** telephone directory, phone book

abbondante abundant; *porzione* generous; *vestito* loose; *nevicata* heavy

abbordabile *persona* approachable; *prezzo* reasonable; **abbordare 1** *v/t persona* approach; F *persona dell'altro sesso* chat up F, Am come on to; *argomento* tackle **2** *v/t* MAR board

abbottonare button up

abbozzo *m* sketch

abbracciare embrace, hug; *fig* take up; **abbracciarsi** embrace, hug; **abbraccio** *m* embrace, hug; **un ~ a fine lettera** love

abbreviare abbreviate; **abbreviazione** *f* abbreviation

abbronzante *m* sun-tan lotion; **lettino** *m* *v/t* sunbed; **abbronzare** *pelle* tan; **abbronzarsi** get a tan; **abbronzato** tanned; **abbronzatura** *f* tan

abbrustolire roast

abbuffarsi stuff o.s. (**di** with)

abdicare abdicate

abete *m* fir

abile good (**in** at); fit (**a** for); **abilità** *f inv* ability

abilitazione *f* qualification

abisso *m* abyss

abitacolo *m* AUTO passenger compartment

abitante *m/f* inhabitant; **abitare 1** *v/t* live in **2** *v/i* live; **abitato 1** *agg* inhabited **2** *m* built-up area; **abitazione** *f* house

abiti *mpl* clothes; **abito** *m* dress; **da uomo** suit; **~ da sera** evening dress

abituale usual; **abituarsi: ~ a** get used to; **abitudinario 1** *agg* of fixed habits **2** *m* creature of habit; **abitudine** *f* habit

abolire abolish; **abolizione** *f* abolition

abominevole abominable

aborigeno *m/agg* aboriginal

abortire MED miscarry; *volontariamente* have an abortion; *fig* fail; **aborto** *m* MED miscarriage; *provocato* abortion

abrogare repeal

abusare: ~ di abuse; (*approfittare*) take advantage of; **~ nel bere** drink to excess; **abusivo** illegal; **abuso** *m* abuse

a.C. (= *avanti Cristo*) BC (= before Christ)

accademia *f* academy; **~ di belle arti** art college; **accademico** academic

accadere happen; **accaduto** *m*: **raccontami l'~** tell me what happened

accaldato overheated

accampamento *m* camp; **accampare 1** *v/t*: **~ scuse** come up with excuses **2** *v/i* e **accamparsi** camp

accanimento *m* (*tenacia*) tenacity; (*furia*) rage; **accanirsi** (*ostinarsi*) persist; **~ contro qu** rage against s.o.; **accanito** *odio* fierce; *fumatore* inveterate

accanto 1 *prp* **~ a** next to **2** *avv* near, nearby; *abitare* next door

accantonare put aside

accappatoio m bathrobe; *da mare* beachrobe

accarezzare caress; *speranza* cherish; *animale* stroke

accasciarsi flop down

accattone m beggar

accavallare cross; **accavallarsi** fig overlap

accecare 1 v/t blind **2** v/i be blinding

accedere: ~ *a* enter

accelerare speed up; AUTO accelerate; **acceleratore** m AUTO accelerator, *Am* gas pedal; **accelerazione** f acceleration

accendere light; RAD, TV turn on; **accendersi** light up; *apparecchio* come on; **accendino** m, **accendisigari** m inv (cigarette) lighter

accennare indicate; *con parole* mention; ~ *a fare qc* show signs of doing sth; **accenno** m (*cenno*) gesture; (*indizio*) sign; (*allusione*) hint

accensione f ignition

accento m accent; **accentuare** accentuate

accertare check; **accertarsi**: ~ *di qc* check sth

acceso *colore* bright; *motore* running; TV, *luce* on

accessibile accessible; *prezzo* reasonable; **accesso** m access; *fig* e MED fit; *divieto d'* ~ no entry

accessori mpl accessories; **accessoriato** AUTO complete with accessories

accetta f axe, *Am* ax

accettabile acceptable; **accettare** accept; **accettazione** f acceptance; *di albergo* reception; ~ *bagagli* check--in

acchiappare catch

acciaio m steel; ~ *inossidabile* stainless steel

accidentale accidental

accidentato *terreno* rough

accidenti F damn! F; *di sorpresa* wow!

accigliato frowning

accingersi: ~ *a fare qc* be about to do sth

acciottolato m cobbles

acciuffare grab

acciuga f anchovy

acclimatarsi get acclimatized

accludere enclose; **accluso** enclosed; *qui* ~ enclosed

accogliere welcoming; **accogliere** welcome; *richiesta* grant

accollarsi take on

accollato *abito* high-necked

accoltellare knife

accolto pp ☞ **accogliere**

accomodante accommodating; **accomodare** (*riparare*) mend; *lite* resolve; **accomodarsi** come o.s. at home; *si accomodi!* come in!; (*sedersi*) have a seat!

accompagnare accompany; **accompagnatore** m, **-trice** f escort; MUS accompanist

acconciatura f hairdo

acconsentire consent (**a** to)

accontentare satisfy; accontentarsi be happy (**di** with)

acconto *m* deposit

accorciare shorten; accorciarsi get shorter

accordare grant; MUS tune; (*armonizzare*) harmonize; accordarsi agree; *di colori* match; accordo *m* agreement; (*armonia*) harmony; MUS chord; *essere d'~* agree; *mettersi d'~* reach an agreement; *d'~!* OK!

accorgersi: ~ **di** notice

accorrere hurry; ~ **in aiuto di qu** rush to help s.o.

accortezza *f* forethought

accorto 1 *pp* ☞ *accorgersi* 2 *agg* shrewd

accostare approach; *porta* leave ajar; accostarsi get close

accreditare confirm; FIN credit; accredito *m* credit

accrescere increase; accrescersi grow bigger

accudire 1 *v/t* look after 2 *v/i*: ~ **a qc** attend to sth

accumulare accumulate; accumulatore *m* battery

accuratezza *f* care; accurato careful

accusa *f* accusation; DIR charge; accusare accuse; DIR charge; accusato *m*, -a *f* accused

acerbo unripe

acero *m* maple

aceto *m* vinegar

acetone *m* nail varnish remover

ACI *m* (= *Automobile Club d'Italia*) Automobile Club of Italy

acidità *f* acidity; ~ **di stomaco** heartburn; acido 1 *agg* acid; *fig* sour 2 *m* acid

acne *f* acne

acqua *f* water; ~ **minerale** mineral water; ~ **potabile** drinking water; ~ **di rubinetto** tap water; ~ **ossigenata** hydrogen peroxide; *-e pl territoriali* territorial waters; *fig* **in cattive -e** in deep water

acquaforte *f* etching

acquaio *m* sink

acquaragia *f* turpentine

acquario *m* aquarium; ASTR *Acquario* Aquarius

acquatico aquatic

acquavite *f* brandy

acquazzone *m* downpour

acquedotto *m* aqueduct

acqueo: *vapore m* ~ water vapour *o Am* vapor

acquerello *m* watercolour, *Am* watercolor

acquirente *m/f* purchaser; acquisizione *f* acquisition; acquistare 1 *v/t* buy; *fig* gain 2 *v/i* improve; acquisto *m* purchase

acquolina *f*: **mi viene l'~ in bocca** my mouth's watering

acre sour; *voce* harsh

acrilico acrylic

acrobata *m/f* acrobat

acustica *f* acoustics; **acustico** acoustic

acuto 1 *agg* intense; *nota, dolore* sharp; *suono, voce* shrill; MED acute **2** *m* MUS high note

ad ☞ **a** (*before vowels*)

adagiarsi lie down; **adagio 1** *avv* slowly; *con cautela* cautiously **2** *m* MUS adagio

adattamento *m* adaptation; (*rielaborazione*) reworking; **adattare** adapt; **adattarsi** (*adeguarsi*) adapt (*a* to); (*addirsi*) be suitable (*a* for); **adattatore** *m* adaptor; **adatto** right (*a* for)

addebitare FIN ~ *qc a qu* debit s.o. with sth; *fig* ascribe sth to s.o.; **addebito** *m* FIN debit; *nota f di* ~ debit note

addensarsi thicken

addestramento *m* training; **addestrare** train

addetto 1 *agg* assigned (*a* to) **2** *m*, -*a f* person responsible; *vietato l'ingresso ai non -i* authorized personnel only

addio 1 *int* goodbye **2** *m* goodbye, farewell

addirittura (*assolutamente*) absolutely; (*perfino*) even

additivo *m* additive; **addizionare** add; **addizione** *f* addition

addobbare decorate; **addobbo** *m* decoration

addolcire sweeten; *fig* soften

addolorare grieve

addome *m* abdomen

addomesticare tame

addominale abdominal

addormentarsi fall asleep; **addormentato** asleep; (*assonnato*) sleepy

addossare (*appoggiare*) lean (*a* on); *fig colpa* put, lay (*a* on); **addossarsi** lean (*a* on); *fig* shoulder; **addosso 1** *prp* on; *vicino* next to **2** *avv* *avere* ~ *vestiti* have on; *avere* ~ *qu* have s.o. breathing down one's neck

adeguarsi conform; **adeguato** adequate

adempiere: ~ *a dovere* carry out, do

aderente 1 *agg vestito* tight **2** *m/f* follower; **aderire:** ~ *a* adhere to; *partito* support; *richiesta* agree to; **adesione** *f* adhesion; (*consenso*) agreement; **adesivo 1** *agg* adhesive **2** *m* sticker

adesso now; *da* ~ *in poi* from now on; *fino a* ~ up to now; *per* ~ for the moment

adiacente adjacent; ~ *a* next to, adjacent to

adirato angry

adolescente *m/f* adolescent, teenager; **adolescenza** *f* adolescence, teens

adoperare use

adorare adore

adottare adopt; **adottivo** *genitori* adoptive; *figlio* adopted; **adozione** *f* adoption

adrenalina *f* adrenalin

adriatico Adriatic; *mare m* **Adriatico** Adriatic Sea

adulare flatter

adulterio *m* adultery; adulto **1** *agg* adult 2 *m*, *-a f* adult

adunare assemble

aerare air; aereo **1** *agg* air *attr*; *fotografia* aerial; *compagnia f -a* airline; *posta f -a* airmail **2** *m* plane

aerobica *f* aerobics *sg*

aerodinamico aerodynamic

aeronautica *f*: ~ *militare* Air Force

aeroplano *m* plane, aeroplane, *Am* airplane

aeroporto *m* airport

aerosol *m inv contenitore* aerosol

aerostazione *f* air terminal

afa *f* closeness, mugginess

affabile affable

affaccendarsi busy o.s. (*in* with); affaccendato busy

affacciarsi appear

affamato starving

affannato breathless; affanno *m* breathlessness; *fig* anxiety

affare *m* matter, business; FIN transaction; *-i pl* business; *non sono -i tuoi* it's none of your business; *uomo m d'-i* businessman

affascinante fascinating; affascinare fascinate

affaticarsi tire o.s. out

affatto completely; *non* ... ~ not ... at all

affermare state; affermarsi become established; affermazione *f* assertion; (*successo*) achievement

afferrare seize, grab; (*comprendere*) grasp; afferrarsi cling (*a* to)

affettare (*tagliare*) slice

affettato[1] *m* sliced meat

affettato[2] *agg* affected

affetto *m* affection; affettuoso affectionate; affezionarsi: ~ *a qu* become fond of s.o.; affezionato: ~ *a qu* fond of s.o.

affibbiare: ~ *qc a qu* saddle s.o. with sth

affidabilità *f* dependability; affidamento *m* trust; *fare su* rely on; affidare entrust; affidarsi: ~ *a* rely on

affiggere *avviso* put up

affilare sharpen; *fig* make thinner; affilato sharp; *naso* thin

affiliato *m*, *-a f* member

affinché so that

affine similar

affinità *f inv* affinity

affiorare *dall'acqua* emerge; *fig* (*mostrarsi*) appear

affissione *f* bill-posting; affisso **1** *pp* ☞ **affiggere 2** *m* bill

affittacamere *m/f* landlord; *donna* landlady; affittare rent; *affittasi* to rent; affitto *m* rent; *dare in* ~ rent (out); *prendere in* ~ rent

affliggere distress; *di malattia* trouble, plague; afflitto distressed

affluente *m* tributary; **affluenza** *f fig* influx

affogare drown

affollare, affollarsi crowd; **affollato** crowded

affondare sink

affrancare free; *posta* frank; **affrancatura** *f* franking; *(tassa di spedizione)* postage

affresco *m* fresco

affrettarsi hurry

affrontare face, confront; *spese* meet

affumicare *stanza* fill with smoke; *alimenti* smoke; **affumicato** smoked

afoso sultry

Africa *f* Africa; **africano 1** *agg* African **2** *m*, **-a** *f* African

afroamericano 1 *agg* African-American **2** *m*, **-a** *f* African-American

afrodisiaco *m/agg* aphrodisiac

agenda *f* diary

agente *m/f* agent; **~ immobiliare** estate agent, *Am* realtor; **~ di pubblica sicurezza** police officer

agenzia *f* agency; **~ di cambio** bureau de change; **~ immobiliare** estate agency, *Am* real estate office.; **~ di viaggi** travel agency

agevolare make easier; **agevolazione** *f* FIN special term

agganciare hook; *cintura, collana* fasten

aggeggio *m* gadget

aggettivo *m* adjective

agghiacciante spine-chilling

aggiornamento *m* updating; *(rinvio)* postponement; **corso m d'~** refresher course; **aggiornare** *(mettere al corrente)* update; *(rinviare)* postpone; **aggiornarsi** keep up to date

aggirare surround; *fig ostacolo* get around

aggirarsi hang around; FIN be in the region of

aggiudicare award; **all'asta** knock down

aggiungere add; **aggiunta** *f* addition

aggiustare *(riparare)* repair; *(sistemare)* settle

agglomerato *m*: **~ urbano** built-up area

aggrapparsi cling, hold on (**a** to)

aggravare *punizione* increase; *(peggiorare)* make worse; **aggravarsi** worsen, deteriorate

aggraziato graceful

aggredire attack; **aggressione** *f* aggression; *(attacco)* attack; **aggressività** *f* aggressiveness; **aggressivo** aggressive; **aggressore** *m* attacker; MIL aggressor

agguato *m* ambush

agguerrito hardened

agiato comfortable, well-off; *(comodo)* comfortable

agibile fit for human habitation

agile agile; **agilità** f agility; *fig* liveliness

agio m ease; **sentirsi a proprio ~** feel at ease

agire act; *di medicina* take effect

agitare shake; *fazzoletto* wave; *fig* (*turbare*) upset, agitate; **agitato** agitated; *mare* rough; **agitazione** f agitation

agli = **a** and *art* **gli**

aglio m garlic

agnello m lamb

agnolotti mpl type of ravioli

ago m needle

agonia f agony

agonistico competitive

agopuntura f acupuncture

agorafobia f agoraphobia

agosto m August

agricolo agricultural; **agricoltore** m farmer; **agricoltura** f agriculture

agrifoglio m holly

agriturismo m farm holidays

agrodolce bittersweet; GASTR sweet and sour

agrumi mpl citrus fruit

aguzzare sharpen; **~ la vista** keep one's eyes peeled; **aguzzo** pointed

ahi! ouch!

ai = **a** and *art* **i**

Aids m o f Aids

airbag m inv airbag

airone m heron

aiuola f flower bed

aiutante m/f assistant; **aiutare** help; **aiuto** m help, assist-

ance; *persona* assistant

aizzare incite

al = **a** and *art* **il**

ala f wing

alabastro m alabaster

alano m Great Dane

alba f dawn; **all'~** at dawn

albanese agg, m/f Albanian; **Albania** f Albania

alberato tree-lined

alberghiero hotel *attr*; **albergo** m hotel

albero m tree; MAR mast; AUTO shaft; **~ genealogico** family tree; **~ di Natale** Christmas tree

albicocca f apricot; **albicocco** m apricot (tree)

albo m notice board, *Am* bulletin board; (*registro*) register; **radiare dall'~** strike off

album m inv album

alcol m alcohol; **alcolico 1** agg alcoholic **2** m alcoholic drink; **alcolismo** m alcoholism; **alcolizzato** m, **-a** f alcoholic; **alcoltest** m inv Breathalyzer®

alcuno 1 agg any; **non ~** no, not any **2** pron any; **-i** pl some, a few

aldilà m: **l'~** the next world

aletta f fin

alfabetico alphabetical; **alfabeto** m alphabet

alfiere m scacchi bishop

alga f seaweed

algebra f algebra

Algeria f Algeria; **algerino 1** agg Algerian **2** m, **-a** f Algerian

aliante *m* glider

alice *f* anchovy

alienato 1 *agg* alienated **2** *m*, -a *f* madman; *donna* madwoman; **alienazione** *f* alienation; ~ **mentale** madness

alimentare 1 *v/t* feed **2** *agg* food *attr*; **generi** *mpl* **-i** foodstuffs; **alimentazione** *f* feeding; **alimento** *m* food; **-i** *pl* DIR alimony

aliquota *f* share; ~ **d'imposta** rate of taxation

aliscafo *m* hydrofoil

alito *m* breath

all. (= **allegato**) enc(l). (= enclosed)

all', alla = **a** *and art* **l', la**

allacciamento *m* TEC connection; **allacciare** fasten; TEC connect

allagamento *m* flooding; **allagare** flood

allargare widen; *vestito* let out; *braccia* open; **allargarsi** widen

allarmare alarm; **allarmarsi** become alarmed; **allarme** *m* alarm; **dare l'**~ raise the alarm

allattare *bambino* feed

alle = **a** *and art* **le**

alleanza *f* alliance; **allearsi** ally o.s.; **alleato 1** *agg* allied **2** *m*, -a *f* ally

allegare *documento* enclose; INFOR attach; **allegato** *m* enclosure; INFOR attachment; **qui** ~ enclosed

alleggerire lighten; *fig: dolore* ease

allegria *f* cheerfulness; **allegro 1** *agg* cheerful; *colore* bright **2** *m* MUS allegro

allenamento *m* training; **allenare**, **allenarsi** train (*per* for; *a* in); **allenatore** *m*, -**trice** *f* trainer

allentare 1 *v/t* loosen **2** *v/i* e **allentarsi** loosen

allergia *f* allergy; **allergico** allergic (*a* to)

allestimento *m* preparation; MAR fitting out; TEA ~ **scenico** sets, scenery; **allestire** prepare; MAR fit out; TEA stage

allevamento *m* BOT, ZO breeding; **allevare** BOT, ZO breed; *bambini* bring up, raise; **allevatore** *m*, -**trice** *f* breeder

alleviare alleviate

allievo *m*, -a *f* pupil, student

alligatore *m* alligator

allineare line up; FIN adjust; TIP align

allo = **a** *and art* **lo**

allodola *f* skylark

alloggiare 1 *v/t* put up **2** *v/i* stay, put up; **alloggio** *m* accommodation; *Am* accommodations; *vitto e* ~ bed and board

allontanarsi go away; *fig* grow apart

allora then; *da* ~ *in poi* from then on; *fin d'*~ since then

alloro *m* laurel; GASTR bay

alluce m big toe

allucinante F incredible, mind-blowing F; **allucinazione** f hallucination

alludere (a ø) allude

alluminio m aluminium, Am aluminum

allungare lengthen; (diluire) dilute; mano put out; **allungarsi** di giorno get longer; di persona stretch out, lie down

allusione f allusion

alluvione f flood

almeno at least

alogena f halogen

Alpi fpl Alps; **alpinismo** m mountaineering; **alpinista** m/f mountain climber; **alpino** Alpine

alquanto 1 agg some **2** avv a little, somewhat

alt stop

altalena f swing

altare m altar

alterare alter; **alterarsi** (guastarsi) go bad ø off; (irritarsi) get angry

alternare, alternarsi alternate; **alternativa** f alternative; **alternativo** alternative; **alternato: corrente** f -a alternating current; **alterno: a giorni** pl -i on alternate days

altezza f height; titolo Highness

alticcio tipsy

altitudine f altitude

alto 1 agg high; persona tall; **a voce -a** in a loud voice; leg-

gere aloud; **in ~** at the top; moto up **2** m top

altoatesino 1 agg South Tyrolean **2** m, -a f South Tyrolean

altoparlante m loudspeaker

altopiano m plateau

altrettanto as much; **-i** pl as many

altrimenti (in modo diverso) differently; (in caso contrario) otherwise

altro 1 agg other; **un ~** another; **l'altr'anno** last year; **l'~ ieri** the day before yesterday **2** pron other; **l'un l'~** one another; **gli altri** other people; **tra l'~** what's more, moreover; **desidera ~?** anything else?; **tutt'~ che** anything but; **qualcun'~** someone ø somebody else

altronde: d'~ on the other hand

altrove elsewhere

altruismo m altruism

altura f hill

alunno m, -a f pupil, student

alzacristallo m inv AUTO window winder

alzare raise; **alzarsi** stand up, rise; da letto get up; di sole rise

amaca f hammock

amalgamare amalgamate

amante m/f lover; **amare** love; amico be fond of

amareggiato embittered

amarena f sour black cherry

amarezza f bitterness; amaro

1 *agg* bitter **2** *m liquore* bitters

ambasciata *f* embassy; **ambasciatore** *m*, **-trice** *f* ambassador

ambedue both

ambientale environmental; **ambientalista 1** *agg* environmental **2** *m/f* environmentalist; **ambientarsi** become acclimatized; **ambiente** *m* environment

ambiguità *f inv* ambiguity; **ambiguo** ambiguous

ambito *m* sphere

ambizione *f* ambition; **ambizioso** ambitious

ambo 1 *agg* both **2** *m lotteria* double

ambulante 1 *agg* travelling, *Am* traveling **2** *m/f* pedlar; **ambulanza** *f* ambulance; **ambulatorio** *m* MED outpatients

America *f* America; **americano 1** *agg* American **2** *m*, **-a** *f* American **3** *m* American English

ametista *f* amethyst

amianto *m* asbestos

amichevole friendly; **amicizia** *f* friendship; **amico 1** *agg* friendly **2** *m*, **-a** *f* friend

amido *m* starch

ammaccare dent; *frutta* bruise; **ammaccatura** *f* dent; *su frutta* bruise

ammaestrare teach; *animali* train

ammalarsi fall sick; **ammala-**

to 1 *agg* sick **2** *m*, **-a** *f* sick person

ammarare *di aereo* put down in the water; *di navetta spaziale* splash down

ammassare, **ammassarsi** mass; **ammasso** *m* pile; GEOL mass

ammazzare kill; *animali* slaughter; **ammazzarsi** (*suicidarsi*) kill o.s.

ammenda *f* (*multa*) fine

ammesso *pp* ☞ **ammettere**; **ammettere** admit; (*supporre*) suppose; (*riconoscere*) acknowledge; **ammesso che** ... supposing (that) ...

amministrare administer; *azienda* manage, run; **amministrativo** administrative; **amministratore** *m*, **-trice** *f* administrator; *di azienda* manager; **amministrazione** *f* administration

ammirare admire; **ammiratore** *m*, **-trice** *f* admirer; **ammirazione** *f* admiration; **ammirevole** admirable

ammobiliare furnish; **ammobiliato** furnished

ammollo: **in ~** soaking

ammonimento *m* reprimand, admonishment; (*consiglio*) warning; **ammonire** reprimand, admonish; (*avvertire*) warn; DIR caution; **ammonizione** *f* reprimand, admonishment; SP warning; DIR caution

ammontare: **~ a** amount to

ammorbidire soften

ammortizzare FIN pay off; **ammortizzatore** m AUTO shock absorber

ammucchiare pile up

ammuffire go mouldy, Am go moldy; fig moulder away, Am molder away

ammutolire be struck dumb

amnesia f amnesia

amnistia f amnesty

amo m hook; fig bait

amore m love; **fare l'~ con qu** make love to s.o.; **amoroso** loving; sguardo amorous; lettera, poesia love attr

ampiezza f di stanza spaciousness; di gonna fullness; fig di cultura breadth; fig ~ **di vedute** broadmindedness; **ampio** stanza spacious, large; abito roomy; gonna full

ampliamento m broadening, widening; di edificio extension; **ampliare** broaden, widen; edificio extend

amplificare TEC suono amplify; **amplificatore** m amplifier

amputare amputate

amuleto m amulet

anabbagliante dipped, Am low-beam

anacronistico anachronistic

anagrafe f ufficio registry office

analcolico 1 agg non-alcoholic **2** m non-alcoholic drink

anale anal

analfabeta m/f illiterate person, person who cannot read or write; **analfabetismo** m illiteracy

analgesico m/agg analgesic

analisi f inv analysis; ~ **del sangue** blood test; **analista** m/f analyst; ~ **programmatore** systems analyst

analizzare analyse, Am analyze

analogia f analogy; **analogo** analogous

ananas m inv pineapple

anarchia f anarchy; **anarchico 1** agg anarchic **2** m, -a f anarchist

anatomia f anatomy; **anatomico** anatomical

anatra f duck

anca f hip

anche too, also; (perfino) even; ~ **se** even if

ancora[1] avv still; di nuovo again; di più (some) more; **non** ~ not yet; ~ **una volta** once more; **dammene** ~ **un po'** give me a bit more

ancora[2] f anchor

andamento m di vendite performance

andare 1 v/i go; (funzionare) work; ~ **via** (partire) leave; di macchia come out; ~ **bene** suit; taglia fit; ~ **a male** go off; **come va?** how are you?; **non mi va** di vestito it doesn't fit me; **non mi va di venire** I don't feel like coming **2** *m*: *a lungo ~* in the long run; **andarsene** go away; **andata** *f* outward journey; (*biglietto m di*) *~* single (ticket), *Am* oneway ticket; (*biglietto m di*) *~ e ritorno* return (ticket), *Am* round-trip ticket; **andatura** *f* walk; SP pace

androne *m* hallway

aneddoto *m* anecdote

anello *m* ring

anemia *f* anaemia, *Am* anemia; **anemico** anaemic, *Am* anemic

anestesia *f* sostanza anaesthetic, *Am* anesthetic; **anestetico** *m* anaesthetic, *Am* anesthetic

anfibio 1 *agg* amphibious **2** *m* ZO amphibian; MIL amphibious vehicle

anfiteatro *m* amphitheatre, *Am* amphitheater

anfora *f* amphora

angelo *m* angel

anglicano 1 *agg* Anglican **2** *m*, **-a** *f* Anglican

angolo *m* corner; MAT angle; *~ cottura* kitchenette; MAT *~ retto* right angle

angoscia *f* anguish; **angoscioso** anguished; *che da angoscia* heart-rending

anguilla *f* eel

anguria *f* water melon

angusto narrow

anice *m* aniseed

anidride *f*: *~ carbonica* carbon dioxide

anima *f* soul

animale *m* animal; *~ domestico* pet

animare give life to; *conversazione* liven up; (*promuovere*) promote; **animato** *strada* busy; *conversazione, persona* animated; **animatore** *m*, **-trice** *f* di gruppo leader; **animazione** *f* animation; INFOR *~ al computer* computer animation

animo *m* nature; (*coraggio*) heart; *perdersi d'~* lose heart

anitra *f* duck

annaffiare water; **annaffiatoio** *m* watering can

annata *f* vintage; (*anno*) year; *importo* annual amount

annegare 1 *v/t* drown **2** *v/i e* **annegarsi** drown

annerire, **annerirsi** turn black, blacken

annessione *f* POL annexation

annidarsi nest

anniversario *m* anniversary

anno *m* year; *buon ~!* Happy New Year!; *quanti -i hai?* how old are you?; *ho 33 -i* I'm 33 (years old)

annodare tie (together); *cravatta* tie, knot

annoiare bore; (*dare fastidio a*) annoy; **annoiarsi** get bored; **annoiato** bored

annotare make a note of; *testo* annotate; **annotazione** *f* note; *in testo* annotation

annuale annual, yearly; *di un*

anno year-long

annuire (*assentire*) assent (*a* to)

annullamento *m* cancellation; *di matrimonio* annulment; **annullare** cancel; *matrimonio* annul; *gol* disallow; (*vanificare*) cancel out

annunciare announce; **annunciatore** *m*, **-trice** *f* RAD, TV announcer; **Annunciazione** *f* REL Annunciation; **annuncio** *m* announcement; *in giornale* advertisement; **-i** *pl* **economici** classifieds

annuo annual, yearly

annusare sniff; *fig* smell

anomalo anomalous

anonimo anonymous

anoressia *f* anorexia; **anoressico** anorexic

anormale abnormal

ansia *f* anxiety

ansimare wheeze

ansioso anxious

antagonismo *m* antagonism; **antagonista** *m/f* antagonist

antartico Antarctic

antecedente 1 *agg* preceding **2** *m* precedent

antenato *m*, **-a** *f* ancestor

antenna *f* RAD, TV aerial, *Am* antenna; (*capra*) **~ parabolica** satellite dish

anteprima *f* preview

anteriore front; *precedente* previous

anti ... anti ...

antibiotico *m/agg* antibiotic

anticamente in ancient times; **antichità** *f inv* antiquity

anticiclone *m* anticyclone

anticipato: pagamento *m* **~** advance payment; **anticipare** anticipate; *denaro* pay in advance; *partenza, riunione ecc* bring forward; **anticipo** *m* advance; (*caparra*) deposit; *in* **~** ahead of time, early

antico ancient; *mobile* antique

anticoncezionale *m/agg* contraceptive

anticonformista *m/f* nonconformist

anticostituzionale unconstitutional

antidoto *m* antidote

antifurto 1 *agg* antitheft **2** *m* anti-theft device

antigas *inv* gas *attr*

antincendio *inv* fire *attr*

antinebbia *m inv* foglamp

antiorario: in senso **~** anticlockwise, *Am* counterclockwise

antipasto *m* starter

antipatia *f* antipathy; **antipatico** disagreeable

antiquariato *m* antique business; **negozio** *m* **di ~** antique shop; **antiquario** *m*, **-a** *f* antique dealer; **antiquato** antiquated

antiriflesso *inv* anti-glare

antiruggine *m* rust inhibitor

antisemitismo *m* anti-Semitism

antisettico *m/agg* antiseptic

antisismico earthquake-proof

antologia *f* anthology

anulare *m* ring finger

anzi in fact; (*o meglio*) (or) better still

anzianità *f* old age; ~ **di servizio** seniority; anziano **1** *agg* elderly; *per servizio* (most) senior **2** *m*, -a *f* old man; *donna* old woman; **gli -i** *pl* the elderly *pl*

anziché rather than

anzitutto first of all

aorta *f* aorta

apatia *f* apathy; apatico apathetic

ape *f* bee

aperitivo *m* aperitif

aperto **1** *pp* ☞ **aprire 2** *agg* open; **all'** ~ **piscina** open-air; **mangiare all'**~ eat in the open air, eat outside; **apertura** *f* opening; FOT aperture

apice *m* apex; *fig* height

apicoltura *f* bee-keeping

apnea *f* SP free diving

apostolo *m* apostle

apostrofo *m* apostrophe

appagare satisfy

appalto *m* (*contratto*) contract; **dare in** ~ contract out; **prendere in** ~ win the contract for; **gara f di** ~ call for tenders

appannarsi *di vetro* mist up; *di vista* grow dim

apparato *m* apparatus; ~ **di-**

gerente digestive system

apparecchiare *tavola* set; (*preparare*) prepare; **apparecchio** *m* TEC device; AVIA F plane; *per denti* brace

apparenza *f* appearance; **apparire** appear; **appariscente** striking

appartamento *m* flat, *Am* apartment

appartarsi withdraw

appartenere belong

appassionare excite; (*commuovere*) move; **appassionarsi** become excited (*a* by); **appassionato** passionate

appassire wither

appellarsi appeal (*a* to; **contro** against); **appello** *m* appeal; **fare** ~ **a qu** appeal to s.o

appena **1** *avv* just **2** *cong* as soon as

appendere hang

appendiabiti *m* hatstand

appendice *f* appendix; **appendicite** *f* appendicitis

Appennini *mpl* Apennines

appesantire make heavier

appeso *pp* ☞ **appendere**

appetito *m* appetite; **buon** ~! enjoy (your meal)!; **appetitoso** appetizing

appiattire flatten

appiccicare stick; **appiccicarsi** stick; **appiccicoso** sticky; *fig* clingy

appiglio *m per mani* fingerhold; *per piedi* toehold; *fig* excuse

applaudire applaud; **applauso** *m* applause

applicare *etichetta* attach; *regolamento* apply; **applicazione** *f* application

appoggiare lean (*a* against); (*posare*) put; *fig* support, back; **appoggiarsi**: ~ *a* lean on; *fig* rely on; **appoggiatesta** *m inv* headrest; **appoggio** *m* support

apporre put; ~ **la firma su qc** put one's signature to sth

apportare bring; *fig* (*causare*) cause

apposito appropriate

apposta deliberately, on purpose; (*specialmente*) specifically

apprendere learn; *notizia* hear

apprendistato *m* apprenticeship

apprensione *f* apprehension; **apprensivo** apprehensive

appreso *pp* ☞ **apprendere**

appresso 1 *prp* close, near; (*dietro*) behind. **2** *avv* near, close by; **portarsi qc ~** bring sth (with one)

apprezzare appreciate

approccio *m* approach

approdare land; *di barca* moor

approdo *m* landing; *luogo* landing stage

approfittare: ~ *di qc* take advantage of sth

approfondire deepen; *fig*

study in depth

appropriarsi: ~ *di qc* appropriate sth; **appropriato** appropriate

approvare approve of; *legge* approve; **approvazione** *f* approval

appuntamento *m* appointment

appuntito pointed; *matita* sharp

appunto 1 *m* note; **prendere -i** take notes **2** *avv*: (**per l'**) ~ exactly

apribottiglie *m inv* bottle opener

aprile *m* April

aprire open; *rubinetto* turn on; **aprirsi** open; **apriscatole** *m inv* can-opener, *Br anche* tin-opener

aquila *f* eagle

aquilone *m* kite

arabesco *m* arabesque; *spir* scrawl, scribble

Arabia Saudita *f* Saudi (Arabia)

arabo 1 *agg* Arab **2** *m*, **-a** *f* Arab **3** *m* Arabic

arachide *f* peanut

aragosta *f* lobster

arancia *f* orange; **aranciata** *f* orangeade

arancio 1 *agg inv* orange **2** *m* *albero* orange tree; *colore* orange; **arancione** *m/agg* orange

arare plough, *Am* plow; **aratro** *m* plough, *Am* plow

arazzo *m* tapestry

arbitrario arbitrary

arbitro *m* arbiter; SP referee

arbusto *m* shrub

arcaico archaic

arcata *f* arch

archeologia *f* archaeology, *Am* archeology; **archeologo** *m*, **-a** *f* archaeologist, *Am* archeologist

archetto *m* MUS bow

architetto *m* architect; **architettonico** architectural

archiviare file; **archivio** *m* archives

arcipelago *m* archipelago

arcivescovo *m* archbishop

arco *m* bow; ARCHI arch; **~ di tempo** period of time; **arcobaleno** *m* rainbow

ardere burn

area *f* surface; *zona* area; **~ di servizio** service area

arena *f* arena

arenarsi run aground; *fig* come to a halt

areo ... ☞ **aereo ...**

argano *m* winch

argentato silver-plated; **argenteria** *f* silver(ware)

Argentina *f* Argentina; **argentino 1** *agg* Argentinian **2** *m*, **-a** *f* Argentinian

argento *m* silver

argilla *f* clay; **argilloso** clayey

arginare embank; **argine** *m* embankment

argomento *m* argument; (*contenuto*) subject

arguto witty; (*perspicace*) shrewd

aria *f* air; (*aspetto*) appearance; MUS tune; *di opera* aria; **~ condizionata** air conditioning; **all'~ aperta** in the fresh air; **mandare all'~ qc** ruin sth; **aver l'~ stanca** look tired; **darsi delle -e** give o.s. airs

arido dry, arid

arieggiare *stanza* air

ariete *m* ZO ram; ASTR **Ariete** Aries

aringa *f* herring

arista *f* GASTR chine of pork

aristocratico 1 *agg* aristocratic **2** *m*, **-a** *f* aristocrat

aritmetica *f* arithmetic

arma *f* weapon; **~ da fuoco** firearm; **chiamare alle -i** call up; *fig* **essere alle prime -i** be a beginner

armadio *m* cupboard; **~ a muro** fitted cupboard

armamento *m* armament; **armarsi** arm o.s. (*di* with); **armato** armed

armatura *f* armour, *Am* armor; (*struttura*) framework

armistizio *m* armistice

armonia *f* harmony

armonica *f* harmonica; **~ a bocca** mouth organ, harmonica

armonioso harmonious

arnese *m* tool

arnia *f* beehive

aroma *m* aroma; **aromaterapia** *f* aromatherapy; **aromatico** aromatic

aromatizzare flavour, *Am*

flavor

arpa *f* harp

arpione *m* harpoon

arrabattarsi do everything one can

arrabbiarsi get angry; **arrabbiato** angry; (*idrofobo*) rabid

arrampicarsi climb; **arrampicata** *f* climb

arrangiarsi (*accordarsi*) agree (**su** on); (*destreggiarsi*) manage

arrecare bring; *fig* cause

arredamento *m* décor; *mobili* furniture; *arte* interior design; **arredare** furnish; **arredatore** *m*, **-trice** *f* interior designer

arrendersi surrender; **arrendevole** soft, yielding

arrestare stop; DIR arrest; **arrestarsi** stop; **arresto** *m* coming to a stop; DIR arrest

arretrato 1 *agg* in arrears; *paese* underdeveloped **2 -i** *mpl* arrears

arricchire *fig* enrich; **arricchirsi** get rich

arricciare *capelli* curl; ~ **il naso** turn up one's nose

arringa *f* DIR closing speech for the defence *o Am* defense

arrivare arrive, come; ~ **a** reach, get to; ~ **a fare qc** manage to do sth

arrivederci, arrivederla goodbye

arrivista *m/f* social climber

arrivo *m* arrival; SP finish line

arrogante arrogant; **arroganza** *f* arrogance

arrossire blush

arrosto *m* roast

arrotolare roll up

arrotondare round off; *stipendio* supplement

arroventato red-hot

arruffato ruffled

arrugginire 1 *v/t* rust **2** *v/i* e **arrugginirsi** rust; *fig* get rusty

arruolarsi enlist

arsenale *m* arsenal; MAR dockyard

arso 1 *pp* ☞ **ardere 2** *agg* burnt; (*secco*) dried-up

arte *f* art; (*abilità*) gift

artefice *m/f* fig author, architect

arteria *f* artery; **arterioso** arterial

artico Arctic

articolazione *f* ANAT joint

articolo *m* item, article; GRAM ~ **determinativo** definite article; GRAM ~ **indeterminativo** indefinite article

artificiale artificial; **artificio** *m* artifice; **artificioso** *maniere* artificial

artigianale handmade; **artigianato** *m* craftsmanship; **artigiano** *m*, **-a** *f* craftsman; *donna* craftswoman

artiglieria *f* artillery

artiglio *m* claw

artista *m/f* artist; **artistico** artistic

arto *m* limb

artrite *f* arthritis

artrosi *f* rheumatism

ascella *f* armpit

ascendente 1 *agg* ascending; *strada* sloping upwards; *movimento* upwards **2** *m* ASTR ascendant; *fig* influence;

ascensione *f* ascent; REL Ascension; **ascensore** *m* lift, *Am* elevator; **ascesa** *f* ascent

ascesso *m* abscess

ascia *f* axe, *Am* ax

asciugacapelli *m* hairdryer; **asciugamano** *m* towel; **asciugare** dry; **asciugarsi** dry o.s.; **~ i capelli** dry one's hair; **asciugatrice** *f* tumble dryer; **asciutto** dry

ascoltare, listen to; **ascoltatore** *m*, **-trice** *f* listener; **ascolto** *m* listening; **dare ~** listen (**a** to)

asettico aseptic

asfaltare asphalt; **asfalto** *m* asphalt

asfissiare asphyxiate

Asia *f* Asia; **asiatico 1** *agg* Asian **2** *m*, **-a** *f* Asian

asilo *m* shelter; **~ politico** political asylum; **~ nido** day nursery, *Am* day care center

asimmetrico asymmetrical

asino *m* ass (*anche fig*)

asma *f* asthma

asociale antisocial

asola *f* buttonhole

asparago *m* spear of aspara-

gus; **-gi** asparagus

aspettare wait for; **~ un bambino** be expecting a baby; **aspettarsi** expect; **aspettativa** *f* expectation; **da lavoro** unpaid leave

aspetto[1] *m* look, appearance; **di problema** aspect

aspetto[2]: **sala f d'~** waiting room

aspirapolvere *m* vacuum cleaner

aspirare 1 *v/t* inhale; TEC suck up **2** *v/i*: **~ a qc** aspire to sth

aspirina *f* aspirin

asportare take away

aspro sour; (*duro*) harsh; *litigio* bitter

assaggiare taste; **assaggio** *m* taste, sample

assai 1 *agg* a lot of **2** *avv con verbo* a lot; *con aggettivo* very; (*abbastanza*) enough

assalire attack

assaltare attack; **assalto** *m* attack; *fig* **prendere d'~** storm

assassinare murder; POL assassinate; **assassinio** *m* murder; POL assassination; **assassino 1** *agg* murderous **2** *m*, **-a** *f* murderer; POL assassin

asse[1] *f* board; **~ da stiro** ironing board

asse[2] *m* TEC axle; MAT axis

assecondare support; (*esaudire*) satisfy

assediare besiege; **assedio** *m* siege

assegnare *premio* award; (*destinare*) assign; **assegno** *m* cheque, *Am* check; **~ in bianco** blank cheque; **~ turistico** traveller's cheque, *Am* traveler's check; **contro ~** cash on delivery, *Am* collect on delivery; **-i familiari** child benefit; **emettere un ~** write a cheque

assemblea *f* meeting

assentarsi go away, leave; **assente** absent, away; *fig* absent-minded; **assenza** *f* absence; **~ di qc** lack of sth

assessore *m* councillor, *Am* councilor; **~ comunale** local councillor

assicurare insure; (*legare*) secure; *lettera, pacco* register; **assicurarsi** make sure, ensure; **assicurata** *f* registered letter; **assicurato 1** *agg* insured; *lettera, pacco* registered **2** *m*, **-a** *f* person with insurance, insured party; **assicurazione** *f* insurance

assideramento *m* exposure

assieme together

assillante nagging; **assillare** pester; **assillo** *m fig*: *persona* pest F, nuisance; (*preoccupazione*) nagging thought

assistente *m/f* assistant; **~ sociale** social worker; **~ di volo** flight attendant; **assistenza** *f* assistance; **~ medica** medical care; **assistere 1** *v/t* assist, help; (*curare*) nurse **2** *v/i* (*essere presente*) be pre-

sent (**a** at)

asso *m* ace

associare take into partnership; *fig* **~ qu a qc** associate s.o. with sth; **associarsi** enter into partnership (**a** with); (*unirsi*) join forces; (*iscriversi*) subscribe (**a** to); (*prendere parte*) join (**a** sth); **associazione** *f* association

assolo *m inv* MUS solo

assolto *pp* ☞ **assolvere**

assolutamente absolutely; **assoluto** absolute; **assoluzione** *f* DIR acquittal; REL absolution; **assolvere** DIR acquit; *da un obbligo* release; *compito* carry out; REL absolve, give absolution to

assomigliare: **~ a qu** be like s.o., resemble s.o.; **assomigliarsi** be like o resemble each other

assonnato sleepy

assorbente 1 *agg* absorbent **2** *m*: **~ igienico** sanitary towel, *Am* sanitary napkin; **assorbire** absorb

assordante deafening; **assordare 1** *v/t* deafen **2** *v/i* go deaf

assortimento *m* assortment

assorto engrossed

assuefatto *pp* ☞ **assuefare**; **assuefazione** *f* resistance, tolerance; *agli alcolici, alla droga* addiction

assumere *impiegato, incarico* take on

assunzione *f di impiegato* employment; REL ***Assunzione*** Assumption

assurdità *f inv* absurdity; **assurdo** absurd

asta *f* pole; FIN auction; ***mettere all'~*** sell at auction

astemio 1 *agg* abstemious **2** *m*, **-a** *f* abstemious person; **astenersi: ~ da** abstain from

asterisco *m* asterisk

astigmatico astigmatic; **astigmatismo** *m* astigmatism

astinenza *f* abstinence

astio *m* rancour, *Am* rancor

astratto abstract

astringente *m/agg* MED astringent

astro *m* star; **astrologia** *f* astrology; **astronauta** *m/f* astronaut; **astronave** *f* spaceship; **astronomia** *f* astronomy; **astronomico** astronomical

astuccio *m* case

astuto astute

ateo *m*, **-a** *f* atheist

atlante *m* atlas

atlantico Atlantic; ***Oceano m Atlantico*** Atlantic Ocean

atleta *m/f* athlete; **atletica** *f* athletics; **~ leggera** track and field (events); **atletico** athletic

atmosfera *f* atmosphere; **atmosferico** atmospheric

atomico atomic; **atomo** *m* atom

atrio *m* foyer, *Am* lobby

atroce atrocious; **atrocità** *f inv* atrocity

attaccabrighe *m* o *f inv* F troublemaker; **attaccante** *m* SP forward; **attaccapanni** *m inv* clothes hook; *a stelo* clothes hanger; **attaccare 1** *v/t* attach; *(incollare)* stick; *(appendere)* hang; *(assalire)* attack **2** *v/i* stick; **attaccarsi** stick; *(aggrapparsi)* hold on (**a** to); **attacco** *m* attack; *(punto di unione)* junction; SCI binding; MED fit

atteggiamento *m* attitude; **atteggiarsi: ~ a** pose as

attendere 1 *v/t* wait for **2** *v/i*: **~ a** attend to

attendibile reliable

attenersi stick (**a** to)

attentare: ~ a attack; **~ alla vita di qu** make an attempt on s.o.'s life; **attentato** *m* attempted assassination

attento 1 *agg* attentive; ***stare ~ a*** be careful of **2** *int* **~!** look out!, (be) careful!

attenuante *f* extenuating circumstance; **attenuare** reduce; *colpo* cushion; **attenuarsi** lessen

attenzione *f* attention; **~!** look out!, (be) careful!; ***far ~ a qc*** mind o watch sth

atterraggio *m* landing; **atterrare 1** *v/t avversario* knock down **2** *v/i* land

attesa *f* waiting; *(tempo d'attesa)* wait; *(aspettativa)* expectation

atteso pp ☞ **attendere**

attestato m certificate

attico m attic

attimo m moment; **un ~!** just a moment!

attirare attract

attitudine f aptitude; **avere ~ per qc** have an aptitude for sth

attivare activate; **attività** f inv activity; pl FIN assets; **attivo 1** agg active **2** m FIN assets; GRAM active (voice)

atto m act; (gesto) gesture; documento deed; **mettere in ~** carry out; **prendere ~ di** note

attorcigliare, attorcigliarsi twist

attore m, **-trice** f actor; donna anche actress

attorno: **~ a qc** around sth; **qui ~** around here

attraccare MAR berth, dock

attraente attractive; **attrarre** attract; **attrattiva** f attraction; **attratto** pp ☞ **attrarre**

attraversare strada, confine cross; **un momento difficile** be going through a bad patch; **attraverso** across

attrazione f attraction

attrezzare equip; **attrezzarsi** get o.s. kitted out; **attrezzato** equipped; **attrezzatura** f equipment, gear F; **attrezzo** m piece of equipment

attribuire attribute

attrice f actress

attuale current; **attualità** f inv

news sg; **d'~** topical; **attuare** put into effect; **attuazione** f putting into effect

audace bold

audioleso 1 agg hearing-impaired **2** m, **-a** f person who is hearing-impaired

audiovisivo audiovisual

audizione f audition

augurare wish; **augurio** m wish; **tanti -ri!** all the best!

aula f di scuola class room; di università lecture room

aumentare increase; **aumento** m increase

aureola f halo

auricolare m earphone

aurora f dawn

ausiliare m/agg auxiliary

australe southern

Australia f Australia; **australiano 1** agg Australian **2** m, **-a** f Australian

Austria f Austria; **austriaco 1** agg Austrian **2** m, **-a** f Austrian

autenticare authenticate; **autentico** authentic

autista m/f driver

auto f inv ☞ **automobile**

autoadesivo 1 agg self-adhesive **2** m sticker

autoambulanza f ambulance

autobiografia f autobiography

autobomba f car bomb

autobus m bus; **~ di linea** city bus

autocarro m truck, Br anche lorry

autocisterna f tanker

autocontrollo m self-control

autodidatta m/f self-taught person

autodifesa f self-defence, Am self-defense

autodromo m motor racing circuit

autogol m inv own goal

autografo m autograph

autogrill m inv roadside café

autolavaggio m car-wash

automa m robot

automatico 1 agg automatic 2 m bottone press-stud, Am snap fastener

automezzo m motor vehicle

automobile f car, Am anche automobile; **automobilismo** m driving; SP motor racing; **automobilista** m/f driver

autonoleggio m car rental; azienda car-rental firm

autonomia f autonomy; TEC battery life; **autonomo** autonomous

autoradio f inv car radio

autore m, **-trice** f author; DIR perpetrator; **autorevole** authoritative

autorimessa f garage

autorità f inv authority; **autoritario** authoritarian; **autorizzare** authorize; **autorizzazione** f authorization

autoscuola f driving school

autostop m: **fare l'~** hitchhike; **autostoppista** m/f hitchhiker

autostrada f motorway, Am highway

autovettura f motor vehicle

autrice f ☞ **autore**

autunno m autumn, Am fall

avambraccio m forearm

avanguardia f avant-garde; azienda leading-edge

avanti 1 avv in front, ahead; **d'ora in ~** from now on; **andare ~ di orologio** be fast; **essere ~ nel programma** be ahead of schedule **2** int **~!** come in!

avanzare 1 v/i advance; fig make progress; (rimanere) be left over **2** v/t put forward

avanzo m remainder; FIN surplus; **gli -i** pl the leftovers

avaria f failure; **avariato** damaged; **cibi** spoiled

avarizia f avarice; **avaro 1** agg miserly **2** m, **-a** f miser

avena f oats

avere 1 v/t have; **~ 20 anni** be 20 (years old); **~ fame / sonno** be hungry / sleepy; **~ caldo / freddo** be hot / cold; **avercela con qu** have it in for s.o **2** v/aus have; **hai visto Tony?** have you seen Tony?; **hai visto Tony ieri?** did you see Tony yesterday? **3** m FIN credit; **-i** mpl wealth

avi mpl ancestors

aviazione f aviation; MIL Air Force

avidità f avidness; **avido** avid

avocado m avocado

avorio *m* ivory

avvalersi: ~ *di qc* avail o.s. of sth

avvantaggiare favour, *Am* favor; avvantaggiarsi: ~ *di qc* take advantage of sth

avveduto astute

avvelenamento *m* poisoning; avvelenare poison; avvelenarsi poison o.s.

avvenimento *m* event; avvenire 1 *v/i (accadere)* happen 2 *m* future

Avvento *m* Advent

avventura *f* adventure; avventurarsi venture; avventuriero *m*, -a *f* adventurer; *donna* adventuress; avventuroso adventurous

avvenuto *pp* ☞ *avvenire*

avverarsi come true

avverbio *m* adverb

avversario 1 *agg* opposing 2 *m*, -a *f* opponent, adversary

avversione *f* aversion (*per* to)

avvertenza *f (ammonimento)* warning; *(premessa)* foreword; *-e pl (istruzioni per l'uso)* instructions

avvertimento *m* warning; avvertire warn; *(percepire)* catch

avviamento *m* introduction; TEC, AUTO start-up; avviare start; avviarsi set out, head off; avviato established

avvicendarsi alternate

avvicinare approach; ~ *qc a*

qc move sth closer to sth; avvicinarsi approach, near (*a* sth)

avvilire depress; *(mortificare)* humiliate; avvilirsi demean o.s.; *(scoraggiarsi)* get depressed; avvilito *(scoraggiato)* depressed

avvio *m*: *dare l'~ a qc* get sth under way

avvisare inform, advise; *(mettere in guardia)* warn; avviso *m* notice; *a mio ~* in my opinion

avvitare screw in; *fissare* screw

avvocato *m* lawyer

avvolgere wrap; avvolgibile *m* roller blind; avvolto *pp* ☞ *avvolgere*

avvoltoio *m* vulture

azienda *f* business; aziendale company *attr*

azionare activate; *allarme* set off; azionario share *attr*; azione *f* action; *(effetto)* influence; FIN share; azionista *m/f* stockholder, shareholder

azoto *m* nitrogen

azzannare bite into

azzardarsi dare; azzardo *m* hazard; *gioco m d'~* game of chance

azzerare TEC reset

azzuffarsi come to blows

azzurro 1 *agg* blue 2 *m* blue; SP *gli -i pl* the Italian national team

B

babbo *m* F dad F, pop F; *Babbo Natale* Santa (Claus), *Br anche* Father Christmas

babordo *m* MAR port (side)

baby-sitter *m/f inv* baby-sitter

bacato wormeaten

bacca *f* berry

baccalà *m inv* dried salt cod

baccano *m* din

bacchetta *f* rod; MUS *del direttore d'orchestra* baton; *per suonare il tamburo* (drum) stick; **~ *magica*** magic wand

bacheca *f* notice board, *Am* bulletin board; *di museo* showcase

baciare kiss; **baciarsi** kiss (each other)

bacillo *m* bacillus

bacinella *f* basin; FOT tray

bacino *m* basin; ANAT pelvis; MAR port

bacio *m* kiss

baco *m* worm; **~ *da seta*** silkworm

bada: *tenere a ~ qu* keep s.o. at bay; **badare:** **~ *a*** look after; *(fare attenzione a)* look out for, mind

baffo *m*: **-i** *pl* moustache, *Am* mustache; *di animali* whiskers

bagagliaio *m* FERR luggage van, *Am* baggage car; AUTO boot, *Am* trunk; **bagaglio** *m*

luggage, baggage; *fare i **-i*** pack

bagliore *m* glare; *di speranza* glimmer

bagnante *m/f* bather; **bagnare** wet; *(immergere)* dip; *(inzuppare)* soak; *(annaffiare)* water; *di fiume* flow through; **bagnarsi** get wet; **bagnato** wet; **bagnino** *m*, **-a** *f* lifeguard; **bagno** *m* bath, *Am* (bath)tub; *stanza* bathroom; *gabinetto* toilet; *fare il ~* have a bath; *mettere a ~* soak; **bagnomaria** *m inv* double boiler, bain marie

baia *f* bay

baita *f* mountain chalet, *Am* mountain lodge

balaustra *f* balustrade

balbettare stammer; *di bambino* babble; **balbettio** *m* stammering; *di bambino* babble, prattle

balbuzie *f* stutter; **balbuziente** *m/f* stutterer

balconata *f* TEA dress circle, *Am* balcony; **balcone** *m* balcony

baldoria *f* revelry; *fare ~* have a riotous time

balena *f* whale

balenare *fig gli è balenata un'idea* an idea flashed through his mind; **baleno** *m* lightning; *in un ~* in a flash

balia f: **in** ~ **di** at the mercy of

balla f bale; fig F (frottola) fib F

ballare dance

ballata f MUS ballad

ballerina f dancer; di balletto ballet dancer; di rivista chorus girl; scarpa ballet shoe; **ballerino** m dancer; di balletto ballet dancer

balletto m ballet

ballo m dance; (il ballare) dancing; (festa) ball; **essere in** ~ persona be involved; (essere in gioco) be at stake; **tirare in** ~ **qc** bring sth up

balneare centro seaside attr

balordo 1 agg ragionamento shaky; idea stupid; tempo, consiglio unreliable **2** m (teppista) lout

balsamico aceto balsamic; aria balmy; **balsamo** m per i capelli hair conditioner

balzare jump, leap; balzo m jump, leap; fig **cogliere la palla al** ~ jump at the chance

bambinaia f nanny; **bambino** m, -a f child; in fasce baby

bambola f doll; **bambolotto** m baby boy doll

bambù m bamboo

banale banal; **banalità** f inv banality

banana f banana

banca f bank; INFOR ~ **dati** data bank

bancarella f stall

bancario 1 agg istituto, segreto

banking attr; deposito, estratto conto bank attr **2** m, -a f bank employee

bancarotta f bankruptcy

banchetto m banquet

banchiere m banker

banchina f FERR platform; MAR quay; di strada verge

banchisa f ice floe

banco m FIN bank; di scuola desk; di bar bar; di chiesa pew; di negozio counter; **bancomat®** m inv (distributore) ATM; carta cash card, debit card

bancone m (work)bench

banconota f banknote, Am bill

banda f band; di delinquenti gang; banda f larga broadband

banderuola f weathercock (anche fig)

bandiera f flag

bandire proclaim; concorso announce; (esiliare) banish; fig (abolire) dispense with; **bandito** m bandit; **bando** m proclamation; (esilio) banishment

bar m inv bar

bara f coffin

baracca f hut; spreg hovel; **baraccopoli** f inv shanty town

barare cheat

baratro m abyss

barattare barter

barattolo m can, Br anche tin; di vetro jar

batticuore

barba f beard; **farsi la~** shave; fig **che ~!** what a pain! F

barbabietola f beetroot, Am red beet; **~ da zucchero** sugar beet

barbarico barbaric; **barbaro 1** agg barbarous **2** m barbarian

barbecue m inv barbecue

barbiere m barber

barboncino m (miniature) poodle

barbone¹ m cane poodle

barbone² m, -a f (vagabondo) tramp, Am hobo

barca f boat; **~ a remi** rowing boat, Am rowboat; **~ a vela** sailing boat, Am sail boat

barcaiolo m boatman

barcollare stagger

barcone m barge

barella f stretcher

barile m barrel

barista m/f barman; donna barmaid; Am bartender; proprietario bar owner

baritono m baritone

barocco m/agg Baroque

barometro m barometer

barone m, -essa f baron; donna baroness

barra f bar

barricata f barricade

barriera f barrier (anche fig)

barzelletta f joke

basare base; **basarsi** be based (**su** on)

basco m (berretto) beret

base f base; fig basis; **in ~ a** on the basis of

basette fpl sideburns

basilica f basilica

basilico m basil

basso 1 agg low; di statura short; MUS bass; fig despicable **2** avv: **in ~** stato down below; **da ~** in una casa downstairs **3** m MUS bass; **basso-piano** m GEOG lowland; **bassorilievo** m bas-relief; **bassotto** m dachshund

basta ☞ **bastare**

bastardo m, -a f cane mongrel; fig bastard

bastare be enough; (durare) last; **basta!** that's enough; **basta che** (purché) as long as

bastonare beat; **bastone** m stick; di pane baguette, French stick

battaglia f battle (anche fig)

battello m boat

battente m di porta wing; di finestra shutter

battere 1 v/i (bussare, dare colpi) knock **2** v/t beat; record break; **~ le mani** clap (one's hands); **~ al computer** key

batteri mpl bacteria

batteria f battery; MUS drums; **batterista** m/f drummer

battersela run off; **battersi** fight

battesimo m christening, baptism; **battezzare** christen, baptize

battibecco m argument; **batticuore** m palpitations; fig **con un gran ~** with great anxiety; **battipanni** *m inv* carpet beater

battistero *m* baptistry

battistrada *m inv* AUTO tread

battito *m* beating, beat; **~ cardiaco** heartbeat

battuta *f* beat; *in dattilografia* keystroke; MUS bar; TEA cue; *nel tennis* service; **~ (di spirito)** wisecrack

baule *m* trunk; AUTO boot, *Am* trunk

bavaglino *m* bib

bavaglio *m* gag

bavero *m* collar

bazzecola *f* trifle

bazzicare 1 *v/t* **un posto** haunt; *persone* associate with **2** *v/i* hang about

beatificare beatify; **beato** happy; REL blessed; **~ te!** lucky you!

beauty-case *m inv* toilet bag

bebè *m inv* baby

beccare peck; F *fig (cogliere sul fatto)* nab F; F *fig: malattia* catch, pick up F; **beccarsi** F *malattia* catch, pick up F

becchino *m* grave digger

becco *m* beak; *di teiera ecc* spout

befana *f kind old witch who brings presents to children on Twelfth Night*, REL Twelfth Night; *fig* old witch

beffa *f* hoax; **farsi ~e di qu** make a fool of s.o.; **beffardo** scornful; **beffare** mock; **beffarsi: ~ di** mock

bega *f (litigio)* fight, argu

ment; *(problema)* can of worms

begli ☞ **bello**

bei ☞ **bello**

belare bleat

belga *agg, m/f* Belgian; **Belgio** *m* Belgium

bellezza *f* beauty

bellico *(di guerra)* war *attr*; *(del tempo di guerra)* wartime *attr*

bello 1 *agg* beautiful; *uomo* handsome; *tempo* fine, nice, beautiful; **questa è ~a!** that's a good one!; **nel bel mezzo** right in the middle **2** *m* beauty; **sul più ~** at the worst possible moment

belva *f* wild beast

belvedere *m inv* viewpoint

bemolle *m* MUS flat

benché although

benda *f* bandage; *per occhi* blindfold; **bendare** MED bandage

bene 1 *avv* well; **~!** good!; *per* **~** properly; **stare ~ di salute** be well; *di vestito* suit; **ben ti sta!** serves you right!; **va ~!** OK!; **andare ~ a qu** *di abito* fit s.o.; *di orario, appuntamento* suit s.o; **sentirsi ~** feel well **2** *m* good; **fare ~ alla salute** be good for you; **per il tuo ~** for your own good; **voler ~ a qu** love s.o; *(amare)* love s.o; **~i** *pl* assets, property; **~i immobili** *pl* real estate

benedetto 1 *pp* ☞ **benedire 2** *agg* blessed; REL **acqua ~a**

holy water; **benedire** bless; **benedizione** f blessing
beneducato well-mannered
beneficenza f charity; **spettacolo** m **di ~** benefit (performance)
beneficio m benefit; **a ~ di** for the benefit of; **benefico** beneficial; **organizzazione**, **istituto** charitable; **spettacolo** charity attr
benessere m well-being; (**agiatezza**) affluence; **benestante 1** agg well-off **2** m/f person with money
benigno MED benign
beninteso of course; **~ che** provided that
benone splendid
benpensante m/f moderate; spreg conformist
bensì but rather
benvenuto 1 agg welcome **2** m welcome; **dare il ~ a qu** welcome s.o.
benvolere: farsi ~ da qu win s.o. over
benzina f petrol, Am gas; **fare ~** get petrol; **benzinaio** m, **-a** f petrol o Am gas station attendant
bere drink; fig swallow
berlina f AUTO saloon, Am sedan
bermuda mpl Bermuda shorts
bernoccolo m bump
berretto m cap
berrò ☞ **bere**
bersaglio m target; fig: di

scherzi butt
bestemmia f swear-word; **bestemmiare 1** v/i swear (**contro** at) **2** v/t curse
bestia f animal; fig **andare in ~** fly into a rage; **bestiale** bestial; F (**molto intenso**) terrible; **bestiame** m livestock
bettola f spreg dive
betulla f birch
bevanda f drink
beve ☞ **bere**
biada f fodder
biancheria f linen; **~ intima** underwear
bianco 1 agg white; **foglio** blank **2** m white; **~ d'uovo** egg white; **mangiare in ~** avoid rich food; **in ~ e nero** film black and white
biasimare blame; **biasimo** m blame
bibbia f bible
biberon m inv baby's bottle
bibita f soft drink
bibliografia f bibliography
biblioteca f library; **mobile** book-case; **bibliotecario** m, **-a** f librarian
bicamerale POL two-chamber
bicarbonato m: **~ (di sodio)** bicarbonate of soda
bicchiere m glass
bicentenario m bicentenary, Am bicentennial
bici f inv F bike f; **bicicletta** f bike, bicycle; **andare in ~** go by bike, Br anche cycle
bidè m inv bidet

bidone

bidone m drum; *della spazzatura* (dust)bin, Am garbage can; F (*imbroglio*) swindle

biennale biennial; (*che dura due anni*) two-year; **biennio** m two-year period

bietola f beet

biforcarsi fork; **biforcazione** f fork

bigamo m, -a f bigamist

bigiotteria f costume jewellery o Am jewelry; *negozio* jeweller's, Am jewelry store

bigliettaio m,-a f ticket seller; *sul treno, tram* conductor, Am guard; **biglietteria** f ticket office; *di cinema, teatro* box office; **biglietto** m ticket; ~ *d'auguri* (greetings) card; ~ *da visita* business card; *un* ~ *da 10 dollari* a ten-dollar bill; *fare il* ~ buy the ticket

bigodino m roller

bigotto 1 agg bigoted **2** m,-a f bigot

bikini m inv bikini

bilancia f scales; ASTR *Bilancia* Libra; **bilanciare** balance; (*pareggiare*) equal; fig weigh up; FIN ~ *un conto* balance an account; **bilanciarsi** balance; **bilancio** m balance; (*rendiconto*) balance sheet; ~ *preventivo* budget; *fare il* ~ draw up a balance sheet; fig take stock

bile f bile; fig rage

biliardo m billiards sg, Am pool

bilico m: *essere in* ~ be precariously balanced; fig be undecided

bilingue bilingual

bilocale m two-room flat o Am apartment

bimbo m, -a f child

bimotore m twin-engine plane

binario 1 agg binary **2** m track; (*marciapiede*) platform

binocolo m binoculars

biochimica f biochemistry

biodegradabile biodegradable

biografia f biography; **biografico** biographical; **biografo** m, -a f biographer

biologia f biology; **biologico** biological; *alimento* organic; **biologo** m, -a f biologist

biondo blonde

biossido m dioxide

birbante m rascal

birichino 1 agg naughty **2** m, -a f little devil

birillo m skittle

biro® f inv ballpoint (pen), Br *anche* biro

birra f beer; ~ *alla spina* draught o Am draft beer; **birreria** f pub that sells only beer; *fabbrica* brewery

bis m inv encore

bisbetico bad-tempered

bisbigliare whisper

bisca f gambling den

biscia f grass snake

biscotto m biscuit, Am cookie

bisessuale bisexual

bisestile: anno *m* ~ leap year

bisnonno *m*, -a *f* great-grandfather; **donna** great-grandmother

bisognare: bisogna farlo it must be done, it needs to be done; **non bisogna farlo** it doesn't have to be done, there's no need to do it; **bisogno** *m* need; (*mancanza*) lack; (*fabbisogno*) requirements; **avere ~ di qc** need sth; **bisognoso** needy

bisonte *m* ZO bison

bistecca *f* steak

bisticciare quarrel; **bisticcio** *m* quarrel

bisturi *m inv* MED scalpel

bitter *m inv* aperitif

bivio *m* junction; *fig* crossroads *sg*

bizantino Byzantine

bizzarro bizarre

bizzeffe: a ~ galore

blando mild, gentle

blatta *f* cockroach

blindato armoured, *Am* armored

blitz *m inv* blitz

bloccare block; MIL blockade; (*isolare*) cut off; *prezzi, conto* freeze; **bloccarsi** *di ascensore, persona* get stuck; *di freni, traffico* jam; **bloccaruota** *m* AUTO wheel clamp, *Am* Denver boot; **mettere il ~ a** clamp; **bloccasterzo** *m* AUTO steering lock

blocchetto *m per appunti* notebook

blocco *m* block; *di carta* pad; **~ stradale** road block

bloc-notes *m inv* writing pad

blu blue

blusa *f* blouse

boa[1] *m inv* ZO boa constrictor

boa[2] *f* MAR buoy

boato *m* rumble

bob *m inv* SP bobsleigh, bobsled; **bobbista** *m/f* bobsledder

bobina *f* spool

bocca *f* mouth; (*apertura*) opening; **in ~ al lupo!** good luck!; **boccaccia** *f* (*smorfia*) grimace; **boccaglio** *m* di maschera per il nuoto mouthpiece

boccale *m* jug; *da birra* tankard

boccetta *f* small bottle

boccheggiare gasp

bocchino *m per sigarette* cigarette holder; MUS, *di pipa* mouthpiece

boccia *f* (*palla*) bowl; **bocciare** (*respingere*) reject, vote down; EDU fail; **boccia** hit, strike; **bocciatura** *f* failure

bocciolo *m* bud

bocconcino *m* morsel; **boccone** *m* mouthful

bocconi face down

body *m inv* body(suit)

boia *m inv* executioner; F **fa un freddo ~** it's freezing

boicottaggio *m* boycott; **boicottare** boycott

bolide m meteor; **come un ~** like greased lightning

bolla[1] f bubble; MED blister

bolla[2] f documento note, docket; MED blister; **~ di consegna** delivery note

bollare stamp; fig brand

bollente boiling hot

bolletta f bill; **~ della luce** electricity bill

bollettino m: **~ meteorologico** weather forecast

bollire boil; **bollito 1** agg boiled **2** m boiled meat; **bollitore** m kettle

bollo m stamp

bomba f bomb; **bombardamento** m shelling, bombardment; (attacco aereo) air raid; fig bombardment; **bombardare** bomb; fig bombard

bombola f cylinder

bomboniera f wedding keepsake

bonaccia f MAR calm

bonaccione m, **-a** f kindhearted person

bonario kind-hearted

bonificare FIN (scontare) discount; (accreditare) credit; AGR reclaim; (prosciugare) drain; **bonifico** m (trasferimento) (money) transfer

bontà f inv goodness; (gentilezza) kindness

bora f bora (a cold north wind)

borbottare mumble

bordello m brothel; fig F bedlam F; (disordine) mess

bordo m (orlo) edge; **a ~** on board

boreale northern; **aurora** f **~** northern lights

borgata f village; (rione popolare) suburb

borghese middle-class; **in ~** in civilian clothes; borghesia f middle classes pl

borgo m village

borraccia f flask

borsa f bag; (borsetta) handbag, Am purse; per documenti briefcase; FIN Stock Market; **~ di studio** scholarship; **borsaiolo** m, **-a** f pickpocket; **borsellino** m purse, Am coin purse; **borsetta** f handbag, Am purse

borsista m/f speculatore speculator; studente scholarship holder

boscaiolo m woodcutter; **bosco** m wood

bossolo m di proiettili (shell) case

botanico 1 agg botanical **2** m, **-a** f botanist

botola f trapdoor

botta f blow; (rumore) bang; **fare a -e** come to blows

botte f barrel

bottega f shop; (laboratorio) workshop; **bottegaio** m, **-a** f shopkeeper; **botteghino** m box office; (del lotto) sales outlet for lottery tickets

bottiglia f bottle

bottino m loot

botto *m* (*rumore*) bang

bottone *m* button; **~ automatico** press-stud, *Am* snap fastener

bovino **1** *agg* bovine **2** *m*: **-i** *pl* cattle *pl*

box *m inv per auto* lock-up (garage); *per bambini* playpen; *per cavalli* loose box

boxe *f* boxing

bozza *f* draft; TIP proof; **bozzetto** *m* sketch

bozzolo *m* cocoon

braccetto *m*: **a ~** arm in arm

bracciale *m* bracelet; (*fascia*) armband; *di orologio* watch strap; **braccialetto** *m* bracelet; **bracciante** *m/f* day labourer, *Am* day laborer

bracciata *f* nel nuoto stroke; **braccio** *m* arm; **portare in ~ qu** carry s.o.; **bracciolo** *m* arm(rest)

bracconiere *m* poacher

brace *f* embers; **alla ~** char-grilled, *Am* char-broiled

braciola *f* GASTR chop

branca *f* branch (*anche fig*)

branchia *f* gill

branco *m di cani, lupi* pack; *di pecore, uccelli* flock; *fig spreg* gang

brancolare grope

branda *f* camp-bed, *Am* cot

brandello *m* shred, scrap; **a -i** in shreds *o* tatters

brano *m di testo, musica* passage

brasato *m di manzo* braised beef

Brasile *m* Brazil; **brasiliano 1** *agg* Brazilian **2** *m*, **-a** *f* Brazilian

bravata *f* boasting; *azione* bravado

bravo good; (*abile*) clever, good; **~!** well done!; **bravura** *f* skill

bretella *f* (*raccordo*) slip road, *Am* ramp; **-e** *pl* braces, *Am* suspenders

breve short; **in ~** briefly, in short

brevettare patent; **brevetto** *m* patent; *di pilota* licence, *Am* license

brezza *f* breeze

bricco *m* jug, *Am* pitcher

briciola *f* crumb; **briciolo** *m* fig grain, scrap

bricolage *m* do-it-yourself, DIY, *Am* home improvement

briga *f*: **darsi la ~ di fare qc** take the trouble to do sth; **attaccar ~ con qu** pick a quarrel with s.o.

brigadiere *m* MIL sergeant

brigante *m* bandit

briglia *f* rein

brillante **1** *agg* sparkling; *colore* bright; *fig* brilliant **2** *m* diamond; **brillare** shine

brillo tipsy

brina *f* hoar-frost

brindare drink a toast (**a** to); **~ alla salute di qu** drink to s.o.'s health; **brindisi** *m inv* toast

brioche *f inv* brioche

britannico 1 *agg* British **2** *m*, -a *f* Briton, Brit F

brivido *m di freddo, spavento* shiver; *di emozione* thrill

brizzolato *capelli* greying, *Am* graying

brocca *f* jug, *Am* pitcher

broccato *m* brocade

broccoli *mpl* broccoli *sg*

brodo *m* (clear) soup; *di pollo, di manzo, di verdura* stock; **brodoso** watery, thin

bronchite *f* bronchitis

broncio *m*: **avere il ~** sulk

broncopolmonite *f* bronchial pneumonia

brontolare grumble; *di stomaco* rumble; **brontolio** *m* grumble; *di stomaco* rumble; **brontolone 1** *agg* grumbling **2** *m*, -a *f* grumbler

bronzo *m* bronze

bruciapelo: **a ~** point-blank; **bruciare 1** *v/t* burn; (*incendiare*) set fire to **2** *v/i* burn; *fig: di occhi* sting; **bruciarsi** burn o.s.; **bruciato** burnt; *dal sole* scorched, parched; **bruciatura** *f* burn; **bruciore** *m* burning sensation; **~ di stomaco** heartburn

bruco *m* grub; (*verme*) worm

brufolo *m* spot

brulicare swarm

brullo bare

bruno brown; *capelli* dark

brusco sharp; *persona, modi* brusque, abrupt; (*improvviso*) sudden

brutale brutal; **brutalità** *f inv* brutality

brutta *f*: (**copia** *f*) **~** rough copy; **bruttezza** *f* ugliness; **brutto** ugly; (*cattivo*) bad; *tempo, tipo, affare* nasty

Bruxelles *f* Brussels

buca *f* hole; (*avvallamento*) hollow; *del biliardo* pocket; **~ delle lettere** letter-box, *Am* mailbox; **bucare** make a hole in; (*pungere*) prick; *biglietto* punch; **~ una gomma** have a flat (tyre); **bucarsi** prick o.s.; *con droga* shoot up

bucato *m* washing, laundry; **fare il ~** do the washing

buccia *f* peel

bucherellare make holes in; **bucherellato dai tarli** riddled with woodworm

buco *m* hole

budello *m* gut; (*vicolo*) alley

budget *m inv* budget

budino *m* pudding

bue *m* ox; *carne* beef

bufalo *m* buffalo

bufera *f* storm

buffet *m inv* buffet; *mobile* sideboard, *Am* buffet

buffo funny; **buffone** *m*, -a *f* buffoon, fool; *di corte* fool, jester

bugia *f* (*menzogna*) lie; **bugiardo 1** *agg* lying **2** *m*, -a *f* liar

buio 1 *agg* dark **2** *m* darkness; **al ~** in the dark

bulbo *m* BOT bulb

Bulgaria *f* Bulgaria; **bulgaro**

1 *agg* Bulgarian **2** *m*, -a *f* Bulgarian

bullone *m* bolt

buoi ☞ **bue**

buon ☞ **buono**

buonafede *f*: **in ~** in good faith

buonanotte good night

buonasera good evening

buongiorno good morning, hello

buongustaio *m*, -a *f* gourmet; **buongusto** *m* good taste; **di ~** in good taste

buono 1 *agg* good; *momento* right; **alla -a** informal, casual **2** *m* good; FIN bond; *(tagliando)* voucher; **~ regalo** gift voucher, *Am* gift certificate; **~ sconto** discount voucher

buonsenso *m* common sense

buonuscita *f* *(liquidazione)* golden handshake

burattino *m* puppet

burbero gruff, surly

burla *f* practical joke, trick; **burlarsi**: **~ di qu** make fun

of s.o.; **burlone** *m*, -a *f* joker

burocratico bureaucratic; **burocrazia** *f* bureaucracy

burrasca *f* storm; **burrascoso** stormy

burro *m* butter

burrone *m* ravine

bussare knock

bussola *f* compass

busta *f* *per lettera* envelope; *per documenti* folder; *(astuccio)* case; **~ paga** pay packet

bustarella *f* bribe

bustina *f*: **~ di tè** tea bag

busto *m* ANAT torso; *scultura* bust; *(corsetto)* girdle

buttafuori *m inv* TEA callboy; *di locale notturno* bouncer; **buttare 1** *v/i* BOT sprout **2** *v/t* throw; **~ via** throw away; *fig* waste; **~ giù** knock down; *lettera* scribble down; *boccone* gulp down; **~ la pasta** put the pasta on; **buttarsi** throw o.s.; *fig* have a go (**in** at)

by-pass *m inv* by-pass

byte *m inv* INFOR byte

C

ca (= **circa**) ca (= circa)

c.a. (= **corrente alternata**) AC (= alternating current)

cabina *f di nave, aereo* cabin; *di ascensore, funivia* cage; **~ telefonica** phone box, *Am* pay phone

cabriolè, cabriolet *m inv* convertible

cacao *m* cocoa

caccia *f* hunting; **cacciagione** *f* GASTR game; **cacciare** hunt; *(scacciare)* drive out; *(ficcare)* shove; **~ via** chase away; **cacciarsi**: **dove ti eri cacciato?** where did you get to?; **cacciatora** f: **alla ~** stewed; **cacciatore** m, **-trice** f hunter; **cacciavite** m inv screwdriver

cachemire m inv cashmere

cactus m inv cactus

cadavere m corpse

cadente: **stella f ~** falling star; **cadere** fall; di edificio fall down; di capelli, denti fall out; di aereo crash; **caduta** f fall

caffè m inv coffee; locale café; **~ corretto** espresso with a shot of alcohol; **~ macchiato** espresso with a splash of milk; **caffeina** f caffeine; **senza ~** caffeine-free; **caffellatte** m inv hot milk with a small amount of coffee; **caffettiera** f (bricco) coffee pot; (macchinetta) coffee maker

cafone m boor

cagna f bitch

calabrese agg. m/f Calabrian

calabrone m hornet

calamari mpl squid

calamità f inv calamity; **~ naturale** natural disaster

calamita f magnet

calante: **luna f ~** waning moon; **calare 1** v/t lower **2** v/i di vento drop; di prezzi, sipario fall; di sole set, go down

calca f throng

calcagno m heel

calcare¹ (pigiare) press down; con i piedi tread; parole emphasize

calcare² m limestone

calcareo chalky

calce f lime

calcestruzzo m concrete

calciatore m football o soccer player

calcina f (malta) mortar; **calcinaccio** m (intonaco) bit of plaster; di muro bit of rubble

calcio¹ m kick; attività football, soccer; MIL butt; **~ di rigore** penalty kick

calcio² m CHIM calcium

calco m mould, Am mould

calcolare calculate; (valutare) weigh up; **calcolatore** m calculator; fig calculating person; elettronico computer; **calcolatrice** f calculator; **calcolo** m calculation

caldaia f boiler

caldarrosta f roast chestnut

caldo 1 agg warm; (molto caldo) hot **2** m warmth; molto caldo heat; **ho ~** I'm warm; I'm hot

calendario m calendar

calibro m calibre, Am caliber; TEC callipers

calice m goblet; REL chalice

calle f a Venezia lane

calligrafia f calligraphy

callo m corn

calma f calm; **prendersela con ~** take it easy; **calmante** m sedative; **calmare** calm; dolore soothe; **calmarsi** di dolore ease (off); **calmo** calm

calo m di peso loss; dei prezzi

drop, fall

calore *m* warmth; *intenso* heat

caloria *f* calorie

caloroso *fig* warm

calpestare walk on; *fig* trample over

calunnia *f* slander

calvario *m* REL Calvary; *fig* ordeal

calvizie *f* baldness; **calvo** bald

calza *f da donna* stocking; *da uomo* sock; **calzamaglia** *f* tights, *Am* pantyhose; *da ginnastica* leotard; **calzare** 1 *v/t scarpe* put on; *(indossare)* wear 2 *v/i fig* fit; **calzascarpe** *m* shoehorn; **calzatoio** *m* shoehorn; **calzature** *fpl* footwear; **calzettone** *m* knee sock; **calzino** *m* sock; **calzolaio** *m* shoemaker

calzoncini *mpl* shorts; ~ *da bagno* (swimming) trunks

calzone *m* GASTR *folded-over pizza*

calzoni *mpl* trousers, *Am* pants

camaleonte *m* chameleon

cambiale *f* bill (of exchange)

cambiamento *m* change; **cambiare** 1 *v/t* change; *(scambiare)* exchange 2 *v/i e* **cambiarsi** change; **cambio** *m* change; FIN, *(scambio)* exchange; AUTO, TEC gear; *in* ~ in exchange (*di* for)

camera *f* room; ~ *da letto* bedroom; ~ *singola* single

room; ~ *matrimoniale* double room; *Camera dei Deputati* House of Commons, *Am* House of Representatives; ~ *d'aria* inner tube; ~ *dell'industria e del commercio* chamber of commerce; **camerata** *f stanza* dormitory; *in ospedale* ward

cameriera *f* waitress; *(domestica)* maid; **cameriere** *m* waiter

camerino *m* dressing room

camice *m di medico* white coat; *di chirurgo* gown; **camicetta** *f* blouse; **camicia** *f* shirt; ~ *da notte* nightdress

caminetto *m* fireplace; **camino** *m* chimney; *(focolare)* fireplace

camion *m inv* truck, *Br anche* lorry; **camioncino** *m* van; **camionista** *m* lorry driver, *Am* truck driver

cammello *m* camel; *stoffa* camel hair

camminare walk; *(funzionare)* work, go; **camminata** *f* walk; **cammino** *m*: *un'ora di* ~ an hour's walk; *mettersi in* ~ set out

camomilla *f* camomile; *(infuso)* camomile tea

camoscio *m* chamois; *scarpe fpl di* ~ suede shoes

campagna *f* country; *fig*, POL campaign

campana *f* bell; **campanello** *m* bell; *della porta* doorbell; **campanile** *m* bell tower

campare 50

campare live
campeggiatore *m* camper;
campeggio *m* camping; *posto* camp site; camper *m inv*
camper van; camping *m*
camp site
campionario *m* samples
campionato *m* champion-
ship
campione *m* sample; (*esemplare*) specimen; SP champion
campo *m* field; ~ *da golf* golf
course; ~ *da calcio* football
o soccer pitch; ~ *da tennis*
tennis court; ~ *profughi* refugee camp; camposanto *m*
cemetery
Canada *m* Canada; canadese 1 *agg* Canadian 2 *m/f* Canadian 3 *f half-litre bottle of
beer*
canale *m* channel; *artificiale*
canal
canapa *f* hemp
canarino *m* canary
cancellare cross out; *con
gomma* erase; INFOR delete;
appuntamento cancel
cancellata *f* railings
cancelleria *f*: *articoli mpl di* ~
stationery
cancelliere *m* chancellor; DIR
clerk of the court
cancello *m* gate
cancerogeno carcinogenic
cancrena *f* gangrene
cancro *m* MED cancer; ASTR
Cancro Cancer
candeggina *f* bleach

candela *f* candle; candelabro
m candelabra; candeliere *m*
candlestick
candidarsi stand (for election), *Am* run; candidato
m, -a *f* candidate; candidatura *f* candidacy, candi-
dature
candido pure white; (*sincero*)
frank; (*innocente*) innocent,
pure; (*ingenuo*) naive
canditi *mpl* candied fruit
cane *m* dog
canestro *m* basket
canguro *m* kangaroo
canile *m* (*casotto*) kennel; *luogo* kennels
canino 1 *agg* dog *attr* 2 *m*
(*dente*) canine (tooth)
canna *f* reed; (*bastone*) stick;
P joint P; ~ *da pesca* fishing
rod
cannella *f* GASTR cinnamon
cannelloni *mpl* cannelloni *sg*
cannibale *m* cannibal
cannocchiale *m* telescope
cannone *m* MIL gun, cannon;
(*asso*) ace
cannuccia *f* straw
canoa *f* canoe
canone *m* FIN rental (fee);
RAD, TV licence (fee); (*norma*) standard
canottaggio *m a pagaie* ca-
noeing; *a remi* rowing
canottiera *f* vest, *Am* undershirt
canotto *m* rowing boat, *Am*
rowboat; ~ *pneumatico* rubber dinghy

cantante *m/f* singer; **cantare** sing; **cantautore** *m*, **-trice** *f* singer-songwriter

cantiere *m* building site; MAR shipyard

cantina *f* cellar; *locale* wine-shop

canto[1] *m* song; (*il cantare*) singing

canto[2] *m*: **d'altro ~** on the other hand

cantone *m* POL canton

canzonare tease

canzone *f* song

caos *m* chaos; **caotico** chaotic

C.A.P. *m* (= *Codice di Avviamento Postale*) postcode, *Am* zip code

capace (*abile*) capable; (*ampio*) large; **~ di fare qc** capable of doing sth; **capacità** *f inv* ability; (*capienza*) capacity

capanna *f* hut; **capannone** *m* shed; AVIA hangar

caparra *f* FIN deposit

capello *m* hair; **-i** *pl* hair

capezzolo *m* nipple

capiente large, capacious; **capienza** *f* capacity

capigliatura *f* hair

capillare MED capillary

capire understand; **capisco** I see; **ho capito** I see

capitale 1 *agg* capital; *fig* major 2 *f città* capital 3 *m* FIN capital; **capitalismo** *m* capitalism; **capitalista** *agg*, *m/f* capitalist

capitaneria *f*: **~ di porto** port authorities

capitano *m* captain

capitare *di avvenimento* happen; *di persona* find o.s.; **~ a proposito** come along at the right time

capitolo *m* chapter

capo *m* head; *persona* head, chief, boss; GEOG cape; **~ di vestiario** item of clothing; **da ~** from the beginning; **andare a ~** start a new paragraph; **capodanno** *m* New Year's Day; **capofamiglia** *m/f* head of the family; **capofitto**: **a ~** headlong; **capogiro** *m* dizzy spell; **capogruppo** *m/f* group leader; POL leader; **capolavoro** *m* masterpiece; **capolinea** *m* terminus; **capoluogo** *m* principal town; **caporeparto** *m/f* di fabbrica foreman; *donna* forewoman; *di ufficio* superintendent; **caposala** *m/f in ospedale* ward sister; *uomo* charge nurse; **capostazione** *m/f* station master; **capostipite** *m/f* founder; **capotavola**: **a ~** at the head of the table; **capotreno** *m/f* guard, *Am* conductor; **capoufficio** *m/f* supervisor; **capoverso** *m* paragraph; TIP indent; **capovolgere** turn upside down; *piani* upset; *situazione* reverse; **capovolgersi** turn upside down; *di barca* capsize; **capovolgimento**

m complete change; **capovolto** *pp* ☞ **capovolgere**

cappa *f* (*mantello*) cloak; *di cucina* hood; **~ del camino** cowl

cappella *f* chapel

cappelletti *mpl* pasta, *shaped like little hats, with meat, cheese and egg filling;* **cappello** *m* hat

cappero *m* caper

cappio *m* noose

cappone *m* capon

cappotto *m* coat

cappuccino *m bevanda* cappuccino

cappuccio *m* hood; *di penna* top, cap

capra *f* (nanny)goat; (*cavalletto*) trestle; **capretto** *m* kid

capriccio *m* whim; *di bambini* tantrum; **fare i -i** have tantrums; **capriccioso** capricious; *bambino* naughty; *tempo* changeable

Capricorno ASTR Capricorn

capriola *f* somersault

capriolo *m* roe deer; GASTR venison; **capro** *m* billy goat; **~ espiatorio** scapegoat

capsula *f* capsule; *di dente* crown

captare RAD pick up

carabiniere *m* police officer

caraffa *f* carafe

caramella *f* sweet

caramello *m* caramel

carato *m* carat

carattere *m* character; (*caratteristica*) characteristic; **-i** *pl*

TIP font; **caratteristica** *f* characteristic; **caratteristico** characteristic; **caratterizzare** characterize

caravan *m inv* caravan

carboidrato *m* carbohydrate

carbone *m* coal; **carbonella** *f* charcoal

carburante *m* fuel

carburatore *m* carburettor, *Am* carburetor

carcassa *f* carcass; TEC (*intelaiatura*) frame; MAR, F wreck

carcerato *m*, **-a** *f* prisoner; **carcerazione** *f* imprisonment; **~ preventiva** preventive detention; **carcere** *m* jail, prison

carciofo *m* artichoke

cardiaco cardiac, heart *attr*

cardinale *m/agg* cardinal

cardiologo *m*, **-a** *f* heart specialist, cardiologist

cardo *m* thistle

carena *f* MAR keel

carenza *f* lack (**di** of)

carestia *f* shortage

carezza *f* caress; **carezzare** caress

cariato: **dente** *m* **~** decayed tooth

carica *f* (*incarico*) office; (*slancio, energia*) drive; TEC load; MIL (*attacco*) charge; SP tackle; **caricare** load; MIL charge; *orologio* wind up; **caricarsi** overload o.s. (**di** with)

caricatura *f* caricature

cartellone

carico 1 *agg* loaded; EL charged **2** *m* load; MAR cargo

carie *f inv* tooth decay

carino (*grazioso*) pretty; (*gentile*) nice

carisma *m* charisma

carità *f* charity

carnagione *f* complexion

carne *f* flesh; GASTR meat; ~ **di maiale / manzo** pork / beef; ~ **tritata** mince, Am ground beef; **carneficina** *f* slaughter

carnevale *m* carnival

carnivoro *m* carnivore

caro 1 *agg* dear; (*costoso*) dear, expensive **2** *avv* a lot; **costare** ~ be very expensive; *fig* have a high price

carogna *f* carrion; F swine

carota *f* carrot

carotide *f* carotid artery

carovana *f* caravan

carovita *m* high cost of living; **indennità** *f* **di** ~ cost of living allowance

carpa *f* carp

carpire: ~ **qc a qu** get sth out of s.o.

carponi on all fours

carrabile → **carraio**

carraio: **passo** *m* ~ driveway

carreggiata *f* roadway

carrello *m* trolley, Am cart; AVIA undercarriage

carretto *m* cart

carriera *f* career

carriola *f* wheelbarrow

carro *m* cart; AST Bear; ~ **ar-**mato tank; ~ **attrezzi** tow truck, Am wrecker

carrozza *f* FERR carriage, Am car; ~ **con cuccette** sleeping car; ~ **ristorante** restaurant car

carrozzella *f* per bambini pram, Am baby carriage; per invalidi wheelchair

carrozzeria *f* bodywork, coachwork; **carrozziere** *m* AUTO (*progettista*) (car) designer; (*costruttore*) coachbuilder; chi fa riparazioni panel beater; **carrozzina** *f* pram, Am baby carriage

carta *f* paper; (*menù*) menu; ~ **geografica** map; ~ **da gioco** (playing) card; ~ **da parati** wallpaper; ~ **di credito** credit card; ~ **d'identità** identity card; ~ **d'imbarco** boarding card; ~ **igienica** toilet paper; ~ **stagnola** silver paper; GASTR tinfoil; ~ **telefonica** phone card; **cartamodello** *m* pattern; **cartapesta** *f* papier-mâché; **cartastraccia** *f* waste paper

cartella *f* (*borsa*) briefcase; di alunno schoolbag; per documenti folder, file; **cartellino** *m* (*etichetta*) label; con prezzo price tag; (*scheda*) card

cartello *m* sign; nelle dimostrazioni placard; FIN cartel; ~ **stradale** road sign

cartellone *m* **pubblicitario** hoarding, Am billboard; TEA bill

cartiera f paper mill

cartilagine f cartilage

cartina f GEOG map; (bustina) packet; per sigarette cigarette paper

cartoccio m paper bag; a cono paper cone; GASTR al ~ baked in tinfoil

cartoleria f stationer's, Am stationery store

cartolina f postcard

cartoncino m (thin) cardboard; (biglietto) card

cartone m cardboard; -i pl animati cartoons

cartuccia f cartridge

casa f edificio house; (abitazione) home; ~ di cura nursing home; ~ editrice publishing house; cambiare ~ move (house); fatto in ~ homemade; andare a ~ go home; essere a ~ be at home; SP giocare in / fuori ~ play at home / away; casalinga f housewife; casalingo domestic; (fatto in casa) home-made; persona home-loving; -ghi mpl household goods

cascare fall; fig cascarci fall for it; **cascata** f waterfall

cascina f (casa colonica) farmhouse; (caseificio) dairy farm

casco m helmet; dal parrucchiere hair dryer

caseggiato m (edificio) block of flats, Am apartment block

caseificio m dairy

casella f di schedario pigeonhole; (quadratino) square; ~ postale post office box; casellario m pigeon holes; (archivi) criminal records (office); casello m autostradale toll booth, pay station

casereccio homemade

caserma f barracks

casinò m inv casino

casino m P brothel; (rumore) din, racket; (disordine) mess

caso m case; (destino) chance; (occasione) opportunity; ~ d'emergenza emergency; per ~ by chance; a ~ at random; in ~ contrario should that not be the case; in ogni ~ in any case, anyway; in nessun ~ under no circumstances

casolare m farmhouse

caspita! good heavens!

cassa f case; di legno crate; di negozio till; sportello cash desk; (banca) bank; ~ toracica ribcage; cassaforte f safe; cassapanca f chest

casseruola f (sauce)pan

cassetta f box; per frutta, verdura crate; (musicassetta) cassette; ~ delle lettere (buca) post box, Am mailbox; (casella) letterbox, Am mailbox

cassetto m drawer; cassettone m chest of drawers

cassiere m, -a f cashier; di

banca teller; *di supermercato* checkout assistant

cassonetto *m* dustbin, *Am* garbage can

casta *f* caste

castagna *f* chestnut; **castagno** *m* chestnut (tree)

castano *capelli* chestnut; *occhi* brown

castello *m* castle

castigo *m* punishment

castità *f* chastity

castoro *m* beaver

castrare castrate; *gatto* neuter; *femmina di animale* spay

casual 1 *agg* casual **2** *m* casual clothes, casual wear; **casuale** chance *attr*, casual

cataclisma *m* disaster

catacomba *f* catacomb

catalizzatore *m* catalyst; AUTO catalytic converter

catalogare catalogue, *Am* catalog; **catalogo** *m* catalogue, *Am* catalog

catapecchia *f* shack

catarifrangente *m* reflector; *lungo la strada* cat's eye, *Am* reflector

catarro *m* catarrh

catasto *m* land register

catastrofe *f* catastrophe; **catastrofico** catastrophic

categoria *f* category; *di albergo* class; **categorico** categoric(al)

catena *f* chain; **-e** *pl* **da neve** snow chains; **~ montuosa** mountain range, chain of mountains

cateratta *f* sluice(gate); (*cascata*) falls

catino *m* basin

catrame *m* tar

cattedra *f* (*scrivania*) desk

cattedrale *f* cathedral

cattiveria *f* wickedness; *di bambini* naughtiness; *azione* nasty thing to do; *parole crudeli* nasty thing to say; **cattivo** bad; *bambino* naughty, bad

cattolicesimo *m* (Roman) Catholicism; **cattolico 1** *agg* (Roman) Catholic **2** *m*, **-a** *f* (Roman) Catholic

cattura *f* capture; (*arresto*) arrest; **catturare** capture; (*arrestare*) arrest

cauccìu *m* rubber

causa *f* cause; (*motivo*) reason; DIR lawsuit; **a ~ di** because of; **causare** cause

cautela *f* caution; (*precauzione*) precaution; **cauto** cautious; **cauzione** *f* (*deposito*) security; *per la libertà provvisoria* bail

cava *f* quarry

cavalcare ride; **cavalcavia** *m inv* flyover, *Am* overpass; **a cavalcioni: a ~** astride; **cavaliere** *m* rider; *accompagnatore* escort; *al ballo* partner

cavalla *f* mare; **cavalletta** *f* grasshopper; **cavalletto** *m* trestle; FOT tripod; *da pittore* easel; **cavallo** *m* horse; *scacchi* knight; *dei pantaloni* crotch; **andare a ~** go riding;

cavallone *m* breaker; **cavalluccio** *m*: **~ marino** sea horse

cavare take out; **cavarsela** manage, get by; **cavarsi: ~ da un impiccio** get out of trouble; **cavatappi** *m inv* corkscrew

caverna *f* cave

cavia *f* guinea pig (*anche fig*)

caviale *m* caviar

caviglia *f* ANAT ankle

cavillo *m* quibble

cavità *f inv* cavity

cavo 1 *agg* hollow 2 *m* cable; (*fune*) rope

cavolfiore *m* cauliflower

cavolo *m* cabbage; **~ di Bruxelles** Brussels sprout

cazzo *m* V prick V; **~!** fuck! V

CC (= **Carabinieri**) Italian police force

cc (= **centimetri cubici**) cc (= cubic centimeters)

c.c. (= **corrente continua**) DC (= direct current)

c/c (= **conto corrente**) current account, *Am* checking account

CD *m inv* CD; **lettore** *m* **~** CD player; **CD-Rom** *m inv* CD-Rom; **drive** *m* **per ~** CD-Rom drive

ce = **ci** (*before* **lo, la, li, le, ne**)

c'è there is

cecchino *m* sniper

cece *m* chickpea

ceco 1 *agg* Czech 2 *m*, -a *f* Czech

cedere 1 *v/t* (*dare*) hand over,

give up; (*vendere*) sell; **~ il posto** give up one's seat 2 *v/i* give in, surrender (**a** to); *muro, terreno* collapse, give way; **non ~!** don't give in!

cedola *f* coupon

cedro *m* **del Libano** cedar

ceffone *m* slap

celebrare celebrate; **celebrazione** *f* celebration; **celebre** famous; **celebrità** *f inv* fame; *persona* celebrity

celeste sky blue; (*divino*) heavenly (*anche fig*)

celibato *m* celibacy; **celibe 1** *agg* single, unmarried **2** *m* bachelor

cella *f* cell

cellula *f* cell; **cellulare 1** *agg* cell *attr*; **telefono** *m* **~** mobile (phone), *Am* cell(ular) phone **2** *m* prison van; *telefono* mobile, *Am* cell (phone); **~ con fotocamera** camera phone

cellulite *f* cellulite

cemento *m* cement; **~ armato** reinforced concrete

cena *f* supper, evening meal; *importante, con ospiti* dinner; **cenacolo** *m* PITT Last Supper; **cenare** have supper; *formalmente* dine

cencio *m* rag; *per spolverare* duster; **bianco come un ~** white as a sheet

cenere *f* ash; **le Ceneri** *fpl* Ash Wednesday

cenno *m* sign; *della mano*

wave; *del capo* nod; *con gli occhi* wink; *(breve notizia)* mention; *(allusione)* hint

cenone *m* feast, banquet

censimento *m* census

censura *f* censorship; **censurare** censor

centenario 1 *agg* hundred-year-old **2** *m persona* centenarian; *anniversario* centenary, *Am* centennial; **centesimo 1** *agg* hundredth **2** *m* FIN cent

centigrado *m* centigrade; **centimetro** *m* centimetre, *Am* centimeter; **~ cubo** cubic centimetre; **~ quadrato** square centimetre; **centinaio** *m* hundred; **un ~ di** about a hundred; **cento** hundred; **per ~** per cent

centrale 1 *agg* central **2** *f station*, plant; **centralinista** *m/f* switchboard operator; **centralino** *m* switchboard; **centrare** centre, *Am* center; **~ il bersaglio** hit the bull's eye

centrifuga 1 *agg* centrifugal **2** *f* spin-dryer; TEC centrifuge; **centrifugare** spin-dry; TEC centrifuge

centro *m* centre, *Am* center; *di bersaglio* bull's eye; **~ commerciale** shopping centre, *Am* downtown; **~ storico** old (part of) town

ceppo *m*: **~ bloccaruota** wheel clamp, *Am* Denver boot

cera *f* wax; *per lucidare* polish

ceramica *f* ceramics *sg*; *oggetto* piece of pottery

cerata *f* oilskins

cerca *f*: **in ~ di ...** in search of ...; **cercare 1** *v/t* look for **2** *v/i*: **~ di fare** try to do

cerchio *m* circle; **cerchione** *m* TEC rim

cereale 1 *agg* grain *attr* **2** **-i** *mpl* grain, cereals

cerebrale: **commozione** *f* **~** concussion

cerimonia *f* ceremony; REL service; **-e** *pl (convenevoli)* pleasantries

cerino *m* (wax) match

cernia *f* grouper

cerniera *f* hinge; **~ lampo** zip (fastener), *Am* zipper

cernita *f* selection, choice

cero *m* (large) candle

cerotto *m* (sticking) plaster, *Am* Bandaid®

certezza *f* certainty

certificare certify; **certificato** *m* certificate

certo 1 *agg (sicuro)* certain, sure; **un ~ signor Federici** a (certain) Mr Federici; **ci vuole un ~ coraggio** it takes (some) courage; **di una ~ età** of a certain age; **-i** some **2** *avv (certamente)* certainly; *(naturalmente)* of course; **~ che ...** surely ... **3** *pron*: **-i, -e** some, some people

certosa *f* Carthusian monastery

cervello *m* brain; GASTR brains

cervo m deer; *carne* venison
cesareo: taglio m ~ Caesarean, *Am* Cesarean
cesoie fpl shears
cespuglio m bush, shrub
cessare stop, cease; **cessate il fuoco** m ceasefire; **cessazione** f *di contratto* termination
cessione f transfer, handover
cesso m P bog P, *Am* john F
cesta f basket
cestinare throw away, bin F; **cestino** m little basket; *per la carta* wastepaper basket, *Am* waste basket; **cesto** m basket
ceto m (social) class; ~ **medio** middle class
cetriolino m gherkin; **cetriolo** m cucumber
che 1 agg what; *a ~ cosa serve?* what is that for?; ~ **brutta giornata!** what a filthy day! 2 pron persona: soggetto who; persona: oggetto who, that, fml whom; cosa that, which; *ciò* ~ what; *non c'è di* ~ don't mention it, you're welcome 3 cong dopo il comparativo than
check-in m inv check-in
chemioterapia f chemotherapy, chemo F
chi who; *di* ~ *è il libro?* whose book is this? *a* ~ *ha venduto la casa?* who did he sell the house to?; *c'è* ~ *dice che* some people say that; ~ ... ~ some ... others

chiacchiera f chat; (maldicenza) gossip; (notizia infondata) rumour, *Am* rumor; **chiacchierare** chat, chatter; spreg gossip; **chiacchierata** f chat; **chiacchierone** 1 agg talkative, chatty; (pettegolo) gossipy 2 m, -a f chatterbox; (pettegolo) gossip
chiamare call; *andare a ~ qu* go and get s.o., fetch s.o.; **chiamarsi** be called; *come ti chiami?* what's your name?; *mi chiamo ...* my name is ...; **chiamata** f call; TELEC (telephone) call, (phone)call
chiara f egg white; **chiarezza** f clarity; **chiarimento** m clarification; **chiarire** clarify; **chiarirsi** become clear; **chiaro** clear; colore light, pale; (luminoso) bright; ~! obviously!; **chiaroscuro** m chiaroscuro
chiasso m din, racket; *fare ~* make a din o racket; **chiassoso** noisy
chiatta f barge; *ponte m di* ~ pontoon bridge
chiave f agg inv key 2 f key; MUS clef; ~ *inglese* spanner, *Am* monkey wrench; **chiavistello** m bolt
chiazza f (macchia) stain; *sulla pelle, di colore* patch
chic inv chic, stylish
chicco m grain; *di caffè* bean; ~ *d'uva* grape
chiedere per sapere ask (di

about); *per avere* ask for; (*esigere*) demand, require; ~ *qc a qu* ask s.o. sth; ~ *di qu* (*chiedere notizie di*) ask about s.o.; *per parlargli* ask for s.o; ~ *un piacere a qu* ask s.o. a favour; ~ *scusa a qu* apologize to s.o.; **chiedersi** wonder (*se* whether)

chiesa *f* church

chiesto *pp* → **chiedere**

chiglia *f* MAR keel

chilo *m* kilo; **chilogrammo** *m* kilogram; **chilometraggio** *m* AUTO mileage; **chilometro** *m* kilometre, *Am* kilometer; **-i** *pl* **all'ora** kilometres per hour

chilowatt *m inv* kilowatt

chimica *f* chemistry; **chimico 1** *agg* chemical **2** *m, -a f* chemist

chinare *testa* bend; *occhi* lower; **chinarsi** stoop, bend down

chincaglierie *fpl* knick-knacks

chioccia *f fig* mother hen

chiocciola *f* snail; *in indirizzo e-mail* at; *scala f a* ~ spiral staircase

chiodato: SP *scarpe fpl* **-e** spikes

chiodo *m* nail

chioma *f* mane; *di cometa* tail

chiosco *m* kiosk

chiostro *m* cloister

chiromante *m/f* palmist

chirurgia *f* surgery; **chirurgo** *m* surgeon

chissà who knows; (*forse*) maybe

chitarra *f* guitar; **chitarrista** *m/f* guitarist

chiudere close, shut; *a chiave* lock; *strada* close off; *gas, luce* turn off; *fabbrica, negozio* shut down; **chiudersi** *di porta, ombrello* close, shut; *di ferita* heal up

chiunque anyone; *relativo* whoever; ~ *lo vede* whoever sees it

chiuso 1 *pp* → **chiudere 2** *agg* closed, shut; *a chiave* locked; *persona* reserved; **chiusura** *f* closing, shutting

choc *m inv* shock

ci 1 *pron* ◇ us; *non* ~ *ha parlato* he didn't speak to us; ~ *siamo divertiti molto* we had a great time; ~ *vogliamo bene* we love each other ◇; ~ *penso* I'm thinking about it **2** *avv* here; (*lì*) there; *c'è* ~ there is ...; ~ *sono* ... there are ...

ciabatta *f* slipper

cialda *f* wafer

ciambella *f* GASTR *type of cake, baked in a ring-shaped mould*; (*salvagente*) lifebelt

cianfrusaglia *f* knick-knack

ciao! hi!; *nel congedarsi* bye!

ciarpame *m* junk

ciascuno 1 *agg* each; (*ogni*) every **2** *pron* everyone

ciber... (*over...*)

cibo *m* food; *-i pl* foodstuffs, foods; ~ *pronto* fast food

cicala f insetto cicada

cicalino m buzzer, bleeper

cicatrice f scar; **cicatrizzare, cicatrizzarsi** heal

cicca f (mozzicone) stub, butt; (gomma da masticare) (chewing) gum

ciccia f (grasso) flab; **ciccione** m, **-a** f fatty

ciclamino m cyclamen

ciclismo m cycling; **ciclista** m/f cyclist; **ciclistico** bike attr, cycle attr; **ciclo** m cycle; **ciclomotore** m moped

ciclone m cyclone

cicloturismo m cycling holidays

cicogna f stork

cicoria f chicory

cieco 1 agg blind; **vicolo** m ∼ dead end, blind alley **2** m, **-a** f blind man; **donna** f blind woman

cielo m sky; REL heaven; **grazie al** ∼ thank heavens

cifra f figure; (monogramma) monogram; (somma) amount, sum; (codice) cipher, code

ciglio m ANAT eyelash; (bordo) edge

cigno m swan

cigolare squeak; **cigolio** m squeak

Cile m Chile

cilecca f: **far** ∼ **di arma da fuoco** misfire

cileno 1 agg Chilean **2** m, **-a** f Chilean

ciliegia f cherry; **ciliegio** m cherry (tree)

cilindro m cylinder; (cappello) top hat

cima f top; **in** ∼ **a** on top of; **da** ∼ **a fondo** from top to bottom; fig from beginning to end

cimentarsi: ∼ **in** embark on

ciminiera f smokestack

cimitero m cemetery

cin cin! F cheers!

Cina f China

cineforum m inv film followed by a discussion; club film club

cinema m inv cinema, luogo cinema, Am movie theater; **cinematografico** film attr, movie attr

cinepresa f cine-camera

cinese agg, m/f Chinese

cinghia f strap; (cintura) belt

cinghiale m wild boar

cinguettare twitter

cinico 1 agg cynical **2** m **-a** f cynic; **cinismo** m cynicism

cinquanta fifty; **cinquantenne** m/f 50-year-old; **cinquantesimo** fiftieth; **cinquantina** f: **una** ∼ **di** about 50; **cinque** five; **cinquecento 1** agg five hundred **2** m: **il Cinquecento** the sixteenth century; **cinquemila** five thousand

cintura f belt; (vita) waist; ∼ **di sicurezza** seatbelt; **cinturino** m strap

ciò (questo) this; (quello) that; ∼ **che** what; ∼ **nonostante**

nevertheless

ciocca *f di capelli* lock
cioccolata *f* chocolate; **cioc-colatino** *m* chocolate; **cioc-colato** *m* chocolate
cioè that is, i.e.
ciondolo *m* pendant
ciotola *f* bowl
ciottolo *m* pebble
cipolla *f* onion; *di pianta* bulb; **cipollina** *f* small onion
cipresso *m* cypress (tree)
cipria *f* (face) powder
circa about
circo *m* circus
circolare 1 *v/i* circulate; *di persone* move along **2** *agg* circular **3** *f lettera* circular; **circolazione** *f* traffic; MED circulation; **mettere in** ~ *voci* spread
circolo *m* circle; (*club*) club
circondare surround
circonferenza *f* circumference
circonvallazione *f* ring road, *Am* beltway
circoscrizione *f* area, district; ~ **elettorale** constituency
circostante surrounding; **circostanza** *f* circumstance; (*occasione*) occasion
circuito *m* SP (*percorso*) track; EL circuit; EL **corto** ~ short circuit
cisterna *f* cistern; (*serbatoio*) tank; **nave** *f* ~ tanker
cisti *f* cyst; **cistifellea** *f* gall bladder; **cistite** *f* cystitis

citare quote; *come esempio* cite, quote; DIR *testimone* summons; **citazione** *f* quotation, quote; DIR summons *sg*
citofono *m* entry phone; *in uffici* intercom
città *f inv* town; *grande* city; **Città del Vaticano** Vatican City; **cittadina** *f* (small) town; **cittadinanza** *f* citizenship; (*popolazione*) citizens; **cittadino 1** *agg* town *attr*, city *attr* **2** *m*, **-a** *f* citizen; (*abitante di città*) city dweller
ciuccio *m* F (*succhiotto*) dummy, *Am* pacifier
ciuffo *m* tuft
civetta *f* ZO (little) owl; *fig* **far la** ~ flirt
civico *della città* municipal, town *attr*; *delle persone* civic
civile 1 *agg* civil; *civilizzato* civilized; (*non militare*) civilian **2** *m* civilian; **civiltà** *f inv* civilization
clacson *m inv* horn
clamoroso *fig* sensational
clandestino 1 *agg* clandestine; (*illegale*) illegal **2** *m*, **-a** *f* stowaway
clarinetto *m* clarinet
classe *f* class; (*aula*) classroom
classico 1 *agg* classical; (*tipico*) classic **2** *m* classic
classifica *f* classification; (*elenco*) list; *sportiva* league standings, league table; *musicale* charts; **classificare**

classify; **classificatore** *m*
(*cartella*) folder; *mobile* filing
cabinet, *Am* file cabinet

classismo *m* class consciousness

clausola *f* clause; (*riserva*)
proviso

claustrofobia *f* claustrophobia

clavicola *f* collar-bone

clero *m* clergy

clessidra *f* hourglass

cliccare INFOR click (**su** on);
~ due volte double-click

cliché *m inv fig* cliché

cliente *m/f* customer; *di professionista* client; *di albergo*
guest; MED patient; **clientela**
f customers, clientele; *di professionista* clients; *di medico*
patients

clima *m* climate; **climatico**
agg climatic; **stazio-
ne *f* climatica** health resort

clinica *f* (*ospedale*) clinic; (*casa di cura*) nursing home; **clinico 1** *agg* clinical **2** *m* clini-
cian

clip *m inv* clip

clonare BIO clone; **clonazione** *f* cloning; **clone** *m* clone

cloro *m* chlorine

clorofilla *f* chlorophyl(l)

cloroformio *m* chloroform

club *m inv* club

coabitare share a flat *o Am*
an apartment

coagularsi *di sangue* coagulate, clot; *di latte* curdle; **coalizione** *f* coalition; **gover-**

no *m di ~ coalition government; **coalizzarsi** join forces; POL form a coalition

cobra *m inv* cobra

cocaina *f* cocaine

coccinella *f* ladybird, *Am* ladybug

coccio *m* earthenware; *frammento* fragment (of pottery);
cocciuto stubborn, obstinate

cocco *m albero* coconut palm

coccodrillo *m* crocodile

coccolare F cuddle; (*viziare*)
spoil

cocktail *m inv* cocktail; *festa*
cocktail party

cocomero *m* water melon

coda *f* tail; (*fila*) queue, *Am*
line; *di veicolo, treno* rear;
MUS coda; **fare la ~** queue
(up), *Am* stand in line

codardo 1 *agg* cowardly **2** *m*,
-a f coward

codice *m* code; **~ di avviamento postale** postcode,
Am zip code; **~ fiscale** tax
code; **~ segreto** PIN; **codifi-
care** *dati* encode; DIR codify

codino *m* .pigtail, plait, *Am*
braid

coerente coherent; *fig* consistent; **coerenza** *f* coher-
ence; *fig* consistency

coetaneo 1 *agg* the same age
(**di** as) **2** *m*, *-a f* contemporary

cofanetto *m* casket

cofano *m* AUTO bonnet, *Am*
hood

cogliere pick; *(raccogliere)* gather; *(afferrare)* seize; *occasione* take, seize; *(capire)* grasp

cognac *m inv* cognac

cognato *m*, **-a** *f* brother-in-law; *donna* sister-in-law

cognizione *f* knowledge; *filosofia* cognition; **parla con ~ di causa** he knows what he's talking about

cognome *m* surname, family name

coi = **con** and *art* **i**

coincidenza *f* coincidence; FERR connection; **coincidere** coincide

coinquilino *m*, **-a** *f* in *condominio* fellow tenant; *in appartamento* flatmate, *Am* roommate

coinvolgere involve; **coinvolto** *pp* ☞ **coinvolgere**

col = **con** and *art* **il**

colapasta *m inv* colander

colare 1 *v/t* strain; *pasta* drain **2** *v/i* drip; *(perdere)* leak; *di naso* run; *di cera* melt; **~ a fondo** *o* **a picco** sink, go down; **colazione** *f prima* breakfast; *di mezzogiorno* lunch; **far ~** have breakfast

colei *pron f* the one; **~ che** the one that

colera *m* cholera

colesterolo *m* cholesterol

colica *f* colic

colino *m* strainer

colla *f* glue; *di farina* paste

collaborare co-operate, collaborate; *con giornale* contribute; **collaboratore** *m*, **-trice** *f* collaborator; *di giornale* contributor; **collaborazione** *f* co-operation, collaboration

collana *f* necklace; *di libri* series sg

collant *m inv* tights, *Am* pantyhose

collare *m* collar

collasso *m* collapse

collaudare test; *fig* put to the test; **collaudo** *m* test

colle *m* hill; *(valico)* pass

collega *m/f* colleague, co-worker

collegamento *m* connection; MIL liaison; RAD, TV link; **collegare** connect, link; **collegarsi** RAD, TV link up

collegio *m* boarding school

collera *f* anger; **essere in ~ con qu** be angry with s.o.

colletta *f* collection; **collettività** *f* community; **collettivo** *m/agg* collective

colletto *m* collar

collezionare collect; **collezione** *f* collection; **fare ~ di qc** collect sth; **collezionista** *m/f* collector; **~ di francobolli** stamp collector

collina *f* hill

collirio *m* eyewash

collisione *f* collision

collo *m* neck; *(bagaglio)* piece of luggage; *(pacco)* package

collocamento *m* placing; *(impiego)* employment;

agenzia f *di* ~ employment agency; **collocare** place, put

colloquiale colloquial

colloquio m talk, conversation; *ufficiale* interview; *(esame)* oral (exam)

colluttazione f scuffle

colmare fill *(di* with); *fig: di gentilezze* overwhelm *(di* with); **colmo** full *(di* of)

colomba f ZO, *fig* dove

colombo m pigeon

colon m colon

colonia f colony; *per bambini* holiday camp, *Am* summer camp; **colonizzare** colonize

colonna f column; ~ *vertebrale* spinal column; **colonnato** m colonnade

colonnello m colonel

colorante m dye; *senza -i* with no artificial colouring o *Am* coloring; **colorare** colour, *Am* color; *disegno* colour in; **colorato** coloured, *Am* colored; **colore** m colour, *Am* color; *carte* suit; *a -i film, televisione* colour *attr*; **colorito 1** *agg volto* rosy-cheeked; *fig (vivace)* colourful, *Am* colorful **2** m complexion

coloro *pron pl* the ones; ~ *che* those who

colossale colossal

colpa f fault; REL sin; *dare a qu la* ~ *di qc* blame s.o. for sth; *per* ~ *tua* because of you; **colpevole 1** *agg* guilty **2** m/f culprit, guilty party

colpire hit, strike; *fig* impress; **colpo** m blow; *di pistola* shot; MED stroke; ~ *di telefono* phonecall; *di* ~ suddenly

coltellata f *ferita* stab wound; **coltello** m knife

coltivare AGR, *fig* cultivate; **coltivazione** f cultivation; *di prodotti agricoli e piante* growing; *campi coltivati* crops

colto[1] cultured, learned

colto[2] *pp* ▶ **cogliere**

coltura f growing; *piante* crop

colui *pron* m the one; ~ *che* the one that

coma m coma

comandante m commander; AVIA, MAR captain; **comandare 1** *v/t (ordinare)* order, command; *esercito* command; *nave* captain, be captain of; TEC control **2** *v/i* be in charge; **comando** m order, command; TEC control

combaciare fit together; *fig* correspond

combattere fight; **combattimento** m fight

combinare combine; *(organizzare)* arrange; ~ *un guaio* make a mess; **combinazione** f combination; *(coincidenza)* coincidence; *per* ~ by chance

combustibile 1 *agg* combustible **2** m fuel

come *avv* as; *(in modo simile o uguale)* like; *interrogativo*, *esclamativo* how; *(prego?)*

pardon?, *Am* pardon me?;
fa' ~ **ti ho detto** do as I told
you; ~ **me** like me; **un cappello** ~ **il mio** a hat like
mine; ~ **sta?** how are you?;
~ **mai?** how come?, why?;
~ **se** as if **2** *cong* (*come se*)
as if, as though; (*appena,
quando*) as (soon as)
cometa *f* comet
comfort *m inv* comfort; **dotato di tutti i** ~ **moderni** with
all mod cons
comico 1 *agg* funny, comical;
genere comic **2** *m*, **-a** *f* comedian; *donna* comedienne
comignolo *m* chimney pot
cominciare start, begin (**a** to)
comitato *m* committee; ~ **direttivo** steering committee;
comitiva *f* group, party
comizio *m* meeting
commedia *f* comedy; *fig* play-
acting; **commediografo** *m*,
-a *f* playwright
commemorare commemo-
rate; **commemorazione** *f*
commemoration
commentare comment on;
commento *m* comment
commerciale commercial;
relazioni, trattative trade *attr;
lettera* business *attr;* **commercialista** *m/f* accountant;
commercializzare market;
commerciante *m/f* merchant; (*negoziante*) shopkeeper, *Am* storekeeper;
commercio *m* trade, business; *di droga* traffic; **essere**

in ~ be available
commesso *m*, **-a** *f* shop assistant, *Am* sales clerk
commestibile 1 *agg* edible **2**
-i *mpl* foodstuffs
commettere commit; *errore*
make
commiserare feel sorry for
commissariato *m*: ~ (**di pubblica sicurezza**) police station; **commissario** *m di polizia* police superintendent,
Am police chief; *membro
di commissione* commission-
er
commissione *f* commission;
(*incarico*) errand; **-i** *pl* shopping
commosso 1 *pp* ☞ **commuovere 2** *agg fig* moved,
touched
commovente moving, touching; **commozione** *f* emotion; ~ **cerebrale** concussion; **commuovere** move,
touch; **commuoversi** be
moved *o* touched
comò *m inv* chest of drawers;
comodino *m* bedside table
comodità *f inv* comfort; (*vantaggio*) convenience
comodo 1 *agg* comfortable;
(*facilmente raggiungibile*)
easy to get to; (*utile*) useful,
handy; F *persona* laidback
F; **stia** ~**!** don't get up! **2** *m*
comfort; **con** ~ at one's convenience; **far** ~ *di denaro*
come in useful; **le fa** ~ **così**
she finds it easier that way;

fare il propio ~ do as one pleases

compagnia f company; (*gruppo*) group; *~ aerea* airline; *far ~ a qu* keep s.o. company

compagno m, *-a* f companion; (*convivente*) partner; POL comrade; *~ di scuola* schoolfriend

comparativo m/agg comparative

comparire appear; (*far figura*) stand out; **comparizione** f: DIR *mandato m di ~* summons sg; **comparsa** f appearance; TEA person with a walk-on part; *in film* extra; **comparso** pp ☞ *comparire*

compartimento m compartment

compassione f compassion, pity; *provare ~ per qu* feel sorry for s.o.

compasso m compass

compatibile compatible; **compatibilità** f compatibility

compatire: *~ qu* feel sorry for s.o.

compatto compact; *folla* dense; *fig* united

compensare (*controbilanciare*) compensate for, make up for; (*ricompensare*) reward; (*risarcire*) pay compensation to; **compenso** m (*ricompensa*, *risarcimento*) compensation; (*retribuzione*)

fee; *in ~* (*d'altra parte*) on the other hand

compera f purchase; *fare le -e* go shopping

competente competent; (*responsabile*) appropriate; **competenza** f (*esperienza*) competence; *essere di ~ di qu* be s.o.'s responsibility

competere (*gareggiare*) compete; **competitivo** competitive; **competizione** f competition

compiacere please; **compiacersi** (*provare piacere*) be pleased (*di* with); **compiaciuto** pp ☞ *compiacere*

compiangere pity; *per lutto* mourn; **compianto** pp ☞ *compiangere*

compiere (*finire*) complete, finish; (*eseguire*) carry out; *~ gli anni* have one's birthday

compilare compile; *modulo* complete

compito m task; EDU *i -i* pl homework

compiuto *lavoro*, *opera* completed, finished; *ha 10 anni -i* he's 10

compleanno m birthday; *buon ~!* happy birthday!

complementare complementary; **complemento** m complement; GRAM object

complessato full of complexes, uptight F; **complessivo** all-in; **complesso 1** agg complex **2** m complex;

MUS group; *di circostanze* set, combination; **in o nel** ~ on the whole

completare complete; **completo 1** *agg* complete; (*pieno*) full; TEA sold out **2** *m* set; (*vestito*) suit; **al** ~ (*pieno*) full (up); TEA sold out

complicare complicate; **complicarsi** get complicated; **complicato** complicated; **complicazione** *f* complication

complice *m/f* DIR accomplice

complimentarsi: ~ **con qu** congratulate s.o. (**per** on); **complimento** *m* compliment; **-i!** congratulations!; **non fare -i!** help yourself!

componente 1 *agg* component **2** *m/f* (*persona*) member; **componibile** modular; *cucina* fitted; **comporre** (*mettere in ordine*) arrange; MUS compose; ~ **un numero** dial a number

comportamento *m* behaviour, *Am* behavior; **comportare** involve; **comportarsi** behave

compositore *m*, **-trice** *f* composer; **composizione** *f* composition; *di fiori* arrangement; DIR settlement

composto 1 *pp* ☞ **comporre 2** *agg* compound; *abiti, capelli* tidy, neat; ~ **da** made up of **3** *m* compound

comprare buy, purchase; (*corrompere*) bribe, buy off;

compratore *m*, **-trice** *f* buyer, purchaser; **compravendita** *f* buying and selling

comprendere (*includere*) comprise, include; (*capire*) understand; **comprensibile** understandable, comprehensible; **comprensione** *f* understanding; **comprensivo** (*tollerante*) understanding; ~ **di** inclusive of; **compreso 1** *pp* ☞ **comprendere 2** *agg* inclusive; (*capito*) understood; **tutto** ~ all in; ~ **te** including you

compressa *f* (*pastiglia*) tablet; *di garza* compress

compresso *pp* ☞ **comprimere**; **comprimere** press; (*reprimere*) repress; FIS compress

compromesso 1 *pp* ☞ **compromettere 2** *m* compromise; **compromettere** compromise; **compromettersi** compromise o.s.

computer *m inv* computer; ~ **portatile** laptop

comunale *del comune* municipal, town *attr*; **comune 1** *agg* common; *amico* mutual; (*ordinario*) ordinary, common; **in** ~ in common; **fuori del** ~ out of the ordinary **2** *m* municipality; **comunemente** te commonly

comunicare 1 *v/t notizia* pass on, communicate; *contagio* pass on; REL give Communion to **2** *v/i* (*esprimersi*) communicate; *di persone* keep in touch, communicate; **comunicato** *m* announcement; ~ **stampa** press release; **comunicazione** *f* communication; *(annuncio)* announcement; TELEC *(collegamento)* connection

comunione *f* REL communion; *di idee* sharing

comunismo *m* Communism; **comunista** *m/f* Communist

comunità *f inv* community; **comunitario** community *attr, dell'Ue* Community *attr*

comunque 1 *cong* however, no matter how **2** *avv (in ogni modo)* in any case, anyhow; *(in qualche modo)* somehow; *(tuttavia)* however

con with; *(mezzo)* by

conato *m*: ~ **di vomito** retching

concedere grant; *premio* award; **concedersi**: ~ **qc** treat o.s. to sth

concentramento *m* concentration; **concentrare**, **concentrarsi** concentrate; **concentrazione** *f* concentration

concentrico concentric

concepibile conceivable; **concepimento** *m* conception; **concepimento** *m* conception; **concepire** conceive

concernere concern

concerto *m* concert; *composizione* concerto

concessionario *m* agent

concesso *pp* ☞ **concedere**

concetto *m* concept; *(giudizio)* opinion

conchiglia *f* shell

conciare *pelle* tan; *(sistemare)* arrange; **come ti sei conciato!** what a state you're in!; ~ **qu per le feste** tan s.o.'s hide

conciliare reconcile; *multa* pay, settle

concimare *pianta* feed; **concime** *m* manure

conciso concise

concittadino *m*, **-a** *f* fellow citizen

concludere conclude; *(portare a termine)* achieve, carry off; ~ **un affare** clinch a deal; **concludersi** end, close; **conclusione** *f* conclusion; **in** ~ in short; **conclusivo** conclusive; **concluso** *pp* ☞ **concludere**

concordare 1 *v/t* agree (on); GRAM make agree **2** *v/i* agree; *(coincidere)* tally; **concorde** in agreement; *(unanime)* unanimous

concorrente 1 *agg (rivale)* competing, rival *attr* **2** *m/f* *in una gara, gioco* competitor, contestant; FIN competitor; **concorrenza** *f* competition; **concorrere** *(contribuire)* concur; *(competere)* compete *(a* for); *di strade* converge; **concorso** *m (competizione)* competition, contest

concreto concrete; *(pratico)* practical

condanna *f* DIR sentence;

condannare condemn (*a* to); DIR sentence (*a* to)

condensare, condensarsi condense

condimento *m* seasoning; *di insalata* dressing; **condire** season; *insalata* dress; **condito** seasoned

condividere share; **condiviso** *pp* ☞ **condividere**

condizionale 1 *m/agg* conditional **2** *f* suspended sentence; **condizionamento** *m* PSI conditioning; **~ dell'aria** air conditioning; **condizionare** PSI condition; **condizionato: con aria -a** air-conditioned; **condizionatore** *m* air conditioner; **condizione** *f* condition; **a ~ che** on condition that

condoglianze *fpl* condolences; **fare le ~ a qu** express one's condolences to s.o.

condominio *m* (*comproprietà*) joint ownership; *edificio* block of flats, *Am* condo(minium); **condomino** *m* owner-occupier, *Am* condo owner

condono *m* remission; **~ fiscale** conditional amnesty for tax evaders

condotta *f* (*comportamento*) behaviour, *Am* behavior, conduct; (*canale*) piping; **condotto 1** *pp* ☞ **condurre 2** *m* pipe; ANAT duct

conducente *m/f* driver; **condurre** lead; (*accompagnare*)

take; *veicolo* drive; **conduttore** *m*, **-trice** *f* RAD, TV presenter; **conduttura** *f* (*condotto*) pipe

confederazione *f* confederation

conferenza *f* conference; **~ stampa** press conference; **conferire 1** *v/t* (*dare*) confer; *premio* award **2** *v/i*: **~ con qu** confer with s.o.

conferma *f* confirmation; **confermare** confirm

confessare, confessarsi confess; **confessione** *f* confession

confetto *m* GASTR sugared almond; MED pill

confettura *f* jam, *Am* jelly

confezione *f* wrapping, packaging; *di abiti* making; **~ regalo** gift wrap; **-i** *pl* (*abiti*) garments

conficcare hammer, drive

confidare 1 *v/t* confide **2** *v/i*: **~ in** trust in, rely on; **confidarsi: ~ con** confide in; **confidenza** *f* (*familiarità*) familiarity, trust; **avere ~ con qu** be familiar with s.o.; **prendere ~ con qc** familiarize o.s. with sth; **confidenziale** (*riservato*) confidential

configurazione *f* configuration

confinante neighbouring, *Am* neighboring

confinare border (*con* sth); *fig* confine; **confine** *m* border; *fra terreni*, *fig* boundary

confisca f seizure; confiscare confiscate

conflitto m conflict

confluire merge

confondere confuse, mix up; (imbarazzare) embarrass; confondersi get mixed up

conformarsi: ~ a conform to; (adattarsi) adapt to; conforme (simile) similar; ~ a in accordance with; conformismo m conformity; conformista m/f conformist; conformità f conformity; in ~ a in accordance with

confortare comfort; confortevole comfortable; conforto m comfort

confrontare compare; confronto m confrontation; (comparazione) comparison; a ~ di, in ~ a compared with; nei -i di towards

confusione f confusion; (disordine) muddle, mess; (baccano) noise; (imbarazzo) embarrassment; confuso 1 pp ☞ confondere 2 agg (non chiaro) confused, muddled; (imbarazzato) embarrassed

congedare dismiss; MIL discharge; congedarsi take leave (da di); congedo m (permesso) leave; MIL ~ assoluto discharge

congelare 1 v/t freeze 2 v/i e congelarsi freeze; congelato frozen; congelatore m freezer

congenito congenital

congestionato congested; volto flushed; congestione f congestion

congettura f conjecture

congiungere join; congiungersi join (up)

congiuntivite f conjunctivitis

congiuntivo m GRAM subjunctive; congiunto 1 pp ☞ congiungere 2 m, -a f relative, relation; congiunzione f GRAM conjunction

congiura f conspiracy, plot

congratularsi: ~ con qu gratulate s.o. (per on); congratulazioni fpl: fare le propie ~ a qu congratulate s.o.; -i! congratulations!

congressista m/f convention participant, Am conventioneer; congresso m convention

conguaglio m balance

coniare mint; fig coin

coniglio m rabbit

coniugare conjugate; coniugato married; coniugazione f conjugation; coniuge m/f spouse; -i pl husband and wife; i -i Rossi Mr and Mrs Rossi

connazionale m/f compatriot

connessione f connection

connotati mpl features

cono m cone; ~ gelato ice-cream cone

conoscente m/f acquaintance; conoscenza f knowledge; persona acquaintance;

(sensi) consciousness; **perdere** ~ lose consciousness, faint; **conoscere** know; *(fare la conoscenza di)* meet; **conosciuto** well-known

conquista *f* conquest; **conquistare** conquer; *fig* win

consacrare consecrate; *sacerdote* ordain; *(dedicare)* dedicate

consanguineo *m*, **-a** *f* blood relative

consapevole: ~ **di** conscious of, aware of; **consapevolezza** *f* consciousness, awareness; **conscio** conscious, aware

consecutivo consecutive; **tre giorni -i** three consecutive days, three days in a row

consegna *f di lavoro*, *documento* handing in; *di prigioniero*, *ostaggio* handover; ~ **bagagli** left luggage, *Am* baggage checkroom; **consegnare** *lavoro*, *documento* hand in; *prigioniero*, *ostaggio* hand over; *merci*, *posta* deliver

conseguenza *f* consequence; **di** ~ consequently; **conseguire** 1 *v/t* achieve; *laurea* obtain 2 *v/i* follow

consenso *m (permesso)* consent, permission; **consentire** 1 *v/i (accondiscendere)* consent 2 *v/t* allow

conserva *f di pomodoro* tomato purée; ~ **di frutta** jam, *Am* jelly; con-

servante *m* preservative; **conservare** keep; GASTR preserve; **conservarsi** keep; *in salute* keep well; **conservatore** *m*, **-trice** *f* conservative; **conservatorio** *m* music school, conservatoire

considerare consider; **considerazione** *f* consideration; *(osservazione)* remark, comment; **prendere in** ~ take into consideration; **considerevole** considerable

consigliare advise; *(raccomandare)* recommend; **consigliarsi** seek advice; **consigliere** *m* adviser; ~ **municipale** town councillor, *Am* councilman; **consiglio** *m* piece of advice; *(organo amministrativo)* council; ~ **d'amministrazione** board (of directors); ~ **dei ministri** Cabinet; **consigli** *pl* advice

consistente substantial; *(denso)* thick; **consistenza** *f (densità)* consistency, thickness; *di materiale* texture; *di argomento* basis; **consistere** consist (**in**, **di** of)

consolare[1] *v/t* console, comfort

consolare[2] *agg* consular

consolarsi console o.s.

consolato *m* consulate

consolazione *f* consolation

console *m diplomatico* consul

consolidare consolidate; **consolidarsi** stabilize

consonante f consonant

consorte m/f spouse; **principe** m ~ prince consort

consorzio m di imprese consortium

constatare ascertain, determine; (notare) note; **constatazione** f statement

consueto usual

consulente m/f consultant; ~ **legale** legal adviser; ~ **tributario** tax consultant; **consulenza** f consultancy; **consultare** consult; **consultarsi: ~ con qu** consult (with) s.o.; **consultazione** f consultation; **consultorio** m family planning clinic

consumare acqua, gas use, consume; (logorare) wear out; (mangiare) eat, consume; (bere) drink; **consumarsi** wear out; **consumatore** m, **-trice** f consumer; **consumazione** f food; (bevanda) drink; **consumismo** m consumerism; **consumo** m consumption; (usura) wear

contabile m/f book-keeper; **contabilità** f FIN disciplina accounting; ufficio accounts department; **tenere la ~** keep the books

contachilometri m inv milometer, Am odometer

contadino 1 agg rural, country attr **2** m, **-a** f farmer; (bracciante) farm labourer o Am laborer

contagiare infect; **contagio** m infection; per contatto diretto contagion; (epidemia) outbreak; **contagioso** infectious; per contatto contagious

contagiri m inv rev(olution) counter; **contagocce** m inv dropper

container m inv container

contaminare contaminate, pollute; **contaminazione** f contamination, pollution

contante m cash; **in -i** cash

contare 1 v/t count **2** v/i count; ~ **di fare qc** plan on doing sth; **contascatti** m inv time meter on phone; **contatore** m meter

contatto m contact

conte m count

contemplare contemplate

contemporaneamente at the same time; **contemporaneo 1** agg contemporary (di with); movimenti simultaneous **2** m, **-a** f contemporary

contendersi contend for, compete for

contenere contain, hold; (reprimere) repress; (limitare) limit; **contenersi** contain o.s.; **contenitore** m container

contentezza f happiness; **contento** pleased (di with); (lieto) glad, happy

contenuto m contents

contesa f dispute

conteso *pp* ☞ *contendere*

contessa *f* countess

contestare protest; DIR serve; **contestazione** *f* protest

contesto *m* context

contiene ☞ *contenere*

continentale continental; **continente** *m* continent

continuare 1 *v/t* continue 2 *v/i* continue, carry on (*a fare* doing); **continuazione** *f* continuation; *di film* sequel; **in ~** over and over again; (*ininterrottamente*) non stop; **continuità** *f* continuity; **continuo** (*ininterrotto*) continuous; (*molto frequente*) continual; **di ~** (*ininterrottamente*) continuously; (*molto spesso*) continually

conto *m* (*calcolo*) calculation; FIN account; *in ristorante* bill, *Am* check; **~ corrente** current account, *Am* checking account; **rendere ~ di qc** account for sth; **rendersi ~ di qc** realize sth; **tenere ~ di qc** take sth into account; **~ alla rovescia** countdown; **in fin dei -i** when all's said and done, after all

contorcersi ~ *dal dolore / dalle risate* roll about in pain / laughing

contorno *m* outline, contour; GASTR accompaniment

contorto twisted

contrabbandare smuggle; **contrabbandiere** *m* smug-

gler; **contrabbando** *m* contraband

contrabbasso *m* MUS double bass

contraccambiare return

contraccettivo *m* contraceptive

contraccolpo *m* rebound; *di arma da fuoco* recoil

contraddire contradict; **contraddizione** *f* contradiction

contraffare (*falsificare*) forge; (*imitare*) imitate; **contraffatto** forged; **voce** imitated; **contraffazione** *f* (*imitazione*) imitation; (*falsificazione*) forgery

contralto *m* MUS contralto

contrappeso *m* counterbalance

contrapporre set against; **contrapposizione** *f* opposition; **mettere in ~** contrast; **contrapposto** *pp* ☞ *contrapporre*

contrariamente: ~ a contrary to

contrariare *piani* thwart, oppose; *persona* irritate, annoy; **contrariato** irritated, annoyed

contrarietà *fpl* difficulties

contrario 1 *agg* contrary; *direzione*; *vento* adverse; **essere ~** be against (*a* sth) 2 *m* contrary, opposite; **al ~** on the contrary

contrarre contract; **contrarsi** contract

contrassegnare mark;

contrassegno *m* mark; FIN (*in*) ~ cash on delivery, *Am* collect on delivery

contrastante contrasting; contrasto *m* contrast; (*litigio, discordia*) dispute

contrattacco *m* counter-attack

contrattare negotiate; *persona* hire

contrattempo *m* hitch

contratto 1 *pp* ☞ **contrarre** 2 *m* contract

contravvenire contravene; contravvenzione *f* contravention; (*multa*) fine

contrazione *f* contraction; (*riduzione*) reduction

contribuente *m/f* taxpayer; contribuire contribute; contributo *m* contribution

contro against

controbattere (*replicare*) answer back; (*confutare*) rebut

controcorrente 1 *agg* nonconformist 2 *avv* against the current; *in fiume* upstream

controffensiva counter-offensive

controfigura *f* in *film* stand-in

controindicazione *f* MED contraindication

controllare control; (*verificare*) check; controllo *m* control; (*verifica*) check; MED check-up; ~ (*dei*) passaporti passport control; controllore *m* controller; *di bus, treno* ticket inspector

controluce *f*: *in* ~ against the light

contromano: *andare a* ~ be going the wrong way

controproducente counterproductive

contrordine *m* counterorder

controsenso *m* contradiction in terms; (*assurdità*) nonsense

controversia *f* controversy, dispute; DIR litigation; controverso controversial

controvoglia unwillingly

contusione *f* bruise; contuso bruised

convalescente 1 *agg* convalescent 2 *m/f* person who is convalescent; convalescenza *f* convalescence; *essere in* ~ be convalescing

convalidare validate

convegno *m* convention; *luogo* meeting place

convenevoli *mpl* pleasantries

conveniente (*vantaggioso*) good; (*opportuno*) appropriate; convenienza *f di prezzo, offerta* good value; *di gesto* appropriateness; *fare qc per* ~ do sth out of self-interest

convenire 1 *v/i* gather, meet; (*concordare*) agree; (*essere opportuno*) be advisable, be better 2 *v/t* (*stabilire*) stipulate

convento *m di monache* con-

vent; *di monaci* monastery
convenuto *pp* ☞ **convenire**
convenzionale conventional; **convenzione** *f* convention; (*accordo*) agreement, convention
convergere converge
conversare talk, make conversation; **conversazione** *f* conversation
conversione *f* conversion; AUTO U-turn; **convertirsi** be converted
convincere convince; **convinto** *pp* ☞ **convincere**; **convinzione** *f* conviction
convivente *m/f* common-law husband; *donna* common-law wife; **convivenza** *f* living together, cohabitation; **convivere** live together
convocare call, convene
convoglio *m* MIL, MAR convoy; FERR train
cooperare co-operate (**a** in); (*contribuire*) contribute (**a** to); **cooperativa** *f*: (*società f*) **~** co-operative; **cooperazione** *f* cooperation
coordinamento *m* co-ordination; **coordinare** co-ordinate; **coordinatore** *m*, **-trice** *f* co-ordinator; **coordinazione** *f* co-ordination
coperchio *m* lid, top
coperta *f* blanket; MAR deck; **copertina** *f* cover; **coperto 1** *pp* ☞ **coprire 2** *agg* covered (**di**) with); *cielo* overcast, cloudy **3** *m* cover, shelter;

piatti e posate place; *prezzo* cover charge; **essere al ~** be under cover, be sheltered
copertone *m* AUTO tyre, *Am* tire
copia *f* copy; **copiare** copy
copione *m per attore* script
copisteria *f* copy centre *o Am* center
coppa *f* cup; (*calice*) glass; **~** (**di**) **gelato** dish of ice-cream; **coppetta** *f di gelato* tub
coppia *f* couple, pair
copricapo *m inv* head covering; **copricostume** *m inv* beachrobe; **coprifuoco** *m* curfew; **copriletto** *m inv* bedspread; **coprire** cover; *errore, suono* cover up; **coprirsi** (*vestirsi*) put something on; (*rannuvolarsi*) become overcast
coraggio *m* courage; (*sfacciataggine*) nerve; **coraggioso** brave, courageous
corallo *m* coral
Corano *m* Koran
corda *f* cord; (*fune*) rope; (*cordicella*), MUS string; **essere giù di ~** feel down; **tagliare la ~** cut and run
cordiale 1 *agg* cordial; **-i saluti** *mpl* kind regards **2** *m* cordial
cordoglio *m* (*dolore*) grief; (*condoglianze*) condolences
cordone *m* cord; *di marciapiedi* kerb, *Am* curb; (*sbarramento*) cordon; **~ ombelica-**

le umbilical cord

coreografo *m*, *-a f* choreographer

coriandolo *m* BOT coriander; *-i mpl* confetti *sg*

coricarsi lie down

cornacchia *f* crow

cornamusa *f* bagpipes

cornea *f* cornea

cornetta *f del telefono* receiver

cornetto *m* (*brioche*) croissant; (*gelato*) cone, cornet

cornice *f* frame

cornicione *m* ARCHI cornice

corno *m* horn; *ramificate* antlers; *fig* F **fare le -a a** qu cheat on s.o.; **facciamo le -a!** touch wood!; **cornuto** F cheated, betrayed

coro *m* chorus; (*cantori*) choir; **in ~** (*insieme*) all together

corona *f* crown; (*rosario*) rosary

corpo *m* body; MIL corps; (*a*) **~ a ~** hand-to-hand; **corporatura** *f* build

corpulento stout, corpulent

corredo *m* equipment; *da sposa* trousseau; *da neonato* layette

correggere correct; **correggersi** correct o.s.

correlazione *f* correlation

corrente 1 *agg* current; *acqua* running; *lingua* fluent; **2** *m*: **essere al ~** know (*di* sth); **tenere qu al ~** keep s.o. up to date, keep s.o. informed **3** *f* current; *fig*: *di opinione*

trend; *fazione* faction; **~ d'aria** draught, *Am* draft

correre 1 *v/t* run; **~ il pericolo** run the risk **2** *v/i* run; (*affrettarsi*) hurry; *di veicolo* speed; *di tempo* fly; **lascia ~!** let it go!; **corre voce** it is rumoured *o Am* rumored

correttezza *f* correctness; (*onestà*) honesty; **corretto 1** *pp* ☞ **correggere 2** *agg* correct; **correzione** *f* correction

corridoio *m* corridor; *in aereo, teatro* aisle

corridore *m* *in auto* racing driver; *a piedi* runner

corriera *f* bus

corriere *m* courier

corrispondente 1 *agg* corresponding **2** *m/f* correspondent; **corrispondenza** *f* correspondence; (*posta*) mail; **corrispondere 1** *v/t* (*pagare*) pay; (*ricambiare*) reciprocate **2** *v/i* correspond; (*coincidere*) coincide; (*equivalere*) be equivalent; **corrisposto 1** *pp* ☞ **corrispondere 2** *agg* reciprocated

corrodere, corrodersi corrode, rust

corrompere corrupt; *con denaro* bribe; **corroso** *pp* ☞ **corrodere**; **corrotto 1** *pp* ☞ **corrompere 2** *agg* corrupt

corrugare wrinkle; **~ la fronte** frown

corruzione *f* corruption; *con denaro* bribery

corsa f run; *attività* running; *di autobus* trip, journey; *(gara)* race; *di* ~ at a run; *in fretta* in a rush; **fare una** ~ rush, dash; **-e** *pl* races

corsia f aisle; *di ospedale* ward; AUTO lane; ~ *di emergenza* emergency lane; ~ *di sorpasso* fast lane; **a tre -e** three-lane

Corsica f Corsica

corsivo m italics

corso[1] 1 *agg* Corsican 2 *m*, -a f Corsican

corso[2] 1 *pp* ☞ **correre** 2 *m* course; *(strada)* main street; FIN *di moneta* circulation; *di titoli* rate; ~ *d'acqua* watercourse; ~ *di lingue* language course; FIN **fuori** ~ out of circulation; **lavori** *mpl* **in** ~ work in progress

corte f court

corteccia f bark

corteggiare court

corteo m procession

cortese polite, courteous; **cortesia** f politeness, courtesy; **per** ~! please!

cortile m courtyard

corto short; **essere a** ~ **di** be short of; **cortocircuito** m short (circuit)

corvo m rook; ~ **imperiale** raven

cosa f thing; *(che)* ~ what; **qualche** ~ something; **dimmi una** ~ tell me something; **una** ~ **da nulla** a trifle

coscia f thigh; GASTR leg

cosciente conscious; **coscienza** f conscience; *(consapevolezza)* consciousness; **coscienzioso** conscientious

così so; *(in questo modo)* like this; ~ ~ so-so; **e** ~ **via** and so on; **per** ~ **dire** so to speak; **proprio** ~! exactly!; **basta** ~! that's enough!; **cosiddetto** so-called

cosmetico m/agg cosmetic

cosmo m cosmos

cosmopolita cosmopolitan

coso m F what-d'you-call-it F

cospargere sprinkle; *(coprire)* cover *(di* with); **cosparso** *pp* ☞ **cospargere**

cospiratore m, **-trice** f conspirator; **cospirazione** f conspiracy

costa f coast, coastline; *(pendio)* hillside; ANAT rib

costante constant, steady; **costanza** f perseverance

costare cost; ~ **caro** be expensive, cost a lot; *fig* cost dear; **quanto costa?** how much is it?

costata f rib steak; ~ **di agnello** lamb chop

costeggiare skirt, hug

costellazione f constellation

costiero coastal

costituire constitute; *società* form, create; **costituirsi** give o.s. up; **costituzionale** constitutional; **costituzione** f constitution

costo m cost; ~ **della vita** cost of living; **ad ogni** ~ at all costs

costola f rib; *di libro* spine; **costoletta** f GASTR cutlet

costoso expensive, costly

costretto *pp* ☞ **costringere**; **costringere** force, compel

costruire build, construct; **costruttivo** *fig* constructive; **costruttore** m, **-trice** f builder; (*fabbricante*) manufacturer; **costruzione** f building, construction; GRAM construction

costume m (*usanza*) custom; (*condotta*) morals; (*indumento*) costume; **~ da bagno** swimming costume, swimsuit; *da uomo* (swimming) trunks

cotechino m kind of pork sausage

cotoletta f cutlet; **~ alla milanese** breaded cutlet fried in butter

cotone m cotton; MED **~ idrofilo** cotton wool, *Am* absorbent cotton

cotta f F crush

cottimo m: **lavorare a ~** do piecework

cotto 1 *pp* ☞ **cuocere** 2 *agg* done, cooked; F *fig* head over heels in love (**di** with); **cottura** f cooking

covare 1 *v/t* sit on, hatch; *fig*: *malattia* sicken for; *rancore* harbour, *Am* harbor 2 *v/i* sit on eggs; *covo* m den; (*nido*) nest; *fig* hideout

covone m sheaf

cozza f mussel

C.P. (= **Casella Postale**) PO Box (= Post Office Box)

crampo m cramp

cranio m skull

cratere m crater

cravatta f tie, *Am anche* necktie

creare create; *fig* (*causare*) cause; **creatività** f creativity; **creativo** 1 *agg* creative 2 m copywriter; **creatore** 1 *agg* creative 2 m Creator 3 m, **-trice** f creator; **creatura** f creature; **creazione** f creation

credente m/f believer

credenza[1] f belief

credenza[2] m mobile dresser

credenziali fpl credentials

credere 1 *v/t* believe; (*pensare*) believe, think; **lo credo bene!** I should think so too!; **credersi** believe *o* think o.s. to be 2 *v/i* believe; **~ a qu** believe in s.o.; **non ci credo** I don't believe it; **credibile** credible; **credibilità** f credibility

credito m credit; *fig* trust; (*attendibilità*) reliability; **creditore** m, **-trice** f creditor

crema f cream; *di latte e uova* custard; **~ da barba** shaving foam; **~ idratante** moisturizer, moisturizing cream; **~ solare** suntan lotion

cremare cremate; **cremazione** f cremation

cren *m* horseradish

crepa *f* crack; **crepaccio** *m* cleft; *di ghiacciaio* crevasse; **crepare** (*spaccarsi*) crack; F (*morire*) kick the bucket F

crêpe *f inv* pancake

crepitare crackle

crepuscolo *m* twilight

crescente growing; *luna* crescent; **crescere 1** *v/t* bring up, raise **2** *v/i* grow

crescione *m* watercress

crescita *f* growth

cresima *f* confirmation

crespo *capelli* frizzy

cresta *f* crest; *di montagna* peak

creta *f* clay

cretino F 1 *agg* stupid, idiotic **2** *m*, **-a** *f* idiot, cretin

cric *m inv* AUTO jack

criminale *agg*, *m/f* criminal; **criminalità** *f* crime; **crimine** *m* crime

criniera *f* mane

cripta *f* crypt

crisantemo *m* chrysanthemum

crisi *f inv* crisis; MED fit

cristallizzare, **cristallizzarsi** crystallize; **cristallo** *m* crystal

cristianesimo *m* Christianity; **cristiano 1** *agg* Christian **2** *m*, **-a** *f* Christian; **Cristo** *m* Christ

criterio *m* criterion; (*buon senso*) common sense

critica *f* criticism; **criticare** criticize; **critico 1** *agg* critical **2** *m*, **-a** *f* critic

croato 1 *agg* Croatian **2** *m*, **-a** *f* Croat, Croatian; **Croazia** *f* Croatia

croccante 1 *agg* crisp, crunchy **2** *m* GASTR nut brittle

crocchetta *f* GASTR potato croquette

croce *f* cross; **Croce Rossa** Red Cross; **crociata** *f* crusade; **crociera** *f* cruise; **crocifiggere** crucify; **crocifisso** *m* crucifix

crollare collapse; **crollo** *m* collapse

cronaca *f* chronicle; *di partita* commentary; *fatto di* ~ news item; ~ **nera** crime news *sg*

cronico chronic

cronista *m/f* reporter; *di partita* commentator

cronologico chronological

cronometrare time; **cronometro** *m* chronometer; SP stopwatch

crosta *f* crust; MED scab; *di formaggio* rind

crostacei *mpl* shellfish *pl*

crostata *f* GASTR tart

crostino *m* GASTR crouton

cruciale crucial

cruciverba *m inv* crossword (puzzle)

crudele cruel; **crudeltà** *f* cruelty

crudo raw

crumiro *m*, **-a** *f* scab

crusca *f* bran

cruscotto *m* dashboard; *scomparto* glove compartment

Cuba f Cuba; **cubano 1** agg Cuban **2** m, **-a** f Cuban

cubetto m (small) cube; **~ di ghiaccio** ice cube; **cubo 1** agg cubic **2** m cube

cuccagna f: (**paese** m **della**) **~** land of plenty

cucchetta f FERR couchette; MAR berth

cucchiaiata f spoonful; **cucchiaino** m teaspoon; **cucchiaio** m spoon; **~ da tavola** tablespoon

cuccia f dog's basket; esterna kennel

cucciolo m cub; di cane puppy

cucina f kitchen; (cibi) food; (il cucinare) cooking; **~ a gas** gas cooker; **cucinare** cook; **cucinino** m kitchenette

cucire sew; **cucito 1** agg sewn **2** m sewing; **cucitura** f seam

cuffia f da piscina swimming cap; RAD, TV headphones; **~ da bagno** shower cap

cugino m, **-a** f cousin

cui persona who, whom fml; cose which; **la casa in ~ abitano** the house they live in, the house in which they live; **il ~ nome** whose name; **per ~** so

culinario cookery attr, culinary; **arte** f **-a** culinary art, cookery

culla f cradle; **cullare** rock

culminante: punto m **~** climax; **culmine** m peak

culo V m arse V, Am ass V

culto m cult; religione religion

cultura f culture; **culturale** cultural; **culturismo** m body-building

cumulativo cumulative; **biglietto** m **~** group ticket; **cumulo** m heap, pile

cuneo m wedge

cunetta f fondo stradale bump

cuocere cook; pane bake; **cuoco** m, **-a** f cook

cuoio m leather; **~ capelluto** scalp

cuore m heart; **carte -i** pl hearts; **di ~** wholeheartedly; **stare a ~ a qu** be very important to s.o.

cupo gloomy; suono deep

cupola f dome

cura f care; MED treatment; **~ dimagrante** diet; **avere ~ di qc** take care of sth; **curabile** curable; **curare** take care of; MED treat; **curarsi** look after o.s.; **non curarti di loro** don't bother about them

curiosare have a look around; spreg pry (in into); **curiosità** f inv curiosity; **curioso** curious

cursore m INFOR cursor

curva f curve; **curvare** curve; schiena bend; **curvarsi** bend; **curvo** curved; persona bent

cuscinetto m TEC bearing; **~ a sfere** ball bearing; POL **stato** m **~** buffer state; **cuscino** m cushion; (guanciale) pillow

custode *m/f* caretaker; *di parco, museo* attendant; **custodia** *f* care; DIR custody; *(astuccio)* case; **custodire**

(conservare) keep

cute *f* skin

CV *m* (= **curriculum vitae**) CV (= curriculum vitae), *Am* résumé

D

da *stato in luogo* at; *moto da luogo* from; *moto a luogo* to; *tempo* since; *con verbo passivo* by; **viene ~ Roma** he comes from Rome; **sono ~ mio fratello** I'm at my brother's (place); **passo ~ Firenze** I'm going via Florence; **vado dal medico** I'm going to the doctor's *o Am* doctor; **~ ieri** since yesterday; **~ oggi in poi** from now on; **~ bambino** as a child; **l'ho fatto ~ me** I did it myself; **qualcosa ~ mangiare** something to eat; **la donna dai capelli grigi** the woman with grey hair

dà *☞* **dare**

daccapo *☞* **capo**

dado *m* dice; GASTR stock cube; TEC nut

dagli = **da** and *art* **gli**

dai[1] = **da** and *art* **i**

dai[2] *☞* **dare**

daino *m* deer; *(pelle)* buckskin

dal = **da** and *art* **il**

dall', dalla, dalle, dallo = **da** and *art* **l', la, le, lo**

daltonico colour-blind, *Am* color-blind

dama *f* lady; *gioco* draughts *sg*, *Am* checkers *sg*

damigiana *f* demijohn

danese 1 *m/agg* Danish **2** *m/f* Dane; **Danimarca** *f* Denmark

danneggiare *(rovinare)* damage; *(nuocere)* harm; **danno** *m* damage; *(a persona)* harm; **dannoso** harmful

danza *f* dance; **~ classica** ballet; **danzare** dance

dappertutto everywhere

dappoco *agg inv* *(inetto)* worthless; *(irrilevante)* minor, unimportant

dapprima at first

dare 1 *v/t* give; **~ qc a qu** give s.o. sth, give sth to s.o.; **~ uno sguardo a qc** have a look at sth; **dammi del tu** call me 'tu' **2** *v/i* *di finestra* overlook *(su* sth); *di porta* lead into *(su* sth) **3** *m* FIN debit; **~ e avere** debit and credit

darsena *f* dock

darsi give each other; *(dedicarsi)* devote o.s. *(a* to); **~ al commercio** go into business; **può ~** perhaps

data *f* date; **~ di nascita** date

of birth; **~ di scadenza** expiry date, *Am* expiration date; **datare 1** *v/t* date **2** *v/i*: **~ da oggi** from today

dato 1 *pp* ☞ **dare 2** *agg* (*certo*) given, particular; (*dedito*) addicted (**a** to); **in -i casi** in certain cases; **~ che** given that **3** *m* piece of data; **-i** *pl* data *sg*

datore *m*, **-trice** *f*: **~ di lavoro** employer

dattero *m* date; (*albero*) date palm

dattilografo *m*, **-a** *f* typist

davanti 1 *prp*: **~ a** in front of **2** *avv* in front; (*dirimpetto*) opposite **3** *m/agg inv* front

davanzale *m* window sill

davanzo more than enough

davvero really

d.C. (= **dopo Cristo**) AD (= anno domini)

dea *f* goddess

debito 1 *agg* due, proper **2** *m* debt; (*dovere*) duty; **avere un ~ con qu** be in debt to s.o.; **debitore** *m*, **-trice** *f* debtor

debole 1 *agg* weak; (*luce*) dim **2** *m* weakness; **avere un ~ per qu** have a soft spot for s.o.; **debolezza** *f* weakness

debutto *m* début

decadente decadent

decaffeinato decaffeinated, decaff *F*

decalcomania *f* transfer, *Am* decal

decappottabile *f/agg* AUTO convertible

decennio *m* decade

decente decent

decentrare decentralize

decesso *m* death

decidere 1 *v/t questione* settle; *data* decide on, settle on; **~ di fare qc** decide to do sth **2** *v/i* decide; **decidersi** decide (**a** to), make up one's mind (**a** to)

decifrare decipher

decimale *m/agg* decimal

decimo tenth

decina *f* MAT ten; **una ~** about ten

decisione *f* decision; (*risolutezza*) decisiveness; **prendere una ~** make a decision; **decisivo** decisive; **deciso 1** *pp* ☞ **decidere 2** *agg* (*definito*) definite; (*risoluto*) determined; (*netto*) clear; (*spiccato*) marked

declinare 1 *v/t* decline; *responsabilità* disclaim **2** *v/i* (*tramontare*) set; (*diminuire*) decline; **declinazione** *f* GRAM declension; **declino** *m* fig decline

decodificatore *m* decoder

decollare take off; **decollo** *m* take-off

decomposizione *f* decomposition; CHIM breaking down

decompressione *f* decompression

decorare decorate; **decoratore** *m*, **-trice** *f* decorator; **decorazione** *f* decoration

decorrenza f: **con immedia-ta ~** with immediate effect; **decorrere** pass; **a ~ da oggi** with effect from today; **decorso** 1 pp ☞ **decorrere** 2 m di malattia course

decrepito decrepit

decreto m decree; **~-legge** m decree passed in exceptional circumstances that has the force of law

dedica f dedication; **dedicare** dedicate; **dedicarsi** dedicate o.s.; **dedito** dedicated (**a** to); a un vizio addicted (**a** to); **dedizione** f dedication

dedurre deduce; FIN deduct; (derivare) derive; **deduzione** f deduction

deficiente 1 agg (mancante) deficient, lacking (**di** in) 2 m/f idiot, moron

deficit m inv deficit; **~ del bilancio pubblico** public spending deficit

definire define; (risolvere) settle; **definitivo** definitive; **definizione** f definition

deflettore m AUTO quarter-light

deformare deform; legno metallo buckle; fig distort; **deformarsi** di legno warp; di metallo buckle; di scarpe lose their shape; **deformazione** f deformation; di legno warping; di metallo buckling; fisica deformity; fig, visuale distortion; defor-me deformed

defunto 1 agg dead; fig defunct 2 m, -a f DIR: il ~ the deceased

degenerare degenerate (**in** into)

degente m/f patient

degli = **di** and art **gli**

degnare 1 v/t: ~ **qu di una parola** deign to speak to s.o. 2 v/i e **degnarsi**: ~ **di** deign to, condescend to

degno worthy; ~ **di nota** noteworthy

degradante degrading; **degradarsi** demean o.s., lower o.s.; CHIM degrade; di ambiente, edifici deteriorate; **degradazione** f degradation; **degrado** m deterioration; ~ **ambientale** damage to the environment

degustazione f tasting

dei[1] = **di** and art **i**

dei[2] (pl di **dio**): **gli** ~ mpl the Gods

del = **di** and art **il**

delega f delegation; (procura) proxy; **delegare** delegate; **delegato** 1 agg: **amministratore** m ~ managing director 2 m, -a f delegate; **sindacale** (trade) union delegate

delfino m dolphin

deliberare 1 v/t decide 2 v/i DIR deliberate (**su** on)

delicatezza f delicacy; **delicato** delicate

delimitare define

delineare outline

delinquente *m/f* criminal; *fig* scoundrel; **delinquenza** *f* crime; **~ minorile** juvenile delinquency; **~ organizzata** organized crime

delirare be in raptures; MED be delirious; **delirio** *m* delirium; *fig* frenzy

delitto *m* crime

delizioso delightful; *cibo* delicious

dell', della, dello = **di** and *art* **l', la, le, lo**

delta *m* delta; **deltaplano** *m* hang-glider; *attività* hanggliding

deludere disappoint; **delusione** *f* disappointment; **deluso** disappointed

demanio *m* State property

demente *m/f* MED person with dementia; F lunatic F

democratico 1 *agg* democratic **2** *m*, **-a** *f* democrat; **democrazia** *f* democracy

demogafico demographic

demolire demolish (*anche fig*); *macchine* crush; **demolizione** *f* demolition; *di macchine* crushing

demonio *m* devil

demoralizzarsi become demoralized, lose heart

demotivato demotivated

denaro *m* money; **~ contante** cash

denaturato CHIM: **alcol** *m* **~** methlyated spirits *sg*

denominare name, call; de-

nominazione *f* name; **~ di origine controllata** term signifying that a wine is of a certain origin and quality

denotare denote, be indicative of

densità *f* density; *della nebbia* thickness, density; **denso** dense; *fumo, nebbia* thick, dense

dentario dental; **dente** *m* tooth; **~ del giudizio** wisdom tooth; **mal** *m* **di -i** toothache; GASTR **al ~** al dente, still slightly firm

dentice *m* fish native to the Mediterranean

dentiera *f* dentures; **dentifricio** *m* toothpaste; **dentista** *m/f* dentist

dentro 1 *prp* in, inside; (*entro*) within **2** *avv* in, inside; (*nell' intimo*) inwardly; **qui / lì ~** in here / there

denuclearizzato nuclearfree, denuclearized

denuncia *f* denunciation; *alla polizia, alla società di assicurazione* complaint, report; *di nascita, morte* registration; **~ dei redditi** income tax return; **denunciare** denounce; *alla polizia, alla società di assicurazione* report; *nascita* register

denutrito undernourished

deodorante *m* deodorant

depilare *con pinzette* pluck; *con rasoio* shave; *con ceretta* wax

depilatorio *m/agg* depilatory

dépliant *m inv* leaflet; *(opuscolo)* brochure

deplorevole deplorable

deporre 1 *v/t* put down; *uova* lay; *re, presidente* depose; **~ il falso** commit perjury **2** *v/i* DIR testify, give evidence (**a favore di** for, **a carico di** against)

deportare deport

depositare deposit; *(posare)* put down, deposit; *(registrare)* register; **depositato: marchio** *m* ~ registered trademark; **deposito** *m* deposit; *(magazzino)* warehouse; *rimessa* depot; FERR ~ **bagagli** left-luggage office, *Am* baggage checkroom

depravato *m*, **-a** *f* depraved person

depressione *f* depression; **depresso 1** *pp* ☞ **deprimere 2** *agg* depressed; **deprimente** depressing; **deprimere** depress; **deprimersi** get depressed

depurare purify; **depuratore** *m* purifier

deputato *m*, **-a** *f* Member of Parliament, *Am* Representative

deragliare FERR go off the rails; **far** ~ derail

deridere deride; **derisione** *f* derision; **deriso** *pp* ☞ **deridere**

deriva *f* MAR drift; **andare alla** ~ drift

derivare 1 *v/t* derive **2** *v/i:* ~ **da** come from, derive from

dermatologo *m*, **-a** *f* dermatologist

derubare rob

descritto *pp* ☞ **descrivere**; **descrivere** describe; **descrizione** *f* description

deserto 1 *agg* deserted **2** *m* desert

desiderare *(volere)* want, wish; *intensamente* long for; *sessualmente* desire; **desidera?** can I help you?; **lascia a** ~ it leaves a lot to be desired; **desiderio** *m* wish *(di* for); *intenso* longing *(di* for); *sessuale* desire *(di* for)

design *m inv* design

designare *(nominare)* appoint, name; *(fissare)* fix

desistere: ~ **da** desist from

desolato desolate; **sono ~!** I am so sorry

dessert *m inv* dessert

destinare destine; *(assegnare)* assign; *con il pensiero* mean, intend; *data* fix; *(indirizzare)* address (**a** to); **destinatario** *m*, **-a** *f di lettera* addressee; **destinazione** *f*: *(luogo m di)* ~ destination

destino *m* destiny

destra *f* right; *(mano)* right hand; **a** ~ to the right

destreggiarsi manœuvre, *Am* maneuver

destrezza *f* skill, dexterity; **destro** right; *(abile)* skilful,

Am skillful, dexterous

detenere hold; **detenuto** *m*, **-a** *f* prisoner; **detenzione** *f* (*imprigionamento*) detention

detergente *m* detergent; *per cosmesi* cleanser

deteriorabile perishable; **deteriorarsi** deteriorate, get worse

determinare determine, establish; (*causare*) cause, lead to; **determinato** certain; (*specifico*) particular, specific; (*risoluto*) determined; **determinazione** *f* determination

detersivo *m* detergent; *per piatti* washing-up liquid, *Am* dishwashing liquid; *per biancheria* detergent, *Br anche* washing powder

detestare hate, detest

detonare detonate

detrarre deduct (**da** from); **detratto** *pp* ☞ **detrarre**; **detrazione** *f* deduction

detrito *m* debris; GEOL detritus

detta: **a ~ di** according to

dettaglio *m* detail; FIN **commercio al** *m* ~ retail trade

dettare dictate; **dettato** *m* dictation

detto 1 *pp* ☞ **dire**; **~ fatto** no sooner said than done; **come non ~** let's forget it **2** *agg* said; (*soprannominato*) known as **3** *m* saying

devastare devastate

deve, devi ☞ **dovere**

deviare 1 *v/t* traffico, sospetti divert **2** *v/i* deviate; **deviazione** *f* deviation; *di traffico* diversion

devo ☞ **dovere**

devoto 1 *agg* devoted; REL devout **2** *m*, **-a** *f* devotee; REL **i -i** the devout *pl*

di 1 *prp* of; *con il comparativo* than; **~ ferro** (made of) iron; **io sono ~ Roma** I'm from Rome; **l'auto ~ mio padre** my father's car; **~ giorno** by day; **parlare ~ politica** talk about politics; **d'estate** in the summer; **di ~** on Sundays; **più bello ~** prettier than **2** *art* some; *interrogativo* any, some; *negativo* any; **del vino** some wine

di' ☞ **dire**

dia ☞ **dare**

diabete *m* diabetes *sg*; **diabetico 1** *agg* diabetic **2** *m*, **-a** *f* diabetic

diadema *m* diadem

diaframma *m* diaphragm

diagnosi *f inv* diagnosis; **diagnosticare** diagnose

diagonale *f/agg* diagonal

diagramma *m* diagram

dialetto *m* dialect

dialisi *f inv* dialysis

dialogo *m* dialogue, *Am* dialog

diamante *m* diamond

diametro *m* diameter

diapason *m inv* tuning fork

diapositiva *f* FOT slide

diario *m* diary

diarrea f diarrhoea, Am diarrhea

diavolo m devil; **mandare qu al ~** tell s.o. to get lost; F **ma che ~ fai?** what the heck are you doing? F

dibattersi struggle; **dibattito** m debate

dicembre m December

diceria f rumour, Am rumor

dichiarare state; *ufficialmente* declare; **dichiararsi** declare o.s.; **dichiarazione** f declaration; **~ dei redditi** income tax statement; **~ doganale** customs declaration

diciannove nineteen; **diciannovesimo** nineteenth; **diciassette** seventeen; **diciassettesimo** seventeenth; **diciottenne** m/f eighteen-year-old; **diciottesimo** eighteenth; **diciotto** eighteen; **dieci** ten; **alle / verso le ~** at / about ten (o'clock)

diesel m diesel

dieta f diet; **essere a ~** be on a diet; **dietetico** diet attr

dietro 1 prp behind; **~ l'angolo** around the corner; **~ di me** behind me 2 avv behind; *in auto* in the back; **di ~** *stanza, porta* back; *zampe* hind; AUTO *rear* m inv back

difatti in fact

difendere defend; (*proteggere*) protect; **difensiva** f defensive; **stare sulla ~** be on the defensive; **difensivo** defensive; **difensore** m defender; **~ d'ufficio** legal aid lawyer, Am public defender; **difesa** f defence, Am defense; **~ dei consumatori** consumer protection; **legittima ~** self-defence; **difeso** pp ◊ **difendere**

difetto m (*imperfezione*) defect; *morale* fault, flaw; (*mancanza*) lack; **difettoso** defective

diffamare slander; *scrivendo* libel; **diffamazione** f defamation of character

differente different (**da** from); **differenza** f difference; **~ di prezzo** difference in price, price difference; **a ~ di** unlike; **differenziarsi** differ (**da** from)

difficile difficult; (*improbabile*) unlikely; **difficoltà** f inv difficulty; **senza ~** easily, without any difficulty

diffidare 1 v/t DIR issue an injunction against; **~ qu dal fare qc** warn s.o. not to do sth 2 v/i: **~ di qu** distrust s.o.; **diffidente** distrustful; **diffidenza** f distrust

diffondere diffuse; *fig* spread; **diffondersi** *fig* spread; (*dilungarsi*) enlarge; **diffusione** f di luce, calore diffusion; di giornale circulation; **diffuso** 1 pp ◊ **diffondere** 2 agg widespread; *luce* diffuse

diga f fluviale dam; *litoranea* dyke; *portuale* breakwater

digerire digest; F (*tollerare*)

stomach F; **digestione** f digestion; **digestivo 1** *agg* digestive **2** *m* after-dinner drink, digestif

digitale digital; **impronta** f ~ fingerprint

digitare INFOR key

digiunare fast; **digiuno 1** *agg* fasting **2** *m* fast; **a** ~ on an empty stomach

dignità f dignity

digrignare gnash

dilagare flood; *fig* spread rapidly

dilaniare tear apart

dilatare expand; *occhi* open wide; **dilatarsi** *di materiali* expand; *di pupilla* dilate

dilazionare defer, delay

dileguarsi vanish, disappear

dilemma *m* dilemma

dilettante *m/f* amateur; *spreg* dilettante; **dilettarsi**: ~ *di qc* dabble in sth, do sth as a hobby; ~ *a fare qc* take delight in doing sth

diligente diligent; *(accurato)* accurate

diluire dilute

dilungarsi *fig* dwell (*su* on)

diluviare pour down; **diluvio** *m* downpour; *fig* deluge

dimagrante: **cura** f ~ diet; **dimagrire** lose weight

dimenarsi throw o.s. about

dimensione f dimension; *(grandezza)* size; *(misure)* dimensions

dimenticanza f forgetfulness, absent-mindedness; *(svista)*

oversight; **dimenticare** forget; **dimenticarsi** forget (*di* sth; *di fare qc* to do sth)

dimestichezza f familiarity

dimettere dismiss (*da* from); *da ospedali* discharge (*da* from); *da carceri* release (*da* from); **dimettersi** resign (*da* from)

dimezzare halve

diminuire 1 *v/t* reduce **2** *v/i* decrease; *di prezzi, valore* fall, go down; *di vento, rumore* die down; **diminuzione** f decrease; *di prezzi, valore* fall, drop (*di* in)

dimissioni *fpl* resignation; **dare le** ~ hand in one's resignation

dimora f residence

dimostrare demonstrate; *(interesse)* show; *(provare)* prove, show; **dimostrarsi** prove to be; **dimostrazione** f demonstration; *(prova)* proof

dinamica f dynamics; **dinamico** dynamic

dinamite f dynamite

dinanzi: ~ *a al cospetto di* before

dinastia f dynasty

dinosauro *m* dinosaur

dintorno 1 *avv* around **2** *m*: **-i** *pl* neighbourhood, *Am* neighborhood

dio *m* god; **grazie a Dio!** thank God!; **per l'amor di Dio** for God's sake

diocesi f *inv* diocese

diossina f dioxin

dipartimento m department

dipendente 1 agg dependent **2** m/f employee; **dipendenza** f dependence; (edificio) annexe, Am annex, **essere alle ~ di** work for; **dipendere: ~ da** (essere subordinato a) depend on; (essere mantenuto da) be dependent on; (essere causato da) be due to; **dipende** it depends; **questo dipende da te** it's up to you; **diposo** pp ☞ **dipendere**

dipingere paint; fig describe, depict; **dipinto 1** pp ☞ **dipingere 2** m painting, picture

diploma m diploma, certificate; **~ di laurea** degree (certificate); **diplomarsi** obtain a diploma

diplomatico 1 agg diplomatic **2** m diplomat; **diplomato 1** agg qualified **2** m, -a f holder of a diploma; **diplomazia** f diplomacy

diporto: imbarcazione f **da ~** pleasure boat

diradare thin out; **diradarsi** thin out; di nebbia clear, lift

dire v/t say; (raccontare) tell; **~ qc a qu** tell s.o. sth; **~ a qu di fare qc** tell s.o. to do sth; **vale a ~** that is, in other words; **a ~ il vero** to tell the truth; **come si dice ... in inglese?** what's the English for ... ?, how do you say ... in English?; **voler ~** mean

2 v/i ~ **bene di qu** speak highly of s.o.; **dico sul serio** I'm serious

direttiva f directive; **direttivo 1** agg managerial; comitato, consiglio, POL executive attr **2** m di società board (of directors); POL leadership

diretto 1 pp ☞ **dirigere 2** agg (immediato) direct; **~ a** aimed at; lettera addressed to; **essere ~ a casa** be heading for home; RAD, TV **in (ripresa)** a live **3** m direct train; SP straight

direttore m, **-trice** f manager; più in alto nella gerarchia direttore; EDU headmaster; donna headmistress; Am principal; di giornale, rivista editor (in chief); **~ generale** CEO; **~ d'orchestra** conductor

direzione f direction; di società management; di partito leadership; ufficio office; **sede generale** head office

dirigente 1 agg classe, partito ruling; personale managerial **2** m/f executive; POL leader; **dirigere** direct; azienda run, manage; orchestra conduct; **dirigersi** head (**a**, **verso** for, toward)

dirigibile m airship, dirigible

diritto 1 agg, avv straight **2** m right; DIR law; **aver ~ a** be entitled to; **di ~** by rights; **~ d'autore** copyright; **~ penale** criminal law; **diritto** fig rectitude; **in ~**

d'arrivo on the home straight

diroccato ramshackle

dirottare *traffico* divert; *aereo* reroute; *con intenzioni criminali* hijack; **dirottatore** *m*, **-trice** *f* hijacker

dirotto: piove a ~ it's pouring

dirupo *m* precipice

disabile 1 *agg* disabled **2** *m/f* disabled person

disabitato uninhabited

disaccordo *m* disagreement

disadattato 1 *agg* maladjusted **2** *m/f* (social) misfit

disagio *m* (*difficoltà*) hardship; (*scomodità*) discomfort; (*imbarazzo*) embarrassment; **essere a ~** be ill at ease

disapprovare disapprove of; **disapprovazione** *f* disapproval

disappunto *m* disappointment

disarmato unarmed; *fig* defenceless, *Am* defenseless; **disarmo** *m* POL disarmament

disastro *m* disaster; **disastroso** disastrous

disattento inattentive; **disattenzione** *f* inattention; *errore* careless mistake

disavanzo *m* deficit

disavventura *f* misadventure

disboscamento *m* deforestation

discapito *m*: **a ~ di qu** to the detriment *o* disadvantage of s.o.

discarica *f* dumping; *luogo* dump

discendente 1 *agg inv* descending **2** *m/f* descendant; **discendere** descend; (*trarre origine*) be descended (**da** from); *da veicoli, da cavallo* get off (**da qc** sth)

discepolo *m* disciple

discesa *f* descent; (*pendio*) slope; *di bus* exit; **strada in ~** street that slopes downward

dischetto *m* INFOR diskette, floppy

disciplina *f* discipline; **disciplinato** disciplined

disco *m* disc, *Am* disk; SP discus; MUS record; INFOR disk; INFOR **~ rigido** hard disk; AUTO **~ orario** parking disc; **~ volante** flying saucer; **discobolo** *m* discus thrower

discolpare clear

discontinuo intermittent; (*disuguale*) erratic

discorde not in agreement, clashing; **discordia** *f* discord; (*differenza di opinioni*) disagreement; (*litigio*) argument

discorrere talk (*di* about); **discorso 1** *pp* ☞ **discorrere 2** *m pubblico, ufficiale* speech; (*conversazione*) conversation, talk

discoteca *f locale* disco; *raccolta* record library

discrepanza *f* discrepancy

discreto (*riservato*) discreet; (*abbastanza buono*) fairly good; (*moderato*) moderate, fair; **discrezione** *f* discretion; **a ~ di** at the discretion of

discriminare 1 *v/i* discriminate **2** *v/t stranieri, donne* discriminate against; **discriminazione** *f* discrimination

discussione *f* discussion; (*litigio*) argument; **discusso** *pp* ☞ **discutere**; **discutere 1** *v/t* discuss, talk about; (*questione*) debate; (*mettere in dubbio*) question; (*contestare*) dispute **2** *v/i* talk; (*litigare*) argue; (*negoziare*) negotiate; **discutibile** debatable

disdegnare disdain

disdetto *pp* ☞ **disdire**; **disdire** *impegno* cancel; *contratto* terminate

disegnare draw; (*progettare*) design; **disegno** *m* drawing; (*progetto*) design; **~ di legge** bill

diserbante *m* weed-killer

diseredare disinherit; **diseredato** underprivileged, disadvantaged

disertare desert; **disertore** *m* deserter; **diserzione** *f* desertion

disfare undo; *letto* strip; (*distruggere*) destroy; **~ la valigia** unpack; **disfarsi di ghiaccio** melt; **~ di** get rid of; **disfatta** *f* defeat; **disfatto** *pp* ☞ **disfare**

disgelo *m* thaw

disgrazia *f* misfortune; (*incidente*) accident; (*sfavore*) disgrace; **per ~** unfortunately; **disgraziato 1** *agg* (*sfortunato*) unlucky **2** *m*, -a *f* poor soul; F (*farabutto*) bastard F

disgregare break up; **disgregarsi** break up, disintegrate

disguido *m* hiccup, hitch

disgustare disgust; **disgusto** *m* disgust; **disgustoso** disgusting

disidratato dehydrated

disillusione *f* disillusionment; **disilluso** disillusioned

disinfettante *m* disinfectant; **disinfettare** disinfect

disinibito uninhibited

disinnescare *bomba* defuse

disinserire disconnect

disinteressarsi take no interest (**di** in); **disinteressato** disinterested; **disinteresse** *m* lack of interest; (*generosità*) unselfishness

disintossicare detoxify; **disintossicazione** *f* treatment for drug / alcohol addiction, detox F

disinvolto confident; **disinvoltura** *f* confidence

dislessia *f* dyslexia; **dislessico** dyslexic

dislivello *m* difference in height, height difference; *fig* difference

disobbedire ☞ **disubbidire**

disoccupato 1 *agg* unemployed, jobless **2** *m*, **-a** *f* unemployed person; **i** *-i* the unemployed *pl*, the jobless *pl*; **disoccupazione** *f* unemployment

disonestà *f* dishonesty; **disonesto** dishonest

disonore *m* dishonour, *Am* dishonor

disopra 1 *avv* above; **al ~ di** above **2** *agg* upper **3** *m inv* top

disordinato untidy, messy; **disordine** *m* untidiness, mess; **in ~** untidy, in a mess; **-i** *pl* riots, public disorder

disorganizzazione *f* disorganization

disorientamento *m* disorientation; **disorientare** disorientate, *Am* disorient; **disorientato** disorientated, *Am* disoriented

disotto 1 *avv* below; **al ~ di** beneath **2** *agg* lower **3** *m* underside

dispari *inv* odd; **disparità** *f inv* disparity

disparte: in ~ aside

dispendio *m* waste; **dispendioso** expensive

dispensa *f* stanza larder; *mobile* cupboard; *pubblicazione* instalment, *Am* installment; DIR exemption; **dispensare** dispense; (*esonerare*) exonerate

disperare despair (*di* of); **far ~ qu** drive s.o. to despair; **disperarsi** despair; **disperato**

desperate; **disperazione** *f* despair, desperation

disperdere disperse; *energie, sostanze* squander; **disperdersi** disperse; **disperso 1** *pp* ☞ **disperdere 2** *agg* scattered; (*sperduto*) lost, missing

dispetto *m* spite; **per ~** out of spite; **a ~ di qc** in spite of sth; **fare i -i a qu** annoy *o* tease s.o.; **dispettoso** mischievous

dispiacere *v/i* (*causare dolore*) upset (*a* s.o.); (*non piacere*) displease (*a* s.o.); **mi dispiace** I'm sorry; **mi dispiace se apro la finestra?** do you mind if I open the window? **2** *m* (*rammarico*) regret, sorrow; (*dolore*) sadness; (*delusione*) disappointment; **-i** *pl* (*preoccupazioni*) worries, troubles

display *m* display

disponibile available; (*cortese*) helpful, obliging; **disponibilità** *f* availability; (*cortesia*) helpfulness

disporre 1 *v/t* arrange; (*stabilire*) order **2** *v/i* (*decidere*) make arrangements; **~ di qc** have sth (at one's disposal)

dispositivo *m* device

disposizione *f* arrangement; (*norma*) provision; (*attitudine*) aptitude (*a* for); **stare / mettere a ~ di qu** be / put at s.o.'s disposal

disposto 1 pp ☞ **disporre 2**
agg: ~ **a** ready to, willing
to; **essere ben ~ verso qu**
be well disposed to s.o.

dispotico despotic

disprezzare despise; **disprezzo** m contempt

disputa f dispute, argument;
disputare 1 v/i argue **2** v/t
SP take part in; **disputarsi
qc** compete for sth

disseminare scatter, dissem-
inate; fig spread

dissenso m dissent; (dissapore) argument, disagreement

dissenteria f dysentery

dissentire disagree (**da** with)

disservizio m poor service;
(inefficienza) inefficiency;
(cattiva gestione) mismanagement

dissestato strada uneven; fi-
nanze precarious

dissetante thirst-quenching;
dissetare: ~ **qu** quench
s.o.'s thirst; **dissetarsi**
quench one's thirst

dissimulare conceal, hide;
dissimulazione f concealment

dissociare dissociate o.s.
(**da** from)

dissolvere dissolve; dubbi,
nebbia dispel; **dissolversi**
dissolve; (svanire) vanish

dissuadere: ~ **qu da fare qc**
dissuade s.o. from doing
sth, persuade s.o. not to do
sth; **dissuaso** pp ☞ **dissuadere**

distaccare detach; SP leave
behind; **distaccarsi da persone** detach o.s. (**da** from);
distacco m detachment (anche fig); (separazione) separation; SP lead

distante distant, far-off; ~ **da**
far from; **distanza** f distance
(anche fig); **distanziare 1** v/t
space out; SP leave behind;
(superare) overtake; **distare:**
l'albergo dista 100 metri
dalla stazione the hotel is
100 metres from the station;
quanto dista da qui? how
far is it from here?

distendere (adagiare) lay;
gambe, braccia stretch out;
muscoli relax; nervi calm; **di-
stendersi** lie down; (rilassarsi) relax

distesa f expanse; **disteso 1**
pp ☞ **distendere 2** agg
stretched out; (rilassato) relaxed

distinguere distinguish; **distintivo 1** agg distinctive **2**
m badge; **distinto** pp ☞ **distinguere 2** agg (diverso)
different, distinct; (chiaro)
distinct; fig distinguished; **-i
saluti** yours faithfully; **distinzione** f distinction

distorsione f distortion; MED
sprain

distrarre distract; (divertire)
entertain; **distrarsi** (non essere attento) get distracted;
(svagarsi) take one's mind
off things; **distratto 1** pp ☞

distrarre 2 *agg* absent-minded; **distrazione** *f* absent-mindedness; (*errore*) inattention; (*svago*) amusement; *che distrae da un'attività* distraction

distribuire distribute; (*premi*) award, present; **distributore** *m* distributor; ~ (**di benzina**) (petrol *o* Am gas) pump; ~ **automatico** vending machine; ~ **automatico di biglietti** ticket machine; **distribuzione** *f* distribution; **posta** delivery

distruggere destroy; **distruttivo** destructive; **distrutto** *pp* ▶ **distruggere**, **distruzione** *f* destruction

disturbare disturb; (*dare fastidio a*) bother; (*sconvolgere*) upset; **disturbarsi**: *non si disturbi* please don't bother; **disturbo** *m* trouble, bother; MED *-i pl di circolazione* circulation problems

disubbidiente disobedient; **disubbidire**: ~ *a* disobey

disumano inhuman

disuso: *in* ~ in disuse, disused

ditale *m* thimble

dito *m* (*pl le dita*) finger; *del piede* toe; *un* ~ *di vino* a drop of wine

ditta *f* company, firm

dittatore *m* dictator; **dittatura** *f* dictatorship

diurno daytime *attr*; *albergo m* ~ place where travellers can have a shower / shave

diva *f* diva

divagare digress

divampare *di rivolta, incendio* break out; *di passione* blaze

divano *m* couch, Br anche sofa; ~ *letto* sofa bed

divaricare open (wide)

divario *m* difference

divenire become

diventare become; *rosso, bianco* turn, go

diverbio *m* argument

divergenza *f* divergence; *di opinioni* difference

diversamente differently; (*altrimenti*) otherwise

diversificare 1 *v/t* diversify **2** *v/i e* **diversificarsi** differ; **diversità** *f inv* difference; (*varietà*) diversity

diversivo *m* diversion, distraction

diverso (*differente*) different; (**da** from; than); *-i pl* several; *da -i giorni* for the past few days

divertente amusing; **divertimento** *m* amusement; *buon* ~! have a good time!, have fun!; **divertire** amuse; **divertirsi** enjoy o.s., have a good time

dividere (*condividere*) share; **dividersi** *di coppia* separate; (*scindersi*) be divided (*in* into)

divieto *m* ban; ~ *di sosta* no parking

divincolarsi twist, wriggle

divinità *f inv* divinity; **divino**

divine

divisa f uniform; FIN currency

divisione f division; **divisorio 1** agg dividing **2** m partition

divo m star

divorare devour

divorziare get a divorce, get divorced; **divorziato** divorced; **divorzio** m divorce

divulgare divulge, reveal; *(rendere accessibile)* popularize

dizionario m dictionary

DNA m inv (= **acido deossiribonucleico**) DNA (= deoxyribonucleic acid)

do[1] ☞ **dare**

do[2] m inv MUS C; *nel solfeggio della scala* doh

dobbiamo ☞ **dovere**

D.O.C., doc (= **Denominazione d'Origine Controllata**) term signifying that a wine is of a certain origin and quality

doccia f shower; **fare la ~** (take) a shower

docente 1 agg teaching **2** m/f teacher

docile docile

documentario m documentary; **documentarsi** collect information; **documentazione** f documentation; **documento** m document

dodicesimo twelfth; **dodici** twelve

dogana f customs; *(dazio)* (customs) duty; **doganale** customs attr

doglie fpl: **avere le -e** be in labour o Am labor

dolce 1 agg sweet; *carattere, voce, pendio* gentle; *acqua* fresh; *clima* mild; *ricordo* pleasant; *suono* soft **2** m portata dessert; *di sapore* sweetness; *torta* cake; **-i** pl sweet things; **dolcezza** f sweetness; *di carattere, voce* gentleness; *di clima* mildness; *di ricordo* pleasantness; *di suono* softness; **dolciastro** sweetish; fig sugary; **dolcificante** m sweetener; **dolciumi** mpl sweets, Am candy

dolente painful, sore; **dolere** hurt, be painful; **mi duole la schiena** my back hurts

dollaro m dollar

dolo m malice

Dolomiti fpl Dolomites

dolore m pain; **doloroso** painful

doloso malicious

domanda f question; *(richiesta)* request; FIN demand; **fare una ~ a qu** ask s.o. a question; **domandare 1** v/t *per sapere: nome, ora, opinione ecc* ask; *per ottenere: informazioni, aiuto ecc* ask for; **~ un favore a qu** ask s.o. a favour; **~ scusa** apologize **2** v/i ask s.o.; **~ di qu** per sapere come sta ask after s.o.; *per parlargli* ask for s.o.; **domandarsi** wonder, ask o.s.

domani m/avv tomorrow; **~ mattina** tomorrow morning;

~ *sera* tomorrow evening; *a* ~! see you tomorrow!

domare tame; *fig* control

domattina tomorrow morning

domenica *f* Sunday

domestico 1 *agg* domestic; *animale* ~ pet **2** *m*, -a *f* servant; *donna* maid

domiciliato: ~ *a* domiciled at; **domicilio** *m* domicile; (*casa*) home

dominante dominant; *idee* prevailing; *classe* ruling; **dominare 1** *v/t* dominate; *materia; passioni* master **2** *v/i* rule (*su* over); *fig: di confusione* reign; **dominio** *m* (*controllo*) control, power; *fig* (*campo*) domain, field; INFOR domain

domino *m* mask, domino

donare donate, give; *sangue* give; **donatore** *m*, **-trice** *f* donor; ~ *di sangue* blood donor

dondolare 1 *v/t culla* rock **2** *v/i* sway; (*oscillare*) swing; **dondolarsi** *su altalena* swing; *su sedia* rock; *fig* hang around; **dondolo** *m*: *cavallo a* ~ rocking horse; *sedia f a* ~ rocking chair

donna *f* woman; *carte da gioco* queen; ~ *di servizio* home help

dono *m* gift

dopo 1 *prp* after; ~ *di te* after you; ~ *mangiato* after eating **2** *avv* (*in seguito*) afterwards,

after, *Am* afterward; (*poi*) then; (*più tardi*) later; *il giorno* ~ the day after **3** *cong:* ~ *che* after; ~ *essere uscito ho visto* ... after I left, I saw ...; **dopobarba** *m inv* aftershave; **dopodomani** the day after tomorrow; **dopoguerra** *m inv* post-war period; **dopopranzo** *m* afternoon; **doposci** *m inv* après-ski; ~ *pl stivali* après-ski boots; **dopotutto** after all

doppiaggio *m di film* dubbing; **doppiare** *film* dub; SP lap; MAR round; **doppiatore** *m*, **-trice** *f* dubber

doppio 1 *agg* double **2** *m* double; SP doubles; **doppietto** *m* double-breasted jacket

dorato 1 *pp* → **dorare 2** *agg* gilded; *sabbia, riflessi* golden; GASTR browned

dormicchiare doze

dormiglione *m*, **-a** *f* late riser

dormire sleep; **dormita** *f* (good) night's sleep; **dormitorio** *m* dormitory; **dormiveglia** *m*: *essere nel* ~ be only half awake

dorso *m* back; (*di libro*) spine; SP backstroke

dosare measure out; *fig* be sparing with; *parole* weigh; **dose** *f* quantity, amount; MED dose

dosso *m di strada* hump; *togliersi gli abiti di* ~ get undressed

dotare provide, supply (*di* with); *fig* provide, endow (*di* with); **dotato** gifted; ~ *di* equipped with; **dote** *f* dowry; *fig* gift

dott. (= *dottore*) Dr (= doctor)

dottore *m* doctor (*in* of); **dottoressa** *f* (woman) doctor

dottrina *f* doctrine

dott.ssa (= *dottoressa*) Dr (= doctor)

dove where; *di* ~ *sei?* where are you from?; *fin* ~? how far?; *per* ~ *si passa?* which way do you go?; *mettilo* ~ *vuoi* put it wherever you like

dovere 1 *v/i* have to, must; *non devo dimenticare* I mustn't forget; *deve arrivare oggi* she is supposed to arrive today; *come si deve* (*bene*) properly; *persona* very decent; *doveva succedere* it was bound to happen; *dovresti avvertirlo* you ought to *o* should let him know 2 *v/t denaro* owe 3 *m* duty

dovunque 1 *avv* (*dappertutto*) everywhere; (*in qualsiasi luogo*) anywhere 2 *cong* wherever

dovuto 1 *pp* ▸ *dovere* 2 *agg* due; ~ *a* because of, due to

dozzina *f* dozen; *una* ~ *di uova* a dozen eggs

dragare dredge

drago *m* dragon; **dragoncello** *m* tarragon

dramma *m* drama; **drammatico** dramatic

drastico drastic

dritto 1 *agg* straight 2 *avv* straight (ahead) 3 *m di indumento, tessuto* right side 4 *m, -a F* crafty devil F; **drizzare** (*raddrizzare*) straighten; (*erigere*) put up, erect; ~ *le orecchie* prick up one's ears; **drizzarsi**: ~ *in piedi* get to one's feet

droga *f* drug; **drogarsi** SP take drugs; **drogato** *m*, *-a f* drug addict

drogheria *f* grocer's, *Am* grocery store

dubbio 1 *agg* doubtful; (*equivoco*) dubious 2 *m* doubt; *essere in* ~ *fra* hesitate between; *mettere qc in* ~ doubt sth; *senza* ~ without a doubt; **dubbioso** doubtful; **dubitare** (*di* sth); *dubito che venga* I doubt whether he'll come

duca *m* duke; **duchessa** *f* duchess

due two; *a* ~ *a* ~ in twos, two by two; *tutt'e* ~ both of them; **duecento** 1 *agg* two hundred 2 *m: il Duecento* the thirteenth century

duello *m* duel

duemila two thousand; **duepezzi** *m inv* bikini; *vestito* two-piece (suit)

duna *f* (sand) dune

dunque 1 *cong* so; (*allora*) well (then) 2 *m: venire al* ~

come to the crunch
duomo *m* cathedral
duplicato *m* duplicate; **duplice** double; **in ~ copia** in duplicate
durante during; **durare** last; (*conservare*) keep, last; **durata** *f* duration, length; *di prodotto* life; **duraturo** last-

ing
duro 1 *agg* hard; *carne, persona* tough; *inverno, voce* harsh; *congegno, meccanismo* stiff; *pane* stale; (*ostinato*) stubborn; **tieni~!** hang in there! **2** *m* tough guy
durone *m* MED callus
DVD *m inv* DVD

E

e and; **sono le due ~ un quarto** it's (a) quarter past two, *Am* it's a quarter after two
è ☞ **essere**
ebano *m* ebony
ebbe, ebbi ☞ **avere**
ebbene well
ebbrezza *f* drunkenness; *fig* thrill
ebraico 1 *agg* Hebrew; *religione* Jewish **2** *m* Hebrew; **ebreo 1** *m*, -**a** *f* Jew; **2** *agg* Jewish
ecc. (= **eccetera**) etc (= et cetera)
eccedente excess; **eccedere 1** *v/t* exceed, go beyond **2** *v/i* go too far; **~ nel bere** drink too much
eccellente excellent
eccentrico eccentric
eccessivo excessive; **eccesso** *m* excess; **~ di velocità** speeding
eccetera et cetera
eccetto except; **eccezionale** exceptional; **eccezional-**

mente exceptionally; **eccezione** *f* exception
ecchimosi *f inv* bruise
eccitante 1 *agg* exciting **2** *m* stimulant; **eccitare** excite; **eccitarsi** get excited; **eccitazione** *f* excitement
ecclesiastico 1 *agg* ecclesiastical **2** *m* priest
ecco (*qui*) here; (*là*) there; **~ come** this is how; **~ fatto** that's that; **~ tutto** that's all; **~mi** here I am; **~li** here they are; **~ti il libro** here's your book
eclissarsi *fig* slip away; **eclisse** *f*, **eclissi** *f inv* eclipse
eco *m/f* echo
ecografia *f* scan
ecologia *f* ecology; **ecologico** ecological
economia *f* economy; *scienza* economics *sg*; **fare ~** economize (**di** on); **-e** *pl* savings; **economico** economic; (*poco costoso*) economical; **economizzare 1** *v/t* save **2** *v/i*

economize (*su* on)

ecosistema *m* ecosystem

eczema *m* eczema

ed and

edera *f* ivy

edicola *f* newspaper kiosk

edificare build; *fig* edify; edi**ficio** *m* building; *fig* structure

edile construction *attr*, building *attr*; edilizia *f* construction, building; (*urbanistica*) town planning

editore 1 *agg* publishing 2 *m*, -trice *f* publisher; (*curatore*) editor; editoria *f* publishing; edizione *f* edition

educare educate; (*allevare*) bring up; *orecchio*, *mente* train; educativo education *attr*, (*istruttivo*) educational; educato: (**ben**) well brought-up; educazione *f* education; *dei figli* upbringing; (*buone maniere*) (good) manners; ~ **fisica** physical education

effervescente effervescent; *aspirina* soluble

effettivamente in fact; *per rafforzare un'affermazione* really, actually; effettivo (*reale*) real, actual; (*efficace*) effective; effetto *m* effect; (*impressione*) impression; fare ~ (*funzionare*) work; (*impressionare*) make an impression; -i pl **personali** personal effects; *in* -*i* in fact; effettuare carry out; *pagamento* make;

effettuarsi take place; *il servizio non si effettua la domenica* there is no Sunday service

efficace effective

efficiente efficient; (*funzionante*) in working order; efficienza *f* efficiency

Egitto *m* Egypt; egiziano 1 *agg* Egyptian 2 *m*, -a *f* Egyptian; egizio ancient Egyptian

egli he

egocentrico egocentric

egoismo *m* selfishness, egoism

egoista 1 *agg* selfish 2 *m/f* selfish person

egr. (= **egregio**) form of address used in correspondence

egregio distinguished; *nelle lettere* ~ **signore** Dear Sir

eguale → **uguale**

ehi! oi!

E.I. (= **Esercito Italiano**) Italian army

elaborare elaborate; *dati* process; *piano* work out; elaborato elaborate; elaboratore *m*: ~ **elettronico** computer; elaborazione *f* elaboration; ~ **elettronica dei dati** electronic data processing; ~ **dei testi** word processing

elastico 1 *agg* elastic; *orari* flexible 2 *m* rubber band

elefante *m* elephant

elegante elegant; eleganza *f* elegance

eleggere elect

elementare elementary; **scuola** f ~ primary school, Am elementary school

elemento m element; (componente) component; **-i** pl (rudimenti) rudiments; (fatti) data sg

elemosina f charity; **chiedere l'~** beg

elencare list; **elenco** m list; ~ **telefonico** phone book, telephone directory

eletto 1 pp ☞ **eleggere** 2 agg chosen; **elettore** m, **-trice** f voter

elettrauto m inv auto electrics garage; persona automobile electrician; **elettricista** m/f electrician; **elettricità** f electricity; **elettrico** electric

elettrocardiogramma m electrocardiogram; **elettrodo** m electrode; **elettrodomestico** m household appliance; **elettromagnetico** electromagnetic

elettrone m electron; **elettronico** electronic; **libro ~** e-book, electronic book; **commercio ~** e-commerce

elettrotecnica 1 agg electrical 2 m electrical engineer

elevare raise; costruzioni erect; (promuovere) promote; fig (migliorare) better; **elevato** high; fig elevated, lofty

elezione f election

eliambulanza f air ambulance

elica f propeller

elicottero m helicopter

eliminare eliminate; **eliminatoria** f SP heat; **eliminazione** f elimination

eliporto m heliport

élite f élite

elmetto m helmet; **elmo** m helmet

elogio m praise

eloquente eloquent

eludere elude; sorveglianza, domanda evade

elvetico Swiss

e-mail f inv e-mail; **inviare un'~ a qc** e-mail s.o., send s.o. an e-mail

emanare 1 v/t give off; legge pass 2 v/i emanate, come (da from)

emanciparsi become emancipated; **emancipazione** f emancipation

emarginare marginalize; **emarginato** m, **-a** f person on the fringes of society

ematoma m haematoma, Am hematoma

embrione m embryo

emergenza f emergency; **emergere** emerge; (distinguersi) stand out; **emerso** pp ☞ **emergere**

emesso pp ☞ **emettere**; **emettere** luce give out, emit; grido, verdetto give; calore give off; FIN issue; TEC emit

emicrania f migraine

emigrante *m/f* emigrant; **emigrare** emigrate; **emigrato** *m*, **-a** *f* person who has emigrated, ex-pat; **emigrazione** *f* emigration

emisfero *m* hemisphere

emissione *f* emission; *di denaro, francobolli* issue; RAD broadcast; **emittente 1** *agg* issuing; *(trasmittente)* broadcasting **2** *f* RAD transmitter; TV channel

emoglobina *f* haemoglobin, *Am* hemoglobin

emorragia *f* haemorrhage, *Am* hemorrhage

emorroidi *fpl* haemorrhoids, *Am* hemorrhoids

emotivo emotional; *(sensibile)* sensitive

emozionante exciting, thrilling; **emozionarsi** get excited; *(commuoversi)* be moved; **emozionato** excited; *(agitato)* nervous; *(commosso)* moved; *(turbato)* upset; **emozione** *f* emotion; *(agitazione)* excitement

emporio *m negozio* department store

emulsione *f* emulsion

enciclopedia *f* encyclopedia

endovenoso intravenous

energetico *consumo ecc* energy *attr*; *alimento* energy-giving; **energia** *f* energy; **energico** strong, energetic

enfasi *f* emphasis

enigma *m* enigma

ennesimo MAT nth; F **per l'-a**

volta for the hundredth time F

enorme enormous

enoteca *f negozio* wine merchant *(specializing in fine wines)*

ente *m* organization; **gli enti locali** the local authorities

entrambi both

entrare *(andare dentro)* go in, enter; *(venire dentro)* come in, enter; *fig* **questo non c'entra** that has nothing to do with it; **~ in una stanza** enter a room, go into / come into a room; **entrata** *f* entrance; *in parcheggio* entrance, way in; *in un paese* entry; FIN **-e** *pl (reddito)* income; *(guadagno)* earnings; **~ libera** admission free

entro within

entroterra *m inv* hinterland

entusiasmare enthuse; **entusiasmo** *m* enthusiasm; **entusiasta** enthusiastic

enumerare enumerate

enzima *m* enzyme

epatite *f* hepatitis

epicentro *m* epicentre, *Am* epicenter; *fig* centre, *Am* center

epidemia *f* epidemic

epidermide *f* skin; MED epidermis

Epifania *f* Epiphany

epilessia *f* epilepsy; **epilettico 1** *agg* epileptic **2** *m*, **-a** *f* epileptic

episodio *m* episode

epoca *f* age; (*periodo*) period, time; *auto f d'~* vintage car; *mobili mpl d'~* period furniture

eppure (and) yet

equatore *m* equator; **equatoriale** equatorial

equazione *f* equation

equilibrare balance; **equilibrato** balanced; **equilibrio** *m* balance; *fig* common sense

equino horse *attr*

equinozio *m* equinox

equipaggiamento *m* equipment; **equipaggio** *m* crew

équipe *f inv* team

equitazione *f* horse riding

equivalente *m/agg* equivalent

equivoco 1 *agg* ambiguous; (*sospetto*) equivocal; (*losco*) shady **F 2** *m* misunderstanding

era *f* (*epoca*) age, era; GEOL era; ~ **atomica** atomic age; ~ **glaciale** Ice Age

era, erano ☞ **essere**

erba *f* grass; GASTR **-e** *pl* herbs; **-e aromatiche** herbs; **erbaccia** *f* weed; **erboristeria** *f* herbalist's, *Am* herbalist store

erede *m/f* heir; *donna* heiress; **eredità** *f* inheritance; BIO heredity; **ereditare** inherit; **ereditarietà** *f* heredity; **ereditario** hereditary; **ereditiera** *f* heiress

eremita *m* hermit

eretico 1 *agg* heretical **2** *m*, **-a** *f* heretic

eretto 1 *pp* ☞ **erigere 2** *agg* erect; **erezione** *f* building; *di pene* erection

ergastolo *m* life sentence

ergonomico ergonomic

erica *f* heather

erigere erect; *fig* (*fondare*) establish, found

eritema *m cutaneo* rash; ~ **solare** sunburn

ermafrodito *m* hermaphrodite

ermellino *m* ermine

ermetico (*a tenuta d'aria*) airtight; *fig* obscure

ernia *f* MED hernia; ~ **del disco** slipped disc

ero ☞ **essere**

eroe *m* hero

erogare *denaro* allocate; *gas, acqua* supply

eroina *f droga* heroin; *donna* eroica heroine

erosione *f* GEOL erosion

erotico erotic; **erotismo** *m* eroticism

errare wander, roam; (*sbagliare*) be mistaken; **errata corrige** *m inv* correction; **erroneamente** mistakenly; **errore** *m* mistake, error; ~ **di ortografia** spelling mistake; ~ **di stampa** misprint, typo; *per* ~ by mistake

erta *f*: *stare all'*~ be on the alert

erudito 1 *agg* erudite, learned **2** *m*, **-a** *f* erudite person, scholar

eruttare *di vulcano* erupt; **eruzione** *f* eruption; MED rash

es. (= **esempio**) eg (= for example)

esagerare 1 *v/t* exaggerate **2** *v/i* exaggerate; *(eccedere)* go too far; **esagerato** exaggerated; *zelo* excessive; *prezzo* exorbitant; **esagerazione** *f* exaggeration

esalare 1 *v/t odori* give off; **~ il respiro** exhale **2** *v/i* come, emanate *(da* from)

esaltare exalt; *(entusiasmare)* elate; **esaltarsi** become elated; **esaltato 1** *agg* elated; *(fanatico)* fanatical **2** *m* fanatic

esame *m* exam(ination); MED *(test)* test; *(visita)* examination; **esaminare** examine *(anche* MED)

esasperante exasperating; **esasperare** *(inasprire)* exacerbate; *(irritare)* exasperate; **esasperazione** *f* exasperation

esattezza *f* accuracy; *per l'~* to be precise; **esatto 1** *pp* ☞ **esigere 2** *agg* exact; *risposta* correct, right; *in punto* exactly; **~!** that's right!

esaudire grant; *speranze* fulfil, *Am* fulfill

esauriente exhaustive; **esaurimento** *m* exhaustion; COM **svendita** *f fino a ~ della merce* clearance sale; **~ ner-**

voso nervous breakdown; **esaurire** exhaust; *merci* run out of; **esaurito** *(esausto)* exhausted; COM sold out; *pubblicazioni* out of print; **esausto** exhausted

esca *f* bait *(anche fig)*

esce ☞ **uscire**

eschimese *agg*, *m/f* Inuit, Eskimo

esclamare exclaim; **esclamazione** *f* exclamation

escludere exclude; **esclusione** *f* exclusion; **esclusiva** *f* exclusive right, sole right; **esclusivo** exclusive; **escluso 1** *pp* ☞ **escludere 2** *agg* excluded; *(impossibile)* out of the question **3** *m*, **-a** *f* person on the fringes of society

esco ☞ **uscire**

escogitare contrive

escoriazione *f* graze

escrementi *mpl* excrement

escursione *f* trip, excursion; *a piedi* hike; **escursionismo** *m* touring; *a piedi* hiking, walking; **escursionista** *m/f* tourist; *a piedi* hiker, walker

esecutivo *m/agg* executive; **esecutore** *m*, **-trice** *f* DIR executor; MUS performer; **esecuzione** *f* *(realizzazione)* carrying out; MUS performance; **~** *(capitale)* execution; **eseguire** carry out; MUS perform

esempio *m* example; *per ~*, *ad ~* for example; **esemplare 1** *agg* exemplary **2** *m* specimen; (*copia*) copy

esentare exempt (**da** from); **esente** exempt; **~ da tasse** tax-free

esercente *m/f* shopkeeper, *Am* storekeeper

esercitare exercise; (*addestrare*) train; *professione* practise, *Am* practice; **esercitarsi** practise, *Am* practice; **esercitazione** *f* exercise

esercito *m* army

esercizio *m* exercise; (*pratica*) practice; (*anno finanziario*) financial year, *Am* fiscal year; FIN *azienda* business; *negozio* shop, *Am anche* store

esibire *documenti* produce; *mettere in mostra* display; **esibirsi** *in uno spettacolo* perform; *fig* show off; **esibizione** *f* exhibition; (*ostentazione*) showing off; (*spettacolo*) performance; **esibizionista** *m/f* show-off; PSI exhibitionist

esigente exacting, demanding; **esigenza** *f* demand; (*bisogno*) need; **esigere** demand; (*riscuotere*) exact

esile slender; *voce* faint

esiliare exile; **esilio** *m* exile

esistente existing; **esistenza** *f* existence; **esistere** exist

esitare hesitate; **esitazione** *f* hesitation

esito *m* result, outcome; FIN sales, turnover

esodo *m* exodus

esofago *m* œsophagus, *Am* esophagus

esonerare exempt (**da** from)

esordiente *m/f* beginner; **esordio** *m* introduction; (*inizio*) beginning; TEA début

esortare (*incitare*) urge; (*pregare*) beg; **esortazione** *f* urging

esotico exotic

espandere expand; **espandersi** expand; (*diffondersi*) spread; **espansivo** FIS, TEC expansive; *fig* warm, friendly

espatriare leave one's country; **espatrio** *m* expatriation

espediente *m* expedient

espellere expel

esperienza *f* experience

esperimento *m* experiment

esperto *m/agg* expert

espirare breathe out, exhale

esplicito explicit

esplodere 1 *v/t colpo* fire **2** *v/i* explode

esplorare explore; **esploratore** *m*, **-trice** *f* explorer; **giovane** *m* **~** boy scout

esplosione *f* explosion; **~ demografica** population explosion; **esplosivo** *m/agg* explosive; **esploso** *pp* ☞ **esplodere**

esponente *m/f* exponent; **esporre** expose (*anche* FOT); *avviso* put up; *in una mostra* exhibit, show; (*riferire*) present; *ragioni, caso* state; *teoria* explain; **esporsi**

expose o.s. (**a** to); (*compro- mettersi*) compromise o.s.

esportare export; **esporta- zione** *f* export

esposizione *f* (*mostra*) exhi- bition; (*narrazione*) presen- tation; FOT exposure; **espo- sto 1** *pp* ☞ **esporre 2** *agg* in mostra on show; ~ **a** ex- posed to; *critiche* open to; ~ **a sud** south facing **3** *m* state- ment; (*petizione*) petition

espressione *f* expression; **espressivo** expressive; **espresso 1** *pp* ☞ **esprimere 2** *agg* express **3** *m* posta ex- press letter; FERR express; (*caffè m*) ~ espresso; **per** ~ express; **esprimere** express; **esprimersi** express o.s.

espropriare expropriate; **esproprio** *m* expropriation

espulsione *f* expulsion; **espulso** *pp* ☞ **espellere**

essa *pron f persona* she; *cosa, animale* it

essenza *f* essence; **essenzia- le 1** *agg* essential **2** *m*: **l'~ è** the main thing is

essere 1 *v/i* be; ~ **di** (*provenire di*) be o come from; ~ **di qu** (*appartenere a*) belong to s:o; **c'è** there is; **ci sono** there are; **sono io** it's me; **cosa c'è?** what's the matter?; **non c'è di che!** don't men- tion it!; **chi è?** who is it; **so- no le tre** it's three o'clock; **siamo in quattro** there are four of us; **se fossi in te** if

I were you; **sarà!** if you say so! **2** *v/aus*: **siamo arrivati al- le due** we arrived at two o'clock; **non siamo ancora arrivati** we haven't arrived yet; **è stato investito** he has been run over **3** *m* being

esso *pron m persona* he; *cosa, animale* it

est *m* east; **a** (*f*)**~ di** (to the) east of

estasi *f* ecstasy

estate *f* summer; **in ~, d'~** in (the) summer

estendere extend; **estender- si** *di territorio* extend; (*allun- garsi*) stretch; fig (*diffonder- si*) spread

estenuante exhausting

esteriore *m/agg* exterior, out- side

esterno 1 *agg* external **2** *m* outside; **all'~** on the outside

estero 1 *agg* foreign **2** *m* for- eign countries; **all'~** abroad

esteso 1 *pp* ☞ **estendere 2** *agg* extensive; (*diffuso*) widespread; **per ~** in full

estetista *f* beautician

estinguere extinguish, put out; *debito* pay off; **estin- guersi** die out; **estinto 1** *pp* ☞ **estinguere 2** *agg* ex- tinct; *debito* paid off **3** *m*, **-a** *f* deceased; **estintore** *m* fire extinguisher; **estinzione** *f* extinction; FIN paying off

estirpare uproot; *dente* ex- tract; fig eradicate

estivo summer *attr*

estorcere *denaro* extort;
estorsione *f* extortion;
estorto *pp* ☞ **estorcere**
estradizione *f* extradition
estraneo 1 *agg* outside (*a qc* sth) **2** *m*, -*a f* stranger; *persona non autorizzata* unauthorized person
estrarre extract; *pistola* pull out; **~ a sorte** draw; **estratto 1** *pp* ☞ **estrarre 2** *m* extract; *documento* abstract; **FIN ~ conto** statement (of account); **estrazione** *f* extraction
estremista *m/f* extremist;
estremità *f inv* extremity;
di corda end; (*punta*) tip; (*punto superiore*) top; **estremo 1** *agg* extreme; (*più lontano*) farthest; (*ultimo nel tempo*) last, final **2** *m* (*estremità*) extreme; **gli -i** *pl* di un documento the main points
estro *m* (*ispirazione artistica*) inspiration
estroverso extrovert(ed)
estuario *m* estuary
esuberante (*vivace*) exuberant
esultare rejoice
età *f inv* age; **all'~ di** at the age of; **avere la stessa ~** be the same age; **di mezz'~** middle-aged
eternità *f* eternity; **eterno** eternal; *questione, problema* age-old; **in ~** for ever and ever

eterogeneo heterogen(e)ous
eterosessuale heterosexual
etica *f* ethics *sg*
etichetta *f* label; *cerimoniale* etiquette
etico ethical
etiope *agg, m/f* Ethiopian; **Etiopia** *f* Ethiopia
etnico ethnic
etrusco 1 *agg* Etruscan **2** *m*, -*a f* Etruscan
ettaro *m* hectare
etto *m* hundred grams; **ettogrammo** *m* hundred grams, hectogram
eucalipto *m* eucalyptus
eucaristia *f* REL Eucharist
euforia *f* euphoria
euro *m inv* euro; **eurodeputato** *m*, -*a f* Euro MP; **Europa** *f* Europe; **europeo 1** *agg* European **2** *m*, -*a f* European; **eurovisione** *f* Eurovision
evacuare evacuate; **evacuazione** *f* evacuation
evadere 1 *v/t* evade; (*sbrigare*) deal with **2** *v/i* escape (*da* from)
evaporare evaporate
evasione *f* escape; *fig* escapism; **~ fiscale** *f* tax evasion;
evasivo evasive; **evaso 1** *pp* ☞ **evadere 2** *m*, -*a f* fugitive; **evasore** *m*: **~ fiscale** tax evader
evenienza *f* eventuality
evento *m* event
eventuale possible; **eventualità** *f inv* eventuality; **eventualmente** if necessary

fallito

evidente evident; evidenziatore *m* highlighter

evitare avoid; **~ il fastidio a qu** spare s.o. the trouble

evoluto **1** *pp* ☞ **evolvere 2** *agg* developed; (*progredito*) progressive, advanced; *senza pregiudizi* open-minded; evoluzione *f* evolution; evolvere **1** *v/t* develop **2** *v/i*

e evolversi evolve, develop

evviva hurray

ex ... ex-, former

extra *m/agg inv* extra

extracomunitario **1** *agg* non-EU **2** *m*, **-a** *f* non-EU citizen

extraconiugale extramarital

extraeuropeo non-European

extraterrestre *agg, m/f* extraterrestrial

F

fa **1** ☞ **fare 2** *avv:* **5 anni ~ 5** years ago **3** *m* MUS F; *nel solfeggio della scala* fa(h)

fabbisogno *m* needs

fabbrica *f* plant, factory; fabbricante *m/f* manufacturer; fabbricare manufacture; ARCHI build; *fig* fabricate; fabbricato *m* building

faccenda *f* matter; faccende *fpl* housework

faccia *f* face; (*risvolto, aspetto*) facet; (*lato*) side; **~ tosta** cheek; **~ a ~** face to face; **gliel'ha detto in ~** he told him to his face; **facciata** *f* ARCHI front, façade; *di foglio* side; *fig* (*esteriorità*) appearance

faccio ☞ **fare**

facile easy; *di carattere* easy-going; (*incline*) prone (**a** to); **è ~ a dirsi** easier said than done; **è ~ che venga** he is likely to come; facilità *f* ease; (*attitudine*) aptitude,

facility; facilitare facilitate; facilmente easily

facoltà *f inv* faculty; (*potere*) power; facoltativo optional

faggio *m* beech (tree)

fagiano *m* pheasant

fagiolini *mpl* green beans; fagiolo *m* bean

fagotto *m* bundle; MUS bassoon; *fig* **far ~** pack up and leave

fai da te *m inv* do-it-yourself, DIY, *Am* home improvement

fai ☞ **fare**

falciatrice *f* lawn-mower

falco *m* hawk

falegname *m* carpenter

falena *f* moth

falla *f* MAR leak

fallimento *m* failure; FIN bankruptcy; fallire **1** *v/t* miss **2** *v/i* fail; FIN go bankrupt; fallito **1** *agg* unsuccessful, failed; FIN bankrupt **2** *m* failure; FIN bankruptcy

fallo *m* fault; (*errore*) error, mistake; *sp* foul

falò *m inv* bonfire

falsario *m* forger; **falsificare** forge; **falso 1** *agg* false; (*sbagliato*) incorrect, wrong; *oro, gioielli* imitation, fake **F** (*falsificato*) forged, fake **F 2** *m* (*falsità*) falsehood; *oggetto falsificato* forgery, fake **F**

fama *f* fame; (*reputazione*) reputation

fame *f* hunger; *aver* ~ be hungry

famiglia *f* family; **familiare 1** *agg* family *attr*, (*conosciuto*) familiar; (*semplice*) informal **2** *m/f* relative, relation; **familiarità** *f* familiarity; **familiarizzarsi** familiarize o.s.

famoso famous

fanale *m* light; (*lampione*) street lamp

fanatico *agg* fanatical **2** *m*, **-a** *f* fanatic

fanciullo *m*, **-a** *f* (young) boy; *ragazza* (young) girl

fango *m* mud; *MED* **-ghi** *pl* mud-baths; **fangoso** muddy

fannullone *m*, **-a** *f* lazy good-for-nothing

fantascienza *f* science fiction

fantasia *f* fantasy; (*immaginazione*) imagination; (*capriccio*) fancy; *MUS* fantasia

fantasma *m* ghost

fantasticare day-dream (*di* about); **fantastico** fantastic

fantoccio *m* puppet (*anche fig*)

farabutto *m* nasty piece of work

faraona *f*: (*gallina f*) ~ guinea fowl

farcire *GASTR* stuff; *torta* fill; **farcito** stuffed; *dolce* filled

fard *m inv* blusher

fardello *m* bundle; *fig* burden

fare 1 *v/t* do; *vestito, dolce, errore* make; *biglietto, benzina* buy, get; ~ *un bagno* have a bath; ~ *il medico* be a doctor; ~ *vedere qc a qu* show sth to s.o.; *farcela* manage; *non c'è la faccio più* I can't take any more; *2 più 2 fa 4* 2 and 2 make(s) 4; *quanto fa?* how much is it?; *far ~ qc a qu* get s.o. to do sth **2** *v/i*: *faccia pure!* go ahead!; *fa freddo / caldo* it's cold / warm

farfalla *f* butterfly

farina *f* flour; **farinaceo 1** *agg* starchy **2** **-cei** *mpl* starchy foodstuffs

faringe *f* pharynx; **faringite** *f* inflammation of the pharynx

farmaceutico pharmaceutical; **farmacia** *f* pharmacy, *Br anche negozio* chemist's; **farmacista** *m/f* pharmacist, *Br anche* chemist; **farmaco** *m* drug

faro *m* *MAR* lighthouse; *AVIA* beacon; *AUTO* headlight

farsi (*diventare*) grow; *F* (*drogarsi*) shoot up; *si sta facendo tardi* it's getting late; ~ *male* hurt o.s.

fascia *f* band; *MED* bandage; ~

oraria (time) slot; **fasciare** MED bandage; **fasciatura** f (*fascia*) bandage; *azione* bandaging

fascicolo m (*opuscolo*) booklet, brochure; (*incartamento*) file

fascino m fascination, charm

fascio m bundle; *di fiori* bunch; *di luce* beam

fascismo m Fascism; **fascista** agg, m/f Fascist

fase f phase; AUTO stroke; *fig* **essere fuori** ~ be out of sorts; ~ **di lavorazione** production stage

fastidio m bother; trouble; **dare** ~ **a qu** bother s.o.; **le dà** ~ **se ... ?** do you mind if ... ?; **fastidioso** (*irritante*) irritating, annoying; (*irritabile*) irritable

fata f fairy

fatale fatal; **fatalità** f inv fate; (*disavventura*) misfortune

fatica f (*sforzo*) effort; (*stanchezza*) fatigue; **a** ~ with a great deal of effort; **faticare** toil; ~ **a** find it difficult to; **faticoso** tiring; (*difficile*) laborious

fatto 1 pp ☞ **fare** 2 agg done; AGR ripe; ~ **a mano** handmade; ~ **di legno** made of wood 3 m fact; (*avvenimento*) event; (*faccenda*) affair, business; **di** ~ agg real; *avv* in fact, actually; **in** ~ **di** as regards

fattore m (*elemento*) factor;

AGR farm manager; ~ **di protezione antisolare** (sun) protection factor

fattoria f farm; *casa* farmhouse

fattorino m messenger; *per consegne* delivery man

fattura f (*lavorazione*) workmanship; *di abiti* cut; FIN invoice; **fatturare** FIN invoice; **fatturato** m FIN (*giro d'affari*) turnover

fauna f fauna

fava f broad bean

favola f (*fiaba*) fairy tale; (*storia*) story; *morale* fable; (*meraviglia*) dream; **favoloso** fabulous

favore m favour, Am favor; **per** ~! please!; **fare un** ~ **a qu** do s.o. a favour; **favorevole** favourable, Am favorable; **favorire** 1 v/t favour, Am favor; (*promuovere*) promote 2 v/i: **vuol** ~? would you care to join me / us?; **favorito** m/agg favourite, Am favorite

fax m inv fax; **faxare** fax

fazione f faction

fazzolettino m: ~ **di carta** tissue; **fazzoletto** m handkerchief; *per la testa* headscarf

febbraio m February

febbre f fever; **ha la** ~ he has a temperature

fecondare fertilize; **fecondazione** f fertilization; ~ **artificiale** artificial insemination

fede f faith; (*fedeltà*) loyalty; *anello* wedding ring; **fedele**

1 agg faithful; (esatto, conforme all'originale) true **2** m REL believer; **i -i** pl the faithful pl

federa f pillowcase

federazione f federation

fegato m liver; fig courage, guts F

felce f fern

felice happy; (fortunato) lucky; **felicità** f happiness; **felicitarsi**: ~ **con qu per qc** congratulate s.o. on sth

felino feline

felpa f sweatshirt

feltro m felt

femmina f (figlia) girl, daughter; ZO, TEC female; **femminile 1** agg feminine; (da donna) women's **2** m GRAM feminine; **femminilità** f femininity; **femminismo** m feminism; **femminista** m/f feminist

femore m femur

fendinebbia m inv fog lamp o light

fenomeno m phenomenon

feriale: **giorno** ~ weekday; **ferie** fpl holiday, Am vacation, **andare in** ~ go on holiday

ferire wound; in incidente injure; fig hurt; **ferirsi** injure o.s.; **ferita** f wound; in incidente injury; **ferito 1** agg wounded; in incidente injured; fig: sentimenti hurt; orgoglio injured **2** m casualty

fermacarte m inv paperweight

fermacravatta m inv tiepin

fermaglio m clasp; per capelli hair slide, Am barrette; (gioiello) brooch

fermare stop; DIR detain; **fermarsi** stop; (restare) stay, remain; **fermata** f stop; ~ **dell' autobus** bus stop

fermentare ferment; **fermento** m yeast; fig ferment

fermo 1 agg still; veicolo stationary; (saldo) firm; mano steady; **star** ~ (non muoversi) keep still **2** int **-1** (alt!) stop!; (immobile!) keep still!

feroce fierce, ferocious; animale wild; (insopportabile) dreadful

ferragosto m August 15 public holiday; periodo August holidays

ferramenta f hardware; negozio hardware store

ferro m iron; (arnese) tool; ~ **da calza** knitting needle; ~ **da stiro** iron; ~ **di cavallo** horseshoe; GASTR **ai -i** grilled, Am broiled; **ferrovia** f railway, Am railroad

fertile fertile; **fertilizzante** m fertilizer

fesso m F idiot F; **far** ~ **qu** con s.o F

fessura f (spaccatura) crack; (fenditura) slit, slot

festa f feast; REL di santo feast day; (ricevimento) party; (compleanno) birthday; ~ **della mamma / del papà** Mother's / Father's Day; ~

filare

nazionale national holiday;
festeggiamenti *mpl* celebrations; **festeggiare** celebrate; *persona* have a celebration for; **festival** *m inv* festival; **festività** *f inv* festival; ~ *pl* celebrations, festivities; **festivo** festive; ***giorno*** ~ holiday
feto *m* fetus, *Br anche* foetus
fetta *f* slice; *a ~ e* sliced
fiaba *f* fairy tale
fiacca *f* weariness; *(svogliatezza)* laziness; ***battere la ~*** be a shirker
fiaccola *f* torch
fiamma *f* flame; MAR pennant; **fiammante: *rosso m ~*** fiery red; ***nuovo ~*** brand new; **fiammifero** *m* match
fiancheggiare border; *fig* support
fianco *m* side; ANAT hip; *~ a ~* side by side; *di ~ a qu* beside s.o.
fiasco *m* flask; *fig* fiasco
fiato *m* breath; ***senza ~*** breathless; ***riprendere ~*** catch one's breath
fibbia *f* buckle
fibra *f* fibre, *Am* fiber; *~ sintetica* synthetic; **fibroso** fibrous
ficcanaso *m/f* F nosy parker F; **ficcare** thrust; F *(mettere)* shove F; **ficcarsi** get; ***dove s'è ficcato?*** where can it / he have got to?
fico *m* fig; *albero* fig (tree); *~ d'India* prickly pear

fidanzamento *m* engagement; **fidanzarsi** get engaged; **fidanzata** *f* fiancée; **fidanzato** *m* fiancé; *i ~ i pl* the engaged couple *pl*
fidarsi: *~ di* trust, rely on; **fidato** trustworthy; **fiducia** *f* confidence; *avere ~ in qu* have faith in s.o.; **fiduciaria** *f ~* FIN trust company; **fiducioso** trusting
fienile *m* barn
fieno *m* hay
fiera *f* *mostra* fair
fiero proud
fifa F *f* jitters F; *aver ~* have the jitters
figlia *f* daughter; **figliastra** *f* stepdaughter; **figliastro** *m* stepson; **figlio** *m* son; *avere -gli il* have children; *essere ~ unico* be an only child; **figlioccia** *f* goddaughter; **figlioccio** *m* godson
figura *f* figure; *(illustrazione)* illustration; *(apparenza)* appearance; *far brutta ~* make a bad impression; **figurare 1** *v/t fig* imagine; ***figurati!*** just imagine! **2** *v/i (apparire)* appear; *(far figura)* make a good impression; **figurato** illustrated; *linguaggio* figurative
fila *f* line, row; *(coda)* queue, *Am* line; ***tre giorni di ~*** three days running; *fare la ~* queue (up), *Am* wait in line; **filare 1** *v/t* spin **2** *v/i di ragionamento* make sense; *di for-*

maggio go stringy; *di veicolo* travel; F (*andarsene*) take off F; **~ diritto** (*comportarsi bene*) behave (o.s.)

filastrocca *f* nursery rhyme

filato 1 *agg* (*logico*) logical; **andare di ~ a casa** go straight home; **per 10 ore filate** for ten hours on the trot **2** *m* yarn; *per cucire* thread

file *m inv* INFOR file

filetto *m* GASTR fillet

filiale *f* branch; (*società affiliata*) affiliate

filigrana *f su carta* watermark; *in oreficeria* filigree

film *m inv* film, movie; **filmare** film; **filmato** *m* short (film)

filo *m* thread; *metallico* wire; *di lama* blade; *d'erba* blade; **~ interdentale** (dental) floss; **~ spinato** barbed wire;

filone *m* MIN vein; *pane* French stick; *fig* tradition

filosofia *f* philosophy; **filosofico** philosophical; **filosofo** *m* philosopher

filtrare 1 *v/t* filter **2** *v/i fig* filter out; **filtro** *m* filter

fin = **fine, fino**

finale 1 *agg* final **2** *m* end **3** *f* SP final; **finalista** *m/f* finalist; **finalmente** (*alla fine*) at last; (*per ultimo*) finally

finanza *f* finance; **finanziamento** *m* funding; **finanziare** fund, finance; **finanziario** financial; **finanziere** *m* financier; (*guardia di finanza*) Customs officer; *lungo le co-*

ste coastguard

finché until; (*per tutto il tempo che*) as long as

fine 1 *agg* fine; (*sottile*) thin; *udito, vista* sharp, keen; (*raffinato*) refined **2** *m* aim; **al ~ di …** in order to … **3** *f* end; **alla ~** in the end; **fine settimana** *m inv* weekend

finestra *f* window; **finestrino** *m* window

fingere 1 *v/t*: **~ sorpresa** pretend to be surprised **2** *v/i*: **~ di** pretend to; **fingersi** pretend to be

finire finish, end; **finiscila!** stop it!; **finito** finished; (*venduto*) sold out

finlandese 1 *m/agg* Finnish **2** *m/f* Finn; **Finlandia** *f* Finland

fino¹ *agg* fine; (*acuto*) sharp; *oro* pure

fino² *prp tempo* till, until; *luogo* as far as; **~ a domani** until tomorrow; **~ a che** (*per tutto il tempo che*) as long as; (*fino al momento in cui*) until; **fin da ieri** since yesterday

fino³ *avv* even; **fin troppo** more than enough

finocchio *m* fennel

finora so far

finta *f* pretence, *Am* pretense, sham; SP feint; **far ~ di** pretend to; **finto 1** *pp* ⇒ **fingere 2** *agg* false; (*artificiale*) artificial; (*simulato*) feigned; **finzione** *f* pretence, *Am* pretense

flotta

fiocco m bow; ~ **di neve** snowflake; **-cchi** pl **d'avena** oat flakes

fioco weak; *luce* dim

fionda f catapult

fioraio m, **-a** f florist; **fiore** m flower; *fig* **il (fior)** ~ the cream; *nelle carte* **i** pl clubs; **fiorente** flourishing

fiorentino 1 *agg* Florentine **2** m, **-a** f Florentine; GASTR *al-la -a* with spinach; *bistecca* charcoal grilled **3** f GASTR T-bone steak

fiorire flower; *fig* flourish

Firenze f Florence

firma f signature; **firmare** sign; **firmatario** m signatory; **firmato** *abito, borsa* designer *attr*

fisarmonica f accordion

fiscale tax *attr*, fiscal; *fig spreg* rigid, unbending

fischiare 1 v/t whistle; ~ **qu** boo s.o. **2** v/i *di vento* whistle; **fischio** m whistle

fisco m tax authorities, Inland Revenue, *Am* IRS, *Am* Internal Revenue Service

fisica f physics; **fisico 1** *agg* physical **2** m physicist; ANAT physique

fisionomia f face; *fig*: *di popolo, città* appearance; *(carattere)* character

fisioterapia f physiotherapy; **fisioterapista** m/f physiotherapist

fissare *(fermare)* fix; *(guarda-*

re intensamente) stare at; *(stabilire)* arrange; *(prenotare)* book; **fissarsi** *(stabilirsi)* settle; *(ostinarsi)* set one's mind **(di** on); *(avere un'idea fissa)* become obsessed **(di** with); **fissazione** f *(mania)* fixation *(di* about); **fisso 1** *agg* fixed; *stipendio, cliente* regular; *lavoro* permanent **2** *avv* fixedly

fitta f sharp pain

fitto *(denso)* thick

fiume m river; *fig* flood, torrent

fiutare smell; *cocaina* snort; ~ **un imbroglio** smell a rat; **fiuto** m sense of smell; *fig* nose

flacone m bottle

flagrante flagrant; **cogliere qu in** ~ catch s.o. red-handed

flash m *inv* FOT flash; *stampa* newsflash

flauto m flute

flemma f calm

flessibile flexible; **flessione** f bending; GRAM inflection; *(diminuzione)* dip, (slight) drop

flipper m *inv* pinball machine

flirtare flirt

F.lli (= **fratelli**) Bros (= brothers)

floppy disk m *inv* floppy (disk)

flora f flora

floscio limp; *muscoli* flabby

flotta f fleet

fluido m/agg fluid

fluorescente fluorescent

flusso m flow

fluttuazione f fluctuation

FMI m (= **Fondo Monetario Internazionale**) IMF (= International Monetary Fund)

foca f seal

focaccia f focaccia; *dolce:* sweet type of bread

foce f mouth

focoso fiery

fodera f *interna* lining; *esterna* cover; **foderare** *all'interno* line; *all'esterno* cover; **fodero** m sheath

foglia f leaf

foglio m sheet

fogna f sewer; **fognatura** f sewers

folata f gust

folclore m folklore; **folcloristico** folk attr

folgorare *di fulmine, idea* strike; *di corrente elettrica* electrocute; **~ qu con lo sguardo** glare at s.o.

folla f crowd; *fig* host

folle[1] agg mad

folle[2] AUTO: **in ~** in neutral

follia f madness

folto thick

fondale m MAR sea bed; TEA backcloth

fondamentalista m/f fundamentalist; **fondamentale** fundamental; **fondamento** m foundation; **senza ~** unfounded; **fondare** found; **fondarsi** be based (**su** on);

fondato founded; **fondatore** m, **-trice** f founder; **fondazione** f foundation

fondere 1 v/t (*liquefare*) melt; *metalli* smelt; *colori* blend **2** v/i melt; **fondersi** melt; FIN merge

fondo 1 agg deep **2** m bottom; (*sfondo*) background; *terreno* property; FIN fund; SP long-distance; SCI cross-country; **-i** pl denaro funds; **a ~** (*profondamente*) in depth; fig in **~** basically; **in ~ alla strada** at the end o bottom of the road; **andare a ~** (*affondare*) sink; (*approfondire*) get to the bottom (**di** of); **fondotinta** m inv foundation

fonduta f cheese fondue

fonetica f phonetics

fontana f fountain

fonte m/f spring; fig source

footing m jogging; **fare ~** go jogging

forare *di proiettile* pierce; *con il trapano* drill; *biglietto* punch; *pneumatico* puncture; **foratura** f *di pneumatico* puncture

forbici fpl scissors

forchetta f fork

forcina f hairpin

foresta f forest

foresteria f guest rooms; **forestiero 1** agg foreign **2** m, **-a** f foreigner

forfait m inv lump sum; **forfettario** flat-rate

forfora f dandruff

forma f form; (*sagoma*) shape; TEC (*stampo*) mould, Am mold; **essere in ~** be in good form

formaggino m processed cheese; **formaggio** m cheese

formale formal; **formalità** f inv formality

formare shape; **formarsi** form; (*svilupparsi*) develop; **formato** m size; di libro format; **formattare** INFOR format; **formazione** f formation; fig: addestramento training; SP line-up

formica[1] f ZO ant

formica[2] ® Formica

formicaio m anthill

formicolare di mano, gamba tingle; fig **~ di** teem with; **formicolìo** m sensazione pins and needles

formidabile (*straordinario*) incredible; (*poderoso*) powerful

formula f formula; **formulare** teoria formulate; (*esprimere*) express

fornaio m baker; negozio bakery; **fornello** m oven

fornire supply (**qc a qu** s.o. with sth); **fornirsi** get (**di** sth); **fornitore** m supplier; **fornitura** f supply

forno m oven; (*panetteria*) bakery; **~ a microonde** microwave (oven); **al ~** carne, patate roast; mele, pasta baked

foro[1] m (*buco*) hole

foro[2] m romano forum; DIR (*tribunale*) (law) court

forse perhaps, maybe

forte 1 agg strong; suono loud; pioggia heavy; taglia, somma large; dolore severe **2** avv (con forza) hard; (ad alta voce) loudly; (*velocemente*) fast **3** m (forza) fort; **fortezza** f MIL fortress

fortuito chance

fortuna f fortune; **avere ~** be successful; (*essere fortunato*) be lucky; **buona ~!** good luck!; **per ~** luckily; **fortunatamente** fortunately; **fortunato** lucky, fortunate

foruncolo m pimple

forza f strength; (*potenza*) power; muscolare force; **a ~ di ...** by dint of ...; **per ~** against my / our will; **per ~!** (*naturalmente*) of course!; **~!** come on!; **-e pl** (**armate**) MIL (armed) forces; **forzare** force

foschìa f haze

fosforescente phosphorescent

fossa f pit, hole; (*tomba*) grave; **fossato** m ditch; di fortezza moat; **fossetta** f dimple

fossile m/agg fossil (*attr*)

fosso m ditch

foto f inv photo

fotocopia f photocopy; **fotocopiatrice** f photocopier

fotografare photograph; **fotografia** f arte photography;

(foto) photograph; **~ a colori** colour photograph; **fotografico** photographic; **macchina** *f* **~a** camera; **fotografo** *m* photographer

fotomontaggio *m* photomontage

fotoromanzo *m* graphic novel

fra between; *più persone o cose* among; *temporale* in; **~ questi ragazzi** out of all these boys; **~ l'altro** what's more; **~ breve** in a very short time, soon; **~ sé e sé** to himself / herself

frac *m inv* tails

fracassare smash; **fracasso** *m* din; *di oggetti che cadono* crash

fradicio rotten; *(bagnato)* soaking wet

fragile fragile; *persona* frail, delicate

fragola *f* strawberry

fragore *m* roar; *di tuono* rumble

fraintendere misunderstand

frammentario fragmentary; **frammento** *m* fragment

frana *f* landslide; **franare** collapse

francamente frankly

francese 1 *m/agg* French **2** *m/f* Frenchman; *donna* Frenchwoman; *i* *-i pl* the French *pl*; **Francia** *f* France

franco franc; FIN free; **farla -a** get away with it; **francobollo** *m* stamp

frangia *f* fringe, *Am* bangs

frantumare shatter; **frantumi** *mpl* splinters; **in ~** in smithereens; **mandare in ~** smash to smithereens

frappé *m inv* milkshake

frase *f* sentence; MUS phrase; **~ fatta** set phrase, idiom

frassino *m* ash (tree)

frastagliato *costa* jagged

frastuono *m* racket

frate *m* REL friar, monk

fratellastro *m* step-brother; **con un genitore in comune** half-brother; **fratello** *m* brother; **-i** *pl fratello e sorella* brother and sister; **fraterno** brotherly, fraternal

frattaglie *fpl* GASTR offal; *di pollo* giblets

frattanto meanwhile, in the meantime

frattempo: **nel ~** meanwhile, in the meantime

frattura *f* fracture; **fratturarsi**: **~ una gamba** break one's leg

frazione *f* fraction; POL small group; *(borgata)* hamlet

freccia *f* arrow; AUTO **~ (di direzione)** indicator, *Am* turn signal

freddo 1 *agg* cold **2** *m* cold; **ho ~** I'm cold; **fa ~** it's cold; **freddoloso**: **essere ~** feel the cold

freezer *m inv* freezer

fregare rub; F *(imbrogliare)* swindle; F *(rubare)* pinch; F P **me ne frego di quello**

che pensano I don't give a damn what they think F; **fregatura** *f* F *(imbroglio)* rip-off F; *(ostacolo, contrarietà)* pain F

fregio *m* ARCHI frieze

frenare AUTO brake; *folla, lacrime, risate* hold back; *impulso* restrain; **frenarsi** *(dominarsi)* restrain o.s.; **frenata** *f* braking; **fare una ~** brake; **freno** *m* AUTO brake; *del cavallo* bit; **~ a mano** handbrake, *Am* parking brake

frequentare *luoghi* frequent; *scuola, corso* attend; *persona* associate with; **frequentato** popular; *strada* busy; **frequente** frequent; **di ~** frequently; **frequenza** *f* frequency; *scolastica* attendance; **un'alta ~ di spettatori** a large audience; **con ~** frequently

fresco 1 *agg* fresh; *temperatura* cool **2** *m* coolness; **fa ~** it's cool; **mettere in ~** put in a cool place

fretta 1 *f* hurry; **aver ~** be in a hurry; **non c'è ~** there's no hurry; **frettoloso** hurried; *lavoro* rushed; *persona* in a hurry

fricassea *f* GASTR fricassée

friggere 1 *v/t* fry **2** *v/i* sizzle; **friggitoria** *f* shop that sells deep fried fish etc

frigo *m* fridge, *Am* refrigerator; **frigorifero 1** *agg* cold

attr; camion refrigerated **2** *m* refrigerator

frittata *f* GASTR omelette, *Am* omelet; **frittella** *f* fritter; **fritto 1** *pp* ☞ **friggere 2** *agg* fried **3** *m* fried food; **~ misto** assortment of deep-fried food

frittura *f metodo* frying; **~ di pesce** fried fish

frivolo frivolous

frizionare rub; **frizione** *f* friction; AUTO clutch

frizzante *bevanda* fizzy, sparkling

frode *f* fraud

frontale frontal; **scontro ~** head-on collision; **fronte 1** *f* forehead; **di ~ a** *(dirimpetto)* opposite, facing; *in presenza di* before; **a confronto di** compared with **2** *m* front; **far ~ agli impegni** face up to one's responsibilities; **fronteggiare** face

frontiera *f* border, frontier

fronzolo *m* frill

frottola *f* F fib F

frugale frugal

frugare 1 *v/i* rummage **2** *v/t (cercare con cura)* search, rummage through

frullare GASTR blend, liquidize; *uova* whisk; **frullato** *m* milkshake; **frullatore** *m* liquidizer, blender; **frullino** *m* whisk

frumento *m* wheat

fruscio *m* rustle

frusta *f* whip; GASTR whisk;

frustare whip; frustino *m* riding crop

frustante frustrating; frustrazione *f* frustration

frutta *f* fruit; **~ secca** nuts

fruttare 1 *v/t* yield 2 *v/i* fruit; frutteto *m* orchard; fruttivendolo *m*, -a *f* greengrocer; frutto *m* fruit; **-i** *pl* **di mare** seafood

FS (= *Ferrovie dello Stato*) Italian State railways

f.to (= *firmato*) signed

fu ☞ *essere*

fucilare shoot; fucile *m* rifle

fuga¹ *f* escape; **~ di gas** gas leak

fuga² *f* MUS fugue

fuggifuggi *m inv* stampede; fuggire flee; fuggitivo *m* fugitive

fuliggine *f* soot

fulminare *di sguardo* glare at; **rimanere fulminato** *da fulmine* be struck by lightning; *da elettricità* be electrocuted; *fig* be thunderstruck; fulminarsi *di lampadina* blow; fulmine *m* lightning; fulmineo fast, rapid

fumare smoke; fumatore *m*, -trice *f* smoker; **scompartimento per -i / non -i** smoking / non-smoking car

fumetto *m* comic strip; **-i** *pl per ragazzi* comics

fumo *m* smoke; (*vapore*) steam; **~ passivo** passive smoking; fumoso smoky; *fig* (*oscuro*) muddled

fune *f* rope; (*cavo*) cable

funebre funeral *attr*; *fig* gloomy, funereal

funerale *m* funeral

fungere act (**da** as)

fungo *m* mushroom; MED fungus

funicolare *f* funicular railway

funivia *f* cableway

funzionamento *m* operation, functioning; funzionare operate, function; **non ~** be out of order; *di orologio* have stopped; funzionario *m* official, civil servant; funzione *f* function; (*carica*) office; REL service; **mettere in ~** put into operation

fuoco *m* fire; FOT focus; **dar ~ a qc** set fire to sth; **~ fuoco** catch fire; **-chi** *pl* **d'artificio** fireworks; MIL **far ~** (open) fire; FOT **mettere a ~** focus

fuorché except

fuori 1 *prp stato* outside, out of; *moto* out of, away from; **~ città** out of town; **~ luogo** out of place; **~ di sé** beside o.s. 2 *avv* outside; **all'aperto** out of doors; SP out; **~!** out!; fuoribordo *m inv* motorboat; *motore* outboard motor; fuorigioco *m inv* offside; **essere nel ~** be offside; fuoriserie 1 *agg* made to order, custom 2 *f inv* AUTO custom-built model; fuoristrada *m inv* off-roader; fuoriuscita *f di gas* leakage; fuorviare **1** v/i go astray **2** v/t lead astray

furbizia f cunning; furbo cunning, crafty

furgoncino m (small) van; furgone m van

furia f fury, rage; a ~ di ... by dint of ...; furibondo furioso, livid; furioso furious; vento, lotta violent; furore m fury, rage; far ~ be all the rage

furto m theft; ~ con scasso burglary

fusa fpl: fare le ~ purr

fuseaux mpl leggings

fusibile m EL fuse

fusione f fusion; FIN merger

fuso[1] pp ☞ fondere; metallo molten; burro melted

fuso[2] m spindle; ~ orario time zone

fusto m (tronco) trunk; (stelo) stem, stalk; di metallo drum; di legno barrel

futile futile

futuristico futuristic; futuro m/agg future

G

gabbia f cage

gabbiano m (sea)gull

gabinetto m toilet, Am rest room

gaffe f blunder, gaffe

gala f (ricevimento) gala

galante gallant

galera f (prigione) jail, prison

galla f: venire a ~ (come to the) surface; fig come to light; (FERR, MIN tunnel; TEA circle, Am balcony

Galles m Wales; gallese **1** m/agg Welsh **2** m/f Welshman; donna Welshwoman

gallina f hen; gallo m cock

gallone m unità di misura gallon

galoppare gallop; galoppo m gallop; al ~ at a gallop

gamba f leg; fig in ~ (capace) smart, bright; persona anziana na sprightly

gamberetto m shrimp; gambero m prawn

gambo m di fiore, bicchiere stem; di pianta, fungo stalk

gamma f range; MUS scale

gancio m hook

gara f competition; di velocità race; fare a ~ compete

garage m inv garage

garantire **1** v/t guarantee; (assicurare) ensure **2** v/i (farsi garante) stand guarantor (per for); garantito guaranteed; garanzia f guarantee; essere in ~ be under guarantee

gareggiare compete

gargarismo m gargle; (collutorio) mouthwash; **fare i -i** gargle

garofano m carnation; GASTR **chiodi di ~** cloves

garza f gauze

gas m inv gas; **a ~** gas attr; **~ lacrimogeno** tear gas; **gasato 1** agg bibita fizzy; F (eccitato) excited **2** m, -a f F bighead F

gasolio m per riscaldamento oil; AUTO diesel

gastrite f gastritis

gastronomia f gastronomy; **gastronomico** gastronomic

gatta f (female) cat; **gattino** m kitten; **gatto** m cat

gay m/agg gay

gazzella f gazelle

gazzetta f gazette

gazzosa f fizzy o Am carbonated drink, Am soda

G.d.F. (= **Guardia di Finanza**) Customs and Excise

gel m inv gel

gelare 1 v/t freeze **2** v/i e gelarsi freeze

gelateria f ice-cream parlour o parlor

gelatina f gelatine; **~ di frutta** fruit jelly

gelato 1 agg frozen **2** m ice cream

gelido freezing

gelo m (brina) frost; fig chill

gelosia f jealousy; **geloso** jealous (**di** of)

gelsomino m jasmine

gemellaggio m twinning; **gemello 1** agg twin **2** m di camicia cuff link **3** m, -a f twin; ASTR **Gemelli** pl Gemini

gemito m groan

gemma f anche fig gem; BOT bud

gene m BIO gene

genealogia f genealogy; **genealogico** genealogical

generale m/agg general; **in ~** in general; **generalità** f inv general nature; **le ~** personal details; **generalizzare** generalize; **generalmente** generally; **generare** (dar vita a) give birth to; (causare) generate, create; sospetti arouse; elettricità, calore generate; **generatore** m EL generator; **generazione** f generation

genere m kind; BIO genus; GRAM gender; **in ~** generally; **-i alimentari** foodstuffs; **~ umano** mankind, humanity; **generico** generic

genero m son-in-law

generoso generous (**con** to)

genetico genetic; **ingegneria** f **-a** genetic engineering

gengiva f gum

geniale ingenious; **genialità** f genius; (ingegnosità) ingeniousness

genio m genius; (inclinazione) talent

genitali mpl genitals

genitori mpl parents

gennaio m January

genocidio m genocide

Genova Genoa; **genovese** *m/agg* Genoese

gentaglia *f* scum

gente *f* people *pl*

gentile kind; *nelle lettere* ~ **Signora** Dear Madam; **gentilezza** *f* kindness

genuino genuine; *prodotto alimentare* traditionally made; *risata* spontaneous

genziana *f* gentian

geografia *f* geography; **geografico** geographic

geologico geological

geometra *m/f* surveyor, *Am* structural engineer; **geometria** *f* geometry

geranio *m* geranium

gerarchia *f* hierarchy

gergo *m* slang; *di una professione anche* jargon

Germania *f* Germany

germe *m* germ; *fig (principio)* seeds; **in** ~ in embryo; **germogliare** sprout; **germoglio** *m* shoot

geroglifico *m* hieroglyph

gesso *m* MIN gypsum; MED, *scultura* plaster cast; *per scrivere* chalk

gesticolare gesticulate

gestione *f* management; **gestire** manage

gesto *m* gesture; *con la testa* nod

gestore *m* manager

Gesù *m* Jesus; ~ **bambino** baby Jesus

gettare throw; *fondamenta* lay; *grido* give, let out; ~

via throw away; **gettarsi** throw o.s.; *di fiume* flow (**in** into)

getto *m* jet; **di** ~ in one go

gettone *m* token; *per giochi* counter; *per giochi d'azzardo* chip

ghetto *m* ghetto

ghiacciaio *m* glacier; **ghiacciato** *lago, stagno* frozen; *bibita* ice-cold; **ghiaccio** *m* ice; *sulla strada* black ice; **ghiacciolo** *m* icicle; *(gelato)* ice lolly, *Am* Popsicle®

ghiaia *f* gravel

ghianda *f* acorn; **ghiandola** *f* gland

ghigliottina *f* guillotine

ghiotto *persona* greedy; *fig: di notizie ecc* avid (**di** for); *(appetitoso)* appetizing

ghirigoro *m* doodle

ghirlanda *f* garland

ghiro *m* dormouse; **dormire come un** ~ sleep like a log

già already; *(ex)* formerly; ~! of course!

giacca *f* jacket; ~ **a vento** windproof jacket

giacché since

giacenza *f* per la vendita stock; *invenduta* unsold goods; *periodo* stock time; ~ **di cassa** cash in hand; **-e** *pl* **di magazzino** stock in hand; **giacimento** *m* MIN deposit

giada *f* jade

giallo *m/agg* yellow; **libro** ~, **film** ~ thriller

Giappone *m* Japan; **giappo-nese** *agg*, *m/f* Japanese

giardinaggio *m* gardening; **giardiniera** *f* gardener; *mobile* plant stand; GASTR (mixed) pickles; **giardiniere** *m* gardener; **giardino** *m* garden; **~ pubblico** park

gigante *m/agg* giant *(attr)*; **gigantesco** gigantic

giglio *m* lily

gilè *m inv* waistcoat, *Am* vest

gin *m inv* gin

ginecologo *m*, **-a** *f* gynaecologist, *Am* gynecologist

ginepro *m* juniper

ginestra *f* broom

gingillarsi fiddle; *(perder tempo)* fool around

ginnastica *f* exercises; *disciplina sportiva* gymnastics; *in palestra* physical education

ginocchio *m* knee; **stare in ~** be on one's knees, be kneeling

giocare 1 *v/i* play; *d'azzardo*, *in Borsa* gamble; *(scommettere)* bet; **~ a tennis**, *flipper* play 2 *v/t* play; *(ingannare)* trick; **giocarsi** *(perdere al gioco)* gamble away; *(beffarsi)* make fun; *carriera* throw away; **giocatore** *m*, **-trice** *f* player; *d'azzardo* gambler; **giocattolo** *m* toy; **gioco** *m* game; **il ~** gambling; **~ d'azzardo** game of chance; **l'ho detto per ~!** I was joking!; **giocoliere** *m* juggler

gioia *f* joy; *(gioiello)* jewel;

gioielleria *f* jeweller's (shop), *Am* jewelry store; **gioiello** *m* jewel

giornalaio *m*, **-a** *f* newsagent, *Am* news vendor; **giornale** *m* (news)paper; *(rivista)* magazine; *(registro)* journal; **~ radio** news (bulletin); **giornaliero** daily; **abbonamento ~** day pass; **giornalino** *m per ragazzi* comic; **giornalismo** *m* journalism; **giornalista** *m/f* journalist, reporter; **giornalistico** journalistic; *agenzia, servizio* news *attr*; **giornata** *f* day; **lo finiremo in ~** we'll finish it today; **giorno** *m* day; **~ feriale** weekday, workday; **~ festivo** (public) holiday; **l'altro ~** the other day; **a -i** *(fra pochi giorni)* in a few days (time); **al ~** a day; **al ~ d'oggi** nowadays; **di ~** by day

giostra *f* carousel, merry-go-round

giovane 1 *agg* young; *(giovanile)* youthful 2 *m/f* young man, youth; *ragazza* young woman, girl; **i -i** young people *pl*, the young *pl*; **giovanotto** *m* young man, youth

giovare *(essere utile)* be useful (**a** to); *(far bene)* be good (**a** for)

Giove *m* Jupiter; **giovedì** *m inv* Thursday

gioventù *f* youth; *(i giovani)* young people *pl*; **giovinezza** *f* youth

gippone m AUTO SUV

giraffa f giraffe

girandola f *fuoco d'artificio* Catherine wheel, Am pinwheel; *(giocattolo)* windmill; *(banderuola)* weather vane;

girare 1 v/t turn; *città, negozi* go around; *paese* travel around; *film* shoot; *(mescolare)* mix; FIN endorse **2** v/i turn; *rapidamente* spin; *(andare in giro)* wander around; *con un veicolo* drive around; **mi gira la testa** I feel dizzy;

girarrosto m GASTR spit; **girasole** m sunflower; **girata** f turn; *(passeggiata a piedi)* walk, stroll; *in macchina* drive; FIN endorsement; **girevole** revolving

girino m tadpole

giro m turn; *(circolo)* circle; *(percorso abituale)* round; *(deviazione)* detour; *(passeggiata a piedi)* walk, stroll; *in macchina* ride; *di pista* lap; *di motore* rev; *(viaggio)* tour; **nel ~ di una settimana** within a week; **essere in ~** *(da qualche parte)* be around somewhere; *(fuori)* be out; **mettere in ~** spread; fig **prendere in ~ qu** pull s.o.'s leg

girocollo m inv: **maglione a ~** crewneck sweater; **gironzolare** hang around; **~ per negozi** wander around the stores; **girovagare** wander around

gita f trip, excursion; **gitante** m/f (day) tripper

giù down; *(sotto)* below; *(da basso)* downstairs; fig **essere ~** be down o depressed; *di salute* be run down; **mandar ~** swallow *(anche fig)*; **su ~** up and down

giubbotto m sports jacket; **~ di salvataggio** life jacket

giudicare judge; **~ male qu** misjudge s.o.; **lo hanno giudicato colpevole** he has been found guilty; **giudice** m judge; **giudizio** m judg(e)ment; *(senno)* wisdom; DIR *(causa)* trial; *(sentenza)* verdict; **a mio ~** in my opinion

giugno m June

giungere arrive *(a* in, at), reach *(a* sth)

giungla f jungle

giunta f addition; POL junta; **~ comunale** town council; **per ~** in addition, moreover;

giunto pp ☞ **giungere**

giuramento m oath; **giurare** swear; **giurato 1** agg sworn **2** m member of the jury; **giuria** f jury

giuridico legal; **giurisprudenza** f jurisprudence

giustificare justify; **giustificazione** f justification

giustizia f justice; **giusto 1** agg just, fair; *(adatto)* right, appropriate; *(esatto)* correct, right **2** avv correctly; *mirare* accurately; *(proprio, per l'appunto)* just; **~!** that's right!

glassa f GASTR icing, Am frosting

gli 1 art mpl the; **avere gli occhi azzurri** have blue eyes **2** pron (a lui) (to) him; (a esso) (to) it; (a loro) (to) them; **dagli i libri** give him / them the books, give the books to him / them

glicemia f glycaemia, Am glycemia

glie: ~la, ~lo, ~li, ~le, ~ne = pron **gli** or **le** with pron **la, lo, li, le, ne**

globale global; **globalizzazione** f globalization; **globo** m globe; **globulo** m globule; MED corpuscle; **~ rosso** red blood cell

gloria f glory

glossario m glossary

glucosio m glucose

gnocchi mpl (di patate) gnocchi (small potato dumplings)

gnorri m F: **fare lo ~** act dumb F

goal m inv SP goal

gobba f hump; **gobbo 1** agg hunchbacked **2** m hunchback

goccia f drop; **a ~ a ~** little by little; **gocciolare** drip

godere v/t enjoy; **godersela** enjoy o.s. **2** v/i (rallegrarsi) be delighted (di at)

goffo awkward, clumsy

gol m inv SP goal

gola f throat; (ingordigia) greed(iness); gluttony; GEOG gorge; **mal** m **di ~** sore throat

golf m inv golf; (cardigan) cardigan; (maglione) sweater

golfo m gulf

goloso greedy; **essere ~ di dolci** have a sweet tooth

golpe m inv coup

gomito m elbow

gomitolo m ball (of wool)

gomma f rubber; per cancellare eraser, Br anche rubber; (pneumatico) tyre, Am tire; **~ da masticare** (chewing) gum; AUTO **~ di scorta** spare tyre; **avere una ~ a terra** have a flat tyre; **gommapiuma®** f foam rubber; **gommista** m tyre o Am tire specialist; **gommone** m rubber dinghy

gondola f gondola; **gondoliere** m gondolier

gonfiare 1 v/t con aria inflate; le guance puff out; fig (esagerare) exaggerate, magnify **2** v/i e **gonfiarsi** swell up; **gonfio** swollen; pneumatico inflated; stomaco bloated; fig puffed up (di with); **gonfiore** m swelling

gonna f skirt

gorgogliare di stomaco rumble; dell'acqua gurgle

gorilla m inv gorilla; F (guardia del corpo) bodyguard, gorilla F

gotico m/agg Gothic

governante 1 f housekeeper **2** m ruler; **governare** POL govern, rule; **governativo** government attr; scuola state

grasso

attr; *governo* m government
gozzovigliare make merry
gracchiare *di corvo* caw; *di rane* croak; *di persona* squawk
gracidare croak
gracile (*debole*) delicate
gradazione f gradation; (*sfumatura*) shade; ~ *alcolica* alcohol(ic) content
gradevole pleasant, agreeable; **gradimento** m liking
gradinata f flight of steps; *stadio* stand; *a teatro* gallery, balcony; **gradino** m step
gradire like; (*desiderare*) wish; **gradisce un po' di vino?** would you like some wine?; **gradito** pleasant; (*bene accetto*) welcome
grado[1] m degree; *in una gerarchia*, MIL rank; *in ~ di lavorare* capable of working, fit for work; *per ~i* by degrees
grado[2] m: *di buon ~* willingly
graduale gradual
graduatoria f list
graffa f TIP brace
graffiare scratch; **graffio** m scratch; **graffiti** mpl graffiti sg o pl
grafica f graphics; **grafico 1** agg graphic **2** m (*diagramma*) graph; (*disegnatore*) graphic artist
grafologia f handwriting analysis, graphology
grammatica f grammar; **grammaticale** grammatical
grammo m gram(me)

Gran Bretagna f Great Britain
gran *☞* **grande**
grana 1 f grain; F (*seccatura*) trouble; F *soldi* dough F, cash **2** m inv cheese similar to Parmesan
granaio m barn
granchio m crab
grande big; (*largo*) wide; *fig* (*intenso, notevole*) great; (*adulto*) grown-up, big; (*vecchio*) old; **grandezza** f (*dimensione*) size; (*larghezza*) width; (*ampiezza*) breadth; (*altezza*) height; *fig* (*eccellenza*) greatness; (*grandiosità*) grandeur
grandinare hail; **grandine** f hail
grandioso grand
granducato m grand duchy
granello m grain; ~ *di pepe* peppercorn; ~ *di polvere* speck of dust
granita f type of ice made of frozen crystals of coffee or fruit syrup
granito m granite
grano m (*chicco*) grain; (*frumento*) wheat; *fig* grain, ounce
granturco m maize, corn
grappa f grappa, *brandy made from the remains of the grapes used in wine-making*
grappolo m bunch
grassetto m TIP bold
grasso 1 agg fat; (*unto*) greasy; *cibo* fatty **2** m fat;

grassoccio plump

grata f grating

gratella f, **graticola** f GASTR grill, Am broiler

gratifica f bonus

gratin m: **al ~** au gratin; **gratinato** au gratin

gratis free (of charge)

gratitudine f gratitude; **grato** grateful

grattacapo m problem, headache f; **grattacielo** m skyscraper; **grattare** scratch; (raschiare) scrape; (grattugiare) grate; F pinch F; **grattugia** f grater; **grattugiare** grate

gratuito free (of charge); (infondato) gratuitous

gravare 1 v/t burden **2** v/i weigh (**su** on); **grave** (pesante) heavy; (serio) serious; (difficile) hard

gravidanza f pregnancy

gravità f seriousness, gravity; FIS (**forza f di**) **~** (force of) gravity

grazia f grace; (gentilezza) favour, Am favor; DIR pardon; **graziare** pardon; **grazie** thank you, thanks; **~ tante**, **~ mille** thank you so much; **~ a** thanks to; **grazioso** charming; (carino) pretty

Grecia f Greece; **greco 1** agg Greek **2** m, -a f Greek

gregge m flock

greggio 1 agg (non lavorato) raw, crude **2** m crude (petroleum)

grembiule m apron; **grembo** m lap; materno womb; fig bosom

gretto (avaro) mean; (di mente ristretta) narrow-minded

gridare 1 v/t shout, yell; **~ aiuto** shout for help **2** v/i shout, yell; (strillare) scream; **grido** m shout, cry

grigio grey, Am gray; fig (triste) sad; (scialbo) dreary

griglia f (grata) grating; GASTR grill; **alla ~** grilled

grilletto m trigger

grillo m cricket; fig (capriccio) fancy, whim

grimaldello m lock pick

grinfie fpl fig clutches

grinta f grit; fig determination

grinza f di stoffa crease; **grinzoso** viso wrinkled; (spiegazzato) creased

grissino m bread stick

grondaia f gutter

grondare 1 v/i (colare) pour; (gocciolare) drip; **~ di sudore** be dripping with sweat **2** v/t drip with

groppa f back

groppo m: **avere un ~ alla gola** have a lump in one's throat

grossezza f (dimensione) size; (spessore) thickness; (l'essere grosso) largeness; **grossista** m/f wholesaler; **grosso 1** agg big, large; (spesso) thick; mare rough; sale, ghiaia coarse; **sbagliarsi di ~** make a big mistake;

farla -a make a fine mess **2** m
bulk; **grossolano** coarse; **errore** serious; **grossomodo**
roughly

grotta f cave; **artificiale** grotto
grottesco grotesque
groviglio m tangle; fig muddle
gru f inv crane
gruccia f crutch; per vestiti
hanger
grumo m clot; di farina lump
gruppo m group; **~ sanguigno** blood group

guadagnare earn; (ottenere)
gain; **guadagno** m gain;
(profitto) profit; (entrate)
earnings
guaina f sheath; (busto) cor-
set
guaio m trouble; (danno)
damage; **essere nei -ai** be
in trouble
guancia f cheek
guanciale m pillow
guanto m glove; **guantone** m:
~ da boxe boxing glove
guardaboschi m inv forest
ranger; **guardacoste** m inv
MAR coastguard; **guardalinee** m inv SP assistant referee, linesman; **guardamac-
chine** m car park attendant,
Am parking lot attendant
guardare **1** v/t look at; (osservare, stare a vedere) watch;
(custodire) watch, look after;
(esaminare) check **2** v/i look;
(controllare) check; di finestra
overlook (**su** sth); **~ a sud**

face south; **guardaroba** m
inv cloakroom, Am check-
room; **armadio** wardrobe;
guardarsi look at o.s.; **~ da**
beware of; (astenersi) refrain
from

guardia f guard; **~ forestale**
forest ranger; **~ di finanza**
Customs official; **~ del corpo** bodyguard; **~ medica,
medico m di ~** duty doctor;
fare la ~ keep guard; **stare in
~** be on one's guard; **guardiano** m, -a f (custode) warden; (portiere) caretaker;
(guardia) guard; di parco
keeper; **~ notturno** night
watchman; **guardone** m
voyeur
guardrail m inv guardrail
guarigione f recovery; **in via
di ~** on the mend; **guarire** **1**
v/t cure **2** v/i recover; di ferita
heal
guarnizione f (abbellimento)
trimming; GASTR garnish;
di rubinetto washer; AUTO **~
del freno** brake lining
guastafeste m/f inv spoilsport; **guastare** spoil, ruin;
meccanismo break; **guastarsi** break down; di tempo
change for the worse; di cibi
go bad; **guasto 1** agg broken; telefono, ascensore out
of order; AUTO broken
down; cibi bad; dente rotten,
decayed **2** m fault, failure;
AUTO breakdown
guerra f war; **guerrafondaio**

m war-monger; **guerriglia** *f* guerrilla warfare; **guerrigliero** *m*, **-a** *f* guerrilla

gufo *m* owl

guida *f* guidance; (*persona, libro*) guide; AUTO driving; **~ telefonica** phone book; **~ turistica** tourist guide; AUTO **~ a destra / a sinistra** right-hand / left-hand

drive; **guidare** guide; AUTO drive; **guidatore** *m*, **-trice** *f* driver

guinzaglio *m* lead, leash

guscio *m* shell

gustare taste; *fig* enjoy; **gusto** *m* taste; (*sapore*) flavour, *Am* flavor; *fig* (*piacere*) pleasure; **buon / cattivo ~** good / bad taste

H

ha¹ (= *ettaro*) ha (= hectare)

ha² ☞ *avere*

habitat *m inv* BIO habitat

habitué *m/f inv* regular

hacker *m/f* INFOR *inv* hacker

hai ☞ *avere*

hall *f inv* foyer

hamburger *m inv* hamburger

handicap *m inv* handicap; **handicappato 1** *agg* disabled, handicapped **2** *m*, **-a** *f* disabled *o* handicapped person

hanno ☞ *avere*

hard disk *m inv* INFOR hard disk

hardware *m inv* INFOR hard-

ware

harem *m inv* harem

hashish *m inv* hashish

henné *m inv* henna

herpes *m inv* herpes

hinterland *m inv* hinterland

hit parade *f inv* hit parade, charts

ho ☞ *avere*

hobby *m inv* hobby

hockey *m inv* hockey; **~ su ghiaccio** ice hockey

hostess *f inv* hostess; **~ di terra** (*guida*) member of ground staff

hot dog *m inv* hot dog

hotel *m inv* hotel

I

i *art mpl* the

iceberg *m inv* iceberg

icona *f* icon

idea *f* idea; (*opinione*) opinion; **cambiare ~** change

one's mind; **non avere la minima ~ di qc** not have the slightest idea about sth; **neanche per ~!** of course not!; **ideale** *m/agg* ideal; **idealiz-**

zare idealize; **ideare** *scherzo, scusa* think up; *metodo, oggetto nuovo* invent; *piano, progetto* devise; **ideatore** *m*, **-trice** *f* originator; *di metodo, oggetto nuovo* inventor

idem ditto

identico identical; **identificare** identify; **identikit** *m inv* Identikit®, *Am* composite drawing; **identità** *f inv* identity

ideologia *f* ideology

idiomatico idiomatic

idiota 1 *agg* idiotic, stupid **2** *m/f* idiot, fool; **idiozia** *f* stupidity; (*assurdità*) nonsense; **un'~** a stupid *o* idiotic thing to do / say

idolo *m* idol

idoneo suitable (**a** for)

idrante *m* hydrant

idratante *della pelle* moisturizing; **idratare** *la pelle* moisturize

idraulico 1 *agg* hydraulic; **impianto** *m* ~ plumbing **2** *m* plumber

idrico water *attr*

idroelettrico hydroelectric; **idrofilo:** *cotone* *m* ~ cotton wool, *Am* absorbent cotton; **idromassaggio** *m* Jacuzzi®, whirlpool; **idroplano** *m* hydroplane

iena *f* hyena

ieri yesterday; ~ **l'altro, l'altro** ~ the day before yesterday; ~ **mattina** yesterday morning

igiene *f* hygiene; **igienico** hygienic; **carta** *f* **-a** toilet paper

ignaro unaware (**di** of); **ignorante** (*non informato*) ignorant; (*incolto*) uneducated; (*maleducato*) rude; **ignoranza** *f* ignorance; **ignorare** (*non considerare*) ignore; (*non sapere*) not know; **ignoto** unknown

il *art m sg* the; ~ **martedì** on Tuesdays; **2 euro** ~ **chilo** 2 euros a kilo; **mi piace il caffè** I like coffee

illegale illegal

illeggibile illegible

illegittimo illegitimate

illeso unhurt

illimitato unlimited

illogico illogical

illudere deceive; **illudersi** delude o.s.

illuminare light up; *fig* enlighten; **illuminazione** *f* lighting; *fig* flash of inspiration

illusione *f* illusion; **illuso 1** *pp* → **illudere 2** *m/f* (*sognatore*) dreamer

illustrare illustrate; **illustratore** *m*, **-trice** *f* illustrator; **illustrazione** *f* illustration

illustre illustrious

imballaggio *m* operazione packing; (*involucro*) package; **imballare** pack; AUTO ~ **il motore** race the engine

imbambolato *occhi, sguardo* blank; *dal sonno* bleary-eyed

imbarazzante embarrassing; **imbarazzare** embarrass; **im-**

barazzato embarrassed; imbarazzo *m* embarrassment; (*disturbo*) trouble; **mettere in ~ qu** embarrass s.o.

imbarcadero *m* landing stage; imbarcarsi go on board, embark; imbarcazione *f* boat; **~ da diporto** pleasure boat; imbarco *m di passeggeri* boarding, embarkation; *di carico* loading; (*banchina*) landing stage

imbattersi: **~ in qu** bump into s.o.

imbattibile unbeatable

imbecille 1 *agg* idiotic, stupid 2 *m/f* imbecile, fool

imbiancare 1 *v/t* whiten; *con pitture* paint; *tessuti* bleach 2 *v/i e* imbiancarsi go white; imbianchino *m* (house) painter

imboccare *persona* feed; *fig* prompt; **~ una strada** turn into a road; imboccatura *f* (*apertura*) opening; (*ingresso*) entrance; MUS mouthpiece; imbocco *m* entrance

imboscata *f* ambush

imbottigliare bottle; *di veicoli* hold up

imbottito stuffed; *panino* filled; imbottitura *f* stuffing; *di giacca* padding

imbranato clumsy

imbrattare soil; (*macchiare*) stain

imbrogliare 1 *v/t* (*raggirare*) take in; (*truffare*) cheat; *fig* confuse 2 *v/i* cheat; imbro-

glio *m* (*truffa*) trick; *fig* (*pasticcio*) mess; imbroglione *m*, -a *f* cheat

imbronciato sulky

imbruttire 1 *v/t* make ugly 2 *v/i* get ugly

imbucare *posta* post, *Am* mail

imburrare butter

imbuto *m* funnel

imitare imitate; imitazione *f* imitation

immaginare imagine; (*supporre*) suppose; immaginario imaginary; immaginazione *f* imagination

immagine *f* image

immangiabile inedible

immaturo *persona* immature; (*precoce*) premature; *frutto* unripe

immedesimarsi identify (**in** with)

immediatamente immediately; immediato immediate; (*pronto*) prompt

immenso immense

immergere immerse; (*lasciare immerso*) soak; immergersi plunge; *di subacqueo, sottomarino* dive; *fig* immerse o.s. (**in** in); immersione *f* immersion; *di subacqueo, sottomarino* dive; immerso 1 *pp* ☞ **immergere** 2 *agg* immersed

immettere introduce (**in** into); INFOR *dati* enter; (*portare*) lead (**in** into); immettersi: **~ in** get into

impedire

immigrante *m/f* immigrant; **immigrare** immigrate; **immigrato** *m*, **-a** *f* immigrant; **immigrazione** *f* immigration; (*immigrati*) immigrants; FIN inflow

imminente imminent; *pericolo* impending; *pubblicazione* forthcoming

immischiarsi meddle (**in** with), interfere (**in** in)

immissione *f* introduction; *di manodopera* intake; INFOR *di dati* entry

immobile 1 *agg* motionless **2** *mpl:* **-i** real estate; **immobiliare:** **agente** *m/f* ~ estate agent, *Am* realtor; **società** *f* ~ *di compravendita* property company; *di costruzione* construction company

immondizia *f* (*gen pl*) rubbish, *Am* trash

immorale immoral

immortale immortal; **immortalità** *f* immortality

immune MED immune (**a** to); (*esente*) free (**da** from); **immunità** *f* immunity; **immunitario:** **sistema** *m* ~ immune system; **immunodeficienza** *f* immunodeficiency

immutato unchanged

impacchettare (*confezionare*) wrap (up); (*mettere in pacchetti*) package

impacciare *movimenti* hamper; *persona* hinder; **impacciato** (*imbarazzato*) embarrassed; (*goffo*) awkward; **impaccio** *m* (*ostacolo*) hindrance; (*situazione difficile*) awkward situation; (*imbarazzo*) awkwardness

impacco *m* MED compress

impadronirsi: ~ *di qc* take possession of sth; *fig* master sth

impalcatura *f* temporanea scaffolding; *fig* framework

impallidire *di persona* turn pale

impanare GASTR coat with breadcrumbs; **impanato** in breadcrumbs, breaded

impaperarsi falter

imparare learn (**a** to)

imparentarsi: ~ **con** *qu* become related to s.o.

impari unequal; MAT odd

impartire give

imparziale impartial; **imparzialità** *f* impartiality

impassibile impassive

impastare mix; *pane* knead; **impasto** *m* GASTR dough; (*mescolanza*) mixture

impatto *m* impact

impaurire frighten; **impaurirsi** get frightened

impaziente impatient; **impazienza** *f* impatience

impazzata: **all'~** correre at breakneck speed; *colpire* wildly

impazzire go mad *o* crazy; **far** ~ *qu* drive s.o. mad *o* crazy

impeccabile impeccable

impedire prevent; (*ostruire*) block, obstruct; (*impacciare*) hinder; **~ a qu di fare qc** prevent s.o. from doing sth, keep s.o. from doing sth

impegnare (*dare come pegno*) pawn; (*riservare*) reserve; *spazio, corsia* take up; **impegnarsi** (*prendersi l'impegno*) commit o.s., undertake (**a** to); (*concentrarsi*) apply o.s. (**in** to); **impegnativo** (*che richiede impegno*) demanding; *pranzo, serata, abito* formal; (*vincolante*) binding; **impegnato** (*occupato*) busy; *fig* (politically) committed; **sono già ~** I've made other arrangements; **impegno** *m* commitment; (*appuntamento*) engagement; **con ~** in earnest

impensabile unthinkable; **impensato** unexpected

imperante (*dominante*) prevailing

imperativo *m/agg* imperative

imperatore *m*, **-trice** *f* emperor; *donna* empress

impercettibile imperceptible

imperdonabile unforgivable

imperfetto *m/agg* imperfect; **imperfezione** *f* imperfection

impermeabile 1 *agg* waterproof **2** *m* raincoat; **impermeabilizzare** waterproof

impero *m* empire; (*potere*) rule

impersonale impersonal; **impersonare** personify; (*interpretare*) play (the part of)

impertinente impertinent; **impertinenza** *f* impertinenza

imperturbabile imperturbabile

imperversare rage; *fig*: *di moda* be all the rage

impeto *m* impetus, force; (*accesso*) outburst; (*slancio*) passion; **parlare con ~** speak forcefully; **impetuoso** impetuoso

impianto *m operazione* installation; (*apparecchiature*) plant; (*sistema*) system; MED implant; *~ elettrico* wiring; *~ di risalita* ski lift; *~ di riscaldamento* heating system

impiccare hang; **impiccarsi** hang o.s.

impicciarsi: ~ di o in qc interfere *o* meddle in sth; **impiccio** *m* (*ostacolo*) hindrance; (*seccatura*) bother; **essere d'~** be in the way; **essere in un ~** be in trouble

impiegare (*usare*) use; *tempo, soldi* spend; (*metterci*) take; (*assumere*) employ; **ho impiegato un'ora** it took me an hour; **impiegato** *m*, **-a** *f* employee; *~ di banca* bank employee; **impiego** *m* (*uso*) use; (*occupazione*) employment; (*posto*) job

impietosire move to pity; **impietosirsi** be moved to pity

impigliare entangle; **impigliarsi** get entangled

impigrire 1 v/t make lazy **2** v/i e **impigrirsi** get lazy

implacabile implacable

implicare (coinvolgere) implicate; (comportare) imply

implicito implicit

implorare implore

impolverato dusty, covered in dust

imponente imposing, impressive

imponibile 1 agg taxable **2** m taxable income

impopolare unpopular

imporre impose; prezzo fix; **imporsi** (farsi valere) assert o.s.; (avere successo) be successful, become established; (essere necessario) be necessary

importante important; **importanza** f importance; **senza ~** not important, unimportant; **importare 1** v/t FIN, INFOR import **2** v/i matter, be important; (essere necessario) be necessary; **non importa** it doesn't matter; **non gliene importa niente** he couldn't care less; **importatore** m, **-trice** f importer; **importazione** f import; **importo** m amount

importunare (assillare) pester; (disturbare) bother; **importuno** troublesome; domanda, osservazione illtimed

impossessarsi: **~ di** seize

impossibile impossible; **impossibilità** f impossibility

imposta¹ f tax; **~ sul reddito** income tax; **~ sul valore aggiunto** value added tax, Am sales tax

imposta² f di finestra shutter

impostare lavoro plan; problema set out; lettera post, Am mail

imposto pp ☞ **imporre**

impostore m impostor

impotente powerless; (inefficace) ineffectual; MED impotent

impraticabile strada impassabile

impratichirsi get practice (**in** in)

imprecare curse, swear (**contro** at); **imprecazione** f curse

imprecisato quantità indeterminate; motivi, circostanze not clear; **imprecisione** f inaccuracy; **impreciso** inaccurate

impregnare impregnate; (imbevere) soak; **impregnarsi** become impregnated (**di** with)

imprenditore m, **-trice** f entrepreneur; **imprenditoriale** entrepreneurial

impreparato unprepared

impresa f (iniziativa) enterprise, undertaking; (azienda) business, firm

impresario m contractor; TEA impresario

impressionante impressive;

(*spaventoso*) frightening; (*sconvolgente*) upsetting, shocking; **impressionare** (*turbare*) upset, shock; (*spaventare*) frighten; (*colpire*) impress; **impressionato** FOT exposed; **~ favorevolmente** (favourably) impressed; **impressione** f impression; (*turbamento*) shock; (*paura*) fright; TIP printing; **impresso** pp ☞ **imprimere**

imprevedibile unforeseeable; *persona* unpredictable; **imprevisto 1** *agg* unexpected **2** *m* unforeseen event; **salvo imprevisti** all being well

imprigionare imprison

imprimere impress; *fig: nella mente* fix firmly, imprint; *movimento* impart; TIP print

improbabile unlikely, improbable

impronta f impression, mark; (*orma*) footprint; (*traccia*) track; *fig* mark; **-e** *pl* **digitali** fingerprints; **-e** *pl* **genetiche** genetic fingerprints

improprio improper

improvvisamente suddenly; **improvvisare** improvize; **improvvisata** f surprise; **improvvisato** improvized, impromptu; **improvviso** sudden; (*inaspettato*) unexpected; **all'~** suddenly; (*inaspettatamente*) unexpectedly

imprudente careless; (*non*

saggio) imprudent, rash; **imprudenza** f carelessness; (*mancanza di saggezza*) imprudence, rashness

impugnare grasp; DIR contest; **impugnatura** f grip; (*manico*) handle

impulsivo impulsive; **impulso** m impulse

impunità f impunity

impuntarsi (*ostinarsi*) dig one's heels in

imputato m, **-a** f accused; **imputazione** f charge

imputridire rot

in in; *moto a luogo* to; **~ casa** at home; **va ~ Inghilterra** he is going to England; **~ italiano** in Italian; **~ campagna** in the country; **viaggiare ~ macchina** travel by car; **nel 1999** in 1999; **~ vacanza** on holiday

inabile unfit (*a* for); (*disabile*) disabled

inaccessibile inaccessible, out of reach; *fig: persona* unapproachable; *prezzi* exorbitant

inaccettabile unacceptable

inacidire, inacidirsi turn sour

inadatto unsuitable (*a* for)

inadeguato inadequate

inalare inhale; **inalatore** m inhaler; **inalazione** f inhalation

inalterabile *sentimento* unchangeable; *colore* fast; *metallo* non-tarnish

inalterato unchanged

inamidare starch

inammissibile inadmissible

inanimato inanimate; (*senza vita*) lifeless

inappetenza *f* lack of appetite

inarcare *schiena* arch; *sopracciglia* raise

inaridire 1 *v/t* parch 2 *v/i* dry up

inaspettato unexpected

inasprimento *m* (*intensificazione*) worsening; *di carattere* embitterment; inasprire exacerbate, make worse; *carattere* embitter

inattendibile unreliable

inatteso unexpected

inattività *f* inactivity; inattivo *persona, capitale* idle, inactive; *vulcano* dormant

inattuabile (*non fattibile*) impracticable; (*non realistico*) unrealistic

inaugurare *mostra* (officially) open, inaugurate; *lapide* unveil; F *oggetto nuovo* christen F; inaugurazione *f di mostra* (official) opening, inauguration; *di lapide* unveiling; F *di oggetto nuovo* christening F

inavvertenza *f* inadvertence

incagliarsi MAR run aground

incalcolabile incalculable

incalzare pursue; *fig*: *con richieste* ply

incamminarsi set out

incandescente incandescent; *fig* heated

incantare enchant; incantarsi (*restare affascinato*) be spellbound; (*sognare a occhi aperti*) be in a daze; TEC jam; incantato *per effetto di magia* enchanted; (*trasognato*) in a daze; (*affascinato*) spellbound; incantesimo *m* spell; incantevole delightful, charming

incanto[1] *m* (*incantesimo*) spell; **come per** ~ as if by magic

incanto[2] *m* COM auction; **mettere all'**~ put up for auction

incapace 1 *agg* incapable (*di* of); (*incompetente*) incompetent 2 *m/f* incompetent person; incapacità *f* (*inabilità*) inability; (*incompetenza*) incompetence

incappare: ~ *in nebbia, difficoltà* run into

incapricciarsi: ~ *di qu* take a liking to s.o.

incarcerare imprison

incaricare (*dare istruzioni a*) instruct; ~ *qu di fare qc* tell *o* instruct s.o. to do sth; incaricarsi: ~ *di qc* see to sth, deal with sth; incaricato *m*, -a *f* (*responsabile*) person in charge; (*funzionario*) official; incarico *m* (*compito*) task, assignment; (*nomina*) appointment

incarnare embody

incartare wrap (up) (in paper)

incassare COM (*riscuotere*) cash; *fig*: colpi, insulti ecc take; **incasso** m (*riscossione*) collection; (*somma incassata*) takings

incastonare set

incastrare fit in; F *fig* (*far apparire colpevole*) frame F; (*mettere in una posizione difficile*) corner F

incastro m joint

incatenare chain

incavato hollow; *occhi* deepset

incendiare set fire to; **incendiario** m, **-a** f arsonist; **incendio** m fire; **~ doloso** arson

incenerire reduce to ashes; **inceneritore** m incinerator

incenso m incense

incensurato irreproachable; DIR **essere ~** have a clean record

incentivare (*incrementare*) boost; **incentivo** m incentive

incerata f oilcloth

incertezza f uncertainty; **incerto 1** *agg* uncertain **2** m uncertainty

incessante incessant

incetta f: **fare ~ di qc** stockpile sth

inchiesta f investigation

inchinarsi bow; *di donna* curtsy; **inchino** m bow; *di donna* curtsy

inchiodare 1 *v/t* nail; *coperchio* nail down **2** *v/i* AUTO jam on the brakes

inchiostro m ink

inciampare trip (*in* over); **~ in qu** run into s.o.

incidentale (*casuale*) accidental; (*secondario*) incidental; **incidente** m (*episodio*) incident; **~ aereo** plane crash; **~ stradale** road accident

incidere[1] *v/i* affect (*su* sth)

incidere[2] *v/t* engrave; (*tagliare*) cut; (*registrare*) record

incinta pregnant

incirca: **all'~** more or less

incisione f engraving; (*acquaforte*) etching; (*taglio*) cut; MED incision; (*registrazione*) recording; **incisivo 1** *agg* incisive **2** m (*dente*) incisor

incitare incite

incivile uncivilized; (*villano*) impolite

inclinare 1 *v/t* tilt **2** *v/i*: **~ a** (*tendere a*) be inclined to; **inclinato** tilted; **inclinazione** f inclination; **incline** inclined (**a** to)

includere include; (*allegare*) enclose; **inclusivo** inclusive; **incluso 1** *pp* ☞ **includere 2** *agg* included; (*compreso*) inclusive; (*allegato*) enclosed

incoerente (*incongruente*) inconsistent; **incoerenza** f inconsistency

incognita f unknown quantity; **incognito** m: **in ~** incognito

incollare stick; *con colla liquida* glue; **incollarsi** stick (**a** to)

incolore colourless, Am col-

orless
incolpare blame
incolto uneducated; (*trascurato*) unkempt; AGR uncultivated
incolume unharmed; **incolumità** f safety
incombente *pericolo* impending; **incombenza** f task
incominciare start, begin (**a** to)
incomodare inconvenience; **incomodarsi** put o.s. out
incompatibile incompatible; **incompatibilità** f incompatibility
incompetente incompetent; **incompetenza** f incompetence
incompiuto unfinished
incompleto incomplete
incomprensibile incomprehensible; **incomprensione** f lack of understanding; (*malinteso*) misunderstanding; **incompreso** misunderstood
inconcepibile inconceivable
inconcludente inconclusive; *persona* ineffectual
inconfondibile unmistakable
inconfutabile indisputable
inconsapevole (*ignaro*) unaware
inconscio m/agg unconscious
inconsistente insubstantial; fig (*infondato*) unfounded; (*vago*) vague

inconsolabile inconsolable
inconsueto unusual
incontentabile hard to please; (*perfezionista*) perfectionist
incontestato undisputed
incontrare 1 v/t meet; *difficoltà* encounter **2** v/i e **incontrarsi** meet (**con** s.o.)
incontrario: all'~ the other way round; (*nel modo sbagliato*) the wrong way round
incontrastato undisputed
incontro 1 m meeting; **~ di calcio** football match o Am game **2** prp: **~ a** towards; **andare ~ a qu** go and meet s.o.; fig meet s.o. halfway
inconveniente m (*svantaggio*) drawback; (*ostacolo*) hitch
incoraggiamento m encouragement; **incoraggiante** encouraging; **incoraggiare** encourage
incorniciare frame
incoronare crown
incorporare incorporate
incorreggibile incorrigible
incorrere: ~ in sanzioni incur; *errore* make
incorruttibile incorruptible
incosciente unconscious; (*irresponsabile*) reckless
incoscienza f unconsciousness; (*insensatezza*) recklessness
incostante changeable; *negli affetti* fickle
incostituzionale unconstitu-

tional

incredibile incredible

incredulo incredulous, disbelieving

incrementare increase; **incremento** *m* increase, growth

increspare *acque* ripple; *capelli* frizz; *tessuto* gather

incriminare indict

incrociare 1 *v/t* cross **2** *v/i* MAR, AVIA cruise; **incrocio** *m* (*intersezione*) crossing; (*crocevia*) crossroads *sg*, *Am* intersection; *di razze animali* cross(-breed)

incubatrice *f* incubator; **incubazione** *f* incubation

incubo *m* nightmare

incudine *f* anvil

incurabile incurable

incurante heedless (**di** of)

incuriosire: ~ qu arouse s.o.'s curiosity

incursione *f* raid; **~ aerea** air raid

incustodito unattended; *passaggio a livello* unmanned

indaco *m*/*agg* indigo

indaffarato busy

indagare investigate (**su**, **intorno a** sth); **indagine** *f* research; *della polizia* investigation; **~ di mercato** market survey

indebitare, indebitarsi get into debt

indebolire weaken

indecente indecent

indecisione *f* indecision, in-

decisiveness; **indeciso** undecided; *abitualmente* indecisive

indefinito indefinite

indelebile indelible; *colore* fast

indenne *persona* uninjured; *cosa* undamaged; **indennità** *f inv* (*gratifica*) allowance, benefit; (*risarcimento*) compensation; **~ di trasferta** travel allowance; **indennizzare** compensate (**per** for); **indennizzo** *m* (*compenso*) compensation

indescrivibile indescribable

indesiderato unwanted

indeterminato *tempo* unspecified, indefinite; *quantità* indeterminate

India *f* India; **indiano 1** *agg* Indian **2** *m*, **-a** *f* Indian

indicare show, indicate; *col dito* point at *o* to; (*consigliare*) suggest, recommend; (*significare*) mean; **indicativo** *m* GRAM indicative; **indicato** (*consigliabile*) advisable; (*adatto*) suitable

indicatore 1 *agg* indicative **2** *m* indicator; AUTO **~ di direzione** indicator, *Am* turn signal; **indicazione** *f* indication; (*direttiva*) direction; (*informazione*) piece of information; MED **-i** *pl* directions (for use); **-i** *pl* **stradali** road signs

indice *m* index; ANAT index finger, forefinger

indicibile indescribable
indietreggiare draw back; *camminando all'indietro* step back; MIL retreat
indietro behind; *tornare, girarsi* back; *essere ~ con il lavoro* be behind; *mentalmente* be backward; *di orologio* be slow; *dare ~ (restituire)* give back; *tirarsi ~* draw back; fig back out; *all'~* backwards
indifeso undefended; *(inerme)* defenceless, *Am* defenseless
indifferente indifferent; *non ~* appreciable, considerable; *per me è ~* it's all the same to me; indifferenza f indifference
indigeno 1 *agg* native, indigenous 2 *m*, -a f native
indigestione f indigestion; indigesto indigestible
indignare: *~ qu* make s.o. indignant; indignarsi get indignant *(per* about)
indimenticabile unforgettable
indipendente independent *(da* of); indipendentemente independently; *~ dall'età* regardless of age; indipendenza f independence
indire *conferenza, elezioni, sciopero* call; *concorso* announce
indiretto indirect
indirizzare direct; *lettera* address; *(spedire)* send; indirizzario *m* address book; per

spedizione mailing list; indirizzo *m* address; *(direzione)* direction; *~ di posta elettronica* e-mail address
indisciplinato undisciplined
indiscreto indiscreet; indiscrezione f indiscretion
indiscriminato indiscriminate
indiscusso unquestioned
indiscutibile unquestionable
indispensabile 1 *agg* indispensable, essential 2 *m* essentials
indispettire irritate; indispettirsi get irritated; indispettito irritated
indisposto *(ammalato)* indisposed
indistinto indistinct
indistruttibile indestructible
indivia f endive
individuale individual; individualista *m/f* individualist; individuo *m* individual
indizio *m* clue; *(segno)* sign; *(sintomo)* symptom; DIR *-i pl* circumstantial evidence
indole f nature
indolente indolent
indolore painless
indomani: *l'~* the next day
indossare *(mettersi)* put on; *(portare)* wear; indossatore *m*, -trice f model
indotto *pp* → *indurre*
indovinare guess; *futuro* predict; indovinato *(ben riuscito)* successful; *(ben scelto)* well chosen; indovinello *m*

riddle; **indovino** m, **-a** f fortune-teller

indubbiamente undoubtedly

indugiare 1 v/t *partenza* delay; **2** v/i *(tardare)* delay; *(esitare)* hesitate; *(attardarsi)* linger; **indugio** m delay; **senza ~** without delay

indulgente indulgent; *giudice, sentenza* lenient; **indulgenza** f indulgence; *di giudice, sentenza* leniency

indumento m item of clothing; **gli -i** pl clothes

indurire 1 v/t harden **2** v/i e **indurirsi** go hard, harden; **indurito** hardened

indurre induce

industria f industry; *(operosità)* industriousness; **industriale 1** agg industrial **2** m industrialist; **industrializzazione** f industrialization

ineccepibile irreproachable; *ragionamento* faultless

inedito unpublished; *fig* novel

inefficace ineffective

inefficiente inefficient; **inefficienza** f inefficiency

ineguagliabile *(senza rivali)* unrivalled, Am unrivaled; *(senza confronto)* incomparable; **ineguale** unequal; *(discontinuo)* uneven

inequivocabile unequivocal

inerte *(inoperoso)* idle; *(immobile)* inert, motionless; *(senza vita)* lifeless; FIS inert; **inerzia** f inertia; *(inattività)* inactivity

inesattezza f inaccuracy; **inesatto** inaccurate

inesauribile inexhaustible

inesperienza f inexperience; **inesperto** inexperienced

inesplorato unexplored

inesploso unexploded

inestimabile inestimable; *bene* invaluable

inetto inept

inevaso pending

inevitabile inevitable

inezia f trifle

infallibile infallible

infame 1 agg *(turpe)* infamous, foul; *spir* horrible **2** m/f P *(delatore)* grass P

infantile *letteratura, giochi* children's; *malattie* childhood; *attr (immaturo)* childish, infantile; **infanzia** f childhood; *(primi mesi)* infancy *(anche fig)*; *(bambini)* children pl

infarinare (dust with) flour; **infarinatura** f fig smattering

infarto m *cardiaco* heart attack

infastidire annoy, irritate

infatti in fact

infatuarsi: ~ di qu become infatuated with s.o.

infedele 1 agg unfaithful; *traduzione* inaccurate **2** m/f REL infidel; **infedeltà** f inv unfaithfulness

infelice unhappy; *(inopportuno)* unfortunate; *(malriuscito)* bad; **infelicità** f unhappiness

inferiore 1 agg lower; fig inferior (*a* to); **essere ~ a qu** be inferior to s.o. **2** m/f inferior; (*subalterno*) subordinate; **inferiorità** f inferiority; **complesso** m **d'~** inferiority complex

infermeria f infirmary; **infermiere** m, -a f nurse; **infermo 1** agg (*ammalato*) ill; (*invalido*) invalid **2** m, -a f invalid

infernale infernal; **inferno** m hell

inferriata f grating; (*cancellata*) railings

infestare infest; **infettarsi** become infected; **infettivo** infectious; **infezione** f infection

infiammabile flammable; **infiammarsi** become inflamed; **infiammazione** f inflammation

infierire di maltempo, malattie rage; **~ su** o **contro** savagely attack

infilare fili, corde, ago thread; (*inserire*) insert, put in; (*indossare*) put on; strada take; **infilarsi** indumento slip on; (*conficcarsi*) stick; (*introdursi*) slip (*in* into); (*stiparsi*) squeeze (*in* into)

infiltrarsi seep; fig infiltrate; **infiltrazione** f infiltration; di liquidi seepage

infilzare pierce; perle thread

infimo lowest

infine (*alla fine*) finally, eventually; (*insomma*) in short

infinità f infinity; **ho un'~ di cose da fare** I've got no end of things to do; **infinito 1** agg infinite **2** m infinity; GRAM infinitive

infischiarsi F: **~ di** not give a hoot about F; **me ne infischio** I couldn't care less F

inflazione f inflation

inflessibile inflexible

infliggere inflict; **inflitto** pp ☞ **infliggere**

influente influential; **influenza** f influence; MED flu, influenza; **influenzabile** easily influenced, impressionable; **influenzare** influence; **influire: ~ su** influence, have an effect on; **influsso** m influence

infondato unfounded

infondere fig instil, Am instill

inforcare occhiali put on; bicicletta get on; mount

informale informal

informare inform (*di* of); **informarsi** find out (*di, su* about); **informatica** f scienza information technology, IT; **informatico 1** agg computer attr, IT **2** m, -a f computer scientist, IT specialist

informato informed; **informatore** m, -trice f informant; della polizia informer; **informazione** f information; **un'~** a piece of information; **-i** information; **ufficio** m **-i** information office

informicolirsi have pins and needles

infortunio *m* accident; **~ sul lavoro** accident at work

infossato *occhi* deep-set, sunken

infrangere break; **infrangibile** unbreakable; **vetro** *m* ~ shatterproof glass

infranto *pp* ☞ **infrangere**

infrarosso infrared

infrasettimanale midweek

infrastruttura *f* infrastructure

infrazione *f* offence, *Am* offense

infreddatura *f* cold

infuocato *(caldissimo)* scorching; *discorso, tramonto* fiery

infuori: **all'~** outwards; **all'~ di** except

infuriarsi fly into a rage; **infuriato** furious

infusione *f*, **infuso** *m* infusion; *(tisana)* herbal tea

ingaggiare *(reclutare)* recruit; *attore, cantante lirico* engage; SP sign (up); *(iniziare)* start, begin; **ingaggio** *m* *(reclutamento)* recruitment; SP signing; *(somma)* fee

ingannare deceive; **~ il tempo** kill time; **inganno** *m* deception, deceit

ingarbugliare tangle; *fig* confuse, muddle; **ingarbugliarsi** get entangled; *fig* get confused

ingegnarsi do one's utmost

(a, per) to)

ingegnere *m* engineer; **ingegneria** *f* engineering; **~ genetica** genetic engineering

ingegno *m* (*mente*) mind; *(intelligenza)* brains; *(genio)* genius; *(inventiva)* ingenuity

ingelosire 1 *v/t* make jealous **2** *v/i* be jealous

ingente enormous

ingenuo ingenuous

ingerire swallow

ingessare put in plaster; **ingessatura** *f* plaster

Inghilterra *f* England

inghiottire swallow

ingiallire turn yellow; **ingiallito** yellowed

inginocchiarsi kneel (down)

ingiù: **all'~** down(wards)

ingiunzione *f* injunction; **~ di pagamento** final demand

ingiuria *f* insult

ingiustificato unjustified

ingiustizia *f* injustice; **ingiusto** unjust, unfair

inglese 1 *m/agg* English **2** *m/f* Englishman; *donna* Englishwoman *f*

ingoiare swallow

ingolfare, ingolfarsi flood

ingombrante cumbersome, bulky; **ingombrare** *passaggio* block; *stanza, mente* clutter (up); **ingombro 1** *agg* *passaggio* blocked; *stanza, mente* cluttered (up) **2** *m* hindrance, obstacle; **essere d'~** be in the way

ingordo greedy

ingorgo *m* blockage; **~ stradale** traffic jam

ingozzare *cibo* devour, gobble up; *persona* stuff (*di* with); **ingozzarsi** stuff o.s (*di* with)

ingranaggio *m* gear; *fig* machine; **ingranare** engage; *fig* **F le cose cominciano a ~** things are beginning to work out

ingrandimento *m* enlargement; *di azienda, città* expansion, growth; **ingrandire** enlarge; *azienda, città* expand, develop; (*esagerare*) exaggerate; **ingrandirsi** grow

ingrassare 1 *v/t animali* fatten (up); (*lubrificare*) grease **2** *v/i* get fat, put on weight

ingratitudine *f* ingratitude; **ingrato** ungrateful; *lavoro, compito* thankless

ingrediente *m* ingredient

ingresso *m* entrance; (*atrio*) hall; (*accesso*) admittance; INFOR input; **~ libero** admission free; **vietato l'~** no entry, no admittance

ingrossare 1 *v/t* make bigger; (*gonfiare, accrescere*) swell **2** *v/i* e **ingrossarsi** get bigger; (*gonfiarsi*) swell; **ingross all'~** (all'incirca) roughly, about; COM wholesale

inguaribile incurable

inguinale groin *attr*; **ernia** *f* **~** hernia; **inguine** *m* ANAT groin

ingurgitare gulp down

inibire prohibit, forbid; PSI inhibit; **inibito** inhibited; **inibizione** *f* PSI inhibition

iniettare inject; **~ qc a qu** inject s.o. with sth; **iniezione** *f* injection

inimicarsi fall out (**con** with); **inimicizia** *f* enmity

inimmaginabile unimaginable

ininterrotto continuous

iniziale *f*/*agg* initial; **iniziare** begin, start; *ostilità, dibattito* open; *fig* initiate; **~ a fare qc** begin *o* start doing sth, begin *o* start to do sth

iniziativa *f* initiative; **di mia ~** on my own initiative

inizio *m* start, beginning; **avere ~** start, begin; **dare ~ a qc** start sth

innaffiare water; **innaffiatoio** *m* watering can

innalzare raise; (*erigere*) erect

innamorarsi fall in love (**di** with); **innamorato 1** *agg* in love (**di** with) **2** *m*, **-a** *f* boyfriend; *donna* girlfriend

innanzi 1 *prp* before; **~ a** in front of; **~ tutto** first of all; (*soprattutto*) above all **2** *avv stato in luogo* in front; (*avanti*) forward; (*prima*) before; **d'ora ~** from now on

innato innate, inborn

innervosire **~ qu** make s.o. nervous; (*irritare*) get on s.o.'s nerves; **innervosirsi** get nervous; (*irritarsi*) get irritated

innestare BOT, MED graft; EL *spina* insert; AUTO *marcia* engage

inno *m* hymn; **~ nazionale** national anthem

innocente innocent; **innocenza** *f* innocence

innocuo innocuous, harmless

innovativo innovative; **innovazione** *f* innovation

inodore odourless, *Am* odorless

inoffensivo harmless, inoffensive

inoltrare forward; **inoltrarsi** advance, penetrate (**in** into); **inoltrato** late; **inoltre** besides

inondare flood; **inondazione** *f* flood

inopportuno (*inadatto*) inappropriate; (*intempestivo*) untimely; *persona* tactless

inorridire 1 *v/t* horrify **2** *v/i* be horrified; **inorridito** horrified

inosservato unobserved, unnoticed; (*non rispettato*) disregarded; **passare ~** go unnoticed

inossidabile stainless

inquadrare *fotografia* frame; *fig* put into context; **inquadratura** *f* frame

inquietante (*che preoccupa*) worrying; (*che turba*) disturbing; **inquieto** restless; (*preoccupato*) worried; (*adirato*) angry

inquilino *m*, **-a** *f* tenant

inquinamento *m* pollution; **inquinante 1** *agg* polluting; **non ~** environmentally friendly; *sostanza f* **~** pollutant **2** *m* pollutant; **inquinare** pollute; DIR *prove* tamper with

insabbiamento *m* di porto silting up; *fig* shelving

insaccati *mpl* sausages

insalata *f* salad; **~ mista** mixed salad; **~ verde** green salad; **insalatiera** *f* salad bowl

insanabile (*incurabile*) incurable; *fig* (*irrimediabile*) irreparable

insanguinato bloodstained

insaponare soap

insapore tasteless; **insaporire** flavour, *Am* flavor

insaputa: all'~ di qu unknown to s.o.

insaziabile insatiable

inscenare stage

inscindibile inseparable

insegna *f* sign; (*bandiera*) flag; (*stemma*) symbol; (*decorazione*) decoration

insegnamento *m* teaching; **insegnante 1** *agg* teaching; *corpo m* **~** (teaching) staff **2** *m/f* teacher; **insegnare** teach; **~ qc a qu** teach s.o. sth

inseguimento *m* chase, pursuit; **inseguire** chase, pursue

inseminazione *f* insemination; **~ artificiale** artificial insemination

insenatura f inlet

insensato 1 agg senseless, idiotic **2** m, -a f fool, idiot

insensibile insensitive (*a* to); *parte del corpo* numb; **insensibilità** f insensitivity; *di parte del corpo* numbness

inseparabile inseparable

inserire insert; (*collegare: in elettrotecnica*) connect; *annuncio* place; **inserirsi** fit in; *in una conversazione* join in; **inserto** m (*pubblicazione*) supplement; **inserviente** m/f attendant

inserzione f insertion; *sul giornale* ad, advertisement

insetticida m insecticide; **insettifugo** m insect repellent; **insetto** m insect

insicurezza f insecurity, lack of security; **insicuro** insecure

insieme 1 avv together; (*contemporaneamente*) at the same time **2** prp: ~ **a,** ~ **con** together with **3** m whole; *di abiti* outfit; **nell'~** on the whole

insignificante insignificant

insinuare insert; fig: *dubbio, sospetto* sow the seeds of; ~ **che** insinuate that; **insinuarsi** penetrate; fig ~ **in** creep into; **insinuazione** f insinuation

insipido insipid

insistente insistent; **insistenza** f insistence; **insiste-** re insist; (*perseverare*) persevere; ~ **a fare qc** insist on doing sth

insoddisfacente unsatisfactory; **insoddisfatto** unsatisfied; (*scontento*) dissatisfied; **insoddisfazione** f dissatisfaction

insofferente intolerant

insolazione f sunstroke

insolente insolent

insolito unusual

insoluto unsolved; *debito* outstanding; **insolvenza** f insolvency

insomma briefly, in short; ~**!** well, really!

insonne sleepless; **insonnia** f insomnia; **insonnolito** sleepy

insopportabile unbearable, intolerable

insorgere rise (up) (*contro* against); *di difficoltà* come up, crop up

insormontabile insurmountable

insorto 1 pp ☞ **insorgere 2** m rebel

insospettabile above suspicion; (*impensato*) unsuspected; **insospettire 1** v/t: ~ **qu** make s.o. suspicious **2** v/i e **insospettirsi** become suspicious

insperato unhoped for; (*inatteso*) unexpected

inspiegabile inexplicable

inspirare breathe in, inhale

instabile unstable; *tempo*

changeable

installare install; **installazione** f installation

instancabile tireless

insù: **all'~** upwards

insuccesso m failure

insufficiente insufficient; (*inadeguato*) inadequate; **insufficienza** f insufficiency; (*inadeguatezza*) inadequacy

insulina f insulin

insulso fig (*privo di vivacità*) dull; (*vacuo*) inane; (*sciocco*) silly

insultare insult; **insulto** m insult

insurrezione f insurrection

intaccare (*corrodere*) corrode; fig (*danneggiare*) damage; *scorte, capitale* make inroads into

intanto (*nel frattempo*) meanwhile; (*per ora*) for the time being; (*invece*) yet; **~ che** while

intasare block; **intasarsi** get blocked; **intasato** blocked

intascare pocket

intatto intact

integrale whole; MAT integral; *edizione* unabridged; **pane** m **~** wholemeal bread, Am wholewheat bread; **integrare** integrate; (*aumentare*) supplement; **integrarsi** integrate; **integrazione** f integration; **cassa** f **~** form of income support

intelaiatura f framework

intelletto m intellect; **intellet-**

tuale agg, m/f intellectual

intelligente intelligent; **intelligenza** f intelligence

intendere (*comprendere*) understand; (*udire*) hear; (*voler dire*) mean; (*avere intenzione*) intend; **s'intende!** of course!; **intendersi** (*capirsi*) understand each other; (*accordarsi*) agree; **~ di qc** know a lot about sth; **intenditore** m, **-trice** f connoisseur, expert

intensificare intensify; **intensificarsi** intensify; **intensità** f inv intensity; EL strength; **intensivo** intensive; **intenso** intense

intento 1 agg engrossed (**a** in), intent (**a** on) **2** m aim, purpose; **intenzionale** intentional; **intenzione** f intention; **avere l'~ di fare qc** intend to do sth

interagire interact

interamente entirely

interattivo interactive

intercalare 1 v/t insert **2** m stock phrase

intercambiabile interchangeable

intercapedine f cavity

intercedere intercede (**presso** with; **per** on behalf of)

intercettare intercept; **intercettazione** f interception; **-i** pl **telefoniche** phone tapping

intercontinentale intercontinental

interdentale: *filo m* ~ (dental) floss

interessante interesting; *in stato* ~ pregnant; **interessare 1** *v/t* interest; *(riguardare)* concern **2** *v/i* matter; **interessarsi** be interested *(a, di* in); *(occuparsi)* take care *(di* of); **interessato 1** *agg* interested *(a* in); *(implicato)* involved *(a* in); *spreg* parere, opinione **interested 2** *m, -a f* person concerned; interested person; **interesse** *m* interest; *(tornaconto)* benefit; *per* ~ out of self-interest; *senza* ~ of no interest

interfaccia *f* INFOR interface

interferenza *f* interference; **interferire** interfere

interiezione *f* interjection

interiora *fpl* entrails

interiore *m/agg* interior

interlocutore *m, -trice f*: *la sua -trice* the woman he was talking to

intermediario *m, -a f* intermediary; **intermedio** intermediate; *bilancio, relazione* interim

interminabile interminable

intermittente intermittent

internazionale international

internet *m* Internet; *navigare su* ~ surf the Net

interno 1 *agg* internal, inside *attr*; GEOG inland; POL, FIN domestic; *fig* inner **2** *m* *(parte interna)* inside, interior; GEOG interior; TELEC exten-

sion; *via Dante n. 6* ~ *9* 6 via Dante, Flat 9; *all'* ~ inside

intero whole, entire; *(completo)* complete; *latte m* ~ whole milk; MAT *numero m* ~ integer

interpellare consult

interpretare interpret; *personaggio* play; MUS play, perform; **interpretazione** *f* interpretation; TEA, MUS, *film* performance; **interprete** *m/f* interpreter; *attore, musicista* performer; *fare da* ~ interpret, act as interpreter

interpunzione *f* punctuation

interrogare question; EDU test; **interrogativo 1** *agg* GRAM interrogative; *occhiata* questioning; *punto m* ~ question mark **2** *m* *(domanda)* question; *(dubbio)* doubt; **interrogatorio** *m* questioning; **interrogazione** *f* questioning; *domanda* question; EDU oral (test)

interrompere interrupt; *(sospendere)* break off, stop; *comunicazioni, forniture* cut off; **interrotto** *pp* ☞ **interrompere**; **interruttore** *m* EL switch; **interruzione** *f* interruption

interurbana *f* long-distance (phone) call; **interurbano** intercity; *chiamata f -a* long-distance (phone) call

intervallo *m* interval; *di scuola, lavoro* break

intervenire intervene; *(parte-*

cipare) take part, participate (*a* in); MED operate; **intervento** *m* intervention; (*partecipazione*) participation; MED operation; **pronto ~** emergency services

intervista *f* interview; **intervistare** interview; **intervistatore** *m*, **-trice** *f* interviewer

intesa *f* (*accordo*) understanding; (*patto*) agreement; SP team work; **inteso 1** *pp* → **intendere 2** *agg* (*capito*) understood; (*destinato*) intended (*a* to); **siamo -i?** agreed

intestare assegno make out (*a* to); *proprietà* register (*a* in the name of); **intestatario** *m*, **-a** *f* di assegno payee; *di proprietà* registered owner

intestazione *f* heading; *su carta da lettere* letterhead

intestinale intestinal; **intestino** *m* intestine, gut

intimare order

intimidazione *f* intimidation; **intimidire** intimidate

intimità *f* privacy; *di un rapporto* intimacy; **intimo 1** *agg* intimate; (*segreto*) private; (*accogliente*) cosy, Am cozy; *amico* close, intimate **2** *m persona* close friend; (*abbigliamento*) underwear

intingere dip

intitolare call, entitle; (*dedicare*) dedicate (*a* to); **intitolarsi** be called

intollerabile intolerable; **intollerante** intolerant; **intol-**

leranza *f* intolerance

intonacare plaster; **intonaco** *m* plaster

intonarsi (*armonizzare*) go well (*a, con* with); **intonato** MUS in tune; **colori** *pl* **-i** colours that go well together

intontito dazed

intoppo *m* (*ostacolo*) hindrance; (*contrattempo*) snag

intorno 1 *prp*: **~ a** around; (*riguardo a*) about **2** *avv* around

intossicare poison; **intossicazione** *f* poisoning; **~ alimentare** food poisoning

intralciare hinder; **intralcio** *m* hindrance

intransigente intransigent

intransitivo intransitive

intraprendente enterprising; **intraprendenza** *f* enterprise; **intraprendere** undertake

intrattabile intractable; *prezzo* fixed, non-negotiable

intrattenere entertain; **~ buoni rapporti con qu** be on good terms with s.o.; **intrattenersi** dwell (*su* on)

intravedere glimpse; *fig* (*presagire*) anticipate, see; **intravisto** *pp* → **intravedere**

intrecciare plait, braid; (*intessere*) weave; **intrecciarsi** intertwine

intreccio *m* *fig* (*trama*) plot

intricato tangled; *disegno* intricate; *fig* complicated

intrigante scheming; (*affasci-*

nante) intriguing; **intrigo** *m* plot

intrinseco intrinsic

introdurre introduce; (*inserire*) insert; **introdursi** get in; **introduzione** *f* introduction

introito *m* income; (*incasso*) takings

intromettersi interfere; (*interporsi*) intervene

introvabile impossible to find

introverso 1 *agg* introverted **2** *m*, **-a** *f* introvert

intrufolarsi sneak in

intruglio *m* concoction

intruso *m*, **-a** *f* intruder

intuire know instinctively; **intuito** *m* intuition; **intuizione** *f* intuition

inumano inhuman

inumidire dampen, moisten; **inumidirsi** get damp

inutile useless; (*superfluo*) unnecessary, pointless; **inutilizzabile** unusable; **inutilmente** pointlessly, needlessly

invadente 1 *agg* nosy **2** *m/f* busybody

invadere invade; (*occupare*) occupy; (*inondare*) flood

invaghirsi: ~ *di* take a liking to

invalido 1 *agg* disabled; DIR invalid **2** *m*, **-a** *f* disabled person

invano in vain

invariato unchanged

invasione *f* invasion (*di* of)

invecchiare 1 *v/t* age **2** *v/i*

age, get older; *di vini, cibi* mature; *fig* (*cadere in disuso*) date

invece instead; (*ma*) but; ~ *di* **fare** instead of doing

inveire: ~ *contro* inveigh against

invenduto unsold

inventare invent

inventario *m* inventory

inventore *m*, **-trice** *f* inventor; **invenzione** *f* invention

invernale winter *attr*, **sport** *mpl* **-i** winter sports; **inverno** *m* winter; *d'*~ in winter

inverosimile improbable, unlikely

inversione *f* (*scambio*) reversal; AUTO ~ *di marcia* U-turn

inverso 1 *agg* reverse **2** *m* opposite

invertire reverse; (*capovolgere*) turn upside down; ~ *la marcia* turn around

investigare investigate; **investigatore** *m*, **-trice** *f* investigator

investimento *m* investment; *di pedone* running over; **investire** *pedone* run over; FIN, *fig* invest

inviare send; **inviato** *m*, **-a** *f* envoy; *di giornale* correspondent

invidia *f* envy; **invidiare** envy; **invidioso** envious

invincibile invincible

invio *m* dispatch

invisibile invisible

invitante *profumo* enticing; *offerta* tempting; **invitare** invite; **invitato** *m*, **-a** *f* guest; **invito** *m* invitation

invocare invoke; *(implorare)* beg for

invogliare induce

involontario involuntary

involtini *mpl* GASTR rolled stuffed slices of meat

involucro *m* wrapping

inzaccherare spatter with mud

inzuppare soak; *(intingere)* dip

io 1 *pron* I; **~ stesso** myself; **sono ~!** it's me! **2** *m inv* ego

iodio *m* iodine

ionico ARCHI Ionic

iosa: a ~ in abundance

iperattivo hyperactive

ipermercato *m* hypermarket, *Am* supermarket

ipersensibile hypersensitive

ipertensione *f* high blood pressure

ipnosi *f* hypnosis; **ipnotizzare** hypnotize

ipocalorico low-calorie

ipocrisia *f* hypocrisy; **ipocrita 1** *agg* hypocritical **2** *m/f* hypocrite

ipoteca *f* mortgage; **ipotecare** mortgage

ipotesi *f inv* hypothesis; **ipotetico** hypothetical; **ipotizzare** hypothesize

ippica *f* (horse) riding; **ippodromo** *m* race-course

ippopotamo *m* hippo(pota-mus)

ira *f* anger

iracheno 1 *agg* Iraqi **2** *m*, **-a** *f* Iraqi

Iran *m* Iran; **iraniano 1** *agg* Iranian **2** *m*, **-a** *f* Iranian

Iraq *m* Iraq

irascibile irritable, irascible

iride *f* (*arcobaleno*) rainbow; ANAT, BOT iris

Irlanda *f* Ireland; **irlandese 1** *agg* Irish **2** *m* Irish Gaelic **3** *m/f* Irishman; *donna* Irish-woman

ironia *f* irony; **ironico** ironic(al); **ironizzare** be ironic

IRPEF *f* (= *Imposta sul Reddito delle Persone Fisiche*) income tax

irraggiungibile unattainable

irragionevole unreasonable

irrazionale irrational

irreale unreal

irrealizzabile unattainable

irregolare irregular; **irregolarità** *f inv* irregularity

irreparabile irreparable

irreperibile impossible to find

irreprensibile irreproachable

irrequieto restless

irresistibile irresistible

irresponsabile irresponsible

irrestringibile shrink-resistant

irrevocabile irrevocable

irriconoscibile unrecognizable

irrigare irrigate

irrigidire stiffen; *fig disciplina* tighten; **irrigidirsi** stiffen

irrilevante irrelevant

irrimediabile irremediable

irripetibile unrepeatable

irrisorio derisive; *quantità, somma di denaro* derisory; *prezzo* ridiculously low

irritabile irritable; **irritabilità** *f* irritability; **irritante** irritating; **irritare** irritate; **irritarsi** get irritated

irruzione *f*: **fare ~ in** burst into; *di polizia* raid

iscritto 1 *pp* ☞ **iscrivere 2** *m*, **-a** *f* member; *a gare, concorsi* entrant; EDU pupil, student **3** *m*: **per ~** in writing; **iscrivere** register; *a gare, concorsi* enter (**a** for, in); EDU enrol (**a** at); **iscriversi** *in un elenco* register; **~ a partito, associazione** join; *gara* enter; EDU enrol at, *Am* enroll at; **iscrizione** *f* inscription

islamico Islamic

Islanda *f* Iceland; **islandese 1** *m/agg* Icelandic **2** *m/f* Icelander

isola *f* island; **~ pedonale** pedestrian precinct

isolamento *m* isolation; TEC insulation; **~ acustico** soundproofing; **isolano** *m*, **-a** *f* islander

isolante 1 *agg* insulating **2** *m* insulator; **isolare** isolate; TEC insulate; **isolarsi** isolate o.s., cut o.s. off; **isolato 1**

agg isolated; TEC insulated **2** *m* outsider; *di case* block

ispettore *m*, **-trice** *f* inspector; **ispezionare** inspect; **ispezione** *f* inspection

ispirare inspire; **ispirarsi** *di artista* get inspiration (**a** from); **ispirazione** *f* inspiration; (*impulso*) impulse; (*idea*) idea

Israele *m* Israel; **israeliano** *m*, **-a** *f* Israeli

istallare ☞ **installare**

istantanea *f* snap; **istantaneo** instantaneous; **istante** *m* instant; **all'~** instantly

istanza *f* (*esigenza*) need; (*domanda*) application; DIR petition

isterico hysterical

istigare instigate

istintivo instinctive; **istinto** *m* instinct

istituire establish; **istituto** *m* institute; *assistenziale* institution, home; **~ di bellezza** beauty salon; **istituzione** *f* institution

istmo *m* isthmus

istruire educate, teach; (*dare istruzioni a, addestrare*) instruct; **istruito** educated; **istruttivo** instructive; **istruttore** *m*, **-trice** *f* instructor; **istruzione** *f* education; (*direttiva*) instruction; **-i** *pl* **per l'uso** instructions (for use)

Italia *f* Italy; **italiano 1** *m/agg* Italian; **parla ~?** do you speak Italian? **2** m, -a f Italian

itinerario m route, itinerary

ittico fish

iuta f jute

IVA f (= **Imposta sul Valore Aggiunto**) VAT (= value-added tax), Am sales tax

J

jazz m jazz; **jazzista** m/f jazz musician

jeans mpl jeans

jeep f inv jeep

jet-lag m inv jet lag

jogging m jogging; **fare ~**, go for a jog

joint-venture f inv joint ven-

ture

jolly m inv joker

joy-stick m inv joystick

judo m inv judo

juke-box m inv jukebox

jumbo m jumbo

junior m/agg junior

K

kamikaze m inv suicide bomber

karatè m karate

killer m inv killer

kit m inv kit

kitsch agg inv, m kitsch

kiwi m inv BOT kiwi (fruit)

kmq (= **chilometri quadrati**) km² (= square kilometres)

k.o.: mettere qu ~ knock s.o. out; fig trounce s.o.

kolossal m inv epic

krapfen m inv GASTR dough-nut, Am donut

L

l (= **litro**) l (= litre)

l' = **lo, la**

là there; **di ~**that way; (in quel luogo) in there; (**al**) **di ~ di** on the other side of; **più in ~** further on; **nel tempo** later on

la[1] art fsg the; **~ signora Rossi** Mrs Rossi; **~ domenica** on

Sundays; **mi piace la birra** I like beer

la[2] pron **1** sg (persona) her; (cosa, animale) it; **~ prenderò** I'll take it **2** anche **La** sg you

la[3] m MUS A; **nel solfeggio della scala** la(h)

labbro m lip

labirinto m labyrinth

laboratorio m lab, laboratory; (officina) workshop

laborioso laborious; persona hard-working

laburista 1 agg Labour **2** m/f Labour Party member; elettore Labour supporter

lacca f lacquer; laccare lacquer

laccio m tie, (draw)string; **-cci** pl **delle scarpe** shoe laces

lacerante dolore, grido piercing; lacero tattered

lacrima f tear; lacrimare water; lacrimevole heart-rending; film m ~ tear-jerker; lacrimogeno: gas m ~ tear gas

lacuna f gap; lacunoso incomplete

ladino 1 agg South Tyrolean **2** m, -a f South Tyrolean

ladro m, -a f thief

laggiù down there; distante over there

laghetto m pond

lagna f (lamentela) whining; persona whiner; (cosa noiosa) bore; lagnarsi complain (di about)

lago m lake

laguna f lagoon

laico 1 agg scuola, stato secular **2** m, -a f layman; laywoman

lama f blade

lamentarsi complain (di about); lamentela f complaint; lamento m whimper

lametta f: ~ (da barba) razor blade

lamiera f metal sheet

lamina f foil; ~ d'oro gold leaf

lampada f lamp; lampadario m chandelier; lampadina f light bulb; ~ tascabile torch, Am flashlight

lampante blindingly obvious

lampeggiare flash; lampeggiatore m AUTO indicator, Am turn signal; FOT flashlight

lampione m streetlight

lampo m lightning

lampone m raspberry

lana f wool; pura ~ vergine pure new wool

lancetta f needle; di orologio hand

lancia f spear; MAR launch; lanciare throw; prodotto launch; ~ un'occhiata glance, take a quick look; ~ un urlo give a shout, shout; lanciarsi rush; ~ contro throw o.s at, attack; F ~ in un'impresa embark on a venture

lancinante dolore piercing

lancio m throwing; di prodotto launch; ~ del disco discus; ~ del giavellotto javelin; ~ del peso putting the shot

languore m languor; ho un ~ allo stomaco I'm feeling peckish

lapide f gravestone; su monumento plaque

lapis m inv pencil

lardo *m* lard

larghezza *f* width, breadth; **largo 1** *agg* wide, broad; *indumento* loose, big; *(abbondante)* large, generous **2** *m* width; *(piazza)* square; **andare al ~** head for the open sea; **farsi ~** elbow one's way through; **stare alla -a da** keep away from

laringe *f* larynx; **laringite** *f* laryngitis

larva *f* ZO larva

lasagne *fpl* lasagne *sg*

lasciapassare *m inv* pass

lasciare leave; *(abbandonare)* give up; *(concedere)* let; *(smettere di tenere)* let go of; **lascia andare!, lascia perdere!** forget it!; **lasciarsi** separate, split; **~ andare** let o.s. go

lascito *m* legacy

laser *m inv, agg inv* laser

lassativo *m/agg* laxative

lasso *m*: **~ di tempo** period of time

lassù up there

lastra *f di pietra* slab; *di metallo, ghiaccio, vetro* sheet; MED X-ray

lastrico *m*: *fig* ridursi sul **~** lose everything

latente latent

laterale lateral

laterizio *m* bricks and tiles

latino 1 *agg* Latin; **~-americano** Latin-American **2** *m* Latin; **~-americano, -a** Latin-American

latitante *m/f* fugitive

latitudine *f* latitude

lato *m* side; **a ~ di, di ~ a** beside

latrato *m* barking

latrina *f* latrine

latta *f can, Br anche* tin

latte *m* milk; **~ intero** whole milk; **~ scremato** skimmed milk; **latteo** milk *attr*; **Via Lattea** Milky Way; **latteria** *f* dairy; **lattice** *m* latex; **latticinio** *m* dairy product

lattina *f can, Br anche* tin

lattuga *f* lettuce

laurea *f* degree; **laurearsi** graduate; **laureato** *m*, **-a** *f* graduate

lava *f* lava

lavabile washable; **~ in lavatrice** machine-washable

lavabo *m* basin

lavaggio *m* washing; **~ a secco** dry-cleaning

lavagna *f* blackboard, *Am* chalkboard; GEOL slate

lavanda *f* BOT lavender

lavanderia *f* laundry; **~ a gettone** launderette, *Am* laundromat®

lavandino *m* basin; *nella cucina* sink

lavapiatti *m/f inv* dishwasher; **lavare** wash; **~ i panni** do the washing; **lavarsi** wash; **~ le mani** wash one's hands; **~ i denti** brush *o* clean one's teeth; **lavastoviglie** *f inv* dishwasher; **lavatrice** *f* washing machine

leopardo

lavello *m* basin; *nella cucina* sink

lavorare 1 *v/i* work 2 *v/t materia prima* process; *legno* carve; *terra* work; lavorativo: *giorno* ~ workday; lavorato legno carved; lavoratore *m*, -trice *f* worker; lavorazione *f di materia prima* processing; *di legno* carving; lavoro *m* work; (*impiego*) job; *per* ~ on business; *-i in corso* roadworks, work in progress; *senza* ~ unemployed, out of work

le¹ *art fpl* the

le² *pron fsg* to her; *fpl* them; *anche* Le you

leader *m/f inv* leader

leale loyal; lealtà *f* loyalty

lebbroso *m*, -a *f* leper

lecca-lecca *m inv* lollipop; leccare lick

leccio *m* holm oak

leccornia *f* delicacy

lecito legal, permissible

lega *f* league; *di metalli* alloy

legale 1 *agg* legal 2 *m/f* lawyer; legalizzare legalize

legame *m* tie, relationship; (*nesso*) link, connection; legamento *m* ANAT ligament; legare tie; *persona* tie up; (*collegare*) link; *fig di lavoro* tie down

legge *f* law; *fuori* ~ illegal

leggenda *f* legend; *di carta geografica ecc* key; leggendario legendary

leggere read

leggerezza *f* lightness; *fig* casualness; *con* ~ thoughtlessly; leggero light; (*lieve, di poca importanza*) slight; (*superficiale*) thoughtless; *caffè* weak; *alla* -a lightly

leggibile legible

leggio *m* lectern; MUS music stand

legislativo legislative; legislatura *f periodo* term of parliament

legittimare approve; legittimo legitimate

legna *f* (fire)wood; legname *m* timber; legno *m* wood; *di* ~ wooden

legumi *mpl* peas and beans; *secchi* pulses

lei *pron fsg soggetto* she; *oggetto, con preposizione* her; ~ *stessa* herself; *anche* Lei you; *dare del* ~ *a qu* address s.o. as 'lei'

lembo *m di gonna* hem, bottom; *di terra* stip

lente *f* lens; *-i pl* glasses, spectacles; *-i* (*a contatto*) contact lenses, contacts F; ~ *d'ingrandimento* magnifying glass

lenticchia *f* lentil

lentiggine *f* freckle

lento slow; (*allentato*) slack; *abito* loose

lenza *f* fishing rod

lenzuolo *m* sheet

leone *m* lion; ASTR *Leone* Leo; leonessa *f* lioness

leopardo *m* leopard

lepre f hare

lesbica f lesbian

lesionare damage; **lesione** f MED injury

lessare boil

lessico m vocabulary; (*dizionario*) glossary

lesso 1 agg boiled **2** m boiled beef

letale lethal

letame m manure, dung

letargo m lethargy

lettera f letter; **alla ~** to the letter; FIN **~ di cambio** bill of exchange; **letterale** literal; **letterario** literary; **letteratura** f literature

lettino m cot, Am crib; *dal medico* bed; *dallo psicologo* couch

letto[1] m bed; **~ a una piazza** single bed; **~ matrimoniale** double bed; **~i pl a castello** bunk beds; **andare a ~** go to bed

letto[2] pp ☞ **leggere**

lettore m, **-trice** f reader; *all'università* lecturer in a foreign language; INFOR disk drive; **~ compact disc, CD** CD player

lettura f reading

leucemia f leukaemia, Am leukemia

leva f lever; MIL call-up, Am draft; AUTO **~ del cambio** gear lever, Am gear shift

levante m east

levare (*alzare*) raise, lift; (*togliere*) take, (re)move; (*ri-*

muovere) take out, remove; *macchia* remove, get out; *dente* take out, extract; **~ l'ancora** weigh anchor; *levarsi di getto* rise; *di sole* rise, come up; *indumento* take off; *levata f di posta* collection; *levatrice* f midwife

levigare smooth down; **levigato** smooth

lezione f lesson; *all'università* lecture

li pron mpl them

lì there; **~ per ~** there and then

libanese agg, m/f Lebanese; **Libano** m (the) Lebanon

libbra f pound

libellula f dragon-fly

liberale 1 agg generous; POL liberal **2** m/f liberal; **liberalizzare** liberalize; **liberalizzazione** f liberalization; **liberamente** freely; **liberare** release, free; (*sgomberare*) empty; *stanza* vacate; *liberarsi ~ di* get rid of; **liberazione** f release; *di nazione* liberation; **libero** free; **libertà** f inv freedom, liberty

Libia f Libya; **libico 1** agg Libyan **2** m, **-a** f Libyan

libreria f bookshop, Am bookstore; (*biblioteca*) library; *mobile* bookcase

libretto m booklet; MUS libretto; **~ degli assegni** cheque book, Am check book; AUTO **~ di circolazione** registration document; **~ di risparmio** bank book

libro *m* book

licenza *f* FIN licence, *Am* license; MIL leave; EDU school leaving certificate; **~ di costruzione** building permit; **~ di esercizio** trading licence; **licenziamento** *m* dismissal; **licenziare** dismiss; **licenziarsi** resign

liceo *m* high school

lido *m* beach

lieto happy; **~ di conoscerla** nice *o* pleased to meet you

lieve light; (*di poca gravità*) slight, minor; *sorriso, rumore* faint

lievitare rise; *fig* rise, be on the increase; **lievito** *m* yeast; **~ in polvere** baking powder

lilla *m/agg* lilac

lima *f* file; **limetta** *f* emery board; *di metallo* nail file

limitare limit (**a** to); **limitato** limited; **limitazione** *f* limitation; **~ delle nascite** birth control; **senza -i** without restriction; **limite** *m* limit; (*confine*) boundary; **~ di velocità** speed limit; **al ~** at most, at the outside

limitrofo bordering

limonata *f* lemonade; **limone** *m* lemon; (*albero*) lemon tree

limpido clear; *acqua* crystal-clear

lince *f* lynx

linciare lynch

linea *f* line; **~ dell'autobus** bus route; **mantenere la ~**

keep one's figure; TELEC **restare in ~** stay on the line, not hang up; INFOR **in ~** on line

lineamenti *mpl* (*fisionomia*) features

lineare linear

lineetta *f* dash

linfonodo *m* lymph node

lingotto *m* ingot

lingua *f* tongue; (*linguaggio*) language; **~ madre** mother tongue; **~ straniera** foreign language; **linguaggio** *m* language

lino *m* BOT flax; *tessuto* linen

liofilizzato freeze-dried

lipidico: a basso contenuto ~ low-fat

liposuzione *f* liposuction

liquidare (*pagare*) pay; *merci* clear; *azienda* liquidate; *fig*: *questione* settle; *problema* dispose of; *persona* F dispose of F; **liquidazione** *f* liquidation; **~ totale** clearance sale; **liquidità** *f* liquid assets, liquidity; **liquido** *m/agg* liquid

liquirizia *f* liquorice

liquore *m* liqueur

lira *f* lira

lirica *f* lyric poem; MUS **la ~** opera; **lirico** lyric; *cantante* opera *attr*

lisca *f* fishbone

lisciare smooth; (*accarezzare*) stroke; *capelli* straighten; **liscio** smooth; *bevanda* straight, neat

liso worn

lista f quarrel, argument; (*elenco*) list; (*striscia*) strip; ~ *d'attesa* waiting list; ~ *dei vini* wine list

listino m: ~ *di borsa* share index; ~ *prezzi* price list

lite f quarrel, argument; **litigare** quarrel, argue; **litigio** m quarrel, argument

litografia f lithography

litorale 1 agg coastal **2** m coast; **litoranea** f coast road; **litoraneo** coast attr, coastal

litro m litre, Am liter

liuto m lute

livella f level; **livello** m level

livido 1 agg livid; *braccio, viso* black and blue; *occhio* black; *per il freddo* blue **2** m bruise

lo 1 art msg the **2** pron msg him; *cosa, animale* it; *non ~ so* I don't know

lobo m lobe

locale 1 agg local **2** m room; *luogo pubblico* place; FERR local train; **località** f inv town; ~ *balneare* seaside resort; **localizzare** localize; (*reperire*) locate

locandina f TEA bill

locatario m, -a f tenant; **locatore** m, -trice f landlord; *donna* landlady; **locazione** f rental

locomotiva f locomotive; **locomozione** f locomotion; *mezzo* m *di* ~ means of transport

locuzione f fixed expression

lodare praise; **lode** f praise

loggia f loggia

loggione m TEA gallery

logica f logic; **logico** logical

logorare wear out; **logorio** m wear and tear; **logoro** *indumento* worn (out)

lombaggine f lumbago

Lombardia f Lombardy; **lombardo 1** agg of Lombardy **2** m, -a f native of Lombardy

lombata f loin

lombo m loin

lombrico m earthworm

Londra f London

longevo long-lived

longitudine f GEOG longitude

lontananza f distance; *tra persone* separation; **lontano 1** agg far; *nel tempo* far-off; *passato, futuro* distant; *parente* distant **2** avv far (away); *da* ~ from a distance; *abita molto* ~? do you live very far away?

lontra f otter

loquace talkative

lordo dirty; *peso, reddito ecc* gross

loro 1 pron soggetto they; *oggetto* them; *forma di cortesia* you **2** possessivo their; *forma di cortesia* your; *il* ~ *amico* their / your friend; *i* ~ *genitori* their / your parents **3** pron: *il* ~ theirs; *forma di cortesia* yours

lotta f struggle; SP wrestling; fig fight; **lottare** wrestle, struggle (*con* with); fig fight (*contro* against; *per* for);

lottatore *m* wrestler

lotteria *f* lottery

lotto *m* lottery; *di terreno* plot

lozione *f* lotion; **~ dopobarba** aftershave

L.st. (= **lira sterlina**) £ (= pound)

lubrificante *m* lubricant; AUTO lubricating oil; **lubrificare** lubricate

lucchetto *m* padlock

luccicare sparkle

luccio *m* pike

lucciola *f* glowworm

luce *f* light; *fig* **far ~ su qc** shed light on sth; AUTO **-i** *pl* **di posizione** side lights; **-i** *pl* **posteriori** rear lights

lucente shining

lucertola *f* lizard

lucidare polish; *disegno* trace; **lucido 1** *agg superficie* shiny; FOT glossy; *persona* lucid **2** *m* polish; *disegno* transparency; **~ da scarpe** shoe polish

lucro *m*: **a scopo di ~** profit-making

luglio *m* July

lugubre sombre, *Am* somber

lui *pron msg soggetto* he; *oggetto* him; **a ~** to him; **~ stesso** himself

lumaca *f* slug

luminosità *f* luminosity; FOT speed; **luminoso** luminous; **stanza** bright

luna *f* moon; **~ crescente / calante** crescent / waning moon; **~ piena** full moon; **~ di miele** honeymoon; **luna-park** *m inv* amusement park

lunario *m*: **sbarcare il ~** make ends meet

lunatico moody

lunedì *m inv* Monday

lunghezza *f* length; **lungo 1** *agg* long; *caffè* weak; **a ~** for a long time; *fig* **alla -a** in the long run; **andare per le -ghe** drag on; *di gran* **-a** by far **2** *prp* along; *(durante)* throughout; **lungolago** *m* lakeside; **lungomare** *m inv* sea front

lunotto *m* AUTO rear window

luogo *m* place; **~ di nascita** birthplace, place of birth; **avere ~** take place, be held; **fuori ~** out of place; **in primo ~** in the first place

lupo *m* wolf

lurido filthy

lusingare flatter

lussazione *f* dislocation

lusso *m* luxury; **albergo** *m* **di ~** luxury hotel; **lussuoso** luxurious

lustrare polish

lutto *m* mourning

M

ma but; (*eppure*) and yet; **~ va!** nonsense!

maccheroni *mpl* macaroni *sg*

macchia *f* spot; *di sporco* stain; (*bosco*) scrub; **macchiare** stain; **macchiato** stained; **caffè** *m* ~ espresso with a splash of milk

macchina *f* machine; (*auto*) car; *fig* machinery; ~ **fotografica** camera; ~ **da cucire** sewing machine; ~ **da scrivere** typewriter; **macchinario** *m* machinery

macedonia *f.* ~ (**di frutta**) fruit salad

macellaio *m*, **-a** *f* butcher; **macelleria** *f* butcher's

macerie *fpl* rubble

macigno *m* boulder

macinacaffè *m inv* coffee mill; **macinapepe** *m inv* pepper mill; **macinare** mill, grind

macrobiotica *f* health food; **negozio** *m* **di** ~ health food store; **macrobiotico** macrobiotic

Madonna *f* Madonna, Our Lady; **madonnaro** *m* pavement artist specializing in sacred images

madre *f* mother; **madrelingua** 1 *f* mother tongue 2 *m/f* native speaker; **madreperla** *f* mother-of-pearl; **ma-**

drina *f* godmother

maestà *f* majesty

maestrale *m* north-west wind

maestro 1 *agg* (*principale*) main 2 *m* master; MUS, PITT maestro, master 3 *m*, **-a** *f* teacher; ~ **di nuoto** swimming teacher *o* instructor; ~ **di sci** ski instructor

mafia *f* Mafia

maga *f* witch

magari 1 *avv* maybe, perhaps 2 *int* ~! if only! 3 *cong* ~ **venisse** if only he would come

magazzino *m* warehouse; *di negozio* stock room; (*emporio*) factory shop; **grandi -i** *pl* department store

maggio *m* May

maggioranza *f* majority; **maggiore** 1 *agg* bigger; (*più vecchio*) older; MUS major; **il** ~ the biggest; *figlio* the oldest; *artista* the greatest; **la maggior parte di …** most of the …, the majority of the …; **andare per la** ~ be a crowd pleaser 2 *m* MIL major; **maggiorenne** adult *attr*; **maggioritario** majority; POL **sistema** *m* ~ first-past-the-post system

magia *f* magic; **magico** magic(al)

magistrato DIR *m* magistrate

maglia *f* top; (*maglione*)

sweater; SP shirt, jersey; *ai ferri* stitch; **lavorare a ~** knit; **maglieria** f knitwear; **maglietta** f T-shirt; **maglione** m sweater

magnetico magnetic

magnifico magnificent

magnolia f magnolia

mago m wizard; **i re -gi** the Three Wise Men, the Magi

magro thin; *cibo* low-fat; *fig: consolazione* small; *guadagno* meagre, Am meager

mai never; *(qualche volta)* ever; **~ più** never again; **più che ~** more than ever; **se ~** if ever; **dove / perché ~?** where / why on earth?

maiale m pig, Am hog; **(carne f di) ~** pork

maiolica f majolica

maionese f mayonnaise

mais m maize

maiuscola f capital (letter); **maiuscolo** capital

mal → **male**

malandato dilapidated; *persona* poorly

malanno m misfortune; *(malattia)* illness

malapena: *a ~* hardly

malato 1 *agg* ill; **essere ~ di cuore** have heart problems; **~ di mente** mentally ill **2** *m*, **-a** f sick person; **malattia** f illness; **essere / mettersi in ~** be / go on sick leave

malavita f underworld

malavoglia f unwillingness, reluctance; *di ~* unwillingly,

reluctantly

malconcio the worse for wear; *persona* not very well

maldestro awkward, clumsy

male 1 m evil; **che c'è ~?** where's the harm in it?; **andare a ~** go bad; MED **mal di gola** sore throat; **mal di testa** headache; **mal di denti** toothache; **mal di mare** seasickness; **far ~ a qu** hurt s.o.; **mi fa ~ il braccio** my arm hurts; **il cioccolato mi fa ~** chocolate doesn't agree with me; **fare ~ alla salute** be bad for you; **farsi ~** hurt o.s. **2** *avv* badly; **capire ~** misunderstand; **meno ~!** thank goodness!; **stare ~** *(essere malato)* be ill; *(essere giù)* be depressed; **il giallo mi sta ~** yellow doesn't suit me

maledetto 1 pp → **maledire 2** agg damn(ed); **maledire** curse; **maledizione** f curse; **~!** damn!

maleducato bad-mannered

malessere m indisposition; *fig* malaise

malfamato disreputable

malfatto *cosa* badly made; *malfattore* m criminal

malformazione f malformation

malgoverno m misgovernment

malgrado 1 prp in spite of; **mio ~** against my will **2** cong although

maligno malicious, spiteful;

MED malignant

malinconia f melancholy;
malinconico melancholic

malincuore: a ~ reluctantly,
unwilling

malintenzionato 1 agg shady,
suspicious **2** m, -a f shady
character

malinteso m misunderstanding

malizioso malicious; **sorriso**
mischievous

malloppo m (refurtiva) loot

malmenare mistreat

malnutrito under-nourished;
malnutrizione f malnutrition

malore m: **è stato colto da un
~** he was suddenly taken ill

malsano unhealthy

maltempo m bad weather

malto m malt

maltrattare ill-treat

malumore m bad mood; **essere di ~** be in a bad mood

malvagio evil, wicked

malvisto unpopular

malvivente m lout

malvolentieri unwillingly, reluctantly

mamma f mother, mum; **~
mia!** goodness!

mammella f breast

mammifero m mammal

mammografia f mammogra-
phy

manager m/f manager; **manageriale** managerial, management attr

mancanza f lack (**di** of); (errore) oversight

mancare 1 v/i be missing; **di
coraggio** fail; (euph: morire)
pass away; **a qu manca qc**
s.o. lacks sth; **mi manchi
molto** I miss you a lot; **mi
mancano 10 euro** I'm 10
euros short; **mancano tre
mesi a Natale** it's three
months to Christmas; **mi
mancano le parole** words
fail me; **c'è mancato poco
che cadesse** he almost fell;
ci mancherebbe altro! no
way!, you must be joking!;
~ di qc (non avere) lack
sth, be lacking in sth **2** v/t
miss; **mancato occasione**
missed, lost; tentativo unsuccessful

mancia f tip; **manciata** f
handful

mancino 1 agg left-handed;
fig **colpo** m **~** dirty trick **2**
m, -a f left-hander

mandante m/f DIR client;
mandare send; **~ qu a prendere qc** send s.o. for sth; fig
~ giù digest, take in

mandarino m BOT mandarin
(orange)

mandato m POL mandate;
DIR warrant; **~ bancario**
banker's order; **~ d'arresto**
arrest warrant

mandibola f jaw

mandolino m mandolin

mandorla f almond; **mandor-
lo** m almond tree

mandria f herd

maneggevole manageable; **maneggiare** handle (*anche fig*); **maneggio** *m* handling; *per cavalli* riding school

manesco a bit too ready with one's fists

manette *fpl* handcuffs

manganello *m* truncheon, *Am* night stick

mangereccio edible

mangiabile edible; **mangiacassette** *m inv*, **mangianastri** *m inv* cassette player; **mangiare 1** *v/t* eat; *fig* squander; **mangiarsi le parole** mumble **2** *m* food; **mangime** *m* fodder; **mangiucchiare** snack

mango *m* mango

mania *f* mania

manica *f* sleeve; **senza -che** sleeveless

Manica *f*: **la ~** the (English) Channel

manicaretto *m* delicacy

manichino *m* dummy

manico *m* handle

manicomio *m* mental home

manicure *f inv* manicure; (*persona*) manicurist

maniera *f* (*modo*) way, manner; (*stile*) manner; **-e pl** manners

manifestante *m/f* demonstrator; **manifestare 1** *v/t* (*esprimere*) express; (*mostrare*) show **2** *v/i* demonstrate; **manifestarsi** appear, show up; *di malattia* manifest itself; **manifestazione** *f* expression; *il mostrare* show; **~ di protesta** demonstration, demo F; **~ sportiva** sporting event; **manifesto 1** *agg* obvious **2** *m* poster

maniglia *f* handle; *di autobus, metro* strap

manipolare manipulate; *vino* adulterate; **manipolato geneticamente** genetically modified

mano *f* hand; **fuori ~** out of the way; *fig* **alla ~** approachable; **di seconda ~** secondhand; **dare una ~ a qu** give s.o. a hand; **tenersi per ~** hold hands; **man ~ che** as (and when); **manodopera** *f* labour, *Am* labor

manomettere tamper with

manopola *f* knob

manoscritto *m* manuscript

manovale *m* hod carrier

manovella *f* starting handle

manovra *f* manoeuvre, *Am* maneuver; **manovrare 1** *v/t* TEC operate; FERR shunt; *fig* manipulate **2** *v/i* manoeuvre, *Am* maneuver

mansarda *f* locale attic

mantello *m* (*cappa*) cloak; *di animale* coat; (*strato*) layer

mantenere keep; *in buono stato* maintain; **mantenersi in forma** keep in shape; **mantenimento** *m* maintenance; *di famiglia* keep

Mantova *f* Mantua; **mantovano 1** *agg* Mantuan **2** *m*, **-a** *f* Mantuan

manuale m/agg manual
manubrio m handlebars
manutenzione f maintenance
manzo m steer, bullock; *carne* ~ beef
mappa f map; **mappamondo** m globe
maratona f marathon; **maratoneta** m/f marathon runner
marca f brand, make; (*etichetta*) label; ~ *da bollo* revenue stamp; **marcare** mark; *goal* score; **marcato** *accento, lineamenti* strong
marchio m COM brand; ~ *depositato* registered trademark
marcia f march; SP walk; TEC AUTO gear; ~ *indietro* reverse; **marciapiede** m pavement, Am sidewalk; FERR platform; **marciare** march
marcio bad, rotten; (*corrotto*) corrupt; **marcire** rot *anche fig*
mare m sea; *in alto ~* on the high seas; **marea** f tide; *fig una ~ di* loads of; *alta ~* high tide; *bassa ~* low tide; **mareggiata** f storm; **maremoto** m tidal wave
margarina f margarine
margherita f daisy
margine m margin; (*orlo*) edge, brink
marina f coast(line); MAR navy; PITT seascape; **marinaio** m sailor
marinare GASTR marinate; F

~ *la scuola* play truant, Am play hooky; **marinato** GASTR marinated
marino sea *attr*, marine
marionetta f puppet, marionette
marito m husband
marittimo maritime
marmellata f jam, Am jelly; ~ *di arance* marmalade
marmitta f AUTO silencer, Am muffler
marmo m marble
marocchino 1 agg Moroccan 2 m, -a f Moroccan; **Marocco** m Morocco
marrone 1 agg (chestnut) brown 2 m colore (chestnut) brown; (*castagno*) chestnut
marsala m Marsala, *dessert wine*
Marte m Mars
martedì m inv Tuesday; ~ *grasso* Shrove Tuesday, Am Mardi Gras
martello m hammer
martire m/f martyr; **martirio** m martyrdom
marzapane m marzipan
marziano m Martian
marzo m March
mascara m inv mascara
mascarpone m mascarpone
mascella f jaw
maschera f mask; *in teatro* usher; *donna* usherette; ~ *antigas* gas mask; **mascherare** mask; *fig* camouflage, conceal; **mascherarsi** put on a mask; (*travestirsi*) dress up

(*da*) as)

maschile spogliatoio, *abito* men's; *caratteristica* male; GRAM masculine; **maschilista** *m/agg* sexist; **maschio 1** *agg* male; **hanno tre figli -i** they have three sons *o* boys **2** *m* (*ragazzo*) boy; (*uomo*) man; ZO male; **mascolino** masculine

mascotte *f inv* mascot

mass media *mpl* mass media

massa *f* mass; EL earth, *Am* ground

massacrare massacre; **massacro** *m* massacre

massaggiare massage; **massaggiatore** *m*, **-trice** *f* masseur; *donna* masseuse; **massaggio** *m* massage

massaia *f* housewife

massiccio 1 *agg* massive; *oro, noce ecc* solid **2** *m* massif

massima *f* saying, maxim; *temperatura* maximum; **in linea** *di* ~ generally speaking; **massimo 1** *agg* greatest, maximum **2** *m* maximum; **al** ~ at most

masso *m* rock

masticare chew

mastice *m* mastic; (*stucco*) putty

mastino *m* mastiff

mastodontico gigantic

masturbarsi, **masturbarsi** masturbate

matematica *f* mathematics, maths, *Am* math; **matematico 1** *agg* mathematical **2** *m*,

-a *f* mathematician

materasso *m* airbed; **materasso** *m* mattress

materia *f* matter; (*materiale*) material; (*disciplina*) subject; ~ **prima** raw material; **materiale 1** *agg* material; (*rozzo*) coarse, rough **2** *m* material; TEC equipment

maternità *f inv* motherhood; *in ospedale* maternity; **materno** maternal; **scuola** *f* **-a** nursery school

matita *f* pencil

matrice *f* matrix

matricola *f* register; *all'università* first-year student

matrigna *f* stepmother

matrimoniale matrimonial; **matrimonio** *m* marriage; *rito* wedding *attr*

mattina *f* morning; *di* ~ in the morning; **mattinata** *f* morning; TEA matinée; **mattiniero: essere** ~ be an early bird; **mattino** *m* morning

matto 1 *agg* mad, crazy (*per* about) **2** *m*, **-a** *f* madman, lunatic; *donna* madwoman, lunatic; **mi piace da -i andare al cinema** I'm mad about the cinema

mattone *m* brick; **mattonella** *f* tile

maturare *interessi* accrue; **maturità** *f* maturity; *diploma*: A levels, *Am* final exams

maturo *frutto* ripe; *persona* mature

mazza *f* club; (*martello*)

sledgehammer; *da baseball*
bat; ~ **da golf** golf club

mazzo *m* bunch; ~ **di carte**
pack *o* deck of cards

me (= *mi before* **lo, la, li, le,
ne**) me; **dammelo** give me
it, give it to me; **per** ~ for me

meccanica *f* mechanics; *di
orologio* mechanism; **meccanicamente** mechanically;
meccanico 1 *agg* mechanical **2** *m* mechanic; **meccanismo** *m* mechanism

mecenate *m/f* sponsor

mèche *f inv* streak, highlight

medaglia *f* medal

medesimo (very) same

media *f* average; **in** ~ on average; **mediano 1** *agg* central,
middle **2** *m* SP half-back;
mediante by (means of);
mediatore *m*, **-trice** *f* mediator; **mediazione** *f* mediation

medicare *persona* treat; *ferita*
clean, disinfect; **medicazione** *f* treatment; (*bende*)
dressing; **medicina** *f* medicine; **medicinale 1** *agg* medicinal **2** *m* medicine; **medico 1** *agg* medical **2** *m* doctor;
~ **di guardia** duty doctor

medievale medieval

medio 1 *agg* middle *attr*; *statura, rendimento* average **2** *m*
middle finger

mediocre mediocre

medioevo *m* Middle Ages

meditare 1 *v/t* think about;
(*progettare*) plan **2** *v/i* medi-

tate; (*riflettere*) think; ~ **su
qc** think about sth; **meditazione** *f* meditation; (*riflessione*) reflection

mediterraneo *m/agg* Mediterranean

medium *m/f inv* medium

medusa *f* ZO jellyfish

meglio 1 *avv* better; ~**!, tanto
~!** good!; **alla** ~ to the best of
one's ability **2** *agg* better; *superlativo* best **3** *m* best; **fare
del proprio** ~ do one's best
4 *f* **avere la** ~ **su** get the better of

mela *f* apple

melagrana *f* pomegranate

melanzana *f* aubergine, *Am*
eggplant

melma *f* mud

melo *m* apple (tree)

melodia *f* melody

melodrammatico melodramatic

melone *m* melon

membrana *f* membrane; ~
del timpano eardrum

membro *m* ANAT limb; *persona* member

memorabile memorable;
memoria *f* memory; **a** ~ by
heart; **-e** *pl* memoirs; **memorizzare** memorize; INFOR
save

menare lead; F (*picchiare*) hit

mendicante *m/f* beggar;
mendicare 1 *v/t* beg for **2**
v/i beg

menefreghismo *m* couldn't-
-care-less attitude

meningite f meningitis

meno 1 avv less; superlativo least; MAT minus; il ~ possibile as little as possible; a ~ che unless; per lo ~ at least; sono le sei ~ un quarto it's a quarter to six, Am it's a quarter of six; sempre ~ less and less; fare a ~ di qc do without sth **2** prp except; menomato damaged; (handicappato) disabled

mensa f di azienda canteen; MIL mess

mensile m/agg monthly; **mensilità** f inv salary

mensola f bracket

menta f mint

mentale mental; **mentalità** f inv mentality; **mentalmente** mentally; **mente** f mind; avere in ~ di fare qc be thinking about doing sth; tenere a ~ qc bear sth in mind; non mi viene in ~ il nome di ... I can't remember the name of ...

mentire lie

mento m chin

mentre while

menù m inv menu (anche INFOR)

menzionare mention

menzogna f lie

meraviglia f wonder; a ~ wonderfully; **meravigliare** astonish; **meravigliarsi**: ~ di be astonished by; **meravigliato** astonished; **meraviglioso** marvellous, Am marvelous, wonderful

mercante m merchant; **mercantile 1** agg nave cargo attr; porto commercial **2** m cargo ship; **mercanzia** f merchandise

mercato m market; ~ coperto indoor market; ~ delle pulci flea market; a buon ~ cheap, inexpensive

merce f goods

merceria f haberdashery, Am notions

mercoledì m inv Wednesday; ~ delle Ceneri Ash Wednesday

mercurio m mercury; AST Mercurio Mercury

merda P shit P

merenda f snack

meridiana f sundial; **meridiano 1** agg midday attr **2** m meridian

meridionale 1 agg southern **2** m/f southerner; **meridione** m south; il Meridione southern Italy

meringa f meringue

meritare 1 v/t deserve **2** v/i: un libro che merita a worthwhile book; **merito** m merit; in ~ a as regards; per ~ suo thanks to him

merletto m lace

merlo m ZO blackbird

merluzzo m cod

meschino mean; (infelice) wretched

mescolanza f mixture; **mescolare** mix; insalata toss;

caffè stir; **mescolarsi** mix, blend

mese *m* month

messa¹: ~ **in piega** set; ~ **in scena** production

messa² *f* REL mass

messaggino *m* text, text message; **messaggio** *m* message

messicano 1 *agg* Mexican **2** *m*, -a *f* Mexican; **Messico** *m* Mexico

messinscena *f* production; fig act

messo *pp* ☞ **mettere**

mestiere *m* trade; (*professione*) profession

mestolo *m* ladle

mestruazione *f* menstruation

meta *f* destination; SP try; fig goal, aim

metà *f inv* half; *punto centrale* middle, centre, *Am* center; *a ~ prezzo* half price; *a ~ strada* halfway; *fare a ~* go halves (*di* on)

metabolismo *m* metabolism

metadone *m* methadone

metafora *f* metaphor; **metaforico** metaphorical

metallico metallic; **metallizzato** metallic; **metallo** *m* metal

metamorfosi *f inv* metamorphosis

metano *m* methane; **metanodotto** *m* gas pipeline

meteora *f* meteor; **meteorite** *m o f* meteorite; **meteorolo-**

gico meteorological, weather er *attr*

meticoloso meticulous

metodico methodical; **metodo** *m* method

metrico metric

metro *m* metre, *Am* meter; ~ **quadrato** square metre; ~ **cubo** cubic metre

metrò *m inv* (*metropolitana*) underground, *Am* subway

metronotte *m inv* night watchman

metropoli *f inv* metropolis; **metropolitana** *f* underground, *Am* subway

mettere put; *vestito* put on; ~ **in moto** start (up); ~ **in ordine** tidy up; **mettiamo che ...** let's assume that ...; **mettersi** *abito, cappello ecc* put on; ~ **a sedere** sit down; AVIA, AUTO ~ **la cintura** fasten one's seat belt; ~ **a fare qc** start to do sth

mezzaluna *f* half moon; GASTR *two-handled chopper*; **mezzanotte** *f* midnight; **mezzo 1** *agg* half; **mezz'ora** half-hour; **le sei e ~** half past six, *Am* six thirty; ~ **chilo** a half kilo; **di ~ età** middle-aged **2** *avv* half **3** *m* (*parte centrale*) middle; (*metà*) half; (*strumento*) means *sg*; (*veicolo*) means *sg* of transport; **per ~ di** by means of; **in ~ a** between; **in ~ a quei documenti** in the middle of those papers, among those papers;

in ~ alla stanza in the middle of the room; **nel ~ di** in the middle of; **giusto ~** happy medium; **mezzobusto** *m* half-length photograph / portrait; **mezzofondo** *m* middle distance; **mezzogiorno** *m* midday; GEOG **Mezzogiorno** south (of Italy)

mi[1] *m* MUS E; *nel solfeggio della scala* me, mi

mi[2] *pron* me; *riflessivo* myself; **eccomi** here I am

miagolare miaow; **miagolio** *m* miaowing

mica: non ho ~ finito I'm nowhere near finished; **non è ~ vero** there's not the slightest bit of truth in it; **~ male** not bad at all

miccia *f* fuse

micidiale *veleno, clima* deadly; *fatica, sforza* exhausting

micio F *m* (pussy) cat

micosi *f inv* mycosis

microbiologia *f* microbiology

microbo *m* microbe

microchip *m inv* microchip

microcamera *f* miniature camera

microchirurgia *f* microsurgery

microfilm *m inv* microfilm

microfono *m* microphone, mike F

microonda *f* microwave; **forno** *m a -e* microwave (oven)

microprocessore *m* micro-

processor

microscopico microscopic; **microscopio** *m* microscope

midollo *m* marrow; **~ spinale** spinal cord

miei *mpl* di **mio** my

miele *m* honey

mietere harvest

migliaio *m* thousand; **un ~** a o one thousand; **a migliaia** in their thousands

miglio[1] *m misura* mile

miglio[2] *m grano* millet

miglioramento *m* improvement; **migliorare 1** *v/t* improve **2** *v/i e* **migliorarsi** improve, get better; **migliore** better; **il ~** the best

mignolo *m* (*o* **dito~**) little finger; *del piede* little toe

-mila thousand; **due~** two thousand

milanese 1 *agg* of Milan **2** *m/f* inhabitant of Milan; **Milano** *f* Milan

miliardario *m*, **-a** *f* billionaire, multimillionaire; **miliardo** *m* billion; **milionario** *m*, **-a** *f* millionaire; *donna* millionairess; **milione** *m* million

militare 1 *agg* military **2** *m* soldier; **milite** *m* soldier; **militesente** exempt from military service; **milizia** *f* militia

mille a thousand

millefoglie *m inv* vanilla slice; **millennio** *m* millennium; **millepiedi** *m inv* millipede; **millesimo** thousandth

milligrammo *m* milligram(me)

millimetro m millimetre, Am millimeter

milza f spleen

mimetizzare MIL camouflage; **mimetizzarsi** camouflage o.s.

mimo m mime

mina f mine; di matita lead

minaccia f threat; **minacciare** threaten; **minaccioso** threatening

minareto m minaret

minato: campo ~ minefield; **minatore** m miner

minatorio threatening

minerale m/agg mineral

minestra f soup; ~ di verdura vegetable soup; **minestrina** f clear soup, broth; **minestrone** m minestrone

miniatura f miniature

miniera f mine (anche fig)

minigolf m inv minigolf

minigonna f mini(skirt)

minimizzare minimize; **minimo 1** agg least, slightest; prezzo lowest; salario, temperatura minimum **2** m minimum

ministero m ministry; **ministro** m minister; ~ degli Esteri Foreign Secretary, Am Secretary of State; ~ degli Interni Home Secretary, Am Secretary of the Interior; primo ~ Prime Minister; consiglio m dei -i Cabinet

minoranza f minority

minorato 1 agg severely handicapped **2** m, -a f severely handicapped person

minore 1 agg minor; di età younger; distanza shorter; più piccolo smaller **2** m/f: vietato ai -i di 18 anni no admittance to those under 18 years of age; film X-rated; **minorenne 1** agg underage **2** m/f minor

minuscola f small letter, lower case letter; **minuscolo** tiny, miniscule

minuto 1 agg tiny, minute; descrizione detailed **2** m minute; minuzioso descrizione detailed; ricerca meticulous

mio 1 agg my; un ~ amico a friend of mine, one of my friends **2** pron: il ~ mine; i miei my parents

miope short-sighted; **miopia** f short-sightedness, myopia

mira f aim; (obiettivo) target; prendere la ~ take aim; fig prendere di ~ qu have it in for s.o.

miracolo m miracle; per ~ by a miracle, miraculously

miraggio m mirage

mirare aim (a at)

mirino m MIL sight; FOT viewfinder

mirtillo m blueberry

mirto m myrtle

miscela f mixture; di caffè, tabacco blend; **miscelatore** m GASTR mixer; rubinetto mixer tap

mischia f (rissa) scuffle; SP,

(folla) scrum; **mischiare** mix; *carte* shuffle; **mischiarsi** mix; **miscuglio** *m* mixture

miseria *f (povertà)* poverty; **costare una ~** cost next to nothing; **F porca ~!** damn and blast! F; **misero** wretched

missile *m* missile

missionario *m*, **-a** *f* missionary; **missione** *f* mission

misterioso mysterious; **mistero** *m* mystery

mistico mystic(al)

misto 1 *agg* mixed **2** *m* mixture; **~ lana** wool mix

misura *f* measurement; *(taglia)* size; *(provvedimento)* fig measure; **su ~** made to measure; **misurare** measure; *vestito* try on; **misurino** *m* measuring spoon

mite mild; *condanna* light

mito *m* myth; **mitologia** *f* mythology; **mitologico** mythological

mitra *m inv*, **mitragliatrice** *f* machine gun

mitt. (= **mittente**) from

mittente *m/f* sender

mixare mix

M.M. (= **Marina Militare**) Italian navy

mobile 1 *agg* mobile; *ripiano, pannello* removeable **2** *m* piece of furniture; **-i** *pl* furniture; **mobilia** *f* furnishings; **mobilificio** *m* furniture factory; **mobilitare** mobilize

moca *m* mocha

mocassino *m* moccasin

moda *f* fashion; **alla ~** fashionable, in fashion; *vestirsi* fashionably; **fuori ~** out of fashion, unfashionable

modalità *f inv* method

modella *f* model; **modellare** model; **modello** *1* *agg* model **2** *m* model; *di vestito* style; *(formulario)* form

modem *m inv* INFOR modem

moderare moderate; **moderato** moderate; **moderazione** *f* moderation

modernizzare modernize; **moderno** modern

modestia *f* modesty; **modesto** modest; *prezzo* very reasonable

modico reasonable

modifica *f* modification; **modificare** modify

modo *m (maniera)* way, manner; *(mezzo)* way; **~ di dire** expression; **per ~ di dire** so to speak; **a ~ mio** in my own way; **ad ogni ~** anyway, anyhow; **di ~ che** so that; **in che ~?** how?

modulo *m* form; *(elemento)* module

mogano *m* mahogany

moglie *f* wife

molare 1 *v/t* grind **2** *m* molar

mole *f (grandezza)* size

molecola *f* molecule

molestare bother; *sessualmente* sexually harass; **molestia** *f* bother, nuisance; **~ sessuale** sexual harassment

molla f spring; fig spur; **-e** pl
tongs; **mollare** corda release,
let go; F **schiaffo, ceffone**
give; F **fidanzato** dump; ~
la presa let go

molle soft; (bagnato) wet

molletta f hairgrip; da bucato
clothes peg, Am clothes pin

mollica f crumb

mollusco m mollusc, Am
mollusk

molo m pier

molteplice multifaceted

moltiplicare, moltiplicarsi
multiply

molto 1 agg a lot of; con nomi
plurali a lot of, many **2** avv a
lot; con aggettivi very; ~ **meglio** much better, a lot better; **da** ~ for a long time;
fra non ~ before long

momentaneo momentary,
temporary; **momento** m
moment; **dal** ~ **che** causale
since; **a -i** sometimes; **per il**
~ for the moment; **sul** ~ at
the time

monaca f nun; **monaco** m
monk

monarchia f monarchy

monastero m monastery; di
monache convent

mondano society attr; (terreno) worldly; **fare vita -a** go
out

mondare frutta peel

mondiale 1 agg world attr; fenomeno, scala worldwide; **di
fama** ~ world-famous **2** m: **i
-i** di calcio the World Cup;

mondo m world; **il più bello
del** ~ the most beautiful in
the world

monello m, **-a** f little devil

moneta f coin; (valuta) currency; (denaro) money; (spiccioli) change; **monetario**
monetary; **Fondo** m ~ **internazionale** International
Monetary Fund

mongolfiera f hot-air balloon

monolocale m bedsit

monopattino m child's scooter

monopolio m monopoly;
monopolizzare monopolize

monoposto m single-seater

monotonia f monotony; **monotono** monotonous

monouso disposable, throw-
away

montacarichi m inv hoist

montaggio m TEC assembly;
di film editing

montagna f mountain; fig **-e**
pl **russe** rollercoaster; **mon-
tagnoso** mountainous;
montanaro m, **-a** f mountain
dweller

montare 1 v/t go up, climb; cavallo get onto, mount; TEC
assemble; film edit; GASTR
whip **2** v/i go up; venire come
up; ~ **in macchina** get into; ~
su scala climb; **pullman** get
on

montarsi: ~ **la testa** get big-
headed

montatura f di occhiali frame;

di gioiello mount; *fig* frame-up F

monte *m* mountain (*anche fig*); **a ~** upstream; *fig* **mandare a ~** ruin

montone *m* ram; *pelle, giacca* sheepskin

montuoso mountainous

monumento *m* monument

moquette *f inv* fitted carpet

mora *f* BOT *del gelso* mulberry; *del rovo* blackberry

morale 1 *agg* moral **2** *f* morals; *di favola etc* moral **3** *m* morale; **essere giù di ~** be feeling a bit down

morbido soft

morbillo *m* measles *sg*

morbo *m* disease; **morboso** *fig* unhealthy; *curiosità* morbid

mordere bite

morena *f* moraine

morfina *f* morphine

moribondo dying

morire die; *fig* **~ di paura** be scared to death

mormorare murmur; (*bisbigliare, lamentarsi*) mutter; **mormorio** *m* murmuring; (*brontolio*) muttering

morsetto *m* TEC clamp; EL terminal

morsicare bite; **morso 1** *pp* ☞ **mordere 2** *m* bite; *di cibo* bit, mouthful; *per cavallo* bit

mortale *malattia* fatal; *offesa, nemico* deadly; *uomo* mortal; **mortalità** *f* mortality

morte *f* death

mortificare mortify

morto 1 *pp* ☞ **morire 2** *agg* dead; **stanco ~** dead tired **3** *m*, **-a** *f* dead man; *donna* dead woman; **i -i** *pl* the dead *pl*

mortorio *m*: F **essere un ~** be deadly boring

mosaico *m* mosaic

mosca *f* fly

moscato 1 *agg* muscat **2** *m* muscatel

moscerino *m* gnat, midge

moschea *f* mosque

moscio thin, flimsy; *fig* washed out

moscone *m* ZO bluebottle; (*imbarcazione*) pedalo

mossa *f* movement; *fig e di judo, karate* move; **mosso 1** *pp* ☞ **muovere 2** *agg mare* rough

mostarda *f* mustard

mosto *m* must, *unfermented grape juice*

mostra *f* show; (*esposizione*) exhibition; *fig* **mettere in ~** show off; **mostrare** show; (*indicare*) point out; **mostrarsi** appear

mostro *m* monster; **mostruoso** monstrous

motel *m inv* motel

motivare cause; *personale* motivate; (*spiegare*) explain; **motivazione** *f* (*spiegazione*) explanation; (*stimolo*) motivation; **motivo** *m* reason; MUS theme, motif; *su tessuto* pattern; **per quale ~?** for what reason?

moto[1] *m* movement; **fare ~** get some exercise; **mettere in ~** *motore* start (up)

moto[2] *f* (motor)bike

motocicletta *f* motorcycle; **motociclista** *m/f* motorcyclist; **motociclo** *m* motorcycling

motore *m* engine; **accendere il ~** start the engine; **motorino** *m* moped; **motorizzato** motorized; F **sei ~** have you got wheels? F

motoscafo *m* motorboat

motto *m* motto

mouse *m inv* INFOR mouse

movente *m* motive

movimento *m* movement; (*vita*) life

mozione *f* motion; **~ di fiducia** vote of confidence

mozzarella *f* mozzarella

mozzicone *m* cigarette end, (cigarette) stub

mozzo *m* TEC hub

mq (= **metro quadrato**) sq m, m² (= square metre)

mucca *f* cow

mucchio *m* pile

muco *m* mucus

muffa *f* mould, *Am* mold; **fare la ~** go mouldy

mugolare whine

mulattiera *f* mule track

mulatto *m*, **-a** *f* mulatto

mulinello *m su canna da pesca* reel; *vortice d'acqua* eddy

mulino *m* mill; **~ a vento** windmill

mulo *m* mule

multa *f* fine; **multare** fine

multiculturale multicultural

multimediale multimedia

multinazionale *f/agg* multinational

multiplo multiple

multisala *m inv* multiplex

multiuso multipurpose

mungere milk

municipale municipal; **municipio** *m* town council, municipality; *edificio* town hall

munire: **~ di** supply with; **munizioni** *fpl* ammunition

muovere 1 *v/t* move **2** *v/i partire* move off (**da** from); **~ incontro a qu** move towards s.o.; **muoversi** move; F (*sbrigarsi*) get a move on F

murare (*chiudere*) wall up; **muratore** *m* bricklayer; **muratura** *f* brickwork

murena *f* moray eel

muro *m* wall; **le -a** *fpl* the (city) walls

muschio *m* BOT moss

muscolare muscular; **strappo** *m* **~** strained muscle; **muscolo** *m* muscle; **muscoloso** muscular

museo *m* museum; **~ etnologico** folk museum; **~ d'arte** art gallery

museruola *f* muzzle

musica *f* music; **musicale** musical; **musicista** *m/f* musician

muso *m di animale* muzzle; **tenere il ~ a qu** be in a huff with s.o.; **musone** *m* sulker

musulmano 1 *agg* Muslim **2** *m*, **-a** *f* Muslim

muta *f di cani* pack; SP wetsuit

mutamento *m* change

mutande *fpl di donna* panties; *di uomo* (under)pants, *Am* briefs; **mutandine** *fpl* panties; **~ (da bagno)** (swimming) trunks, *Am* swimsuit

mutare change

mutilato *m* disabled ex-serviceman

muto 1 *agg* dumb; (*silenzioso*) silent, dumb; **film** *m* **~** silent movie **2** *m*, **-a** *f* mute

mutua *f fund that pays out sickness benefit;* **medico** *m* **della ~a** *doctor recognized by the 'mutua';* **mutuato** *m*, **-a** *f person entitled to sickness benefit*

mutuo 1 *agg* mutual **2** *m* mortgage

N

n. (= *numero*) No. (= number)

nacchere *fpl* castanets

nafta *f* naphtha

nano 1 *agg* dwarf **2** *m*, **-a** *f* dwarf

napoletano 1 *agg* Neapolitan **2** *m*, **-a** *f* Neapolitan; **Napoli** *f* Naples

nappa *f* tassel; *pelle* nappa (*type of soft leather*)

narcotico *m* narcotic

narice *f* nostril

narrare tell, narrate; **narratore, -trice** *f* narrator

nascere be born; BOT, *di sole* come up; *fig* develop; **sono nato a Roma** I was born in Rome; **nascita** *f* birth

nascondere hide; **nascondersi** hide; **nascondiglio** *m* hiding place; **nascosto 1** *pp* ☞ **nascondere 2** *avv*: **di ~** in secret; **di ~ a qu** unbeknownst to s.o.

nasello *m pesce* hake

naso *m* nose

nastro *m* tape; *per capelli, di decorazione* ribbon; **~ adesivo** adhesive tape, Sellotape®, *Am* Scotch tape®

Natale *m* Christmas; **buon ~!** Merry Christmas!; **natalità** *f* birth rate; **natalizio** Christmas

natante 1 *agg* floating **2** *m* boat

nativo 1 *agg* native **2** *m*, **-a** *f* native

NATO *f* (= **Organizzazione del Trattato nord-atlantico**) NATO (= North Atlantic Treaty Organization)

nato ☞ **nascere**

natura *f* nature; PITT **~ morta** still life; **naturale** natural; **naturalezza** *f* naturalness; **con ~** naturally; **naturaliz-**

zare: **è naturalizzato americano** he's a naturalized American; **naturalmente** naturally

naufragare *di nave* be wrecked; *di persona* be shipwrecked; **fig** be ruined; **naufragio** *m* shipwreck; *fig* ruin; **fare ~ di nave** be wrecked; *di persona* be shipwrecked; **naufrago** *m*, **-a** *f* survivor of a shipwreck

nausea *f* nausea; **avere la ~** feel sick, *Am* feel nauseous; **nauseare** nauseate (*anche fig*)

nautico nautical

navale naval; **cantiere m ~** shipyard

navata *f* ARCHI: **~ centrale** nave; **~ laterale** aisle

nave *f* ship; **~ da carico** cargo ship; **~ passeggeri** passenger ship; **~ traghetto** ferry; **navetta 1** *agg inv*: **bus m ~** shuttle bus **2** *f* shuttle; **~ spaziale** space shuttle

navigabile navigable; **navigare** sail; INFOR navigate; **~ in Internet** surf the Net; **navigatore** *m* navigator

nazionale 1 *agg* national **2** *f* national team; **nazionalismo** *m* nationalism; **nazionalista** *m/f* nationalist; **nazionalità** *f inv* nationality; **nazione** *f* nation

ne 1 *pron* (*di lui*) about him; (*di lei*) about her; (*di loro*) about them; (*di ciò*) about

it; **~ sono contento** I'm happy about it; **~ ho abbastanza** I have enough **2** *avv* from there; **~ vengo adesso** I've just come back from there

né: ~ ... ~ neither ... nor; **non l'ho trovato ~ a casa ~ in ufficio** I couldn't find him either at home or in the office

neanche neither; **neanch'io** neither am I, me neither; **non l'ho ~ visto** I didn't even see him

nebbia *f* fog; **nebbioso** foggy

nebulosa *f* AST nebula

necessaire *m inv*: **~ (da viaggio)** beauty case; **necessario 1** *agg* necessary **2** *m*: **il ~ per vivere** the basic necessities; **necessità** *f inv* need; **in caso di ~** if need be; **per ~** out of necessity

nefrite *f* MED nephritis

negare deny; (*rifiutare*) refuse; **negativa** *f* negative; **negativo** *m/agg* negative; **negato: essere ~ per qc** be hopeless at sth

negli = in and *art* **gli**

negligente careless, negligent; **negligenza** *f* carelessness, negligence

negoziante *m/f* shopkeeper, *Am* storekeeper; **negoziare** negotiate FIN **~ in** trade in; **negoziato** *m* negotiation; **~i pl di pace** peace negotiations; **negozio** *m* shop, *Am* store

negro 1 *agg* black **2** *m*, **-a** *f*

black (man / woman)

nei, nell, nell', nella, nelle, **nello** = **in** and *art* **i, il, l', la, le, lo**

nemico 1 *agg* enemy *attr* 2 *m*, -a *f* enemy

nemmeno neither; **~ io** me neither; **~ per idea!** don't even think about it!

neo *m* mole; *fig* flaw

neonato *m*, -a *f* infant, new-born baby

neppure not even; **non ci vado – ~ io** I'm not going – neither am I, me neither

nero 1 *m/agg* black (*anche fig*) 2 *m*, -a *f* black (man / woman)

nervo *m* nerve; **dare sui -i a qu** get on s.o.'s nerves; **nervosismo** *m* nervousness; **nervoso** 1 *agg* nervous; (*irritabile*) edgy 2 *m* F: **mi viene il ~** this is getting on my nerves

nespola *f* medlar; **nespolo** *m* medlar (tree)

nessuno 1 *agg* no; **non chiamare in nessun caso** don't call in any circumstances; **c'è -a notizia?** is there any news? 2 *pron* nobody, no one; **hai visto ~?** did you see anyone or anybody?

nettezza *f* cleanliness; **~ urbana** cleansing department; **netto** clear; (*chiaro*) clear; *reddito, peso* net

neurologico neurological; **neurologo** *m*, -a *f* neurologist

neutrale neutral; **neutralizzare** neutralize; **neutro** 1 *agg* neutral; GRAM neuter

neve *f* snow; **nevicare** snow; **nevicata** *f* snowfall

nevralgia *f* neuralgia; **nevralgico** neuralgic; **punto ~** specially painful point; *fig* weak point

nevrotico 1 *agg* neurotic; F short-tempered 2 *m*, -a *f* neurotic

nicchia *f* niche

nicotina *f* nicotine

nido *m* nest

niente 1 *pron* nothing 2 *avv* nothing; **non ho ~** I don't have anything, I have nothing; **non ho per ~ fame** I'm not at all hungry; **non fa niente** it doesn't matter; **niente(di)meno** no less; **~!** that's incredible!

ninfea *f* water-lily

nipote *m/f di zio* nephew; *donna, ragazza* niece; *di nonno* grandson; *donna, ragazza* granddaughter

nitido clear; FOT sharp

nitrire neigh

NO (= **nord-ovest**) NW (= northwest)

no no; **come ~!** of course!; **se ~** otherwise; **dire di ~** say no; **credo di ~** I don't think so

nobile 1 *agg* noble 2 *m/f* aristocrat; **nobiltà** *f* nobility

nocca *f* knuckle

nocciola *f* hazelnut; (*color m*) **~** hazel; **nocciolina** *f*: **~**

(*americana*) peanut

nocciolo[1] *m albero* hazel (tree)

nocciolo[2] *m di frutto* stone; *di questione* kernel

noce 1 *m* walnut (tree); *legno* walnut **2** *f* walnut; **~ di cocco** coconut; **~ moscata** nutmeg; **nocepesca** *f* nectarine

nocivo harmful

nodo *m* knot; *fig* crux; FERR junction

no-global *m/f inv* anti-globalist

noi *pron soggetto* we; *con prp* us; **a ~** to us; **con ~** with us

noia *f* boredom; **-e** *pl* trouble; **dar ~ a qu** annoy s.o.; **noioso** boring; (*molesto*) annoying

noleggiare rent, *Br anche* hire; (dare a noleggio) rent out, *Br* hire out; **noleggio** *m* rent, *Br anche* hire; **nolo** *m* rent, *Br anche* hire; **prendere a ~** rent; **dare a ~** rent out

nome *m* name; GRAM noun; **~ di battesimo** Christian name; **~ e cognome** full name; **in ~ di** in the name of

nomina *f* appointment; **nominare** (*menzionare*) mention; *a un incarico* appoint (**a** to)

non not; **~ ho fratelli** I don't have any brothers, I have no brothers

non stop *inv* nonstop

non vedente *m/f* blind person

nonché let alone; (*e anche*) as well as

noncurante nonchalant; **~ di** heedless of

nondimeno nevertheless

nonno *m*, **-a** *f* grandfather; *donna* grandmother; **-i** *pl* grandparents

nonnulla *m inv* trifle

nono ninth

nonostante despite; **ciò ~** however

nord *m* north; **a(l) ~ di** (to the) north of; **nordest** *m* northeast; **nordico** northern; *lingue* Nordic; **nordovest** *m* north-west

norma *f* (*precetto*) rule; TEC standard; **a ~ di legge** up to standard; **normale** normal; **normalità** *f* normality

norvegese *agg*, *m/f* Norwegian; **Norvegia** *f* Norway

nostalgia *f* nostalgia; **avere ~ di casa** feel homesick; **avere ~ di qu** miss s.o.

nostrano local, home *attr*

nostro 1 *agg* our; **i -i genitori** our parents; **un ~ amico** a friend of ours **2** *pron*: **il ~** ours

nota *f* note; FIN bill; **~ spese** expense account; **prendere ~ di qc** make a note of sth; *situazione* take note of sth; **notaio** *m* notary (public);

notare (*osservare*) notice; (*annotare*) make a note of; *con segni* mark; **notarile** notarial; **notevole** (*degno di nota*) notable, noteworthy; (*grande*) considerable; **notificare** serve (**a** on)

notizia *f* piece of news; ***avere -e di qu*** have news of s.o., hear from s.o.; **notiziario** *m* RAD, TV news *sg*

noto well-known; **rendere** ~ announce; **notorietà** *f* fame; *spreg* notoriety

nottambulo *m*, **-a** *f* night owl; **nottata** *f* night; **fare la** ~ stay up all night; **notte** *f* night; *di* ~ at night; **buona** ~*!* good night!; **notturno** *agg* night(-time) *attr*; *animale* nocturnal

novanta ninety; **novantesimo** ninetieth; **nove** nine; **novecento 1** *agg* nine hundred **2** *m*: **il Novecento** the twentieth century

novella *f* short story

novembre *m* November

novità *f inv* novelty; (*notizia*) piece of news

nozione *f* notion, idea; *-i pl di base* rudiments

nozze *fpl* wedding; ~ *d'argento* silver wedding (anniversary)

ns. (= *nostro*) our(s), *used in correspondence*

nube *f* cloud; **nubifragio** *m* cloudburst

nubile single, unmarried

nuca *f* nape of the neck

nucleare nuclear; **nucleo** *m* FIS nucleus (*anche fig*)

nudismo *m* naturism, nudism; **nudista** *m/f* naturist, nudist; **nudo 1** *agg* nude, naked; (*spoglio*) bare **2** *m* PITT nude

nulla nothing; **è una cosa da** ~ it's nothing; **per** ~ for nothing; **nullaosta** *m*: *fig* **ottenere il** ~ get the green light; **nullo** invalid; *gol* disallowed; *voto* spoiled

numerale *m* numeral; **numerare** number; **numerato** numbered; **numero** *m* number; *arabo, romano* numeral; *di scarpa* size; ~ *di targa* registration number, *Am* license number; ~ *di telefono* phone number; ~ *di volo* flight number; ~ *verde* 0800 number, *Am* toll-free number; F **dare i** -*i* talk nonsense; **numeroso** numerous; *famiglia, classe* large

nuocere: ~ **a** harm

nuora *f* daughter-in-law

nuotare swim; **nuotata** *f* swim; **nuoto** *m* swimming

nuovamente again; **nuovo 1** *agg* new; *di* ~ again **2** *m*: **che c'è di** ~? what's new?

nutriente nourishing; **nutrimento** *m* food; **nutrire** feed; **nutrirsi:** ~ *di* live on; **nutritivo** nutritious

nuvola *f* cloud; *fig* **cadere dalle -e** be taken aback; **nuvoloso** cloudy

O

O (= *ovest*) W (= west)

o or; **~ ... ~** either ... or

oasi *f inv* oasis

obbedire ☞ **ubbidire**

obbligare: **~ qu a fare qc** oblige s.o. to do sth; **obbligatorio** obligatory; **obbligazione** *f* obligation; FIN bond; **obbligo** *m* obligation; **d'~** obligatory

obesità *f* obesity; **obeso** obese

obiettare *object* (*a* to); **obiettivo 1** *agg* objective **2** *m* aim, objective; FOT lens; **obiettore** *m*: **~ di coscienza** conscientious objector; **obiezione** *f* objection

obliquo oblique

obliterare *biglietto* punch

oblò *m inv* MAR porthole

oca *f* goose; *fig* silly woman

occasionale casual; **occasionalmente** occasionally; **occasione** *f* (*opportunità*) opportunity, chance; (*evento*) occasion; (*affare*) bargain; **automobile** *f* **d'~** second-hand car; **cogliere l'~** seize the opportunity; **all'~** if necessary; **in ~ di** on the occasion of

occhiaie *fpl* bags under the eyes

occhiali *mpl* glasses; **~ da sole** sunglasses; **occhiata** *f* look; **dare un'~ a** have a look at; (*sorvegliare*) keep an eye on; **occhiello** *m* buttonhole; **occhio** *m* eye; **a ~ nudo** to the naked eye; **a ~ e croce** roughly; **dare nell'~** attract attention; **a quattr' ~i** in private

occidentale western; **occidente** *m* west; **a ~ di** (to the) west of

occorrente 1 *agg* necessary **2** *m* necessary materials; **occorrenza** *f*: **all'~** if necessary, if need be; **occorrere** *be* necessary; (*accadere*) occur; **mi occorre** I need; **non occorre!** there's no need!

occupare *spazio* take up, occupy; *tempo* occupy, fill; *posto* have; *persona* keep busy; **occuparsi** take care (*di* of), deal (*di* with); **occupati degli affari tuoi!** mind your own business!; **occupato** TELEC busy, Br *anche* engaged; *posto, appartamento* taken; *gabinetto* engaged, Am occupied; *persona* busy; *città, nazione* occupied; **occupazione** *f di città, paese* occupation; (*attività*) pastime; (*impiego*) job

oceano *m* ocean; **Oceano Atlantico** Atlantic Ocean; **Oceano Pacifico** Pacific

Ocean

oculista *m/f* ophthalmologist

od = **o** (*before a vowel*)

odiare hate, detest

odierno modern-day *attr*, today's *attr*

odio *m* hatred; **odioso** hateful, odious

odontotecnico *m*, *-a f* dental technician

odorare smell (**di** of); **odorato** *m* sense of smell; **odore** *m* smell, odour, *Am* odor; **-i** *pl* GASTR herbs

offendere offend; **offendersi** take offense *o Am* offense; **offensiva** *f* offensive; **offensivo** offensive

offerente *m* bidder; **maggior** ~ highest bidder; **offerta** *f* offer; FIN supply; REL offering; (**dono**) donation; **in asta** bid; ~ **d'impiego** job offer; ~ **speciale** special offer

offesa *f* offence, *Am* offense; **offeso** *pp* ☞ **offendere**

officina *f* workshop; **per macchine** garage

offrire offer; **ti offro da bere** I'll buy you a drink; **posso offrirti qualcosa?** can I get you anything?

oggettivo objective; **oggetto** *m* object

oggi today; **d'~** of today; **da ~ in poi** from now on; ~ **stesso** today, this very day; ~ **come ~** at the moment; ~ **pomeriggio** this afternoon; **oggigiorno** nowadays

ogni every; ~ **tanto** every so often; ~ **sei giorni** every six days; **Ognissanti** *m inv* All Saints Day; **ognuno** everyone, everybody

Olanda *f* Holland; **olandese** **1** *agg* Dutch **2** *m/f* Dutchman; **donna** Dutchwoman

oleandro *m* oleander

oleoso oily

olfatto *m* sense of smell

oliera *f* type of cruet for oil and vinegar bottles

Olimpiadi *fpl* Olympic Games, Olympics; ~ **invernali** Winter Olympics

olio *m* oil; ~ **extra-vergine d'oliva** extra-virgin olive oil; ~ **solare** suntan oil

oliva *f* olive; **olivo** *m* olive (tree)

oltraggio *m* offense, *Am* offense, outrage

oltre 1 *prp* after, past; (**più di**) over; **vai** ~ **il semaforo** go past the traffic lights; ~ **a** apart from **2** *avv* **nello spazio** further; **nel tempo** longer

omaggio *m* homage; (**dono**) gift; **copia** (**in**) ~ free *o* complimentary copy; **essere in** ~ **con** come free with

ombelico *m* navel

ombra *f* shadow; **zona non illuminata** shade; **all'~** in the shade; **ombrello** *m* umbrella; **ombrellone** *m* parasol; **sulla spiaggia** beach umbrella; **ombretto** *m* eye shadow

omeopatico 1 *agg* homeopathic 2 *m*, -a *f* homeopath

omero *m* humerus

omesso *pp* ☞ *omettere*; omettere omit, leave out

omicida 1 *agg* murderous 2 *m/f* murderer; omicidio *m* murder

omogeneizzato *m* baby food; omogeneo homogeneous

omonimo 1 *agg* of the same name 2 *m* homonym 3 *m*, -a *f* namesake

omosessuale *agg, m/f* homosexual

on. (= *onorevole*) Hon (= honourable)

onda *f* wave; -e *pl corte* short wave; -e *pl lunghe* long wave; -e *pl medie* medium wave; RAD *andare in* ~ go on the air; ondata *f* wave; ~ *di caldo* heat wave; ~ *di freddo* cold spell; ondeggiare *di barca* rock; *di bandiera* flutter; ondulato *capelli* wavy; *superficie* uneven; *cartone, lamiera* corrugated

onestà *f* honesty; onesto honest; *prezzo, critica* fair

onice *m* onyx

onomastico *m* name day

onorare be a credit to; ~ *qu di qc* honour *o Am* honor s.o. with sth; onorario 1 *agg* honorary *Am* fee; onore *m* honour, *Am* honor; *in* ~ *di* in honour of; onorevole 1 *agg* honourable, *Am* honorable 2 *Onorevole m/f*

Member of Parliament

ONU *f* (= *Organizzazione delle Nazioni Unite*) UN (= United Nations)

opaco opaque; *calze, rossetto* dark

opera *f* work; MUS opera; ~ *d'arte* work of art; *mettersi all'*~ set to work; operaio 1 *agg* working 2 *m*, -a *f* worker; ~ *specializzato* skilled worker; operare 1 *v/t cambiamento* make; *miracoli* work; MED operate on 2 *v/i* act; operativo operational; *ricerca* applied; *ordine* operative; *piano m* ~ plan of operations; operatore *m*, -trice *f* operator; *televisivo, cinematografico* cameraman; ~ *di Borsa* market trader; ~ *sociale* social worker; ~ *turistico* tour operator; operazione *f* operation

opinione *f* opinion

oppio *m* opium

opporre offer; opporsi be opposed

opportunista *m/f* opportunist; opportunità *f inv* opportunity; *di decisione* timeliness; opportuno suitable

opposizione *f* opposition; opposto 1 *pp* ☞ *opporre* 2 *agg* opposite 3 *m* POL opposition

oppressione *f* oppression; oppresso 1 *pp* ☞ *opprimere* 2 *agg* oppressed; opprimere oppress

oppure or (else)

optare: ~ **per** choose, opt for

opuscolo *m* brochure

opzione *f* option

ora[1] *f* time; *unità di misura* hour; *che ~ è?, che -e so-no?* what's the time?; ~ *le-gale* daylight saving time; ~ *locale* local time; ~ *di punta* rush hour; TELEC peak time; *di buon'~* early

ora[2] *1 avv* now; *per ~* for the moment, for the time being; ~ *come ~* at the moment; *d'~ in poi* from now on 2 *cong* now

orale *m/agg* oral

orario 1 *agg tariffa* hourly; *ve-locità* per hour **2** *m di treno, bus* timetable, *Am* schedule; *di negozio* business hours; *al lavoro* hours of work; ~ *di apertura / chiusura* open-ing / closing time; *in ~* on time

orata *f* bream

orbita *f* AST orbit; ANAT eye-socket; *in ~* in orbit

orchestra *f* orchestra; *luogo (orchestra)* pit

orchidea *f* orchid

ordigno *m* device

ordinale *m/agg* ordinal

ordinamento *m* rules and regulations; ~ *sociale* rules governing society; *ordinare* order; *stanza* tidy up

ordinario ordinary; *mediocre* pretty average

ordinato tidy; **ordinazione** *f*

order; *ordine m* order; *met-tere in ~* tidy up; *di prim'~* first-rate; ~ *del giorno* agen-da; *l'~ dei medici* the medical association

orecchino *m* earring; *orec-chio m* ear; MUS *a ~* by ear; *orecchioni mpl* mumps *sg*

oreficeria *f* goldsmith work; *(gioielleria)* jeweller's, *Am* jewelry store

orfano 1 *agg* orphan *2 m*, -a *f* orphan; *orfanotrofio m* or-phanage

organismo *m* organism; *fig* body

organizzare organize; *orga-nizzazione f* organization

organo *m* organ

orgasmo *m* orgasm

orgoglio *m* pride; *orgoglio-so* proud

orientale 1 *agg* eastern; *(del-l'Oriente)* Oriental **2** *m/f* Ori-ental

orientamento *m*: *senso d'~* sense of direction; ~ *pro-fessionale* professional ad-vice; *orientarsi* get one's bearings

oriente *m* east; *l'Oriente* the Orient; *Medio Oriente* Mid-dle East; *Estremo Oriente* Far East; *ad ~ di* (to the) east of

origano *m* oregano

originale *m/agg* original; *ori-ginalmente* originally; *ori-ginario* original; *essere ~*

di come from; *popolo* originate in; **origine** *f* origin; *in*
~ originally

origliare eavesdrop

orizzontale horizontal; **orizzonte** *m* horizon

orlo *m* edge; *di vestito* hem

orma *f* footprint; *fig* **seguire
le -e di qu** follow in s.o.'s
footsteps

ormai by now

ormonale hormonal; **ormone** *m* hormone

ornamentale ornamental;
ornamento *m* ornament; **ornare** decorate

oro *m* gold; **d'~** (made of)
gold

orologiaio *m* (clock- and)
watch-maker; **orologio** *m*
clock; *da polso* watch

oroscopo *m* horoscope

orrendo horrendous

orribile horrible

orrore *m* horror (**di** of)

orsacchiotto *m* bear cub;
giocattolo teddy (bear)

orso *m* bear; *fig* hermit; **~
bianco** polar bear

ortaggio *m* vegetable

ortica *f* nettle; **orticaria** *f* nettle rash

orto *m* vegetable garden,
kitchen garden; **~ botanico**
botanical gardens

ortodosso orthodox

ortografia *f* spelling

ortopedico 1 *agg* orthopae-
dic, *Am* orthopedic **2** *m*, **-a**
f orthopaedist, *Am* orthope-

dist

orzaiolo *m* stye

orzo *m* barley

osare dare

osceno obscene

oscillare *di corda* sway,
swing; *di barca* rock; FIS os-
cillate; *fig: di persona* waver;
di prezzi fluctuate

oscurare obscure; *luce* block
out; **oscurità** *f* darkness; *fig*
obscurity; **nell'~** in the dark;
oscuro 1 *agg* dark; *(sconosciuto)* obscure **2** *m*: **essere
all'~ di qc** be in the dark
about sth

ospedale *m* hospital

ospitale hospitable; **ospitalità** *f* hospitality; **ospitare** put
up; **ospite** *m/f* guest; *chi
ospita* host; *donna* hostess;
ospizio *m* old folk's home

osservare *(guardare)* look at,
observe; *(notare)* see, observe; *(far notare)* point
out; *(seguire)* obey; **~ una
dieta** keep to a diet; **osservatore** *m*, **-trice** *f* observer;
osservatorio *m* AST observatory; **osservazione** *f* observation

ossessione *f* obsession (**di**
with); **avere l'~ di** be obsessed with; **ossessivo** obsessive

ossia or rather

ossidare tarnish

ossigeno *m* oxygen

osso *m* bone; **~ sacro** sa-
crum; **in carne e -a** in the

flesh; **ossobuco** *m* marrow-bone; GASTR ossobuco, *stew made with knuckle of veal*

ostacolare hinder; **ostacolo** *m* obstacle; *nell'atletica* hurdle; *nell'equitazione* fence, jump; *fig* stumbling block, obstacle

ostaggio *m* hostage; **prendere qu in ~** take s.o. hostage

ostello *m:* **~ della gioventù** youth hostel

osteoporosi *f* osteoporosis

osteria *f* inn

ostetrica *f* obstetrician; *(levatrice)* midwife; **ostetrico 1** *agg* obstetric(al) **2** *m* obstetrician

ostia *f* Host

ostile hostile; **ostilità** *f inv* hostility

ostinarsi dig one's heels in; **~ a fare qc** persist in doing sth; **ostinato** obstinate

ostrica *f* oyster

ostruire block, obstruct; **ostruito** blocked

otite *f* ear infection

otorinolaringoiatra *m/f* ear, nose and throat specialist

ottagono *m* octagon; **ottanta** eighty; **ottantesimo** eighti-

eth; **ottavo** eighth

ottenere get, obtain; **ottengo** ☞ **ottenere**

ottica *f* optics; *fig* viewpoint; **ottico 1** *agg* optical **2** *m* optician

ottimismo *m* optimism; **ottimista** *m/f* optimist

ottimizzare optimize; **ottimo** excellent

otto eight

ottobre *m* October

ottocento 1 *agg* eight hundred **2** *m:* **l'Ottocento** the nineteenth century

ottone *m* brass; MUS **-i** *pl* brass

otturare block; *dente* fill; **otturatore** *m* FOT shutter; **otturazione** *f* blocking; *di dente* filling

ottuso obtuse

ovaia *f* ANAT ovary

ovale *m/agg* oval

overdose *f inv* overdose

ovest *m* west; **a(l) ~ di** (to the) west of

ovini *mpl* sheep

ovunque everywhere

ovvero or rather; *(cioè)* that is

ovvio obvious

ozio *m* laziness, idleness

ozono *m* ozone; **la fascia d'~** the ozone layer

P

pacato calm, unhurried

pacchetto *m* package; *di sigarette, biscotti* packet

pacchiano vulgar, in bad taste

pacco *m* parcel, package; **~ postale** parcel

pace *f* peace; *lasciare in ~ qu* leave s.o. alone *o* in peace

pacifista *m/f* pacifist

padano of the Po; *pianura ~a* Po Valley

padella *f di cucina* frying pan

padiglione *m* pavilion; *~ auricolare* auricle

Padova *f* Padua; **padovano 1** *agg* Paduan **2** *m*, **-a** Paduan

padre *m* father; **padrino** *m* godfather; **padronanza** *f* control; (*conoscenza*) mastery; *~ di sé* self-control; **padrone** *m*, **-a** *f* boss; (*proprietario*) owner; *di cane* master; *donna mistress*; *~ di casa* man / lady of the house; *per inquilino* landlord; *donna* landlady

paesaggio *m* scenery; PITT, GEOG landscape; **paesaggista** *m/f* PITT landscape painter; **paese** *m* country; (*villaggio*) village; (*territorio*) region; *i Paesi Bassi pl* the Netherlands; *~ pl in via di sviluppo* developing countries

paga *f* pay; **pagabile** payable; **pagamento** *m* payment; **pagare 1** *v/t* pay for; *conto, fattura* pay; *gliela faccio ~* he'll pay for this **2** *v/i* pay

pagella *f* report, *Am* report card

paghetta *f* pocket money

pagina *f* page; *-e gialle* Yellow Pages; *~ web* webpage

paglia *f* straw

paio *m*: *un ~ di* a pair of; *un ~ di volte* a couple of times

pala *f* shovel; *di elica, turbina* blade

palasport *m inv* indoor sports arena

palato *m* palate

palazzina *f* luxury home; **palazzo** *m* palace; (*edificio*) building; *con appartamenti* block of flats, *Am* apartment block; *~ di giustizia* courthouse; *~ dello sport* indoor sports arena

palco *m* dais; TEA stage; **palcoscenico** *m* stage

palese obvious

Palestina *f* Palestine; **palestinese** *agg, m/f* Palestinian

palestra *f* gym

paletta *f* shovel; *per la spiaggia* spade; **paletto** *m* tent peg

palla *f* ball; *~ di neve* snowball; **pallacanestro** *f* basketball; **pallanuoto** *f* water po-

papero

lo; **pallavolo** f volley ball

palliativo m palliative

pallido pale

pallina f di vetro marble; **~ da golf** golf ball; **~ da tennis** tennis ball; **pallino** m nel biliardo cue ball; nelle bocce jack; munizione pellet; fig **avere il ~ della pesca** be mad about fishing; **a -i** fig spotted; **palloncino** m balloon; **pallone** m ball; (calcio) football, soccer; AVIA balloon; **pallottola** f pellet; di pistola bullet

palma f palm

palmare m PDA

palmo m hand's breadth; ANAT palm

palo m pole; nel calcio (goal)-post

palombaro m diver

palpare feel; MED palpate

palpebra f eyelid

paltò m inv overcoat

palude f swamp; **paludoso** swampy; **palustre** swampy; **pianta** swamp attr

panca f bench; in chiesa pew

pancarré m sliced loaf

pancetta f pancetta, cured belly of pork

panchetto m footstool; **panchina** f bench

pancia f m stomach; **mal m di ~** stomach-ache; **panciotto** m waistcoat, Am vest

pancreas m inv pancreas

pane m bread; **~ integrale** wholemeal o Am whole-

wheat bread; **panetteria** f bakery; **panettiere** m/f baker; **panettone** m panettone, cake made with candied fruit

panfilo m yacht; **~ a motore** motor yacht

pangrattato m breadcrumbs

panico m panic

paniere m basket

panificio m bakery

panino m roll; **~ imbottito** filled roll; **paninoteca** f sandwich shop

panna f cream; **~ montata** whipped cream

panne f: **essere in ~** have broken down

pannello m panel; **~ solare** solar panel

panno m (pezzo di stoffa) cloth; **-i** pl clothes; **se fossi nei tuoi -i** if I were in your shoes

pannocchia f cob

pannolino m nappy, Am diaper; per donne sanitary towel, Am sanitary napkin

panorama m panorama; fig overview

pantaloncini mpl shorts; **pantaloni** mpl trousers, Am pants

pantera f ZO panther

pantofola f slipper

papà m inv daddy, dad

papa m Pope

papavero m poppy

papera f fig (errore) slip of the tongue

papero m, **-a** f gosling

papillon m inv bow tie

pappa f food

pappagallo m parrot

paprica f paprika

parabola f TV satellite dish

parabrezza m inv windscreen, Am windshield

paracadute m inv parachute; **paracadutista** m/f parachutist

paracarro m post

paradiso m heaven, paradise

paradossale paradoxical; **paradosso** m paradox

parafango m AUTO wing; di bici mudguard

parafulmine m lightning rod

paraggi mpl neighbourhood, Am neighborhood; **nei ~ di** (somewhere) near

paragonare compare; **paragone** m comparison

paragrafo m paragraph

paralisi f paralysis; **paralizzare** paralyze

parallela f parallel line; **-e** pl parallel bars; **parallelo** m/agg parallel

paralume m lampshade

parametro m parameter

paranoia f paranoia; **paranoico** paranoid

paranormale m/agg paranormal

paraocchi mpl blinkers (anche fig)

parapetto m parapet; MAR rail

paraplegico 1 agg paraplegic **2** m, **-a** f paraplegic

parare 1 v/t ornare decorate; proteggere shelter; occhi shield; scansare parry **2** v/i save

parassita m/f parasite (anche fig)

parata f parade

paraurti m inv bumper

parcheggiare park; **parcheggio** m parking; luogo car park, Am parking lot

parchimetro m parking meter

parco m park; **~ naturale** nature reserve

parecchio 1 agg a lot of **2** pron **parecchi** mpl, **parecchie** fpl quite a few **3** avv quite a lot

pareggiare 1 v/t even up; (uguagliare) match; conto balance **2** v/i SP draw, Am tie; **pareggio** m SP draw, Am tie

parente m/f relative

parentesi f bracket, Am parenthesis

parere 1 v/i seem, appear; **che te ne pare?** what do you think?; **non ti pare?** don't you think?; **a quanto pare** by all accounts **2** m opinion; **a mio ~** in my opinion

parete f wall

pari 1 agg equal; numero even; **alla ~** the same; SP **finire alla ~** end in a draw o Am tie **2** m (social) equal, peer

Parigi Paris; **parigino** Parisian

parità f equality, parity; **~ di diritti** equal rights; **a ~ di condizioni** all things being equal

parlamentare 1 agg Parliamentary **2** v/i negotiate **3** m/f Member of Parliament, MP; **parlamento** m Parliament

parlare talk, speak (**a qu** to s.o.; **di qc** about sth); **parla inglese?** do you speak English?

parmigiano m formaggio Parmesan

parodia f parody

parola f word; facoltà speech; **~ d'ordine** password; **-e** pl **crociate** crossword; **~ chiave** keyword; **essere di ~** keep one's word; **parolaccia** f swear word

parquet m parquet floor

parrocchia f parish; **parroco** m parish priest

parrucca f wig; **parrucchiere** m, **-a** f hairdresser; **~ per signora** ladies' hairdresser

part time 1 agg part-time **2** avv part time

parte f part; (porzione) portion; (lato) side; DIR party; **prendere ~ a** take part in; **a ~** separate; **mettere da ~ qc** put sth aside; **da nessuna ~** nowhere; **da tutte le -i** everywhere; **da ~ mia** regalo ecc from me; **in ~** in part, partly

partecipante m/f participant;

partecipare 1 v/t announce **2** v/i: **~ a gara** take part in; **dolore, gioia** share; **partecipazione** f (intervento) participation; (annunzio) announcement; FIN holding; **~ agli utili** profit-sharing

partenza f departure; SP start

participio m participle

particolare 1 agg particular; segretario private; **in ~** in particular **2** m particular, detail; **particolareggiato** detailed; **particolarità** f inv special nature

partigiano m, **-a** f partisan

partire leave; AUTO, SP start

partita f SP match; di carte game; di merce shipment; **~ IVA** VAT registration number

partito m POL party

partner m/f inv partner

parto m birth; **partorire** give birth to

parziale partial; fig biased

Pasqua f Easter; **pasquale** Easter attr; **Pasquetta** f Easter Monday

passaggio m passage; **in macchina** lift, Am ride; atto passing; SP pass; **essere di ~** be passing through; **~ a livello** level crossing, Am grade crossing; **dare un ~ a qu** give s.o. a lift; **passante** m/f passer-by; **passaporto** m passport; **passare 1** v/i (trasferirsi) go (**in** into); SP pass; di legge be passed; di *tempo* go by, pass; **~ da / per Milano** go through Milan; **~ dal panettiere** drop by the baker's; **mi è passato di mente** it slipped my mind; **~ per imbecille** be taken for a fool 2 *v/t* confine cross; (*sorpassare*) overstep; (*porgere*) pass; (*trascorrere*) spend; TELEC **ti passo Claudio** here's Claudio; **passata** *f* quick wipe; GASTR **~ (di pomodoro)** passata, sieved tomato pulp; **passatempo** *m* pastime, hobby; **passato 1** *agg* past; *alimento* puréed; **l'anno ~** last year **3** *m* past; GASTR purée

passeggero 1 *agg* passing, short-lived **2** *m*, *-a f* passenger; **passeggiare** stroll, walk; **passeggiata** *f* stroll, walk; (*percorso*) walk; **passeggino** *m* pushchair, *Am* baby buggy; **passeggio** *m*: **andare a ~** go for a walk

passe-partout *m inv* chiave master key

passerella *f* (foot)bridge; MAR gangway; AVIA ramp; *per sfilate* catwalk, *Am* runway

passero *m* sparrow

passionale passionate; *delitto* of passion; **passione** *f* passion; REL Passion

passivo 1 *agg* passive **2** *m* GRAM passive; FIN liabilities

passo *m* step; (*impronta*) footprint; *di libro* passage;

GEOG pass; **~ carrabile** driveway; **fare due -i** go for a walk *o* a stroll; *fig* **fare il primo ~** take the first step

pasta *f* paste; (*pastasciutta*) pasta; (*impasto*) dough; (*dolce*) pastry; **frolla** shortcrust pastry; **~ sfoglia** puff pastry; **pastasciutta** *f* pasta; **pastella** *f* batter

pastello *m* pastel

pasticca *f* pastille

pasticceria *f* pastries, cakes; *negozio* cake shop; **pasticcino** *m* pastry; **pasticcio** *m* GASTR pie; *fig* mess; **essere nei -i** be in a mess

pastiglia *f* MED tablet, pill

pasto *m* meal

pastore *m*, *-a f* shepherd **2** *m* REL: **~ (evangelico)** pastor; **pastorizzato** pasteurized

patata *f* potato; **-e pl fritte** (French) fries; **patatine** *fpl* crisps, *Am* chips; (*fritte*) French fries

patente *f*: **~ (di guida)** driving licence, *Am* driver's license

paternità *f* paternity; **paterno** paternal, fatherly

patetico pathetic

patire 1 *v/i* suffer (**di** from) **2** *v/t* suffer (from); **patito 1** *agg* of suffering **2** *m*, *-a f* fan

patria *f* homeland

patrigno *m* stepfather

patrimonio *m* estate; **~ artistico** artistic heritage

patriottismo *m* patriotism

patrocinio *m* support, patronage

patrono *m*, -a *f* REL patron saint

patteggiare negotiate

pattinaggio *m* skating; ~ *su ghiaccio* ice skating; *pattinare* skate; AUTO skid; *pattinatore* *m*, -*trice* *f* skater; *pattino* *m* SP skate; ~ *a rotelle* roller skate; ~ *in linea* roller blade

patto *m* pact; *a* ~ *che* on condition that

pattuglia *f* patrol

pattumiera *f* dustbin, *Am* trashcan

paura *f* fear; *avere* ~ *di* be frightened of; *mettere* ~ *a qu* frighten s.o.; *pauroso* fearful; *(che fa paura)* frightening

pausa *f* pause; *durante il lavoro* break

pavimento *m* floor

pavone *m* peacock

paziente be patient; *paziente* *agg*, *m/f* patient; *pazienza* *f* patience

pazzesco crazy; *pazzia* *f* madness; *pazzo* **1** *agg* mad, crazy; *andare* ~ *per* be mad *o* crazy about **2** *m*, -a *f* madman; *donna* madwoman

p.c. (= *per conoscenza*) cc (= carbon copy)

peccare sin; ~ *di* be guilty of; *peccato* *m* sin; *(che)* ~ *!* what a pity!

pecora *f* sheep

pecorino *m/agg*: *(formaggio* *m)* ~ pecorino *(ewe's milk cheese)*

peculiarità *f inv* special feature, peculiarity

pedaggio *m* toll

pedalare pedal; *pedale* *m* pedal; *pedalò* *m inv* pedalo

pedana *f* footrest; SP springboard

pedata *f* kick; *impronta* footprint

pediatra *m/f* paediatrician, *Am* pediatrician

pedicure **1** *m/f* chiropodist, *Am* podiatrist **2** *m inv* pedicure

pedina *f* draughtsman, *Am* draftsman; *fig* cog in the wheel; *pedinare* shadow, follow

pedofilo *m*, -a *f* paedophile, *Am* pedophile

pedonale pedestrian; *pedone* *m* pedestrian

peggio **1** *avv* worse **2** *m*: *il* ~ *è che* the worst of it is that; *avere la* ~ get the worst of it; *peggioramento* *m* deterioration, worsening; *peggiorare* **1** *v/t* make worse, worsen **2** *v/i* get worse, worsen; *peggiore* worse; *superlativo* worst; *il* ~ the worst

pelare peel; *pollo* pluck; *fig* F fleece F

pelle *f* skin; *avere la* ~ *d'oca* have gooseflesh

pellegrinaggio *m* pilgrimage; **pellegrino** *m*, **-a** *f* pilgrim

pelletteria *f* leatherwork

pellicano *m* pelican

pelliccia *f* fur; *cappotto* fur coat

pellicola *f* film

pelo *m* hair, coat; *(pelliccia)* coat; *fig* **per un ~** by the skin of one's teeth

pena *f (sofferenza)* pain, suffering; *(punizione)* punishment; **~ di morte** death penalty; **stare in ~ per qu** worry about s.o.; **non ne vale la ~** it's not worth it; **mi fa ~** I feel sorry for him / her; **penale 1** *agg* criminal; *codice* **penale 2** *f* penalty; **penalità** *f inv* penalty; **penalizzare** penalize

pendenza *f* slope; **pendere** hang; *(essere inclinato)* slope; **pendio** *m* slope

pendolare *m/f* commuter

pendolo *m* pendulum

pene *m* penis

penetrante *dolore, freddo* piercing; *fig: sguardo* piercing, penetrating; *analisi* penetrating; **penetrare 1** *v/t* penetrate **2** *v/i:* **~ in** enter

penisola *f* peninsula

penitenza *f* REL penance; *in gioco* forfeit; **penitenziario** *m* prison

penna *f* pen; *di uccello* feather; **~ stilografica** fountain pen; **pennarello** *m* felt-tip (pen); **pennello** *m* brush

penombra *f* half-light

penoso painful

pensare think; **~ a** think about *o* of; **~ a fare qc** *(ricordarsi di)* remember to do sth; **~ di fare qc** think of doing sth; **ci penso io** I'll take care of it; **pensiero** *m* thought; *(preoccupazione)* worry; **stare in ~** be worried *(per* about); **pensieroso** pensive

pensile hanging

pensilina *f* shelter

pensionamento *m* retirement; **pensionato** *m*, **-a** *f* pensioner, retired person; *alloggio* boarding house; **pensione** *f* pension; *albergo* boarding house; **~ completa** full board; **mezza ~** half board; **andare in ~** retire

Pentecoste *f* Pentecost, *Br anche* Whitsun

pentirsi *di peccato* repent; **~ di aver fatto qc** be sorry for doing sth

pentola *f* pot, pan

penultimo last but one, penultimate

penzolare dangle; **penzoloni** dangling

pepare pepper; **pepato** peppered; **pepe** *m* pepper; **peperone** *m* pepper

per for; *mezzo* by; **~ qualche giorno** for a few days; **~ tutta la notte** throughout the night; **dieci ~ cento** ten per cent; **uno ~ uno** one by one; **~ fare qc** (in order) to do sth; **stare ~** be about to

pera f pear

peraltro however

perbene 1 agg respectable **2** avv properly

percento 1 m percentage **2** avv per cent; **percentuale** f agg percentage

percepire perceive; (*riscuotere*) cash

perché because; (*affinché*) so that; **~?** why?

perciò so, therefore

percorrere *distanza* cover; *strada, fiume* travel along; **percorso 1** pp ☞ **percorrere 2** m (*tragitto*) route

percossa f blow; **percosso** pp ☞ **percuotere**; **percuotere** strike

percussione f percussion; MUS **-i** pl percussion

perdere v/t lose; *treno, occasione* miss; **~ tempo** waste time **2** v/i lose; *di rubinetto, tubo* leak; **perdersi** get lost; **~ d'animo** lose heart; **mi sono perduto** I'm lost; **perdita** f loss; *di gas, di acqua* leak; **~ di tempo** waste of time; **perditempo 1** m/f inv idler **2** m inv waste of time

perdonare forgive; **perdono** m forgiveness

perenne eternal; BOT perennial

perfettamente perfectly; **perfetto** perfect; **perfezionamento** m perfection, further improvement; **corso m di ~** further training; **per-**

fezionare perfect; **perfezione** f perfection; **perfezionista** m/f perfectionist

perfido treacherous

perfino even

perforare drill through

pergolato m pergola

pericolante on the verge of collapse; **pericolo** m danger; (*rischio*) risk; **fuori ~** out of danger; **pericoloso** dangerous

periferia f periphery; *di città* outskirts; **periferico** peripheral; *quartiere* outlying; IN-FOR **unità** f inv **-a** peripheral

perifrasi f inv circumlocution

periodico 1 agg periodic **2** m periodical; **~ mensile** monthly; **periodo** m period

peripezia f misadventure

perito 1 agg expert **2** m, **-a** f expert

peritonite f peritonitis

perizia f skill, expertise; *esame* examination (by an expert)

perla f pearl; **perlina** f bead

perlomeno at least

perlopiù usually

perlustrare patrol

permaloso easily offended, touchy

permanente 1 agg permanent **2** f perm; **permanenza** f permanence; **in un luogo** stay

permesso 1 pp ☞ **permettere 2** m permission; (*breve licenza*) permit; MIL leave; **~**

di soggiorno residence permit; (*è*) *~?* may I?; permettere allow, permit; permettersi afford

pernacchia *f* F raspberry F, *Am* bronx cheer F

perno *m* pivot

pernottamento *m* night, overnight stay

però but

pero *m* pear (tree)

perpendicolare *f/agg* perpendicular

perplesso perplexed

perquisire search; perquisizione *f* search; *~ personale* body search; *mandato m di ~* search warrant

persecuzione *f* persecution; *mania f di ~* persecution complex; perseguitare persecute; perseguitato *m: ~ politico* person persecuted for their political views

perseverante persevering; perseverare persevere

persiana *f* shutter

persino *☞ perfino*

persistente persistent; persistere persist

perso *pp ☞ perdere*

persona *f* person; *a (o per) ~* a head, each; *in ~, di ~* in person; personaggio *m* character; (*celebrità*) personality; personale **1** *agg* personal **2** *m* staff, personnel; personalità *f inv* personality; personalmente personally

perspicace shrewd

persuadere persuade, convince; *~ qu a fare qc* persuade s.o. to do sth; persuasivo persuasive; persuaso *pp ☞ persuadere*

pertanto and so, therefore

pertinente relevant, pertinent

perturbazione *f* disturbance

Perù *m* Peru; peruviano **1** *agg* Peruvian **2** *m, -a f* Peruvian

pervenire arrive; *far ~* send

p.es. (= *per esempio*) eg (= for example)

pesante heavy; fig: *libro, film* boring; pesantezza *f* heaviness; *~ di stomaco* indigestion; pesapersone *f inv* scales; *in negozio ecc* weighing machine; pesare weigh

pesca[1] *f frutto* peach

pesca[2] *f* fishing

pescare fish for; (*prendere*) catch; fig dig up; *ladro, svaligiatore ecc* catch (red-handed); pescatore *m* fisherman; pesce *m* fish; *~ d'aprile* April Fool; ASTR *Pesci pl* Pisces; pescecane *m* shark; peschereccio *m* fishing boat; pescheria *f* fishmonger's, *Am* fish store; pescivendolo *m, -a f* fishmonger, *Am* fish seller

pesco *m* peach (tree)

peso *m* weight; *a ~* by weight

pessimismo *m* pessimism; pessimista **1** *agg* pessimistic **2** *m/f* pessimist

pessimo very bad, terrible

pestaggio *m* F going-over F;
pestare *carne*, *prezzemolo*
pound; *con piede* step on;
(*picchiare*) beat up
peste *f* plague; *persona* pest F
pesticida *m* pesticide
pesto *m* pesto, *paste* of basil,
olive oil and pine nuts
petalo *m* petal
petardo *m* fire-cracker
peto *m* fart F
petroliera *f* (oil) tanker; petrolifero oil *attr*, petrolio *m*
oil, petroleum
pettegolezzo *m* piece of gossip; pettegolo 1 *agg* gossipy
2 *m*, -a *f* gossip
pettinare comb; pettinarsi
comb one's hair; pettinatura
f hairstyle, hairdo; pettine *m*
comb
petto *m* chest; (*seno*) breast; ~
di pollo chicken breast; *a
doppio ~* double-breasted
pezza *f* cloth; (*toppa*) patch
pezzo *m* piece; *di motore* part;
da / per un ~ for a long
time; ~ *di ricambio* spare
(part); *andare in ~* break into pieces
piacere 1 *v/i*: *le piace il vino?*
do you like wine?; *non mi
piace il cioccolato* I don't
like chocolate; *mi piacereb-
be saperlo* I'd really like to
know 2 *m* pleasure; (*favore*)
favour, *Am* favor; ~! pleased
to meet you!; *mi fa ~* I'm
happy to; *con ~* with pleasure; *per ~* please; piacevole

pleasant; piacimento: *a ~* as
much as you like
piaga *f* (*ferita*) wound
piallare plane
pianerottolo *m* landing
pianeta *m* planet
piangere 1 *v/i* cry, weep 2 *v/t*
mourn
pianificare plan
pianista *m/f* pianist; piano 1
agg flat 2 *avv* (*adagio*) slowly;
(*a voce bassa*) quietly 3 *m*
plan; (*pianura*) plane; *di e-
dificio* floor; MUS piano; ~
rialzato mezzanine; *primo ~*
foreground; FOT close-up;
pianoforte *m* piano
pianta *f* plant; *di città* map; *del
piede* sole; piantare plant;
chiodo hammer in; F *pianta-
la!* cut it out! F; F ~ *qu* dump
s.o. F
pianterreno *m* ground floor,
Am first floor
pianto 1 *pp* ☞ *piangere* 2 *m*
crying, weeping; (*lacrime*)
tears
pianura *f* plain
piastra *f* plate; piastrella *f* tile
piattaforma *f* platform; ~ *di
lancio* launch pad; piattino
m saucer; piatto 1 *agg* flat
2 *m* plate; GASTR dish; MUS
-i pl cymbals; *primo ~* first
course; ~ *del giorno* day's
special
piazza *f* square; COM market
(place); piazzale *m* large
square; *in autostrada* toll-
booth area; piazzare place,

put; (*vendere*) sell; **piazzola** *f* small square; **~ di sosta** layby

piccante spicy, hot

picchiare beat

piccione *m* pigeon

picco *m* peak; MAR **colare a ~** sink

piccolo 1 *agg* small, little; **di statura** short 2 *m*, **-a** *f* child; **la gatta con i suoi -i** the cat and her young; **da ~** as a child

piccozza *f* ice axe, *Am* ice ax

picnic *m inv* picnic

pidocchio *m* louse

piede *m* foot; **a -i** on foot; **stare in -i** stand; **a -i nudi** barefoot, with bare feet

piedistallo *m* pedestal

piega *f* wrinkle; **di pantaloni** crease; **di gonna** pleat; **piegare 1** *v/t* bend; (*ripiegare*) fold 2 *v/i* bend; **piegarsi** bend; *fig* **~ a** comply with; **pieghevole** sedia folding

Piemonte *m* Piedmont; **piemontese** *agg*, *m/f* Piedmontese

piena *f* flood; *a teatro* full house; **pieno 1** *agg* full (**di** of); (*non cavo*) solid 2 *m*: AUTO **fare il ~** fill up

pietà *f* pity (**di** for); PITT pietà; **avere ~ di qu** take pity on s.o.

pietanza *f* dish

pietra *f* stone; **pietrina** *f* flint; **pietroso** stony

pigiama *m* pyjamas, *Am* pajamas

pigiare crush

pigliare catch

pigna *f* pinecone

pignolo pedantic

pigrizia *f* laziness; **pigro** lazy

pila *f* EL battery; (*catasta*) pile

pilastro *m* pillar

pillola *f* pill; **prendere la ~** be on the pill

pilone *m* pier; EL pylon

pilota *m/f* AVIA, MAR pilot; AUTO driver; **pilotare** pilot; AUTO drive

pinacoteca *f* art gallery

pineta *f* pine forest

ping-pong *m* ping-pong

pinna *f di pesce* fin; SP flipper

pino *m* pine; **pinolo** *m* pine nut

pinza *f* pliers; **pinzare** staple; **pinzatrice** *f* stapler; **pinzette** *fpl* tweezers

pioggia *f* rain

piombare fall; *precipitarsi* rush (**su** at); **mi è piombato in casa** he dropped in unexpectedly; **piombino** *m* sinker; **piombo** *m* lead

pioppo *m* poplar

piovere rain; **piovigginare** drizzle; **piovoso** rainy

piovra *f* octopus

pipa *f* pipe

pipì *f* F pee F; F **fare la ~** go for a pee F

pipistrello *m* bat

piramide *f* pyramid

pirata *m* pirate

pirofila *f* oven-proof dish

piroscafo *m* steamer

pisciare P piss P

piscina *f* (swimming) pool; ~ **coperta** indoor pool

pisello *m* pea

pisolino *m* nap

pista *f* di atletica track; *(traccia)* trail; ~ **d'atterraggio** runway; ~ **da ballo** dance floor; ~ **da sci** ski slope; ~ **ciclabile** bike path

pistacchio *m* pistachio

pistola *f* pistol

pittore *m*, **-trice** *f* painter; **pittura** *f* painting; **pitturare** paint

più 1 *avv* more *(di, che* than); *superlativo* most; MAT plus; ~ **grande** bigger; *il* ~ **grande** the biggest; *di* ~ more; *non* ~ no more; *tempo* no longer; ~ **o meno** more or less; *per di* ~ what's more; *mai* ~ never again; *al* ~ **presto** as soon as possible; *al* ~ **tardi** at the latest **2** *agg* more; *superlativo* most; ~ **volte** several times **3** *m* most; ~ **mainly**; *i* ~, *le* ~ the majority

piuma *f* feather

piumino *m* down; *giacca* ~ quilted jacket

piumone® *m* Continental quilt, duvet

piuttosto rather

pizza *f* pizza; **pizzaiolo** *m* pizza maker; **pizzeria** *f* pizzeria

pizzicare 1 *v/t braccio, persona* pinch; F *ladro* catch (redhanded) **2** *v/i* pinch; **pizzico**

m pinch; **pizzicotto** *m* pinch

pizzo *m* *(merletto)* lace

placare placate; *dolore* ease

placca *f* plate; *(targhetta)* plaque; ~ **dentaria** plaque; **placcare** plate; *nel rugby* tackle; **placcato d'oro** gold-plated

planetario 1 *agg* planetary **2** *m* planetarium

plasma *m* plasma; ~ **sanguigno** blood plasma; **plasmare** mould, *Am* mold

plastica *f* plastic; MED plastic surgery; **plastico 1** *agg* plastic **2** *m* ARCHI scale model; **esplosivo** *m* *al* ~ plastic bomb

plastilina *f* Plasticine®

platano *m* plane (tree)

platea *f* TEA stalls

platino *m* platinum

plausibile plausible

plenilunio *m* full moon

plettro *m* plectrum

pleurite *f* pleurisy

plico *m* envelope

plurale *m/agg* plural

plutonio *m* plutonium

pneumatico 1 *agg* pneumatic **2** *m* tyre, *Am* tire

po': *un* ~ a little *(di* sth), a little bit *(di* of); *un bel* ~ quite a lot

poco 1 *agg* little; *con nomi plurali* few **2** *avv* not much; *con aggettivi* not very; **senti un po'!** just listen!; *a* ~ *a* ~ little by little, gradually; ~ **fa** a little while ago; *fra* ~

in a little while, soon; **~ dopo** a little while later, soon after; **per ~** cheap; (*quasi*) almost, nearly

podere *m* farm

podio *m* podium

podismo *m* walking

poesia *f* poetry; *componimento* poem; **poeta** *m*, **-essa** *f* poet; **poetico** poetic

poggiare lean; (*posare*) put, place; **poggiatesta** *m inv* head rest

poi then; **d'ora in ~** from now on

poiché since

polacco 1 *m/agg* Polish **2** *m*, **-a** *f* Pole

polare Polar; **circolo** *m* **~ artico / antartico** Arctic / Antarctic circle

polemica *f* argument; **polemico** argumentative; **polemizzare** argue

polenta *f* polenta, *kind of porridge made from cornmeal*

policlinico *m* general hospital

poliglotta 1 *agg* multilingual **2** *m/f* polyglot

poligono *m* MAT polygon; MIL **~ di tiro** firing range

poliomielite *f* poliomyelitis

polipo *m* polyp

politica *f* politics; (*strategia*) policy; **politico 1** *agg* political **2** *m*, **-a** *f* politician

polizia *f* police; **poliziesco** police *attr*; **romanzo** *m* **~** detective story; **poliziotto 1** *m*

policeman **2** *agg*: **donna** *f* **-a** policewoman; **cane** *m* **~** police dog

polizza *f* policy

pollame *m* poultry

pollice *m* thumb; **unità di misura** inch

polline *m* pollen

pollo *m* chicken

polmone *m* lung; **polmonite** *f* pneumonia

polo¹ *m* GEOG pole; **~ nord** North Pole; **~ sud** South Pole

polo² *m* SP polo **2** *f inv* polo shirt

Polonia *f* Poland

polpa *f* flesh; *di manzo, vitello* meat

polpaccio *m* calf

polpastrello *m* fingertip

polpetta *f di carne* meatball; **polpettone** *m* meat loaf

polpo *m* octopus

polsino *m* cuff; **polso** *m* ANAT wrist; *di camicia* cuff; *pulsazione* pulse

poltiglia *f* mush

poltrire laze around

poltrona *f* armchair; TEA stall (seat)

poltrone *m*, **-a** *f* lazybones *sg*

polvere *f* dust; (*sostanza polverizzata*) powder; **latte** *m* **in ~** powdered milk; **polverina** *f* powder; **polveroso** dusty

pomata *f* cream

pomello *m* cheek; *di porta* knob

pomeridiano afternoon *attr*; pomeriggio *m* afternoon; *di* ~, *nel* ~ in the afternoon

pomice *f*lag*g*: (*pietra f*) ~ pumice (stone)

pomo *m* knob; ~ *d'Adamo* Adam's apple

pomodoro *m* tomato

pompa¹ *f* pomp; *impresa f di -e funebri* undertaker's, *Am* mortician

pompa² *f* TEC pump

pompelmo *m* grapefruit

pompiere *m* fireman; -*i pl* fire brigade, *Am* fire department

pone ☞ *porre*

ponente *m* west

pongo ☞ *porre*

ponte *m* bridge; ARCHI scaffolding; *Am* deck; *fare il* ~ make a long weekend of it

pontefice *m* pontiff

ponteggio *m* scaffolding

pontificio papal; *Stato m* ~ Papal States

pontile *m* jetty

pop: *musica f* ~ pop (music)

popolare 1 *agg* popular; *quartiere* working-class; *ballo m* ~ folk dance 2 *v/t* populate; popolarità *f* popularity; popolato populated; (*abitato*) inhabited; (*pieno*) crowded; popolazione *f* population; popolo *m* people

poppa *f* MAR stern

porcellana *f* porcelain, china

porcellino *m* piglet; ~ *d'India* guinea-pig

porcheria *f* disgusting thing; *è una* ~ it's disgusting; -*e pl* junk food; porchetta *f* suckling pig, *roasted whole in the oven*

porcile *m* pigsty, *Am* pigpen

porcino *m* cep

porco *m* pig; porcospino *m* porcupine

porgere *mano, oggetto* hold out; *aiuto, saluto ecc* offer

porno *m/agg* F porn F; pornografico pornographic

poro *m* pore

porre place, put; *domanda* ask; *poniamo che* ... let's suppose that ...

porro *m* leek; MED wart

porta *f* door

portabagagli *m inv* luggage rack; AUTO roof rack; portacenere *m inv* ashtray; portachiavi *m inv* keyring; portafinestra *f* French window; portafoglio *m* wallet; portafortuna *m inv* good luck charm

portale *m* door; INFOR portal

portamonete *m inv* purse; portaombrelli *m inv* umbrella stand; portapacchi *m inv di macchina* roof rack; *di bicicletta* carrier; portapenne *m inv* pencil case

portare (*trasportare*) carry; (*accompagnare*) take; (*avere addosso*) wear; (*condurre*) lead; ~ *via* take away; *mi ha portato un regalo* he brought me a present; *por-*

tale un regalo take her a present; *essere portato per qc / per fare qc* have a gift for sth / for doing sth

portasci *m inv* AUTO ski rack

portata *f* GASTR course; *di cannocchiale* range; *alla ~ di film, libro ecc* suitable for; *a ~ di mano* within reach

portatile portable; (*computer m*) ~ portable (computer); (*telefono m*) ~ mobile (phone), *Am* cell(ular) phone

portatore *m*, **-trice** *f* bearer; *di malattia* carrier

portauovo *m inv* eggcup

portavoce *m/f inv* spokesperson

portico *m* porch; *-i pl* arcades

portiera *f* door; **portiere** *m* doorman; (*portinaio*) caretaker; SP goalkeeper

portinaio *m*, **-a** *f* caretaker; **portineria** *f* caretaker's flat, *Am* superintendent's apartment

porto[1] *pp* ▷ *porgere*

porto[2] *m posta* postage; ~ *d'armi* gun licence *o Am* license

porto[3] *m* MAR port

Portogallo *m* Portugal; **portoghese** *agg*, *m/f* Portuguese

portone *m* main entrance

porzione *f* share; GASTR portion

posa *f di cavi, tubi* laying; FOT exposure; FOT *mettersi in ~*

pose; **posacenere** *m inv* ashtray; **posare 1** *v/t* put, place **2** *v/i* pose; ~ *su* rest on; *fig* ~ *da intellettuale* pose as an intellectual; **posarsi** alight; **posate** *fpl* cutlery, *Am* flatware

positivo positive

posizione *f* position

possedere own, possess; **possessivo** possessive; **possesso** *m* possession

possiamo ▷ *potere*

possibile possible; *il più presto ~* as soon as possible **2** *m*: *fare il ~* do everything one can; **possibilità** *f inv* possibility; (*occasione*) opportunity, chance; **possibilmente** if possible

posso ▷ *potere*

posta *f* mail, *Br anche* post; (*ufficio postale*) post office; ~ *aerea* airmail; *per* ~ by post; INFOR ~ *elettronica* e-mail; ~ *lumaca* snail mail; **postale** postal

postdatare postdate

posteggiare park; **posteggio** *m* carpark, *Am* parking lot; ~ *dei taxi* taxi rank, *Am* cab stand

posteriore back *attr*, rear *attr*; (*successivo*) later

posticipare postpone; **posticipato**: *pagamento m* ~ payment in arrears

postino *m*, **-a** *f* postman, *Am* mailman; *donna* postwoman, *Am* mailwoman

posto[1] *pp* ☞ *porre*; ~ *che* supposing that

posto[2] *m* place; (*lavoro*) job, position; *mettere a ~ stanza* tidy up; ~ *macchina* parking space; ~ *finestrino / corridoio* window / aisle seat; ~ *a sedere* seat; ~ *di polizia* police station; *vado io al ~ tuo* I'll go in your place, I'll go instead of you; *fuori ~* out of place

postoperatorio postoperative

postumo posthumous

potabile fit to drink; *acqua f ~* drinking water

potare prune

potente *m/f* (*efficace*) potent; **potenza** *f* power; ~ *mondiale* world power; ~ *del motore* engine power; **potenziare** strengthen

potere 1 *v/i* can, be able to; *non posso andare* I can't go; *non ho potuto farlo* I couldn't do it, I wasn't able to do it; *può darsi* perhaps, maybe **2** *m* power

poveraccio *m*, **-a** *f* poor thing; **poverino** *m*, poverino *m* poor man; **povero 1** *agg* poor **2** *m*, **-a** *f* poor man; *donna* poor woman; *i -i pl* the poor *pl*; **povertà** *f* poverty

pozzanghera *f* puddle

pozzo *m* well; ~ *petrolifero* oil well

PP.TT. (= *Poste e Telecomu-*

nicazioni) Italian Post Office

pranzare have lunch; *la sera* have dinner; **pranzo** *m* lunch; *la sera* dinner

prassi *f inv* standard procedure

pratica *f* practice; (*esperienza*) experience; (*atto*) file; *mettere in ~* put into practice; *-che pl* papers; *in ~* in practice; *avere ~ di qc* have experience of sth; **praticabile** *sport* which can be done; *strada* passable; **praticantato** *m* apprenticeship; **praticare** *professione* practise; *locale* frequent; ~ *molto sport* do a lot of sport; **pratico** practical; *essere ~ di conoscere bene* know a lot about

prato *m* meadow

preavviso *m* notice

precauzione *f* caution; *-i pl* precautions

precedente *agg* preceding **2** *m* precedent; *avere dei -i penali* have a record; **precedenza** *f* precedence; *avere la ~* AUTO have right of way; *dare la ~* AUTO give way, *Am* yield; **precedere** precede

precipitare 1 *v/t* throw; *fig* rush **2** *v/i* fall, plunge; **precipitarsi** (*affrettarsi*) rush; **precipitazione** *f* (*fretta*) haste; *-i pl atmosferiche* atmospheric precipitation; **precipitoso** hasty

precipizio *m* precipice

precisamente precisely; **precisare** specify; **precisione** *f* precision; **con ~** precisely; **preciso** accurate; **persona precisa** precise

precoce precocious; **pianta precoce** early

precotto *m* ready-made, pre-cooked

preda *f* prey

predica *f* sermon

prediletto 1 *pp* ☞ **prediligere 2** *agg* favourite, *Am* favorite; **prediligere** prefer

predire predict

predisporre draw up in advance; **~ a** encourage; **predisposto** *pp* ☞ **predisporre**

predominare predominate; **predominio** *m* predominance

prefabbricato 1 *agg* prefabricated **2** *m* prefabricated building

prefazione *f* preface

preferenza *f* preference; **preferenziale** preferential; **preferire** prefer

preferito favourite, *Am* favorite

prefettura *f* prefecture

prefiggersi set o.s.; **prefisso 1** *pp* ☞ **prefiggersi 2** *m* TELEC code

pregare beg (**di fare** to do); **divinità** pray to; **ti prego di ascoltarmi** please listen to me

preghiera *f* request; REL prayer

pregiato *pietra* precious

pregio *m* (*qualità*) good point

pregiudicato *m*, **-a** *f* previous offender; **pregiudizio** *m* prejudice

prego please; **~?** I'm sorry (what did you say)?; **grazie! – ~!** thank you! - you're welcome!, not at all!

preistoria *f* prehistory; **preistorico** prehistoric

prelavaggio *m* pre-wash

prelevamento *m*, **di sangue**, **campione** taking; FIN withdrawal; **~ in contanti** cash withdrawal; **prelevare** *sangue*, *campione* take; *denaro* withdraw

prelibato exquisite

prelievo *m* (*prelevamento*) taking; FIN withdrawal; **~ del sangue** blood sample

pre-maman 1 *agg* maternity *attr* **2** *m inv* maternity dress

prematuro premature

premeditato premeditated

premere press

premessa *f* introduction

premesso *pp* ☞ **premettere**; **premettere** say first

premiare give an award *o* prize to; *onestà, coraggio* reward; **premiazione** *f* awards ceremony; **premio** *m* prize, award; FIN premium

premura *f* (*fretta*) hurry, rush; **mettere ~ a qu** hurry s.o. along; **premuroso** attentive

prenatale prenatal

prestarsi

prendere 1 v/t take; *malattia,
treno* catch; *cosa prendi?*
what will you have; *andare / venire a ~ qu* fetch
s.o.; *il sole* sunbathe; *prendersela* get upset (*per*
about; *con* with); *che ti
prende?* what's got into
you? **2** v/i: *~ a destra* turn
right; *prendisole m inv* sun-
dress

prenotare book, reserve;
prenotazione f booking,
reservation

preoccupare worry; **preoccuparsi** worry; **preoccupato** worried; **preoccupazione** f worry

preparare prepare; **prepararsi** get ready (*a* to), prepare
(*a* to); **preparativi** mpl pre-
parations; **preparazione** f
preparation

preposizione f preposition

prepotente domineering; *bisogno* pressing

presa f grip, hold; EL: *~ di corrente* socket, Am outlet; *essere alle -e con qc* be grap-
pling with sth

presagio m omen

presbite far-sighted

prescindere: *~ da* have nothing to do with

prescritto pp ☞ **prescrivere**

prescrivere prescribe

presentare *documenti, biglietto* show, present; *domanda*
submit; *scuse* make; TEA present; (*contenere*) contain; (*far*
conoscere) introduce (*a* to);
presentarsi look; (*esporre*)
show itself; *occasione* occur;
presentatore m, **-trice** f presenter; **presentazione** f
presentation; *di richiesta*
submission; *fare le -i* make
the introductions; **presente
1** agg present; *hai ~ il negozio ... ?* do you know the
shop ... ? **2** m present; *i -i*
pl those present

presentimento m premoni-
tion

presenza f presence; *alla* (*o
in*) *~ di* in the presence of

presepe m, **presepio** m na-
tivity (scene)

preservare protect, keep (*da*
from); **preservativo** m condom

presidente m/f chairman;
POL President; *~ del Consi-
glio (dei ministri)* Prime
Minister

preso pp ☞ **prendere**

pressappoco more or less

pressione f pressure; *far ~ su*
put pressure on, pressure

presso 1 prp (*vicino a*) near;
nella sede di on the premises
of; *posta* care of; *vive ~ i genitori* he lives with his parents; *lavoro ~ la FIAT* I work
for FIAT **2** m: *nei -i di* in the
vicinity of; **pressoché** almost

prestare lend; *~ ascolto / aiuto a qu* listen to /
help s.o.; **prestarsi** offer

one's services; (*essere adatto*)
lend itself (*a* to); **prestazio-
ne** *f* service; **prestito** *m* loan;
in ~ on loan; **dare in ~** lend;
prendere in ~ borrow

presto (*fra poco*) soon; (*in
fretta*) quickly; (*di buon'ora*)
early; **a ~!** see you soon!;
far ~ be quick

presumere presume; **presuntuoso** presumptuous

prete *m* priest

pretendere claim; **pretesa** *f*
pretension

pretesto *m* pretext

pretura *f* magistrates' court,
Am circuit court

prevalenza *f* prevalence; **in ~**
prevalently; **prevalere** prevail

prevedere foresee, predict;
tempo forecast; *di legge* provide for; **prevedibile** predictable

prevendita *f* advance sale

prevenire *domanda, desiderio*
anticipate; (*evitare*) prevent;
preventivo *1 agg* preventive
2 *m* estimate; **prevenzione** *f*
prevention

previdenza *f* foresight; **~ sociale** social security, *Am*
welfare

previsione *f* forecast; **-i** *pl del
tempo* weather forecast;
previsto *pp* ☞ **prevedere**

prezioso precious

prezzemolo *m* parsley

prezzo *m* price; **a buon ~**
cheap

prigione *f* prison; **prigioniero**
m, **-a** *f* prisoner

prima[1] *avv* before; (*in primo
luogo*) first; **~ di** before; **~
di fare qc** before doing sth;
~ o poi sooner or later; **~
che** before; **~ quanto** as
soon as possible

prima[2] *f* FERR first class;
AUTO first; TEA first night

primavera *f* spring

primitivo primitive; (*iniziale*)
original

primizia *f* early crop

primo *1 agg* first **2** *m*, **-a** *f* first;
ai -i del mese at the begin-
ning of the month; **sulle -e**
in the beginning, at first **3**
m GASTR first course, starter; **primogenito 1** *agg* first-
born **2** *m*, **-a** *f* first-born

principale 1 *agg* main **2** *m*
boss

principato *m* principality;
principe *m* prince; **principessa** *f* princess

principiante *m/f* beginner;
principio *m* start, beginning; (*norma*) principle; **al
~** at the start, in the beginning; **per ~** as a matter of
principle

privare deprive (*di* of); **pri-
varsi** deprive o.s. (*di* of)

privatizzare privatize; **privato 1** *agg* private; **in ~** in private **2** *m* private citizen

privilegiare favour, *Am* favor,
prefer; **privilegiato** privileged; **privilegio** *m* privilege

privo: ~ *di* lacking in; ~ *di grassi* fat-free

pro 1 *m inv:* **i ~ e i contro** the pros and cons; **a che ~?** what's the point? 2 *prp* for; ~ *capite* per capita, each

probabile probable; **probabilità** *f inv* probability

problema *m* problem

proboscide *f* trunk

procedere carry on; *fig (agire)* proceed; **procedimento** *m* process

procedura *f* procedure; DIR proceedings

processare try

processione *f* procession

processo *m* process; DIR trial

procinto *m:* **essere in ~** *di* be about to

proclamare proclaim

procura *f* power of attorney; **Procura di Stato** public prosecutor's office; *per* ~ by proxy; **procurare** *(causare)* cause; ~ *qc a qu* cause s.o. sth; **procurarsi** get hold of; **procuratore** *m*, *-trice f* person with power of attorney; DIR lawyer for the prosecution; ~ *generale* Attorney General

prodotto 1 *pp* ☞ **produrre** 2 *m* product; **produco** ☞ **produrre**; **produrre** produce; *danni* cause; **produttivo** productive; **produttore** *m*, *-trice f* producer; **produzione** *f* production

prof. ssa (= **professoressa**)

Prof. (= Professor)

profanare desecrate

professionale professional; *scuola, corso* vocational; **professione** *f* profession; **professionista** *m/f* professional; **libero** ~ self-employed person

professore *m*, *-essa f* teacher; *d'università* professor

proficuo profitable

profilattico prophylactic

profilo *m* profile

profitto *m (vantaggio)* advantage

profondità *f inv* depth; FOT ~ *di campo* depth of field; **profondo** deep

profugo *m*, *-a f* refugee

profumare perfume; **profumeria** *f* perfume shop; **profumo** *m* perfume

progettare plan; **progetto** *m* design; *di costruzione* project; ~ *di legge* bill

prognosi *f inv* prognosis

programma *m* programme, *Am* program; INFOR program; ~ *televisivo* TV programme; **avere in** ~ have planned; **programmare** plan; INFOR program; **programmatore** *m*, *-trice f* programmer; **programmazione** *f* programming; FIN ~ *economica* economic planning; INFOR **linguaggio** *m* *di* ~ programming language

progredire progress; **progressivo** progressive; **pro-**

gresso *m* progress; *fare -i* make progress

proibire ban, prohibit; *~ a qu di fare qc* forbid s.o. to do sth

proiettare throw; *film* screen, show; *fig* project; proiettile *m* projectile

proiettore *m* projector; *~ per diapositive* slide projector

proletario 1 *agg* proletariat 2 *m* proletarian

pro loco *f inv* local tourist board

prologo *m* prologue

prolunga *f* EL extension cord; prolungare extend; *nel tempo* prolong, extend; prolungarsi *di strada* extend; *di riunione* go on

promemoria *m inv* memo

promessa *f* promise; promesso *pp* ☞ *promettere*; promettere promise; *~ bene* look promising

promontorio *m* promontory, headland

promosso *pp* ☞ *promuovere*; promozione *f* promotion; EDU year; *~ delle vendite* sales promotion; promuovere promote; EDU move up

pronome *m* pronoun

prontezza *f* readiness, promptness; *(rapidità)* speediness, promptness; *~ di spirito* quick thinking; pronto *(preparato)* ready (*a fare qc* to do sth; *per qc*

for sth); TELEC *~!* hello!; *~ soccorso* first aid; *in ospedale* accident and emergency, A&E

pronuncia *f* pronunciation; pronunciare pronounce; pronunciarsi give an opinion (*su* on)

propaganda *f* propaganda; propagare propagate; *fig* spread; propagarsi spread (*anche fig*)

propenso inclined (*a fare qc* to do sth)

propongo ☞ *proporre*; proporre propose; proporsi stand (*come* as); *~ di fare qc* intend to do sth

proporzionato in proportion (*a* to); proporzione *f* proportion; *in ~* in proportion (*a, con* to)

proposito *m* intention; *a ~* by the way; *a ~ di* about, with reference to; *di ~* on purpose

proposizione *f* GRAM sentence

proposta *f* proposal; proposto *pp* ☞ *proporre*

proprietà *f inv* property; *diritto* ownership; proprietario *m*, -a *f* owner

proprio 1 *agg* own; *(caratteristico)* typical; *(adatto)* proper; *nome m ~* proper noun; *amor m ~* pride 2 *avv (davvero)* really 3 *m (beni)* personal property; *lavorare in ~* be self-employed

propulsore *m* propeller

prora f prow

proroga f postponement; (prolungamento) extension; **prorogare** (rinviare) postpone; (prolungare) extend

prosa f prose

prosciogliere release; DIR acquit

prosciugare drain; di sole dry up

prosciutto m ham; **~ cotto** cooked ham; **~ crudo** salted air-dried ham

proseguimento m continuation; **proseguire 1** v/t continue 2 v/i continue, carry on

prospettiva f perspective; (panorama) view; (possibilità) prospect; fig point of view

prospetto m disegno elevation; (facciata) facade; (tabella) table

prossimamente shortly, soon; **prossimità** f inv proximity; **in ~** near; **prossimo 1** agg close; **la ~a volta** the next time 2 m fellow human being

prostituta f prostitute

protagonista m/f protagonist

proteggere protect (da from)

proteina f protein

protesi f inv prosthesis; **~ dentaria** false teeth

protesta f protest; **protestante** agg, m/f Protestant; **protestare** protest

protetto pp ☞ **proteggere**; **protezione** f protection

prova f (esame) test; (tentativo) attempt; (testimonianza) proof; di abito fitting; SP heat; TEA **-e pl** rehearsal; TEA **-e pl generali** dress rehearsal; **mettere alla ~** put to the test; **provare** test, try out; vestito try (on); (dimostrare) prove; TEA rehearse; **~ a fare qc** try to do sth

provengo ☞ **provenire**; **provenienza** f origin; **provenire come** (da from); **proventi** mpl income

proverbio m proverb

provetta f test-tube

provincia f province; **provinciale 1** agg provincial 2 m/f provincial 3 f A road, Am highway

provino m screen-test; (campione) sample

provocante provocative; **provocare** (causare) cause; (sfidare) provoke; invidia arouse

provvedere 1 v/t provide (di with) 2 v/i: **~ a** take care of; **provvedimento** m measure

provvigione f commission

provvisorio provisional

provvista f: **far ~ di qc** stock up on sth; **provvisto 1** pp ☞ **provvedere 2** agg: **essere ~ di** be provided with

prozio m, **-a** f great-uncle; donna great-aunt

prua f prow

prudente careful, cautious;

prudenza f care, caution
prudere: **mi prude la mano** my hand itches
prugna f plum; **~ secca** prune
prurito m itch
P.S. (= **Pubblica Sicurezza**) police; (= **post scriptum**) PS (= post scriptum)
pseudo ... pseudo ...
pseudonimo m pseudonym
psicanalisi f psychoanalysis; **psicanalista** m/f psychoanalyst
psiche f psyche
psichiatra m/f psychiatrist
psicologia f psychology; **psicologico** psychological; **psicologo** m, **-a** f psychologist
psicosi f inv psychosis
psicoterapia f psychotherapy
P.T.P. (= **Posto Telefonico Pubblico**) public telephone
pubblicare publish; **pubblicazione** f publication; **-i** pl (**matrimoniali**) banns; **pubblicità** f inv publicity; annuncio advert; **fare ~ a** evento publicize; **prodotto** advertise; **pubblicitario 1** agg advertising **2** m, **-a** f publicist
pubblico 1 agg public **2** m public; (spettatori) audience; **in ~** in public
pube m pubis
pubertà f puberty
pudore m modesty
pugilato m boxing; **pugile** m boxer
pugnalare stab; **pugnale** m dagger

pugno m fist; (colpo) punch; quantità handful; **fare a ~i** come to blows
pulce f flea
pulcino m chick
puledro m, **-a** f colt; femmina filly
pulire clean; **pulito** clean; fig cleaned-out; **pulitura** f cleaning; **~ a secco** dry cleaning; **pulizia** f cleanliness; **fare le -e** do the cleaning
pullman m inv bus, Br anche coach
pullover m inv pullover
pullulare: **~ di** be swarming with
pulpito m pulpit
pulsante m button; **pulsazione** f pulsation
pungere prick; di ape sting; **pungiglione** m sting
punibile punishable (**con** by); **punire** punish; **punizione** f punishment; SP (**calcio** m di) **~** free kick
punta f di spillo, coltello point; di dita, lingua tip; GEOG peak; fig touch, trace; **puntare 1** v/t pin (**su** to); (dirigere) point (**verso** at); (scommettere) bet (**su** on); fig **~ i piedi** dig one's heels in **2** v/i: **~ a** successo aspire to; **puntata** f installment, Am installment; (scommessa) bet
punteggiatura f punctuation; **punteggio** m score
puntiglioso punctilious

puntina *f di giradischi* stylus; ~ **(da disegno)** drawing pin, *Am* thumbtack; **puntino** *m* dot; **a** ~ perfectly; **punto 1** *pp* ☞ **pungere 2** *m* point; MED, *(maglia)* stitch; ~ **di vista** point of view; ~ **cardinale** point of the compass; **fino a che** ~ **sei arrivato?** how far have you got?; **alle dieci in** ~ at ten o'clock exactly *o* on the dot; ~ **(fermo)** full stop, *Am* period; **due -i** colon; ~ **e virgola** semi-colon; ~ **esclamativo** exclamation mark, *Am* exclamation point; ~ **interrogativo** question mark; **essere sul** ~ **di fare qc** be on the point of doing sth

puntuale punctual; **puntualità** *f* punctuality; **puntualizzare** make clear

puntura *f di ape* sting; *di ago* prick

punzecchiare prick; *fig (provocare)* tease

può, puoi ☞ **potere**

pupazzo *m* puppet; ~ **di neve** snowman

pupilla *f* pupil

purché provided

pure 1 *cong* even if; *(tuttavia)* (and) yet **2** *avv* too, as well; **pur di** in order to; **venga** ~ **avanti!** do come in!

purè *m inv* purée

purga *f* purge; **purgante** *m* laxative

puro pure

purtroppo unfortunately

pus *m* pus

pustola *f* pimple

puttana *f* P whore

puzza *f* stink; **puzzare** stink (**di** *of*); **puzzo** *m* stink; **puzzola** *f* ZO polecat; **puzzolente** stinking

p.v. (= **prossimo venturo**) next

Q

q (= **quintale**) 100 kilos

qua here; **passa di** ~ come this way; **al di** ~ **di** on this side of

quaderno *m* exercise book

quadrante *m* quadrant; *di orologio* dial

quadrare *di conti* balance; *fig* **i conti non quadrano** there's something fishy going on; **quadrato** *m/agg* square

quadrifoglio *m* four-leaf clover

quadro 1 *agg* square **2** *m* painting, picture; MAT square; **a -i** check *attr*, *Am* checkered

quadruplo *m/agg* quadruple

quaggiù down here

quaglia *f* quail

qualche a few; *(un certo)*

some; *interrogativo* **any; ~ co-sa** something; **~** **volta** sometime; *alcune volte* a few times; *a volte* sometimes; *in ~ luogo* somewhere; *in ~ modo* somehow

qualcosa something; *interrogativo* anything, something; **qualcos'altro** something else; **~ da mangiare** something to eat; **~ di bello** something beautiful

qualcuno someone, somebody; *in interrogazioni anche* anyone, anybody; *c'è ~?* is anybody there?

quale 1 *agg* what; *~ libro vuoi?* which book do you want? **2** *pron*: *prendi un libro – ~?* take a book – which one?; *il / la ~ persona* who, that; *cosa* which, that; *la persona della ~ stai parlando* the person you're talking about **3** *avv* as

qualifica *f* qualification; **qualificare** qualify; *(definire)* describe; **qualificarsi** give one's name *(come* as); *a esame, gara* qualify; **qualificato** qualified

qualità *f inv* quality; *di prima ~* top quality

qualora in the event that

qualsiasi any; *non importa quale* whatever; **~ persona** anyone; **~ cosa faccia** whatever I do

qualunque any; *uno ~* any one; **~ cosa** anything; **~ co-**

sa faccia whatever I do; *in ~ stagione* whatever the season

qualvolta: ogni ~ every time that

quando when; *da ~?* how long?; *~ vengo* when I come; *ogni volta che* whenever I come

quantità *f inv* quantity, amount; **quantitativo** *m* quantity, amount

quanto 1 *agg* how much; *con nomi plurali* how many; *tutti -i pl* every single one *sg*; *-i ne abbiamo oggi?* what is the date today? **2** *avv*: *~ dura ancora?* how long will it go on for?; *~ a me* as for me; *~ costa?* how much is it; *in ~* since, because; *per ~ ne sappia* as far as I know

quaranta forty

quarantena *f* quarantine

quarantenne 1 *agg* forty or so **2** *m/f* person in his / her forties; **quarantesimo** fortieth

quaresima *f* Lent

quarta *f* AUTO fourth (gear)

quartiere *m* district; MIL quarters; **~ generale** headquarters

quarto 1 *agg* fourth **2** *m* fourth; *(quarta parte)* quarter; **~ d'ora** quarter of an hour

quarzo *m* quartz

quasi almost; **~ mai** hardly ever

quassù up here

quattordicesimo fourteenth;
quattordici fourteen
quattrini *mpl* money
quattro four; *farsi in ~ per fare qc* go to a lot of trouble to
do sth; **quattrocchi**: *a ~* in
private; **quattrocento 1** *agg*
four hundred **2** *m*: *il Quattrocento* the fifteenth century; **quattromila** four thousand
quegli, quei *☞* **quello**
quello 1 *agg* that, *pl* those **2**
pron that (one), *pl* those
(ones); *~ che* the one that;
tutto ~ che all (that), everything (that)
quercia *f* oak
querela *f* legal action; *sporgere ~ contro qc* take legal
action against s.o.
quesito *m* question
questi *☞* **questo**
questionario *m* questionnaire; **questione** *f* question;
è fuori ~ it is out of the question
questo 1 *agg* this, *pl* these **2**
pron this (one), *pl* these
(ones); *~ qui* this one here;
per ~ for that reason; *-a*

poi! well I'm blowed
questore *m* chief of police;
questura *f* police headquarters
qui here; *~ vicino* near here;
passa di ~! come this
way!; *di ~ a un mese* a
month from now
quiete *f* peace and quiet
quindi 1 *avv* then **2** *cong*
therefore
quindicesimo fifteenth;
quindici fifteen; **quindicina**
f: *una ~* about fifteen; **quinta** *f* AUTO fifth (gear); TEA *le
-e* the wings; **quintale** *m*
hundred kilos; **quinto** fifth
quota *f* share, quota; (*altitudine*) altitude; **quotare** (*valutare*) value; FIN **quotate in borsa** listed *o* quoted on the
Stock Exchange; **quotato**
respected; **quotazione** *f di
azioni* value, price; *~ d'acquisto* bid price; *~ di vendita* offer price
quotidianamente daily;
quotidiano 1 *agg* daily **2** *m*
daily (newspaper)
quoziente *m*: *~ d'intelligenza*
IQ

R

rabarbaro *m* rhubarb
rabbia *f* rage; (*stizza*) anger;
MED rabies *sg*; *fare ~ a qu*
make s.o. angry
rabbino *m* rabbi

rabbioso *gesto, sguardo* of
rage; *cane* rabid
rabbrividire shudder; *per paura* shiver
raccapricciante appalling

raccattare (*tirar su*) pick up

racchetta *f* racquet; **~ da sci** ski pole

raccogliere (*tirar su*) pick up; (*radunare*) gather; AGR harvest; **raccoglitore** *m* ring binder; **~ del vetro** bottle bank; **raccolgo** ☞ **raccogliere**; **raccolta** *f* collection; AGR harvest; **fare la ~ di francobolli** collect stamps; **raccolto 1** *pp* ☞ **raccogliere 2** *m* harvest

raccomandabile: **un tipo poco ~** a shady character; **raccomandare 1** *v/t* recommend **2** *v/i*: **~ a qu di fare qc** tell s.o. to do sth; **raccomandata** *f* recorded delivery (letter), *Am* certified mail; **raccomandazione** *f* recommendation

raccontare tell; **racconto** *m* story

raccordo *m* TEC connection; **strada** *f* slip road, *Am* ramp; **~ anulare** ring road, *Am* beltway

radar *m inv* radar

raddoppiare double; **sforzi** redouble

raddrizzare straighten

radere shave; (*sfiorare* skim; **~ al suolo** raze to the ground; **radersi** shave

radiare strike off

radiatore *m* radiator

radicale radical; **radice** *f* root; **~ quadrata** square root

radio *f inv* radio; (*stazione*) ra-

dio station; **radioascoltatore** *m*, **-trice** *f* (radio) listener; **radioattività** *f* radioactivity; **radioattivo** radioactive; **radiocronaca** *f* (radio) commentary; **radiofonico** radio *attr*; **radiografia** *f* X-ray; **radiosveglia** *f* clock radio; **radiotaxi** *m inv* taxi, cab; **radiotelefono** *m* radio; **radioterapia** *f* radiation treatment; **radiotrasmittente** *f apparecchio* radio transmitter; **stazione** radio station

rado *pettine* wide-toothed; *alberi, capelli* sparse; **di ~** seldom

radunare, **radunarsi** collect, gather; **raduno** *m* rally

rafano *m* horseradish

raffermo *pane* stale

raffica *f* gust; **di mitragliatrice** burst

raffigurare represent

raffinatezza *f* refinement; **raffinato** *fig* refined; **raffineria** *f* refinery

rafforzare strengthen

raffreddare cool; **raffreddarsi** cool down; MED catch cold; **raffreddato**: **essere ~** have a cold; **raffreddore** *m* cold; **~ da fieno** hay fever

rag. (= *ragioniere*) accountant

ragazza *f* girl; **la mia ~** my girlfriend

ragazzo *m* boy; **il mio ~** my boyfriend

raggio *m* ray; MAT radius; **~**

d'azione range; *fig* duties; **-i** *pl* **X** X-rays

raggirare fool, take in; **raggiro** *m* trick

raggiungere *luogo* reach, get to; *persona* join; *scopo* achieve

raggomitolarsi curl up

raggrinzito wrinkled

ragionamento *m* reasoning; **ragionare** reason; **ragione** *f* reason; *(diritto)* right; **aver ~** be right; **dare ~ a qu** admit that s.o. is right; **ragioneria** *f* book-keeping; EDU *high school specializing in business studies*; **ragionevole** reasonable; **ragioniere** *m*, **-a** *f* accountant

ragnatela *f* spider's web; **ragno** *m* spider

ragù *m inv* meat sauce for pasta

rallegramenti *mpl* congratulations; **rallegrare** cheer up; **rallegrarsi** cheer up; **~ con qu di qc** congratulate s.o. on sth

rallentare slow down; **rallentatore**: **al ~** in slow motion

ramanzina *f* lecture

rame *m* copper

rammaricarsi be disappointed *(di* at)

rammendare darn

ramo *m* branch; **ramoscello** *m* twig

rampa *f* flight; **~ d'accesso** slip road, *Am* ramp; **rampicante 1** *agg* climbing; **pianta**

f **~** climber **2** *m* climber

rampone *m* crampon

rana *f* frog

rancore *m* rancour, *Am* rancor

randagio stray

rango *m* rank

rannicchiarsi huddle up

rannuvolarsi cloud over

ranocchio *m* frog

rapa *f* turnip

rapace 1 *m* bird of prey **2** *agg fig* predatory

rapida *f* rapids; **rapidità** *f* speed, rapidity; **rapido 1** *agg* quick, fast; *crescita, aumento* rapid **2** *m* **(treno** *m***) ~** intercity train

rapimento *m* abduction, kidnapping

rapina *f* robbery; **rapinare** rob; **rapinatore** *m*, **-trice** *f* robber

rapire abduct, kidnap; **rapitore** *m*, **-trice** *f* abductor, kidnapper

rappacificazione *f* reconciliation

rapporto *m* *(resoconto)* report; *(relazione)* relationship; *(nesso)* connection; **in ~ a** in connection with

rappresentante *m/f* representative; **rappresentanza** *f* agency; **~ esclusiva** sole agency; **rappresentare** represent; TEA perform; **rappresentazione** *f* representation; TEA performance

rarità *f inv* rarity; **raro** rare

rasare shave; **rasatura** *f* shaving

raschiare scrape; *ruggine, sporco* scrape off; **raschiarsi**: ~ **la gola** clear one's throat

rasentare *(sfiorare)* scrape; *fig (avvicinarsi)* verge on; ~ **il muro** hug the wall; **rasente**: ~ **a** very close to

rasoio *m* razor

rassegna *f* festival; *di pittura ecc* exhibition; **passare in** ~ review; **rassegnarsi** resign o.s *(a* to)

rasserenarsi *di tempo* clear up

rassicurare reassure

rassomigliare: ~ **a** look like, resemble; **rassomigliarsi** look like *o* resemble each other

rastrellare rake; *fig* comb; **rastrelliera** *f* rack; ~ **per biciclette** bike rack; **rastrello** *m* rake

rata *f* instalment, *Am* installment; **a -e** in instalments; **rateale**: **pagamento** *m* ~ payment in instalments *o Am* installments; **vendita** *f* ~ hire purchase, *Am* installment plan

ratto *m* ZO rat

rattoppare patch; **rattoppo** *m* patch

rattrappito stiff

rattristare sadden; **rattristarsi** become sad

raucedine *f* hoarseness; **rau-**co hoarse

ravanello *m* radish

ravioli *mpl* ravioli *sg*

ravvicinare move closer; *(riappacificare)* reconcile

ravvivare revive

razionale rational; **razionare** ration; **razione** *f* ration

razza *f* race; *fig* sort, kind; ZO breed

razzia *f* raid

razziale racial; **razzismo** *m* racism; **razzista** *agg*, *m/f* racist

razzo *m* rocket

re *m inv* king; MUS D

reagire react *(a* to)

reale *(vero)* real; *(regale)* royal; **realista** *m/f* realist

realizzabile feasible; **realizzare** realize; *progetto* carry out; **realizzarsi** *di sogno* come true; *di persona* find, find fulfilment *o Am* fulfillment

realmente really; **realtà** *f inv* reality; **in** ~ in fact, actually

reato *m* (criminal) offence *o Am* offense

reattore *m* AVIA jet engine; *aereo* jet; ~ **nucleare** nuclear reactor; **reazione** *f* reaction

recapitare deliver; **recapito** *m* delivery; *(indirizzo)* address; ~ **telefonico** phone number

recarsi go

recensione *f* review; **recensire** review

recente recent; **recentemen-**

te recently

recintare enclose; **recinto** *m* enclosure; *steccato* fence

recipiente *m* container, recipient

reciproco mutual, reciprocal

recita *f* performance; recitare 1 *v/t* recite; TEA play (the part of); *preghiera* say 2 *v/i* act

reclamare 1 *v/i* complain 2 *v/t* claim

réclame *f inv* advert; reclamizzare advertise

reclamo *m* complaint

reclusione *f* seclusion

record *m inv* record

recuperare ☞ **ricuperare**

redatto *pp* ☞ **redigere**; redattore *m*, **-trice** *f* editor; *di articolo* writer; **~ capo** editor-in-chief

reddito *m* income

redigere *testo*, *articolo* write; *lista* draw up

redini *fpl* reins

referendum *m inv* referendum

referenza *f* reference

referto *m* (official) report

refettorio *m* refectory

refurtiva *f* stolen property

regalare give; regalino *m* little gift o present; regalo *m* gift, present

regata *f* (boat) race

reggere 1 *v/t* (*sostenere*) support; (*tenere in mano*) hold; (*sopportare*) bear 2 *v/i di ragionamento* stand up; reg-

gersi stand

reggia *f* palace

reggipetto *m*, reggiseno *m* bra, *Am* brassiere

regia *f* production; *di film* direction

regime *m* régime; MED diet

regina *f* queen

regionale regional; regione *f* region

regista *m/f* director; TEA producer

registrare record; (*rilevare*) show, register; registratore *m*: **~ a cassetta**) cassette recorder; registrazione *f* recording; registro *m* register

regno *m* kingdom; *periodo* reign

regola *f* rule; **in ~** in order; regolabile adjustable; regolamento *m* regulation; regolare 1 *v/t* regulate; *spese* cut down on; TEC adjust; *questione* sort out; *conto*, *debito* settle 2 *agg* regular

regredire regress

relativo relative (**a** to); (*corrispondente*) relevant; relatore *m*, **-trice** *f* speaker; relazione *f* relationship; (*esposizione*) report; **avere una ~ con qu** have a relationship with s.o.

religione *f* religion; religiosa *f* nun; religioso 1 *agg* religious 2 *m* monk

relitto *m* wreck

remare row; remo *m* oar

remoto remote

remunerare pay; **remunerazione** f payment, remuneration

rendere (restituire) give back, return; (fruttare) yield; senso, idea render; **~ felice** make happy; **rendimento** m di macchina, impiegato performance; **rendita** f income

rene m kidney

reparto m department

repentaglio: **mettere a ~** risk, endanger

reperibile available; **difficilmente ~** difficult to find; **reperire** find; **reperto** m find; DIR exhibit

replica f replica; TV, TEA repeat; (risposta) answer, reply; **replicare** repeat; (ribattere) reply, answer

reportage m inv report

represso pp ☞ **reprimere**; **reprimere** repress

repubblica f republic

reputare consider; **reputarsi** consider o.s.; **reputazione** f reputation

requisire requisition; **requisito** m requirement

resa f surrender; (restituzione) return; **~ dei conti** settling of accounts

residence m inv block of service flats o Am apartments; **residente** resident; **residenza** f (official) address; (sede) seat; (soggiorno) stay; **residenziale** residential; **zona** f **~** residential area

residuo m remainder

resina f resin

resistente sturdy, strong; **resistere** al freddo ecc stand up to; (opporsi) resist

reso pp ☞ **rendere**

resoconto m report

respingere richiesta reject, turn down; nemico, attacco repel; **respinto** pp ☞ **respingere**

respirare 1 v/t breathe (in) **2** v/i breathe; fig draw breath; **respiratore** m respirator; per apnea snorkel; **respirazione** f breathing; **~ artificiale** artificial respiration; **respiro** m breathing; **trattenere il ~** hold one's breath

responsabile responsible (di for); DIR liable (di for); **responsabilità** f inv responsibility; DIR liability

ressa f crowd

restare stay, remain; (avanzare) be left; **~ indietro** stay behind; **~ perplesso / vedovo** be puzzled / widowed

restaurare restore; **restauro** m restoration

restituire return; salute restore

resto m rest, remainder; (soldi) change; **~ i pl** remains; **del ~** anyway, besides

restringere narrow; vestito take in; **restringersi** di strada narrow; di stoffa shrink

rete f per pescare ecc net; SP goal; INFOR, TELEC, FERR

network
retina *f* ANAT retina
retribuire pay; **retribuzione** *f*
payment
retroattivo retroactive
retrobottega *m inv* back shop
retrocedere retreat; *fig* lose
ground
retrodatare backdate
retromarcia *f* AUTO reverse
(gear)
retroscena *mpl fig* background
retrospettivo *mostra* retrospective
retroterra *m inv* hinterland
retrovisivo: *specchietto* **~** *m*
rearview mirror
retta[1] *f somma* fee
retta[2] *f* MAT straight line
retta[3] *f*: *dare* **~** *a qu* listen to
s.o.
rettangolare rectangular; **rettangolo** *m* rectangle
rettificare correct
rettile *m* reptile
rettilineo straight
rettore *m* rector
reumatismo *m* rheumatism
revisionare *conti* audit; *automobile* MOT; *testo* revise; **revisione** *f di conti* audit; *di
automobile* MOT; *di testo* revision
revoca *f* repeal; **revocare** repeal
ri- re-
riabilitazione *f* rehabilitation
riacquistare get back, regain;
casa buy back

riagganciare TELEC hang up
riallacciare *re*fasten; TELEC
reconnect
rialzare (*alzare di nuovo*) pick
up; (*aumentare*) raise, increase; **rialzo** *m* rise, increase
rianimare *speranze, entusiasmo* revive; (*rallegrare*) cheer
up; MED resuscitate; **riani-
mazione** *f* resuscitation;
centro **m** *di* **~** intensive care
unit
riapertura *f* reopening; **riaprire** reopen
riassumere re-employ; (*riepilogare*) summarize; **riassunto** 1 *pp* ☞ **riassumere** 2 *m*
summary
riavere get back, regain
ribaltabile folding; **ribaltare**
overturn
ribassare 1 *v/t* lower 2 *v/i* fall,
drop; **ribasso** *m* fall, drop;
(*sconto*) discount
ribattere (*replicare*) answer
back; (*insistere*) insist
ribellarsi rebel (*a* against); **ribelle** 1 *agg* rebellious 2 *m/f*
rebel; **ribellione** *f* rebellion
ribes *m inv* currant; **~** *nero*
blackcurrant; **~** *rosso* red-
currant
ribrezzo *m* horror; *fare* **~** *a*
disgust
ricadere fall; (*cadere di nuovo*) fall back; *fig* relapse; **ricaduta** *f* relapse
ricamare embroider
ricambiare change; (*contrac-*

cambiare) return, reciprocate; **ricambio** *m* change; (*sostituzione*) replacement; *pezzo* (spare) part

ricamo *m* embroidery

ricapitolare sum up, recapitulate

ricaricare *batteria* recharge

ricattare blackmail; **ricatto** *m* blackmail

ricavare *denaro* get; **ricavato** *m* di vendita proceeds

ricchezza *f* wealth

riccio[1] *m* ZO hedgehog; **~ di mare** sea urchin

riccio[2] **1** *agg* curly **2** *m* curl

ricciolo *m* curl

ricco 1 *agg* rich; **~ di** rich in **2** *m*, **-a** *f* rich man / woman

ricerca *f* research; *di persona scomparsa, informazione ecc* search (for); EDU project; **alla ~ di** in search of; **ricercare** (*cercare di nuovo*) look again for; (*cercare con cura*) search for; **ricercato 1** *agg* oggetto, *artista* sought-after **2** *m* man wanted by the police

ricetta *f* prescription; GASTR recipe

ricevere receive; *di medico* see patients; **ricevimento** *m* receipt; *festa* reception; **ricevitore** *m* receiver; **ricevuta** *f* receipt

richiamare (*chiamare di nuovo*) call again; (*chiamare indietro*) call back; (*attirare*)

draw; *fig* (*rimproverare*) reprimand

richiedere ask for again; (*necessitare di*) take, require; *documento* apply for; **richiesta** *f* request (*di qc* for sth); **a** (*o* **su**) **~ di** at the request of; **richiesto** *pp* ☞ **richiedere**

riciclare recycle; **riciclabile** recyclable

ricompensa *f* reward; **ricompensare** reward (**qu di** *o* **per qc** s.o. for sth)

riconciliarsi be reconciled

riconoscente grateful; **riconoscenza** *f* gratitude; **riconoscere** recognise; **riconoscimento** *m* recognition

riconquistare reconquer

ricordare remember; (*menzionare*) mention; **~ qc a qu** remind s.o. of sth; **ricordarsi** remember (**di qc** sth; **di fare qc** to do sth); **ricordo** *m* memory; *oggetto* memento; **~** (**di viaggio**) souvenir

ricorrenza *f* recurrence; *di evento* anniversary; **ricorrere** *di date, di festa* take place; **~ a qu** turn to s.o.; **~ a qc** have recourse to sth; **ricorso 1** *pp* ☞ **ricorrere 2** *m* DIR appeal; **avere ~ a** *avvocato, medico* see

ricostruire rebuild; *fig* reconstruct; **ricostruzione** *f* rebuilding; *fig* reconstruction

ricotta *f* ricotta, soft cheese made from ewe's milk

ricoverare admit; **ricovero** *m*

in ospedale admission; *(refugio)* shelter

ricreazione *f* recreation; *nelle scuole* break, *Am* recess

ricredersi change one's mind

ricuperare 1 *v/t* get back, recover; *libertà, fiducia* regain; *spazio* gain; *tempo* make up **2** *v/i* catch up; **recupero** *m* recovery; **~ del centro storico** development of the old town; **~ di debiti** debt collection; EDU *corso m di* ~ remedial course; *materiale m di* **~** scrap; SP *partita f di* **~** rescheduled match

ridare *(restituire)* give back, return; *fiducia, forze* restore

ridere laugh *(di* at*)*

ridicolo 1 *agg* ridiculous **2** *m* ridicule

ridimensionare downsize; *fig* put into perspective

ridotto 1 *pp* ☞ **ridurre 2** *agg:* **a prezzi -i** at reduced prices; **riduco** ☞ **ridurre; ridurre** reduce *(a* to*)*; *prezzi* reduce, cut; *personale* reduce, cut back; **ridursi** decrease; **~ a fare qc** be reduced to doing sth; **~ male** be in a bad way; **~ in miseria** ruin o.s.; **riduzione** *f* reduction, cut

riempire fill (up); *formulario* fill in

rientrare come back; *a casa* come home; **questo non rientrava nei miei piani** that didn't come in to the plan; **rientro** *m* return; **al tuo ~**

when you get back

rifare do again; *(rinnovare)* do up; *stanza* tidy up; *letto* make; **rifarsi** rebuild; *casa* renovate; *guardaroba* replace; **~ di qc** make up for sth

riferimento *m* reference; **riferire** report; **riferirsi: ~ a** refer to

rifiutare, rifiutarsi refuse; **rifiuto** *m* refusal; **-i** *pl* waste, refuse; *(spazzatura)* rubbish

riflessione *f anche* FIS reflection; **riflessivo** thoughtful; GRAM reflexive; **riflesso 1** *pp* ☞ **riflettere 2** *m* reflection; *(gesto istintivo)* reflex *(movement)*; **riflettere 1** *v/t* reflect **2** *v/i* think; **~ su qc** think about sth, reflect on sth; **riflettersi** be reflected; **riflettore** *m* floodlight

riforma *f* reform; **riformare** *(rifare)* re-shape, re-form; *(cambiare)* reform; MIL declare unfit

rifornimento *m* AVIA refuelling, *Am* refueling; **-i** *pl* supplies; **fare ~ di cibo** stock up on food; **fare ~ di benzina** fill up; **rifornire** *macchina* fill up; *frigo* restock, fill *(di* with*)*; **~ il magazzino** restock; **rifornirsi** stock up *(di* on*)*

rifugiarsi take refuge; **rifugiato** *m*, **-a** *f* refugee; **rifugio** *m* shelter; **~ alpino** mountain hut

riga f line; (fila) row; (regolo) rule; in stoffa stripe; nei capelli parting, Am part; **stoffa f a -ghe** striped fabric

rigatoni mpl rigatoni sg

rigenerare regenerate; **rigenerazione** f regeneration

rigetto m MED rejection; fig mental block

rigido (duro) rigid; muscolo, articolazione stiff; clima harsh; fig (severo) strict

rigirare 1 v/i walk around **2** v/t turn over and over; denaro launder; ~ il discorso change the subject; **rigirarsi** turn around; nel letto toss and turn

riglioglioso lush, luxurian

rigore m di clima harshness; (severità) strictness; SP (calcio m di) ~ penalty (kick); rigoroso rigorous

riguardare look at again; (rivedere) review, look at; (riferirsi) be about; non ti riguarda it doesn't concern you; riguardarsi take care of o.s.; **riguardo** m (attenzione) care; (rispetto) respect; ~ a as regards

rilasciare release; documento issue; rilascio m release; di passaporto issue

rilassare, rilassarsi relax; rilassato relaxed

rilegare libro bind

rilevare (ricavare) find; (osservare) notice; ditta buy up

rilievo m relief; fig dare ~ a

qc, mettere qc in ~ emphasize o highlight sth

rima f rhyme; far ~ rhyme

rimandare send again; (restituire) send back; palla return; (rinviare) postpone

rimanente 1 agg remaining **2** m rest, balance; rimanere stay, remain; (avanzare) be left (over); **rimanerci male** be hurt; rimango ☞ **rimanere**

rimarginare, rimarginarsi heal

rimasto pp ☞ **rimanere**

rimbalzare bounce

rimboccare coperte tuck in; **rimboccarsi le maniche** roll up one's sleeves

rimborsare reimburse, pay back; **rimborso** m reimbursement, repayment; ~ spese reimbursement of expenses

rimboschire reforest

rimediare 1 v/i: ~ a make up for, remedy **2** v/t find, scrape together; **rimedio** m remedy; MED medicine

rimescolare mix again; più volte mix thoroughly; caffè stir again

rimessa f di auto garage; degli autobus depot; SP ~ **laterale** throw-in

rimettere put back, return; (affidare) refer; (vomitare) bring up; ~ a posto put back; **ci ho rimesso molti soldi** I lost a lot of money; rimettersi *di tempo* improve; **~ da qc** get over sth

rimodernare modernize

rimorchiare AUTO tow (away); **rimorchiatore** *m* MAR tug; **rimorchio** *m* AUTO tow; *veicolo* trailer

rimorso *m* remorse

rimozione *f* removal

rimpatriare 1 *v/t* repatriate **2** *v/i* go home

rimpiangere regret (**di avere fatto qc** doing sth); *tempi passati, giovinezza* miss; **rimpianto 1** *pp* ☞ **rimpiangere 2** *m* regret

rimpiazzare replace

rimpicciolire 1 *v/t* make smaller **2** *v/i* become smaller, shrink

rimproverare scold; *impiegato* reprimand; **~ qc a qu** reproach s.o. for sth; **rimprovero** *m* scolding

rimuovere remove; (*muovere di nuovo*) move again

rinascere be born again; *di passione, speranza* be revived; *fig* **sentirsi~** feel rejuvenated; **Rinascimento** *m* Renaissance

rincarare 1 *v/t* increase, put up; **~ la dose** make matters worse **2** *v/i* increase in price; **rincaro** *m* price increase

rincasare *venire* come home; *andare* go home

rinchiudere shut up; **rinchiudersi** shut o.s. up

rincorrere run after; **rincorsa**

f run-up; **rincorso** *pp* ☞ **rincorrere**

rincrescere: mi rincresce I'm sorry

rinfacciare: ~ qc a qu cast sth up to s.o.

rinforzare strengthen; **rinforzo** *m* reinforcement; MIL **-i** *pl* reinforcements

rinfrescare cool down; **rinfrescarsi** freshen up; **rinfresco** *m* buffet (*party*)

rinfusa: alla~ any which way, all higgledy-piggledy

ringhiare growl

ringhiera *f* railing

ringiovanire 1 *v/t* make feel younger; *di aspetto* make look younger **2** *v/i* feel younger; *di aspetto* look younger

ringraziamento: un~ a word of thanks; **i miei ~-i** *pl* my thanks; **ringraziare** thank (**di** for)

rinnovare renovate; *guardaroba* replace; *abbonamento* renew; (*ripetere*) renew, repeat; **rinnovarsi** renew itself; (*ripetersi*) be repeated; **rinnovo** *m* renovation; *di guardaroba* replacement; *di abbonamento* renewal; *di richiesta* repetition

rintracciare track down

rinuncia *f* renunciation (**a** of); **rinunciare** give up (**a** sth)

rinvenire 1 *v/t* recover; *resti* discover **2** *v/i* regain consciousness, come round

rinviare (*mandare indietro*) return; (*posticipare*) postpone; *letteratura* refer; **rinvio** *m* return; *di riunione* postponement; *in un testo* cross-reference

rione *m* district

riordinare tidy up

riorganizzare reorganize

riparare 1 *v/t* (*proteggere*) protect (*da* from); (*aggiustare*) repair; *un torto* make up for **2** *v/i* escape; **ripararsi dalla pioggia** take shelter (*da* from); *riparato* sheltered; **riparazione** *f* repair; *fig di torto* putting right; **riparo** *m* shelter; **mettersi al ~** take shelter

ripartire¹ *v/i* leave again

ripartire² *v/t* divide up

ripassare 1 *v/i* ☞ **passare 2** *v/t col ferro* iron; *lezione* revise, *Am* review

ripensamento *m*: **avere un ~** have second thoughts; **ripensare**: **~ a qc** think about sth again; **ci ho ripensato** I've changed my mind

ripetere repeat; **ripetizione** *f* repetition; **dare -i a qu** tutor s.o.

ripido steep

ripiegare 1 *v/t* fold up again **2** *v/i* fall back; **ripiego** *m* makeshift (solution)

ripieno 1 *agg* full; GASTR stuffed **2** *m* stuffing

riporre put away; *speranze* place

riportare take back; (*riferire*) report; *vittoria, successo* achieve; MAT carry over; *danni* sustain

riposarsi rest; **riposo** *m* rest

ripostiglio *m* boxroom, storeroom

riprendere take again; (*prendere indietro*) take back; *lavoro* go back to; FOT record; **~ a fare qc** start doing sth again; **riprendersi**: **~ da qc** get over sth; **ripresa** *f* resumption; *di vestito* alteration; *film* shot; AUTO acceleration; **a più -e** several times

riproduco ☞ **riprodurre**; **riprodurre** reproduce; **riprodursi** *di animali* breed, reproduce; *di situazione* happen again; **riproduzione** *f* reproduction; **~ vietata** copyright

riprovare 1 *v/t* feel again; *vestito* try on again **2** *v/i* try again

ripugnante disgusting, repugnant; **ripugnare**: **~ a qu** disgust s.o.

ripulire clean again; (*rimettere in ordine*) tidy (up)

risa *fpl* laughter

risalire 1 *v/t scale* go back up **2** *v/i* (*rincarare*) go back up; **~ a** go back to; **risalita** *f* ascent; **impianti** *mpl* **di ~** ski lifts

risaltare stand out; **risalto**:

mettere in ~, dare ~ a highlight

risanamento *m* redevelopment; FIN improvement

risarcimento *m* compensation; **risarcire** *persona* compensate (**di** for); *danno* compensate for

risata *f* laugh

riscaldamento *m* heating; **~ della temperatura terrestre** global warming

riscaldare heat *o* warm up; **riscaldarsi** warm o.s.

rischiararsi clear (up); *di cielo* clear (up); **~ in volto** cheer up

rischiare 1 *v/t* risk **2** *v/i:* **~ di sbagliare** risk making a mistake; **rischio** *m* risk; **rischioso** risky

riscontrare (*confrontare*) compare; (*controllare*) check; (*incontrare*) come up against; *errori* come across

riscuotere FIN *soldi* draw; *assegno* cash; *fig* earn

risentimento *m* resentment; **risentire 1** *v/t* hear again **2** *v/i* feel the effects; **risentirsi** TELEC talk again; (*offendersi*) take offence *o Am* offense

riserva *f* reserve; *fig* reservation; AUTO **essere in ~** be running out of fuel; **fare ~ di** stock up on; **riservare** keep; (*prenotare*) book, reserve; **riservarsi** reserve; **mi riservo di non accettare**

I reserve the right to not accept; **riservato** reserved; (*confidenziale*) confidential

risiedere be resident, reside

riso[1] *pp* ☞ **ridere 2** *m* laughing

riso[2] *m* rice

risolto *pp* ☞ **risolvere**; **risoluto** determined; **risoluzione** *f* resolution; (*soluzione*) solution; *di contratto* cancellation; **prendere una ~** make a decision; **risolvere** solve; (*decidere*) resolve; **risolversi** be solved; (*decidersi*) decide, resolve; **~ in nulla** come to nothing

risorgere rise; *fig: di industria ecc* experience a rebirth; **Risorgimento** *m* Risorgimento, *the reunification of Italy*

risorsa *f* resource

risotto *m* risotto

risparmiare save; *fig* spare; **risparmio** *m* saving, **-i** *pl* savings

rispettare respect; *legge, contratto* abide by; **rispettivo** respective; **rispetto 1** *m* respect **2** *prp:* **~ a** (*confronto a*) compared with; (*in relazione a*) as regards

risplendere shine, glitter

rispondere answer (**a** sth), reply (**a** to); (*reagire*) respond; *saluto* acknowledge; **~ di qc** be accountable for sth (**a** to); **risposta** *f* answer, reply; (*reazione*) response

rissa *f* brawl

ristabilire *ordine* restore; *regolamento* re-introduce; **ristabilirsi** recover

ristampa *f* reprint

ristorante *m* restaurant

ristretto: *caffè m inv* ~ very strong coffee

ristrutturare restructure; **ristrutturazione** *f* restructuring

risultare result; (*rivelarsi*) turn out; **risultato** *m* result

risurrezione *f* REL Resurrection

risvegliare, **risvegliarsi** *fig* reawaken

ritardare 1 *v/t* delay **2** *v/i* be late; *di orologio* be slow; **ritardatario** *m*, -a *f* latecomer; **ritardo** *m* delay; *essere in* ~ be late

ritenere (*credere*) believe; **ritenersi**: *si ritiene molto intelligente* he' thinks he is very intelligent; **ritenuta** *f* deduction

ritirare withdraw, pull back; (*tirare di nuovo*) throw again; *proposta* withdraw; (*prelevare*) collect; **ritirarsi** (*restringersi*) shrink; ~ *da gara, esame ecc* withdraw from; **ritiro** *m* withdrawal

ritmo *m* rhythm

rito *m* ceremony

ritoccare touch up

ritornare *venire* get back, come back, return; *andare* go back, return; *su argomento* go back (*su* over); ~ *verde*

turn green again

ritornello *m* refrain

ritorno *m* return; *essere di* ~ be back

ritrarre pull away; PITT paint

ritrattare retract

ritratto *m* portrait

ritrovare find; (*riacquistare*) regain; **ritrovarsi** meet again; (*capitare*) find o.s.; (*orientarsi*) get one's bearings; **ritrovo** *m* meeting; *luogo* meeting place

riunione *f* meeting; *di amici, famiglia* reunion; **riunire** gather; **riunirsi** meet

riuscire succeed; (*essere capace*) manage; *non riesco a capire* I can't understand; ~ *in qc* be successful in sth; **riuscita** *f* success; **riuscito** successful

riutilizzare re-use

riva *f* shore

rivale *m/f, agg* rival *attr*, **rivalità** *f inv* rivalry

rivalutare revalue; *persona* change one's mind about

rivedere see again; (*ripassare*) review, look at again; (*verificare*) check

rivelare reveal

rivendere resell

rivendicare demand

rivendita *f negozio* retail outlet; **rivenditore** *m*, **-trice** *f* retailer; ~ *specializzato* dealer

rivestimento *m* covering; **rivestire** (*foderare*) cover; *ruo-*

lo play; *carica* fill

rivincita *f* return game; **prendersi la ~** get one's revenge

rivista *f* magazine; TEA revue; MIL review

rivolgere turn; *domanda* address (*a qu* to s.o.); **~ la parola a qu** speak to s.o., address s.o; **rivolgersi: ~ a qu** apply to s.o. (**per** for)

rivolta revolt; **rivoltare** turn; (*mettere sottosopra*) turn upside down; (*disgustare*) revolt; **rivoltella** *f* revolver; **rivoluzione** *f* revolution

rizzare put up; *bandiera* raise; *orecchie* prick up; **rizzarsi** straighten up; **mi si sono rizzati i capelli in testa** my hair stood on end

roba *f* things, stuff; **~ da matti!** would you believe it!

robot *m inv* robot; *da cucina* food processor

robusto sturdy

rocca *f* fortress

roccia *f* rock; **roccioso** rocky

rock *m inv* MUS rock

roco hoarse

rodaggio *m* running in; *fig* **sono ancora in ~** I'm still finding my feet

rodere gnaw at; **rodersi:** **~ dalla gelosia** be eaten up with jealousy; **roditore** *m* rodent

rogna *f* F *di cane* mange; *problema* hassle

rognone *m* *di animale* kidney

Roma *f* Rome

Romania *f* Romania

romanico Romanesque; **romano 1** *agg* Roman **2** *m*, **-a** *f* Roman

romantico 1 *agg* romantic **2** *m*, **-a** *f* romantic

romanzo 1 *agg* Romance **2** *m* novel; **~ giallo** thriller

rombo[1] *m* rumble

rombo[2] *m* MAT rhombus

romeno 1 *agg* Romanian **2** *m*, **-a** *f* Romanian

rompere 1 *v/t* break; F **~ le scatole a qu** get on s.o.'s nerves F **2** *v/i* F be a pain F; rompersi break; **~ un braccio** break one's arm

rompicapo *m inv* puzzle; (*problema*) headache

rondine *f* swallow

ronzare buzz; **ronzio** *m* buzzing

rosa 1 *f* rose **2** *m/agg inv* pink; **rosario** *m* REL rosary; **rosato** *m* rosé; **rosmarino** *m* rosemary

rosolare brown

rosolia *f* German measles *sg*

rosone *m* ARCHI rose window

rospo *m* toad

rossetto *m* lipstick

rosso 1 *agg* red **2** *m* red; **~ d'uovo** egg yolk; **passare col ~** go through a red light

rosticceria *f* rotisserie (*shop selling roast meat*)

rotaia *f* rail

rotatoria *f* roundabout, *Am* traffic circle

rotella *f* castor

rotolare roll; **rotolarsi** roll (around); **rotolino** m FOT film; **rotolo** m roll; FOT film; **andare a -i** go to rack and ruin

rotondo round

rotta f MAR, AVIA course

rottame m wreck

rotto 1 pp ☞ **rompere 2** agg broken; **rottura** f breaking; F *tra innamorati* break-up; F **che ~!** what a pain! F

rotula f kneecap

roulotte f inv caravan, Am trailer

routine f routine

rovesciare *liquidi* spill; *oggetto* knock over; (*capovolgere*) overturn; **rovesciarsi** overturn, capsize; **rovescio** reverse; in *tennis* backhand; **mettersi una maglia al ~** put a sweater on inside out

rovina f ruin; **andare in ~** go to rack and ruin; **rovinare** ruin; **rovinarsi** ruin o.s.

rovo m bramble

rozzo rough and ready

ruba: **andare a ~** sell like hot cakes; **rubare** steal

rubinetto m tap, Am faucet

rubino m ruby

rubrica f *di libro* table of contents; *quaderno* address book; *di giornale* column; TV report

rudere m ruin

rudimentale rudimentary

ruga f wrinkle, line

ruggine f rust

ruggire roar

rugiada f dew

rullino m FOT film; **rullo** m roll

rum m rum

rumore m noise; **rumoroso** noisy

ruolo m role

ruota f wheel; **~ di scorta** spare wheel

rupe f cliff

rupestre rock attr; **arte** f **~** wall painting

ruscello m stream

russare snore

Russia f Russia; **russo 1** agg Russian 2 m, **-a** f Russian

rustico rural, rustic; *fig* unsophisticated

ruttare belch; **rutto** m belch

ruvido rough

ruzzolare fall; **ruzzolone** m fall; **fare un ~** fall

S

S. (= **santo**) St (= Saint)

sa ☞ **sapere**

sabato *m* Saturday

sabbia *f* sand; **sabbioso** sandy

sabotaggio *m* sabotage; **sabotare** sabotage

sacca *f* bag; ANAT, BIO sac

saccheggiare sack; *spir* raid

sacchetto *m* bag; **sacco** *m* sack; *fig* **F un ~ di** piles of F; **costa un ~** it costs a fortune; **~ a pelo** sleeping bag; **saccopelista** *m/f* backpacker

sacerdote *m* priest

sacramento *m* sacrament

sacrificare sacrifice; **sacrificarsi** sacrifice o.s.; **sacrificio** *m* sacrifice

sacro sacred

sadico 1 *agg* sadistic **2** *m*, -a *f* sadist

safari *m inv* safari

saggio¹ 1 *agg* wise **2** *m* wise man, sage

saggio² *m* test; (*campione*) sample; *scritto* essay; *di danza, musica* end of term show

Sagittario *m* ASTR Sagittarius

sahariana *f* safari jacket

sala *f* room; (*soggiorno*) living room; **~ da pranzo** dining room; **~ giochi** amusement arcade; **~ operatoria** (operating) theatre, *Am* operating room

salame *m* salami

salamoia *f*: **in ~** in brine

salariale pay *attr*; **salario** *m* salary, wages

salatino *m* savoury, *Am* savory; **salato** savoury, *Am* savory; *acqua* salt; *cibo* salted; F (*caro*) steep F; **troppo ~** salty

saldare weld; *ossa* set; *fattura* pay; **saldo 1** *m* steady, secure **2** *m* payment; *in svendita* sale item; (*resto*) balance; **-i** *pl* **di fine stagione** end-of--season sales

sale *m* salt

salgo ☞ **salire**

salice *m* willow; **~ piangente** weeping willow

saliera *f* salt cellar; **salina** *f* salt works

salire 1 *v/i* climb; *di livello, prezzi, temperatura* rise; **~ in macchina** get in; **~ su scala** climb; *treno, autobus* get on **2** *v/t scale* climb; **salita** *f* climb; *strada* slope; **strada** *f* **in ~** steep street

saliva *f* saliva

salma *f* corpse, body

salmastro 1 *agg* briny **2** *m* salt

salmone *m* salmon; **~ affumicato** smoked salmon

salone *m* living room; (*esposi-*

zione) show

salotto *m* lounge

salpare sail

salsa *f* sauce; **~ di pomodoro** tomato sauce

salsiccia *f* sausage

saltare 1 *v/t* jump; (*omettere*) skip; **~ (in padella)** sauté 2 *v/i* di bottone come off; di fusibile blow; F di impegno be canceled o *Am* canceled; **~ fuori** turn up

saltellare hop

salto *m* jump; (*dislivello*) change in level; **~ in alto** high jump; **~ in lungo** long jump, *Am* broad jump; **faccio un ~ da te** I'll drop in

saltuariamente occasionally; **saltuario** occasional

salumeria *f* shop that sells 'salumi'; **salumi** *mpl* cold meat

salutare 1 *agg* healthy 2 *v/t* say hello to, greet; **salute** *f* health; **~!** cheers!; **saluto** *m* wave; **tanti -i** greetings

salvagente *m inv* lifebelt; (*giubbotto*) life jacket; *per bambini* ring; (*isola spartitraffico*) traffic island; **salvaguardare** protect, safeguard; **salvaguardia** *f* protection; **salvare** save, rescue; **salvataggio** *m* salvage; **barca** *f* **di ~** lifeboat; **salve!** hello!; **salvezza** *f* salvation

salvia *f* sage

salvietta *f* napkin

salvo 1 *agg* safe 2 *prp* except;

~ che unless; **~ imprevisti** all being well 3 *m*: **mettersi in ~** take shelter

San = **Santo**

sandalo *m* sandal; BOT sandalwood

sangue *m* blood; **a ~ freddo** in cold blood; GASTR **al ~** rare; **sanguigno**: **gruppo** *m* **~** blood group; **sanguinare** bleed; **sanguinoso** bloody; **sanguisuga** *f* leech

sanità *f* health; **amministrazione** *f* **~** health care; **sanitario** health *attr*, **assistenza** *f* **-a** health care

sanno ☞ **sapere**

sano healthy; **~ e salvo** safe and sound

santo 1 *agg* holy 2 *m*, **-a** *f* saint; *davanti al nome* St

santuario *m* sanctuary

sanzione *f* sanction

sapere 1 *v/t* know; (*essere capace di*) be able to; (*venire a*) **~** hear; **sai nuotare?** can you swim?; **lo so** I know 2 *v/i*: **far ~ qc a qu** let s.o. know sth; **~ di** (*avere sapore di*) taste of 3 *m* knowledge

sapone *m* soap; **saponetta** *f* toilet soap

sapore *m* taste; **-i pl** aromatic herbs; **saporito** tasty

saracinesca *f* roller shutter

sarcastico sarcastic

sarcofago *m* sarcophagus

Sardegna *f* Sardinia

sardina *f* sardine

sardo 1 *agg* Sardinian 2 *m*, **-a**

f Sardinian

sarò *☞* **essere**

sarto *m*, -a *f* tailor; *per donne* dressmaker; sartoria *f* tailor's; *per donne* dressmaker's

sasso *m* stone

sassofono *m* saxophone

satellite *m* satellite

satira *f* satire; satirico satirical

saturo saturated

sauna *f* sauna

sazietà *f*: **mangiare a ~** eat one's fill; sazio full (up)

sbadato absent-minded

sbadigliare yawn; sbadiglio *m* yawn

sbagliare 1 *v/i e* sbagliarsi make a mistake 2 *v/t* make a mistake in; TELEC **sbagliare ~** dial the wrong number; **~ strada** go the wrong way; sbagliato wrong; sbaglio *m* mistake; *per ~* by mistake

sbalordire amaze; sbalorditivo amazing

sbalzare throw; sbalzo *m* jump; **~ di temperatura** sudden change in temperature

sbandare AUTO skid; FERR, *fig* go off the rails; sbandata *f* AUTO skid; *fig* **prendersi una ~ per qu** get a crush on s.o.

sbarazzare clear; sbarazzarsi: **~ di** get rid of

sbarcare 1 *v/t merci* unload; *persone* disembark 2 *v/i* disembark; sbarco *m di merci* unloading; *di persone* disembarkation

sbarra *f* bar

sbarramento *m* fence; (*ostacolo*) barrier; sbarrare bar; *assegno* cross; *occhi* open wide; *sbarrato* assegno crossed; *occhi* wide open

sbattere 1 *v/t porta* slam, bang; (*urtare*) bang; GASTR beat 2 *v/i* bang

sberla *f* F slap

sbiadire fade; sbiadito faded

sbilanciarsi lose one's balance; *fig* commit o.s.

sbizzarrirsi indulge o.s.

sbloccare clear; *macchina* unblock; *prezzi* deregulate

sboccare: **~ in** *di fiume* flow into; *di strada* lead to

sbocciare open (out)

sbocco *m di situazione* way out

sbornia *f* F: **prendersi una ~** get drunk

sborsare F cough up F

sbottonare unbutton; sbottonarsi: **la giacca** unbutton one's jacket

sbraitare shout, yell

sbranare tear apart

sbriciolarsi crumble

sbrigare attend to; sbrigarsi hurry up; sbrigativo (*rapido*) hurried, rushed; (*brusco*) brusque

sbrinare *frigorifero* defrost; sbrinatore *m* defrost control

sbrogliare untangle; **sbrogliarsela** sort things out

sbronza f F hangover; **sbronzarsi** F get drunk; **sbronzo** F tight F

sbucare emerge; **da dove sei sbucato?** where did you spring from?

sbucciare frutta, patate peel; **sbucciarsi le ginocchia** skin one's knees; **sbucciatura** f graze

scabroso rough, uneven; fig offensive

scacchiera f chessboard

scacciare chase away

scacco m (chess) piece; **-cchi** pl chess; **a -cchi** checked, Am checkered

scadente 1 ⇒ **scadere 2** agg second-rate; **scadenza** f deadline; su alimento best before date; **scadere** di passaporto expire; di cambiale fall due; (perdere valore) decline (in quality); **scaduto** expired; alimento past its sell-by date

scaffale m shelves

scaglia f flake; di legno chip; di pesce scale

scagliare hurl; **scagliarsi contro** attack

scala f staircase; GEOG, MUS scale; **~ (a pioli)** ladder; **~ mobile** escalator; disegno m in **~** scale drawing; **fare le -e** climb the stairs; **scalare** climb; **scalata f** climb; **~ al successo** rise to fame; **scalatore** m, **-trice** f climber

scaldabagno m water heater; **scaldare** heat (up); **scaldarsi** warm up; fig get worked up

scalinata f steps; **scalino** m step

scalo m AVIA stop; MAR port of call; **fare ~ a** call at

scalogna f bad luck; **portare ~** be unlucky; **scalognato** unlucky

scaloppina f escalope

scalpello m chisel

scalzo barefoot

scambiare (confondere) mistake (**per** for); (barattare) exchange, swap F (**con** for); **scambio** m exchange; di persona mistake; FERR points; **-i pl commerciali** trade

scampagnata f day out in the country

scampanellata f ring

scampi mpl scampi

scampo m escape, way out

scampolo m remnant

scandagliare sound; fig sound out

scandalistico scandal-mongering; **scandalizzare** scandalize; **scandalizzarsi** be scandalized (**di** by); **scandalizzato** scandalized; **scandalo** m scandal; **scandaloso** scandalous

scandinavo 1 agg Scandinavian 2 m, **-a** f Scandinavian

scanner m inv INFOR scanner; **scannerizzare** INFOR scan

scansare (allontanare) move;

(*evitare*) avoid; **scansarsi** move out of the way

scansionare scan

scantinato *m* cellar

scapito: *a ~ di* to the detriment of

scapola *f* shoulder blade, ANAT scapula

scapolo 1 *agg* single, unmarried **2** *m* bachelor

scappamento *m* TEC exhaust

scappare (*fuggire*) run away; (*affrettarsi*) rush, run

scappatella *f di bambino* escapade; *fare delle -lle* get into mischief

scappatoia *f* way out

scarabocchiare scribble; **scarabocchio** *m* scribble

scarafaggio *m* cockroach

scaraventare throw, hurl; **scaraventarsi** throw *o* hurl o.s. (*contro* at)

scarcerare release; **scarcerazione** *f* release

scarica *f* discharge; **scaricamento** *m* INFOR download; **scaricare** unload; *batteria* run down; *rifiuti, sostanze nocive* dump; *responsabilità* offload; INFOR download; **scaricarsi** *di batteria* run down; **scarico 1** *agg camion* empty; *batteria* run-down **2** *m di merci* unloading; *luogo* dump; *divieto di ~* no dumping

scarlattina *f* scarlet fever

scarpa *f* shoe

scarpata *f* (*burrone*) escarp-ment

scarpinata *f* trek

scarpone *m* (heavy) boot; *~ da sci* ski boot

scarseggiare become scarce; *~ di qc* be short of sth; **scarso** scarce, in short supply; *quattro chilometri -si* barely four kilometres

scartare (*svolgere*) unwrap; (*eliminare*) reject; **scarto** *m* rejection; (*cosa scartata*) reject

scassare F ruin, wreck; **scassarsi** F give up the ghost F; **scassato** F done for F

scassinare force open; **scasso** *m* forced entry; *furto m con ~* breaking and entering

scatenare FIG unleash; **scatenarsi** *di tempesta* break; *di collera* break out; *di persona* let one's hair down

scatola *f* box; *di tonno, piselli* can, *Br anche* tin; *in ~ cibo* canned, *Br anche* tinned

scattare 1 *v/t* FOT take **2** *v/i* go off; *di serratura* catch; (*arrabbiarsi*) lose one's temper; *di atleta* put on a spurt; **scatto** *m* click; SP spurt; FOT exposure; *di foto* taking; TEL unit; *uno ~ di rabbia* an angry gesture

scavalcare *muro* climb (over)

scavare *con pala* dig; *con trivella* excavate; **scavi** *mpl* archeologici dig

scegliere choose, select;

scelgo ☞ **scegliere**; **scelta** f choice, selection; **di prima ~** first-rate; **scelto 1** pp ☞ **scegliere 2** agg handpicked; merce, pubblico (specially) selected

scemo 1 agg stupid, idiotic **2** m, -a f idiot

scena f theatre, Am theater; (scenata) scene; **scenata** f scene

scendere 1 v/i andare go down, descend; venire come down, descend; da cavallo get down, dismount; dal treno, dall'autobus get off; dalla macchina get out; di temperatura, prezzi go down, drop **2** v/t: **~ le scale** andare go down the stairs; venire come down the stairs

sceneggiatura f screenplay

scenografo m, -a f set designer

scettico 1 agg sceptical, Am skeptical **2** m, -a f sceptic, Am skeptic

scheda f card; (formulario) form; **~ telefonica** phonecard; **schedario** m file; **schedina** f pools coupon

scheggia f sliver

scheletro m skeleton

schema m diagram; (abbozzo) outline; **schematico** general; disegno schematic

scherma f fencing

schermo m screen; (riparo) shield

scherzare play; (burlare)

joke; **scherzo** m joke; **-i a parte** joking aside; **per ~** fare, dire qc as a joke

schiaccianoci m inv nutcrackers; **schiacciare 1** v/t crush; noce crack **2** v/i SP smash the ball; **schiacciato** crushed, squashed

schiaffeggiare slap; **schiaffo** m slap

schiamazzo m yell, scream

schiantare, **schiantarsi** crash

schiarire lighten; **schiarirsi** brighten up; **schiarita** f bright spell

schiavitù f slavery; **schiavo 1** agg: **essere ~ di** be a slave to **2** m, -a f slave

schiena f back; **mal** m **di ~** back ache; **schienale** m di sedile back

schiera f group; **a ~** in ranks; **schierarsi**: **~ in favore di qu** come out in favour o Am favor of s.o.

schietto pure; fig frank

schifezza: **che ~!** how disgusting!; **schifo** m disgust; **fare ~ a qu** disgust s.o.; **schifoso** disgusting; (pessimo) dreadful

schiuma f foam; **~ da bagno** bubble bath; **~ da barba** shaving foam

schivare avoid, dodge F; **schivo** shy

schizzare 1 v/t (spruzzare) squirt; (abbozzare) sketch **2** v/i squirt; (saltare) jump

scollatura

schizzinoso fussy

schizzo m squirt; (abbozzo) (lightning) sketch

sci m inv ski; attività skiing; ~ **acquatico** water ski / skiing; ~ **di fondo** cross-country ski / skiing

sciacquare rinse

sciagura f disaster; **sciagurato** unfortunate

scialle m shawl

scialuppa f dinghy; ~ **di salvataggio** lifeboat

sciame m swarm

sciare ski

sciarpa f scarf

sciatica f sciatica

sciatore m, **-trice** f skier

sciatto untidy, sloppy

scientifico scientific; **scienza** f science; **scienziato** m, **-a** f scientist

scimmia f monkey; **scimmiottare** ape

scimpanzè m inv chimpanzee, chimp F

scintilla f spark; **scintillante** sparkling; **scintillare** sparkle

sciocchezza f (idiozia) stupidity; **sciocco 1** agg silly **2** m, **-a** f silly thing

sciogliere untie; capelli let down; neve melt; dubbio, problema clear up; **sciogliersi di corda, nodo** come undone; di burro, neve melt; **scioglilingua** m inv tongue-twister

scioltezza f nimbleness; fisica agility

sciolto 1 pp ☞ **sciogliere 2** agg ghiaccio melted

scioperare strike; **sciopero** m strike; **fare** ~ go on strike

sciovia f ski-lift

scippatore m, **-trice** f bag-snatcher; **scippo** m bag-snatching

scirocco m sirocco

sciroppo m syrup

scissione f splitting

sciupare (logorare) wear out; salute ruin; tempo, denaro waste; **sciupato** persona drawn; cosa worn out

scivolare slide; (cadere) slip; **scivolo** m slide; gioco chute; **scivoloso** slippery

sclerosi f inv MED sclerosis; ~ **multipla** multiple sclerosis, MS

scocciare F bother, hassle F; **scocciatore** F m, **-trice** f pest F, nuisance; **scocciatura** F f nuisance

scodella f bowl

scogliera f cliff; **scoglio** m rock

scoiattolo m squirrel

scolapasta m inv colander; **scolare** drain

scolaro m, **-a** f schoolboy; ragazza schoolgirl; **scolastico** school attr

scoliosi f inv curvature of the spine

scollato low-necked; donna wearing a low neckline; **scollatura** f neck(line);

scollo m neck

scolo m drainage

scolorire, scolorirsi fade; **scolorito** faded

scolpire *statua* sculpt; *legno* carve; *fig* engrave

scommessa f bet; **scommesso** pp ☞ **scommettere**; **scommettere** bet

scomodare disturb; **scomodarsi** put o.s. out; **non si scomodi** please don't go to any bother; **scomodo** uncomfortable; (*non pratico*) inconvenient

scomparire disappear; **scomparsa** f disappearance; **scomparso** pp ☞ **scomparire**

scompartimento m compartment

scompigliare *persona* ruffle the hair of; *capelli* ruffle; **scompiglio** m confusion

scomporre break down; **scomporsi**: **senza~** without showing any emotion

sconcertante disconcerting

sconcio indecent; *parola* filthy

sconclusionato incoherent

sconfiggere defeat

sconfinato vast, boundless

sconfitta f defeat; **sconfitto** pp ☞ **sconfiggere**

sconforto m discouragement

scongelare thaw

scongiurare beg; *pericolo* avert

sconosciuto 1 agg unknown

2 m, -a f stranger

sconsigliare advise against; **~ qc a qu** advise s.o. against sth

scontare FIN deduct, discount; *pena* serve; **scontato** discounted; (*previsto*) expected; **~ del 30%** with a 30% discount

scontento 1 agg unhappy, not satisfied (**di** with) **2** m unhappiness, dissatisfaction

sconto m discount

scontrarsi collide (**con** with); *fig* clash (**con** with)

scontrino m receipt

scontro m AUTO collision; *fig* clash; **scontroso** unpleasant, disagreeable

sconvolgente upsetting, distressing; *di un'intelligenza ~* incredibly intelligent; **sconvolgere** upset; **sconvolto 1** pp ☞ **sconvolgere 2** agg *paese in upheaval*

scopa f broom; **scopare** sweep; P shag P

scoperchiare *pentola* take the lid off

scoperta f discovery; **scoperto 1** pp ☞ **scoprire 2** agg: **assegno ~** m ~ dud cheque **3** m: **allo ~** in the open

scopo m aim, purpose; **allo ~ di fare qc** in order to do sth

scoppiare *di bomba* explode; *di palloncino, pneumatico* burst; **~ in lacrime** burst into tears; **~ a ridere** burst out laughing; **scoppio** m explosion; *di palloncino* bursting; *fig* outbreak

scoprire *contenitore* take the lid off; (*denudare*) uncover; *piani, verità* discover

scoraggiare discourage; **scoraggiarsi** become discouraged, lose heart; **scoraggiato** discouraged

scorciatoia *f* short cut

scordare, scordarsi di forget; **scordato** MUS out of tune

scoreggia *f* F fart F; **scoreggiare** F fart F

scorgere see, make out

scoria *f* waste

scorpione *m* scorpion; ASTR **Scorpione** Scorpio

scorrere 1 *v/i* flow, run; *di tempo* go past, pass **2** *v/t giornale* skim

scorretto (*errato*) incorrect; (*non onesto*) unfair

scorrevole *porta* sliding; *stile* flowing

scorso 1 *pp* ☞ **scorrere 2** *agg:* **l'anno ~** last year

scorta *f* escort; (*provvista*) supply; **scortare** escort

scortese rude, discourteous; **scortesia** *f* rudeness

scorto *pp* ☞ **scorgere**

scorza *f* peel; *fig* exterior

scossa *f* shake; **~ di terremoto** (earth) tremor; **~ elettrica** electric shock; **scosso** *pp* ☞ **scuotere**

scostare move away (**da** from); **scostarsi** move

(aside)

scottare 1 *v/t* burn; GASTR *verdure* blanch **2** *v/i* burn; **scotta!** it's hot!; **scottato** *verdure* blanched; **scottatura** *f* burn

Scozia *f* Scotland; **scozzese 1** *agg* Scottish **2** *m/f* Scot

screditare discredit

scremato skimmed

screpolare, screpolarsi crack; **screpolatura** *f* crack

scricchiolare creak; **scricchiolio** *m* creak

scritta *f* inscription; **scritto 1** *pp* ☞ **scrivere 2** *m* writing; **scrittore** *m*, **-trice** *f* writer; **scrittura** *f* writing; REL scripture

scrivania *f* desk; **scrivere** write; (*annotare*) write down; **come si scrive ... ?** how do you spell ... ?

scroccare F scrounge F

scrollare shake; **~ le spalle** shrug (one's shoulders)

scrosciare *di pioggia* fall in torrents

scrupolo *m* scruple; **scrupolosità** *f* scrupulousness; **scrupoloso** scrupulous

scrutare look at intently; *orizzonte* scan

scrutinio *m* POL counting; EDU *teachers' meeting to discuss pupils' performance*

scucire unpick; **F scuci i soldi!** cough up! F; **scucirsi** come apart at the seams

scuderia *f* stable

scudetto *m* SP championship; **scudo** *m* shield

sculacciare spank

scultore *m*, **-trice** *f* sculptor; **scultura** *f* sculpture

scuola *f* school; ~ **media** secondary school; ~ **superiore** high school; ~ **guida** driving school; **andare a** ~ go to school

scuotere shake

scure *f* axe, *Am* ax

scurire darken; **scuro** dark

scusa *f* excuse; **chiedere** ~ apologize; **scusare** forgive; (*giustificare*) excuse; **mi scusi** I'm sorry; **scusi, scusa** excuse me; **scusarsi** apologize

sdebitarsi pay one's debts

sdegno *m* moral indignation

sdentato toothless

sdoganare clear through customs

sdolcinato sloppy

sdraiarsi lie down; **sdraiato** lying down; **sdraio** *m*: (**sedia** *f* **a**) ~ deck chair

sé oneself; *lui* himself; *lei* herself; *loro* themselves; *esso, essa* itself; **da** ~ (by) himself / herself / themselves

se[1] *cong* if; **~ mai** if need be; **~ mai arrivasse ...** should he arrive ...; **come** ~ as if; **~ no** if not

se[2] *pron* = **si** in front of **lo, la, li, le, ne**

sebbene even though

secca *f* shallows

seccante *fig* annoying; **seccare 1** *v/t* dry; *fig* annoy **2** *v/i* dry; **seccarsi** dry; *fig* get annoyed; **seccatore** *m*, **-trice** *f* nuisance, pest F; **seccatura** *f* nuisance

secchio *m* bucket

secco dry; *fiori, pomodori* dried; *tono* curt

secolo *m* century

seconda *f* AUTO second (gear); FERR second class; EDU second year; **secondario** secondary; **secondo 1** *agg* second; **di -a mano** second-hand; ~ **fine** ulterior motive **2** *prp* according to; ~ **me** in my opinion **3** *m* second; GASTR main course

sedano *m* celery

sedare calm (down); **sedativo** *m* sedative

sede *f* headquarters

sedentario sedentary; **sedere 1** *m* F rear end F **2** *v/i e* **sedersi** sit down; **sedia** *f* chair; ~ **a dondolo** rocking chair; ~ **a rotelle** wheelchair

sedicesimo sixteenth; **sedici** sixteen

sedile *m* seat

seducente attractive; **sedurre** seduce; (*attrarre*) attract

seduta *f* session; **seduto** seated

seduzione *f* seduction

sega *f* saw

segale *f* rye

segare saw; **segatura** *f* sawdust

seggio m seat; ~ (**elettorale**) polling station; **seggiola** f chair; **seggiolino** m di bicicletta child's seat; **seggiolone** m high chair; **seggiovia** f chair lift

segnalare signal; (annunciare) report; **segnale** m signal; (segno) sign; ~ **d'allarme** alarm; **segnaletica** f signs; **segnalibro** m bookmark; **segnare** (marcare) mark; (annotare) note down; SP score; **segno** m sign; (traccia) mark, trace; (cenno) gesture, sign

segretaria f secretary; **segretario** m secretary; **segreteria** f carica secretaryship; ufficio administrative office; attività secretarial duties; ~ **telefonica** answering machine, voicemail

segreto m/agg secret

seguace m/f disciple, follower; **seguente** next, following; **seguire 1** v/t follow; corso take **2** v/i follow (**a qc** sth); **seguito** m persone retinue; (sostenitori) followers; di film sequel; **di** ~ one after the other, in succession; **in** ~ after that

sei¹ → **essere**

sei² six

seicento 1 agg six hundred **2** m: **il Seicento** the seventeenth century

selciato m paving

selezione f selection

self-service m inv self-service (café)

sella f saddle; **sellino** m saddle

seltz m: **acqua f di** ~ soda (water)

selvaggina f game; **selvaggio 1** agg animale, fiori wild; tribù, omicidio savage **2** m, -a f savage; **selvatico** wild

semaforo m traffic lights

sembrare seem; (assomigliare a) look like

seme m seed

semestre m six months; EDU term, Am semester

semicerchio m semi-circle; **semicircolare** semi-circular

semifinale f semi-final

semifreddo m soft ice cream

seminare sow

seminario m seminar

seminudo half-naked

seminuovo practically new

semolino m semolina

semplice simple; (non doppio) single; (spontaneo) natural; **semplicità** f simplicity; **semplificare** simplify

sempre always; **per** ~ for ever; ~ **più** more and more; ~ **più vecchio** older and older; **piove... di più** the rain's getting heavier and heavier; ~ **che** as long as

senape f mustard

senato m senate; **senatore** m, -trice f senator

senno m common sense; **uscire di** ~ lose one's mind;

(*arrabbiarsi*) lose control

seno m breast

sensato sensible

sensazionale sensational; **sensazione** f sensation, feeling; (*impressione*) feeling; **fare ~** cause a sensation

sensibile sensitive; (*evidente*) significant; **sensibilità** f sensitivity; **sensibilizzare** make more aware (**a** of)

senso m sense; (*significato*) meaning; (*direzione*) direction; **buon ~** common sense; **~ unico** one way; **~ vietato** no entry; **in ~ orario** clockwise; **perdere i -i** faint; **sensore** m TEC sensor

sensuale sensual

sentenza f DIR verdict

sentiero m path

sentimentale sentimental; **sentimento** m feeling, sentiment

sentire feel; (*udire*) hear; (*ascoltare*) listen to; *odore* smell; *cibo* taste; **sentirsi** feel; **sentirsela di fare qc** feel up to doing sth

senza without; **senz'altro** definitely; **~ di me** without me; **~ ridere** without laughing; **senzatetto** m/f inv homeless person; **i -i** pl the homeless pl

separare separate; **separarsi** separate, split up F; **separazione** f separation

sepolto pp **▷ seppellire**; **sepoltura** f burial; **seppellire**

bury

seppia f cuttlefish

seppure even if

sequestrare confiscate; DIR impound, seize; (*rapire*) kidnap; **sequestro** m kidnap(ping); DIR impounding, seizure

sera f evening; **di ~** in the evenings; **serale** evening *attr*; **serata** f evening; *festa* party

serbatoio m tank

Serbia f Serbia

serbo¹1 *agg* Serbian **2** m, **-a** f Serb

serbo² m: **avere qc in ~** have sth in store

serenata f serenade

sereno serene; *fig* relaxed, calm

sericoltura f silk-worm farming

serie f inv series sg

serietà f seriousness; **serio 1** *agg* serious; (*affidabile*) reliable **2** m: **sul ~** seriously

serpe f grass snake; **serpente** m snake

serra f greenhouse

serramanico m: **coltello** m **a ~** flick knife, Am switchblade

serranda f shutter; **serrare** close; *denti, pugni* clench; **serratura** f lock

servire 1 v/i be useful; **non mi serve** I don't need it; **a che serve questo?** what's this for? **2** v/t serve; **~ da bere a qu** pour s.o. a drink; **ser-**

virsi (*usare*) use (*di* sth); **prego, si serva!** a tavola please help yourself!

servizio *m* service; (*favore*) favour, *Am* favor; (*dipartimento*) department; *in giornale* feature (story); **~ militare** military service; **~ da tavola** dinner service; **fuori ~** out of order; **in ~** on duty; **-zi** *pl* (**igienici**) toilets, *Am* rest room

servofreno *m* servo brake; **servosterzo** *m* power steering

sesamo *m* sesame

sessanta sixty; **sessantenne** sixty-year-old; **sessantesimo** sixtieth; **sessantina** *f*: **una ~** about sixty (*di* sth)

sesso *m* sex; **sessuale** sexual

sesto sixth

seta *f* silk

sete *f* thirst; **aver ~** be thirsty

setta *f* sect

settanta seventy; **settantenne** seventy-year-old; **settantesimo** seventieth; **settantina** *f*: **una ~** about seventy (*di* sth)

settare *macchina, computer* set up

sette seven; **settecento 1** *agg* seven hundred **2** *m*: **il Settecento** the eighteenth century

settembre *m* September

settentrionale 1 *agg* northern **2** *m/f* northerner; **settentrione** *m* north

setticemia *f* septicaemia, *Am* septicemia

settimana *f* week; **~ santa** Easter week, Holy week; **settimanale** *m/agg* weekly

settimo seventh

settore *m* sector

severo severe

sezione *f* section

sfacchinata *f* backbreaking job

sfacciato cheeky, *Am* fresh

sfamare feed

sfarzo *m* splendour, *Am* splendor

sfarzoso magnificent

sfasciare smash; **sfasciarsi** smash

sfavore *m* disadvantage; **sfavorevole** unfavourable, *Am* unfavorable

sfera *f* sphere

sfida *f* challenge; **sfidare** challenge

sfiducia *f* distrust

sfigurare 1 *v/t* disfigure **2** *v/i* look out of place; **sfigurato** disfigured

sfilare 1 *v/t* unthread; (*togliere*) take off **2** *v/i* parade; **sfilata** *f*: **~ di moda** fashion show

sfinimento *m* exhaustion; **sfinito** exhausted

sfiorare brush; *argomento* touch on

sfitto empty, not rented

sfocato *foto* blurred, out of focus

sfociare flow

sfogare *rabbia, frustrazione* vent, get rid of (**con, su** on); **sfogarsi** vent one's feelings; **~ con qu** confide in s.o.

sfoglia: *pasta f* **~** puff pastry; *sfogliare libro* leaf through

sfogo *m* outlet; MED rash

sfoltire thin

sfondare break; *porta* break down; *pavimento* break through

sfondo *m* background

sformare stretch out of shape; **sformato** *m* GASTR soufflé

sfortuna *f* bad luck, misfortune; **sfortunatamente** unfortunately; **sfortunato** unlucky, unfortunate

sforzare strain; **sforzarsi** try very hard; **sforzo** *m* effort; *fisico* strain; **fare uno ~** make an effort

sfrattare evict; **sfratto** *m* eviction

sfregare rub

sfruttamento *m* exploitation; **sfruttare** exploit

sfuggire (*scampare*) escape (*a* from); *mi è sfuggito di mente* it slipped my mind; **sfuggita:** *di* **~** in passing

sfumatura *f* nuance; *di colore* shade

sfuriata *f* (angry) tirade

sfuso loose; *vino* in bulk

sgabello *m* stool

sgabuzzino *m* cupboard

sgambetto *m:* *fare lo* **~** *a qu*

trip s.o. up

sganciare unhook; F *soldi* fork out F; **sganciarsi** come unhooked

sgarbato rude

sgobbare slave; **sgobbone** *m, -a f* F swot F

sgocciolare drip

sgombero ☞ **sgombrare**; **sgombrare** *strada, stanza* clear; *ostacolo* remove

sgombro[1] *agg strada, stanza* empty

sgombro[2] *m* mackerel

sgomentarsi be frightened

sgonfiare 1 *v/t* let the air out of **2** *v/i e* **sgonfiarsi** become deflated; *il braccio si è sgonfiato* the swelling in the arm has gone down; **sgonfio** flat; MED not swollen

sgradevole unpleasant

sgradito unwelcome

sgranchire, sgranchirsi: **~** *le gambe* stretch one's legs

sgraziato awkward

sgridare scold, tell off F

sguaiato raucous

sguardo *m* look; (*occhiata*) glance

sguazzare splash about; *fig* F **~** *nei soldi* be rolling in it F

sgusciare 1 *v/t* shell **2** *v/i* slip away; *mi è sgusciato di mano* it slipped out of my hand

shampoo *m inv* shampoo

shock *m inv* shock

sì yes; *dire di* **~** say yes; *penso di* **~** I think so

si[1] *pron* oneself; *lui* himself; *lei* herself; *esso, essa* itself; *loro* themselves; *reciproco* each other; **spazzolarsi i capelli** brush one's hair; **~ dice** they say; **cosa ~ può dire?** what can one say?, what can I say?

si[2] *m* MUS B

sia: ~ ... ~ ... both ... and ...; *(o l'uno o l'altro)* either ... or ...; **~ che ... ~ che ...** whether ... or whether ...

siamo ☞ **essere**

sibilare hiss; *di vento* whistle

sicario *m* hired killer, hit man F

sicché (and) so

siccità *f inv* drought

siccome since

Sicilia *f* Sicily; **siciliano 1** *agg* Sicilian **2** *m*, **-a** *f* Sicilian

sicura *f* safety catch

sicurezza *f* security; *(protezione)* safety; *(certezza)* certainty; **sicuro 1** *agg* safe; *(certo)* sure; **~ di sé** sure of o.s.; **di ~** definitely **2** *m*: **mettere al ~** put in a safe place

sidro *m* cider

siedo ☞ **sedere**

siepe *f* hedge

siero *m* MED serum; **sieropositivo** HIV positive

siesta *f* siesta

siete ☞ **essere**

sig. (= **signore**) Mr (= mister)

sigaretta *f* cigarette; **sigaro** *m* cigar

sigg. (= **signori**) Messrs

sigillare seal; **sigillo** *m* seal

sigla *f* initials *pl*; *musicale* theme (tune)

sig.na (= **signorina**) Miss, Ms

significare mean; **significato** *m* meaning

signora *f* lady; **mi scusi, ~!** excuse me!; **la ~ Rossi** Mrs Rossi; **-e e signori** ladies and gentlemen

signore *m* gentleman; **mi scusi, ~!** excuse me!; **il signor** Mr Rossi; **i -i Rossi** Mr and Mrs Rossi

signorina *f* young lady; **la ~ Rossi** Miss Rossi

sig.ra (= **signora**) Mrs

silenziatore *m* silencer, *Am* muffler

silenzio *m* silence; **silenzioso** silent

sillaba *f* syllable

siluro *m* MAR torpedo

simboleggiare symbolize; **simbolico** symbolic; **simbolismo** *m* symbolism; **simbolo** *m* symbol

simile similar

simmetria *f* symmetry; **simmetrico** symmetrical

simpatia *f* liking; *(affinità)* sympathy; **simpatico** likeable; **simpatizzare** become friends

simulare feign; TEC simulate; **simulazione** *f* pretence, *Am* pretense; TEC simulation

sinagoga *f* synagogue

sinceramente sincerely; *(in verità)* honestly; **sincerità** *f* sincerity; **sincero** sincere

sindacalista *m/f* trade unionist, *Am* labor unionist; **sindacato** *m* trade union, *Am* labor union

sindaco *m* mayor

sinfonia *f* symphony; **sinfonico** symphonic

singhiozzare sob; **singhiozzo** *m*: **avere il ~** have hiccups; **-zi** *pl* sobs

single *m/f inv* single

singolare 1 *agg* singular; (*insolito*) unusual; (*strano*) strange **2** *m* singular; SP singles; **singolo 1** *agg* individual; *camera, letto* single **2** *m* individual; SP singles

sinistra *f* left; **a** ~ on the left; *andare* to the left; **sinistro 1** *agg* left, left-hand; *fig* sinister **2** *m* accident

sino ☞ **fino**

sinonimo 1 *agg* synonymous **2** *m* synonym

sintesi *f inv* synthesis; (*riassunto*) summary; **sintetico** synthetic; (*riassunto*) brief; **sintetizzare** synthesize; (*riassumere*) summarize

sintomo *m* symptom

sintonia *f* RAD tuning; *fig* **essere in ~** be on the same wavelength (**con** as); **sintonizzare** RAD tune; **sintonizzarsi** tune in (**su** to)

sinusite *f* sinusitis

sipario *m* curtain

sirena *f* siren; *mitologica* mermaid; **~ d'allarme** alarm

siringa *f* MED syringe

sismico seismic

sistema *m* system; **sistemare** put; (*mettere in ordine*) arrange; *casa* do up; **sistemarsi** tidy o.s. up; (*trovare casa, sposarsi*) settle down; **sistemazione** *f* place; (*lavoro*) job; *in albergo* accommodation, *Am* accommodations

sito site; **in ~** on the premises

situato: **essere ~** be situated; **situazione** *f* situation

sito web *m* website

slacciare undo

slalom *m* slalom

slanciato slender

slancio *m* impulse

slavo 1 *agg* Slav, Slavonic **2** *m*, **-a** *f* Slav

sleale disloyal

slegare untie

slip *m inv* underpants, *Am* briefs; *da donna* panties

slitta *f* sledge

slittino *m* sled; SP bobsleigh

slogan *m inv* slogan

slogare dislocate; **slogarsi**: **~ una caviglia** sprain one's ankle; **slogatura** *f* sprain

sloggiare move out

Slovacchia *f* Slovakia; **slovacco1** *agg* Slovak(ian) **2** *m*, **-a** *f* Slovak(ian)

Slovenia *f* Slovenia; **sloveno 1** *agg* Slovene **2** *m*, **-a** *f* Slovene

smacchiare take the stains out of; **smacchiatore** *m* stain remover

soffiarsi

smagliatura f ladder, Am
run; MED stretch mark
smaltire dispose of
smalto m enamel; per ceramiche glaze; ~ per unghie nail
varnish
smantellare dismantle
smarrimento m loss; smarrirse lose; smarrirsi get lost;
smarrito 1 pp → smarrire
2 agg lost
smascherare unmask
smemorato forgetful
smentire prove to be wrong;
smentita f denial
smeraldo m/agg emerald
smesso pp → smettere;
smettere 1 v/t stop; abiti stop
wearing 2 v/i stop (di fare qc
doing sth)
smilitarizzare demilitarize
sminuire problema downplay; persona belittle
smisurato boundless
smontabile which can be taken apart, Am knockdown;
smontare 1 v/i da cavallo
dismount 2 v/t dismantle
smorfia f grimace; smorfioso
affected
smorzare colore tone down;
luce dim; entusiasmo dampen
SMS m inv text, text message;
mandare un ~ a qc text s.o.,
send s.o. a text
smuovere shift, move
snello slim, slender
snervante irritating
snob 1 agg snobbish 2 m/f inv
snob

SO (= sud-ovest) SW (=
southwest)
so → sapere
sobborgo m suburb
sobrio sober
Soc. (= società) Co (= company); soc. (= society)
socchiudere half-close; socchiuso 1 pp → socchiudere
2 agg half-closed; porta ajar
soccorrere help; soccorritore m rescue worker; soccorso 1 pp → soccorrere 2 m
rescue; pronto ~ first aid; ~
stradale breakdown service,
Am wrecking service
sociale social; socialismo m
socialism; socialista agg,
m/f socialist; socializzare
socialize
società f inv company; (associazione) society; ~ per azioni joint stock company
socievole sociable
socio m, -a f member; FIN
partner
soddisfacente satisfying;
soddisfare satisfy; soddisfatto 1 pp → soddisfare 2
agg satisfied; essere ~ di
qu be satisfied with s.o.;
soddisfazione f satisfaction
sodo uovo hard-boiled
sofà m inv sofa
sofferenza f suffering
soffermarsi dwell (su on)
sofferto pp → soffrire
soffiare blow; F swipe F; soffiarsi: ~ il naso blow one's

nose

soffice soft

soffio *m* puff

soffitta *f* attic

soffitto *m* ceiling

soffocante suffocating; **soffocare** suffocate

soffriggere fry gently

soffrire 1 *v/t* suffer; *persone* bear, stand 2 *v/i* suffer (*di* from)

soffritto *pp* ☞ **soffriggere**

sofisticato sophisticated

software *m inv* software

soggettivo subjective; **soggetto** 1 *agg* subject; *essere ~ a qc* suffer from sth 2 *m* GRAM subject; **soggezione** *f* subjection

soggiornare stay; **soggiorno** *m* stay

soglia *f* threshold

sogliola *f* sole

sognare, **sognarsi** dream (*di* about, of); **sognatore** *m*, *-trice f* dreamer; **sogno** *m* dream

soia *f* soya

sol *m inv* MUS G

solaio *m* attic, loft

solamente only

solare solar

solco *m* furrow

soldato *m* soldier

soldi *mpl* money

sole *m* sun; *c'è il ~* it's sunny; *prendere il ~* sunbathe; **soleggiato** sun-dried

solenne solemn

solere: *~ fare* be in the habit of doing

soletta *f* insole

solidale *fig* in agreement; **solidarietà** *f* solidarity

solido solid; (*robusto*) sturdy

solista *m/f* soloist

solitario 1 *agg* solitary; *luogo* lonely 2 *m* solitaire; *gioco* patience, *Am* solitaire

solito 1 *agg* usual, same 2 *m di ~* usually; *come al ~* as usual

solitudine *f* solitude

sollecitare (*stimolare*) urge; *risposta* ask for

solletico *m* tickling; *fare il ~ a qu* tickle s.o.; *soffrire il ~* be ticklish

sollevamento *m* lifting; (*insurrezione*) rising; *~ pesi* weightlifting; **sollevare** lift; *obiezione* bring up; **sollevarsi** *di popolo* rise up; AVIA climb

sollievo *m* relief

solo 1 *agg* lonely; (*non accompagnato*) alone; (*unico*) only; MUS solo; *da ~* by myself / yourself etc, on my / your etc own 2 *avv* only 3 *m* MUS solo

solstizio *m* solstice

soltanto only

solubile soluble; **soluzione** *f* solution; **solvente** 1 *agg* FIN solvent 2 *m* CHIM solvent

somigliante similar; **somiglianza** *f* resemblance; **somigliare**: *~ a qu* resemble s.o.

somma f (*addizione*) addition; (*risultato*) sum; (*importo*) amount, sum; **sommare** add; **sommario 1** agg summary **2** m summary; *di libro* table of contents; **sommato**: **tutto ~** all things considered

sommergere submerge; fig overwhelm (**di** with); **sommergibile** m submarine; **sommerso** pp ☞ **sommergere**

somministrare MED administer

sommossa f uprising

sondaggio m: **~** (**d'opinione**) (opinion) poll

sondare sound; fig test

sonnambulo m, **-a** f sleepwalker; **sonnecchiare** doze; **sonnifero** m sleeping pill; **sonno** m sleep; **aver ~** be sleepy; **sonnolenza** f drowsiness

sono ☞ **essere**

sonoro sound attr; risa, applausi loud; **colonna** f **-a** sound-track

sontuoso sumptuous

soppesare weigh; fig weigh up

sopportabile bearable, tolerable; **sopportare** peso bear; fig bear, stand F

soppressione f deletion; *di regola* abolition; **soppresso** pp ☞ **sopprimere**; **sopprimere** delete; *regola* abolish

sopra 1 prp on; (*più in alto di*) above; **l'uno ~ l'altro** one on top of the other; **i bambini ~ cinque anni** children over five; **al di ~ di qc** over sth **2** avv on top; (*al piano superiore*) upstairs; **vedi ~** see above

soprabito m (over)coat

sopracciglio m eyebrow

sopraccoperta f di letto bedspread; *di libro* dustjacket

sopraffare overwhelm

sopraggiungere di persona turn up; di difficoltà come up

sopralluogo m inspection (of the site)

soprammobile m ornament

soprannaturale supernatural

soprannome m nickname

soprannumero: **in ~** overcrowded

soprano m soprano; **mezzo ~** mezzo(-soprano)

soprappensiero ☞ **sovrapensiero**

soprattassa f surcharge

soprattutto particularly, above all

sopravvalutare overvalue; fig overestimate

sopravvento m: **avere** o **prendere il ~** have the upper hand

sopravvissuto 1 agg surviving **2** m, **-a** f survivor; **sopravvivenza** f survival; **sopravvivere** survive, outlive (**a qu** s.o.)

soprintendente m/f supervisor

sopruso *m* abuse of power

soqquadro *m*: **mettere a ~** turn upside down

sorbetto *m* sorbet

sorbirsi put up with

sordina *f* mute; **in ~** in secret, on the quiet

sordità *f* deafness; **sordo** deaf; **sordomuto** deaf and dumb

sorella *f* sister; **sorellastra** *f* stepsister

sorgente *f* spring; *fig* source; **sorgere** *di sole* rise, come up; *fig* arise, come up

sorpassare go past; AUTO pass, *Br anche* overtake; *fig* exceed; **sorpassato** out of date; **sorpasso** *m*: **fare un ~** pass, *Br anche* overtake

sorprendente surprising; **sorprendere** surprise; (*cogliere sul fatto*) catch; **sorpresa** *f* surprise; **sorpreso** *pp* ☞ **sorprendere**

sorridere smile; **sorriso** 1 *pp* ☞ **sorridere** 2 *m* smile

sorseggiare sip

sorso *m* mouthful

sorta *f* sort, kind

sorte *f* fate; **tirare a ~** draw lots; **sorteggiare** draw

sorto *pp* ☞ **sorgere**

sorveglianza *f* supervision; *di edificio* security; **sorvegliare** supervise; *bagagli ecc* look after

sorvolare 1 *v/t* AVIA fly over 2 *v/i fig*: **~ su** skim over; (*omettere*) skip

sosia *m inv* double

sospendere suspend; (*appendere*) hang; **sospensione** *f* suspension; **sospeso** 1 *pp* ☞ **sospendere** 2 *agg* hanging; *fig*: *questione* pending; **tenere in ~** *persona* keep in suspense

sospettare suspect; **~ qu o di qu** suspect s.o.; **sospetto** 1 *agg* suspicious 2 *m*, -a *f* suspect; **sospettoso** suspicious

sospirare 1 *v/i* sigh 2 *v/t* long for; **sospiro** *m* sigh

sosta *f* stop; (*pausa*) break, pause; **divieto di ~** no parking

sostantivo *m* noun

sostanza *f* substance

sostare stop

sostegno *m* support

sostenere support; (*affermare*) maintain; **sostengo** ☞ **sostenere**; **sostenitore** *m*, **-trice** *f* supporter

sostituibile replaceable; **sostituire**: **~ X con Y** replace X with Y, substitute Y for X; **sostituto** *m*, **-a** *f* substitute, replacement; **sostituzione** *f* substitution, replacement

sottaceti *mpl* pickles

sottana *f* slip, underskirt; (*gonna*) skirt; REL cassock

sotterraneo 1 *agg* underground *attr* 2 *m* cellar

sotterrare bury

sottile fine; *fig* subtle; *udito* keen

sottintendere imply; **sottinteso 1** *pp* ☞ **sottintendere 2** *m* allusion

sotto 1 *prp* under; **5 gradi ~ zero** 5 degrees below (zero); **al di ~ di qc** under sth **2** *avv* below; *(più in basso)* lower down; *(al di sotto)* underneath; *(al piano di ~)* downstairs

sottobanco under the counter

sottobraccio: camminare ~ walk arm-in-arm; **prendere qu ~** take s.o.'s arm

sottocchio: tenere ~ qc keep an eye on sth

sottoesposto FOT underexposed

sottofondo *m* background

sottolineare *anche fig* underline

sottomarino 1 *agg* underwater *attr* **2** *m* submarine

sottomesso 1 *pp* ☞ **sottomettere 2** *agg* submissive; *popolo* subject *attr*; **sottomettere** submit; *popolo* subdue

sottopassaggio *m* underpass

sottoporre submit; **sottoporsi: ~ a** undergo

sottoscritto 1 *pp* ☞ **sottoscrivere 2** *m* undersigned; **sottoscrivere** *documento* sign; *teoria* subscribe to; *abbonamento* take out; **sottoscrizione** *f* signing; *(abbonamento)* subscription

sottosopra *fig* upside-down

sottosuolo *m* subsoil

sottosviluppato underdeveloped

sottovalutare undervalue; *persona* underestimate

sottoveste *f* slip, underskirt

sottovoce quietly, sotto voce

sottrarre MAT subtract; *denaro* embezzle; **sottrarsi: ~ a qc** avoid sth; **sottratto** *pp* ☞ **sottrarre**; **sottrazione** *f* MAT subtraction; *di denaro* embezzlement

souvenir *m inv* souvenir

sovrabbondante overabundant

sovraccarico 1 *agg* overloaded *(di* with) **2** *m* overload

sovrano 1 *agg* sovereign **2** *m*, -a *f* sovereign

sovrappensiero: essere ~ be lost in thought

sovrappeso 1 *agg* overweight **2** *m* excess weight

sovrappopolato overpopulated

sovrapporre overlap

sovrastare overlook, dominate

sovrintendente *m/f* ☞ **soprintendente**

sovrumano superhuman

sovvenzionare give a grant to; **sovvenzione** *f* grant

sovversivo subversive

S.P. (= **Strada Provinciale**) A road, *Am* highway

S.p.A. *f* (= **Società per Azio-**

ni) joint stock company

spaccare break in two; *legna* split, chop; **spaccarsi** break in two

spacciare *droga* deal in, push F; **spacciarsi: ~ per** pass o.s. off as; **spacciatore** *m*, **-trice** *f di droga* dealer; **spaccio** *m di droga* dealing; *negozio* general store

spacco *m in gonna* slit; *in giacca* vent; **spaccone** *m*, **-a** *f* braggart

spada *f* sword

spaesato disoriented, confused

spaghetti *mpl* spaghetti *sg*

Spagna *f* Spain; **spagnolo** *1* *m/agg* Spanish **2** *m*, **-a** *f* Spaniard

spago *m* string

spalancare open wide

spalla *f* shoulder; *era di e-e* he had his back to me

spalliera *f* wallbars

spallina *f* shoulder pad

spalmare spread

spalti *mpl* terraces

spandere spread; **spandersi** spread; **spanto** *pp* ☞ **spandere**

sparare *1* *v/i* shoot (*a* at) *2* *v/t*: **~ un colpo** fire a shot; **sparatoria** *f* gunfire

sparecchiare clear

spareggio *m* SP play-off

spargere spread; *lacrime, sangue* shed

sparire disappear; **sparizione** *f* disappearance

sparo *m* (gun)shot

sparpagliare scatter

sparso 1 *pp* ☞ **spargere 2** *agg* scattered

spartire divide (up), split; **spartito** *m* score; **spartitraffico** *m* traffic island

spasimante *m/f* admirer

spasmo *m* MED spasm

spasso *m* fun; *andare a ~* go for a walk; *è uno ~* he / it's a good laugh; **spassoso** very funny

spavaldo cocky, over-confident

spaventapasseri *m inv* scarecrow; **spaventare** frighten, scare; **spaventarsi** be frightened, be scared; **spavento** *m* fright, scare; **spaventoso** frightening

spaziale space *attr*

spazientirsi get impatient

spazio *m* space; **spazioso** spacious

spazzaneve *m inv* snowplough, *Am inv* snowplow; **spazzare** sweep; **spazzatura** *f* rubbish, *Am* garbage; **spazzino** *m*, **-a** *f* street sweeper; **spazzola** *f* brush; **spazzolare** brush; **spazzolino** *m* brush; **~ da denti** toothbrush

specchiarsi look at o.s.; (*riflettersi*) be mirrored; **specchietto** *m* mirror; (*prospetto*) table; AUTO **~ retrovisore** rear-view mirror; **specchio** *m* mirror

speciale special; **specialista** *m/f* specialist; **specialità** *f inv* speciality, *Am* specialty; **specializzarsi** specialize; **specialmente** especially

specie 1 *f inv* species *sg*; **una ~ di** a sort *o* kind of **2** *avv* especially

specificare specify; **specifico** specific

speculatore *m*, -**trice** *f* speculator; **speculazione** *f* speculation

spedire send; **spedizione** *f* dispatch; *di merce* shipping; *(viaggio)* expedition; **spedizioniere** *m* courier

spegnere put out; *luce, motore, radio* turn off, switch off; **spegnersi** *di fuoco* go out; *di motore* stop

spellare skin; **spellarsi** peel

spendere spend; *fig* invest

spennare *pollo* pluck

spensierato carefree

spento *pp* ☞ **spegnere**

speranza *f* hope; **sperare 1** *v/t* hope for **2** *v/i* trust (**in** in)

sperduto lost; *luogo* isolated

sperimentare try; *in laboratorio* test; *fig: fatica, dolore* feel; *droga* experiment with

sperma *m* sperm

sperperare fritter away, squander

spesa *f* expense; **fare la ~ do** the shopping; **fare -e** go shopping; **a proprie -e** at one's own expense

spesso 1 *agg* thick **2** *avv* often, frequently; **spessore** *m* thickness

spett. (= **spettabile**) Messrs; *in lettera* **Spett. Ditta** Dear Sirs

spettacolare spectacular; **spettacolo** *m* show; *(panorama)* spectacle, sight; **~ teatrale** show

spettare: questo spetta a te this is yours; **non spetta a te giudicare** it's not up to you to judge

spettatore *m*, -**trice** *f* spectator; TEA member of the audience

spettinare: ~ qu ruffle s.o.'s hair

spettro *m* ghost; FIS spectrum

spezie *fpl* spices

spezzare break in two; **spezzarsi** break; **spezzatino** *m* stew; **spezzato 1** *agg* broken (in two) **2** *m* co-ordinated two-piece suit; **spezzettare** break up

spia *f* spy; TEC pilot light; **fare la ~** tell, sneak

spiacente: essere ~ be sorry; **spiacere: mi spiace** I am sorry

spiacevole unpleasant

spiaggia *f* beach

spiare spy on

spiazzo *m* empty space

spiccato strong

spicchio *m di frutto* section; **~ d'aglio** clove of garlic

spicciarsi hurry up

spiccioli *mpl* (small) change

spiedo *m* spit; **allo ~** spit-roasted

spiegare (*stendere*) spread; (*chiarire*) explain; **spiegarsi** explain what one means; **spiegazione** *f* explanation

spiegazzare crease

spietato pitiless

spiga *f di grano* ear; **spigato** herring-bone *attr*

spigliato confident

spigola *f* sea bass

spigolo *m* corner

spilla *f gioiello* brooch; **~ da balia** safety pin

spillo *m* pin

spina *f* BOT thorn; ZO spine; *di pesce* bone; EL plug; ANAT **~ dorsale** spine

spinaci *mpl* spinach

spinale spinal

spinello F *m* joint F

spingere push; *fig* drive

spinoso thorny

spinta *f* push

spinterogeno *m* AUTO distributor

spinto *pp* ☞ **spingere**

spionaggio *m* espionage

spiraglio *m* crack; *di luce, speranza* glimmer

spirale *f* spiral; *contraccettivo* coil

spirare blow; *fig* die

spirito *m* spirit; (*disposizione*) mind; (*umorismo*) wit; **spiritoso** witty; **spirituale** spiritual

splendente bright; **splendere** shine; **splendido** wonderful, splendid

spogliare undress; (*rubare*) rob; **spogliarello** *m* striptease; **spogliarsi** undress, strip; **spogliatoio** *m* dressing room, locker room; **spoglio** bare

spola *f*: **fare la ~ da un posto all'altro** shuttle backwards and forwards between two places

spolverare dust

sponda *f di letto* edge, side; *di fiume* bank; *nel biliardo* cushion

sponsor *m inv* sponsor; **sponsorizzare** sponsor

spontaneo spontaneous

sporadico sporadic

sporcare dirty; **sporcarsi** get dirty; **sporcizia** *f* dirt; **sporco 1** *agg* dirty **2** *m* dirt

sporgere 1 *v/t* hold out; *denuncia* make **2** *v/i* jut out; **sporgersi** lean out

sport *m inv* sport

sportello *m* door; **~ automatico** ATM, cash dispenser

sportivo 1 *agg* sports *attr*; *persona* sporty **2** *m*, **-a** *f* sportsman; *donna* sportswoman

sporto *pp* ☞ **sporgere**

sposa *f* bride; **sposare** marry; **sposarsi** get married; **sposato** married; **sposo** *m* bridegroom; **-i** *pl* newlyweds

spostare (*trasferire*) move, shift; (*rimandare*) postpone; **spostarsi** move

spranga *f* bar; **sprangare** bar

sprecare waste, squander; **spreco** *m* waste

spregevole despicable

spremere squeeze; **spremilimoni** *m inv* lemon squeezer; **spremuta** *f* juice; **~ d'arancia** orange juice

sprofondare sink

sproporzionato out of proportion (**a** to)

sproposito *m* blunder; **costare uno ~** cost a fortune; **a ~** out of turn

sprovveduto inexperienced

sprovvisto: ~ di lacking; **alla -a** unexpectedly

spruzzare spray; **spruzzatore** *m* spray; **spruzzo** *m* spray; **di fango** splatter

spudorato shameless

spugna *f* sponge

spuma *f* foam; **spumante:** (**vino** *m*) **~** sparkling wine

spuntare stick out; BOT come up; **di sole** appear; **di giorno** break

spuntino *m* snack

spunto *m* suggestion; **prendere ~ da** be inspired by

sputare 1 *v/i* spit 2 *v/t* spit out; **sputo** *m* spittle

squadra *f* *strumento* set square; (*gruppo*) squad; SP team

squalifica *f* disqualification; **squalificare** disqualify

squallido squalid; **squallore** *m* squalor

squalo *m* shark

squama *f* flake; **di pesce** scale

squarcio *m* *in stoffa* rip, tear; *in nuvole* break

squilibrato 1 *agg* insane **2** *m*, **-a** *f* lunatic; **squilibrio** *m* imbalance

squillare ring; **squillo** *m* ring

squisito *cibo* delicious

sradicare uproot; *fig* (*eliminare*) eradicate; *persona, pianta* uproot

S.r.l. *f* (= **Società a responsabilità limitata**) Ltd (= limited)

SS. (= **santi**) Saints

stabile 1 *agg* steady; (*duraturo*) stable; *tempo* settled **2** *m* building

stabilimento *m* (*fabbrica*) plant, *Br* factory

stabilire *data, obiettivi, record* set; (*decidere*) decide, settle; **stabilirsi** settle; **stabilità** *f* steadiness; **di relazione, moneta** stability

staccare remove, detach; EL unplug

stadio *m* stage; SP stadium

staffa *f* stirrup; **perdere le -e** blow one's top

staffetta *f* SP relay; **corsa** *f* **a ~** relay race

stage *m inv* training period

stagionale seasonal; **stagionare** age, mature; *legno* season; **stagionato** aged, mature; *legno* seasoned; **stagione** *f* season; **alta ~** high season; **bassa ~** low season

stagnante *f* SP stagnant

stagno 1 *m* pond; TEC tin **2**

agg watertight

stalla *f per bovini* cowshed; *per cavalli* stable

stamani, **stamattina** this morning

stambecco *m* ibex

stampa *f* press; *tecnica* printing; FOT print; *posta* **-e** *pl* printed matter; **stampante** *f* INFOR printer; **~ a getto di inchiostro** ink-jet printer; **stampare** print; **stampatello** *m* block letters; **stampato** *m* INFOR printout, hard copy

stampella *f* crutch

stampo *m* mould, *Am* mold

stancare tire (out); **stancarsi** get tired, tire; **stanchezza** *f* tiredness; **stanco** tired; **~ morto** dead beat

stanghetta *f* leg

stanotte tonight; *(la notte scorsa)* last night

stanza *f* room

stanziare *somma di denaro* allocate, earmark

stanzino *m* boxroom

stappare take the top off

stare be; *(restare)* stay; *(abitare)* live; **~ in piedi** stand; **~ bene** be well; *di vestiti* suit; **~ per fare qc** be about to do sth; **lascialo ~** let him be; **~ telefonando** be making a phonecall; **come sta?** how are you?, how are things?; **ben ti sta!** serves you right!

starnutire sneeze; **starnuto** *m* sneeze

stasera this evening, tonight

statale 1 *agg* state *attr* **2** *m/f* civil servant **3** *f* main road; **Stati Uniti d'America** *mpl* United States of America, USA

statistica *f* statistics

stato 1 *pp* ☞ **essere** *e* **stare 2** *m anche* POL state; **~ civile** marital status

statua *f* statue

statunitense 1 *agg* US *attr*, American **2** *m/f* US citizen

statura *f* height; *fig* stature

stavolta this time

stazionario stationary; **stazione** *f* station; **~ di servizio** service station; **~ balneare** seaside resort; **~ termale** spa

stecca *f di biliardo* cue; *di sigarette* carton; MED splint; MUS wrong note; **stecchino** *m* toothpick

stella *f* star; **~ di mare** starfish

stelo *m* stem, stalk

stemma *m* coat of arms

stendere spread; *braccio* stretch out; *biancheria* hang up; *verbale* draw up; **stendersi** stretch out; **stendibiancheria** *m inv* clothes dryer

stenodattilografa *f* shorthand typist

stentare **~ a fare qc** find it hard to do sth; **stento: a ~** with difficulty

stereo *m inv* stereo

stereotipo 1 *agg* stereotypical **2** *m* stereotype

sterile sterile; sterilità *f* sterility; sterilizzare sterilize; sterilizzazione *f* sterilization

sterlina *f* sterling

sterminare exterminate

sterminato vast

sterminio *m* extermination

sterno *m* breastbone, ANAT sternum

sterzare steer; sterzata *f* swerve; sterzo *m* AUTO steering

steso *pp* ☞ **stendere**

stesso same; **lo ~, la stessa** the same one; **è lo ~** it's all the same; **oggi ~** this very day; **io ~** myself; **se ~** himself

stile *m* style

stilografica *f* fountain pen

stima *f* (*ammirazione*) esteem; (*valutazione*) estimate; stimare *persona* esteem; *oggetto* value; (*ritenere*) consider; stimato respected

stimolante 1 *agg* stimulating 2 *m* stimulant; stimolare stimulate

stinco *m* shin

stingere, stingersi fade; stinto *pp* ☞ **stingere**

stipare cram; stipato crammed (**di** with)

stipendiato *m*, -a *f* salary-earner; stipendio *m* salary

stipulare stipulate

stiramento *m* MED pulled muscle

stirare iron; stirarsi pull; stiro: **ferro** *m* **da ~** iron; **non ~**

non-iron

stirpe *f* (*origine*) birth

stitichezza *f* constipation

stivale *m* boot; **-i** *pl* **di gomma** wellingtons, *Am* rubber boots

sto ☞ **stare**

stoccafisso *m* stockfish (*air-dried cod*)

stoffa *f* material

stomaco *m* stomach

stonare *di cantante* sing out of tune; *fig* be out of place; *di colori* clash; stonato *persona* tone deaf; *nota* false; *strumento* out of tune

stop *m inv* AUTO brake light; *cartello* stop sign; stoppare stop

storcere twist; **~ il naso** make a face; storcersi bend; **~ un piede** twist one's ankle

stordimento *m* dizziness; stordire stun; stordito stunned

storia *f* history; (*narrazione*) story; **non far -e!** don't make a scene!; storico 1 *agg* historical; (*memorabile*) historic 2 *m*, -a *f* historian

stormo *m di uccelli* flock

storpio 1 *agg* crippled 2 *m* -a *f* cripple

storta *f*: **prendere una ~** twist one's ankle; storto crooked

stoviglie *fpl* dishes

strabico cross-eyed; strabismo *m* strabismus

stracarico overloaded

stracciare tear up

stracciatella f type of soup; *gelato* chocolate chip
stracciato in shreds
straccio m *per pulire* cloth; *per spolverare* duster
strada f road; **per ~** down the road; **sono (già) per ~** I'm on my way; **a metà ~** half-way; *stradale* road *attr*; **stra-dario** m street-finder, street map
strafare exaggerate
strage f slaughter
stragrande: **la ~ maggioran-za** the vast majority
strangolare strangle
straniero 1 *agg* foreign **2** *m*, -a *f* foreigner
strano strange
straordinario 1 *agg* special; *(eccezionale)* extraordinary **2** *m* overtime
strapazzare treat badly; **stra-pazzarsi** overdo it; **strapaz-zo** m strain; **essere uno ~** be exhausting; **da ~** third-rate
strapieno crowded
strapiombo: **a ~** overhanging
strappare tear, rip; *(staccare)* tear down; *(togliere)* snatch *(a qu* from s.o.); **strappo** m tear, rip; MED torn ligament
strapripare overflow its banks
strascico m train; *fig* after-effects
stratagemma m stratagem
strategia f strategy; **strategi-co** strategic
strato m layer
stravagante extravagant

stravecchio ancient
stravedere: **~ per qu** worship s.o.
stravolgere change radically; *(travisare)* twist; *(stancare)* exhaust; **stravolto 1** *pp* ☞ **stra-volgere 2** *agg (stanco)* exhausted
strazio m: **era uno ~** it was painful
strega f witch; **stregone** m wizard
stremare exhaust; **stremato** exhausted
stress m *inv* stress; **stressan-te** stressful; **stressare** stress
stretta f hold; **~ di mano** handshake; **mettere qu alle -e** put s.o. in a tight corner; **strettamente** closely; **tene-re qc ~ (in mano)** clutch sth (in one's hand); **stretto 1** *pp* ☞ **stringere 2** *agg* narrow; *vestito* too tight; **lo ~ ne-cessario** the bare minimum **3** *m* GEOG strait; **strettoia** f bottleneck
stridere *di porta* squeak; *di colori* clash
stridulo shrill
strillare scream; **strillo** m scream
striminzito skimpy
strimpellare strum
stringa f lace
stringere 1 *v/t* make narrower; *abito* take in; *vite* tighten; **~ amicizia** become friends **2** *v/i di tempo* press; **stringersi** *intorno a tavolo*

squeeze up

striscia f strip; *dipinta* stripe; **-sce** pl **pedonali** zebra crossing, *Am* crosswalk; **a -sce** striped

strisciare 1 v/t *piedi* scrape; (*sfiorare*) brush, smear (**contro** against) **2** v/i crawl; **striscio** *m* MED smear

striscione *m* banner

strizzare wring; **~ l'occhio a qu** wink at s.o.

strofa f verse

strofinaccio *m* dish towel; **strofinare** rub

stroncare *vita* snuff out; F *idea* shoot down

stropicciare crush, wrinkle

strozzare strangle

strozzino *m*, **-a** f loan shark F

strumentalizzare make use of; **strumento** *m* instrument

strutto *m* lard

struttura f structure

struzzo *m* ZO ostrich

stuccare plaster; **stucco** *m* plaster

studente *m*, **-essa** f student; **studiare** study; **studio** *m* study; *di artista*, RAD, TV studio; *di professionista* office; *di medico* surgery, *Am* office

stufa f stove; **~ elettrica / a gas** electric / gas heater

stufare GASTR stew; *fig* bore; **stufarsi** get bored (**di** with); **stufato** *m* stew; **stufo: esse-re ~ di qc** be bored with sth

stuolo *m* host

stupefacente 1 agg amazing,

stupefying **2** *m* narcotic; **stu-pefatto** amazed, stupefied; **stupendo** stupendous

stupidaggine f stupidity; **stupidità** f stupidity; **stupi-do 1** agg stupid **2** *m*, **-a** f idiot

stupire 1 v/t amaze **2** v/i **e stu-pirsi** be amazed; **stupore** *m* amazement

stuprare rape; **stupro** *m* rape

sturare clear, unblock

stuzzicadenti *m* inv tooth-pick

stuzzicare tease; *appetito* whet

su 1 prp on; *argomento* about; (*circa*) about; **sul tavolo** on the table; **sul mare** by the sea; **sui trecento euro** about three hundred euros; **nove volte ~ dieci** nine times out of ten **2** avv up; (*al piano di sopra*) upstairs; **~!** come on!; **guardare in ~** look up

sub *m/f* inv skin diver

subacqueo 1 agg underwater **2** *m*, **-a** f skin diver

subaffittare sublet; **subaffit-to** *m* sublet

subentrare: ~ a qu take s.o.'s place

subire *danni*, *perdita* suffer

subito immediately

suburbano suburban

succedere (*accadere*) happen; **~ a in carica** succeed; **suc-cessione** f succession; **suc-cessivo** successive

successo 1 pp ☞ **succedere** **2** *m* success; **di ~** successful;

successore m successor

succhiare suck; **succo** m juice; **~ d'arancia** orange juice

succursale f branch

sud m south; **a(l)~ di** (to the) south of;**~ ovest** south-west; **~ est** south-east; **a ~ di** (to the) south of

sudare perspire, sweat; **sudato** sweaty

suddividere subdivide

sudicio 1 agg dirty **2** m dirt; **sudiciume** m dirt

sudore m perspiration, sweat

sufficiente sufficient; **sufficienza** f sufficiency; **a ~** enough

suffragio m suffrage

suggerimento m suggestion; **suggerire** suggest; TEA prompt; **suggeritore** m TEA prompter; **suggestionare** influence; **suggestivo** picturesque

sughero m cork

sugli = su and art **gli**

sugo m sauce; **di arrosto** juice

sui = su and art **i**

suicida m/f suicide (victim); **suicidarsi** commit suicide, kill o.s.; **suicidio** m suicide

suino porc attr

sul = su and art **il**

sull', sulla, sulle, sullo = su and art **l', la, le, lo**

suo 1 agg ◇ **di lui** his; **di lei** her; **di cosa** its; **il ~ maestro** his / her teacher; **questo libro è ~** this is his / her book

◇ **forma di cortesia** your; **il ~, la sua, i suoi, le sue** your **2** pron: **il ~, la sua, i suoi, le sue di lui** his; **di lei** hers; **di cosa** its; **forma di cortesia** yours

suocera f mother-in-law; **suocero** m father-in-law; **-i** pl mother- and father-in-law, in-laws F

suola f sole

suolo m ground; (*terreno*) soil

suonare 1 v/t play; **campanello** ring; **2** v/i play; **alla porta** ring; **suono** m sound

suora f REL nun

super f inv F 4-star, *Am* premium

superare go past; *fig* overcome; **esame** pass

superbo haughty

superficiale superficial; **superficie** f surface

superfluo superfluous

superiore 1 agg top; **qualità** superior **2** m superior; **superiorità** f superiority

superlativo m/agg superlative

supermarket m inv, **supermercato** m supermarket

superstite 1 agg surviving **2** m/f survivor

superstizione f superstition; **superstizioso** superstitious

superstrada f motorway, *Am* highway

supergiù about

supplementare supplementary; **supplemento** m supplement; **supplente** *m/f* replacement; EDU supply teacher

supplicare beg

suppongo ☞ **supporre**; **supporre** suppose

supporto *m* TEC support

supposizione *f* supposition

supposta *f* MED suppository

supposto *pp* ☞ **supporre**

suppurare MED suppurate

surf *m inv* surfboard; **fare ~** surf, go surfing; **surfista** *m/f* surfer

surgelato 1 *agg* frozen **2** *m*: **-i** *pl* frozen food

suscettibile touchy

suscitare arouse

susina *f* plum

sussidio *m* grant, allowance

sussultare start, jump; **sussulto** *m* start, jump

sussurrare whisper

svagarsi take one's mind off things; **svago** *m* distraction

svaligiare burgle, *Am* burglarize

svalutare devalue; **svalutazione** *f* devaluation

svanire vanish

svantaggio *m* disadvantage; **svantaggioso** disadvantageous

svariato varied

svedese 1 *m/agg* Swedish **2** *m/f* Swede

sveglia *f* alarm clock; **sve-**gliare wake (up); **svegliarsi** waken up; **sveglio** awake; *fig* alert

svelare *segreto* reveal

svelto quick; **alla -a** quickly

svendere sell at a reduced price; **svendita** *f* clearance

svenire faint

sventolare wave

svenuto *pp* ☞ **svenire**

svestire undress; **svestirsi** get undressed, undress

Svezia *f* Sweden

sviare deflect; *fig* divert

svignarsela slip away

sviluppare develop; **svilupparsi** develop; **sviluppato** developed; **sviluppo** *m* development

svincolo *m di strada* junction

svista *f* oversight

svitare unscrew; **svitato** unscrewed; *fig* F **essere ~** have a screw loose F

Svizzera *f* Switzerland; **svizzero 1** *agg* Swiss **2** *m*, **-a** *f* Swiss

svogliato lazy

svolgere *rotolo* unwrap; *tema* develop; *attività* carry out; **svolgersi** happen; *di film* be set

svolta *f* turning; *fig* turning point; **svoltare**: **~ a destra** turn right; **svolto** *pp* ☞ **svolgere**

svuotare empty

T

tabaccheria f tobacconist's, Am tobacco store; **tabacco** m tobacco

tabella f table; **tabellina** f multiplication table

tabellone m board; per avvisi notice board, Am bulletin board

tabù m/agg inv taboo

tabulato m printout

taccagno mean, stingy F

tacchino m turkey

tacco m heel

taccuino m notebook

tacere 1 v/t keep quiet about, say nothing about 2 v/i not say anything, be silent

tachicardia f tachycardia

tachimetro m speedometer

taciturno taciturn

tafano m ZO horsefly

tafferuglio m scuffle

taglia f (misura) size; ~ **unica** one size; **tagliacarte** m inv paper-knife; **tagliando** m coupon; AUTO service; **tagliare** cut; albero cut down; legna chop; **tagliarsi i capelli** have one's hair cut; fig ~ **la strada a qu** cut in front of s.o.; tagliarsi col o.s.: **mi sono tagliata un dito** I've cut my finger; **tagliatelle** fpl tagliatelle sg; **tagliente** sharp; **tagliere** m chopping board; **taglierini** mpl type of noo-

dles; **taglio** m cut

tailleur m inv suit

talco m talcum powder

tale such a; -i pl such; ~ **e quale** just like; **un** ~ someone

talento m talent

talloncino m coupon

tallone m heel

talmente so

talora sometimes

talpa f mole

talvolta sometimes

tamburo m drum

tamponamento m AUTO collision; ~ **a catena** multi-vehicle pile-up; **tamponare** falla plug; AUTO collide with; **tampone** m MED swab; per donne tampon; per timbri (ink) pad

tana f den

tandem m inv tandem

tangente f MAT tangent; F (bustarella) bribe; **tangenziale** f ring road

tanica f container

tanto 1 agg so much; -i pl so many; **-i saluti** best wishes; **-e grazie** thank you so much 2 pron much; **-i pl** many 3 avv (così) so; con verbi so much; **di ~ in ~** from time to time; ~ **quanto** as much as; **è da ~ (tempo) che non lo vedo** I haven't seen him for a long time

tappa *f* stop; *di viaggio* stage; **tappare** *f* plug; *bottiglia* put the cork in; **tapparella** *f* rolling shutter

tappeto *m* carpet

tappezzare (wall)paper; **tappezzeria** *f* wallpaper; *di sedili* upholstery

tappo *m* cap, top; *di sughero* cork; *di lavandini, vasche* plug

tarchiato stocky

tardare 1 *v/t* delay **2** *v/i* be late; **tardi** late; **più** ~ later (on); **al più** ~ at the latest; **a più** ~! see you!; **far** ~ (*arrivare in ritardo*) be late; (*stare alzato*) stay up late; *in ufficio* work late; **tardo** late

targa *f* nameplate; AUTO numberplate, *Am* license plate; **targhetta** *f* tag; *su porta* nameplate

tariffa *f* rate; *nei trasporti* fare

tarlato worm-eaten

tarlo *m* woodworm

tarma *f* (clothes) moth

tartaro *m* tartar

tartaruga *f* tortoise; *aquatica* turtle

tartina *f* canapé

tartufo *m* truffle

tasca *f* pocket; **tascabile 1** *agg* pocket *attr* **2** *m* paperback

tassa *f* tax; **tassametro** *m* meter; **tassare** tax

tassello *m* nel muro plug

tassista *m/f* taxi driver, cab driver

tasso *m* FIN rate; ~ **d'interesse** interest rate

tastare feel; *fig* ~ **il terreno** see how the land lies

tastiera *f* keyboard; **tasto** *m* key

tattica *f* tactics

tatto *m* (*senso*) touch; *fig* tact

tatuaggio *m* tattoo

tavola *f* table; (*asse*) plank, board; *in libro* plate; ~ **calda** snackbar; **mettersi a** ~ sit down to eat; **tavoletta** *f*: ~ **di cioccolata** bar of chocolate; **tavolo** *m* table

taxi *m inv* taxi, *esp Am* cab

tazza *f* cup; **tazzina** *f* espresso cup

tè *m inv* tea; ~ **freddo** iced tea

te you

teatrale theatre *attr*, *Am* theater *attr*; *fig* theatrical; **rappresentazione** *f* ~ play; **teatro** *m* theatre, *Am* theater; ~ **lirico** opera (house)

tecnica *f* technique; (*tecnologia*) technology; **tecnico 1** *agg* technical **2** *m* technician; **tecnologia** *f* technology; **alta** ~ high tech; **tecnologico** technological

tedesco 1 *m/agg* German **2** *m*, *-a f* German

tegame *m* (sauce)pan

teglia *f* baking tin

tegola *f* tile

teiera *f* teapot

tela *f* cloth; PITT canvas; ~ **cerata** oilcloth

telaio *m* loom; *di automobile*

chassis; *di bicicletta, finestra* frame

telecamera *f* television camera

telecomando *m* remote control

telecomunicazioni *fpl* telecommunications, telecomms

teleferica *f* cableway

telefilm *m inv* television film

telefonare (tele)phone, call (*a qu* s.o.); **telefonata** *f* (tele)phone call; **fare una ~ a qu** phone *o* call s.o.; **telefonico** (tele)phone *attr*; **telefonino** *m* mobile (phone), *Am* cell(ular) phone; **telefono** *m* (tele)phone; **~ a scheda (magnetica)** cardphone; **~ cellulare** mobile phone, *Am* cellular phone

telegiornale *m* news *sg*

telelavoro *m* teleworking

teleobiettivo *m* telephoto lens

telepatia *f* telepathy

teleschermo *m* TV screen

telescopio *m* telescope

telespettatore *m*, **-trice** *f* TV viewer

televisione *f* television, TV; **televisivo** television *attr*, TV *attr*; **televisore** *m* television (set), TV (set)

tema *m* theme, subject

temere be afraid *o* frightened of

temperamatite *m inv* pencil sharpener

temperamento *m* temperament

temperare *acciaio* temper; *matita* sharpen; **temperato** *acciaio* tempered; *clima* temperate

temperatura *f* temperature; **~ ambiente** room temperature

tempesta *f* storm

tempia *f* temple

tempio *m* temple

tempo *m* time; *meteorologico* weather; **~ meteorologico** weather; *a ~ pieno* full-time; *in ~* in time; *un ~* once, long ago; *lavora da molto* he has been working for a long time; *fa bel / brutto ~* the weather is lovely / nasty

temporale *m* thunderstorm; **temporaneo** temporary

tenace tenacious

tenaglie *fpl* pincers

tenda *f* curtain; *da campeggio* tent

tendenza *f* tendency; **tendere 1** *v/t elastico, muscoli* stretch; *corde del violino* tighten; *mano* hold out; *fig: trappola* lay; **2** *v/i:* **~ a** (*aspirare a*) aim at; (*essere portati a*) tend to; (*avvicinarsi a*) verge on

tendina *f* net curtain

tendine *m* tendon

tenente *m* lieutenant

tenere 1 *v/t* hold; (*conservare, mantenere*) keep; (*gestire*) run; *conferenza* give; **~ d'oc-**

chio keep an eye on **2** *v/i* hold (on); **~ a** (*dare importanza a*) care about; SP support

tenero tender; *pietra, legno* soft

tenersi (*reggersi*) hold on (**a** to); (*mantenersi*) keep o.s.; **~ in piedi** stand (up)

tengo ☞ *tenere*

tennis *m* tennis; **~ da tavolo** table tennis; **tennista** *m/f* tennis player

tenore *m* MUS tenor

tensione *f* voltage; *fig* tension

tentare try, attempt; (*allettare*) tempt; **tentativo** *m* attempt; **tentazione** *f* temptation

tenuta *f* (*capacità*) capacity; (*resistenza*) stamina; (*divisa*) uniform; (*abbigliamento*) outfit; AGR estate

teologo *m*, **-a** *f* theologian

teorema *m* theorem; **teoria** *f* theory; **teorico** theoretical

tepore *m* warmth

teppista *m/f* hooligan

terapia *f* therapy

tergicristallo *m* AUTO windscreen *o* Am windshield wiper

termale thermal; **terme** *fpl* baths

terminal *m inv* AVIA terminal; **terminale** *m/agg* terminal; **terminare** end, terminate; **termine** *m* end; (*confine*) limit; FIN (*scadenza*) deadline; (*parola*) term; **a breve / lungo ~** in the short / long term

termocoperta *f* electric blanket

termometro *m* thermometer

termos *m inv* thermos®

termosifone *m* radiator

termostato *m* thermostat

terra *f* earth; (*regione, proprietà, terreno agricolo*) land; (*superficie del suolo*) ground; (*pavimento*) floor; **a ~** on the ground; AVIA, MAR **scendere a ~** get off; **terracotta** *f* terracotta; **terraferma** *f* dry land, terra firma

terrazza *f*, **terrazzo** *m* balcony, terrace

terremoto *m* earthquake

terreno 1 *agg* earthly; *piano* ground, *Am* first **2** *m* (*superficie*) ground; (*suolo, materiale*) soil; (*appezzamento*) plot of land; *fig* (*settore, tema*) field, area; **terrestre** terrestrial

terribile terrible

terrina *f* bowl

territorio *m* territory

terrore *m* terror; **terrorismo** *m* terrorism; **terrorista** *m/f* terrorist; **terrorizzare** terrorize

terza *f* AUTO third (gear); **terziario** *m* tertiary sector, services; **terzino** *m* SP back; **terzo** third

teschio *m* skull

tesi *f inv*: **~ (di laurea)** thesis

teso 1 *pp* ☞ *tendere* **2** *agg* taut; *fig* tense

tesoro *m* treasure; (*tesoreria*)

treasury

tessera f card

tessile 1 agg textile **2** -i mpl textiles

tessuto m fabric, material

test m inv test

testa f head; **a** ~ a head; **essere in** ~ lead, be ahead

testamento m will

testardo stubborn

testata f (giornale) newspaper; di letto headboard

teste m/f witness

testicolo m testicle

testimone m/f witness; **testimoniare 1** v/i testify, give evidence **2** v/t fig testify to; DIR ~ **il falso** commit perjury

testo m text

tetano m tetanus

tetro gloomy

tetto m roof; **tettoia** f roof

Tevere m Tiber

TG m (= **Telegiornale**) TV news sg

thermos ☞ **termos**

ti you; riflessivo yourself

tibia f shinbone, tibia

tic m inv di orologio tick; MED tic

ticket m inv MED prescription charge

tiene ☞ **tenere**

tiepido lukewarm, tepid

tifo m MED typhus; fig **fare il** ~ **per** be a fan o supporter of; **tifoso** m, **-a** f fan, supporter

tigre f tiger

timbrare stamp; **timbro** m stamp; MUS timbre; ~ **posta-**

le postage stamp

timidezza f shyness, timidity; **timido** shy, timid

timo m BOT thyme

timone m MAR, AVIA rudder

timore m fear

timpano m MUS kettledrum; ANAT eardrum

tingere ☞ **tingere**

tinta f (colorante) dye; (colore) colour, Am color; **tintarella** f (sun)tan

tinto pp ☞ **tingere**

tintoria f dry-cleaner's

tintura f dyeing; (colorante) dye; ~ **di iodio** iodine

tipico typical

tipo m sort, type; F fig guy

tipografia f printing; stabilimento printer's

tir m heavy goods vehicle, Am truck

tiranno m tyrant

tirare 1 v/t pull; (tendere) stretch; (lanciare) throw; (sparare) fire; (tracciare) draw; ~ **fuori** take out; ~ **su da terra** pick up; bambino bring up; ~ **giù** take down **2** v/i pull; di abito be too tight; di vento blow; (sparare) shoot; **tirarsi**: ~ **indietro** back off; fig back out; **tiratura** di libro print run; di giornale circulation

tirchio 1 agg mean **2** m, **-a** f miser, skinflint F

tiro m (lancio) throw; (sparo) shot; ~ **con l'arco** archery

tirocinante m/f trainee; **tiro-**

cinio *m* training
tiroide *f* thyroid
tirolese *agg*, *m/f* Tyrolean, Tyrolese; Tirolo *m* Tyrol
tisana *f* herbal tea, tisane
titolare *m/f* owner; titolo *m* title; *dei giornali* headline; FIN security; ~ *di studio* qualification
titubare hesitate
tizio *m*, -a *f*: *un* ~ somebody, some man; *una* -*a* somebody, some woman
toccare 1 *v/t* touch; (*riguardare*) be about 2 *v/i* happen (*a* to); *tocca a me* it's my turn; *mi tocca partire* I have to go; tocco *m* touch
togliere take (away), remove; (*eliminare*) take off; (*revocare*) take out, extract; ~ *di mezzo* get rid of; togliersi giacca take off, remove; (*spostarsi*) take o.s. off; ~ *dai piedi* get out of the way; tolgo ☞ *togliere*
tollerante tolerant; tollerare tolerate
tolto *pp* ☞ *togliere*
tomba *f* grave
tombola *f* bingo
tonaca *f* habit
tonalità *f inv* tonality
tondo round
tonfo *m in acqua* splash
tonificare tone up
tonnellata *f* tonne
tonno *m* tuna
tono *m* tone
tonsille *fpl* ANAT tonsils; ton-

sillite *f* tonsillitis
topazio *m* topaz
topo *m* mouse; Topolino *m* Mickey Mouse
toppa *f* (*serratura*) keyhole; (*rattoppo*) patch
torace *m* chest
torbido *liquido* cloudy
torcere twist; *biancheria* wring; torchio *m* press
torcia *f* torch
torcicollo *m* stiff neck
tordo *m* thrush
torinese *m* of Turin; Torino *f* Turin
tormenta *f* snowstorm; tormentare torment; tormentarsi torment o.s.
tornaconto *m* benefit
tornante *m* hairpin bend
tornare *venire* come back, return; *andare* go back, return; (*quadrare*) balance; ~ *utile* prove useful
torneo *m* tournament
tornio *m* lathe
toro *m* bull; ASTR *Toro* Taurus
torre *f* tower
torrefazione *f* roasting
torrente *m* stream
torrido torrid
torrone *m* nougat
torso *m* torso
torsolo *m* core
torta *f* cake; tortellini *mpl* tortellini *sg*
torto *m* wrong; *aver* ~ be wrong; *a* ~ wrongly
tortora *f* turtledove
tortuoso (*sinuoso*) winding;

tortura															264

(ambiguo) devious

tortura f torture; **torturare** torture

tosaerba f o m lawnmower; **tosare** *pecore* shear

Toscana f Tuscany; **toscano** Tuscan

tosse f cough; **aver la ~** have a cough

tossico 1 agg toxic **2** m, -a f F druggie F; **tossicodipendente** m/f drug addict; **tossicodipendenza** f drug addiction; **tossicomane** m/f drug addict

tossire cough

tostapane m toaster; **tostare** *pane* toast; *caffè* roast

totale m/agg total; **totalità** f *(interezza)* totality; **nella ~ dei casi** in all cases

totip m competition similar to football pools, based on horse racing

totocalcio m competition similar to football pools

tovaglia f tablecloth; **tovagliolo** m napkin, serviette

tozzo 1 agg stocky **2** m *di pane* crust

tra ☞ **fra**

traballare stagger; *di mobile* wobble

traboccare overflow *(anche fig)*

traccia f *(orma)* footprint; *di veicolo* track; *(indizio)* clue; *(segno)* trace; *(abbozzo)* sketch; **tracciare** *linea* draw; *(delineare)* outline; *(abbozza-*

re) sketch

trachea f windpipe

tracolla f (shoulder) strap; **a ~** slung over one's shoulder; **borsa f a ~** shoulder bag

tradimento m betrayal; **tradire** betray; **coniuge** be unfaithful to; **tradirsi** give o.s. away; **traditore 1** agg *(infedele)* unfaithful **2** m, -trice traitor

tradizionale traditional; **tradizione** f tradition

tradotto pp ☞ **tradurre**; **tradurre** translate *(in* into); **traduttore** m, -trice f translator; **traduzione** f translation

trafficante m/f spreg dealer; **~ di droga** drug dealer; **trafficare** deal, trade *(in* in); spreg traffic *(in* in); *(armeggiare)* tinker; *(affaccendarsi)* bustle about; **traffico** m traffic

traforo m tunnel

tragedia f tragedy

traghetto m ferry

tragico tragic

tragitto m journey

traguardo m finishing line

traiettoria f trajectory

trainare *(rimorchiare)* tow; *di animali* pull, draw; **traino** m towing; *veicolo* vehicle on tow; **a ~** on tow

tralasciare *(omettere)* omit, leave out; *(interrompere)* interrupt

traliccio m EL pylon; TEC trellis

tram m inv tram

trama f fig plot

tramandare hand down

tramare fig plot

trambusto m (confusione)
bustle; (tumulto) commotion

tramezzino m sandwich

tramite 1 m (collegamento)
link; (intermediario) go-between 2 prp through

tramontana f north wind

tramontare set; tramonto m
sunset; fig decline

trampolino m diving board;
SCI ski jump

tranello m trap

tranne except

tranquillante m tranquillizer,
Am tranquilizer; tranquillità
f peacefulness, tranquillity;
tranquillizzare: ~ qu set
s.o.'s mind at rest; tranquillo
calm, peaceful

transatlantico 1 agg transatlantic 2 m liner

transazione f DIR settlement;
FIN transaction

transenna f barrier

transgenico genetically
modified

transitabile strada passable

transitivo GRAM transitive

transito m transit; divieto di
~ no thoroughfare

trantran m F routine

tranviere m (manovratore)
tram driver; (controllore)
tram conductor

trapanare drill; trapano m
drill

trapezio m trapeze; trapezi-

sta m/f trapeze artist

trapiantare transplant; trapianto m transplant

trappola f trap

trapunta f quilt

trarre conclusioni draw; vantaggio derive

trasalire jump

trasandato scruffy; lavoro
slipshod

trasbordo m transfer

trascinare drag; (travolgere)
sweep away; fig (entusiasmare) carry away

trascorrere 1 v/t spend 2 v/i
pass, go by; trascorso pp
☞ trascorrere

trascrivere transcribe

trascurabile unimportant; trascurare neglect; (trala-
sciare) ignore; trascurato
careless, negligent; (trasandato) slovenly; (ignorato) neglected

trasferibile transferable; trasferimento m transfer; trasferire transfer; trasferirsi
move; trasferta f transfer;
SP away game

trasformare transform; TEC
process; trasformarsi
change, turn (in into); trasformatore m transformer;
trasformazione f transformation

trasfusione f transfusion

trasgredire disobey; tra-
sgressore m transgressor

traslocare move; trasloco m
move

trasmettere pass on; RAD, TV broadcast, transmit; tra*smissione* f transmission; RAD, TV broadcast, transmission; (*programma*) programme, Am program

trasparente 1 agg transparent **2** m transparency

trasportare transport; tra*sporto* m transport; *-i pl* **pubblici** public transport, Am mass transit

trasversale 1 agg transverse **2** f MAT transversal

tratta f trade; FIN draft

trattamento m treatment; trat*tare* **1** v/t treat; TEC treat, process; FIN deal in; (*negoziare*) negotiate **2** v/i deal; ~ *di* be about; trattarsi: *di che si tratta?* what's it about?; trattative fpl negotiations, talks; trattato m treatise; DIR, POL treaty

trattenere (*far restare*) keep, hold; (*far perder tempo*) hold up; (*frenare*) restrain; *fiato, respiro* hold; *lacrime* hold back; *somma* withhold; trattenersi (*rimanere*) stay; (*frenarsi*) restrain o.s.; ~ *dal fare qc* refrain from doing sth; trattenuta f deduction

trattino m dash; *in parole composte* hyphen; tratto **1** pp ☞ **trarre 2** m di spazio, tempo stretch; *di penna* stroke; (*linea*) line; *a un* ~ all of a sudden; *-i pl* (*lineamenti*) features

trattore m tractor

trattoria f restaurant

trauma m trauma; traumati*co* traumatic

travaglio m MED labour, Am labor

travasare decant

trave f beam

traversa f crossbeam; traver*sare* cross; traversata f crossing; traverso: *andare di* ~ *di cibi* go down the wrong way

travestire disguise; travestir*si* disguise o.s., dress up (*da* as); travestito m transvestite

travolgere carry away (*anche fig*); *con un veicolo* run over; travolto pp ☞ **travolgere**

trazione f TEC traction; AUTO ~ *anteriore* / *posteriore* front- / rear-wheel drive

tre three

treccia f plait

trecento 1 agg three hundred **2** m: *il Trecento* the fourteenth century; tredicesimo thirteenth; tredici thirteen

tregua f truce; *fig* break, let-up

trekking m hiking

tremare tremble, shake (*di, per* with)

tremendo terrible, tremendous

tremila three thousand

treno m train; *in* ~ by train

trenta thirty; trentenne agg, m/f thirty-year-old; trentesimo thirtieth; trentina: *una* ~

about thirty

treppiedi *m inv* tripod

triangolare triangular; **triangolo** *m* triangle; AUTO warning triangle

tribù *f inv* tribe

tribuna *f* platform; **tribunale** *m* court

tributo *m* tax; *fig* tribute

tricheco *m* walrus

triciclo *m* tricycle

tricolore *m* Italian flag

triennale *contratto* three-year; *mostra* three-yearly; **triennio** *m* three-year period

trifoglio *m* clover

triglia *f* red mullet

trillo *m* trill

trimestrale quarterly

trincea *f* trench

trio *m* trio

trionfare triumph (**su** over); **trionfo** *m* triumph

triplicare triple; **triplo 1** *agg* triple **2** *m*: **il ~** three times as much (**di** as)

trippa *f* tripe

triste sad; **tristezza** *f* sadness

tritare mince, *Am* ground meat; **tritatutto** *m inv* mincer, *Am* meat grinder

trittico *m* triptych

triturare grind

trivella *f* drill

triviale trivial

trofeo *m* trophy

tromba *f* MUS trumpet; **~ d'aria** whirlwind; **~ delle scale** stairwell

trombone *m* trombone

trombosi *f* thrombosis

troncare cut off; *fig* break off

tronco *m* ANAT, BOT trunk; FERR section

trono *m* throne

tropicale tropical; **tropici** *mpl* tropics

troppo 1 *agg* too much; **-i** *pl* too many **2** *avv* too much; *con agg* too; **è ~ tardi** it's too late

trota *f* trout

trottare trot; **trotto** *m* trot

trovare find; (*inventare*) find, come up with; **andare a ~ qu** (go and) see s.o.; **trovarsi** be; **~ bene** be happy; **trovata** *f* good idea

truccare make up; *motore* soup up F; *partita, elezioni* fix; **truccarsi** put on one's make-up; **trucco** *m* make-up; (*inganno, astuzia*) trick

truffa *f* fraud; **truffare** defraud (**di** of); **truffatore** *m*, **-trice** *f* trickster, con artist F

truppa *f* troops

tu you; **dammi del ~** call me 'tu'

tubatura *f*, **tubazione** *f* pipes, piping

tubercolosi *f* tuberculosis

tubetto *m* tube

tubo *m* pipe; *flessibile* hose; AUTO **~ di scappamento** exhaust (pipe)

tuffarsi (*immergersi*) dive; (*buttarsi dentro*) throw o.s. (*anche fig*); **tuffo** *m* dip; SP dive

tugurio m hovel

tulipano m tulip

tumore m tumour, Am tumor

tumulto m tumult

tunica f tunic

Tunisia f Tunisia; **tunisino** 1 agg Tunisian 2 m, -a f Tunisian

tunnel m inv tunnel

tuo 1 agg your; **il ~ amico** your friend; **un ~ amico** a friend of yours 2 pron: **il ~** yours

tuonare thunder; **tuono** m thunder

tuorlo m yolk

turbante m turban

turbare upset, disturb; **turbolenza** f turbulence

turchese m/agg turquoise

Turchia f Turkey; **turco** 1 m/agg Turkish 2 m, -a f Turk

turismo m tourism; **turista** m/f tourist; **turistico** tourist attr

turno m turn; di lavoro shift; **a ~** in turn; **~ di riposo** rest day; **darsi il ~** take turns

tuta f da lavoro overalls; **~ da ginnastica** track suit, Am sweats; **~ da sci** ski suit

tutela f protection; DIR guardianship; **tutelare** protect; **tutore** m, **-trice** f guardian

tuttavia still

tutto 1 agg whole; **-i, -e** pl all; **~ il libro** the whole book; **-i i giorni** every day; **-i e tre** all three; **noi -i** all of us 2 avv all; **era ~ solo** he was all alone; **del ~** quite; **in ~** altogether, in all 3 pron all; gente everybody, everyone; cose everything

tuttora still

TV f inv TV

U

ubbidiente obedient; **ubbidire** obey

ubriacare: **~ qu** get s.o. drunk; **ubriacarsi** get drunk; **ubriaco** 1 agg drunk 2 m, -a f drunk

uccello m bird

uccidere kill; **uccidersi** kill o.s.; **ucciso** pp ☞ **uccidere**

udienza f audience; DIR hearing; **udire** hear; **udito** m hearing

Ue f (= **Unione europea**) EU (= European Union)

ufficiale 1 agg official 2 m official; MIL officer; **ufficio** m office; **~ cambi** bureau de change; **~ postale** post office; **~ turistico** tourist information office; **ufficioso** unofficial

ufo m UFO

uguaglianza f equality; **uguagliare** make equal; (livellare) level; (essere pari a) equal; **uguale** equal; (lo stes-

so) the same; *terreno* level

ulcera *f* ulcer

ulteriore further

ultimamente recently; **ultimare** complete; **ultimatum** *m inv* ultimatum; **ultimo 1** *agg* last; (*più recente*) latest; ~ **piano** top floor **2** *m*, -a *f* last; **fino all'~** to the end

ultrasuono *m* ultrasound

ultravioletto ultraviolet

ululare howl

umanità *f* humanity; **umanitario** humanitarian; **umano** human; *trattamento ecc* humane

umidificatore *m* humidifier; **umidità** *f* dampness; *di clima* humidity; **umido 1** *agg* damp **2** *m* dampness; GASTR **in** ~ stewed

umile (*modesto*) humble; *mestiere* menial; **umiliante** humiliating; **umiliare** humiliate; **umiliazione** *f* humiliation; **umiltà** *f* humility

umore *m* mood; **di buon** ~ in a good mood; **di cattivo** ~ in a bad mood

umorismo *m* humour, *Am* humor

un, una ☞ **uno**

unanime unanimous; **unanimità** *f* unanimity; **all'~** unanimously

uncinetto *m* crochet hook; **uncino** *m* hook

undicesimo eleventh; **undici** eleven

ungere grease

ungherese *agg*, *m/f* Hungarian; **Ungheria** *f* Hungary

unghia *f* nail

unico only; (*senza uguali*) unique

unifamiliare: **casa** *f* ~ detached house

unificazione *f* unification

uniformare standardize; **uniformarsi**: ~ **a** conform to; *regole* comply with; **uniforme** *f* agg uniform

unione *f* union; *fig* unity; **Unione europea** European Union; **unire** unite; (*congiungere*) join; **unirsi** unite; **unità** *f inv* unit; INFOR ~ **disco** disk drive; ~ **di misura** unit of measurement; **unito** united

universale universal; **università** *f inv* university; **universitario 1** *agg* university *attr* **2** *m*, -a *f* university student; (*professore*) university lecturer; **universo** *m* universe

uno 1 *art* a; *before a vowel or silent h* an; **un uovo** an egg **2** *agg* a, one **3** *m* one; ~ **e mezzo** one and a half **4** *pron* one; **a** ~ **a** ~ one by one; **l'un l'altro** each other, one another

unto 1 *pp* ☞ **ungere 2** *agg* greasy **3** *m* grease

uomo *m* man; ~ **d'affari** businessman; **da** ~ *abbigliamento ecc* for men, men's

uovo *m* egg; ~ **alla coque** soft-boiled egg; ~ **di Pasqua** Easter egg; ~ **al tegame**

fried egg; **-a** *pl* **strapazzate** scrambled eggs

uragano *m* hurricane

uranio *m* uranium

urbano urban; *fig* urbane

urgente urgent; **urgenza** *f* urgency; **in caso d'~** in an emergency

urina *f* urine

urlare scream; **urlo** *m* scream

urna *f* urn; *elettorale* ballot box

urrà! hooray!

urtare bump into; *fig* offend

urto *m* bump; (*scontro*) collision

usa: ~ e getta disposable, throw-away

usanza *f* custom, tradition; **usare** 1 *v/t* use 2 *v/i* use; (*essere di moda*) be in fashion; **usato** used; (*di seconda mano*) second-hand

uscire come out; (*andare fuo-*

ri) go out; **uscita** *f* exit, way out; **~ di sicurezza** emergency exit

usignolo *m* nightingale

uso *m* use; (*abitudine*) custom; **fuori ~** out of use; **per ~ esterno** not to be taken internally

ustionarsi burn o.s.; **ustione** *f* burn

usuale usual

usufruire: ~ di qc have the use of sth

usuraio *m* loan shark

utensile *m* utensil

utente *m/f* user

utero *m* womb

utile 1 *agg* useful **2** *m* FIN profit; **utilità** *f* usefulness; **utilitaria** *f* economy car; **utilizzare** use; **utilizzazione** *f* use

utopia *f* utopia

uva *f* grapes; **~ passa** raisins *pl*; **~ spina** gooseberry

V

V. (= *via*) St (= *street*)

va ☞ **andare**

vacanza *f* holiday, *Am* vacation; **andare in ~** go on holiday

vacca *f* cow

vaccinare vaccinate; **vaccinazione** *f* vaccination; **vaccino** *m* vaccine

vado ☞ **andare**

vagabondo 1 *agg* (*girovago*) wandering; (*fannullone*) idle

2 *m*, **-a** *f* (*giramondo*) wanderer; (*fannullone*) idler, layabout F; (*barbone*) tramp, *Am* hobo; **vagare** wander (aimlessly)

vagina *f* ANAT vagina

vaglia *m inv:* **~ (postale)** postal order

vago vague

vagone *m* carriage, car; *per merci* wagon; **~ letto** sleeper; **~ ristorante** dining car

vegetariano

vai ☞ *andare*

valanga *f* avalanche

valere be worth; (*essere valido*) be valid; *far ~ diritti, autorità* assert; **valersi: ~ di qc** avail o.s. of sth; **valevole** valid

valgo ☞ *valere*

valico *m* pass

validità *f* validity; **valido** valid; *persona* fit

valigia *f* suitcase; *fare le ~* pack

valle *f* valley

valore *m* value; (*coraggio*) bravery, valour, *Am* valor; *-i pl* securities; *di ~* valuable; **valorizzare** increase the value of; (*far risaltare*) show off

valuta *f* currency; **valutare** value

valvola *f* valve; EL fuse

valzer *m inv* waltz

vandalo *m* vandal

vanga *f* spade

vangelo *m* gospel

vaniglia *f* vanilla

vanità *f* vanity; **vanitoso** vain

vanno ☞ *andare*

vano 1 *agg* minacce, promesse empty; (*inutile*) vain **2** *m* (*spazio vuoto*) hollow; (*stanza*) room

vantaggio *m* advantage; *in gara* lead; **vantaggioso** advantageous

vantarsi boast (*di* about)

vapore *m* vapour, *Am* vapor; MAR steamer; *~ (acqueo)* steam; **vaporetto** *m* water

bus; **vaporoso** floaty; (*vago*) woolly, *Am* wooly

variabile 1 *agg* changeable **2** *f* MAT variable; **variare** vary; **variazione** *f* variation

varice *f* varicose vein

varicella *f* chickenpox

varietà 1 *f inv* variety **2** *m inv* variety, *Am* vaudeville; **(spettacolo** *m* **di) ~** (variety o *Am* vaudeville) show; **vario** varied; *-ri pl* various

variopinto multicoloured, *Am* multicolored

vasca *f* (*serbatoio, cisterna*) tank; (*lunghezza di piscina*) length; *di fontana* basin; *~* **(da bagno)** bath, (bath)tub

vaselina *f* vaseline

vasellame *m* dishes

vaso *m* pot; ANAT vessel

vassoio *m* tray

vasto vast

V.d.F. (= *vigili del fuoco*) fire brigade, *Am* fire department

ve ☞ *vi* (*before lo, la, li, le, ne*)

vecchiaia *f* old age; **vecchio 1** *agg* old **2** *m*, *-a f* old man; *donna* old woman

vece *f*: *fare le -i di qu* take s.o.'s place

vedere see; *far ~* show

vedovo 1 *agg* widowed **2** *m*, *-a f* widower; *donna* widow

veduta *f* view (*su* of)

vegetale 1 *agg* vegetable *attr*; *vita* plant *attr* **2** *m* vegetable; **vegetariano 1** *agg* vegetarian *attr* **2** *m*, *-a f* vegetarian;

vegetazione f vegetation

vegeto *vecchio* spry; *vivo e ~* hale and hearty

veglia f (*l'essere svegli*) wakefulness; (*il vegliare*) vigil

veicolo m vehicle

vela f sail; *attività* sailing

veleno m poison; *di animali* venom (*anche fig*); **velenoso** poisonous; *fig* venomous

veliero m sailing ship

velina: *carta f ~ per imballaggio* tissue paper

velista m/f sailor

velluto m velvet; *~ a coste* corduroy

velo m veil

veloce fast, quick; **velocemente** quickly; **velocità** f inv speed

vena f vein

vendemmia f (grape) harvest; **vendemmiare** harvest

vendere sell

vendetta f revenge; **vendicare** avenge; **vendicarsi** get one's revenge (*di qu* on s.o.; *di qc* for sth)

vendita f sale; **venditore** m, **-trice** f salesman; *donna* saleswoman

venerare revere

venerdì m inv Friday; *Venerdì Santo* Good Friday

Venere f Venus

Venezia f Venice; **veneziano** 1 agg Venetian 2 m, -a f Venetian

vengo ☞ **venire**; **venire** come; (*riuscire*) turn out; *co-*

me ausiliare be; *mi sta venendo fame* I'm getting hungry

ventaglio m fan

ventenne agg, m/f twenty-year-old; **ventesimo** twentieth; **venti** twenty

ventilatore m fan

ventina f: *una ~* about twenty; **ventiquattrore** f inv valigetta overnight bag

vento m wind; *c'è ~* it's windy; **ventoso** windy

ventre m stomach

venuta f arrival; **venuto** pp ☞ **venire**

veramente really

veranda f veranda

verbale 1 agg verbal 2 m record; *di riunione* minutes

verbo m GRAM verb

verde 1 agg green 2 m green; POL *i* -*i* pl the Greens

verdetto m verdict

verdura f vegetables

vergine 1 agg virgin attr 2 f virgin; ASTR *Vergine* Virgo

vergogna f shame; (*timidezza*) shyness; **vergognarsi** be ashamed; (*essere timido*) be shy; **vergognoso** ashamed; (*timido*) shy; *azione* shameful

verifica f check; **verificare** check; **verificarsi** (*accadere*) occur, take place; (*avverarsi*) come true

verità f inv truth

verme m worm

vermut m vermouth

vernice *f* paint; *trasparente* varnish; *pelle* patent leather; **~ fresca** wet paint; **verniciare** paint; *con vernice trasparente* varnish

vero 1 *agg* true; *(autentico)* real; **sei contento, ~?** you're happy, aren't you?; **ti piace il gelato, ~?** you like ice cream, don't you? **2** *m* truth

veronese 1 *agg* of Verona **2** *m/f* inhabitant of Verona

verosimile likely

verruca *f* wart

versamento *m* payment

versante *m* slope

versare *vino* pour; *denaro* pay; *(rovesciare)* spill

versione *f* version; *(traduzione)* translation

verso 1 *prp* towards; **andare ~ casa** head for home; **~ le otto** about eight o'clock **2** *m* *di poesie* verse

vertebra *f* vertebra; **vertebrale: colonna** *f* **~** spinal column

verticale 1 *agg* vertical **2** *f* vertical (line); *in ginnastica* handstand

vertice *m* summit

vertigine *f* vertigo, dizziness; **ho le ~i** I feel dizzy; **vertiginoso** *altezza* dizzy; *prezzi* sky-high; *velocità* breakneck

verza *f* savoy (cabbage)

vescica *f* ANAT bladder

vescovo *m* bishop

vespa *f* ZO wasp

vestaglia *f* dressing gown,

Am robe

veste *f* fig *(capacità, funzione)* capacity; *in ~ ufficiale* in an offical capacity; **vestiario** *m* wardrobe; **vestire** dress; *(portare)* wear; **vestirsi** get dressed; *in un certo modo* dress; **~ da** *(travestirsi)* dress up as; **vestito** *m* da uomo suit; *da donna* dress; *(capo di vestiario)* item of clothing, garment; *-i pl* clothes; *-i pl da uomo* menswear

veterinario *m*, *-a f* veterinary surgeon, vet F

veto *m* veto; **porre il ~ a** veto

vetrata *f* *finestra* large window; *porta* glass door; *di chiesa* stained-glass window; **vetrina** *f* (shop) window; *mobile* display cabinet; *di museo*, fig showcase; **vetrinista** *m/f* window dresser; **vetro** *m* glass; *di finestra, porta pane*; **di ~** glass *attr*

vetta *f* top; *di montagna* peak

vettura *f* AUTO car; FERR carriage, car

vi 1 *pron* you; *riflessivo* yourselves; *reciproco* each other **2** *avv* ☞ **ci**

via 1 *f* street, road; fig way; **per ~ di** by; *(a causa di)* because of **2** *m* off, starting signal; SP **dare il ~** give the off **3** *avv* away; **andar ~** go away, leave; **e così ~** and so on; **~!** per scacciare go away!; *(suvvia)* come on! **4** *prp* via, by way of

viabilità f road conditions; (*rete stradale*) road network; (*traffico stradale*) road traffic

viadotto m viaduct

viaggiare travel; **viaggiatore** m, **-trice** f traveller, Am traveler; **viaggio** m journey; ~ **di nozze** honeymoon; ~ **d'affari** business trip; ~ **di studio** study trip; **essere in** ~ be away, be travelling

viale m avenue

viavai m inv coming and going

vibrare vibrate; **vibrazione** f vibration

vice m/f inv deputy

vice- prefisso vice-

vicedirettore m assistant manager

vicenda f (*episodio*) event; (*storia*) story; **a** ~ (*a turno*) in turn; (*scambievolmente*) each other, one another

viceversa vice versa

vicinanza f nearness, proximity; **-e** pl neighbourhood, Am neighborhood, vicinity; **vicinato** m neighbourhood, Am neighborhood, (*persone*) neighbours, Am neighbors; **vicino 1** agg near, close; ~ **a** near, close to; (*accanto a*) next to; **da** ~ esaminare closely; **visto** close up **2** avv nearby, close by **3** m, **-a** f neighbour, Am neighbor

vicolo m lane; ~ **cieco** dead end

videata f INFOR display

video m video; F (*schermo*) screen; **videocamera** f videocamera, camcorder; **videocassetta** f video (cassette); **videogioco** m video game; **videoregistratore** m video (recorder); **videoteca** f video library; **negozio** m video shop o Am store; **videotel** m inv Italian Videotex®; **videotelefono** m videophone

vietare forbid; ~ **a qu di fare qc** forbid s.o. to do sth; **vietato** forbidden; ~ **fumare** no smoking

vigilanza f vigilance; **sotto** ~ under surveillance; **vigile 1** agg watchful **2** m/f: ~ (**urbano**) local police officer; ~ **del fuoco** firefighter; **vigilia** f night before, eve; ~ **di Natale** Christmas Eve

vigliacco 1 agg cowardly **2** m, **-a** f coward

vigna f (small) vineyard; **vigneto** m vineyard

vignetta f cartoon

vigore m vigour, Am vigor

vile 1 agg vile; (*codardo*) cowardly **2** m coward

villa f villa

villaggio m village; ~ **turistico** holiday village

villeggiatura f holiday, Am vacation

villino m house

vincere v/t win; *avversario* defeat, beat; *difficoltà* overcome **2** v/i win; **vincita** f win; **vincitore** *m*, **-trice** *f* winner

vincolare bind; *capitale* tie up; **vincolo** *m* bond

vino *m* wine; **~ bianco** white wine; **~ rosso** red wine

vinto *pp* ☞ **vincere**

viola 1 *m/agg inv* purple **2** *f* MUS viola; BOT violet

violare violate; *legge* break; **violazione** *f* violation; *di leggi, accordi* breach; **~ di domicilio** unlawful entry

violentare rape; **violento** violent; **violenza** *f* violence

violino *m* violin; **violoncello** *m* cello

vipera *f* viper

virgola *f* comma; MAT decimal point

virile manly, virile

virtù *f inv* virtue

virus *m inv* virus

vischio *m* mistletoe

viscido slimy

viscosa *f* viscose

visibile visible; **visibilità** *f* visibility

visiera *f di berretto* peak; *di casco* visor

visione *f* sight, vision

visita *f* visit; **~ medica** medical (examination); **far ~ a qu** visit s.o.; **visitare** visit; MED examine; **visitatore** *m*, **-trice** *f* visitor

visivo visual

viso *m* face

visone *m* mink

vissuto *pp* ☞ **vivere**

vista *f* sight; (*veduta*) view; **a prima ~** at first sight; **conoscere qu di ~** know s.o. by sight; *fig* **perdere qu di ~** lose touch with s.o.; **visto 1** *pp* ☞ **vedere**; **~ che** seeing that **2** *m* visa; **vistoso** eye-catching

visuale 1 *agg* visual **2** *f* (*veduta*) view

vita *f* life; (*durata della vita*) lifetime; ANAT waist; **vitale** vital; *persona* lively

vitamina *f* vitamin

vite[1] *f* TEC screw

vite[2] *f* AGR vine

vitello *m* calf; GASTR veal

viticoltura *f* vinegrowing

vitreo *fig*: *sguardo* glazed

vittima *f* victim

vitto *m* diet food; **~ e alloggio** bed and board

vittoria *f* victory

viva voce *m inv* speakerphone, hands-free phone

vivace lively; *colore* bright

vivaio *m di pesci* tank; *di piante* nursery; *fig* breeding ground

vivanda *f* food

vivente living; **vivere 1** *v/i* live (*di* on) **2** *v/t* (*passare, provare*) experience; *vita* live, lead; **viveri** *mpl* food (supplies)

vivisezione *f* vivisection

vivo 1 *agg* (*in vita*) alive; (*vivente*) living; *colore* bright; **farsi ~** get in touch; (*arrivare*) turn up **2** *m*: **dal ~** *trasmissione* live; **i -i** *pl* the living *pl*

viziare *persona* spoil; **viziato** *persona* spoiled; **aria** *f* **-a** stale air; **vizio** *m* vice; (*cattiva abitudine*) (bad) habit; (*dipendenza*) addiction; **vizioso** *persona* dissolute; **circolo** *m* ~ vicious circle

v.le (= *viale*) St (= street)

vocabolario *m* vocabulary; (*dizionario*) dictionary; **vocabolo** *m* word

vocale 1 *agg* vocal **2** *f* vowel

vocazione *f* vocation

voce *f* voice; *fig* rumour, *Am* rumor; **in dizionario, elenco** entry

voglia *f* (*desiderio*) wish, desire; (*volontà*) will; **sulla pelle** birthmark; **avere ~ di fare qc** feel like doing sth; **contro ~, di mala ~** unwillingly; **voglio** ☞ **volere**

voi *pron; riflessivo* yourselves; **reciproco** each other

volano *m* shuttlecock

volante 1 *agg* flying **2** *m* AUTO (steering) wheel; **volantino** *m* leaflet; **volare** *f/v* fly

volentieri willingly; **~!** with pleasure!

volere 1 *v/t & v/i* want; **vorrei ...** I would *o* I'd like ...; **vorrei partire** I'd like to leave; **~ dire** mean; **~ bene a qu** (*amare*) love s.o.; **ci vogliono dieci mesi** it takes ten months; **senza ~** without meaning to **2** *m* will

volgare vulgar

volgere 1 *v/t*: **~ le spalle** turn

one's back **2** *v/i*: **~ al termine** draw to a close

volo *m* flight; (*caduta*) fall; **~ di linea** scheduled flight; *fig* **afferrare qc al ~** be quick to grasp sth

volontà *f* will; **a ~** as much as you like; **buona ~** goodwill; **volontariato** *m* voluntary work; **volontario 1** *agg* voluntary **2** *m*, **-a** *f* volunteer

volpe *f* fox; **femmina** vixen

volt *m inv* volt

volta *f* time; (*turno*) turn; ARCHI vault; **una ~** once; **due ~e** twice; **qualche ~** sometimes; **poco per ~** little by little; **un'altra ~** (*ancora una volta*) one more time; **lo faremo un'altra ~** we'll do it some other time

voltaggio *m* voltage

voltare turn; **~ a destra** turn right; **voltarsi** turn (round)

volto¹ *m* face

volto² *pp* ☞ **volgere**

volume *m* volume; **voluminoso** bulky

vomitare vomit; **vomito** *m* vomit

vongola *f* ZO, GASTR clam

vortice *m* whirl; **in acqua** whirlpool; **di vento** whirlwind

vostro 1 *agg* your; **i -i amici** your friends **2** *pron*: **il ~** yours; **questi libri sono -i** these books are yours

votare vote; **votazione** *f* vote; **voto** *m* POL vote; EDU mark,

Am grade; REL vow
v.r. (= *vedi retro*) see over
v.s. (= *vedi sopra*) see above
Vs. (= *vostro*) your
V.U. (= *Vigili Urbani*) police
vulcanico volcanic; vulcano *m* volcano
vulnerabile vulnerable

vuole ☞ *volere*
vuotare empty; vuotarsi empty; vuoto 1 *agg* empty; (*non occupato*) vacant 2 *m* (*spazio*) empty space; (*recipiente*) empty; FIS vacuum; *fig* void; *andare a ~* fall through

W

W (= *watt*) W (= watt); (= *viva*) long live
walkman *m inv* Walkman®
watt *m inv* watt
WC *m inv* WC
week-end *m inv* weekend

western *m inv* Western
whisky *m inv* whisky
windsurf *m inv* (*tavola*) sailboard; *attività* windsurfing; *fare ~* go windsurfing

X

X, x *f* x; *raggi mpl ~* X-rays
xenofobia *f* xenophobia

xilofono *m* xylophone

Y

yacht *m inv* yacht
yoga *m* yoga

yogurt *m inv* yoghurt

Z

zafferano *m* saffron
zaffiro *m* sapphire
zaino *m* rucksack, backpack
zampa *f* ZO (*piede*) paw; *di uccello* claw; (*arto*) leg; GASTR *di maiale* trotter

zampillare gush; zampillo *m* spurt
zampone *m* GASTR stuffed pig's trotter
zanzara *f* mosquito; zanzariera *f* mosquito net; *su fine-*

stre insect screen

zappa *f* hoe; **zappare** hoe

zapping *m inv*: **fare lo ~** zap, channel-punch

zattera *f* raft

zebra *f* zebra

zecca[1] *f* ZO tick

zecca[2] *f* Mint

zelo *m* zeal

zenzero *m* ginger

zeppo: **pieno ~** crammed (**di** with)

zerbino *m* doormat

zero *m* zero; *nel tennis* love; *nel calcio* nil; **2 gradi sotto ~** 2 degrees below zero

zigomo *m* cheekbone

zigzag *m inv* zigzag

zimbello *m* decoy; *fig* laughing stock

zinco *m* zinc

zingaro *m*, **-a** *f* gipsy

zio *m*, **-a** *f* uncle; *donna* aunt

zitto quiet; **sta ~!** be quiet!

zoccolo *m* clog; ZO hoof

zodiacale: **segni** *mpl* **-i** signs of the Zodiac

zolfo *m* sulphur, *Am* sulfur

zona *f* zone, area; **~ disco** short-stay parking area; **~ industriale** industrial area; **~ pedonale** pedestrian precinct

zoo *m inv* zoo

zoppicare limp; *di mobile* wobble

zoppo lame; (*zoppicante*) limping; *mobile* wobbly

zucca *f* marrow; *fig* F (*testa*) nut F

zuccherare sugar; **zucchero** *m* sugar

zucchini *mpl* courgettes, *Am* zucchini(s)

zuffa *f* scuffle

zuppa *f* soup; **~ inglese** trifle

zuppo soaked

A

a [ə] un *m*, una *f*; *masculine before s + consonant, gn, ps, x, y, z* uno; *feminine before vowel* un'; *five flights ~ day* cinque voli al giorno

aback [ə'bæk]: *taken ~* preso alla sprovvista

abandon [ə'bændən] abbandonare; *scheme* rinunciare a

abate [ə'beɪt] *of storm* calmarsi

abbey ['æbɪ] abbazia *f*

abbreviate [ə'briːvɪeɪt] abbreviare; **abbreviation** abbreviazione *f*

abdicate ['æbdɪkeɪt] abdicare

abdomen ['æbdəmən] addome *m*

abduct [əb'dʌkt] sequestrare

◆ **abide by** [ə'baɪd] attenersi a

ability [ə'bɪlətɪ] abilità *f inv*

ablaze [ə'bleɪz] in fiamme

able ['eɪbl] (*skilful*) capace; *be ~ to do sth* poter fare qc

abnormal [æb'nɔːml] anormale

aboard [ə'bɔːd] **1** *prep* a bordo di **2** *adv* a bordo

abolish [ə'bɒlɪʃ] abolire; **abolition** abolizione *f*

abort [ə'bɔːt] annullare; *program* interrompere; **abortion** aborto *m*; *have an ~* abortire; **abortive** fallito

about [ə'baut] **1** *prep* (*concerning*) su; *talk ~ sth* parlare di qc; *be angry ~ sth* essere arrabbiato per qc; *what's it ~?* *of book, film* di cosa parla?; *of complaint, problem* di cosa si tratta? **2** *adv* (*roughly*) intorno a; (*nearly*) quasi; *it's ~ ready* è quasi pronto; *be ~ to ...* (*be going to*) essere sul punto di ...; *be ~* (*somewhere near*) essere nei paraggi; *there are a lot of people ~* c'è un sacco di gente qui

above [ə'bʌv] sopra; *on the floor ~* al piano di sopra; **above-mentioned** suddetto

abrasive [ə'breɪsɪv] *personality* ruvido

abreast [ə'brest] fianco a fianco; *keep ~ of* tenere al corrente di

abridge [ə'brɪdʒ] ridurre

abroad [ə'brɔːd] all'estero

abrupt [ə'brʌpt] brusco

abscess ['æbsɪs] ascesso *m*

absolute ['æbsəlu:t] assoluto; *idiot* totale; **absolutely** (*completely*) assolutamente; *do you agree? – ~* sei d'accordo? – assolutamente sì; **absolution** REL assoluzione *f*; **absolve** assolvere

absorb [əb'sɔ:b] assorbire; **absorbent** assorbente; **sorbent cotton** *Am* cotone *m* idrofilo; **absorbing** avvincente

abstain [əb'steɪn] *from voting* astenersi; **abstention** *in voting* astensione *f*

abstract ['æbstrækt] astratto

absurd [əb'sɜ:d] assurdo; **absurdity** assurdità *f inv*

abundance [ə'bʌndəns] abbondanza *f*; **abundant** abbondante

abuse[1] [ə'bju:s] *n* abuso *m*; (*ill treatment*) maltrattamento *m*; (*insults*) insulti *mpl*

abuse[2] [ə'bju:z] *v/t* abusare di; (*treat badly*) maltrattare; (*insult*) insultare

abusive [ə'bju:sɪv] *language* offensivo; **become ~** diventare aggressivo

abysmal [ə'bɪzml] F (*very bad*) pessimo

academic [ækə'demɪk] **1** *n* docente *m/f* universitario, -a **2** *adj* accademico; *person* portato per lo studio; **academy** accademia *f*

accelerate [ək'seləreɪt] accelerare; **acceleration** accelerazione *f*; **accelerator** acce-

leratore *m*

accent ['æksənt] accento *m*; **accentuate** accentuare

accept [ək'sept] accettare; **acceptable** accettabile; **acceptance** accettazione *f*

access ['ækses] **1** *n* accesso *m* **2** *v/t* accedere a; **accessible** accessibile

accessory [ək'sesərɪ] *for wearing* accessorio *m*; LAW complice *m/f*

accident ['æksɪdənt] incidente *m*; **by ~** per caso; **accidental** accidentale; **accidentally** accidentalmente

acclimatize [ə'klaɪmətaɪz] acclimatarsi

accommodate [ə'kɒmədeɪt] ospitare; *needs* tenere conto di; **accommodation**, *Am* **accommodations** sistemazione *f*

accompaniment [ə'kʌmpənɪmənt] MUS accompagnamento *m*; **accompany** accompagnare

accomplice [ə'kʌmplɪs] complice *m/f*

accomplished [ə'kʌmplɪʃt] dotato; **accomplishment** *of task* realizzazione *f*; (*talent*) talento *m*; (*achievement*) risultato *m*

accord [ə'kɔ:d] accordo *m*; *of his own ~* di sua spontanea volontà

accordance [ə'kɔ:dəns]: *in ~ with* conformemente a

according [ə'kɔ:dɪŋ]: *~ to* secondo; **accordingly** di conseguenza

accordion [əˈkɔːdɪən] fisarmonica f

account [əˈkaʊnt] *financial* conto m; (*report, description*) resoconto m; **give an ~ of** fare un resoconto di; **on no ~** per nessuna ragione; **on ~ of** a causa di; **take into ~** tenere conto di

◆ **account for** (*explain*) giustificare; (*make up*) ammontare a

accountable [əˈkaʊntəbl] responsabile; **accountant** contabile m/f; **running own business** commercialista m/f; **account number** numero m di conto; **accounts** contabilità f

accumulate [əˈkjuːmjʊleɪt] **1** v/t accumulare **2** v/i accumularsi; **accumulation** accumulazione f

accuracy [ˈækjʊrəsɪ] precisione f; **accurate** preciso; **accurately** con precisione

accusation [ækjuːˈzeɪʃn] accusa f; **accuse**: **~ s.o. of sth** accusare qn di qc; **accused** LAW accusato m, -a f; **accusing** accusatorio

accustom [əˈkʌstəm]: **get ~ed to** abituarsi a

ace [eɪs] *in cards* asso m; (*in tennis: shot*) ace m inv

ache [eɪk] **1** n dolore m **2** v/i fare male

achieve [əˈtʃiːv] realizzare;

success ottenere; **achievement** *of ambition* realizzazione f; (*thing achieved*) successo m

acid [ˈæsɪd] acido m

acknowledge [əkˈnɒlɪdʒ] riconoscere; **~ receipt of** accusare ricezione di; **acknowledg(e)ment** riconoscimento m; (*letter*) lettera f di accusata ricezione

acorn [ˈeɪkɔːn] ghianda f

acoustics [əˈkuːstɪks] acustica f

acquaint [əˈkweɪnt]: **be ~ed with** fml conoscere; **acquaintance** *person* conoscenza f

acquire [əˈkwaɪə(r)] acquisire; **acquisition** acquisizione f

acquit [əˈkwɪt] LAW assolvere; **acquittal** LAW assoluzione f

acre [ˈeɪkə(r)] acro m (4.047m²)

acrobat [ˈækrəbæt] acrobata m/f

across [əˈkrɒs] **1** prep *on other side of* dall'altro lato di; **walk ~ the street** attraversare la strada; **a bridge ~ the river** un ponte sul fiume; **~ Europe** all over in tutta Europa **2** adv *to other side* dall'altro lato; **10 m ~** largo 10 m; **swim ~** attraversare a nuoto

act [ækt] **1** v/i agire; THEA recitare **2** n (*deed*) atto m; *of play* atto m; *in variety show* numero m; (*pretence*) finta f; (*law*) atto *m*

action ['ækʃn] azione *f*; **take ~** agire; **action replay** TV replay *m inv*

active ['æktɪv] attivo; **activist** POL attivista *m/f*; **activity** attività *f inv*

actor ['æktə(r)] attore *m*; **actress** attrice *f*

actual ['æktjʊəl] reale; *cost* effettivo; **actually** in realtà; *expressing surprise* veramente; *stressing the converse* a dire il vero

acute [ə'kjuːt] acuto

ad [æd] ☞ **advertisement**

AD [eɪ'diː] (= *anno domini*) d.C. (= dopo Cristo)

adamant ['ædəmənt] categorico

adapt [ə'dæpt] **1** *v/t* adattare **2** *v/i of person* adattarsi; **adaptability** adattabilità *f*; **adaptable** adattabile; **adaptation** *of play etc* adattamento *m*; **adapter** *electrical* adattatore *m*

add [æd] **1** *v/t* aggiungere; MATH addizionare **2** *v/i of person* fare le somme

♦ **add on** aggiungere

♦ **add up 1** *v/t* sommare **2** *v/i fig* quadrare

addict ['ædɪkt] *to football, chess* maniaco *m, -a f*; **drug ~** tossicomane *m/f*, **TV ~** teledipendente *m/f*; **addicted** dipendente; **be ~ to** *drugs, alcohol* essere dedito a; **addiction** dipendenza *f*; **addic-**

tive: **be ~** provocare dipendenza

addition [ə'dɪʃn] MATH addizione *f*; *to list, company etc* aggiunta *f*; **in ~ to** in aggiunta a; **additional** aggiuntivo; **additive** additivo *m*; **add-on** complemento *m*

address [ə'dres] **1** *n* indirizzo *m* **2** *v/t letter* indirizzare; *audience* tenere un discorso a; **address book** indirizzario *m*; **addressee** destinatario *m*, -a *f*

adequate ['ædɪkwət] adeguato; **adequately** adeguatamente

♦ **adhere to** [æd'hɪə(r)] *surface* aderire a; *rules* attenersi a

adhesive [əd'hiːsɪv] adesivo *m*

adjacent [ə'dʒeɪsnt] adiacente

adjective ['ædʒɪktɪv] aggettivo *m*

adjoining [ə'dʒɔɪnɪŋ] adiacente

adjourn [ə'dʒɜːn] aggiornare; **adjournment** aggiornamento *m*

adjust [ə'dʒʌst] **1** *v/t* regolare **2** *v/i: ~ to* adattarsi a; **adjustable** regolabile; **adjustment** regolazione *f*; *psychological* adattamento *m*

ad lib [æd'lɪb] **1** *adj* a braccio F **2** *v/i* improvvisare

administer [əd'mɪnɪstə(r)] *country* governare; **adminis-**

tration amministrazione *f*; (*government*) governo *m*; administrative amministrativo; administrator amministratore *m*, -trice *f*

admirable ['ædmərəbl] ammirevole

admiral ['ædmərəl] ammiraglio *m*

admiration [ædmə'reɪʃn] ammirazione *f*; admire ammirare; admirer ammiratore *m*, -trice *f*; admiring ammirativo; admiringly con ammirazione

admissible [əd'mɪsəbl] ammissibile; admission (*confession*) ammissione *f*; **~ free** entrata *f* libera; admit ammettere; *to a place* lasciare entrare; *to school, club etc* ammettere; *to hospital* ricoverare; admittance: **no ~** vietato l'accesso

adolescence [ædə'lesns] adolescenza *f*; adolescent **1** *n* adolescente *m/f* **2** *adj* adolescenziale

adopt [ə'dɒpt] adottare; adoption adozione *f*

adorable [ə'dɔ:rəbl] adorabile; adoration adorazione *f*; adore adorare

adrenalin [ə'drenəlɪn] adrenalina *f*

adrift [ə'drɪft] alla deriva; *fig* sbandato

adult ['ædʌlt] **1** *n* adulto *m*, -a *f* **2** *adj* adulto; adultery adulterio *m*

advance [əd'vɑːns] **1** *n* (*money*) anticipo *m*; *in science etc* progresso *m*; MIL avanzata *f*; **in ~** in anticipo; **make ~s** (*progress*) fare progressi; *sexually* fare delle avances **2** *v/i* MIL avanzare; (*make progress*) fare progressi **3** *v/t* theory avanzare; *money* anticipare; *knowledge, cause* fare progredire; *advanced* avanzato; *learner* di livello avanzato

advantage [əd'vɑːntɪdʒ] vantaggio *m*; take ~ of *opportunity* approfittare di; advantageous vantaggioso

adventure [əd'ventʃə(r)] avventura *f*; adventurous avventuroso

adverb ['ædvɜːb] avverbio *m*

adversary ['ædvəsərɪ] avversario *m*, -a *f*

adverse ['ædvɜːs] avverso

advertise ['ædvətaɪz] **1** *v/t* job mettere un annuncio per; *product* reclamizzare **2** *v/i* *for job* mettere un annuncio; *for product* fare pubblicità; advertisement annuncio *m*; *for product* pubblicità *f* *inv*; advertiser *in newspaper etc* inserzionista *m/f*; advertising pubblicità *f*; advertising agency agenzia *f* pubblicitaria; advertising campaign campagna *f* pubblicitaria

advice [əd'vaɪs] consigli *mpl*; **a bit of ~** un consiglio;

advisable consigliabile; advise *person* consigliare a

advocate ['ædvəkeɪt] propugnare

aerial ['eərɪəl] antenna *f*; aerial photograph fotografia *f* aerea

aerobics [eə'rəʊbɪks] aerobica *f*

aerodynamic [eərəʊdaɪ'næmɪk] aerodinamico

aeronautical [eərəʊ'nɔːtɪkl] aeronautico

aeroplane ['eərəpleɪn] aeroplano *m*

aerosol ['eərəsɒl] spray *m inv*

aesthetic [iːs'θetɪk] estetico

affair [ə'feə(r)] (*matter*) affare *m*; (*love*) relazione *f*

affect [ə'fekt] *v/t* colpire; (*influence*) influire su; (*concern*) riguardare

affection [ə'fekʃn] affetto *m*; affectionate affettuoso; affectionately affettuosamente

affirmative [ə'fɜːmətɪv] affermativo

affluence ['æfluəns] benessere *m*; affluent benestante

afford [ə'fɔːd]: be able to ~ sth potersi permettere qc; affordable abbordabile

afloat [ə'fləʊt] *boat* a galla

afraid [ə'freɪd]: be ~ avere paura (of di); I'm ~ *expressing regret* sono spiacente

afresh [ə'freʃ] da capo

Africa ['æfrɪkə] Africa *f*; African 1 *n* africano *m*, -a *f* 2 *adj*

africano; African-American 1 *n* afroamericano *m*, -a *f* 2 *adj* afroamericano

after ['ɑːftə(r)] 1 *prep* dopo; ~ her / me dopo di lei / me; ~ all dopo tutto; ~ that dopo; the day ~ tomorrow dopodomani 2 *adv* dopo; the day ~ il giorno dopo 3 *conj*: after I left, I saw ... dopo essere uscito ho visto ...; after I left, she saw ... dopo che io sono uscito, lei ha visto ...; aftermath ['ɑːftəmæθ] di guerra il dopoguerra; in the ~ nel periodo immediatamente successivo a; afternoon pomeriggio *m*; this ~ oggi pomeriggio; good ~ buon giorno; after sales service servizio *m* dopovendita; aftershave dopobarba *m inv*; afterwards dopo

again [ə'geɪn] di nuovo; I never saw him ~ non l'ho mai più visto

against [ə'geɪnst] contro

age [eɪdʒ] 1 *n* (*also* era) età *f inv*; she's five years of ~ ha cinque anni; I've been waiting for ~s F ho aspettato un secolo F 2 *v/i* invecchiare; aged: a boy ~ 16 un ragazzo di 16 anni; he was ~ 16 aveva 16 anni; age group fascia *f* d'età; age limit limite *m* d'età

agency ['eɪdʒənsɪ] agenzia *f*

agenda [ə'dʒendə] ordine *m* del giorno

agent ['eɪdʒənt] agente m/f

aggravate ['ægrəveɪt] aggravare; (annoy) seccare

aggression [ə'greʃn] aggressione f; **aggressive** aggressivo; **aggressively** con aggressività

aghast [ə'gɑːst] inorridito

agile ['ædʒaɪl] agile; **agility** agilità f

agitated ['ædʒɪteɪtɪd] agitato; **agitation** agitazione f; **agitator** agitatore m, -trice f

agnostic [æg'nɒstɪk] agnostico m, -a f

ago [ə'gəʊ]: **2 days** ~ due giorni fa; **long** ~ molto tempo fa

agonize ['ægənaɪz] angosciarsi (**over** per); **agonizing** angosciante; **agony** agonia f; **mental agonia** f

agree [ə'griː] **1** v/i essere d'accordo; of figures quadrare; (reach agreement) mettersi d'accordo; **I** ~ sono d'accordo **2** v/t price concordare; **agreeable** (pleasant) piacevole; **agreement** accordo m

agricultural [ægrɪ'kʌltʃərəl] agricolo; **agriculture** agricoltura f

ahead [ə'hed] davanti; (in advance) avanti; **be** ~ of essere davanti a; **plan** ~ programmare per tempo

aid [eɪd] **1** n aiuto m **2** v/t aiutare

aide [eɪd] assistente m/f

Aids [eɪdz] Aids m

ailing ['eɪlɪŋ] economy malato

ailment ['eɪlmənt] disturbo m

aim [eɪm] **1** n (objective) obiettivo m **2** v/i in shooting mirare; ~ **to do sth** aspirare a fare qc **3** v/t: **be** ~**ed at** of remark etc essere rivolto a; of guns essere puntato contro; **aimless** senza obiettivi; wandering senza meta

air [eə(r)] **1** n aria f; **by** ~ travel in aereo; send mail per via aerea; **in the open** ~ all'aperto; **on the** ~ RAD, TV in onda **2** v/t room arieggiare; views rendere noto; **airbag** airbag m inv; **air-conditioned** con aria condizionata; **air-conditioning** aria f condizionata; **aircraft** aereo m; **aircraft carrier** portaerei f inv; **air fare** tariffa f aerea; **air force** aeronautica f militare; **air hostess** hostess f inv; **airline** compagnia f aerea; **airliner** aereo m di linea; **airmail: by** ~ per via aerea; **airplane** Am aeroplano m; **airport** aeroporto m; **air rage** comportamento di estrema irascibilità dei passeggeri di un aereo; **air terminal** terminal m; **air-traffic control** controllo m del traffico aereo; **air-traffic controller** controllore m di volo

aisle [aɪl] corridoio m; in supermarket corsia f; in church navata f laterale

ajar [ə'dʒɑː(r)]: **be** ~ essere socchiuso

alarm [əˈlɑːm] **1** n allarme m **2** v/t allarmare; **alarm clock** sveglia f; **alarming** allarmante; **alarmingly** in modo allarmante

Albania [ælˈbeɪnɪə] Albania f; **Albanian 1** adj albanese **2** n albanese m/f; language albanese m

album [ˈælbəm] album m inv

alcohol [ˈælkəhɒl] alcol m; **alcoholic 1** n alcolizzato m, -a f **2** adj alcolico

alert [əˈlɜːt] **1** n (signal) allarme m **2** v/t mettere in guardia **3** adj all'erta inv

A-level [ˈeɪlevl] diploma di scuola media superiore in Gran Bretagna che permette di accedere all'università

alibi [ˈælɪbaɪ] alibi m inv

alien [ˈeɪlɪən] **1** n straniero m, -a f; from space alieno m, -a f **2** adj estraneo; **alienate** alienarsi

align [əˈlaɪn] allineare

alike [əˈlaɪk] **1** adj simile; **be ~** assomigliarsi **2** adv: **old and young ~** vecchi e giovani allo stesso tempo

alimony [ˈælɪmənɪ] alimenti mpl

alive [əˈlaɪv]: **be ~** essere vivo

all [ɔːl] **1** adj tutto; (any whatever) qualsiasi; **~ day** tutto il giorno; **beyond ~ doubt** al di là di qualsiasi dubbio **2** pron tutto; **~ of us / them** tutti noi / loro; **he ate ~ of it** lo ha mangiato tutto; **for**

~ I know per quel che ne so; **~ at once** tutto in una volta; (suddenly) tutt'a un tratto; **~ but** (nearly) quasi; **~ but John agreed** (except) erano tutti d'accordo tranne John; **~ the better** molto meglio; **they're not at ~ alike** non si assomigliano affatto; **not at ~!** niente affatto!; **two ~** sp due pari; **~ right** ☞ **alright**

allegation [ælɪˈgeɪʃn] accusa f; **allege** dichiarare; **alleged** presunto; **allegedly** a quanto si suppone

allegiance [əˈliːdʒəns] fedeltà f inv

allergic [əˈlɜːdʒɪk] allergico (**to** a); **allergy** allergia f

alleviate [əˈliːvɪeɪt] alleviare

alley [ˈælɪ] vicolo m

alliance [əˈlaɪəns] alleanza f

allocate [ˈæləkeɪt] assegnare; **allocation** assegnazione f; (amount) parte f

allot [əˈlɒt] assegnare

allow [əˈlaʊ] permettere; (calculate for) calcolare; **it's not ~ed** è vietato

◆ **allow for** tenere conto di

allowance [əˈlaʊəns] (money) sussidio m; (pocket money) paghetta f

alloy [ˈælɔɪ] lega m

'all-purpose multiuso inv; **all-round** generale; person eclettico; **all-time**: **be at an ~ low** aver raggiunto il minimo storico

◆ **allude to** [əˈluːd] alludere a

alluring [əˈluːrɪŋ] attraente

'all-wheel drive quattro per quattro *m inv*

ally [ˈælaɪ] alleato *m*, -a *f*

almond [ˈɑːmənd] mandorla *f*

almost [ˈɔːlməust] quasi

alone [əˈləʊn] solo

along [əˈlɒŋ] **1** *prep* lungo; **walk ~ the street** camminare lungo la strada **2** *adv*: **~ with** insieme con; **all ~** (*all the time*) per tutto il tempo; **alongside di** lungo fianco a; *per-son* al fianco di

aloof [əˈluːf] in disparte

aloud [əˈlaʊd] ad alta voce

alphabet [ˈælfəbet] alfabeto *m*; **alphabetical** alfabetico

alpine [ˈælpaɪn] alpino; **Alps** Alpi *fpl*

already [ɔːlˈredɪ] già

alright [ɔːlˈraɪt]: **I'm ~** (*not hurt*) sto bene; (*have enough*) va bene così; **is the monitor ~?** (*in working order*) funziona il monitor?; **is it ~ with you if I ...?** ti va bene se ...?; **~, you can have one!** va bene, puoi averne uno!; **that's ~** (*don't mention it*) non c'è di che; (*I don't mind*) non fa niente; **~, that's enough!** basta così!

Alsatian [ælˈseɪʃn] pastore *m* tedesco

also [ˈɔːlsəʊ] anche

altar [ˈɔːltə(r)] altare *m*

alter [ˈɒltə(r)] modificare; *clothes* aggiustare; *altera-*

tion modifica *f*

alternate [ˈɒltəneɪt] *v/i* alternare **2** [ˈɒltənət] *adj* alternato; **on ~ Mondays** un lunedì su due; **alternative 1** *n* alternativa *f* **2** *adj* alternativo; **alternatively** alternativamente

although [ɔːlˈðəʊ] benché (+ *subj*), sebbene (+ *subj*)

altitude [ˈæltɪtjuːd] altitudine *f*

altogether [ɔːltəˈɡeðə(r)] (*completely*) completamente; (*in all*) complessivamente

altruism [ˈæltruːɪzm] altruismo *m*; **altruistic** altruistico

aluminium [æljʊˈmɪnɪəm], *Am* **aluminum** [əˈluːmɪnəm] alluminio *m*

always [ˈɔːlweɪz] sempre

a.m. [eɪˈem] (= *ante meridiem*) di mattina

amass [əˈmæs] accumulare

amateur [ˈæmətə(r)] *n* (*un-skilled*) dilettante *m/f*; SP non professionista *m/f*; **amateurish** *pej* dilettantesco

amaze [əˈmeɪz] stupire; **amazed** stupito; **amazement** stupore *m*; **amazing** sorprendente; F (*good*) incredibile; **amazingly** incredibilmente

ambassador [æmˈbæsədə(r)] ambasciatore *m*, -trice *f*

amber [ˈæmbə(r)] *n* ambra *f*; **at ~** giallo

ambience [ˈæmbɪəns] atmosfera *f*

ambiguity [æmbɪˈgjuːətɪ] ambiguità f inv; ambiguous ambiguo

ambition [æmˈbɪʃn] ambizione f; ambitious ambizioso

ambivalent [æmˈbɪvələnt] ambiguo

amble [ˈæmbl] camminare con calma

ambulance [ˈæmbjuləns] ambulanza f

ambush [ˈæmbuʃ] 1 n agguato m 2 v/t tendere un agguato a

amend [əˈmend] emendare; amendment emendamento m; amends: make~ fare ammenda

amenities [əˈmiːnətɪz] comodità fpl

America [əˈmerɪkə] America f; American 1 n americano m, -a f 2 adj americano

amicable [ˈæmɪkəbl] amichevole; amicably amichevolmente

ammunition [æmjuˈnɪʃn] munizioni fpl

amnesia [æmˈniːzɪə] amnesia f

amnesty [ˈæmnəstɪ] amnistia f

among(st) [əˈmʌŋ(st)] tra

amoral [eɪˈmɒrəl] amorale

amount [əˈmaunt] quantità f inv; (sum of money) importo m

♦ amount to ammontare a; (be equal to) equivalere a

amphibian [æmˈfɪbɪən] anfi-

bio m

ample [ˈæmpl] abbondante

amplifier [ˈæmplɪfaɪ(r)] amplificatore m; amplify sound amplificare

amputate [ˈæmpjuteɪt] amputare; amputation amputazione f

amuse [əˈmjuːz] (make laugh etc) divertire; (entertain) intrattenere; amusement (merriment) divertimento m; (entertainment) intrattenimento m; amusement park parco m giochi; amusing divertente

an [æn] ☞ a

anaemia [əˈniːmɪə] anemia f; anaemic anemico

anaesthetic [ænəsˈθetɪk] anestetico m

analog [ˈænəlɒg] COMPUT analogico; analogy analogia f

analyse, Am analyze [ˈænəlaɪz] analizzare; (psychoanalyse) psicanalizzare; analysis analisi f inv; analyst PSYCH analista m/f; analytical analitico

anarchy [ˈænəkɪ] anarchia f

ancestor [ˈænsestə(r)] antenato m, -a f

anchor [ˈæŋkə(r)] 1 n NAUT ancora f 2 v/i NAUT gettare l'ancora; anchorman conduttore m; anchorwoman conduttrice f

ancient [ˈeɪnʃənt] antico

and [ænd] e

anemia Am ☞ **anaemia**

anesthetic Am ☞ **anaesthetic**

angel ['eɪndʒl] angelo m

anger ['æŋgə(r)] 1 n rabbia f 2 v/t fare arrabbiare

angle ['æŋgl] n angolo m; (position, fig) angolazione f

angry ['æŋgrɪ] arrabbiato

animal ['ænɪml] animale m

animated ['ænɪmeɪtɪd] animato; **animated cartoon** cartone m animato; **animation** animazione f

animosity [ænɪ'mɒsətɪ] animosità f inv

ankle ['æŋkl] caviglia f

annexe, Am **annex** [ə'neks] state annettere

annihilate [ə'naɪəleɪt] annientare; **annihilation** annientamento m

anniversary [ænɪ'vɜːsərɪ] anniversario m

announce [ə'naʊns] annunciare; **announcement** annuncio m; **announcer** TV, RAD annunciatore m, -trice f

annoy [ə'nɔɪ] infastidire; **annoyance** (anger) irritazione f; (nuisance) fastidio m; **annoying** irritante

annual ['ænjʊəl] annuale

annul [ə'nʌl] annullare; **annulment** annullamento m

anonymous [ə'nɒnɪməs] anonimo

anorak ['ænəræk] giacca f a vento

anorexia [ænə'reksɪə] anores-

sia f

another [ə'nʌðə(r)] 1 adj un altro m, un'altra f 2 pron un altro m, un'altra f; **one ~** l'un l'altro; **do they know one ~?** si conoscono?

answer ['ɑːnsə(r)] 1 n risposta f 2 v/t rispondere a; **~ the door** aprire la porta; **answering machine**, **answerphone** segreteria f telefonica

ant [ænt] formica f

antagonism [æn'tægənɪzm] antagonismo m; **antagonistic** ostile; **antagonize** contrariare

Antarctic [ænt'ɑːktɪk] Antartico m

antenatal [æntɪ'neɪtl]: **~ classes** corso m di preparazione al parto; **~ clinic** clinica f per gestanti

antenna [æn'tenə] antenna f

antibiotic [æntɪbaɪ'ɒtɪk] antibiotico m

anticipate [æn'tɪsɪpeɪt] prevedere; **anticipation** previsione f

anticlockwise ['æntɪklɒkwaɪz] 1 adj antiorario 2 adv in senso antiorario

antics ['æntɪks] buffonate fpl

antidote ['æntɪdəʊt] antidoto m

antifreeze ['æntɪfriːz] antigelo m inv

anti-globalist [æntɪ'gləʊbəlɪst] no-global m/f inv

antipathy [æn'tɪpəθɪ] antipatia f

antiquated ['æntɪkweɪtɪd] antiquato

antique [æn'ti:k] n pezzo m d'antiquariato

antiseptic [æntɪ'septɪk] **1** adj antisettico **2** n antisettico m

antisocial [æntɪ'səʊʃl] asociale

antivirus program [æntɪ'vaɪrəs] COMPUT programma m antivirus

anxiety [æŋ'zaɪətɪ] ansia f; anxious ansioso

any ['enɪ] **1** adj qualche; **are there ~ glasses?** ci sono dei bicchieri?; **is there ~ bread?** c'è del pane?; **is there ~ improvement?** c'è qualche miglioramento?; **there isn't ~ bread** non c'è pane; **take ~ one you like** prendi quello che vuoi **2** pron: **do you have ~?** ne hai?; **there aren't ~ left** non ce ne sono più; **there isn't ~ left** non ce n'è più; **~ of them could be guilty** chiunque di loro potrebbe essere colpevole **3** adv un po'; **is that ~ easier?** è un po' più facile?

anybody ['enɪbɒdɪ] qualcuno; with negative nessuno; (whoever) chiunque; **there wasn't ~ there** non c'era nessuno; **~ could do it** lo potrebbe fare chiunque

anyhow ['enɪhaʊ] comunque

anyone ['enɪwʌn] ☞ any-

body

anything ['enɪθɪŋ] qualcosa; with negatives niente, nulla; **I didn't hear ~** non ho sentito niente or nulla; **~ but** per niente

anyway ['enɪweɪ] ☞ **anyhow**

anywhere ['enɪweə(r)] da qualche parte; with negative da nessuna parte; (wherever) dovunque; **I can't find it ~** non riesco a trovarlo da nessuna parte

apart [ə'pɑːt] in distance distante; **~ from** (excepting) a parte; (in addition to) oltre a

apartment [ə'pɑːtmənt] appartamento m; apartment block Am palazzo m (d'appartamenti)

ape [eɪp] scimmia f

Apennines ['æpənaɪnz] Appennini mpl

aperitif [ə'perɪtiːf] aperitivo m

apologize [ə'pɒlədʒaɪz] scusarsi (**to s.o.** con qu); apology scusa f

apostrophe [ə'pɒstrəfɪ] GRAM apostrofo m

appalling [ə'pɔːlɪŋ] sconvolgente

apparatus [æpə'reɪtəs] apparecchio m

apparent [ə'pærənt] evidente; (seeming) apparente; apparently apparentemente

appeal [ə'piːl] (charm) attrattiva f; for funds etc, LAW appello m

◆ **appeal for** fare un appello per

◆ **appeal to** (*be attractive to*) attirare

appealing [ə'pi:lɪŋ] *idea, offer* allettante

appear [ə'pɪə(r)] apparire; *in court* comparire; *it ~s that ...* sembra che ...; **appearance** apparizione *f*, *in court* comparizione *f*; (*look*) aspetto *m*

appendicitis [əpendɪ'saɪtɪs] appendicite *f*; **appendix** [ə'pendɪks] MED, *of book etc* appendice *f*

appetite ['æpɪtaɪt] appetito *m*; **appetizer** *food* stuzzichino *m*; *drink* aperitivo *m*; **appetizing** appetitoso

applaud [ə'plɔːd] applaudire; **applause** applauso *m*; (*praise*) approvazione *f*

apple ['æpl] mela *f*; **apple pie** torta *f* di mele

appliance [ə'plaɪəns] apparecchio *m*; *household* elettrodomestico *m*

applicable [ə'plɪkəbl] applicabile; **applicant** candidato *m*, -a *f*; **application** *for job etc* candidatura *f*; *for passport* domanda *f*; *for university* domanda *f* di iscrizione; **apply 1** *v/t* applicare **2** *v/i of rule* applicarsi

◆ **apply for** *job, passport* fare domanda per; *university* fare domanda di iscrizione a

◆ **apply to** (*contact*) rivolgersi a; (*affect*) applicarsi a

appoint [ə'pɔɪnt] *to position* nominare; **appointment** *to position* nomina *f*; (*meeting*) appuntamento *m*

appraisal [ə'preɪz(ə)l] valutazione *f*

appreciable [ə'priːʃəbl] notevole; **appreciate 1** *v/t* apprezzare; (*acknowledge*) rendersi conto di **2** *v/i* FIN rivalutarsi; **appreciative** (*showing gratitude*) riconoscente; (*showing pleasure*) soddisfatto

apprehensive [æprɪ'hensɪv] apprensivo

approach [ə'prəʊtʃ] **1** *n* avvicinamento *m*; (*proposal*) contatto *m*; *to problem* approccio *m* **2** *v/t* (*get near to*) avvicinarsi a; (*contact*) contattare; *problem* abbordare; **approachable** abbordabile

appropriate [ə'prəʊprɪət] appropriato

approval [ə'pruːvl] approvazione *f*; **approve** approvare

◆ **approve of** approvare

approximate [ə'prɒksɪmət] approssimativo; **approximately** approssimativamente

apricot ['eɪprɪkɒt] albicocca *f*

April ['eɪprəl] aprile *m*

apt [æpt] *remark* appropriato; **aptitude** attitudine *f*

aqualung ['ækwəlʌŋ] autorespiratore *m*

aquarium [ə'kweərɪəm] acquario *m*

Aquarius [əˈkweərɪəs] ASTR Acquario m

Arab [ˈærəb] **1** n arabo m, -a f **2** adj arabo; **Arabic 1** n arabo m **2** adj arabo

arbitrary [ˈɑːbɪtrərɪ] arbitrario

arbitrate [ˈɑːbɪtreɪt] arbitrare; **arbitration** arbitrato m

arch [ɑːtʃ] arco m

archaeological [ɑːkɪəˈlɒdʒɪk] archeologico; **archaeologist** archeologo m, -a f; **archaeology** archeologia f

archaic [ɑːˈkeɪɪk] arcaico

archbishop [ɑːtʃˈbɪʃəp] arcivescovo m

archeology Am ☞ **archaeology**

architect [ˈɑːkɪtekt] architetto m; **architectural** architettonico; **architecture** architettura f

archives [ˈɑːkaɪvz] archivi mpl

Arctic [ˈɑːktɪk] Artico m

ardent [ˈɑːdənt] ardente

arduous [ˈɑːdjʊəs] arduo

area [ˈeərɪə] area f; (region) zona f; **area code** TELEC prefisso m telefonico

arena [əˈriːnə] SP arena f

Argentina [ɑːdʒənˈtiːnə] Argentina f; **Argentinian 1** adj argentino **2** n argentino m, -a f

arguably [ˈɑːgjʊəblɪ] probabilmente; **it was ~ ...** si può dire che ...; **argue** (quarrel) litigare; (reason) so-

stenere; **argument** (quarrel) litigio m; (reasoning) argomento m; **argumentative** polemico

arid [ˈærɪd] land arido

Aries [ˈeəriːz] ASTR Ariete m

arise [əˈraɪz] of situation emergere

aristocracy [ærɪˈstɒkrəsɪ] aristocrazia f; **aristocrat** aristocratico m, -a f; **aristocratic** aristocratico

arithmetic [əˈrɪθmətɪk] aritmetica f

arm[1] [ɑːm] n braccio m; of chair bracciolo m

arm[2] [ɑːm] v/t armare

armaments [ˈɑːməmənts] armamenti mpl

armchair [ˈɑːmtʃeə(r)] poltrona f

armed [ɑːmd] armato; **armed forces** forze fpl armate; **armed robbery** rapina f a mano armata

armour, Am **armor** [ˈɑːmə(r)] armatura f; metal plates blindatura f

armpit ascella f

arms [ɑːmz] (weapons) armi fpl

army [ˈɑːmɪ] esercito m

around [əˈraʊnd] **1** prep (in circle, roughly) intorno a; room, world attraverso; **it's ~ the corner** è dietro l'angolo **2** adv (in the area) qui intorno; (encircling) intorno; **he lives ~ here** abita da queste parti; **walk ~** andare in giro; **she has been ~** (*has travelled, is experienced*) ha girato; **he's still ~** F (*alive*) è ancora in circolazione

arouse [əˈraʊz] suscitare; (*sexually*) eccitare

arrange [əˈreɪndʒ] (*put in order*) sistemare; *music* arrangiare; *meeting, party etc* organizzare; *time and place combinare*; **I've ~d to meet her** ho combinato di incontrarla; **arrangement** (*agreement*) accordo *m*; *of party, meeting* organizzazione *f*; *of furniture etc* disposizione *f*; *of music* arrangiamento *m*; **~s for party, meeting** preparativi *mpl*

arrears [əˈrɪəz] arretrati *mpl*

arrest [əˈrest] **1** *n* arresto *m*; **be under ~** essere in arresto **2** *v/t* arrestare

arrival [əˈraɪvl] arrivo *m*; **arrive** arrivare

♦ **arrive at** arrivare a

arrogance [ˈærəgəns] arroganza *f*; **arrogant** arrogante

arrow [ˈærəʊ] freccia *f*

arse [ɑːs] P culo *m* P

arson [ˈɑːsn] incendio *m* doloso

art [ɑːt] arte *f*

artery [ˈɑːtəri] arteria *f*

'**art gallery** galleria *f* d'arte

arthritis [ɑːˈθraɪtɪs] artrite *f*

artichoke [ˈɑːtɪtʃəʊk] carciofo *m*

article [ˈɑːtɪkl] articolo *m*

articulate [ɑːˈtɪkjʊlət] chiaro; **be ~** *of person* esprimersi bene

artificial [ɑːtɪˈfɪʃl] artificiale; (*not sincere*) finto

artillery [ɑːˈtɪləri] artiglieria *f*

artist [ˈɑːtɪst] artista *m/f*; **artistic** artistico

'**arts degree** laurea *f* in discipline umanistiche

as [æz] **1** *conj* (*while, when*) mentre; (*because*) dato che; (*like*) come; **~ if** come se; **~ usual** come al solito **2** *adv*: **~ high ~ ...** alto come ...; **~ much ~ that?** così tanto?; **run ~ fast ~ you can** corri più veloce che puoi **3** *prep* come; **~ a child** da bambino; **dressed ~ a policeman** vestito da poliziotto; **work ~ a translator** essere traduttore; **~ for** quanto a; **~ Hamlet** nel ruolo di Amleto

Ascension [əˈsenʃn] REL Ascensione *f*; **ascent** *path* salita *f*; *of mountain* ascensione *f*; *fig* ascesa *f*

ash [æʃ] cenere *f*

ashamed [əˈʃeɪmd]: **be ~ of** vergognarsi di

ashore [əˈʃɔː(r)] a terra; **go ~** sbarcare

ashtray [ˈæʃtreɪ] portacenere *m*; **Ash Wednesday** mercoledì *m inv* delle Ceneri

Asia [ˈeɪʃə] Asia *f*; **Asian 1** *n* asiatico *m*, -a *f*; (*Indian, Pakistani*) indiano *m*, -a *f* **2** *adj* asiatico; (*Indian, Pakistani*) indiano; **Asian-American** americano *m*, -a *f* di origine asiatica

aside [ə'said] da parte; **~ from** a parte

ask [ɑ:sk] **1** v/t person chiedere a; (invite) invitare; question fare; favour chiedere; **~ s.o. for ...** chiedere a qu ...; **~ s.o. to ...** chiedere a qu di ... **2** v/i chiedere

♦ **ask after** person chiedere di

♦ **ask for** chiedere; person chiedere di

♦ **ask out** chiedere di uscire a

asleep [ə'sli:p]: **he's ~** sta dormendo; **fall ~** addormentarsi

asparagus [ə'spærəgəs] asparagi mpl

aspect ['æspekt] aspetto m

aspirations [æspə'reɪnz] aspirazioni fpl

aspirin ['æsprɪn] aspirina f

ass¹ [æs] F (idiot) cretino m, -a

ass² [æs] Am P (bum) culo m P

assassin [ə'sæsɪn] assassino m, -a f; **assassinate** assassinare; **assassination** assassinio m

assault [ə'sɔlt] **1** n assalto m **2** v/t aggredire

assemble [ə'sembl] **1** v/t parts assemblare **2** v/i of people radunarsi; **assembly** assemblea f; of parts assemblaggio m; **assembly line** catena f di montaggio

assent [ə'sent] acconsentire

assertive [ə'sɜ:tɪv] person si-

curo di sé

assess [ə'ses] valutare; **assessment** valutazione f

asset ['æset] FIN attivo m; fig: thing vantaggio m; person elemento m prezioso

assign [ə'saɪn] person destinare; thing assegnare; **assignment** (task) compito m

assimilate [ə'sɪmɪlert] assimilare; person into group integrare

assist [ə'sɪst] assistere; **assistance** assistenza f; **assistant** assistente m/f; in shop commesso m, -a f; **assistant manager** vice-responsabile m/f; of hotel, restaurant vice-direttore m

associate 1 [ə'səʊʃɪeɪt] v/t associare **2** [ə'səʊʃɪət] n socio m, -a f; **association** associazione f

assortment [ə'sɔːtmənt] assortimento m

assume [ə'sjuːm] (suppose) supporre; **assumption** supposizione f

assurance [ə'ʃʊərəns] assicurazione f; (confidence) sicurezza f; **assure** (reassure) ~ **s.o. of sth** assicurare qc a qu

asterisk ['æstərɪsk] asterisco m

asthma ['æsmə] asma f

astonish [ə'stɒnɪʃ] sbalordire; **astonishing** sbalorditivo; **astonishment** stupore m

astound [ə'staʊnd] stupefare

astride [ə'straɪd] a cavalcioni

di
astrology [əˈstrɒlədʒɪ] astrologia *f*

astronaut [ˈæstrənɔːt] astronauta *m/f*

astronomer [əˈstrɒnəmə(r)] astronomo *m*, -a *f*; **astronomical** *price etc* astronomico; **astronomy** astronomia *f*

astute [əˈstjuːt] astuto

asylum [əˈsaɪləm] *mental* manicomio *m*; *political* asilo *m*

at [æt] *(with places)* a; **he works ~ the hospital** lavora in ospedale; **~ the baker's** dal panettiere, in panetteria; **~ Joe's** da Joe; **~ the door** alla porta; **~ 10 pounds** a 10 sterline; **~ the age of 18** all'età di 18 anni; **~ 5 o'clock** alle cinque; **~ night** di notte; **~ 150 km / h** a 150 km/h; **be good / bad ~ sth** essere / - non essere bravo in qc

atheist [ˈeɪθɪɪst] ateo *m*, -a *f*

athlete [ˈæθliːt] atleta *m/f*; **athletic** atletico; **athletics** atletica *f*

Atlantic [ətˈlæntɪk] Atlantico *m*

atlas [ˈætləs] atlante *m*

ATM [eɪtiːˈem] (= **automatic teller machine**) (sportello *m*) Bancomat® *m*

atmosphere [ˈætməsfɪə(r)] atmosfera *f*

atom [ˈætəm] atomo *m*; **atom bomb** bomba *f* atomica; **atomic** atomico

◆ **atone for** [əˈtəʊn] scontare

atrocious [əˈtrəʊʃəs] atroce; **atrocity** atrocità *f inv*

attach [əˈtætʃ] attaccare; *importance* attribuire; *document, file* allegare; **attachment** *to email* allegato *m*

attack [əˈtæk] **1** *n* aggressione *f*; MIL attacco *m* **2** *v/t* aggredire; MIL attaccare

attempt [əˈtempt] **1** *n* tentativo *m* **2** *v/t* tentare

attend [əˈtend] partecipare a; *school* frequentare

◆ **attend to** *(deal with)* sbrigare; *customer, patient* assistere

attendance [əˈtendəns] partecipazione *f*; *at school* frequenza *f*; **attendant** *in museum etc* sorvegliante *m/f*

attention [əˈtenʃən] attenzione *f*; **pay ~** fare attenzione; **attentive** attento

attic [ˈætɪk] soffitta *f*

attitude [ˈætɪtjuːd] atteggiamento *m*

attorney [əˈtɜːnɪ] avvocato *m*

attract [əˈtrækt] attirare; **attraction** attrazione *f*; **attractive** attrattivo; *person* attraente

aubergine [ˈəʊbəʒiːn] melanzana *f*

auction [ˈɔːkʃn] asta *f*

audacity [ɔːˈdæsətɪ] audacia *f*

audible [ˈɔːdəbl] udibile

audience [ˈɔːdɪəns] pubblico *m*; TV telespettatori *mpl*; *with the Pope etc* udienza *f*

audio [ˈɔːdɪəʊ] audio *inv*;

audiovisual audiovisivo

audit ['ɔːdɪt] **1** *n* revisione *f* contabile **2** *v/t* verificare

audition [ɔː'dɪʃn] **1** *n* audizione *f* **2** *v/i* fare un'audizione

auditor ['ɔːdɪtə(r)] revisore *m* contabile

auditorium [ɔːdɪ'tɔːrɪəm] *of theatre* sala *f*

August ['ɔːgəst] agosto *m*

aunt [ɑːnt] zia *f*

au pair [əʊ'peə(r)] ragazza *f* alla pari

aura ['ɔːrə]: **she has an ~ of confidence** emana sicurezza

auspicious [ɔː'spɪʃəs] propizio

austere [ɔː'stɪə(r)] austero; austerity austerità *f inv*

Australia [ɔː'streɪlɪə] Australia *f*; Australian **1** *adj* australiano **2** *n* australiano *m*, -a *f*

Austria ['ɒstrɪə] Austria *f*; Austrian **1** *adj* austriaco **2** *n* austriaco *m*, -a *f*

authentic [ɔː'θentɪk] autentico; authenticity autenticità *f*

author ['ɔːθə(r)] autore *m*, autrice *f*

authoritarian [ɔːθɒrɪ'teərɪən] autoritario; authoritative autoritario; *information* autorevole; authority autorità *f inv*; *(permission)* autorizzazione *f*; authorization autorizzazione *f*; authorize autorizzare

autistic [ɔː'tɪstɪk] autistico

autobiography [ɔːtəbaɪ'ɒgrəfɪ] autobiografia *f*

autocratic [ɔːtə'krætɪk] autocratico

autograph ['ɔːtəgrɑːf] autografo *m*

automate ['ɔːtəmeɪt] automatizzare; automatic **1** *adj* automatico **2** *n car* macchina *f* con il cambio automatico; automatically automaticamente; automation automazione *f*

automobile [ˈɔːtəməbiːl] automobile *f*

autonomous [ɔː'tɒnəməs] autonomo

autopilot [ˈɔːtəʊpaɪlət] pilota *m* automatico

autopsy ['ɔːtɒpsɪ] autopsia *f*

autumn ['ɔːtəm] autunno *m*

auxiliary [ɔːg'zɪlɪərɪ] ausiliario

available [ə'veɪləbl] disponibile

avalanche ['ævəlɑːnʃ] valanga *f*

avenue ['ævənjuː] corso *m*; *fig* strada *f*

average ['ævərɪdʒ] **1** *adj* medio; *(mediocre)* mediocre **2** *n* media *f*; **on ~** in media

◆ average out at risultare in media *f*

averse [ə'vɜːs]: **not be ~ to** non avere niente contro; aversion avversione *f* (**to** per)

avid ['ævɪd] avido

avocado [ævə'kɑːdəʊ] avocado *m inv*

avoid [ə'vɔid] evitare

await [ə'weit] attendere

awake [ə'weik] sveglio; *it's keeping me ~* mi impedisce di dormire

award [ə'wɔːd] **1** *n (prize)* premio *m* **2** *v/t* assegnare; *damages* riconoscere; **awards ceremony** cerimonia *f* di premiazione

aware [ə'weə(r)] conscio; *become ~ of* rendersi conto di; **awareness** consapevolezza *f*

away [ə'wei] via; SP fuori casa; *be ~ travelling, sick etc* essere via; *run ~* correre via; *look ~*

guardare da un'altra parte; *it's 2 miles ~* dista 2 miglia; **away game** SP partita *f* fuori casa

awesome ['ɔːsm] F *(terrific)* fantastico

awful ['ɔːful] tremendo, terribile; **awfully** F *(very)* da matti F

awkward ['ɔːkwəd] *(clumsy)* goffo; *(difficult)* difficile; *(embarrassing)* scomodo; *feel ~* sentirsi a disagio

axe, *Am* **ax** [æks] **1** *n* scure *f*, accetta *f* **2** *v/t project, job* sopprimere

axle ['æksl] asse *f*

B

BA [biːˈei] (= *Bachelor of Arts) (degree)* laurea *f* in lettere; *(person)* laureato *m*, -a *f* in lettere

baby ['beibi] *n* bambino *m*, -a *f*; **baby-sit** fare il / la baby-sitter

bachelor ['bætʃələ(r)] scapolo *m*

back [bæk] **1** *n of person* schiena *f*; *of animal, hand* dorso *m*; *of car, bus* parte *f* posteriore; *of book, house* retro *m*; *of clothes* rovescio *m*; *of drawer* fondo *m*; *of chair* schienale *m*; SP terzino *m*; *in the ~ (of the car)* (nei sedili) di dietro; *at the ~ of the bus* in fondo all'auto-

bus; *~ to front* al contrario **2** *adj door, steps* di dietro; *wheels, legs* posteriore; *garden* sul retro **3** *adv*: *please move ~* indietro, per favore; *give sth ~ to s.o.* restituire qc a qu; *she'll be ~ tomorrow* sarà di ritorno domani **4** *v/t (support)* appoggiare; *car* guidare in retromarcia; *horse* puntare su

◆ **back down** fare marcia indietro

◆ **back off** spostarsi indietro; *from danger* tirarsi indietro

◆ **back out** *of commitment* tirarsi indietro

◆ **back up 1** *v/t (support)* confermare; *claim, argument* supportare; *file* fare un back-up di **2** *v/i in car* fare retro-marcia

'backache mal *m inv* di schiena; **backbone** spina *f* dorsale; **backdate** retrodatare; **backdoor** porta *f* di dietro; **backer** FIN finanziatore *m*, -trice *f*; **background** sfondo *m*; *of person* background *m inv*; *of story* retroscena *mpl*; **backhand** *in tennis* rovescio *m*; **backing** *moral* appoggio *m*; MUS accompagnamento *m*; **backing group** gruppo *m* d'accompagnamento; **backlash** reazione *f* violenta; **backlog**: ~ *of work* lavoro *m* arretrato; **backpack** zaino *m*; **backpacker** sacco-pelista *m/f*; **back seat** sedile *m* posteriore; **backside** F sedere *m*; **backspace** **(key)** (tasto di) ritorno *m*; **back streets** vicoli *mpl*; **backstroke** SP dorso *m*; **backtrack** tornare indietro; **backup** **(support)** rinforzi *mpl*; COMPUT backup *m inv*; **backup disk** COMPUT disco *m* di backup; **backward** *child* tardivo; *society* arretrato; *glance* all'indietro; **backwards** indietro; **backyard** cortile *m*

bacon ['beikn] pancetta *f*

bacteria [bæk'tɪərɪə] batteri *mpl*

bad [bæd] *news, manners* cattivo; *weather, headache* brutto; *mistake* grave; *food* guasto; *it's not* ~ non è male; *that's too* ~ *shame* peccato!

badge [bædʒ] distintivo *m*

bad 'language parolacce *fpl*; **badly** male; *injured* gravemente; *he* ~ *needs* ... ha urgente bisogno di ...

badminton ['bædmɪntən] badminton *m*

bad-tempered [bæd'tempəd] irascibile

baffle ['bæfl]: **be ~d** essere perplesso

bag [bæg] borsa *f*; *plastic, paper* busta *f*

baggage ['bægɪdʒ] bagagli *mpl*; **baggage check** *Am* deposito *m* bagagli; **baggage trolley** carrello *m*

baggy ['bægɪ] senza forma

bail [beɪl] LAW cauzione *f*; *on* ~ su cauzione

bait [beɪt] esca *f*

bake [beɪk] cuocere al forno; **baked potatoes** *patate cotte al forno con la buccia*; **baker** fornaio *m*, -a *f*; **bakery** panetteria *f*

balance ['bæləns] **1** *n* equilibrio *m*; *(remainder)* resto *m*; *of bank account* saldo *m* **2** *v/t* tenere in equilibrio **3** *v/i* stare in equilibrio; *of accounts* quadrare; **balanced** *(fair)* obiettivo; *diet, personality* equilibrato; **balance sheet** bilancio *m* (di esercizio)

balcony ['bælkənɪ] balcone

banner

m; in theatre prima galleria *f*

bald [bɔːld] *man* calvo; **balding** stempiato

Balkans [ˈbɔːlkənz]: **the ~** i Balcani *mpl*

ball [bɔːl] palla *f; football* pallone *m;* **be on the ~** essere sveglio; **play ~** *fig* collaborare; **the ~'s in his court** la prossima mossa è sua

ballad [ˈbæləd] ballata *f*

ballerina [bæləˈriːnə] ballerina *f*

ballet [ˈbæleɪ] *art* danza *f* classica; *dance* balletto *m;* **ballet dancer** ballerino *m* classico, ballerina *f* classica

'ball game F: **that's a different ~** è un altro paio di maniche

ballistic missile [bəˈlɪstɪk] missile *m* balistico

balloon [bəˈluːn] *child's* palloncino *m; for flight* mongolfiera *f*

ballot [ˈbælət] **1** *n* votazione *f* **2** *v/t members* consultare tramite votazione; **ballot box** urna *f* elettorale

'ballpark F: **be in the right ~** essere nell'ordine corretto di cifre; **ballpark figure** F cifra *f* approssimativa; **ballpoint (pen)** penna *f* a sfera

balls [bɔːlz] V palle *fpl* V

bamboo [bæmˈbuː] bambù *m inv*

ban [bæn] **1** *n* divieto *m* (**on** di) **2** *v/t* proibire

banal [bəˈnɑːl] banale

banana [bəˈnɑːnə] banana *f*

band [bænd] banda *f; pop* gruppo *m; of material* nastro *m*

bandage [ˈbændɪdʒ] **1** *n* benda *f* **2** *v/t* bendare

'Band-Aid® *Am* cerotto *m*

B&B [biːnˈbiː] (= **bed and breakfast**) pensione *f* familiare, bed and breakfast *m inv*

bandit [ˈbændɪt] brigante *m*

bandy [ˈbændɪ] *legs* storto

bang [bæŋ] **1** *n* colpo *m* **2** *v/t door* chiudere violentemente; *(hit)* sbattere

bangle [ˈbæŋgl] braccialetto *m*

bangs [bæŋz] *Am* frangia *f*

banisters [ˈbænɪstəz] ringhiera *fsg*

banjo [ˈbændʒəʊ] banjo *m inv*

bank¹ [bæŋk] *of river* riva *f*

bank² [bæŋk] FIN banca *f*

♦ **bank on** contare su

'bank account conto *m* bancario; **banker** banchiere *m;* **banker's card** carta *f* assegni; **bank holiday** giorno *m* festivo; **banking** professione *f* bancaria; **bank loan** prestito *m* bancario; **bank manager** direttore *m* di banca; **bank rate** tasso *m* ufficiale di sconto; **bankroll** finanziare; **bankrupt** fallito; **go ~** fallire; **bankruptcy** bancarotta *f*

banner [ˈbænə(r)] striscione *m*

banquet ['bæŋkwɪt] banchetto *m*

baptism ['bæptɪzm] battesimo *m*; **baptize** battezzare

bar[1] [bɑː(r)] *n* of iron spranga *f*; of chocolate tavoletta *f*; for drinks bar *m inv*; (counter) bancone *m*

bar[2] [bɑː(r)] *v/t* vietare l'ingresso a

barbaric [bɑː'bærɪk] barbaro

barbecue ['bɑːbɪkjuː] **1** *n* barbecue *m inv* **2** *v/t* cuocere al barbecue

barbed 'wire [bɑːbd] filo *m* spinato

barber ['bɑːbə(r)] barbiere *m*

'bar code codice *m* a barre

bare [beə(r)] (naked) nudo; room) spoglio; **barefoot: be ~** essere scalzo; **bare-headed** senza cappello; **barely** appena

bargain ['bɑːgɪn] **1** *n* (deal) patto *m*; (good buy) affare *m* **2** *v/i* tirare sul prezzo

barge [bɑːdʒ] NAUT chiatta *f*
◆ **barge into** piombare su

baritone ['bærɪtəʊn] *n* baritono *m*

bark[1] [bɑːk] **1** *n* of dog abbaiare *m* **2** *v/i* abbaiare

bark[2] [bɑːk] *n* of tree corteccia *f*

'barmaid barista *f*; **barman** barista *m*

barn [bɑːn] granaio *m*

barometer [bə'rɒmɪtə(r)] also fig barometro *m*

barracks ['bærəks] MIL caser-

ma *fsg*

barrel ['bærəl] (container) barile *m*

barren ['bærən] land arido

barrette [bə'ret] *Am* molletta *f*

barricade [bærɪ'keɪd] barricata *f*

barrier ['bærɪə(r)] barriera *f*

barrister ['bærɪstə(r)] avvocato *m*

'bar tender barista *m/f*

barter [bɑː'tə(r)] **1** *n* baratto *m* **2** *v/i* barattare

base [beɪs] **1** *n* base *f* **2** *v/t* basare (**on** su); **baseball** baseball *m*; ball palla *f* da baseball; **baseball cap** berretto *m* da baseball; **baseboard** *Am* battiscopa *m inv*; **basement** seminterrato *m*

basic ['beɪsɪk] (rudimentary) rudimentale; salary di base; beliefs fondamentale; **basically** essenzialmente

basin ['beɪsn] for washing lavandino *m*

basis ['beɪsɪs] base *f*

bask [bɑːsk] crogiolarsi

basket ['bɑːskɪt] cestino *m*; in basketball cesto *m*; **basketball** basket *m*, pallacanestro *f*; ball pallone *m* da pallacanestro

bass [beɪs] (part) voce *f* di basso; (singer, guitar) basso *m*; (double bass) contrabbasso *m*

bastard ['bɑːstəd] F bastardo *m*, -a *f* F

bear

bat¹ [bæt] **1** n mazza f; *for table tennis* racchetta f **2** v/i SP battere

bat² [bæt] *animal* pipistrello m

batch [bætʃ] n *of students* gruppo m; *of goods* lotto m; *of bread* infornata f

bath [bɑːθ] bagno m

bathe [beɪð] *(swim, have bath)* fare il bagno; bathing costume m da bagno

'bathrobe accappatoio m; bathroom *(stanza f da)* bagno m; bath towel asciugamano m da bagno; bathtub vasca f da bagno

batter ['bætə(r)] pastella f; battered maltrattato; *suitcase etc* malridotto

battery ['bætrɪ] pila f; MOT batteria f

battle ['bætl] **1** n *also fig* battaglia f **2** v/i *against illness etc* lottare; battleship corazzata f

bawl [bɔːl] *(shout)* urlare; *(weep)* strillare

bay [beɪ] *(inlet)* baia f; bay window bovindo m

BC [biː'siː] (= *before Christ*) a. C. (= avanti Cristo)

be [biː] ◇ essere; *it's me* sono io; *how much is* quant'è / quanto sono ...?; *there is, there are* ...?; c'è, ci sono; *don't ~ sad* non essere triste; *how are you?* come stai?; *he's very well* sta bene; *I'm hot / cold* ho freddo / caldo; *it's hot / cold* fa

freddo / caldo; *he's seven* ha sette anni ◇ *has the postman been?* è passato il postino?; *I've never been to Japan* non sono mai stato in Giappone; *I've been here for hours* sono qui da tanto ◇ *tags: that's right, isn't it?* giusto, no?; *she's American, isn't she?* è americana, vero? ◇ v/aux: *I am thinking* sto pensando; *he's working in London* lavora a Londra ◇ *obligation: you are to do what I tell you* devi fare quello che ti dico ◇ *passive* essere; *he was killed* è stato ucciso

beach [biːtʃ] spiaggia f; beachwear abbigliamento m da spiaggia

beads [biːdz] perline fpl

beak [biːk] becco m

'be-all: *the ~ and end-all* la cosa più importante

beam [biːm] **1** n *in ceiling etc* trave f **2** v/i *(smile)* fare un sorriso radioso **3** v/t *(transmit)* trasmettere

bean [biːn] *(vegetable)* fagiolo m; *of coffee* chicco m; *be full of ~s* F essere particolarmente vivace

bear¹ [beə(r)] n *animal* orso m

bear² [beə(r)] **1** v/t *weight* portare; *costs* sostenere; *(tolerate)* sopportare; *child* dare alla luce **2** v/i: *bring pressure to ~ on* fare pressione su

bearable ['beərəbl] sopportabile

beard [bɪəd] barba f

beat [bi:t] **1** n of heart battito m; of music ritmo m **2** v/i of heart battere; of rain picchiettare; **~ about the bush** menar il can per l'aia **3** v/t in competition battere; (hit) picchiare; drum suonare; **~ it!** F fila!; **it ~s me** non capisco

◆ **beat up** picchiare

beaten ['bi:tən]: **off the ~ track** fuori mano; **beating** physical botte fpl; **beat-up** F malconcio

beautiful ['bju:tɪfʊl] bello; **thanks, that's just ~!** grazie, così va bene; **beautifully** stupendamente; **beauty** bellezza f; **beauty salon** istituto m di bellezza

beaver ['bi:və(r)] castoro m

because [bɪ'kɒz] perché; **~ of** a causa di

become [bɪ'kʌm] diventare; **what's ~ of her?** che ne è stato di lei?; **becoming** grazioso

bed [bed] letto m; **~ of flowers** aiuola f; **go to ~** andare a letto; **bedding** materasso m e lenzuola fpl; **bedridden** costretto a letto; **bedroom** camera f da letto; **bed-sit, bed-sitter** monolocale m; **bedtime** ora f di andare a letto

bee [bi:] ape f

beech [bi:tʃ] faggio m

beef [bi:f] manzo m; **beefbur-**ger hamburger m inv

beep [bi:p] **1** n bip m inv **2** v/i suonare

beer [bɪə(r)] birra f

beet [bi:t] barbabietola f

beetle ['bi:tl] coleottero m

before [bɪ'fɔ:(r)] **1** prep prima di **2** adv prima; **I've seen this film ~** questo film l'ho già visto **3** conj prima che (+ subj); **I saw him ~ he left** l'ho visto prima che partisse; **I saw him ~ I left** l'ho visto prima di partire; **beforehand** prima

befriend [bɪ'frend] fare amicizia con

beg [beg] **1** v/i mendicare **2** v/t: **~ s.o. to ...** pregare qu di ...; **beggar** mendicante m/f

begin [bɪ'gɪn] cominciare; **beginner** principiante m/f; **beginning** inizio m; (origin) origine f

behalf [bɪ'hɑ:f]: **on ~ of** a nome di

behave [bɪ'heɪv] comportarsi; **~ (yourself)!** comportati bene!; **behaviour**, Am **behavior** comportamento m

behind [bɪ'haɪnd] **1** prep dietro; in order dietro a; **be ~** (responsible for) essere dietro a; (support) appoggiare **2** adv (at the back) dietro; **she had to stay ~** è dovuta rimanere; **be ~ in match** essere in svantaggio

beige [beɪʒ] beige inv

being ['bi:ɪŋ] (*existence*) esistenza *f*; (*creature*) essere *m*

belated [bɪ'leɪtɪd] in ritardo

belch [beltʃ] **1** *n* rutto *m* **2** *v/i* ruttare

Belgian ['beldʒən] **1** *adj* belga **2** *n* belga *m/f*; **Belgium** Belgio *m*

belief [bɪ'li:f] convinzione *f*; *in God* fede *f*; **believe** credere

◆ **believe in** *God, person* credere in; *ghost, person* credere a

believer [bɪ'li:və(r)] REL credente *m/f*; **I'm a great ~ in ...** credo fermamente in ...

bell [bel] *in church, school* campana *f*; *on door, bicycle* campanello *m*; **bellhop** *Am* fattorino *m* d'albergo

belligerent [bɪ'lɪdʒərənt] bellicoso

bellow ['beləʊ] urlare; *of bull* muggire

belly ['belɪ] pancia *f*

belong [bɪ'lɒŋ] *v/i*: **where does this ~?** dove va questo?; **I don't ~ here** mi sento un estraneo

◆ **belong to** appartenere a

be'longings cose *fpl*

beloved [bɪ'lʌvɪd] adorato

below [bɪ'ləʊ] **1** *prep* sotto **2** *adv* di sotto; *in text* sotto **10 degrees ~** 10 gradi sotto zero

belt [belt] cintura *f*

bench [bentʃ] *seat* panchina *f*; **benchmark** punto *m* di riferimento

bend [bend] **1** *n* curva *f* **2** *v/t* piegare **3** *v/i* curvarsi; *of person* inchinarsi

◆ **bend down** chinarsi

beneath [bɪ'ni:θ] **1** *prep* sotto **2** *adv* di sotto

benefactor ['benɪfæktə(r)] benefattore *m*, -trice *f*

beneficial [benɪ'fɪʃl] vantaggioso

benefit ['benɪfɪt] **1** *n* vantaggio *m* **2** *v/t* andare a vantaggio di **3** *v/i* trarre vantaggio (*from* da)

benevolent [bɪ'nevələnt] benevolo

benign [bɪ'naɪn] benevolo; MED benigno

bequeath [bɪ'kwi:ð] *also fig* lasciare in eredità

bequest [bɪ'kwest] lascito *m*

bereaved [bɪ'ri:vd] **1** *adj* addolorato **2** *n*: **the ~** i familiari *mpl* del defunto

beret ['bereɪ] berretto *m*

berry ['berɪ] bacca *f*

berth [bɜ:θ] *on ship, train* cuccetta *f*; *for ship* ormeggio *m*

beside [bɪ'saɪd] accanto a; *be ~ o.s.* essere fuori di sé; *that's ~ the point* questo non c'entra

besides [bɪ'saɪdz] **1** *adv* inoltre **2** *prep* (*apart from*) oltre a

best [best] **1** *adj* migliore **2** *adv* meglio; *it would be ~ if ...* sarebbe meglio se ...; *I like her ~* lei è quella che mi piace di più **3** *n*: *do one's*

~ fare del proprio meglio; **the** ~ il meglio; (*outstanding thing or person*) il / la migliore; **they've done the** ~ **they can** hanno fatto tutto il possibile; **make the** ~ **of** cogliere il lato buono di; **all the** ~**!** tanti auguri!; best before date scadenza *f*; best man at *wedding* testimone *m* dello sposo

bet [bet] **1** *n* scommessa *f* **2** *v/i* scommettere; **you** ~**!** ci puoi scommettere!

betray [bɪ'treɪ] tradire; **betrayal** tradimento *m*

better ['betə(r)] **1** *adj* migliore; **get** ~ migliorare **2** *adv* meglio; **you'd** ~ **ask permission** faresti meglio a chiedere il permesso; **I'd really** ~ **not** sarebbe meglio di no; **all the** ~ **for us** tanto meglio per noi; **I like her** ~ lei mi piace di più; **better off be** ~ stare meglio finanziariamente

between [bɪ'twiːn] tra

beware [bɪ'weə(r)]: ~ **of** …! (stai) attento a …!

bewilder [bɪ'wɪldə(r)] sconcertare; **bewilderment** perplessità *f*

beyond [bɪ'jɒnd] oltre, al di là di

bias ['baɪəs] *against* pregiudizio *m*; *in favour of* preferenza *f*; bias(s) parziale

Bible ['baɪbl] bibbia *f*; **biblical** biblico

bicentenary [baɪsen'tiːnərɪ] bicentenario *m*

bicker ['bɪkə(r)] bisticciare

bicycle ['baɪsɪkl] bicicletta *f*

bid [bɪd] **1** *n at auction* offerta *f*; (*attempt*) tentativo *m* **2** *v/t & v/i at auction* offrire; **bidder** offerente *m/f*

biennial [baɪ'enɪəl] biennale

big [bɪg] **1** *adj* grande; **my** ~ **brother / sister** mio fratello / mia sorella maggiore **2** *adv*: **talk** ~ sparare grosse

bigamist ['bɪgəmɪst] bigamo *m*, -a *f*

'bighead F pallone *m* gonfiato F

bigot ['bɪgət] fanatico *m*, -a *f*

bike [baɪk] F *bici* f inv F **2** *v/i* andare in bici; **biker** motociclista *m/f*; (*courier*) corriere *m*

bikini [bɪ'kiːnɪ] bikini *m* inv

bilingual [baɪ'lɪŋgwəl] bilingue

bill [bɪl] **1** *n in hotel, restaurant* conto *m*; (*gas / electricity* ~) bolletta *f*; (*invoice*) fattura *f*; Am: *money* banconota *f*; POL disegno *m* di legge; (*poster*) avviso *m*

'billboard Am tabellone *m* per affissioni pubblicitarie; **billfold** Am portafoglio *m*

billiards ['bɪljədz] biliardo *m*

billion ['bɪljən] (*1,000,000,000*) miliardo *m*

bin [bɪn] bidone *m* f; **bin lorry** camion *m* della nettezza urbana bind [baɪnd] *also fig* legare; LAW obbligare; **binding** *agreement* vincolante

binoculars [bɪ'nɒkjʊləz] binocolo *mpl*

biodegradable [baɪəʊdɪ'greɪdəbl] biodegradabile

biographer [baɪ'ɒɡrəfə(r)] biografo *m*, -a *f*; **biography** biografia *f*

biological [baɪə'lɒdʒɪkl] biologico; **biology** biologia *f*; **biotechnology** biotecnologia *f*

bird [bɜːd] uccello *m*

biro® ['baɪrəʊ] biro *f*

birth [bɜːθ] *also fig* nascita *f*; (*labour*) parto *m*; **give ~ to child** partorire; **date of ~** data di nascita; **birth certificate** certificato *m* di nascita; **birth control** controllo *m* delle nascite; **birthday** compleanno *m*; **happy ~!** buon compleanno!; **birthplace** luogo *m* di nascita

biscuit ['bɪskɪt] biscotto *m*

bisexual ['baɪseksjʊəl] bisessuale

bishop ['bɪʃəp] vescovo *m*

bit [bɪt] *n* (*piece*) pezzo *m*; (*part*) parte *f*; **a ~** (*a little*) un po'; **a ~ of advice** un consiglio; **~ by ~** poco a poco; **I'll be there in a ~** (*in a little while*) sarò lì tra poco

bitch [bɪtʃ] **1** *n dog* cagna *f*; F *woman* bastarda *f* **2** *v/i* F (*complain*) lamentarsi

bite [baɪt] **1** *n* morso *m* **2** *v/t*

mordere; **one's nails** mangiarsi 3 *v/i* mordere

bitter ['bɪtə(r)] *taste* amaro; *person* amareggiato

black [blæk] **1** *adj* nero; *tea* senza latte **2** *n colour* nero *m*; *person* nero *m*, -a *f*

◆ **black out** (*faint*) svenire

'blackberry mora *f* di rovo; **blackbird** merlo *m*; **blackboard** lavagna *f*; **black box** scatola *f* nera; **black coffee** caffè *m* nero; **black economy** economia *f* sommersa; **black eye** occhio *m* nero; **blacklist** lista *f* nera; **blackmail 1** *n* ricatto *m* **2** *v/t* ricattare; **black market** mercato *m* nero; **blackness** oscurità *f*; **blackout** ELEC black-out *m inv*; MED svenimento *m*

bladder ['blædə(r)] vescica *f*

blade [bleɪd] *of knife* lama *f*; *of helicopter* pala *f*; *of grass* filo *m*

blame [bleɪm] **1** *n* colpa *f*; (*responsibility*) responsabilità *f* **2** *v/t*: **~ s.o. for sth** ritenere qu responsabile di qc

bland [blænd] *smile* insulso; *food* insipido

blank [blæŋk] **1** *adj* (*not written on*) bianco; *tape* vergine; *look* vuoto **2** *n* (*empty space*) spazio *m*; **blank cheque,** *Am* **blank check** assegno *m* in bianco

blanket ['blæŋkɪt] coperta *f*

blasphemy ['blæsfəmɪ] bestemmia *f*

blast [blɑːst] **1** n (*explosion*) esplosione f; (*gust*) raffica f **2** v/t far esplodere; **~!** accidenti!; **blast-off** lancio m

blatant ['bleɪtənt] palese

blaze [bleɪz] **1** n (*fire*) incendio m **2** v/i of fire ardere

blazer ['bleɪzə(r)] blazer m inv

bleach [bliːtʃ] **1** n for clothes varechina f; for hair acqua f ossigenata **2** v/t hair ossigenarsi

bleak [bliːk] countryside desolato; weather cupo; future deprimente

bleary-eyed ['blɪərɪaɪd]: **be ~** avere lo sguardo appannato

bleat [bliːt] of sheep belare

bleed [bliːd] sanguinare; **bleeding** emorragia f

bleep [bliːp] **1** n blip m inv **2** v/i suonare

blemish ['blemɪʃ] on skin imperfezione f; on fruit ammaccatura f

blend [blend] **1** n miscela f **2** v/t miscelare; **blender** machine frullatore m

bless [bles] benedire; **~ you!** (in response to sneeze) salute!; **blessing** benedizione f

blind [blaɪnd] **1** adj cieco **2** n: **the ~** i ciechi **3** v/t accecare; **blind alley** vicolo m cieco; **blind date** appuntamento m al buio; **blindfold 1** n benda f **2** v/t bendare (gli occhi a); **blinding** atroce; light accecante; **blindly** a tastoni; fig ciecamente; **blind spot** in road punto m cieco

blink [blɪŋk] of person sbattere le palpebre; of light tremolare

blister ['blɪstə(r)] vescichetta f

blizzard ['blɪzəd] bufera f di neve

bloc [blɒk] POL blocco m

block [blɒk] **1** n blocco m; in town isolato m; of flats palazzo m (d'appartamenti) **2** v/t bloccare

◆ **block out** light impedire

blockage ['blɒkɪdʒ] ingorgo m; **blockbuster** successone m; **block letters** maiuscole fpl

bloke [bləʊk] F tipo m F

blond [blɒnd] biondo; **blonde** woman bionda f

blood [blʌd] sangue m; **blood donor** donatore m, -trice f di sangue; **blood group** gruppo m sanguigno; **blood poisoning** setticemia f; **blood pressure** pressione f del sangue; **blood sample** prelievo m di sangue; **bloodshed** spargimento m di sangue; **bloodshot** iniettato di sangue; **bloodstained** macchiato di sangue; **blood test** analisi f inv del sangue; **bloodthirsty** assetato di sangue; **bloody 1** adj hands etc insanguinato; F maledetto; **~ hell!** porca miseria! F; **you're a ~ genius!** sei un geniaccio! F **2** adv: **I'm ~ tired**

sono stanco morto
bloom [bluːm] *also fig* fiorire
blossom ['blɒsəm] **1** *n* fiori *mpl*; *fig* fiore *m* **2** *v/i also fig* fiorire
blot [blɒt] macchia *f*
♦ **blot out** *memory* cancellare; *view* nascondere
blouse [blauz] camicetta *f*
blow¹ [bləu] *n* colpo *m*
blow² [bləu] **1** *v/t of wind* spingere; *smoke* soffiare; ~ *a whistle* fischiare; ~ *one's nose* soffiarsi il naso **2** *v/i of wind, person* soffiare; *of fuse* saltare; *of tyre* scoppiare
♦ **blow out 1** *v/t candle* spegnere **2** *v/i of candle* spegnersi
♦ **blow over 1** *v/t* abbattere **2** *v/i* rovesciarsi; *of storm, argument* calmarsi
♦ **blow up 1** *v/t with explosives* far saltare; *balloon* gonfiare; *photograph* ingrandire **2** *v/i also fig* esplodere
'blow-dry asciugare col phon;
blow-out *of tyre* scoppio *m*
blue [bluː] **1** *adj* blu; *film* porno; **blue chip** sicuro; *company* di alto livello; **blues** MUS blues *m inv*; **have the ~** essere giù
bluff [blʌf] **1** *n* (*deception*) bluff *m inv* **2** *v/i* bluffare
blunder ['blʌndə(r)] **1** *n* errore *m* **2** *v/i* fare un errore
blunt [blʌnt] spuntato; *person* diretto; **bluntly** senza mezzi termini
blur [blɜː(r)] **1** *n* massa *f* indi-

stinta **2** *v/t* offuscare
blurt out [blɜːt] spiattellare
blush [blʌʃ] **1** *n* rossore *m* **2** *v/i* arrossire; **blusher** *cosmetic* fard *m inv*
blustery ['blʌstərɪ] ventoso
BO [biːˈəu] (= *body odour*) odori *mpl* corporei
board [bɔːd] **1** *n* asse *f*; *for chess* scacchiera *f*; *for notices* tabellone *m*; ~ (*of directors*) consiglio *m* (d'amministrazione); *on* ~ a bordo **2** *v/t aeroplane etc* salire a bordo di **3** *v/i of passengers* salire a bordo
♦ **board up** chiudere con assi
boarder ['bɔːdə(r)] pensionante *m/f*; EDU convittore *m*, -trice *f*; **board game** gioco *m* da tavolo; **boarding card** carta *f* d'imbarco; **boarding pass** carta *f* d'imbarco; **boarding school** collegio *m*; **board meeting** riunione *f* di consiglio; **board room** sala *f* del consiglio
boast [bəust] vantarsi
boat [bəut] (*small, for leisure*) barca *f*; (*ship*) nave *f*
bodily ['bɒdɪlɪ] **1** *adj* corporale **2** *adv eject* di peso; **body** corpo *m*; *dead* cadavere *m*; **body double** controfigura *f*; **bodyguard** guardia *f* del corpo; **body language** linguaggio *m* del corpo; **bodywork** MOT carrozzeria *f*
bogus ['bəugəs] fasullo

boil

boil¹ [bɔɪl] *n* (*swelling*) foruncolo *m*

boil² [bɔɪl] **1** *v/t* far bollire **2** *v/i* bollire

◆ **boil down to** ridursi a

boiler ['bɔɪlə(r)] caldaia *f*

boisterous ['bɔɪstərəs] turbolento

bold [bəʊld] **1** *adj* (*brave*) audace **2** *n print* neretto *m*; **in ~** in neretto

bolster ['bəʊlstə(r)] *confidence* rafforzare

bolt [bəʊlt] **1** *n* on door catenaccio *m*; (*metal pin*) bullone *m* **2** *adv*: **~ upright** diritto come un fuso **3** *v/t* (*fix with bolts*) fissare con bulloni; (*close*) chiudere col catenaccio **4** *v/i* (*run off*) scappare via

bomb [bɒm] **1** *n* bomba *f* **2** *v/t* bombardare; (*blow up*) far saltare; **bombard** *also fig* bombardare; **bomb attack** attacco *m*; **bomber** *airplane* bombardiere *m*; *terrorist* dinamitardo *m*, -a *f*; **bomb scare** allarme-bomba *m*; **bombshell** *fig*: *news* bomba *f*

bond [bɒnd] **1** *n* (*tie*) legame *m*; FIN obbligazione *f* **2** *v/i* aderire

bone [bəʊn] osso *m*; *in fish* lisca *f*

bonfire ['bɒnfaɪə(r)] falò *m inv*

bonnet ['bɒnɪt] *of car* cofano *m*

bonus ['bəʊnəs] *money* gratifica *f*; (*something extra*) vantaggio *m* in più

boo [buː] **1** *n* fischio *m* **2** *v/t & v/i* fischiare

boob¹ [buːb] F (*mistake*) errore *m*

boob² [buːb] P (*breast*) tetta *f* P

booboo ['buːbuː] F gaffe *f inv*

book [bʊk] **1** *n* libro *m* **2** *v/t* (*reserve*) prenotare; *of policeman* multare; SP ammonire; **bookcase** scaffale *m*; **booked up** tutto esaurito; *person* occupatissimo; **bookie** F allibratore *m*; **booking** (*reservation*) prenotazione *f*; **booking office** biglietteria *f*; **bookkeeper** contabile *m/f*; **bookkeeping** contabilità *f*; **booklet** libretto *m*; **bookmaker** allibratore *m*; **books** (*accounts*) libri *mpl* contabili; **bookseller** libraio *m*, -a *f*; **bookshop**, *Am* **bookstore** libreria *f*

boom¹ [buːm] **1** *n* boom *m inv* **2** *v/i of business* andare a gonfie vele

boom² [buːm] *n* (*bang*) rimbombo *m*

boost [buːst] **1** *n* spinta *f* **2** *v/t sales* incrementare; *confidence* aumentare

boot¹ [buːt] stivale *m*; (*climbing ~*) scarpone *m*; *for football* scarpetta *f*

◆ **boot up** COMPUT inizializzare

booth [buːð] *at market, fair* bancarella *f*; *(telephone ~)* cabina *f*

booze [buːz] F alcolici *mpl*; **booze-up** F bevuta *f*

border[1] ['bɔːdə(r)] **1** *n* confine *m*; *(edge)* bordo *m* **2** *v/t country* confinare con

◆ **border on** *country* confinare con; *(be almost)* rasentare

bore[1] [bɔː(r)] *v/t hole* praticare

bore[2] [bɔː(r)] **1** *n person* persona *f* noiosa **2** *v/t* annoiare

bored [bɔːd] annoiato; **I'm ~** mi sto annoiando; **boredom** noia *f*; **boring** noioso

born [bɔːn]: **be ~** essere nato

borrow ['bɒrəʊ] prendere in prestito

bosom ['bʊzm] *of woman* seno *m*

boss [bɒs] boss *m inv*

◆ **boss around** dare ordini a

bossy ['bɒsɪ] prepotente

botanical [bə'tænɪkl] botanico; **botany** botanica *f*

botch [bɒtʃ] fare un pasticcio con

both [bəʊθ] **1** *adj pron* entrambi, tutti *mpl* e due, tutte *fpl* e due; tutti e due; *~ (of the)* **brothers were there** tutt'e due i fratelli erano lì; *~ of them* entrambi *m* **2** *adv*: *~ my mother and I* sia mia madre che io; *is it business or pleasure? - ~* per piacere o per affari? - tutt'e due

bother ['bɒðə(r)] **1** *n* disturbo *m*; *it's no ~* non c'è problema **2** *v/t (disturb)* disturbare; *(worry)* preoccupare **3** *v/i*: **don't ~** *(you needn't do it)* non preoccuparti

bottle ['bɒtl] bottiglia *f*; *for baby* biberon *m*

◆ **bottle up** *feelings* reprimere

'bottle bank contenitore *m* per la raccolta del vetro; **bottled water** acqua *f* in bottiglia; **bottleneck** ingorgo *m*; **bottle-opener** apribottiglie *m inv*

bottom ['bɒtəm] **1** *adj* più basso **2** *n* fondo *m*; *(buttocks)* sedere *m*; **at the ~ of the screen** in basso sullo schermo; **at the ~ of the page** in fondo alla pagina

◆ **bottom out** toccare il fondo

bottom 'line *financial* risultato *m* finanziario; **the ~** *(the real issue)* l'essenziale *m*

boulder ['bəʊldə(r)] macigno *m*

bounce [baʊns] **1** *v/t ball* far rimbalzare **2** *v/i ball* rimbalzare; *on sofa etc* saltare; *of cheque* essere protestato; **bouncer** buttafuori *m inv*

bound[1] [baʊnd] *adj*: **be ~ to do sth** *(sure to)* dover fare per forza qc; *(obliged to)* essere obbligato a fare qc; **the train is ~ to be late** il treno sarà senz'altro in ritardo

bound² [baʊnd] *adj*: **be ~ for**
of ship essere diretto a

bound³ [baʊnd] *n* (*jump*) balzo *m*

boundary ['baʊndərɪ] confine
m

bouquet [bʊ'keɪ] bouquet *m
inv*

bourbon ['bɜːbən] bourbon
m inv

bout [baʊt] MED attacco *m*; *in
boxing* incontro *m*

bow¹ [baʊ] **1** *n as greeting* inchino *m* **2** *v/i* inchinarsi **3**
v/t head chinare

bow² [baʊ] *n* (*knot*) fiocco *m*;
MUS archetto *m*

bow³ [baʊ] *n of ship* prua *f*

bowels ['baʊəlz] intestino
msg

bowl¹ [bəʊl] *n container* bacinella *f*; *for soup, cereal* ciotola *f*; *for cooking, salad* terrina
f

bowl² [bəʊl] **1** *n ball* boccia *f* **2**
v/i in bowling lanciare

bowling ['bəʊlɪŋ] bowling *m*;
bowling alley pista *f* da
bowling; **bowls** *nsg* (*game*)
bocce *fpl*

bow 'tie (cravatta *f* a) farfalla
f

box¹ [bɒks] *n container* scatola *f*; *on form* casella *f*

box² [bɒks] *v/i* fare pugilato

boxer ['bɒksə(r)] pugile *m*;
boxing pugilato *m*, boxe *f*;
Boxing Day Santo Stefano;
boxing glove guantone *m*
da pugile; **boxing match** in-

contro *m* di pugilato

'box number *at post office* casella *f*; **box office** botteghino *m*

boy [bɔɪ] *child* bambino *m*;
youth ragazzo *m*; *son* figlio *m*

boycott ['bɔɪkɒt] **1** *n* boicottaggio *m* **2** *v/t* boicottare

'boyfriend ragazzo *m*; **boy-
scout** boy-scout *m inv*

bra [brɑː] reggiseno *m*

bracelet ['breɪslɪt] braccialetto *m*

bracket ['brækɪt] *for shelf*
staffa *f*; *in text* parentesi *f inv*

brag [bræg] vantarsi

braid [breɪd] *trimming* passa-
maneria *f*; *Am in hair* treccia
f

braille [breɪl] braille *m*

brain [breɪn] cervello *m*;
brainless F deficiente;
brains (*intelligence*) cervello
msg; **brain surgeon** neuro-
chirurgo *m*; **brain tumour**,
Am **brain tumor** tumore *m*
al cervello; **brainwash** fare
il lavaggio del cervello a;
brainy F geniale

brake [breɪk] **1** *n* freno **2** *v/i*
frenare; **brake light** MOT fanalino *m* d'arresto; **brake
pedal** MOT pedale *m* del freno

branch [brɑːntʃ] *of tree* ramo
m; *of company* filiale *f*

♦ **branch out** diversificarsi

brand [brænd] **1** *n* marca *f* **2**
v/t: **be ~ed a traitor** essere
tacciato di tradimento;

brand image brand image *f inv*

brandish ['brændɪʃ] brandire

brand 'leader marca *f* leader di mercato; **brand name** marca *f*; **brand-new** nuovo di zecca

brandy ['brændɪ] brandy *m inv*

brass [brɑːs] *(alloy)* ottone *m*; **the ~** MUS gli ottoni; **brass band** fanfara *f*

brassière [brə'zɪə(r)] reggiseno *m*

brat [bræt] *pej* marmocchio *m*

brave [breɪv] coraggioso; **bravery** coraggio *m*

brawl [brɔːl] **1** *n* rissa *f* **2** *v/i* azzuffarsi

Brazil [brə'zɪl] Brasile *m*; **Brazilian 1** *adj* brasiliano **2** *n* brasiliano *m*, -a *f*

breach [briːtʃ] *(violation)* violazione *f*; *in party* rottura *f*; **breach of contract** inadempienza *f* di contratto

bread [bred] pane *m*

breadth [bredθ] larghezza *f*

'breadwinner: be the ~ mantenere la famiglia

break [breɪk] **1** *n* also fig rottura *f*; *(rest)* pausa *f* EDU intervallo *m* **2** *v/t china, egg, bone* rompere; *rules, law* violare; *promise* non mantenere; *news* comunicare; *record* battere **3** *v/i of china, egg, toy* rompersi; *of news* diffondersi; *of storm* scoppiare

◆ **break down 1** *v/i of vehicle, machine* avere un guasto; *of talks* arenarsi; *in tears* scoppiare in lacrime; *mentally* avere un esaurimento **2** *v/t door* buttare giù; *figures* analizzare

◆ **break even** coprire le spese

◆ **break in** *(interrupt)* interrompere; *of burglar* entrare con la forza

◆ **break off** *v/t* staccare; *engagement* rompere; **they've broken it off** si sono lasciati **2** *v/i (stop talking)* interrompersi

◆ **break up 1** *v/t into parts* scomporre; *fight* far cessare **2** *v/i of ice* spaccarsi; *of couple* separarsi; *of band, meeting* sciogliersi

breakable ['breɪkəbl] fragile; **breakage** danni *mpl*; **breakdown** *of vehicle, machine* guasto *m*; *of talks* rottura *f*; *(nervous ~)* esaurimento *m* (nervoso); *of figures* analisi *f inv*; **breakdown lorry** carro *m* attrezzi; **breakdown service** servizio *m* di soccorso stradale; **breakdown truck** carro *m* attrezzi

breakfast ['brekfəst] colazione *f*; **have ~** fare colazione

'break-in furto *m* (con scasso); **breakthrough** *in negotiations* passo *m* avanti; *of technology* scoperta *f*; **breakup** *of partnership* rottura *f*

breast [brest] seno *m*; **breast-feed** allattare; **breaststroke** nuoto *m* a rana

breath [breθ] respiro *m*; **be out of ~** essere senza fiato

breathe [briːð] respirare

◆ **breathe in** inspirare

◆ **breathe out** espirare

breathing ['briːðɪŋ] respiro *m*

breathless ['breθlɪs] senza fiato; **breathtaking** mozzafiato

breed [briːd] **1** *n* razza *f* **2** *v/t* allevare; *fig* generare **3** *v/i* *of animals* riprodursi; **breeding** allevamento *m*; *of person* educazione *f*

breeze [briːz] brezza *f*; **breezy** ventoso; *fig* brioso

brew [bruː] **1** *v/t beer* produrre **2** *v/i of storm* prepararsi; **there's trouble ~ing** ci sono guai in vista; **brewery** fabbrica *f* di birra

bribe [braɪb] **1** *n* bustarella *f* **2** *v/t* corrompere; **bribery** corruzione *f*

brick [brɪk] mattone *m*

bride [braɪd] sposa *f*; **bridegroom** sposo *m*; **bridesmaid** damigella *f* d'onore

bridge [brɪdʒ] **1** *n* ponte *m*; *of ship* ponte *m* di comando **2** *v/t gap* colmare

◆ **brighten up** ['braɪtn] **1** *v/t* ravvivare **2** *v/i of weather* schiarirsi; *of face, person* rallegrarsi

bridle ['braɪdl] briglia *f*

brief[1] [briːf] *adj* breve

brief[2] [briːf] **1** *n* (*mission*) missione *f* **2** *v/t*: **~ s.o. on sth** *instruct* dare istruzioni a qu su qc; *inform* mettere qu al corrente di qc

'**briefcase** valigetta *f*; **briefing** briefing *m inv*; **briefly** brevemente; (*to sum up*) in breve; **briefs** slip *m inv*

bright [braɪt] *colour* vivace; *smile, future* radioso; (*sunny*) luminoso; (*intelligent*) intelligente; **~ red** rosso vivo; **brightly** *smile* in modo radioso; *shine, lit* intensamente; *coloured* in modo sgargiante

brilliance ['brɪljəns] *of person* genialità *f*; *of colour* vivacità *f*; **brilliant** *sunshine etc* sfolgorante; (*very good*) eccezionale; (*very intelligent*) brillante

brim [brɪm] *of container* orlo *m*; *of hat* falda *f*

bring [brɪŋ] portare

◆ **bring back** (*return*) restituire; (*re-introduce*) reintrodurre; *memories* risvegliare

◆ **bring down** *also fig government* abbattere; *price* far scendere

◆ **bring on** *illness* provocare

◆ **bring out** *book* pubblicare; *new product* lanciare

◆ **bring up** *child* allevare; *subject* sollevare; (*vomit*) vomitare

brink [brɪŋk] orlo *m*

brisk [brɪsk] *person, tone* spiccio; *walk* svelto; *trade* vivace

bristles ['brɪslz] peli *mpl*

Brit [brɪt] F britannico *m*, -a *f*; **Britain** Gran Bretagna *f*; **British 1** *adj* britannico **2** *n*: **the ~** i britannici

brittle ['brɪtl] fragile

broad [brɔːd] largo; (*general*) generale; **in ~ daylight** in pieno giorno; **broadband** banda *f* larga; **broadcast** [-] **1** *n* trasmissione *f* **2** *v/t* trasmettere; **broadcaster** giornalista *m/f* radiotelevisivo, -a; **broad jump** *Am* salto *m* in lungo; **broadly**: **~ speaking** parlando in senso lato; **broadminded** di larghe vedute

broccoli ['brɒkəlɪ] broccoli *mpl*

brochure ['brəʊʃə(r)] dépliant *m inv*, opuscolo *m*

broil [brɔɪl] *Am* fare alla griglia; **broiler** *Am on stove* grill *m inv*

broke [brəʊk] al verde; **broken 1** *adj* rotto; *English* stentato; *marriage* fallito; **she's from a ~ home** i suoi sono separati; **broken-hearted** col cuore spezzato; **broker** mediatore *m*, -trice *f*

bronchitis [brɒŋ'kaɪtɪs] bronchite *f*

bronze [brɒnz] bronzo *m*

brooch [brəʊtʃ] spilla *f*

brothel ['brɒθl] bordello *m*

brother ['brʌðə(r)] fratello *m*; **brother-in-law** cognato *m*;

brotherly fraterno

brow [braʊ] (*forehead*) fronte *f*; *of hill* cima *f*

brown [braʊn] **1** *n* marrone *m* **2** *adj* marrone; *eyes, hair* castano; (*tanned*) abbronzato; **Brownie** giovane esploratrice *f*; **brownie** *Am* dolcetto *m* al cioccolato con noci; **brown sugar** zucchero *m* non raffinato

browse [braʊz] *in shop* curiosare; COMPUT navigare; **~ through a book** sfogliare un libro; **browser** COMPUT browser *m inv*

bruise [bruːz] livido *m*; *on fruit* ammaccatura *f*

brunette [bruː'net] brunetta *f*

brunt [brʌnt]: **bear the ~ of ...** subire il peggio di ...

brush [brʌʃ] **1** *n* spazzola *f*; (*paint~*) pennello *m*; (*tooth~*) spazzolino *m* da denti; (*conflict*) scontro *m* **2** *v/t* spazzolare; (*touch lightly*) sfiorare

♦ **brush aside** ignorare

♦ **brush up** ripassare

brusque [brʊsk] brusco

Brussels 'sprout ['brʌslz] cavolino *m* di Bruxelles

brutal ['bruːtl] brutale; **brutality** brutalità *f inv*; **brutally** brutalmente; **brute** bruto *m*

bubble ['bʌbl] bolla *f*

buck¹ [bʌk] *n Am* F (*dollar*) dollaro *m*

buck² [bʌk] *v/i of horse* sgroppare

bucket ['bʌkɪt] secchio *m*

buckle¹ ['bʌkl] **1** *n* fibbia *f* **2** *v/t belt* allacciare

buckle² ['bʌkl] *v/i* of wood, metal piegarsi

bud [bʌd] BOT bocciolo *m*

buddy ['bʌdɪ] F amico *m*, -a *f*

budge [bʌdʒ] **1** *v/t* smuovere **2** *v/i* muoversi

budgerigar ['bʌdʒərɪgɑː(r)] pappagallino *m*

budget ['bʌdʒɪt] budget *m inv*; of company bilancio *m* preventivo; of state bilancio *m* dello Stato

buff [bʌf] appassionato *m*, -a *f*

buffalo ['bʌfələʊ] bufalo *m*

buffer ['bʌfə(r)] RAIL respingente *m*; COMPUT buffer *m inv*; fig cuscinetto *m*

buffet ['bʊfeɪ] meal buffet *m inv*

bug [bʌg] **1** *n* (insect) insetto *m*; (virus) virus *m inv*; (spying device) bug *m inv* **2** *v/t room* installare microspie in; telephone mettere sotto controllo; F (annoy) seccare

buggy ['bʌgɪ] for baby passeggino *m*

build [bɪld] **1** *n* of person corporatura *f* **2** *v/t* costruire
◆ **build up 1** *v/t relationship* consolidare; **build up one's strength** rimettersi in forze **2** *v/i* of tension, traffic aumentare

builder ['bɪldə(r)] muratore *m*; company impresario *m* edile; **building** edificio *m*,

palazzo *m*; (activity) costruzione *f*; **building site** cantiere *m* edile; **building society** istituto *m* di credito immobiliare; **building trade** edilizia *f*; **build-up** of traffic, pressure aumento *m*; of arms, forces ammassamento *m*; (publicity) pubblicità *f inv*; **built-in** wardrobe a muro; flash incorporato; **built-up area** abitato *m*

bulb [bʌlb] BOT bulbo *m*; (light ~) lampadina *f*

bulge [bʌldʒ] **1** *n* rigonfiamento *m* **2** *v/i* sporgere

bulky ['bʌlkɪ] voluminoso

bull [bʊl] toro *m*; **bulldozer** bulldozer *m inv*

bullet ['bʊlɪt] proiettile *m*, pallottola *f*

bulletin ['bʊlɪtɪn] bollettino *m*; **bulletin board** COMPUT bulletin board *m inv*; Am: on wall bacheca *f*

'bullet-proof a prova di proiettile

'bull's-eye centro *m* del bersaglio; **hit the ~** fare centro; **bullshit** V stronzate *fpl* V

bully ['bʊlɪ] **1** *n* prepotente *m/f* **2** *v/t* tiranneggiare; **bullying** prepotenze *fpl*

bum [bʌm] **1** *n* F worthless person mezza calzetta *f* F; (bottom) sedere *m*; (Am: tramp) barbone *m* **2** *v/t* F cigarette etc scroccare

bump [bʌmp] **1** *n* (swelling) gonfiore *m*; (lump) bernoc-

business school

colo *m; on road* cunetta *f* **2** *v/t* battere

♦ **bump into** *table* battere contro; (*meet*) incontrare

bumper ['bʌmpə(r)] MOT paraurti *m inv;* **bumpy** *road* accidentato; *flight* movimentato

bunch [bʌntʃ] *of people* gruppo *m; of keys, flowers* mazzo *m;* **a ~ of grapes** un grappolo d'uva; **thanks a ~** *ironic* grazie tante!

bungalow ['bʌŋgələʊ] bungalow *m inv*

bungle ['bʌŋgl] pasticciare

bunk [bʌŋk] cuccetta *f;* **bunk beds** letti *mpl* a castello

buoy [bɔɪ] NAUT boa *f;* **buoyant** allegro; *economy* sostenuto

burden ['bɜːdn] **1** *n also fig* peso *m* **2** *v/t:* **~ s.o. with sth** *fig* opprimere qu con qc

bureau ['bjʊərəʊ] (*office*) ufficio *m*

bureaucracy [bjʊə'rɒkrəsɪ] burocrazia *f;* **bureaucrat** ['bjʊərəkræt] burocrate *m/f;* **bureaucratic** [bjʊərə'krætɪk] burocratico

burger ['bɜːgə(r)] hamburger *m inv*

burglar ['bɜːglə(r)] ladro *m;* **burglar alarm** antifurto *m;* **burglarize** *Am* svaligiare; **burglary** furto *m* (con scasso); **burgle** svaligiare

burial ['berɪəl] sepoltura *f*

burn [bɜːn] **1** *n* bruciatura *f* **2** *v/t* bruciare; *of sun* scottare **3**
v/i ardere; *of house* bruciare; *of toast, get sunburnt* scottarsi, bruciarsi

♦ **burn down 1** *v/t* dare alle fiamme **2** *v/i* essere distrutto dal fuoco

burp [bɜːp] **1** *n* rutto *m* **2** *v/i* ruttare

burst [bɜːst] **1** *n in pipe* rottura *f* **2** *adj tyre* bucato **3** *v/t balloon* far scoppiare **4** *v/i of balloon, tyre* scoppiare; **~ into tears** scoppiare in lacrime; **~ out laughing** scoppiare a ridere

bury ['berɪ] seppellire; *hide* nascondere

bus [bʌs] autobus *m inv;* (*long distance*) pullman *m inv;* **bus driver** autista *m/f* di autobus

bush [bʊʃ] *plant* cespuglio *m; land* boscaglia *f;* **bushy** *eyebrows* irsuto

business ['bɪznɪs] (*trade*) affari *mpl;* (*company*) impresa *f;* (*work*) lavoro *m;* (*affair, matter*) faccenda *f;* (*as subject of study*) economia *f* aziendale; **on ~** per affari; **mind your own ~!** fatti gli affari tuoi!; **business card** biglietto *m* da visita (della ditta); **business class** business class *f;* **business hours** orario *msg* di apertura; **businesslike** efficiente; **businessman** uomo *m* d'affari; **business meeting** riunione *f* d'affari; **business school** istituto *m* commerciale;

business studies (*course*)
economia *f* aziendale; business trip viaggio *m* d'affari; businesswoman donna *f* d'affari

'bus station autostazione *f*; bus stop fermata *f* dell'autobus

bust¹ [bʌst] *n of woman* petto *m*

bust² [bʌst] *adj* F (*broken*) scassato

'bust-up F rottura *f*; busty prosperoso

busy ['bɪzɪ] 1 *adj also* TELEC occupato; *day* intenso; *street* animato; *shop, restaurant* affollato; busybody impiccione *m*, -a *f*

but [bʌt] 1 *conj* ma 2 *prep*: all ~ him tutti tranne lui; the last ~ one il penultimo; ~ for you se non fosse per te; nothing ~ the best solo il meglio

butcher ['bʊtʃə(r)] macellaio *m*, -a *f*; butcher's macelleria *f*

butt [bʌt] 1 *n of cigarette* mozzicone *m*; *Am* P (*backside*)

culo *m* P 2 *v/t* dare una testata a

butter ['bʌtə(r)] burro *m*; buttercup ranuncolo *m*; butterfly *also swimming* farfalla *f*

buttocks ['bʌtəks] natiche *fpl*

button ['bʌtn] bottone *m*; *on machine* pulsante *m*

buy [baɪ] comprare

◆ buy out COM rilevare

buyer ['baɪə(r)] acquirente *m/f*

buzz [bʌz] 1 *n* ronzio *m* 2 *v/i of insect* ranzare; buzzer cicalino *m*

by [baɪ] *agency* da; (*near, next to*) vicino a; (*no later than*) entro, per; (*past*) davanti a; (*mode of transport*) in; ~ day di giorno; ~ bus in autobus; ~ my watch secondo il mio orologio; a book ~ ... un libro di ...; ~ myself / herself da solo

bye(-bye) [baɪ] ciao

'bypass circonvallazione *f*; MED by-pass *m inv*; by-product sottoprodotto *m*; bystander astante *m/f*

C

cab [kæb] taxi *m inv*; *of truck* cabina *f*

cabbage ['kæbɪdʒ] cavolo *m*

'cab driver *esp Am* tassista *m/f*

cabin ['kæbɪn] *of plane, ship* cabina *f*; cabin attendant

assistente *m/f* di volo; cabin crew equipaggio *m*

cabinet ['kæbɪnət] armadietto *m*; POL Consiglio *m* dei ministri; cabinet minister membro *m* del Consiglio dei ministri cable ['keɪbl] ELEC, *for securing* cavo *m*; ~ **(TV)** TV *f* via cavo; cable car funivia *f*; cable television televisione *f* via cavo

'cab stand *Am* stazione *f* dei taxi

cactus ['kæktəs] cactus *m inv*

cadaver [kə'dævə(r)] *Am* cadavere *m*

caddie ['kædɪ] *in golf* portamazze *m inv*

Caesarean [sɪ'zeərɪən] parto *m* cesareo

café ['kæfeɪ] caffè *m inv*, bar *m*; cafeteria tavola *f* calda

caffeine ['kæfi:n] caffeina *f*

cage [keɪdʒ] gabbia *f*; cagey evasivo

cake [keɪk] **1** *n* dolce *m*, torta *f* **2**

calamity [kə'læmətɪ] calamità *f inv*

calcium ['kælsɪəm] calcio *m*

calculate ['kælkjʊleɪt] calcolare; calculating calcolatore; calculation calcolo *m*; calculator calcolatrice *f*

calendar ['kælɪndə(r)] calendario *m*

calf[1] [kɑ:f] *young cow* vitello *m*

calf[2] [kɑ:f] *of leg* polpaccio *m*

call [kɔ:l] **1** *n (phone ~)* telefonata *f*; *(shout)* grido *m*; *(demand)* richiesta *f*; *(visit)* visita *f* **2** *v/t on phone*, *(summon)* chiamare; *(shout)* gridare; meeting convocare; **be ~ed** chiamarsi **3** *v/i on phone* chiamare; *(shout)* gridare;

(visit) passare

◆ **call back 1** *v/t also* TELEC richiamare **2** *v/i on phone* richiamare; *(make another visit)* ripassare

◆ **call for** *(collect)* passare a prendere; *(demand)* reclamare; *(require)* richiedere

◆ **call off** *strike* revocare; *wedding* disdire

◆ **call out** *(shout)* chiamare ad alta voce; *(summon)* chiamare

'call centre, *Am* call center centro *m* chiamate

caller ['kɔ:lə(r)] *on phone* persona *f* che ha chiamato; *(visitor)* visitatore *m*, -trice *f*

callous ['kæləs] freddo, insensibile

calm [kɑ:m] **1** *adj* calmo **2** *n* calma *f*

◆ **calm down 1** *v/t* calmare **2** *v/i* calmarsi

calmly ['kɑ:mlɪ] con calma

calorie ['kælərɪ] caloria *f*

camcorder ['kæmkɔ:də(r)] videocamera *f*

camera ['kæmərə] macchina *f* fotografica; *(video ~)* videocamera *f*; *(television ~)* telecamera *f*; cameraman cameraman *m inv*; camera phone cellulare *m* con fotocamera

camouflage ['kæməflɑ:ʒ] **1** *n* mimetizzazione *f*; *of soldiers* tuta *f* mimetica **2** *v/t* mimetizzare

camp [kæmp] **1** *n* campo *m* **2**

v/i accamparsi

campaign [kæm'peɪn] **1** *n* campagna *f* **2** *v/i* militare

'camp-bed letto *m* da campo; **camper** *person* campeggiatore *m*, -trice *f*; *vehicle* camper *m inv*; **camping** campeggio *m*; **campsite** camping *m inv*, campeggio *m*

campus ['kæmpəs] campus *m inv*

can[1] [kæn] ◇ *(ability)* potere; **~ you hear me?** mi senti?; **I can't see** non vedo; **~ you speak French?** sai parlare il francese?; **as well as you** ~ meglio che puoi ◇ *(permission)* potere; **~ I help you?** posso aiutarla?; **~ you help me?** mi può aiutare?

can[2] [kæn] *for drinks* lattina *f*; *for food* scatola *f*

Canada ['kænədə] Canada *m*; **Canadian 1** *adj* canadese **2** *n* canadese *m/f*

canal [kə'næl] *(waterway)* canale *f*

canary [kə'neərɪ] canarino *m*

cancel ['kænsl] annullare; **cancellation** annullamento *m*

cancer ['kænsə(r)] cancro *m*

Cancer ['kænsə(r)] ASTR Cancro *m*

candid ['kændɪd] franco

candidacy ['kændɪdəsɪ] candidatura *f*; **candidate** candidato *m*, -a *f*

candle ['kændl] candela *f*

candour, *Am* candor

candy ['kændɪ] *Am (sweet)* caramella *f*; *(sweets)* dolciumi *mpl*; **candy floss** zucchero *m* filato

cane [keɪn] canna *f*; *for walking* bastone *m*

canister ['kænɪstə(r)] barattolo *m*; *spray* bombola *f*

cannabis ['kænəbɪs] hashish *m*

canned [kænd] *in scatola*; *(recorded)* registrato

cannot ['kænɒt] → **can not**

canny ['kænɪ] *(astute)* arguto

canoe [kə'nu:] canoa *f*

'can opener apriscatole *m inv*

can't [kɑ:nt] → **can not**

canteen [kæn'ti:n] *in factory* mensa *f*

canvas ['kænvəs] tela *f*

canyon ['kænjən] canyon *m inv*

cap [kæp] *hat* berretto *m*; *for lens* coperchio *m*

capability [keɪpə'bɪlətɪ] *of person* capacità *f inv*; **capable** capace

capacity [kə'pæsətɪ] capacità *f inv*; *of engine* potenza *f*

capital ['kæpɪtl] *of country* capitale *f*; *capital letter* maiuscola *f*; *money* capitale *m*; **capitalism** capitalismo *m*; **capitalist 1** *adj* capitalista **2** *n* capitalista *m/f*; **capital letter** lettera *f* maiuscola; **capital punishment** pena *f* capitale

carpet

Capricorn ['kæprɪkɔːn] ASTR Capricorno *m*

capsize [kæp'saɪz] ribaltarsi

capsule ['kæpsjʊl] *of medicine* cachet *m inv*; *(space ~)* capsula *f*

captain ['kæptɪn] capitano *m*

caption ['kæpʃn] didascalia *f*

captivate ['kæptɪveɪt] affascinare; **captive** prigioniero; **captivity** cattività *f*; **capture 1** *n of building, city* occupazione *f*; *of city* presa *f*; *of criminal, animal* cattura *f* **2** *v/t person, animal* catturare; *city, building* occupare; *city* prendere; *market share* conquistare

car [kɑː(r)] macchina *f*, auto *f inv*; *of train* vagone *m*; **by ~** in macchina

caravan ['kærəvæn] roulotte *f inv*

'car bomb autobomba *f*

carbon monoxide [kɑːbən-ˈmɒnˈɒksaɪd] monossido *m* di carbonio

carburetor [kɑːbjʊˈretə(r)] carburatore *m*

carcass ['kɑːkəs] carcassa *f*

card [kɑːd] *to mark special occasion* biglietto *m*; *(post~)* cartolina *f*; *(business ~)* biglietto *m (da visita)*; *(playing ~)* carta *f*; COMPUT scheda *f*; **cardboard** cartone *m*

cardiac ['kɑːdɪæk] cardiaco; **cardiac arrest** arresto *m* cardiaco

cardinal ['kɑːdɪnl] REL cardi-

nale *m*

care [keə(r)] **1** *n of baby, pet* cure *fpl*; *of the elderly* assistenza *f*; *of the sick* cura *f*; *(worry)* preoccupazione *f*; **take ~** *(be cautious)* fare attenzione; **take ~ (of yourself)!** *(goodbye)* stammi bene; **take ~ of** *baby, dog* prendersi cura di; *tool, house, garden* tenere bene; *(deal with)* occuparsi di **2** *v/i* interessarsi; **I don't ~!** non mi importa

◆ **care about** interessarsi a

◆ **care for** *(look after)* prendersi cura di

career [kəˈrɪə(r)] carriera *f*; *(path through life)* vita *f*

careful ['keəfʊl] **(be) ~!** (stai) attento!; **carefully** con cautela; **careless** incurante; *driver, worker* sbadato; *work* fatto senza attenzione; **carelessly** senza cura; **carer** accompagnatore *m*, -trice *f*

caress [kəˈres] accarezzare

'car ferry traghetto *m* (per le macchine)

cargo ['kɑːgəʊ] carico *m*

'car hire autonoleggio *m*

caricature ['kærɪkətʊə(r)] caricatura *f*

carnation [kɑːˈneɪʃn] garofano *m*

carnival ['kɑːnɪvl] carnevale *m*

'car park parcheggio *m*

carpenter ['kɑːpɪntə(r)] falegname *m*

carpet ['kɑːpɪt] tappeto *m*;

(fitted ~) moquette f inv

'**car phone** telefono m da automobile; **car rental** autonoleggio m

carrier ['kærɪə(r)] (company) compagnia f di trasporto; of disease portatore m sano, portatrice f sana

carrot ['kærət] carota f

carry ['kærɪ] **1** v/t portare; of ship, bus etc trasportare **2** v/t of sound sentirsi

◆ **carry on 1** v/i (continue) andare avanti, continuare **2** v/t (conduct) portare avanti

◆ **carry out** survey etc effettuare; orders etc eseguire

cart [kɑːt] carretto m; Am: in supermarket, at airport carrello m

carton ['kɑːtn] cartone m; of cigarettes stecca f

cartoon [kɑː'tuːn] fumetto m; on TV, film cartone m animato

cartridge ['kɑːtrɪdʒ] for gun, printer cartuccia f

carve [kɑːv] meat tagliare; wood intagliare

case[1] [keɪs] for glasses, pen astuccio m; of wine cassa f; (suitcase) valigia f

case[2] [keɪs] (instance, for police), MED caso m; LAW causa f; **in** ~ ... in caso; **in any** ~ in ogni caso

cash [kæʃ] **1** n contanti mpl; (money) soldi mpl **2** v/t cheque incassare; **cash desk** cassa f; **cash flow** flusso m

di cassa; **cashier** in shop etc cassiere m, -a f; **cash machine, cashpoint** (sportello m) Bancomat® m; **cash register** cassa f

casino [kə'siːnəʊ] casinò m inv

casket ['kæskɪt] Am (coffin) bara f

casserole ['kæsərəʊl] meal stufato m; container casseruola f

cassette [kə'set] cassetta f; **cassette recorder** registratore m (a cassette)

cast [kɑːst] **1** n of play cast m inv; (mould) stampo m **2** v/t doubt, suspicion far sorgere (**on** su); metal colare (in uno stampo)

cast 'iron ghisa f

castle ['kɑːsl] castello m

casual ['kæʒʊəl] (chance) casuale; (offhand) disinvolto; remark poco importante; clothes casual inv; **casually** dressed (in modo) casual; say con disinvoltura; **casualty** dead person vittima f; injured ferito m

cat [kæt] gatto m

catalogue, Am **catalog** ['kætəlɒg] catalogo m

catalyst ['kætəlɪst] catalizzatore m

catastrophe [kə'tæstrəfɪ] catastrofe f; **catastrophic** catastrofico

catch [kætʃ] **1** n presa f; of fish pesca f; on bag, box chiusura *f; on door, window* fermo *m; (problem)* inghippo *m* **2** *v/t ball, escapee, bus, fish, illness* prendere; *(hear)* afferrare

◆ **catch on** *(become popular)* fare presa; *(understand)* afferrare

◆ **catch up** recuperare; *catch up with s.o.* raggiungere qu; *catch up with sth work, studies* mettersi in pari con qc

catching ['kætʃɪŋ] *also fig* contagioso; *catchy tune* orecchiabile

categoric [kætə'gɒrɪk] categorico; **category** categoria *f*

caterer ['keɪtərə(r)] ristoratore *m*, -trice *f*

caterpillar ['kætəpɪlə(r)] bruco *m*

cathedral [kə'θiːdrəl] cattedrale *f*, duomo *m*

Catholic ['kæθəlɪk] **1** *adj* cattolico **2** *n* cattolico *m*, -a *f*; **Catholicism** cattolicesimo *m*

cattle ['kætl] bestiame *m*

cauliflower ['kɒlɪflaʊə(r)] cavolfiore *m*

cause [kɔːz] **1** *n* causa *f*; *(grounds)* motivo *m* **2** *v/t* causare

caution ['kɔːʃn] **1** *n* *(carefulness)* cautela *f*, prudenza *f* **2** *v/t* *(warn)* mettere in guardia; **cautious** cauto, prudente; **cautiously** con cautela

cave [keɪv] caverna *f*, grotta *f*

caviar ['kævɪɑː(r)] caviale *m*

cavity ['kævətɪ] cavità *f inv; in tooth* carie *f inv*

CD [siː'diː] (= *compact disc*) CD *m inv;* **CD player** lettore *m* CD; **CD-ROM** CD-ROM *m inv*

cease [siːs] cessare; **cease-fire** cessate il fuoco *m inv*

ceiling ['siːlɪŋ] soffitto *m; (limit)* tetto *m*, plafond *m inv*

celeb ['seleb] vip *m/f inv*

celebrate ['selɪbreɪt] festeggiare; **celebrated** acclamato; **celebration** celebrazione *f*, festeggiamento *m*; **celebrity** celebrità *f inv*

celibate ['selɪbət] *man* celibe; *woman* nubile

cell [sel] *for prisoner* cella *f*, BIO cellula *f; in spreadsheet* casella *f*, cella *f*

cellar ['selə(r)] cantina *f; of wine* collezione *f* di vini

cellist ['tʃelɪst] violoncellista *m/f;* **cello** violoncello *m*

'cell phone, cellular phone ['seljuːlə(r)] *Am* telefono *m* cellulare, cellulare *m*

cement [sɪ'ment] cemento *m*

cemetery ['semətrɪ] cimitero *m*

censor ['sensə(r)] censurare; **censorship** censura *f*

census ['sensəs] censimento *m*

cent [sent] centesimo *m*

centenary [sen'tiːnərɪ] centenario *m*

center *Am* ☞ **centre**

centigrade ['sentɪgreɪd] centigrado

centimetre, *Am* **centimeter** ['sentɪmi:tə(r)] centimetro *m*

central ['sentrəl] centrale; **central heating** riscaldamento *m* autonomo; **centralize** accentrare; **central locking** MOT chiusura *f* centralizzata; **central reservation** MOT banchina *f* spartitraffico

centre ['sentə(r)] **1** *n* centro *m* **2** *v/t* centrare

century ['sentʃərɪ] secolo *m*

CEO [si:i:'əʊ] (= *Chief Executive Officer*) direttore *m* generale

ceramic [sɪ'ræmɪk] ceramico

cereal ['sɪərɪəl] cereale *m*; (*breakfast* ~) cereali *mpl*

ceremonial [serɪ'məʊnɪəl] **1** *adj* da cerimonia **2** *n* cerimoniale *m*; **ceremony** cerimonia *f*

certain ['sɜ:tn] (*sure, particular*) certo; **certainly** certamente; ~ *not!* certo che no!; **certainty** certezza *f*; **it's a** ~ è una cosa certa

certificate [sə'tɪfɪkət] *qualification* certificazione *f*; *official paper* certificato *m*; **certify** ['sɜ:tɪfaɪ] dichiarare ufficialmente

Cesarean *Am* ☞ **Caesarean**

chain [tʃeɪn] **1** *n* catena *f* **2** *v/t*: ~ *sth to sth* incatenare qc a qc; **chain reaction** reazione *f* a catena

chair [tʃeə(r)] **1** *n* sedia *f*; (*arm* ~) poltrona *f*; *at university* cattedra *f* **2** *v/t meeting* presiedere; **chair lift** seggiovia *f*; **chairman** presidente *m*; **chairmanship** presidenza *f*; **chairperson** presidente *m/f*

chalet ['ʃæleɪ] chalet *m inv*

chalk [tʃɔ:k] gesso *m*

challenge ['tʃælɪndʒ] **1** *n* sfida *f* **2** *v/t* sfidare; (*call into question*) mettere alla prova; **challenger** sfidante *m/f*; **challenging** *job, undertaking* stimolante

chambermaid ['tʃeɪmbəmeɪd] cameriera *f*; **Chamber of Commerce** Camera *f* di Commercio

champagne [ʃæm'peɪn] champagne *m inv*

champion ['tʃæmpɪən] **1** *n* SP campione *m*, -essa *f* **2** *v/t cause* difendere; **championship** *event* campionato *m*; *title* titolo *m* di campione

chance [tʃɑ:ns] (*possibility*) probabilità *f inv*; (*opportunity*) opportunità *f inv*; (*luck*) caso *m*; **by** ~ per caso; **take a** ~ correre un rischio

change [tʃeɪndʒ] **1** *n* cambiamento *m*; *small coins* moneta *f*; *from purchase* resto *m*; **for a** ~ per cambiare **2** *v/t* cambiare **3** *v/i* cambiare; (*put on different clothes*) cambiarsi; **changeable** incostante; *weather* variabile; **change-**

over passaggio *m*; *period* fase *f* di transizione; **changing room** SP spogliatoio *m*; *in shop* camerino *m*

channel ['tʃænl] *on* TV, *in water* canale *m*; **Channel Tunnel** tunnel *m* della Manica

chant [tʃɑːnt] **1** *n* slogan *m inv*; REL canto *m* **2** *v/i* gridare; *of demonstrators* gridare slogan; REL cantare

chaos ['keɪɒs] caos *m*; **chaotic** caotico

chap [tʃæp] *n* F tipo *m* F

chapel ['tʃæpl] cappella *f*

chapter ['tʃæptə(r)] capitolo *m*

character ['kærɪktə(r)] carattere *m*; (*person*) tipo *m*; *in book* personaggio *m*; **characteristic 1** *n* caratteristica *f* **2** *adj* caratteristico; **characterize** caratterizzare

charge [tʃɑːdʒ] **1** *n* (*fee*) costo *m*; LAW accusa *f*; *free of ~* gratis; *be in ~* essere responsabile **2** *v/t sum of money* far pagare; *Am* (*put on account*) addebitare; LAW accusare; *battery* caricare **3** *v/i* (*attack*) attaccare; **charge account** conto *m* (spese); **charge card** carta *f* di addebito

charisma [kærˈɪzmæ] carismatico

charitable ['tʃærɪtəbl] *institution* di beneficenza; *person* caritatevole; **charity** carità *f*; *organization* associazione *f* di beneficenza

charm [tʃɑːm] **1** *n* fascino *m*; *on bracelet etc* ciondolo *m* **2** *v/t* (*delight*) conquistare; **charming** affascinante; *house, village* incantevole

charred [tʃɑːd] carbonizzato

chart [tʃɑːt] *n* diagramma *m*; (*map*) carta *f*

'charter flight volo *m* charter *inv*

chase [tʃeɪs] **1** *n* inseguimento *m* **2** *v/t* inseguire

◆ **chase away** cacciare (via)

chassis ['ʃæsɪ] *of car* telaio *m*

chat [tʃæt] **1** *n* chiacchierata *f* **2** *v/i* chiacchierare

◆ **chat up** F abbordare F

'chatline chat line *f inv*; **chat room** chat room *f inv*; **chat show** talk show *m inv*

chatter ['tʃætə(r)] **1** *n* parlantina *f* **2** *v/i talk* fare chiacchiere; *of teeth* battere; **chatterbox** chiacchierone *m*, -a *f*

chauffeur ['ʃəʊfə(r)] autista *m/f*

chauvinist ['ʃəʊvɪnɪst] (*male ~*) maschilista *m*

cheap [tʃiːp] economico; (*nasty*) cattivo; (*mean*) tirchio

cheat [tʃiːt] **1** *n* imbroglione *m*, -a *f* **2** *v/t* imbrogliare **3** *v/i* imbrogliare; *in cards* barare

check[1] [tʃek] **1** *adj shirt* a quadri **2** *n* quadro *m*

check[2] [tʃek] *n Am* FIN assegno *m*

check[3] [tʃek] **1** *n to verify sth* verifica *f* **2** *v/t & v/i* verificare

◆ **check in** registrarsi

◆ **check out 1** v/i *of hotel* saldare il conto **2** v/t (*look into*) verificare; *club, restaurant etc* provare

◆ **check up on** fare dei controlli su

checked ['tʃekt] *material* a quadri

checkered ['tʃekərd] *Am material* a quadri; **checkers** *Am* dama f

'**check-in** (**counter**) banco m dell'accettazione; **checking account** conto m corrente; **check-in time** check in m *inv*; **checklist** lista f di verifica; **checkmark** *Am* segno m; **check-mate** n scacco m matto; **check-out** cassa f; **check-point** posto m di blocco; **checkroom** *Am for coats* guardaroba m *inv*; **checkup** *medical* check up m *inv*; *dental* visita f di controllo

cheek [tʃiːk] guancia f; (*impudence*) sfacciataggine f; **cheeky** sfacciato

cheer [tʃɪə(r)] **1** n acclamazione f; **~s!** (*toast*) salute!; **~s!** F (*thanks*) grazie! **2** v/t acclamare **3** v/i fare acclamazioni

◆ **cheer up 1** v/i consolarsi; **cheer up!** su con la vita! **2** v/t tirare su

cheerful ['tʃiəful] allegro; **cheering** acclamazioni fpl

cheerio [tʃɪərɪ'əʊ] F ciao F

'**cheerleader** ragazza f pon

pon

cheese [tʃiːz] formaggio m; **cheesecake** dolce m al formaggio

chef [ʃef] chef m/f *inv*

chemical ['kemɪkl] **1** adj chimico **2** n sostanza f chimica; **chemist** farmacista m/f; *in laboratory* chimico m, -a f; **chemistry** chimica f

chemotherapy [kiːməʊ'θerəpɪ] chemioterapia f

cheque [tʃek] assegno m; **chequebook** libretto m degli assegni

cherry ['tʃerɪ] *fruit* ciliegia f; *tree* ciliegio m

chess [tʃes] scacchi mpl

chest [tʃest] *of person* petto m; (*box*) cassa f

chew [tʃuː] masticare; *of dog, rats* rosicchiare; **chewing gum** gomma f da masticare

chic [ʃiːk] chic *inv*

chick [tʃik] pulcino m; F (*girl*) ragazza f

chicken ['tʃikɪn] **1** n pollo m; **chickenpox** varicella f

chief [tʃiːf] **1** n principale m/f; *of tribe* capo m **2** adj principale; **chiefly** principalmente

child [tʃaɪld] (*pl* **children** ['tʃɪldrən]) *also pej* bambino m, -a f; **they have two children** hanno due figli; **childhood** infanzia f; **childish** *pej* infantile, puerile; **childlike** innocente; **childminder** baby-sitter m/f *inv*

children ['tʃɪldrən] pl ☞ **child**

Chile ['tʃɪlɪ] Cile *m*; **Chilean 1** *adj* cileno **2** *n* cileno *m*, -a *f*

chill [tʃɪl] **1** *n in air* freddo *m*; *illness* colpo *m* di freddo; ***there's a ~ in the air*** l'aria è fredda **2** *v/t wine* mettere in fresco

◆ **chill out** rilassarsi

chilli (pepper) ['tʃɪlɪ] peperoncino *m*

chilly ['tʃɪlɪ] *weather, welcome* freddo

chimney ['tʃɪmnɪ] camino *m*

chimpanzee [tʃɪmpæn'ziː] scimpanzé *m inv*

chin [tʃɪn] mento *m*

china ['tʃaɪnə] porcellana *f*

China ['tʃaɪnə] Cina *f*; **Chinese 1** *adj* cinese **2** *n language* cinese *m*; *person* cinese *m/f*

chip [tʃɪp] **1** *n fragment* scheggia *f*; *damage* scheggiatura *f*; *in gambling* fiche *f inv*; COMPUT chip *m inv*; **~s** patate *fpl* fritte; *Am* patatine *fpl* **2** *v/t damage* scheggiare

chisel ['tʃɪzl] scalpello *m*

chlorine ['klɔːriːn] cloro *m*

chock-full ['tʃɒkful] F strapieno

chocolate ['tʃɒkələt] cioccolato *m*; *in box* cioccolatino *m*; **chocolate cake** dolce *m* al cioccolato

choice [tʃɔɪs] **1** *n* scelta *f*; *I had no ~* non avevo scelta **2** *adj* (*top quality*) di prima scelta

choir ['kwaɪə(r)] coro *m*

choke [tʃəuk] **1** *n* MOT starter *m inv* **2** *v/t & v/i* soffocare

cholesterol [kə'lestərɒl] colesterolo *m*

choose [tʃuːz] scegliere; **choosey** F selettivo

chop [tʃɒp] **1** *n meat* braciola *f* **2** *v/t wood* spaccare; *meat, vegetables* tagliare a pezzi

◆ **chop down** *tree* abbattere

chord [kɔːd] MUS accordo *m*

chore [tʃɔː(r)] *household* faccenda *f* domestica

choreographer [kɒrɪ'ɒgrəfə(r)] coreografo *m*, -a *f*; **choreography** coreografia *f*

chorus ['kɔːrəs] *singers, of song* coro *m*

Christ [kraɪst] Cristo *m*; **~!** Cristo!

christen ['krɪsn] battezzare

Christian ['krɪstʃən] **1** *n* cristiano *m*, -a *f* **2** *adj* cristiano; **Christianity** cristianesimo *m*; **Christian name** nome *m* di battesimo

Christmas ['krɪsməs] Natale *m*; ***Merry ~!*** Buon Natale!; **Christmas card** biglietto *m* di auguri natalizi; **Christmas Day** giorno *m* di Natale; **Christmas Eve** vigilia *f* di Natale; **Christmas present** regalo *m* di Natale; **Christmas tree** albero *m* di Natale

chrome, chromium [krəum, 'krəumɪəm] cromo *m*

chronic ['krɒnɪk] cronico

chrysanthemum [krɪ'sænθəməm] crisantemo *m*

chubby ['tʃʌbɪ] paffuto

chuck [tʃʌk] F buttare

chuckle ['tʃʌkl] **1** *n* risatina *f* **2** *v/i* ridacchiare

chunk [tʃʌŋk] pezzo *m*

church [tʃɜːtʃ] chiesa *f*; **church service** funzione *f* religiosa; **churchyard** cimitero *m* (di una chiesa)

chute [ʃuːt] scivolo *m*; *for waste disposal* canale *m* di scarico

cider ['saɪdə(r)] sidro *m*

cigar [sɪ'gɑː(r)] sigaro *m*

cigarette [sɪgə'ret] sigaretta *f*; **cigarette lighter** accendino *m*

cinema ['sɪnɪmə] cinema *m inv*; **cinema goer** frequentatore *m*, -trice *f* di cinema

cinnamon ['sɪnəmən] canella *f*

circle ['sɜːkl] *n* cerchio *m*; (*group*) cerchia *f* **2** *v/i of plane* girare in tondo; *of bird* volteggiare

circuit ['sɜːkɪt] ELEC circuito *m*; (*lap*) giro *m*; **circuit board** COMPUT circuito *m* stampato

circular ['sɜːkjʊlə(r)] **1** *n giving information* circolare *f* **2** *adj* circolare; **circulate 1** *v/i* circolare **2** *v/t memo* far circolare; **circulation** BIO circolazione *f*; *of newspaper* tiratura *f*

circumstances ['sɜːkəmstənsɪz] circostanze *fpl*; (*financial*) situazione *fsg* (eco-

nomica)

circus ['sɜːkəs] circo *m*

cistern ['sɪstən] cisterna *f*; *of WC* serbatoio *m*

citizen ['sɪtɪzn] cittadino *m*, -a *f*; **citizenship** cittadinanza *f*

city ['sɪtɪ] città *f inv*; **city centre**, *Am* **city center** centro *m* (della città); **city hall** sala *f* municipale

civic ['sɪvɪk] civico

civil ['sɪvl] civile; **civil ceremony** cerimonia *f* civile; **civil engineer** ingegnere *m* civile; **civilian 1** *n* civile *m/f* **2** *adj* clothes civile; **civilization** civilizzazione *f*; **civilize** civilizzare; **civil rights** diritti *mpl* civili; **civil servant** impiegato *m*, -a *f* statale; **civil service** pubblica amministrazione *f*; **civil war** guerra *f* civile

claim [kleɪm] **1** *n* (*request*) richiesta *f*; (*right*) diritto *m*; (*assertion*) affermazione *f* **2** *v/t* (*ask for as a right*) rivendicare; *damages* richiedere; (*assert*) affermare; *lost property* reclamare; **claimant** richiedente *m/f*

clairvoyant [kleə'vɔɪənt] chiaroveggente *m/f*

clam [klæm] vongola *f*

clammy ['klæmɪ] *hands* appiccicaticcio; *weather* afoso

clamp [klæmp] *fastener* morsa *f*; *for wheel* ceppo *m* (bloccaruote)

◆ **clamp down** usare il pu-

cleavage

gno di ferro
◆ **clamp down on** mettere un freno a
clandestine [klænˈdestɪn] clandestino
clap [klæp] (*applaud*) applaudire
clarification [klærɪfɪˈkeɪʃn] chiarimento *m*; **clarify** chiarire
clarinet [klærɪˈnet] clarinetto *m*
clarity [ˈklærɪtɪ] chiarezza *f*
clash [klæʃ] **1** *n* scontro *m* **2** *v/i* scontrarsi; *of opinions* essere in contrasto; *of colours* stonare; *of events* coincidere
clasp [klɑːsp] **1** *n fastener* chiusura *f* **2** *v/t in hand* stringere
class [klɑːs] **1** *n* (*lesson*) lezione *f*; (*group of people, category*) classe *f* **2** *v/t* classificare
classic [ˈklæsɪk] **1** *adj* classico **2** *n* classico *m*; **classical** classico; **classification** classificazione *f*; **classified** *information* riservato; **classified ad**(**vertisement**) inserzione *f*, annuncio *m*; **classify** (*categorize*) classificare
'**classroom** aula *f*; **classy** F d'alta classe
clause [klɔːz] *in agreement* articolo *m*; GRAM proposizione *f*
claustrophobia [klɔːstrəˈfəʊbɪə] claustrofobia *f*
claw [klɔː] **1** *n* artiglio *m*; *of lobster* chela *f* **2** *v/t* (*scratch*)

graffiare
clay [kleɪ] argilla *f*
clean [kliːn] **1** *adj* pulito **2** *adv* F (*completely*) completamente **3** *v/t* pulire; *teeth* lavarsi; *car, hands, face* lavare; *clothes* lavare *o* pulire a secco
cleaner [ˈkliːnə(r)] *male* uomo *m* delle pulizie; *female* donna *f* delle pulizie; (*dry ~*) lavanderia *f*, tintoria *f*
cleanse [klenz] *skin* detergere; **cleanser** *for skin* detergente *m*; **cleansing cream** latte *f* detergente
clear [klɪə(r)] **1** *adj* chiaro; *sky* sereno; *water, eyes* limpido; *skin* uniforme; *conscience* pulito **2** *v/t roads etc* sgomb(e)rare; (*acquit*) scagionare; (*authorize*) autorizzare **3** *v/i of sky* schiarirsi; *of mist* diradarsi
◆ **clear off** F filarsela F
◆ **clear out 1** *v/t cupboard* sgomb(e)rare **2** *v/i* sparire
◆ **clear up 1** *v/i* (*tidy up*) mettere in ordine; *of weather* schiarirsi; *of illness* sparire **2** *v/t* (*tidy*) mettere in ordine; *mystery* risolvere
clearance [ˈklɪərəns] *space* spazio *m* libero; (*authorization*) autorizzazione *f*; **clearance sale** liquidazione *f*; **clearing** *in woods* radura *f*; **clearly** chiaramente
cleavage [ˈkliːvɪdʒ] décolleté *m inv*

clench [klentʃ] serrare

clergy ['klɜːdʒɪ] clero *m*; clergyman ecclesiastico *m*

clerk [klɑːk, *Am* klɜːk] impiegato *m*, -a *f*; *Am in store* commesso *m*, -a *f*

clever ['klevə(r)] intelligente; *gadget* ingegnoso

click [klɪk] **1** *n* COMPUT click *m inv* **2** *v/i of camera etc* scattare

♦ **click on** COMPUT cliccare su

client ['klaɪənt] cliente *m/f*; **clientele** clientela *f*

cliff [klɪf] scogliera *f*

climate ['klaɪmət] clima *m*; **climate change** mutazione *f* climatica

climax ['klaɪmæks] punto *m* culminante

climb [klaɪm] **1** *n up mountain* scalata *f*, arrampicata *f* **2** *v/t* salire su **3** *v/i* salire; **climber** alpinista *m/f*

clinch [klɪntʃ] *deal* concludere

cling [klɪŋ] *of clothes* essere attillato

♦ **cling to** *of child* avvinghiarsi a; *tradition* aggrapparsi a

clingy ['klɪŋɪ] *person* appiccicoso

clinic ['klɪnɪk] clinica *f*; **clinical** clinico

clip[1] [klɪp] **1** *n fastener* fermaglio *m*; *for hair* molletta *f* **2** *v/t*: ~ **sth to sth** attaccare qc a qc

clip[2] [klɪp] *n from film* spez-

zone *f* **2** *v/t hair, grass* tagliare

clipping ['klɪpɪŋ] *from newspaper* ritaglio *m*

cloakroom ['kləʊkruːm] *for coats* guardaroba *m inv*

clock [klɒk] orologio *m*; **clock radio** radiosveglia *f*; **clockwise** in senso orario

clone [kləʊn] **1** *n* clone *m* **2** *v/t* clonare; **cloning** clonazione *f*

close[1] [kləʊs] **1** *adj family, friend* intimo **2** *adv* vicino; ~ **at hand** a portata di mano; ~ **by** nelle vicinanze

close[2] [kləʊz] **1** *v/t* chiudere **2** *v/i of door, eyes* chiudersi; *of shop* chiudere

closed-circuit 'television televisione *f* a circuito chiuso; **close-knit** affiatato; **closely** *listen, watch* attentamente; *cooperate* fianco a fianco

closet ['klɒzɪt] *Am* armadio *m*

close-up ['kləʊsʌp] primo piano *m*

closing date ['kləʊzɪŋ] termine *m*

closure ['kləʊʒə(r)] chiusura *f*

clot [klɒt] **1** *n of blood* grumo *m* **2** *v/i of blood* coagularsi

cloth [klɒθ] tessuto *m*; *for cleaning* straccio *m*

clothes [kləʊðz] vestiti *mpl*; **clothes hanger** attaccapanni *m inv*; **clothes peg** molletta *f* per i panni; **clothing** abbigliamento *m*

coffee shop

cloud [klaʊd] *n* nuvola *f*
♦ cloud over rannuvolarsi
cloudless ['klaʊdlɪs] sereno; cloudy nuvoloso
clout [klaʊt] *fig (influence)* impatto *m*
clove of 'garlic [kləʊv] spicchio *m* d'aglio
clown [klaʊn] *also pej* pagliaccio *m*
club [klʌb] *weapon* clava *f*; *in golf* mazza *f*; *organization* club *m inv*
clue [kluː] indizio *m*
clumsiness ['klʌmzɪnɪs] goffaggine *f*; clumsy goffo, maldestro
cluster ['klʌstə(r)] gruppo *m*
clutch [klʌtʃ] 1 *n* MOT frizione *f* 2 *v/t* stringere
♦ clutch at cercare di afferrare
Co. (= *Company*) Cia (= compagnia)
c/o (= *care of*) presso
coach [kəʊtʃ] 1 *n (trainer)* allenatore *m*, -trice *f*; *on train* vagone *m*; *(bus)* pullman *m inv* 2 *v/t* allenare; coaching allenamento *m*; coach station stazione *f* dei pullman
coagulate [kəʊˈægjʊleɪt] coagularsi
coal [kəʊl] carbone *m*
coalition [kəʊəˈlɪʃn] coalizione *f*
'coalmine miniera *f* di carbone
coarse [kɔːs] *skin, fabric* ruvido; *hair* spesso; *(vulgar)*

grossolano; *coarsely (vulgarly)* grossolanamente; *ground* a grani grossi
coast [kəʊst] costa *f*; *coastal* costiero
'coastguard *organization, person* guardia *f* costiera; coastline costa *f*, litorale *m*
coat [kəʊt] 1 *n (over~)* cappotto *m*; *of animal* pelliccia *f*; *of paint etc* mano *f* 2 *v/t (cover)* ricoprire; coathanger attaccapanni *m inv*, gruccia *f*; coating strato *m*
coax [kəʊks] convincere con le moine
cobweb ['kɒbweb] ragnatela *f*
cocaine [kəˈkeɪn] cocaina *f*
cock [kɒk] *chicken* gallo *m*; *any male bird* maschio *m* (di uccelli); cockpit *of plane* cabina *f* (di pilotaggio); cockroach scarafaggio *m*; cocktail cocktail *m inv*
cocoa ['kəʊkəʊ] *drink* cioccolata *f* calda
coconut ['kəʊkənʌt] cocco *m*; coconut palm palma *f* di cocco
code [kəʊd] codice *m*
coeducational [kəʊedjʊ-ˈkeɪʃnl] misto
coerce [kəʊˈɜːs] costringere
coexist [kəʊɪgˈzɪst] coesistere; coexistence coesistenza *f*
coffee ['kɒfɪ] caffè *m inv*; coffee maker caffettiera *f*; coffee pot caffettiera *f*; coffee

shop caffetteria *f*
coffin ['kɒfɪn] bara *f*
cog [kɒg] dente *m*
cohabit [kəʊ'hæbɪt] convivere
coherent [kəʊ'hɪərənt] coerente
coil [kɔɪl] **1** *n* of rope rotolo *m* **2** *v/t:* **~ (up)** avvolgere
coin [kɔɪn] moneta *f*
coincide [kəʊɪn'saɪd] coincidere; **coincidence** coincidenza *f*
Coke® [kəʊk] Coca® *f*
cold [kəʊld] **1** *adj* freddo; *I'm* **~** ho freddo; *it's* **~** *of weather* fa freddo **2** *n* freddo *m*; MED raffreddore *m*; **cold-blooded** *also* murder a sangue freddo; *person* spietato; **cold calling** porta-a-porta *m*; **by phone** televendita *fpl*; **coldly** freddamente; **coldness** freddezza *f*; **cold sore** febbre *f* del labbro
collaborate [kə'læbəreɪt] collaborare; **collaboration** collaborazione *f*; *with enemy* collaborazionismo *m*; **collaborator** collaboratore *m*, -trice *f*; *with enemy* collaborazionista *m/f*
collapse [kə'læps] crollare; *of person* accasciarsi; **collapsible** pieghevole
collar ['kɒlə(r)] collo *m*, colletto *m*; *of dog* collare *m*; **collar-bone** clavicola *f*
collateral [kə'lætərəl] *for loan* garanzia *f* collaterale; **collat-**

eral damage danni *mpl* collaterali
colleague ['kɒliːg] collega *m/f*
collect [kə'lekt] **1** *v/t person* andare / venire a prendere; *tickets, cleaning etc* ritirare; *as hobby* collezionare; (*gather*) raccogliere **2** *v/i* (*gather together*) radunarsi **3** *adv* Am: *call* **~** telefonare a carico del destinatario; **collection** collezione *f*; *in church* colletta *f*; *of poems, stories* raccolta *f*; **collective** collettivo; **collector** collezionista *m/f*
college ['kɒlɪdʒ] istituto *m* di studi superiori; *for professional training* scuola *f* professionale; *of British university* college *m inv*; *technical college* istituto *m* tecnico
collide [kə'laɪd] scontrarsi; **collision** collisione *f*, scontro *m*
colon ['kəʊlən] *punctuation* due punti *mpl*
colonel ['kɜːnl] colonnello *m*
colonial [kə'ləʊnɪəl] coloniale; **colonize** colonizzare; **colony** colonia *f*
color Am ☞ **colour**
colossal [kə'lɒsl] colossale
colour ['kʌlə(r)] colore *m*; **colour-blind** daltonico; **coloured** *person* di colore; **colourful** pieno di colori; *account* pittoresco
colt [kəʊlt] puledro *m*

column ['kɒləm] colonna f; *in newspaper* rubrica f; **columnist** giornalista m/f che cura una rubrica

coma ['kəumə] coma m inv

comb [kəum] **1** n pettine m **2** v/t pettinare; *area* rastrellare

combat ['kɒmbæt] **1** n combattimento m **2** v/t combattere

combination [kɒmbɪ'neɪʃn] combinazione f

combine [kəm'baɪn] **1** v/t unire; *ingredients* mescolare **2** v/i combinarsi

come [kʌm] venire; *of train, bus* arrivare

♦ **come about** (*happen*) succedere

♦ **come across** (*find*) trovare

♦ **come along** (*come too*) venire; (*turn up*) presentarsi; (*progress*) fare progressi

♦ **come back** ritornare

♦ **come down** venire giù; *in price, amount etc,* (*descend*) scendere; *of rain, snow* cadere

♦ **come for** (*attack*) assalire; (*collect*) venire a prendere

♦ **come forward** farsi avanti

♦ **come from** venire da; **where do you come from?** di dove sei?

♦ **come in** entrare; *of train, in race* arrivare; *of tide* salire

♦ **come in for** attirare; **come in for criticism** attirare delle critiche

♦ **come off** *of handle etc* staccarsi

♦ **come on** (*progress*) fare progressi; **how's the work coming on?** come sta venendo il lavoro?; **come on!** dai!; *in disbelief* ma dai!

♦ **come out** *of person, book, sun* uscire; *of results, product* venir fuori; *of stain* venire via

♦ **come to 1** v/t *place* arrivare a; **that comes to £70** fanno 70 sterline **2** v/i (*regain consciousness*) rinvenire

♦ **come up** salire; *of sun* sorgere

♦ **come up with** *new idea etc* venir fuori con

'comeback ritorno m; **make a ~** tornare alla ribalta

comedian [kə'mi:dɪən] comico m, -a f; pej buffone m; **comedy** commedia f

comfort ['kʌmfət] **1** n comodità f inv; (*consolation*) conforto m **2** v/t confortare; **comfortable** *chair, room* comodo

comic ['kɒmɪk] **1** n *to read* fumetto m; (*comedian*) comico m, -a f **2** adj comico; **comical** comico; **comic book** fumetto m; **comic strip** striscia f (di fumetti)

comma ['kɒmə] virgola f

command [kə'mɑːnd] **1** n comando m **2** v/t person comandare a

commandeer [kɒmən'dɪə(r)]

appropriarsi di

commander [kə'mɑːndə(r)] comandante *m*; **commander-in-chief** comandante *m* in capo

commemorate [kə'meməreɪt] commemorare

commence [kə'mens] cominciare

commendable [kə'mendəbl] lodevole; **commendation** *for bravery* riconoscimento *m*

comment ['kɒment] **1** *n* commento *m* **2** *v/i* fare commenti; **commentary** cronaca *f*; **commentator** *on TV* telecronista *m/f*; *on radio* radiocronista *m/f*

commerce ['kɒmɜːs] commercio *m*; **commercial** **1** *adj* commerciale **2** *n* (*advert*) pubblicità *f inv*; **commercial break** interruzione *f* pubblicitaria; **commercialize** *Christmas etc* commercializzare

commission [kə'mɪʃn] (*payment*, *committee*) commissione *f*; (*job*) incarico *m*

commit [kə'mɪt] *crime* commettere; *money* assegnare; **~ o.s.** impegnarsi; **commitment** impegno *m*; **committee** comitato *m*

commodity [kə'mɒdətɪ] prodotto *m*

common ['kɒmən] comune; **have sth in ~ with s.o.** avere qc in comune con qu; commonly comunemente; **common sense** buon senso *m*

commotion [kə'məʊʃn] confusione *f*

communal ['kɒmjʊnl] comune

communicate [kə'mjuːnɪkeɪt] comunicare; **communication** comunicazione *f*; **communications** comunicazioni *fpl*; **communicative** comunicativo

Communion [kə'mjuːnɪən] REL comunione *f*

Communism ['kɒmjʊnɪzm] comunismo *m*; **Communist** **1** *adj* comunista **2** *n* comunista *m/f*

community [kə'mjuːnɪtɪ] comunità *f inv*

commute [kə'mjuːt] **1** *v/i* fare il / la pendolare **2** *v/t* LAW commutare; **commuter** pendolare *m/f*; **commuter traffic** traffico *m* dei pendolari; **commuter train** treno *m* dei pendolari

compact **1** [kəm'pækt] *adj* compatto **2** ['kɒmpækt] *n* MOT compact *m inv*

companion [kəm'pænjən] compagno *m*, -a *f*

company ['kʌmpənɪ] compagnia *f*; COM società *f inv*; **company car** auto *f inv* della ditta

comparable ['kɒmpərəbl] paragonabile; (*similar*) simile; **comparative** **1** *adj* (*relative*) relativo; *study*, *method* comparato; **comparatively** relativamente; **compare 1** *v/t* paragonare (**with** a); **~d with ...** rispetto a ... **2** *v/i*: **how did he ~?** com'era rispetto agli altri?; **comparison** paragone *m*, confronto *m*

compartment [kəm'pɑːtmənt] scomparto *m*

compass ['kʌmpəs] bussola *f*; *for geometry* compasso *m*

compassion [kəm'pæʃn] compassione *f*; **compassionate** compassionevole

compatibility [kəmpætə'bɪlɪtɪ] compatibilità *f*; **compatible** compatibile

compel [kəm'pel] costringere

compensate ['kɒmpənseɪt] **1** *v/t with money* risarcire **2** *v/i*: **~ for** compensare; **compensation** *money* risarcimento *m*; *reward* vantaggio *m*; *comfort* consolazione *f*

compete [kəm'piːt] competere; (*take part*) gareggiare; **~ for** contendersi

competence ['kɒmpɪtəns] competenza *f*; **competent** competente

competition [kɒmpə'tɪʃn] (*contest*) concorso *m*; SP gara *f*; (*competing, competitors*) concorrenza *f*; **competitive** competitivo; *sport* agonistico; *price, offer* concorrenziale; **competitiveness** competitività *f*; **competitor** *in contest* concorrente *m/f*; **our ~s** COM la concorrenza

complacent [kəm'pleɪsənt] compiaciuto

complain [kəm'pleɪn] lamentarsi; *to shop* reclamare; **complaint** lamentela *f*; *to shop* reclamo *m*; MED disturbo *m*

complementary [kɒmplɪ'mentərɪ] complementare

complete [kəm'pliːt] **1** (*total*) completo; (*finished*) terminato **2** *v/t task, building etc* completare; *form* compilare; **completely** completamente; **completion** completamento *m*

complex ['kɒmpleks] **1** *adj* complesso **2** *n also* PSYCH complesso *m*; **complexion** *facial* carnagione *f*; **complexity** complessità *f inv*

compliance [kəm'plaɪəns] conformità *f*

complicate ['kɒmplɪkeɪt] complicare; **complicated** complicato; **complication** complicazione *f*

compliment ['kɒmplɪmənt] **1** *n* complimento *m* **2** *v/t* fare i complimenti a; **complimentary** lusinghiero; (*free*) in omaggio

comply [kəm'plaɪ] ubbidire; **~ with** osservare; *of products, equipment* essere conforme a

component [kəm'pəʊnənt] componente *m*

compose [kəm'pəʊz] *also* MUS comporre; **composed**

(*calm*) calmo; **composer**
MUS compositore *m*, -trice
f; **composition** *also* MUS
composizione *f*; (*essay*) tema
m; **composure** calma *f*

compound ['kɒmpaʊnd] *n*
CHEM composto *m*

comprehend [kɒmprɪ'hend]
(*understand*) capire; **com-
prehension** comprensione
f; **comprehensive** esauriente; **comprehensive insurance** polizza *f* casco

compress ['kɒmpres] comprimere; *information* condensare

comprise [kəm'praɪz] comprendere; (*make up*) costituire; **be ~d of** essere composto da

compromise ['kɒmprəmaɪz]
1 *n* compromesso *m* **2** *v/i* arrivare a un compromesso **3**
v/t (*jeopardize*) compromettere; **~ o.s.** compromettersi

compulsion [kəm'pʌlʃn]
PSYCH coazione *f*; **compul-
sive** *behaviour* patologico;
reading avvincente; **compul-
sory** obbligatorio

computer [kəm'pju:tə(r)]
computer *m inv*; **computer
game** computer game *m
inv*; **computerize** compute-
rizzare; **computer literate**
che ha dimestichezza con il
computer; **computer sci-
ence** informatica *f*; **computer scientist** informatico *m*,
-a *f*; **computing** informatica

f

comrade ['kɒmreɪd] *also* POL
compagno *m*, -a *f*; **comrade-
ship** cameratismo *m*

conceal [kən'si:l] nascondere; **concealment** occultazio-
ne *f*

conceit [kən'si:t] presunzione *f*; **conceited** presuntuoso

conceivable [kən'si:vəbl]
concepibile; **conceive** *of
woman* concepire

concentrate ['kɒnsəntreɪt] **1**
v/i concentrarsi **2** *v/t energies*
concentrare; **concentration**
concentrazione *f*

concept ['kɒnsept] concetto
m; **conception** *of child* concepimento *m*

concern [kən'sɜ:n] **1** *n* (*anxiety*) preoccupazione *f*; (*care*)
interesse *m*; (*business*) affare
m; (*company*) impresa *f* **2** *v/t*
(*involve*) riguardare; (*worry*)
preoccupare; **concerned**
(*anxious*) preoccupato; (*car-
ing*) interessato; (*involved*)
in questione; **as far as I'm
~** per quanto mi riguarda;
concerning riguardo a

concert ['kɒnsət] concerto *m*;
concerted congiunto

concession [kən'seʃn] (*compromise*) concessione *f*

concise [kən'saɪs] conciso

conclude [kən'klu:d] concludere (**from** da); **conclusion**
conclusione *f*; **conclusive**
conclusivo

concrete ['kɒŋkri:t] concreto

concussion [kənˈkʌʃn] commozione f cerebrale

condemn [kənˈdem] condannare; **condemnation** condanna f

condensation [kɒndenˈseɪʃn] *on walls, windows* condensa f

condescend [kɒndɪˈsend]: *he ~ed to speak to me* si è degnato di rivolgermi la parola; **condescending** borioso

condition [kənˈdɪʃn] **1** n *(state, requirement)* condizione f; MED malattia f; *in / out of ~* in / fuori forma **2** v/t PSYCH condizionare; **conditioner** *for hair* balsamo m; *for fabric* ammorbidente m; **conditioning** PSYCH condizionamento m

condo [ˈkɒndəʊ] Am condominio m

condolences [kənˈdəʊlənsɪz] condoglianze fpl

condom [ˈkɒndəm] preservativo m

condominium [kɒndəˈmɪniəm] Am condominio m

condone [kənˈdəʊn] *actions* scusare

conduct 1 [ˈkɒndʌkt] n *(behaviour)* condotta f **2** [kənˈdʌkt] v/t *(carry out)*, ELEC condurre; MUS dirigere; **conducted tour** visita f guidata; **conductor** MUS direttore m d'orchestra; *on bus* bigliettaio m; PHYS conduttore m

cone [kəʊn] cono m; *of pine*

tree pigna f

conference [ˈkɒnfərəns] congresso m; **conference room** sala f riunioni

confess [kənˈfes] **1** v/t confessare **2** v/i confessare; REL confessarsi; **confession** confessione f

confide [kənˈfaɪd] **1** v/t confidare **2** v/i: *~ in s.o.* confidarsi con qu; **confidence** *(assurance)* sicurezza f (di sé); *(trust)* fiducia f; *in ~* in confidenza; **confident** sicuro; *person* sicuro di sé; **confidential** riservato, confidenziale; *adviser* di fiducia; **confidently** con sicurezza

confine [kənˈfaɪn] *(imprison)* richiudere; *(restrict)* limitare; **confined** *space* ristretto

confirm [kənˈfɜːm] confermare; **confirmation** conferma f

confiscate [ˈkɒnfɪskeɪt] sequestrare

conflict 1 [ˈkɒnflɪkt] n conflitto m **2** [kənˈflɪkt] v/i *of statements* essere in conflitto; *of dates* coincidere

conform [kənˈfɔːm] conformarsi; *~ to of products, acts etc* essere conforme a

confront [kənˈfrʌnt] *(face)* affrontare; *~ s.o. with sth* mettere qu di fronte a qc; **confrontation** scontro m

confuse [kənˈfjuːz] confondere; *~ s.o. with s.o.* confondere qu con qu; **confused** confuso; **confusing** che confonde; **confusion** confusione *f*

congested [kən'dʒestɪd] congestionato; **congestion** congestione *f*

congratulate [kən'grætjʊleɪt] congratularsi con; **congratulations** congratulazioni *fpl*

congregate ['kɒŋɡrɪɡeɪt] (*gather*) riunirsi; **congregation** REL fedeli *mpl*

congress ['kɒŋɡres] (*conference*) congresso *m*; ***Congress in USA* il Congress; Congressional del Congresso; Congressman membro *m* del Congresso

conjecture [kən'dʒektʃə(r)] (*speculation*) congettura *f*

conjurer, conjuror ['kʌndʒərə(r)] (*magician*) prestigiatore *m*, -trice *f*

con man ['kɒnmæn] F truffatore *m*

connect [kə'nekt] (*join, link*) collegare; *to power supply* allacciare; **connected: be well-~** avere conoscenze influenti; **be ~ with ...** essere collegato con; **connecting flight** coincidenza *f* (volo); **connection** (*link*) collegamento *m*; *when travelling* coincidenza *f*; (*personal contact*) conoscenza *f*; **in ~ with** a proposito di

connoisseur [kɒnə'sɜː(r)] intenditore *m*, -trice *f*

conquer ['kɒŋkə(r)] conqui-

stare; *fear etc* vincere; **conqueror** conquistatore *m*, -trice *f*; **conquest** conquista *f*

conscience ['kɒnʃəns] coscienza *f*; **conscientious** coscienzioso; **conscientiousness** coscienziosità *f*

conscious ['kɒnʃəs] (*aware*) consapevole; (*deliberate*) conscio; MED cosciente; **consciously** consapevolmente; **consciousness** consapevolezza *f*; **lose / regain ~** perdere / riprendere conoscenza

consecutive [kən'sekjʊtɪv] consecutivo

consensus [kən'sensəs] consenso *m*

consent [kən'sent] **1** *n* consenso *m* **2** *v/i* acconsentire

consequence ['kɒnsɪkwəns] conseguenza *f*; **consequently** di conseguenza

conservation [kɒnsə'veɪʃn] tutela *f*; **conservationist** ambientalista *m/f*; **conservative 1** *adj* (*conventional*) conservatore; *clothes* tradizionale; *estimate* cauto; **Conservative** Br POL conservatore **2** *n* Br POL **Conservative** conservatore *m*, -trice *f*; **conserve 1** *n* (*jam*) marmellata **2** *v/t energy* risparmiare

consider [kən'sɪdə(r)] considerare; (*show regard for*) tener conto di; (*think about*) pensare a; **considerable** considerevole; **considerably** considerevolmente; **considerate** premuroso; **be ~ of** avere riguardo per; **considerately** premurosamente; **consideration** (*thought*) considerazione *f*; (*thoughtfulness, concern*) riguardo *m*; (*factor*) fattore *m*; **take sth into ~** prendere in considerazione qc

consignment [kənˈsaɪnmənt] COM consegna *f*

◆ **consist of** [kənˈsɪst] consistere in

consistency [kənˈsɪstənsɪ] (*texture*) consistenza *f*; (*unchangingness*) coerenza *f*; **consistent** coerente

consolidate [kənˈsɒlɪdeɪt] consolidare

consonant [ˈkɒnsənənt] GRAM consonante *f*

conspicuous [kənˈspɪkjʊəs]: **be / look ~** spiccare

conspiracy [kənˈspɪrəsɪ] cospirazione *f*; **conspirator** cospiratore *m*, -trice *f*; **conspire** cospirare

constant [ˈkɒnstənt] costante; **constantly** costantemente

constipated [ˈkɒnstɪpeɪtɪd] stitico; **constipation** stitichezza *f*

constituency [kənˈstɪtjʊənsɪ] POL circoscrizione *f* elettorale

constitute [ˈkɒnstɪtjuːt] costi-

tuire; **constitution** costituzione *f*; **constitutional** POL costituzionale

constraint [kənˈstreɪnt] restrizione *f*

construct [kənˈstrʌkt] costruire; **construction** costruzione *f*; **construction industry** edilizia *f*; **construction worker** operaio *m* edile; **constructive** costruttivo

consul [ˈkɒnsl] console *m*; **consulate** consolato *m*

consult [kənˈsʌlt] (*seek advice of*) consultare; **consultancy** (*company*) società *f inv* di consulenza; (*advice*) consulenza *f*; **consultant** consulente *m/f*; **consultation** consultazione *f*

consume [kənˈsjuːm] consumare; **consumer** consumatore *m*, -trice *f*; **consumer confidence** fiducia *f* dei consumatori; **consumption** consumo *m*

contact [ˈkɒntækt] **1** *n* contatto *m*; (*person*) conoscenza *f* **2** *v/t* mettersi in contatto con; **contact lens** lente *f* a contatto

contagious [kənˈteɪdʒəs] contagioso

contain [kənˈteɪn] contenere; **container** contenitore *m*; COM container *m inv*; **container ship** nave *f* portacontainer

contaminate [kənˈtæmɪneɪt]

contaminare; **contamination** contaminazione f

contemporary [kən'tempərə-rɪ] **1** adj contemporaneo **2** n coetaneo m, -a f

contempt [kən'tempt] disprezzo m; **contemptible** spregevole; **contemptuous** sprezzante

contender [kən'tendə(r)] concorrente m/f; against champion sfidante m/f; POL candidato m, -a f

content[1] ['kɒntent] n contenuto m

content[2] [kən'tent] **1** adj contento **2** v/t: ~ **o.s. with** accontentarsi di

contented [kən'tentɪd] contento; **contentment** soddisfazione f

contents ['kɒntents] of container contenuto m

contest[1] ['kɒntest] n (competition) concorso m; (struggle, for power) lotta f

contest[2] [kən'test] v/t leadership etc essere in lizza per; will impugnare

contestant [kən'testənt] concorrente m/f

context ['kɒntekst] contesto m

continent ['kɒntɪnənt] continente m; **the ~** l'Europa continentale; **continental** continentale

continual [kən'tɪnjʊəl] continuo; **continually** continuamente; **continuation** segui-

to m; **continue** continuare (**doing** a fare); **continuous** ininterrotto; **continuously** ininterrottamente

contort [kən'tɔːt] contorcere

contraception [kɒntrə'sepʃn] contraccezione f; **contraceptive** anticoncezionale m, contraccettivo m

contract[1] ['kɒntrækt] n contratto m

contract[2] [kən'trækt] **1** v/i (shrink) contrarsi **2** v/t illness contrarre

contractor [kən'træktə(r)] appaltatore m, -trice f; **building ~** ditta f di appalti (edili)

contractual [kən'træktjʊəl] contrattuale

contradict [kɒntrə'dɪkt] contraddire; **contradiction** contraddizione f; **contradictory** contraddittorio

contrary[1] ['kɒntrərɪ] **1** adj contrario; **~ to** contrariamente a **2** n: **on the ~** al contrario

contrary[2] [kən'treərɪ]: **be ~** (perverse) essere un bastian contrario

contrast ['kɒntrɑːst] **1** n contrasto m **2** v/t contrastare **3** v/i contrastare; **contrasting** contrastante

contravene [kɒntrə'viːn] contravvenire a

contribute [kən'trɪbjuːt] **1** v/i contribuire; **to magazine** collaborare (**to** con); **to discus-**

sion intervenire (**to** in) **2** *v/t money* contribuire con; **contribution:** *money* offerta *f*; *to political party, church* donazione *f*; *of time, effort* contributo *m*; *to debate* intervento *m*; *to magazine* collaborazione *f*; **contributor** *of money* finanziatore *m*, -trice *f*; *to magazine* collaboratore *m*, -trice *f*

control [kən'trəʊl] **1** *n* controllo *m*; **be in ~ of sth** tenere qc sotto controllo; **~s** *of aircraft, vehicle* comandi; **~s** (*restrictions*) restrizioni **2** *v/t* (*govern*) controllare; (*regulate*) regolare; **~ o.s.** controllarsi

controversial [kɒntrə'vɜːʃl] controverso; **controversy** polemica *f*

convalescence [kɒnvə'lesns] convalescenza *f*

convenience [kən'viːnɪəns] comodità *f inv*; **at your ~** a tuo comodo; **convenience store** negozio *m* alimentari; **convenient** comodo; **whenever it's ~** quando ti va bene

convent ['kɒnvənt] convento *m*

convention [kən'venʃn] (*tradition*) convenzione *f*; (*conference*) congresso *m*; **conventional** convenzionale; *method* tradizionale

conversation [kɒnvə'seɪʃn] conversazione *f*; **conversational** colloquiale

conversely [kən'vɜːslɪ] per contro

conversion [kən'vɜːʃn] conversione *f*; *of house* trasformazione *f*; **convert 1** *n* convertito *m*, -a *f* **2** *v/t* convertire; **convertible** *car* cabriolet *f inv*, decappottabile *f*

convey [kən'veɪ] (*transmit*) comunicare; (*carry*) trasportare; **conveyor belt** nastro *m* trasportatore

convict ['kɒnvɪkt] *n* carcerato *m*, -a *f* **2** [kən'vɪkt] *v/t* LAW condannare; **conviction** LAW condanna *f*; (*belief*) convinzione *f*

convince [kən'vɪns] convincere

convoy ['kɒnvɔɪ] convoglio *m*

cook [kʊk] **1** *n* cuoco *m*, -a *f* **2** *v/t food* cucinare; *meal* preparare **3** *v/i of person* cucinare; *of food* cuocere; **cookbook** ricettario *m*; **cooker** cucina *f*; **cookery** cucina *f*; **cookie** *Am* biscotto *m*; **cooking** cucina *f*

cool [kuːl] **1** *n* F: **keep one's ~** conservare la calma **2** *adj* fresco; (*calm*) calmo; (*unfriendly*) freddo; F (*great*) grande **3** *v/i of food* raffreddarsi; *of tempers* calmarsi; *of interest* raffreddarsi **4** *v/t* F: **~ it!** calma!

◆ **cool down 1** *v/i* raffreddarsi; *of weather* rinfrescare; *fig: of tempers* calmarsi **2** *v/t food* raffreddare; *fig* calmare

cooperate [kəʊˈɒpəreɪt] cooperare; **cooperation** cooperazione f; **cooperative** (helpful) disponibile (a collaborare)

coordinate [kəʊˈɔːdɪneɪt] coordinare; **coordination** of activities coordinamento m; of body coordinazione f

cop [kɒp] F poliziotto m

cope [kəʊp] farcela; ~ **with** farcela con

copier [ˈkɒpɪə(r)] machine fotocopiatrice f

copper [ˈkɒpə(r)] metal rame m

copy [ˈkɒpɪ] **1** n copia f **2** v/t copiare

cord [kɔːd] (string) corda f; (cable) filo m; **cordless** (phone) cordless m inv

cordon [ˈkɔːdn] cordone m

cords [kɔːdz] trousers pantaloni mpl di velluto a coste

corduroy [ˈkɔːdərɔɪ] velluto m a coste

core [kɔː(r)] **1** n of fruit torsolo m; of problem nocciolo m; of organization, party cuore m **2** adj issue essenziale

cork [kɔːk] in bottle tappo m di sughero; (material) sughero m; **corkscrew** cavatappi m inv

corn [kɔːn] grain frumento m; Am (maize) granturco m

corner [ˈkɔːnə(r)] **1** n of page, room, street angolo m; of table spigolo m; in football calcio m d'angolo, corner m

inv; **in the** ~ nell'angolo; **on the** ~ of street all'angolo **2** v/t person bloccare; ~ **a market** prendersi il monopolio di un mercato **3** v/i of driver, car affrontare una curva

coronary [ˈkɒrənərɪ] **1** adj coronario **2** n infarto m

coroner [ˈkɒrənə(r)] ufficiale pubblico che indaga sui casi di morte sospetta

corporal [ˈkɔːpərəl] caporale m maggiore; **corporal punishment** punizione f corporale

corporate [ˈkɔːpərət] COM aziendale; **sense of** ~ **loyalty** corporativismo m; **corporation** (business) corporation f inv

corpse [kɔːps] cadavere m

correct [kəˈrekt] **1** adj giusto; **she's** ~ ha ragione **2** v/t correggere; **correction** correzione f; **correctly** giustamente

correspond [kɒrɪˈspɒnd] (match, write) corrispondere; **correspondence** corrispondenza f; **correspondent** corrispondente m/f

corridor [ˈkɒrɪdɔː(r)] corridoio m

corroborate [kəˈrɒbəreɪt] corroborare

corrosion [kəˈrəʊʒn] corrosione f

corrupt [kəˈrʌpt] **1** adj also COMPUT corrotto **2** v/t mor-

als, youth traviare; *(bribe)* corrompere; **corruption** corruzione *f*

Corsica ['kɔːsɪkə] Corsica *f*; **Corsican 1** *adj* corso **2** *n* corso *m*, -a *f*

cosmetic [koz'metik] cosmetico; *surgery* estetico; *fig* di facciata; **cosmetics** cosmetici *mpl*; **cosmetic surgery** chirurgia *f* estetica

cosmopolitan [kozmə'pɒlɪtən] cosmopolitano

cost [kɒst] **1** *n also fig* costo *m* **2** *v/t* costare; FIN *proposal* fare il preventivo di; **how much does it ...?** quanto costa?; **cost-effective** conveniente; **cost of living** costo *m* della vita; **cost price** prezzo *m* di costo

costume ['kɒstjuːm] *for actor* costume *m*

cosy ['kəʊzɪ] *(comfortable)* gradevole; *(intimate and friendly)* intimo

cot [kɒt] *for child* lettino *m*; *Am (camp-bed)* letto *m* da campo

cottage ['kɒtɪdʒ] cottage *m inv*

cotton ['kɒtn] **1** *n* cotone *m* **2** *adj* di cotone; **cotton candy** *Am* zucchero *m* filato; **cotton wool** ovatta *f*

couch [kaʊtʃ] divano *m*

couchette [kuː'ʃet] cuccetta *f*

couch po'tato *F* teledipendente *m/f*

cough [kɒf] **1** *n* tosse *f* **2** *v/i*

tossire; to get attention tossicchiare; **cough medicine**, **cough syrup** sciroppo *m* per la tosse

could [kʊd]: **~ I have my key?** mi dà la chiave?; **~ you help me?** mi puoi dare una mano?; **you ~ be right** magari hai ragione; **you ~ have warned me!** avresti potuto avvisarmi!; **I ~n't say for sure** non potrei giurarci

council ['kaʊnsl] *(assembly)* consiglio *m*; *(city ~)* comune *m*; **councillor**, *Am* **councilor** consigliere *m*, -a *f* (*comunale*)

counsel ['kaʊnsl] **1** *n (advice)* consiglio *m*; *(lawyer)* avvocato *m* **2** *v/t action* consigliare; *person* offrire consulenza a; **counselling**, *Am* **counseling** terapia *f*; **counsellor**, *Am* **counselor** *(adviser)* consulente *m/f*

count [kaʊnt] **1** *n* conteggio *m* **2** *v/t & v/i* contare; **~ yourself lucky** considerati fortunato

◆ **count on** contare su

'countdown conto *m* alla rovescia

counter ['kaʊntə(r)] *in shop, café* banco *m*; *in game* segnalino *m*

'counteract neutralizzare; **counter-attack 1** *n* contrattacco *m* **2** *v/i* contrattaccare; **counterclockwise** *Am* **1** *adj* antiorario **2** *adv* in senso antiorario; **counterespionage** controspionaggio *m*; **counterfeit 1** *v/t* falsificare **2** *adj* falso; **counterpart** *person* omologo *m*, -a *f*; **counterproductive** controproducente

countess ['kauntes] contessa *f*

countless ['kauntlɪs] innumerevole

country ['kʌntrɪ] paese *m*; *as opposed to town* campagna *f*; **countryside** campagna *f*

county ['kauntɪ] contea *f*

coup [kuː] POL colpo *m* di stato, golpe *m inv*; *fig* colpo *m*

couple ['kʌpl] coppia *f*; *just a* ~ solo un paio; *a* ~ *of* un paio di

coupon ['kuːpɒn] buono *m*

courage ['kʌrɪdʒ] coraggio *m*; **courageous** coraggioso

courgette [kʊə'ʒet] zucchino *m*

courier ['kʊrɪə(r)] *(messenger)* corriere *m*; *with tourist party* accompagnatore *m* turistico, accompagnatrice *f* turistica

course [kɔːs] *of lessons* corso *m*; *of meal* portata *f*; *of ship, plane* rotta *f*; *for golf* campo *m*; *for race, skiing* pista *f*; *of* ~ *(certainly)* certo; *(naturally)* ovviamente; *of* ~ *not* certo che no; *first* ~ primo *m*

court [kɔːt] LAW corte *f*; *(courthouse)* tribunale *m*; SP campo *m*; *take s.o. to* ~ fare causa a qu; *out of* ~ in via

amichevole; **court case** caso *m (giudiziario)*

courtesy ['kɜːtəsɪ] cortesia *f*

'**courthouse** tribunale *m*, palazzo *m* di giustizia; **courtroom** aula *f* del tribunale; **courtyard** cortile *m*

cousin ['kʌzn] cugino *m*, -a *f*

cover ['kʌvə(r)] **1** *n protective* fodera *f*, *of book, magazine* copertina *f*; *(shelter)* riparo *m*; *insurance* copertura *f* **2** *v/t* coprire; *distance* percorrere

♦ **cover up 1** *v/t* coprire; *fig* insabbiare **2** *v/i*: **cover up for s.o.** coprire qu

coverage ['kʌvərɪdʒ] *by media* copertura *f*

covert ['kʌvɜːt] segreto

'**cover-up** insabbiamento *m*

cow [kau] mucca *f*

coward ['kauəd] vigliacco *m*, -a *f*; **cowardice** vigliaccheria *f*

'**cowboy** cow-boy *m inv*

co-worker ['kəʊwɜːkə(r)] collega *m/f*

cozy *Am* ☞ **cosy**

crab [kræb] granchio *m*

crack [kræk] **1** *n* crepa *f*; *(joke)* battuta *f* **2** *v/t cup, glass* incrinare; *nut* schiacciare; *code* decifrare; F *(solve)* risolvere **3** *v/i* incrinarsi

♦ **crack down on** prendere serie misure contro

cracked [krækt] *cup* incrinato; **cracker** *to eat* cracker *m inv*

cradle ['kreɪdl] *for baby* culla *f*

craft[1] [krɑːft] NAUT imbarcazione *f*

craft[2] [krɑːft] *(skill)* attività *f inv* artigiana; *(trade)* mestiere *m*

'craftsman artigiano *m*

crafty ['krɑːftɪ] astuto

crag [kræg] *rock* rupe *f*

cram [kræm] *papers, food* infilare; *people* stipare

cramps [kræmps] crampo *m*

crane [kreɪn] **1** *n machine* gru *f inv* **2** *v/t* ~ **one's neck** allungare il collo

crank [kræŋk] *person* tipo *m* strambo; **cranky** *Br (eccentric)* strampalato; *Am (bad-tempered)* irascibile

crap [kræp] P merda *f*; **don't talk ~** non dire cazzate

crash [kræʃ] **1** *n noise* fragore *m*; *accident* incidente *m*; COM crollo *m*; COMPUT crash *m inv* **2** *v/i fall noisily* fracassarsi; *of car* schiantarsi; *of two cars* scontrarsi, schiantarsi; *of plane* precipitare; *of market* crollare; COMPUT fare un crash **3** *v/t car* avere un incidente con; **crash course** corso *m* intensivo; **crash diet** dieta *f* lampo; **crash helmet** casco *m* (di protezione); **crash-land** fare un atterraggio di fortuna

crate [kreɪt] cassetta *f*

crater ['kreɪtə(r)] cratere *m*

crave [kreɪv] smaniare dalla voglia di; **craving** voglia *f*;

pej smania *f*

crawl [krɔːl] **1** *n in swimming* crawl *m* **2** *v/i on floor* andare (a) carponi; *(move slowly)* avanzare lentamente

crayon ['kreɪən] matita *f* colorata; *wax* pastello *m* a cera

craze [kreɪz] moda *f*; **crazy** pazzo

creak [kriːk] scricchiolare; **creaky** che scricchiola

cream [kriːm] *n for skin* crema *f*; *for coffee, cake* panna *f*; *colour* color *m* panna **2** *adj* color panna

crease [kriːs] **1** *n grinza f*; *deliberate* piega *f* **2** *v/t accidentally* sgualcire

create [kriː'eɪt] creare; **creation** creazione *f*; **creative** creativo; **creator** creatore *m*, -trice *f*

creature ['kriːtʃə(r)] creatura *f*

credibility [kredə'bɪlɪt] credibilità *f*; **credible** credibile

credit ['kredɪt] **1** *n* FIN credito *m*; *(honour)* merito *m* **2** *v/t amount* accreditare; **creditable** lodevole; **credit card** carta *f* di credito; **credit limit** limite *m* di credito; **creditor** creditore *m*, -trice *f*; **creditworthy** solvibile

creep [kriːp] **1** *n pej* tipo *m* odioso *f* **2** *v/i quietly* avanzare quatto quatto; *slowly* avanzare lentamente; **creepy** F che dà i brividi

cremate [krɪ'meɪt] cremare; **cremation** cremazione *f* crest [krest] *of hill, bird* cresta *f*

crevasse [krə'væs] voragine *f*

crevice ['krevɪs] crepa *f*

crew [kru:] *of ship, plane* equipaggio *m*; crew cut taglio *m* a spazzola

crib [krɪb] *Am for baby* lettino *m*

crime [kraɪm] reato *m*; (*criminality*) criminalità *f*; (*shameful act*) crimine *m*; criminal 1 *n* delinquente *m/f*; LAW penale; (*shameful*) vergognoso

crimson ['krɪmzn] cremisi *inv*

cripple ['krɪpl] 1 *n* invalido *m*, -a *f* 2 *v/t person* rendere invalido; *fig* paralizzare

crisis ['kraɪsɪs] crisi *f inv*

crisp [krɪsp] *weather, lettuce, new shirt* fresco; *bacon, toast* croccante; crisps patatine *fpl*

criterion [kraɪ'tɪərɪən] criterio *m*

critic ['krɪtɪk] critico *m*, -a *f*; critical critico; criticism critica *f*; criticize criticare

Croatia [krəʊ'eɪʃə] Croazia *f*; Croatian 1 *adj* croato 2 *n* croato *m/f*; *language* croato *m*

crockery ['krɒkərɪ] stoviglie *fpl*

crocodile ['krɒkədaɪl] coccodrillo *m*

crony ['krəʊnɪ] F amico *m*, -a *f*

crook [krʊk] truffatore *m*, -trice *f*; crooked *streets* tortuoso; *picture* storto; (*dishonest*) disonesto

crop [krɒp] 1 *n* raccolto *m*; *type of grain etc* coltura *f* 2 *v/t hair, photo* tagliare
◆ crop up saltar fuori

cross [krɒs] 1 *adj* (*angry*) arrabbiato 2 *n* croce *f* 3 *v/t* (*go across*) attraversare; ~ o.s. REL farsi il segno della croce 4 *v/i* (*go across*) attraversare; *of lines* intersecarsi
◆ cross off, cross out depennare

'crosscheck 1 *n* controllo *m* incrociato 2 *v/t* fare un controllo incrociato su; cross-country (*skiing*) sci *m* di fondo; cross-examine LAW interrogare in contraddittorio; cross-eyed strabico; crossing NAUT traversata *f*; crossroads incrocio *m*; *fig* bivio *m*; crosswalk *Am* passaggio *m* pedonale; crossword (puzzle) cruciverba *m inv*

crotch [krɒtʃ] *of person* inguine *m*; *of trousers* cavallo *m*

crouch [kraʊtʃ] accovacciarsi

crow [krəʊ] *bird* corvo *m*; as the ~ flies in linea d'aria

crowd [kraʊd] folla *f*; crowded affollato

crown [kraʊn] corona *f*; *on tooth* capsula *f*

crucial ['kru:ʃl] essenziale

crucifix ['kru:sɪfɪks] crocifisso *m*; **crucifixion** crocifissione *f*; **crucify** REL crocifiggere; *fig* fare a pezzi

crude [kru:d] **1** *adj* (*vulgar*) volgare; (*unsophisticated*) rudimentale **2** *n*: ~ (*oil*) (petrolio *m*) greggio *m*

cruel ['kru:əl] crudele; **cruelty** crudeltà *f inv*

cruise [kru:z] **1** *n* crociera *f* **2** *v/i of people* fare una crociera; *of car, plane* viaggiare a velocità di crociera

crumb [krʌm] briciola *f*

crumble ['krʌmbl] *of bread* sbriciolarsi; *of stonework* sgretolarsi; *fig: of opposition etc* crollare

crumple ['krʌmpl] **1** *v/t* (*crease*) sgualcire **2** *v/i* (*collapse*) accasciarsi

crush [krʌʃ] **1** *n* (*crowd*) ressa *f* **2** *v/t* schiacciare; (*crease*) sgualcire

crust [krʌst] *on bread* crosta *f*

crutch [krʌtʃ] *for injured person* stampella *f*

cry [kraɪ] **1** *n* (*call*) grido *m* **2** *v/t* (*call*) gridare **3** *v/i* (*weep*) piangere

◆ **cry out** gridare

cryptic ['krɪptɪk] sibillino

crystal ['krɪstl] cristallo *m*

cube [kju:b] cubo *m*; **cubic** cubico

cubicle ['kju:bɪkl] cabina *f*

cucumber ['kju:kʌmbə(r)] cetriolo *m*

cuddle ['kʌdl] coccolare

cue [kju:] *for actor etc* imbec-

cata *f*; *for pool* stecca *f*

cuff [kʌf] *of shirt* polsino *m*; (*blow*) schiaffo *m*; *Am* (*of trousers*) risvolto *m*

culminate ['kʌlmɪneɪt]: ~ *in* culminare in; **culmination** culmine *m*

culprit ['kʌlprɪt] colpevole *m/f*

cult [kʌlt] culto *m*

cultivate ['kʌltɪveɪt] *land* coltivare; *person* coltivarsi; **cultivated** *person* colto; **cultivation** *of land* coltivazione *f*

cultural ['kʌltʃərəl] culturale; **culture** cultura *f*; **cultured** colto

cumulative ['kju:mjʊlətɪv] cumulativo

cunning ['kʌnɪŋ] **1** *n* astuzia *f* **2** *adj* astuto

cup [kʌp] tazza *f*; (*trophy*) coppa *f*

cupboard ['kʌbəd] armadio *m*

'cup final finale *f* di coppa

curb [kɜ:b] **1** *n on powers etc* freno *m* **2** *v/t* tenere a freno

cure [kjʊə(r)] **1** *n* MED cura *f* **2** *v/t* MED guarire; *by drying* essiccare; *by salting* salare; *by smoking* affumicare

curiosity [kjʊərɪˈɒsɪtɪ] curiosità *f inv*; **curious** (*inquisitive*) curioso; (*strange*) strano

curl [kɜ:l] **1** *n in hair* ricciolo *m*; *of smoke* spirale *f* **2** *v/t* arricciare **3** *v/i of hair* arricciarsi; *of leaf etc* accartocciarsi

◆ **curl up** acciambellarsi

curly ['kɜːlɪ] *hair* riccio; *tail* a ricciolo

currant ['kʌrənt] *uva f* passa

currency ['kʌrənsɪ] *money* valuta *f*; **foreign ~** valuta estera; **current 1** *n in sea*, ELEC corrente *f* **2** *adj* (*present*) attuale; **current account** conto *m* corrente; **current affairs** attualità *f*

curry ['kʌrɪ] *dish* piatto *m* al curry; *spice* curry *m*

curse [kɜːs] **1** *n spell* maledizione *f*; (*swearword*) imprecazione *f* **2** *v/t* maledire; (*swear at*) imprecare contro **3** *v/i* (*swear*) imprecare

cursor ['kɜːsə(r)] COMPUT cursore *m*

cursory ['kɜːsərɪ] di sfuggita

curt [kɜːt] brusco

curtain ['kɜːtn] tenda *f*; THEA sipario *m*

curve [kɜːv] **1** *n* curva *f* **2** *v/i* (*bend*) fare una curva

cushion ['kʊʃn] **1** *n* cuscino *m* **2** *v/t blow, fall* attutire

custody ['kʌstədɪ] *of children* custodia *f*; **in ~** LAW in detenzione preventiva

custom ['kʌstəm] usanza *f*; COM clientela *f*; **customer** cliente *m/f*; **customer service** servizio *m* assistenza al cliente

customs ['kʌstəmz] dogana *f*; **Customs and Excise** Ufficio *m* Dazi e Dogana; **customs officer** doganiere *m*, -a *f*

cut [kʌt] **1** *n with knife, of hair, clothes* taglio *m*; (*reduction*) riduzione *f* **2** *v/t* tagliare; (*reduce*) ridurre; **get one's hair ~** tagliarsi i capelli

◆ **cut down 1** *v/t tree* abbattere **2** *v/i in smoking etc* limitarsi

◆ **cut off** tagliare; (*isolate*) isolare

◆ **cut up** *meat etc* sminuzzare

'**cutback** *in production* riduzione *f*; *in spending* taglio *m*

cute [kjuːt] **1** (*pretty*) carino; (*smart, clever*) furbo

cutlery ['kʌtlərɪ] posate *fpl*

'**cut-off date** scadenza *f*; '**cut-price** *goods* a prezzo ridotto; *store* di articoli scontati; '**cut-throat** *competition* spietato; **cutting 1** *n from newspaper etc* ritaglio *m* **2** *adj remark* tagliente

CV [siː'viː] (= **curriculum vitae**) curriculum vitae *m inv*

cycle ['saɪkl] **1** *n* (*bicycle*) bicicletta *f*; *of events* ciclo *m* **2** *v/i to work* andare in bicicletta; **cycling** ciclismo *m*; **cyclist** ciclista *m/f*

cylinder ['sɪlɪndə(r)] cilindro *m*; **cylindrical** cilindrico

cynic ['sɪnɪk] cinico *m*, -a *f*; **cynical** cinico; **cynicism** cinismo *m*

cypress ['saɪprəs] cipresso *m*

Czech [tʃek] **1** *adj* ceco; **the ~ Republic** la Repubblica Ceca **2** *n person* ceco *m*, -a *f*; *language* ceco *m*

D

DA Am (= **district attorney**) procuratore m distrettuale

♦ **dabble in** dilettarsi di

dad [dæd] papà m inv

daddy ['dædɪ] papà m inv; **daddy longlegs** zanzarone m

daffodil ['dæfədɪl] trombone m

daft [dɑːft] stupido

dagger ['dægə(r)] pugnale m

daily ['deɪlɪ] **1** n (paper) quotidiano m **2** adj quotidiano

'dairy products latticini mpl

daisy ['deɪzɪ] margherita f

dam [dæm] for water diga f

damage ['dæmɪdʒ] **1** n also fig danno m **2** v/t danneggiare; fig: reputation etc compromettere; **damages** LAW risarcimento msg; **damaging** nocivo

damn [dæm] **1** int F accidenti **2** adj F maledetto **3** adv F incredibilmente; **damning** evidence schiacciante; report incriminante

damp [dæmp] umido

dance [dɑːns] **1** n ballo m **2** v/i ballare; of ballerina danzare; **dancer** (performer) ballerino m, -a f; **be a good ~** ballare bene; **dancing** ballo m, danza f

dandelion ['dændɪlaɪən] dente m di leone

dandruff ['dændrʌf] forfora f

Dane [deɪn] danese m/f

danger ['deɪndʒə(r)] pericolo m; **dangerous** pericoloso

dangle ['dæŋgl] **1** v/t dondolare **2** v/i pendere

Danish ['deɪnɪʃ] **1** adj danese **2** n (language) danese m; **Danish pastry** dolcetto ripieno

dare [deə(r)] **1** v/i osare; **~ to do sth** osare fare qc; **how ~ you!** come osi! **2** v/t: **~ s.o. to do sth** sfidare qu a fare qc; **daring** audace

dark [dɑːk] **1** n buio m, oscurità f **2** adj room, night buio; hair, eyes, colour scuro; **dark glasses** occhiali mpl scuri; **darkness** oscurità f

darling ['dɑːlɪŋ] tesoro m

dart [dɑːt] **1** n for throwing freccetta f **2** v/i scagliarsi; **darts** game freccette fpl

dash [dæʃ] **1** n in punctuation trattino m; of whisky, milk goccio m; of salt pizzico m **2** v/i precipitarsi **3** v/t hopes stroncare; **dashboard** cruscotto m

data ['deɪtə] dati mpl; **database** base f dati; **data protection** protezione f dati

date¹ [deɪt] (fruit) dattero m

date² [deɪt] data f; (meeting) appuntamento m; **what's**

the ~ today? quanti ne abbiamo oggi?; *out of ~ clothes* fuori moda; *passport* scaduto; *up to ~* aggiornato; (*fashionable*) attuale; dated superato

daughter ['dɔːtə(r)] figlia *f*; **daughter-in-law** nuora *f*

dawdle ['dɔːdl] ciondolare

dawn [dɔːn] alba *f*; *fig: of new age* albori *mpl*

day [deɪ] giorno *m*; *emphasizing duration* giornata *f*; **the ~ after** il giorno dopo; **the ~ after tomorrow** dopodomani; **the ~ before** il giorno prima; **the ~ before yesterday** l'altro ieri; *in those ~s* a quei tempi; **the other ~** (*recently*) l'altro giorno; **daybreak: at ~** allo spuntare del giorno; **daydream 1** *n* sogno *m* a d occhi aperti **2** *v/i* essere sovrappensiero; **daylight** luce *f* del giorno; **daytime: in the ~** durante il giorno; **day return** biglietto *m* di andata e ritorno in giornata; **daytrip** gita *f* di un giorno

dazed [deɪzd] *by news* sbalordito; *by blow* stordito

dazzle ['dæzl] *of light, fig* abbagliare

dead [ded] **1** *adj* morto; *battery* scarica; *phone* muto **2** *adv* F (*very*) da matti F; *~ beat, ~ tired* stanco morto **3** *n*: **the ~** (*dead people*) i morti; **dead end** *street* vicolo *m* cieco; **dead heat** pareggio

m; **deadline** scadenza *f*; *for newspaper* termine *m* per l'invio in stampa; **deadlock** *in talks* punto *m* morto; **deadly** mortale

deaf [def] sordo; **deafening** assordante; **deafness** sordità *f*

deal [diːl] **1** *n* accordo *m*; *a great ~ of* un bel po' di **2** *v/t cards* distribuire

♦ deal in trattare; *drugs* trafficare

♦ deal with (*handle*) occuparsi di; *situation* gestire; (*do business with*) trattare con

dealer ['diːlə(r)] (*merchant*) commerciante *m/f*; (*drug ~*) spacciatore *m*, -trice *f*; **dealing** (*drug ~*) spaccio *m*; **dealings** (*business*) rapporti *mpl*

dear [dɪə(r)] caro; *Dear Sir* Egregio Signore

death [deθ] morte *f*; **death penalty** pena *f* di morte; **death toll** numero *m* delle vittime

debatable [dɪ'beɪtəbl] discutibile; **debate 1** *n* dibattimento *m*; POL dibattito *m* **2** *v/i* dibattere **3** *v/t* dibattere su

debit ['debɪt] **1** *n* addebito *m* **2** *v/t* addebitare; **debit card** bancomat *m inv*

debris ['debriː] *of plane* rottami *mpl*; *of building* macerie *fpl*

debt [det] debito *m*; *be in ~*

avere dei debiti; **debtor** debitore *m*, -trice *f*

debug [diːˈbʌg] COMPUT togliere gli errori da

decade [ˈdekeɪd] decennio *m*, decade *f*

decadent [ˈdekədənt] decadente

decaffeinated [diːˈkæfɪneɪtɪd] decaffeinato

decay [dɪˈkeɪ] **1** *n of matter* decomposizione *f*; *of civilization* declino *m*; *(decayed matter)* marciume *m*; *in teeth* carie *f* **2** *v/i of organic matter* decomporsi; *of civilization* declinare; *of teeth* cariarsi

deceased [dɪˈsiːst]: **the ~** il defunto *m*, la defunta *f*

deceit [dɪˈsiːt] falsità *f*, disonestà *f*; **deceitful** falso, disonesto; **deceive** ingannare

December [dɪˈsembə(r)] dicembre *m*

decency [ˈdiːsənsɪ] decenza *f*; **decent** *price, proposition* corretto; *meal, sleep* decente; **a ~ guy** un uomo per bene

decentralize [diːˈsentrəlaɪz] decentralizzare

deception [dɪˈsepʃn] inganno *m*; **deceptive** ingannevole; **deceptively**: *it looks ~ simple* sembra semplice solo all'apparenza

decide [dɪˈsaɪd] decidere (**to do** di fare); **decided** *(definite)* deciso

decimal [ˈdesɪml] decimale *f*

decipher [dɪˈsaɪfə(r)] decifra-

re

decision [dɪˈsɪʒn] decisione *f*; **decisive** risoluto; *(crucial)* decisivo

deck [dek] *of ship* ponte *m*; *of bus* piano *m*; *of cards* mazzo *m*; **deckchair** sedia *f* a sdraio, sdraio *f inv*

declaration [dekləˈreɪʃn] dichiarazione *f*; **declare** dichiarare

decline [dɪˈklaɪn] **1** *n in number, standards* calo *m*; *in health* peggioramento *m* **2** *v/t invitation* declinare; **~ to comment** esimersi dal commentare **3** *v/i (refuse)* declinare; *(decrease)* diminuire; *of health* peggiorare

decode [diːˈkəʊd] decodificare

decompose [diːkəmˈpəʊz] decomporsi

décor [ˈdeɪkɔː(r)] arredamento *m*

decorate [ˈdekəreɪt] *with paint* imbiancare; *with paper* tappezzare; *(adorn)*, MIL decorare; **decoration** *paint* vernice *f*; *paper* tappezzeria *f*; *(ornament)* addobbi *mpl*; MIL decorazione *f*; **decorator** *(interior ~)* imbianchino *m*

decoy [ˈdiːkɔɪ] *n* esca *f*

decrease [ˈdiːkriːs] **1** *n* diminuzione *f* **2** *v/t* ridurre **3** *v/i* ridursi

dedicate [ˈdedɪkeɪt] *book etc* dedicare; **dedicated** dedito;

dedication *in book* dedica *f*; *to cause, work* dedizione *f*

deduce [dɪ'djuːs] dedurre

deduct [dɪ'dʌkt] detrarre (**from** da); **deduction** *from salary* trattenuta *f*; (*conclusion*) deduzione *f*

deed [diːd] (*act*) azione *f*; LAW atto *m*

deep [diːp] profondo; *colour* intenso; **deepen 1** *v/t* rendere più profondo **2** *v/i* diventare più profondo; *of crisis* aggravarsi; *of mystery* infittirsi; **deep freeze** congelatore *m*

deer [dɪə(r)] cervo *m*

deface [dɪ'feɪs] vandalizzare

defamation [defə'meɪʃn] diffamazione *f*; **defamatory** diffamatorio

default ['dɪfɒlt] COMPUT di default

defeat [dɪ'fiːt] **1** *n* sconfitta *f* **2** *v/t* sconfiggere

defect ['diːfekt] difetto *m*; **defective** difettoso

defence [dɪ'fens] difesa *f*; **defenceless** indifeso

defend [dɪ'fend] difendere; **defendant** accusato *m*, -a *f*; *in criminal case* imputato *m*, -a *f*; **defense** *Am* **defence**; **Defense Secretary** *Am* POL ministro *m* della difesa; **defensive 1** *n*: **go on the** mettersi sulla difensiva **2** *adj weaponry* difensivo; *person* sulla difensiva

deference ['defərəns] deferenza *f*

defiance [dɪ'faɪəns] sfida *f*; **defiant** provocatorio

deficiency [dɪ'fɪʃənsɪ] carenza *f*

deficit ['defɪsɪt] deficit *m inv*

define [dɪ'faɪn] definire

definite ['definɪt] *date, time, answer* preciso; *improvement* netto; (*certain*) certo; **definite article** GRAM articolo *m* determinativo; **definitely** senza dubbio; *smell, hear* distintamente

definition [defɪ'nɪʃn] definizione *f*

definitive [dɪ'fɪnətɪv] *biography* più completo; *performance* migliore

deformity [dɪ'fɔːmɪtɪ] deformità *f inv*

defrost [diː'frɒst] *food* scongelare; *fridge* sbrinare

defuse [diː'fjuːz] *bomb* disinnescare; *situation* placare

defy [dɪ'faɪ] (*disobey*) disobbedire

degrading [dɪ'greɪdɪŋ] degradante

degree [dɪ'griː] grado *m*; *from university* laurea *f*

dehydrated [diːhaɪ'dreɪtɪd] disidratato

deign [deɪn]: ~ **to** ... degnarsi di ...

dejected [dɪ'dʒektɪd] sconfortato

delay [dɪ'leɪ] **1** *n* ritardo **2** *v/t* ritardare; **be** ~**ed** (*be late*) essere in ritardo **3** *v/i* tardare delegate ['delɪgeɪt] **1** *n* delegato *m*, -a *f* **2** *v/t* delegare; **delegation** *of task* delega *f*; (*people*) delegazione *f*

delete [dɪ'liːt] cancellare; **delete key** COMPUT tasto *m* cancella; **deletion** *act* cancellazione *f*; *that deleted* cancellatura *f*

deliberate **1** [dɪ'lɪbərət] *adj* deliberato **2** [dɪ'lɪbəreɪt] *v/i* riflettere; **deliberately** deliberatamente

delicate ['delɪkət] delicato

delicatessen [delɪkə'tesn] gastronomia *f*

delicious [dɪ'lɪʃəs] delizioso, ottimo

delight [dɪ'laɪt] gioia *f*; **delighted** lieto; **delightful** molto piacevole

deliver [dɪ'lɪvə(r)] consegnare; *message* trasmettere; *baby* far nascere; *speech* tenere; **delivery** *of goods, mail* consegna *f*; *of baby* parto *m*; **delivery date** termine *m* di consegna; **delivery van** furgone *m* delle consegne

de luxe [də'lʌks] di lusso

demand [dɪ'mɑːnd] **1** *n* rivendicazione *f*; COM domanda *f*; **in** ~ richiesto **2** *v/t* esigere; (*require*) richiedere; **demanding** *job* impegnativo; *person* esigente

demented [dɪ'mentɪd] demente

demo ['deməʊ] (*protest*) manifestazione *f*; *of video etc* dimostrazione *f*

democracy [dɪ'mɒkrəsɪ] democrazia *f*; **democrat** democratico *m*, -a *f*; **democratic** democratico

demolish [dɪ'mɒlɪʃ] demolire; **demolition** demolizione *f*

demonstrate ['demənstreɪt] **1** *v/t* (*prove*) dimostrare; *machine* fare una dimostrazione di **2** *v/i politically* manifestare; **demonstration** dimostrazione *f*; (*protest*) manifestazione *f*; **demonstrator** (*protester*) manifestante *m/f*

demoralized [dɪ'mɒrəlaɪzd] demoralizzato; **demoralizing** demoralizzante

demote [dɪ'məʊt] retrocedere; MIL degradare

den [den] (*study*) studio *m*

denial [dɪ'naɪəl] negazione *f*

denim ['denɪm] denim *m*; **denims** (*jeans*) jeans *m inv*

Denmark ['denmɑːk] Danimarca *f*

denomination [dɪnɒmɪ'neɪʃn] *of money* banconota *f*; REL confessione *f*

dense [dens] fitto; **density** *of population* densità *f inv*

dent [dent] **1** *n* ammaccatura *f* **2** *v/t* ammaccare

dental ['dentl] *treatment* dentario, dentale; *hospital* dentistico

dented ['dentɪd] ammaccato

dentist ['dentɪst] dentista *m/f*; **dentures** dentiera *f*

Denver boot ['denvə(r)] *Am* ceppo *m* bloccaruote

deny [dɪ'naɪ] negare; *rumour* smentire

deodorant [di:'əʊdərənt] deodorante *m*

depart [dɪ'pɑːt] partire; ~ *from* (*deviate from*) allontanarsi da

department [dɪ'pɑːtmənt] *of university* dipartimento *m*; *of government* ministero *m*; *of store, company* reparto *m*; **Department of State** *Am* Ministero *m* degli esteri; **department store** grande magazzino *m*

departure [dɪ'pɑːtʃə(r)] partenza *f*; (*deviation*) allontanamento *m*; **departure lounge** sala *f* partenze; **departure time** ora *f* di partenza

depend [dɪ'pend] **that ~s** dipende; **it ~s on the weather** dipende dal tempo; **dependable** affidabile; **dependence, dependency** dipendenza *f*; **dependent 1** *n* persona *f* a carico; **a married man with ~s** un uomo sposato con famiglia a carico **2** *adj* dipendente; ~ **children** figli *mpl* a carico

depict [dɪ'pɪkt] raffigurare

deplorable [dɪ'plɔːrəbl] deplorevole; **deplore** deplorare, lamentarsi di

deploy [dɪ'plɔɪ] (*use*) spiegare; (*position*) schierare

deport [dɪ'pɔːt] deportare; **deportation** deportazione *f*

deposit [dɪ'pɒzɪt] **1** *n in bank* versamento *m*, deposito *m*; *of mineral* deposito *m*; *on purchase* acconto *m*; (*against loss, damage*) cauzione *f* **2** *v/t money* versare, depositare; (*put down*) lasciare; *silt, mud* depositare; **deposit account** libretto *m* di risparmio

depot ['depəʊ] (*bus station*) rimessa *f* degli autobus; *for storage* magazzino *m*; *Am* (*train station*) stazione *f* ferroviaria

depreciate [dɪ'priːʃɪeɪt] FIN svalutarsi; **depreciation** FIN svalutazione *f*

depress [dɪ'pres] *person* deprimere; **depressed** depresso; **depressing** deprimente; **depression** depressione *f*

deprivation [deprɪ'veɪʃn] privazione *f*; (*lack: of sleep, food*) carenza *f*; **deprive**: **s.o. of sth** privare qu di qc; **deprived** socialmente svantaggiato

depth [depθ] profondità *f inv*; **in** ~ (*thoroughly*) a fondo

deputy ['depjʊtɪ] vice *m/f inv*; **deputy leader** *of party* vice segretario *m*

derail [dɪ'reɪl]: **be ~ed** *of train* essere deragliato

derelict ['derɪlɪkt] desolato

deride [dɪ'raɪd] deridere; **derision** derisione *f*; **derisory**

amount irrisorio

derivative [dɪˈrɪvətɪv] derivato; **derive** trarre; *be ~d from* of word derivare da

dermatologist [dɜːməˈtɒlədʒɪst] dermatologo *m*, -a *f*

derogatory [dɪˈrɒgətrɪ] peggiorativo

descend [dɪˈsend] **1** *v/t* scendere; *be ~ed from* discendere da **2** *v/i* scendere; *of mood, darkness* calare; **descendant** discendente *m/f*; **descent** discesa *f*; *(ancestry)* discendenza *f*

describe [dɪˈskraɪb] descrivere; **description** descrizione *f*

desegregate [diːˈsegrəgeɪt] eliminare la segregazione in

desert[1] [ˈdezət] *n* deserto *m*

desert[2] [dɪˈzɜːt] **1** *v/t (abandon)* abbandonare **2** *v/i of soldier* disertare

deserted [dɪˈzɜːtɪd] deserto; **deserter** MIL disertore *m*; **desertion** abbandono *m*; MIL diserzione *f*

deserve [dɪˈzɜːv] meritare

design [dɪˈzaɪn] **1** *n* design *m*; *technical* progettazione *f*; *(pattern)* motivo *m* **2** *v/t house, car* progettare; *clothes* disegnare

designate [ˈdezɪgneɪt] *person* designare

designer [dɪˈzaɪnə(r)] designer *m/f inv*; *of building, car, ship* progettista *m/f*; **fashion ~** stilista *m/f*; **designer**

clothes abiti *mpl* firmati

desirable [dɪˈzaɪrəbl] desiderabile; *(advisable)* preferibile; **desire** desiderio *m*

desk [desk] scrivania *f*; *in hotel* reception *f inv*; **desk clerk** receptionist *m/f inv*; **desktop publishing** editoria *f* elettronica

desolate [ˈdesələt] *place* desolato

despair [dɪˈspeə(r)] **1** *n* disperazione *f*; *in ~* disperato **2** *v/i* disperare; **desperate** disperato; *be ~ for sth* morire dalla voglia di qc; **desperation** disperazione *f*

despicable [dɪsˈpɪkəbl] deplorevole; **despise** disprezzare

despite [dɪˈspaɪt] malgrado, nonostante

dessert [dɪˈzɜːt] dolce *m*, dessert *m inv*

destination [destɪˈneɪʃn] destinazione *f*

destiny [ˈdestɪnɪ] destino *m*

destitute [ˈdestɪtjuːt] indigente

destroy [dɪˈstrɔɪ] distruggere; **destroyer** NAUT cacciatorpediniere *m*; **destruction** distruzione *f*; **destructive** distruttivo; *child* scalmanato

detach [dɪˈtætʃ] staccare; **detached** *(objective)* distaccato; **detached house** villetta *f*; **detachment** *(objectivity)* distacco *m*

detail [ˈdiːteɪl] dettaglio *m*; *in*

~ dettagliatamente; **detailed** dettagliato

detain [dɪ'teɪn] trattenere; **detainee** detenuto *m*, -a *f*

detect [dɪ'tekt] rilevare; *anxiety, irony* cogliere; **detection of crime** investigazione *f*; *of smoke etc* rilevamento *m*; **detective** agente *m/f* investigativo; **detector** rilevatore *m*

détente ['deɪtɒnt] POL distensione *f*

deter [dɪ'tɜː(r)] dissuadere

detergent [dɪ'tɜːdʒənt] detergente *m*

deteriorate [dɪ'tɪərɪəreɪt] deteriorarsi

determination [dɪtɜːmɪ'neɪʃn] (*resolution*) determinazione *f*; **determine** (*establish*) determinare; **determined** determinato, deciso

deterrent [dɪ'terənt] deterrente *m*

detest [dɪ'test] detestare; **detestable** detestabile

detour ['diːtʊə(r)] deviazione *f*

◆ **detract from** [dɪ'trækt] *merit, value* sminuire; *enjoyment* rovinare

devaluation [diːvæljʊ'eɪʃn] svalutazione *f*; **devalue** svalutare

devastate ['devəsteɪt] *also fig* devastare

develop [dɪ'veləp] **1** *v/t film, business* sviluppare; *land, site* valorizzare; (*originate*) sco-

prire; *illness* contrarre **2** *v/i* (*grow*) svilupparsi; *~ into* diventare; **developing country** paese *m* in via di sviluppo; **development** sviluppo *m*; *of land, site* valorizzazione *f*; (*origination*) scoperta *f*

device [dɪ'vaɪs] (*tool*) dispositivo *m*

devil ['devl] diavolo *m*

devious ['diːvɪəs] (*sly*) subdolo

devise [dɪ'vaɪz] escogitare

devoid [dɪ'vɔɪd]: **be ~ of** essere privo di

devolution [diːvə'luːʃn] POL decentramento *m*

devote [dɪ'vəʊt] dedicare; **devoted** *son etc* devoto; **devotion** *to a person* attaccamento *m*; *to one's job* dedizione *f*

devour [dɪ'vaʊə(r)] *food, book* divorare

devout [dɪ'vaʊt] devoto; **a ~ Catholic** un cattolico fervente

dew [djuː] rugiada *f*

diabetes [daɪə'biːtiːz] diabete *m*; **diabetic** diabetico *m*, -a *f*

diagnose ['daɪəgnəʊz] diagnosticare; **diagnosis** diagnosi *f inv*

diagonal [daɪ'ægənl] diagonale; **diagonally** diagonalmente

diagram ['daɪəgræm] diagramma *m*

dial ['daɪəl] **1** *n of clock, meter* quadrante *m* **2** *v/i* TELEC

dining room

comporre il numero **3** *v/t* TELEC comporre

dialect ['daɪəlekt] dialetto *m*

'dialling tone, *Am* **'dial tone** segnale *m* di linea libera

dialogue, *Am* **dialog** ['daɪəlɒɡ] dialogo *m*

diameter [daɪ'æmɪtə(r)] diametro *m*

diamond ['daɪəmənd] diamante *m*; (*shape*) losanga *f*; ~**s** *in cards* quadri *mpl*

diaper ['daɪəpə(r)] *Am* pannolino *m*

diaphragm ['daɪəfræm] diaframma *m*

diarrhoea, *Am* **diarrhea** [daɪə'riːə] diarrea *f*

diary ['daɪərɪ] *for thoughts* diario *m*; *for appointments* agenda *f*

dice [daɪs] dado *m*

dictate [dɪk'teɪt] dettare; dic**tator** POL dittatore *m*; dic**tatorship** dittatura *f*

dictionary ['dɪkʃənrɪ] dizionario *m*

die [daɪ] morire

◆ **die down** *of noise, fire* estinguersi; *of storm, excitement* placarsi

◆ **die out** *of custom* scomparire; *of species* estinguersi

diesel ['diːzl] (*fuel*) diesel *m*

diet ['daɪət] **1** *n* dieta *f* **2** *v/i to lose weight* essere a dieta

differ ['dɪfə(r)] differire; (*disagree*) non essere d'accordo; **difference** differenza *f*; (*disagreement*) divergenza *f*; dif**ferent** diverso, different; **differentiate** distinguere; ~ **between** *things* distinguere tra; *people* fare distinzioni tra; **differently** diversamente, differentemente

difficult ['dɪfɪkəlt] difficile; **difficulty** difficoltà *f inv*; **with** ~ a fatica

dig [dɪɡ]) scavare

digest [daɪ'dʒest] *also fig* digerire; **digestion** digestione *f*

digit ['dɪdʒɪt] cifra *f*; **digital** digitale

dignified ['dɪɡnɪfaɪd] dignitoso; **dignity** dignità *f*

dilapidated [dɪ'læpɪdeɪtɪd] rovinato; *house* cadente

dilemma [dɪ'lemə] dilemma *m*

dilute [daɪ'luːt] diluire

dim [dɪm] **1** *adj room* buio; *light* fioco; *outline* indistinto; (*stupid*) idiota; *prospects* vago **2** *v/i of lights* abbassarsi

dime [daɪm] *Am* moneta da dieci centesimi

dimension [daɪ'menʃn] dimensione *f*

diminish [dɪ'mɪnɪʃ] diminuire

din [dɪn] baccano *m*

dine [daɪn] cenare

dinghy ['dɪŋɡɪ] *small yacht* dinghy *m*; *rubber boat* gommone *m*

dining car ['daɪnɪŋ] RAIL vagone *m* ristorante; **dining room** *in house* sala *f* da pranzo; *in hotel* sala *f* ristorante

dinner ['dɪnə(r)] *in the evening* cena *f; at midday* pranzo *m; formal gathering* ricevimento *m;* **dinner jacket** smoking *m inv;* **dinner party** cena *f*

dinosaur ['daɪnəsɔ:(r)] dinosauro *m*

dip [dɪp] **1** *n for food* salsa *f; in road* pendenza *f* **2** *v/i of road* scendere

diploma [dɪ'pləʊmə] diploma *m*

diplomacy [dɪ'pləʊməsɪ] diplomazia *f;* **diplomat** diplomatico *m,* -a *f;* **diplomatic** diplomatico

direct [daɪ'rekt] **1** *adj* diretto **2** *v/t play* mettere in scena; *film* curare la regia di; **could you please ~ me to ...?** mi può per favore indicare la strada per ...?; **direction** direzione *f; of film, play* regia *f;* **~s** (*instructions*), *to a place* indicazioni *fpl; for use* istruzioni *fpl;* **directly** (*straight*) direttamente; (*soon, immediately*) immediatamente; **director** *of company* direttore *m,* -trice *f; of play, film* regista *m/f;* **directory** elenco *m;* TELEC guida *f* telefonica

dirt [dɜ:t] sporco *m,* sporcizia *f;* **dirty 1** *adj* sporco; (*pornographic*) sconcio **2** *v/t* sporcare

disability [dɪsə'bɪlətɪ] handicap *m inv,* invalidità *f inv;* **disabled** handicappato *m,* -a *f;* **the ~** i disabili

disadvantage [dɪsəd'vɑ:ntɪdʒ] svantaggio *m;* **disadvantaged** penalizzato

disagree [dɪsə'gri:] *of person* non essere d'accordo

◆ **disagree with** *of person* non essere d'accordo con; *of food* fare male a

disagreeable [dɪsə'gri:əbl] sgradevole; **disagreement** disaccordo *m;* (*argument*) discussione *f*

disallow [dɪsə'laʊ] *goal* annullare

disappear [dɪsə'pɪə(r)] sparire, scomparire; **disappearance** sparizione *f,* scomparsa *f*

disappoint [dɪsə'pɔɪnt] deludere; **disappointed** deluso; **disappointing** deludente; **disappointment** delusione *f*

disapproval [dɪsə'pru:vl] disapprovazione *f;* **disapprove** disapprovare; **~ of** disapprovare; **disapproving** di disapprovazione

disarm [dɪs'ɑ:m] **1** *v/t* disarmare **2** *v/i* disarmarsi; **disarmament** disarmo *m*

disaster [dɪ'zɑ:stə(r)] disastro *m;* **disastrous** disastroso

disband [dɪs'bænd] **1** *v/t* sciogliere **2** *v/i* sciogliersi

disbelief [dɪsbə'li:f] incredulità *f*

disc [dɪsk] disco *m*

discard [dɪ'skɑ:d] sbarazzarsi di

disciplinary [dɪsɪˈplɪnərɪ] disciplinare; discipline disciplina f

'disc jockey disc jockey m/f inv

disclaim [dɪsˈkleɪm] negare; responsibility declinare

disclose [dɪsˈkləʊs] svelare, rivelare

disco [ˈdɪskəʊ] discoteca f

discomfort [dɪsˈkʌmfət] disagio m; (pain) fastidio m

disconcert [dɪskənˈsɜːt] sconcertare

disconnect [dɪskəˈnekt] (detach) sconnettere; supply, telephones staccare

disconsolate [dɪsˈkɒnsələt] sconsolato

discontent [dɪskənˈtent] malcontento m; discontented scontento

discontinue [dɪskənˈtɪnjuː] interrompere; be a ~d line essere fuori produzione

discotheque [ˈdɪskətek] discoteca f

discount [ˈdɪskaʊnt] sconto m

discourage [dɪsˈkʌrɪdʒ] (dissuade) scoraggiare

discover [dɪsˈkʌvə(r)] scoprire; discovery scoperta f

discredit [dɪsˈkredɪt] screditare

discreet [dɪsˈkriːt] discreto

discrepancy [dɪsˈkrepənsɪ] incongruenza f

discretion [dɪsˈkreʃn] discrezione f

discriminate [dɪsˈkrɪmɪneɪt]: ~ against discriminare; discriminating esigente; discrimination sexual, racial etc discriminazione f

discus [ˈdɪskəs] SP object disco m; event lancio m del disco

discuss [dɪsˈkʌs] discutere; of article trattare di; discussion discussione f

disease [dɪˈziːz] malattia f

disembark [dɪsɪmˈbɑːk] sbarcare

disentangle [dɪsənˈtæŋgl] districare

disfigure [dɪsˈfɪgə(r)] sfigurare; fig deturpare

disgrace [dɪsˈgreɪs] 1 n vergogna f 2 v/t disonorare; disgraceful vergognoso

disgruntled [dɪsˈgrʌntld] scontento

disguise [dɪsˈgaɪz] 1 n travestimento m 2 v/t voice etc camuffare; fear, anxiety dissimulare; ~ o.s. as travestirsi da

disgust [dɪsˈgʌst] 1 n disgusto m 2 v/t disgustare; disgusting disgustoso

dish [dɪʃ] piatto m; for cooking recipiente m

dishearten [dɪsˈhɑːtnɪŋ] demoralizzante

disheveled [dɪˈʃevld] person, appearance arruffato; after effort scompigliato

dishonest [dɪsˈɒnɪst] disonesto; dishonesty disonestà f

dishonor etc Am ☞ **dishonour** etc

dishonour [dɪsˈɒnə(r)] disonore m; **dishonourable** disdicevole

'dishwasher *machine* lavastoviglie f *inv; person* lavapiatti m/f *inv*; **dishwashing liquid** Am detersivo m per i piatti

disillusion [dɪsɪˈluːʒn] disilludere; **disillusionment** disillusione f

disinfect [dɪsɪnˈfekt] disinfettare; **disinfectant** disinfettante m

disinherit [dɪsɪnˈherɪt] diseredare

disintegrate [dɪsˈɪntɪɡreɪt] disintegrarsi; *of marriage, building* andare in pezzi

disinterested [dɪsˈɪntrəstɪd] (*unbiased*) disinteressato

disjointed [dɪsˈdʒɔɪntɪd] sconnesso

disk [dɪsk] disco m; (*diskette*) dischetto m; **disk drive** COMPUT lettore m or drive m *inv* di dischetti; **diskette** dischetto m

dislike [dɪsˈlaɪk] **1** n antipatia f **2** v/t: **I ~ cats** non mi piacciono i gatti

dislocate ['dɪsləkeɪt] lussare

disloyal [dɪsˈlɔɪəl] sleale; **disloyalty** slealtà f

dismal ['dɪzməl] *weather, news* deprimente; *person* (*sad*), *failure* triste; *person* (*negative*) ombroso

dismantle [dɪsˈmæntl] smontare; *organization* demolire

dismay [dɪsˈmeɪ] costernazione f

dismiss [dɪsˈmɪs] *employee* licenziare; *suggestion* scartare; *idea* accantonare; **dismissal** *of employee* licenziamento m

disobedience [dɪsəˈbiːdɪəns] disobbidienza f; **disobedient** disobbidiente; **disobey** disobbidire a

disorder [dɪsˈɔːdə(r)] (*untidiness*) disordine m; (*unrest*) disordini mpl; MED disturbo m

disorganized [dɪsˈɔːɡənaɪzd] disorganizzato

disoriented [dɪsˈɔːrɪəntɪd], **disorientated** [dɪsˈɔːrɪənteɪtɪd] disorientato

disown [dɪsˈəʊn] disconoscere

disparaging [dɪˈspærɪdʒɪŋ] dispregiativo

disparity [dɪˈspærətɪ] disparità f *inv*

dispassionate [dɪˈspæʃənət] spassionato

dispatch [dɪˈspætʃ] (*send*) spedire

disperse [dɪˈspɜːs] *of crowd* disperdersi; *of mist* dissiparsi

display [dɪˈspleɪ] **1** n esposizione f, mostra f; *in shop window* articoli mpl in esposizione; COMPUT visualizzazione f **2** v/t *emotion* manifestare; *at exhibition* esporre;

(*for sale*) esporre in vendita; COMPUT visualizzare

displease [dɪs'pliːs] contrariare; **displeasure** disappunto *m*

disposable [dɪ'spəʊzəbl] usa e getta *inv*; **disposable income** reddito *m* disponibile; **disposal** eliminazione *f*; *of waste* smaltimento *m*; **put sth at s.o.'s** ~ mettere qc a disposizione di qu

◆ **dispose of** [dɪ'spəʊz] (*get rid of*) sbarazzarsi di

disposed [dɪ'spəʊzd]: **be ~ to do sth** (*willing*) essere disposto a fare qc; **be well ~ towards** essere ben disposto verso

disprove [dɪs'pruːv] smentire

dispute [dɪ'spjuːt] **1** *n* controversia *f*; *industrial* contestazione *f* **2** *v/t* contestare; (*fight over*) contendersi

disqualification [dɪskwɒlɪfɪ'keɪʃn] squalifica *f*; **disqualify** squalificare

disregard [dɪsrə'gɑːd] **1** *n* mancanza *f* di considerazione **2** *v/t* ignorare

disreputable [dɪs'repjʊtəbl] depravato; *area* malfamato

disrespect [dɪsrə'spekt] mancanza *f* di rispetto; **disrespectful** irriverente

disrupt [dɪs'rʌpt] *train service* creare disagi a; *meeting, class* disturbare; **disruption** *of train service* disagio *m*; *of meeting, class* disturbo *m*

dissatisfaction [dɪssætɪs-'fækʃn] insoddisfazione *f*; **dissatisfied** insoddisfatto

dissident ['dɪsɪdənt] dissidente *m/f*

dissimilar [dɪs'sɪmɪlə(r)] dissimile

dissolute ['dɪsəluːt] *adj* dissoluto

dissolve [dɪ'zɒlv] **1** *v/t substance* sciogliere **2** *v/i of substance* sciogliersi

distance ['dɪstəns] distanza *f*; **in the** ~ in lontananza; **distant** lontano

distaste [dɪs'teɪst] avversione *f*; **distasteful** spiacevole

distinct [dɪ'stɪŋkt] (*clear*) netto; (*different*) distinto; **distinction** (*differentiation*) distinzione *f*; **hotel of** ~ hotel d'eccezione; **distinctive** caratteristico; **distinctly** (*decidedly*) decisamente

distinguish [dɪ'stɪŋgwɪʃ] (*see*) distinguere; ~ **between X and Y** distinguere tra X e Y; **distinguished** (*famous*) insigne; (*dignified*) distinto

distort [dɪ'stɔːt] distorcere

distract [dɪ'strækt] *person* distrarre; *attention* distogliere

distraught [dɪ'strɔːt] affranto

distress [dɪ'stres] **1** *n* sofferenza *f* **2** *v/t* (*upset*) angosciare; **distressing** sconvolgente

distribute [dɪ'strɪbjuːt] distribuire; **distribution** distribuzione f; **distributor** COM distributore m

district ['dɪstrɪkt] quartiere m; **district attorney** Am procuratore m distrettuale

distrust [dɪs'trʌst] diffidenza f

disturb [dɪ'stɜːb] disturbare; **disturbance** (interruption) fastidio m; ~**s** (civil unrest) disordini mpl; **disturbed** turbato; psychologically malato di mente; **disturbing** inquietante

disused [dɪs'juːzd] inutilizzato

ditch [dɪtʃ] **1** n fosso m **2** v/t F boyfriend scaricare F; F car sbarazzarsi di

dive [daɪv] **1** n tuffo m; underwater immersione f; of plane picchiata f; F bar etc bettola f F **2** v/i tuffarsi; underwater fare immersione; of submarine immergersi; of plane scendere in picchiata; **dive off board** tuffatore m, -trice f; underwater sub m/f inv, sommozzatore m, -trice f

diverge [daɪ'vɜːdʒ] divergere

diversification [daɪvɜːsɪfɪ'keɪʃn] COM diversificazione f; **diversify** COM diversificare; **diversion** for traffic deviazione f; to distract attention distogliere m; **diversity** varietà f inv

divert [daɪ'vɜːt] traffic deviare; attention sviare

divide [dɪ'vaɪd] dividere

dividend ['dɪvɪdend] FIN dividendo m

divine [dɪ'vaɪn] REL, F divino

diving ['daɪvɪŋ] from board tuffi mpl; underwater immersione f; **diving board** trampolino m

division [dɪ'vɪʒn] divisione f; of company sezione f

divorce [dɪ'vɔːs] **1** n divorzio m **2** v/t divorziare da **3** v/i divorziare; **divorced** divorziato; **divorcee** divorziato m, -a f

divulge [daɪ'vʌldʒ] divulgare

DIY [diːaɪ'waɪ] (= **do it yourself**) fai da te m inv, bricolage m

dizziness ['dɪzɪnɪs] giramento m di testa, vertigini fpl; **dizzy** stordito; **I feel ~** mi gira la testa

DJ [diː'dʒeɪ] (= **disc jockey**) dj m/f inv; (= **dinner jacket**) smoking m inv

DNA [diːen'eɪ] (= **deoxyribonucleic acid**) DNA m inv (= acido m deossiribonucleico)

do [duː] **1** v/t fare; one's hair farsi; 100mph etc andare a; ~ **the ironing / cooking** stirare / cucinare; **have one's hair done** farsi fare i capelli **2** v/i (be suitable, enough) andare bene; **that will ~!** basta così!; ~ **well** (do a good job) essere bravo; (be in good health) stare bene; of busi-

ness andare bene; **well done!** bravo!; **how ~ you ~?** molto piacere
◆ **do away with** abolire
◆ **do up** (*renovate*) restaurare; (*fasten*) allacciare
◆ **do with: I could do with ...** mi ci vorrebbe ...
◆ **do without 1** *v/i* farne a meno **2** *v/t* fare a meno di

docile ['dəʊsaɪl] docile

dock[1] [dɒk] **1** *n* NAUT bacino *m* **2** *v/i of ship* entrare in porto; *of spaceship* agganciarsi

dock[2] [dɒk] LAW banco *m* degli imputati

doctor ['dɒktə(r)] MED dottore *m*, -essa *f*; **doctorate** dottorato *m*

doctrine ['dɒktrɪn] dottrina *f*

document ['dɒkjʊmənt] documento *m*; **documentary** documentario *m*; **documentation** documentazione *f*

dodge [dɒdʒ] *blow* schivare; *person, issue* evitare; *question* aggirare

dog [dɒg] **1** *n* cane *m* **2** *v/t of bad luck* perseguitare

dogged ['dɒgɪd] accanito

dogma ['dɒgmə] dogma *m*; **dogmatic** dogmatico

'dog-tired F stravolto

do-it-yourself [du:ɪtʃə'self] fai da te *m*

doldrums ['dɒldrəmz]: **be in the ~** *of economy* essere in stallo; *of person* essere giù di corda

doll [dɒl] *toy*, F *woman* bam-

bola *f*

dollar ['dɒlə(r)] dollaro *m*

Dolomites ['dɒləmaɪts] Dolomiti *mpl*

dolphin ['dɒlfɪn] delfino *m*

dome [dəʊm] *of building* cupola *f*

domestic [də'mestɪk] domestico; *news, policy* interno; **domestic flight** volo *m* nazionale

dominant ['dɒmɪnənt] dominante; *member* principale; **dominate** dominare; **domination** dominio *m*; **domineering** autoritario

donate [dəʊ'neɪt] donare; **donation** donazione *f*

donkey ['dɒŋkɪ] asino *m*

donor ['dəʊnə(r)] donatore *m*, -trice *f*

donut ['dəʊnʌt] *Am* bombolone *m*, krapfen *m inv*

doodle ['du:dl] scarabocchiare

doom [du:m] (*fate*) destino *f*; (*ruin*) rovina *f*; **doomed** *project* condannato al fallimento

door [dɔ:(r)] porta *f*; *of car* portiera *f*; **doorbell** campanello *m*; **doorman** usciere *m*; **doorway** vano *m* della porta

dope [dəʊp] (*drugs*) droga *f* leggera; F (*idiot*) cretino *m*, -a *f*

dormant ['dɔ:mənt]: **~ volcano** vulcano *m* inattivo

dormitory ['dɔ:mɪtrɪ] dormitorio *m*; *Am* casa *f* dello studente

dose [dəʊs] dose *f*

dot [dɒt] puntino *m*; *in email address* punto *m*

double ['dʌbl] **1** *n amount* doppio; *(person)* sosia *m inv*; *of film star* controfigura *f* **2** *adj* doppio **3** *adv*: **~ the amount** il doppio della quantità **4** *v/t & v/i* raddoppiare; **double-bass** contrabbasso *m*; **double bed** letto *m* matrimoniale; **doublecheck** ricontrollare; **double-click** cliccare due volte (**on** su); **doublecross** fare il doppio gioco con; **double glazing** doppi vetri *mpl*; **double park** parcheggiare in doppia fila; **double room** camera *f* doppia; **with double bed** camera *f* matrimoniale; **doubles** *in tennis* doppio *msg*

doubt [daʊt] **1** *n* dubbio *m*; **be in ~** essere in dubbio; **no ~** *(probably)* senz'altro **2** *v/t* dubitare di; **doubtful** *look* dubbio; **be ~** *of person* essere dubbioso; **doubtless** senza dubbio

dough [dəʊ] impasto *m*; **doughnut** bombolone *m*, krapfen *m inv*

dove [dʌv] colomba *f*; *fig* pacifista *m/f*

down [daʊn] **1** *adv* (*downwards*) giù; **~ there** laggiù; **£200 ~** *as deposit* un acconto

di £200; **~ south** a sud; **be ~** *of price, rate* essere diminuito; *(not working)* non funzionare; F *(depressed)* essere giù **2** *prep* giù da; *(along)* lungo; **walk ~ a street** percorrere una strada; **down-and-out** senza tetto *m/f inv*; **downhill** in discesa; **go ~** *fig* peggiorare; **downhill skiing** discesa *f* libera; **download** COMPUT **1** *v/t* scaricare **2** *n* scaricamento *m*; **downmarket** di fascia medio-bassa; **down payment** deposito *m*, acconto *m*; **downplay** minimizzare; **downpour** acquazzone *m*; **downright 1** *adj*: **it's a ~ lie** è una bugia bella e buona; **he's a ~ idiot** è un perfetto idiota **2** *adv dangerous etc* assolutamente; **downscale** *Am* di fascia medio-bassa; **downside** *(disadvantage)* contropartita *f*; **downsize** *company* ridimensionare; **the ~ed version** *of car* la versione ridotta; **downstairs** al piano di sotto; **downtown** in centro; **downwards** verso il basso

doze [dəʊz] fare un sonnellino

♦ **doze off** assopirsi

dozen ['dʌzn] dozzina *f*

drab [dræb] *adj* scialbo

draft [drɑːft] *of document* bozza *f*; *Am* MIL leva *f*; *Am* ☞ **draught 2** *v/t document* fare una bozza di; *Am* MIL arruolare; **draft dodger** *Am* MIL renitente *m* alla leva

drag [dræg] **1** *v/t* (*pull*) trascinare; (*search*) dragare **2** *v/i* of time non passare mai; of show, film trascinarsi

drain [dreɪn] **1** *n* (*pipe*) tubo *m* di scarico; under street tombino *m* **2** *v/t* water fare colare; oil fare uscire; vegetables scolare; land drenare; glass, tank svuotare; (*exhaust: person*) svuotare; **drainage** (*drains*) fognatura *f*; of water from soil drenaggio *m*; **drainpipe** tubo *m* di scarico

drama ['drɑːmə] arte *f* drammatica; (*excitement*) dramma *m*; (*play: on TV*) sceneggiato *m*; **dramatic** drammatico; (*exciting*) sorprendente; gesture teatrale; **dramatist** drammaturgo *m*, -a *f*; **dramatize** story adattare; fig drammatizzare

drapes [dreɪps] *Am* tende *fpl*

drastic ['dræstɪk] drastico

draught [drɑːft] of air corrente *f* (d'aria); ~ (*beer*) birra *f* alla spina; **draught beer** birra *f* alla spina; **draughts** game dama *f*; **draughtsman** disegnatore *m* industriale; of plan disegnatore *m*, -trice *f*; **draughty** pieno di correnti d'aria

draw [drɔː] **1** *n* in game pareggio *m*; in lottery estrazione *f*; (*attraction*) attrazione *f* **2** *v/t* picture disegnare; curtain, ti-

rare; in lottery, gun, knife estrarre; (*attract*) attirare; (*lead*) tirare; from bank account ritirare **3** *v/i* disegnare; in game pareggiare

◆ **draw back 1** *v/i* (*recoil*) tirarsi indietro **2** *v/t* hand ritirare; curtains aprire

◆ **draw out** wallet etc estrarre; money from bank ritirare

◆ **draw up 1** *v/t* document redigere; chair accostare **2** *v/i* of vehicle fermarsi

'drawback inconveniente *m*

drawer [drɔː(r)] of desk etc cassetto *m*

drawing ['drɔːɪŋ] disegno *m*; **drawing pin** puntina *f*

drawl [drɔːl] pronuncia *f* strascicata

dread [dred] aver il terrore di; **dreadful** terribile; **dreadfully** F (*extremely*) terribilmente; behave malissimo

dream [driːm] **1** *n* sogno *m* **2** *v/i* sognare; I ~t about you ti ho sognato

◆ **dream up** sognare

dreary ['drɪərɪ] deprimente; (*boring*) noioso

dredge [dredʒ] canal dragare

◆ **dredge up** fig scovare

dregs [dregz] of coffee fondi *mpl*; **the ~ of society** la feccia della società

dress [dres] **1** *n* for woman vestito *m*; (*clothing*) abbigliamento *m* **2** *v/t* person vestire; wound medicare; salad condire; **get ~ed** vestirsi **3** *v/i* vestirsi

◆ **dress up** vestirsi elegante; (*wear a disguise*) travestirsi

'**dress circle** prima galleria *f*; **dresser** *in kitchen* credenza *f*; **dressing** *for salad* condimento *m*; *for wound* medicazione *f*; **dressing gown** vestaglia *f*; **dress rehearsal** prova *f* generale

dribble ['dribl] *of person* sbavare; *of water* gocciolare; SP dribblare

dried [draɪd] *fruit etc* essicato

drier ['draɪr] ☞ **dryer**

drift [drɪft] *of snow* accumularsi; *of ship* andare alla deriva; (*go off course*) uscire dalla rotta; *of person* vagabondare

◆ **drift apart** *of couple* allontanarsi (l'uno dall'altro)

drifter ['drɪftə(r)] vagabondo *m*, -a *f*

drill [drɪl] **1** *n* (*tool*) trapano *m*; (*exercise*), MIL esercitazione *f* **2** *v/t tunnel* scavare; ~ **a hole** fare un foro col trapano **3** *v/i for oil* trivellare; MIL addestrarsi

drily ['draɪlɪ] *remark* ironicamente

drink [drɪŋk] **1** *n* bevanda *f*; **non-alcoholic** ~ bibita *f* (analcolica); **a** ~ **of ...** un bicchiere di ... **2** *v/t & v/i* bere

◆ **drink up 1** *v/i* (*finish drink*) finire il bicchiere **2** *v/t* (*drink completely*) finire di bere

drinkable ['drɪŋkəbl] potabi-

le; **drinker** bevitore *m*, -trice *f*; **drinking water** acqua *f* potabile

drip [drɪp] **1** *n* goccia *f*; MED flebo *f inv* **2** *v/i* gocciolare

drive [draɪv] **1** *n outing* giro *m* in macchina; (*driveway*) viale *m*; (*energy*) grinta *f*; COMPUT lettore *m*; (*campaign*) campagna *f* **2** *v/t vehicle* guidare; (*take in car*) portare (in macchina); TECH azionare **3** *v/i* guidare; **I** ~ **to work** vado al lavoro in macchina

◆ **drive in** *nail* piantare

drivel ['drɪvl] sciocchezze *fpl*

driver ['draɪvə(r)] guidatore *m*, -trice *f*, conducente *m/f*; *of train* macchinista *m/f*; COMPUT driver *m inv*; **driver's license** *Am* patente *f* (di guida); **driveway** viale *m*; **driving 1** *n* guida *f* **2** *adj rain* violento; **driving lesson** lezione *f* di guida; **driving licence** patente *f* (di guida); **driving school** scuola *f* guida; **driving test** esame *m* di guida

drizzle ['drɪzl] **1** *n* pioggerella *f* **2** *v/i* piovigginare

drop [drɒp] **1** *n of rain* goccia *f*; *in price, temperature* calo *m* **2** *v/t* far cadere; *from plane* sganciare; (*driveway*) lasciare; *person from car* lasciare; *person from team* scartare; (*stop seeing*) smettere di frequentare; *charges, demand etc* abbandonare; (*give up*) lasciare perdere **3**

v/i cadere; (*decline*) calare

◆ **drop in** passare

◆ **drop off 1** *v/t person, goods* lasciare **2** *v/i* (*fall asleep*) addormentarsi; (*decline*) calare

◆ **drop out** *from competition, school* ritirarsi

drought [draʊt] siccità *f inv*

drown [draʊn] annegare

drowsy ['draʊzɪ] sonnolento

drug [drʌg] **1** *n* droga *f*; **be on ~s** drogarsi **2** *v/t* drogare; **drug addict** tossicodipendente *m/f*; **drug dealer** spacciatore *m*, -trice *f* (di droga); **druggist** *Am* farmacista *m/f*; **drugstore** *Am* negozio-bar che vende articoli vari, inclusi medicinali; **drug trafficking** traffico *m* di droga

drum [drʌm] MUS tamburo *m*; (*container*) bidone *m*; **~s** in pop music batteria *f*; **drummer** batterista *m/f*; in brass band percussionista *m/f*; **drumstick** MUS bacchetta *f*

drunk [drʌŋk] **1** *n* ubriacone *m*, -a *f* **2** *adj* ubriaco; **get ~** ubriacarsi; **drunk driving** guida *f* in stato di ebbrezza

dry [draɪ] **1** *adj* secco **2** *v/t & v/i* asciugare; **dry-clean** pulire *or* lavare a secco; **dry cleaner** tintoria *f*; **dryer** machine asciugatrice *f*

dual ['dju:əl] doppio; **dual carriageway** carreggiata *f* a due corsie

dub [dʌb] movie doppiare

dubious ['dju:bɪəs] equivoco; (*having doubts*) dubbioso

duchess ['dʌtʃɪs] duchessa *f*

duck [dʌk] **1** *n* anatra *f* **2** *v/i* piegarsi

dud [dʌd] F (*false bill*) falso *m*

due [dju:] dovuto; **the rent is ~ tomorrow** domani scade la rata dell'affitto

duke [dju:k] duca *m*

dull [dʌl] weather grigio; sound, pain sordo; (*boring*) noioso

duly ['dju:lɪ] (*as expected*) come previsto; (*properly*) debitamente

dumb [dʌm] (*mute*) muto; *Am* F (*stupid*) stupido

dummy ['dʌmɪ] for clothes manichino *m*; for baby succhiotto *m*

dump [dʌmp] **1** *n* for rubbish discarica *f*; (*unpleasant place*) postaccio *m* **2** *v/t* (*deposit*) lasciare; (*dispose of*) scaricare; waste sbarazzarsi di

dune [dju:n] duna *f*

duplex (**apartment**) ['du:pleks] appartamento *m* su due piani

duplicate ['dju:plɪkət] duplicato *m*

durable ['djʊərəbl] material resistente

during ['djʊərɪŋ] durante

dusk [dʌsk] crepuscolo *m*

dust [dʌst] **1** *n* polvere *f* **2** *v/t* spolverare; **dustbin** bidone *m* della spazzatura; **duster**

straccio m (per spolverare); **dustpan paletta** f; **dusty table** impolverato; **road** polveroso

Dutch [dʌtʃ] **1** adj olandese **2** n language olandese m; **the** ~ gli Olandesi

duty ['djuːtɪ] dovere m; on goods tassa f doganale, dazio m; **be on** ~ essere di servizio; **duty free** duty free inv

DVD [diːviː'diː] (= **digital versatile disk**) DVD m inv

dwarf [dwɔːf] **1** n nano m, -a f

2 v/t fare scomparire

dwindle ['dwɪndl] diminuire

dye [daɪ] **1** n tintura f; for food colorante m **2** v/t colorare, tingere

dying ['daɪɪŋ] morente; tradition in via di disparizione

dynamic [daɪ'næmɪk] dinamico; **dynamism** dinamismo m

dynasty ['dɪnəstɪ] dinastia f

dyslexic [dɪs'leksɪk] **1** adj dislessico **2** n dislessico m, -a f

E

each [iːtʃ] **1** adj ogni **2** adv ciascuno; **they're £1.50** ~ costano £1,50 ciascuno **3** pron ciascuno m, -a f, ognuno m, -a f; ~ **other** l'un l'altro m, l'una l'altra f; **we know** ~ **other** ci conosciamo

eager ['iːgə(r)] entusiasta; **be** ~ **to do sth** essere ansioso di fare qc; **eagerly** ansiosamente; **eagerness** smania f

eagle ['iːgl] aquila f; **eagle-eyed**: **be** ~ **eyed** avere l'occhio di falco

ear[1] [ɪə(r)] orecchio m

ear[2] [ɪə(r)] of corn spiga f

'earache mal m d'orecchi

early ['ɜːlɪ] **1** adj (not late) primo; arrival anticipato; (farther back in time) antico; ~ **October** inizio ottobre; ~ **at an** ~ **age** in giovane età; **let's**

have an ~ **supper** ceniamo presto **2** adv (not late) presto; (ahead of time) in anticipo; **early bird** (early riser) persona f mattiniera

earmark ['ɪəmɑːk] riservare

earn [ɜːn] guadagnare; interest fruttare; holiday, respect etc guadagnarsi

earnest ['ɜːnɪst] serio

earnings ['ɜːnɪŋz] guadagno m

'earphones cuffie fpl (d'ascolto); **earring** orecchino m; **earshot**: **within** ~ a portata d'orecchio; **out of** ~ fuori dalla portata d'orecchio

earth [ɜːθ] **1** n also ELEC terra f **2** v/t ELEC mettere a terra; **earthenware** terracotta f; **earthly** terreno; **it's no** ~

use ... F è perfettamente
inutile ...; **earthquake** terremoto *m*; **earth-shattering**
sconvolgente

ease [i:z] **1** *n* facilità *f*; *feel at
~* sentirsi a proprio agio **2** *v/t*
(*relieve*) it will ... *my
mind* mi darà sollievo **3** *v/i of
pain* alleviarsi

♦ **ease off 1** *v/t* (*remove*) togliere con cautela **2** *v/i of
pain, rain* diminuire

easel ['i:zl] cavalletto *m*

easily ['i:zəlɪ] facilmente; (*by
far*) di gran lunga

east [i:st] **1** *n* est *m* **2** *adj*
orientale **3** *adv travel* a est;
~ of a est di

Easter ['i:stə(r)] Pasqua *f*;
Easter Day il giorno *or* la
domenica di Pasqua; **Easter
egg** uovo *m* di Pasqua

easterly ['i:stəlɪ]: *~ wind* vento *m* dell'est; *in an ~ direction* verso est

Easter 'Monday lunedì *m inv*
di Pasqua, Pasquetta *f*

eastern ['i:stən] orientale

Easter 'Sunday il giorno *or*
la domenica di Pasqua

eastward ['i:stwəd] verso est

easy ['i:zɪ] facile; (*relaxed*)
tranquillo; **easy chair** poltrona *f*; **easy-going**: *he's
very ~* gli va bene quasi tutto

eat [i:t] mangiare

♦ **eat out** mangiare fuori

eatable ['i:təbl] commestibile; *lunch, dish* mangiabile

eavesdrop ['i:vzdrɒp]: *~ on*

s.o. origliare qu

ebb [eb] *of tide* rifluire

e-book ['i:bʊk] e-book *m inv*,
libro *m* elettronico; **e-busi-
ness** e-commerce *m*, commercio *m* elettronico

eccentric [ɪk'sentrɪk] **1** *adj*
eccentrico **2** *n* eccentrico
m, -a f; **eccentricity** eccen-
tricità *f inv*

echo ['ekəʊ] **1** *n* eco *f* **2** *v/i* risuonare **3** *v/t words* ripetere;
views condividere

eclipse [ɪ'klɪps] **1** *n* eclissi *f
inv* **2** *v/t fig* eclissare

ecofriendly ['i:kəʊfrendlɪ]
ecologico

ecological [i:kə'lɒdʒɪkl] ecologico; **ecologically** ecolo-
gicamente; **ecologically
friendly** ecologico; **ecolo-
gist** ecologista *m/f*; **ecology**
ecologia *f*

economic [i:kə'nɒmɪk] economico, **economical**
(*cheap*) economico; (*thrifty*)
parsimonioso; **economics**
science economia *f*; *financial
aspects* aspetti *mpl* economici; **economist** economista
m/f; **economize** risparmiare, fare economia

♦ **economize on** risparmiare su

economy [ɪ'kɒnəmɪ] economia *f*; **economy class** classe
f economica

ecosystem ['i:kəʊsɪstm] ecosistema *m*; **ecotourism** agriturismo *m*

ecstasy ['ekstəsı] estasi *f inv*; **ecstatic** in estasi

eczema ['eksmə] eczema *m*

edge [edʒ] **1** *n of knife* filo *m*; *of table, seat, lawn* bordo *m*; *of road* ciglio *m*; *of cliff* orlo *m*; **on ~** teso **2** *v/i (move slowly)* muoversi con cautela; **edgeways:** *I couldn't get a word in* **~** non sono riuscito a piazzare una parola; **edgy** teso

edible ['edɪbl] commestibile

edit ['edɪt] *text* rivedere; *prepare for publication* curare; *newspaper* dirigere; *TV program, film* montare; COMPUT editare; **edition** edizione *f*; **editor** *of text* revisore *m*; *of publication* curatore *m*, *-trice f*; *of newspaper* direttore *m*, *-trice*; *of TV program* responsabile *m/f* del montaggio; *of film* tecnico *m* del montaggio; **editorial 1** *adj* editoriale; **the ~ staff** la redazione **2** *n* editoriale *m*

educate ['edjukeɪt] *child* istruire; *consumers* educare; **he was ~d at …** ha studiato a …; **educated** istruito; **education** istruzione *f*; **the ~ system** la pubblica istruzione; **educational** didattico; *(informative)* istruttivo

eerie ['ɪərɪ] inquietante

effect [ɪ'fekt] effetto *m*; **effective** efficace; *(striking)* d'effetto

effeminate [ɪ'femɪnət] effeminato

efficiency [ɪ'fɪʃənsɪ] efficienza *f*; *of machine* rendimento *m*; **efficient** efficiente; *machine* ad alto rendimento; **efficiently** con efficienza

effort ['efət] sforzo *m*; **effortless** facile

e.g. [i:'dʒi:] ad *or* per esempio

egg [eg] uovo *m*; **eggcup** portauovo *m inv*; **egghead** F intellettualoide *m/f*; **eggplant** *Am* melanzana *f*

ego ['i:gəʊ] ego *m*; **egocentric** egocentrico; **egoism** egoismo *m*; **egoist** egoista *m/f*

eiderdown ['aɪdədaʊn] *(quilt)* piumino *m*

eight [eɪt] otto; **eighteen** diciotto; **eighteenth** diciottesimo; **eighth** ottavo; **eighth note** *Am* MUS croma *f*; **eightieth** ottantesimo; **eighty** ottanta

either ['aɪðə(r)] **1** *adj* l'uno o l'altro; *(both)* entrambi *pl* **2** *pron* l'uno o l'altro *m*, l'una o l'altra *f* **3** *adv* neppure, nemmeno; *I won't go* **~** non vado nemmeno *or* neppure io **4** *conj:* **~** *my mother or my sister* mia madre o mia sorella; **he doesn't like ~ wine or beer** non gli piacciono né il vino, né la birra

eject [ɪ'dʒekt] **1** *v/t* espellere **2** *v/i from plane* eiettarsi

♦ **eke out** [i:k] usare con parsimonia; *grant etc* arrotondare; *eke out a living* tirare avanti

el [el] *Am* ferrovia *f* sopraelevata

elaborate 1 [ɪˈlæbərət] *adj* elaborato **2** [ɪˈlæbəreit] *v/i* fornire particolari

elapse [ɪˈlæps] trascorrere

elastic [ɪˈlæstik] **1** *adj* elastico **2** *n* elastico *m*; elasticità *f* elasticizzato; **elastic band** elastico *m*

Elastoplast® [ɪˈlæstəpla:st] cerotto *m*

elated [ɪˈleitid] esultante; **elation** esultanza *f*

elbow [ˈelbəu] gomito *m*

elder [ˈeldə(r)] **1** *adj* maggiore **2** *n* maggiore *m/f*; **elderly 1** *adj* anziano; **2** *npl* **the ~ gli** anziani; **eldest 1** *adj* maggiore **2** *n* maggiore *m/f*

elect [ɪˈlekt] eleggere; **elected** eletto; **election** elezione *f*; **election campaign** campagna *f* elettorale; **election day** giorno *m* delle elezioni; **electorate** elettorato *m*

electric [ɪˈlektrik] *also fig* elettrico; **electrical** elettrico; **electric chair** sedia *f* elettrica; **electrician** elettricista *m/f*; **electricity** elettricità *f*; **electrify** elettrificare; *fig* elettrizzare

electrocute [ɪˈlektrəkju:t] fulminare

electron [ɪˈlektrɒn] elettrone *m*; **electronic** elettronico;

electronics elettronica *f*

elegance [ˈeligəns] eleganza *f*; **elegant** elegante

element [ˈelimənt] elemento *m*; **elementary** elementare; **elementary school** *Am* scuola *f* elementare

elephant [ˈelifənt] elefante *m*

elevate [ˈeliveit] elevare; **elevated railroad** *Am* ferrovia *f* sopraelevata; **elevation** (*altitude*) altitudine *f*; **elevator** *Am* ascensore *m*

eleven [ɪˈlevn] undici; **eleventh** undicesimo

eligible [ˈelidʒəbl]: **be ~ to do sth** avere il diritto di fare qc

eliminate [ɪˈlimineit] eliminare; **elimination** eliminazione *f*

elite [eiˈli:t] **1** *n* elite *f inv* **2** *adj* elitario

eloquence [ˈeləkwəns] eloquenza *f*; **eloquent** eloquente

else [els]: *anything ~* qualcos'altro; *nothing ~* nient'altro; *nobody ~* nessun altro; *everyone ~ is going* tutti gli altri vanno; *someone ~* qualcun altro; *something ~* qualcos'altro; *let's go somewhere ~* andiamo da qualche altra parte; *or ~* altrimenti; *elsewhere* altrove

elude [ɪˈlu:d] sfuggire a; **elusive** *person* difficile da trovare; *quality* raro

emaciated [ɪˈmeisieitid] emaciato

e-mail ['i:meɪl] **1** *n* e-mail *m inv* **2** *v/t person* mandare un e-mail a; *text* mandare per e-mail; **e-mail address** indirizzo *m* e-mail

emancipation [ɪmænsɪ'peɪʃn] emancipazione *f*

embalm [ɪm'bɑ:m] imbalsamare

embankment [ɪm'bæŋkmənt] *of river* argine *m*; RAIL massicciata *f*

embargo [em'bɑ:gəʊ] embargo *m inv*

embark [ɪm'bɑ:k] imbarcarsi

embarrass [ɪm'bærəs] imbarazzare; **embarrassed** imbarazzato; **embarrassing** imbarazzante; **embarrassment** imbarazzo *m*

embassy ['embəsɪ] ambasciata *f*

embezzle [ɪm'bezl] appropriarsi indebitamente di; **embezzlement** appropriazione *f* indebita

emblem ['embləm] emblema *f*

embodiment [ɪm'bɒdɪmənt] incarnazione *f*; **embody** incarnare

embrace [ɪm'breɪs] **1** *n* abbraccio *m* **2** *v/t* (*hug, include*) abbracciare **3** *v/i of two people* abbracciarsi

embroider [ɪm'brɔɪdə(r)] ricamare; *fig* ricamare su

embryo ['embrɪəʊ] embrione *m*; **embryonic** *fig* embrionale

emerald ['emərəld] smeraldo *m*; *colour* verde *m* smeraldo

emerge [ɪ'mɜ:dʒ] (*appear*) emergere; **it has ~d that ...** è emerso che ...

emergency [ɪ'mɜ:dʒənsɪ] emergenza *f*; **emergency exit** uscita *f* di sicurezza; **emergency landing** atterraggio *m* di fortuna; **emergency services** servizi *mpl* di soccorso

emigrant ['emɪgrənt] emigrante *m/f*; **emigrate** emigrare; **emigration** emigrazione *f*

Eminence ['emɪnəns]: REL **His ~** Sua Eminenza; **eminent** eminente

emission [ɪ'mɪʃn] *of gases* emanazione *f*; **emit** *heat, gases* emanare; *light, smoke* emettere; *smell* esalare

emotion [ɪ'məʊʃn] emozione *f*; **emotional** *problems, development* emozionale; (*causing emotion*) commovente; (*showing emotion*) commosso

emperor ['empərə(r)] imperatore *m*

emphasis ['emfəsɪs] enfasi *f*; *on word* rilievo *m*; **emphasize** enfatizzare; *word* dare rilievo a; **emphatic** enfatico

empire ['empaɪə(r)] impero *m*

employ [ɪm'plɔɪ] dare lavoro a; (*take on*) assumere; (*use*) impiegare; **employee** dipendente *m/f*; **employer** datore *m*, -trice *f* di lavoro; **employment** occupazione *f*; *(work)* impiego *m*

emptiness ['emptinis] vuoto *m*; **empty 1** *adj* vuoto **2** *v/t* vuotare **3** *v/i* of room, street svuotarsi

emulate ['emjʊleɪt] emulare

enable [ɪ'neɪbl] *person* permettere a; *thing* permettere

enchanting [ɪn'tʃɑːntɪŋ] incantevole

encircle [ɪn'sɜːkl] circondare

enclose [ɪn'kləʊz] *in letter* allegare; *area* recintare; **enclosure** *with letter* allegato *m*

encore ['ɒŋkɔː(r)] bis *m inv*

encounter [ɪn'kaʊntə(r)] **1** *n* incontro *m* **2** *v/t* incontrare

encourage [ɪn'kʌrɪdʒ] incoraggiare; **encouragement** incoraggiamento *m*; **encouraging** incoraggiante

encyclopedia [ɪnsaɪklə'piːdɪə] enciclopedia *f*

end [end] **1** *n* (*conclusion, purpose*) fine *m*; (*extremity*) estremità *f inv*; **in the ~** alla fine **2** *v/t* terminare **3** *v/i* finire

♦ **end up** finire

endanger [ɪn'deɪndʒə(r)] mettere in pericolo; **endangered species** specie *f* in via d'estinzione

endeavour *Am* **endeavor** [ɪn'devə(r)] **1** *n* tentativo *m* **2** *v/t* tentare

endemic [en'demɪk] endemico

ending ['endɪŋ] finale *m*; GRAM desinenza *f*; **endless** interminabile

endorse [en'dɔːs] *candidacy* appoggiare; *product* fare pubblicità a; **endorsement** *of candidacy* appoggio *m*; *of product* pubblicità *f*

end 'product prodotto *m* finale

endurance [ɪn'djʊərəns] resistenza *f*; **endure 1** *v/t* sopportare **2** *v/i* (*last*) resistere; **enduring** durevole

end-'user utente *m* finale

enemy ['enəmɪ] nemico *m*, -a *f*

energetic [enə'dʒetɪk] energico; **energy** energia *f*; **energy supply** rifornimento *m* di energia elettrica

enforce [ɪn'fɔːs] far rispettare

engage [ɪn'geɪdʒ] **1** *v/t* (*hire*) ingaggiare **2** *v/i* TECH ingranare; **engaged:** *to be married* fidanzato; **get ~** fidanzarsi; TELEC occupato; **engagement** (*appointment*) impegno *m*; *to be married* fidanzamento *m*; MIL scontro *m*; **engagement ring** anello *m* di fidanzamento

engine ['endʒɪn] motore *m*; **engineering** ingegneria *f*; **engineer** ingegnere *m*; *for sound, software* tecnico *m*; NAUT macchinista *m*

England ['ɪŋglənd] Inghilterra *f*; **English 1** *adj* inglese **2** *n* (*language*) inglese *m*;

***the* ~** gli inglesi; **English Channel** Manica *f*; **English-man** inglese *m*; **English-woman** inglese *f*

engrave [ɪn'ɡreɪv] incidere; **engraving** *(drawing)* stampa *f*; *(design)* incisione *f*

engrossed [ɪn'ɡrəʊst]: **~ in** assorto in

engulf [ɪn'ɡʌlf] avvolgere

enhance [ɪn'hɑːns] accrescere; *performance*, *reputation* migliorare

enigma [ɪ'nɪɡmə] enigma *m*

enjoy [ɪn'dʒɔɪ]: **did you ~ the film?** ti è piaciuto il film?; ***I ~ reading*** mi piace leggere; **~ (your meal)** buon appetito!; **~ o.s.** divertirsi; **enjoyable** piacevole; **enjoyment** piacere *m*, divertimento *m*

enlarge [ɪn'lɑːdʒ] ingrandire; **enlargement** ingrandimento *m*

enlighten [ɪn'laɪtn] illuminare

enlist [ɪn'lɪst] MIL arruolarsi

enmity ['enmɪtɪ] inimicizia *f*

enormous [ɪ'nɔːməs] enorme; **enormously** enormemente

enough [ɪ'nʌf] **1** *adj* sufficiente, abbastanza *inv* **2** *pron* abbastanza; **will £50 be ~?** saranno sufficienti £50?; **that's ~!** basta! **3** *adv* abbastanza; **strangely ~** per quanto strano

enquire [ɪn'kwaɪə(r)] chiedere informazioni, informarsi

enrol, *Am* **enroll** [ɪn'rəʊl] iscriversi

en suite (bathroom) ['ɒn-swiːt] bagno *m* in camera

ensure [ɪn'ʃʊə(r)] assicurare

entail [ɪn'teɪl] comportare

entangle [ɪn'tæŋɡl] *in rope* impigliare

enter ['entə(r)] **1** *v/t room*, *house* entrare in; *competition* iscriversi a; COMPUT inserire **2** *v/i* entrare; *in competition* iscriversi **3** *n* COMPUT invio *m*

enterprise ['entəpraɪz] *(initiative)* intraprendenza *f*; *(venture)* impresa *f*; **enterprising** intraprendente

entertain [entə'teɪn] *(amuse)* intrattenere; *(consider: idea)* considerare; **entertainer** artista *m/f*; **entertaining** divertente; **entertainment** divertimento *m*

enthusiasm [ɪn'θjuːzɪæzm] entusiasmo *m*; **enthusiast** appassionato *m*, -a *f*; **enthusiastic** entusiasta; **enthusiastically** con entusiasmo

entire [ɪn'taɪə(r)] intero; **entirely** interamente

entitle [ɪn'taɪtl] dare il diritto a; **be ~d to** avere il diritto di fare qc

entrance ['entrəns] entrata *f*, ingresso *m*; THEA entrata *f* in scena

entranced [ɪn'trɑːnst] incantato

'entrance exam(ination)

erosion

esame *m* di ammissione

entrant ['entrənt] concorrente *m/f*

entrepreneur [ɒntrəprə'nɜ:] imprenditore *m*, -trice *f*; **entrepreneurial** imprenditoriale

entrust [in'trʌst] affidare

entry ['entri] (*way in*) entrata *f*; *in diary* annotazione *f*; *in accounts, dictionary* voce *f*; **entryphone** citofono *m*

envelop [in'veləp] avviluppare

envelope ['envələup] busta *f*

enviable ['enviəbl] invidiabile; **envious** invidioso; **be ~ of s.o.** essere invidioso di qu

environment [in'vaiərənmənt] ambiente *m*; **environmental** ambientale; **environmentalist** ambientalista *m/f*; **environmentally friendly** ecologico; **environmental protection** tutela *f* dell'ambiente; **environs** dintorni *mpl*

envisage [in'vizidʒ] prevedere

envoy ['envoi] inviato *m*, -a *f*

envy ['envi] **1** *n* invidia *f* **2** *v/t*: **~ s.o. sth** invidiare qc a qu

epic ['epik] **1** *n* epopea *f* **2** *adj journey* mitico

epicentre, *Am* **epicenter** ['episentr] epicentro *m*

epidemic [epi'demik] epidemia *f*

episode ['episəud] episodio *m*

epitaph ['epita:f] epitaffio *m*

epoch ['i:pɒk] epoca *f*

equal ['i:kwl] **1** *adj* uguale **2** *n*: **be the ~ of** essere equivalente a; **treat s.o. as his ~** trattare qualcuno allo stesso *3* *v/t* (*be as good as*) uguagliare; **equality** uguaglianza *f*, parità *f*; **equalize 1** *v/t* uniformare **2** *v/i* SP pareggiare; **equalizer** SP gol *m inv* del pareggio; **equally** ugualmente; **equal rights** parità *f* di diritti

equation [i'kweiʒn] MATH equazione *f*

equator [i'kweitə(r)] equatore *m*

equip [i'kwip] equipaggiare; **equipment** equipaggiamento *m*; *electrical, electronic* apparecchiature *fpl*

equity ['ekwəti] FIN capitale *m* azionario

equivalent [i'kwivələnt] **1** *adj* equivalente **2** *n* equivalente *m*

era ['iərə] era *f*

eradicate [i'rædikeit] sradicare

erase [i'reiz] cancellare; **eraser** gomma *f* (da cancellare)

erect [i'rekt] **1** *adj* eretto **2** *v/t* erigere; **erection** erezione *f*

ergonomic [ɜ:gəʊ'nɒmik] ergonomico

erode [i'rəud] erodere; *fig* intaccare; **erosion** erosione *f*; *fig* diminuzione *f* erotic [ɪˈrɒtɪk] erotico

errand [ˈerənd] commissione f

erratic [ɪˈrætɪk] irregolare

error [ˈerə(r)] errore m; **error message** COMPUT messaggio m di errore

erupt [ɪˈrʌpt] of volcano eruttare; of violence esplodere; of person dare in escandescenze; **eruption** of volcano eruzione f; of violence esplosione f

escalate [ˈeskəleɪt] of costs aumentare; of war intensificarsi; **escalation** escalation f inv; **escalator** scala f mobile

escape [ɪˈskeɪp] 1 n of prisoner, animal, gas fuga f 2 v/i of prisoner, animal scappare, fuggire; of gas fuoriuscire

escort 1 [ˈeskɔːt] n accompagnatore m, -trice f; (guard) scorta f 2 [ɪˈskɔːt] v/t socially accompagnare; act as guard to scortare

especially [ɪˈspeʃlɪ] specialmente

espionage [ˈespɪənɑːʒ] spionaggio m

espresso (coffee) [esˈpresəʊ] espresso m

essay [ˈeseɪ] saggio m; in school tema m

essential [ɪˈsenʃl] essenziale

establish [ɪˈstæblɪʃ] company fondare; (create, determine) stabilire; **establishment** firm azienda f; restaurant locale m

estate [ɪˈsteɪt] land tenuta f; of dead person patrimonio m; **estate agent** agente m/f immobiliare; **estate car** giardiniera f

esthetic Am ☞ **aesthetic**

estimate [ˈestɪmət] 1 n stima f, valutazione f; COM preventivo m 2 v/t stimare

estuary [ˈestjʊərɪ] estuario m

etc [etˈsetrə] (= **et cetera**) ecc. (= eccetera)

eternal [ɪˈtɜːnl] eterno; **eternity** eternità f inv

ethical [ˈeθɪkl] etico; **ethics** etica f

ethnic [ˈeθnɪk] etnico; **ethnic minority** minoranza f etnica

e-ticket [ˈiːtɪkɪt] biglietto m acquistato su Internet

EU [iːˈjuː] (= **European Union**) UE f (= Unione europea)

euphemism [ˈjuːfəmɪzm] eufemismo m

euro [ˈjʊərəʊ] euro m inv; **Euro MP** eurodeputato m, -a f

Europe [ˈjʊərəp] Europa f; **European 1** adj europeo 2 n europeo m, -a f; **European Parliament** Parlamento m europeo; **European Union** Unione f europea

euthanasia [juːθəˈneɪzɪə] eutanasia f

evacuate [ɪˈvækjʊeɪt] evacuare

evade [ɪˈveɪd] eludere; taxes evadere

exceed

evaluate [ɪˈvæljʊeɪt] valutare; **evaluation** valutazione *f*

evaporate [ɪˈvæpəreɪt] evaporare; *of confidence* svanire; **evaporation** evaporazione *f*

evasion [ɪˈveɪʒn] elusione *f*; *of taxes* evasione *f*; **evasive** evasivo

eve [iːv] vigilia *f*

even [ˈiːvn] **1** *adj* (*regular*) omogeneo; *breathing* regolare; *surface* piano; (*number*) pari *inv*; *players, game* alla pari; **get ~ with ...** farla pagare a ... **2** *adv* persino; **~ bigger** ancora più grande; **not ~** nemmeno, neppure; **~ so** nonostante questo; **~ if** anche se **3** *v/t:* **~ the score** pareggiare

evening [ˈiːvnɪŋ] sera *f*; **in the ~** di sera; **this ~** stasera; **good ~** buona sera; **evening class** corso *m* serale; **evening dress** *for woman* vestito *m* da sera; *for man* abito *m* scuro

evenly [ˈiːvnlɪ] (*regularly*) in modo omogeneo; *breathe* regolarmente

event [ɪˈvent] evento *m*, avvenimento *m*; SP prova *f*; **eventful** movimentato

eventually [ɪˈventjʊəlɪ] finalmente, alla fine

ever [ˈevə(r)] mai; **have you been to ...?** sei mai stato in ...?; **for ~** per sempre; **as ~** come sempre; **~ since he**

left da quando è partito; **everlasting** eterno

every [ˈevrɪ] ogni; **~ other day** un giorno sì, uno no; **~ now and then** ogni tanto; **everybody** tutti; **everyday** di tutti i giorni; **everyone** tutti *pl*; **everything** tutto; **everywhere** dovunque, dappertutto; (*wherever*) dovunque

evict [ɪˈvɪkt] sfrattare

evidence [ˈevɪdəns] prova *f*; **give ~** testimoniare; **evident** evidente; **evidently** evidentemente

evil [ˈiːvl] **1** *adj* cattivo **2** *n* male *m*

evolution [iːvəˈluːʃn] evoluzione *f*; **evolve** evolvere

ex [eks] F *wife / husband* ex *m/f inv*

exact [ɪgˈzækt] esatto; **exacting** *task* impegnativo; *employer* esigente; *standards* rigido; **exactly** esattamente

exaggerate [ɪgˈzædʒəreɪt] esagerare; **exaggeration** esagerazione *f*

exam [ɪgˈzæm] esame *m*; **examination** esame *m*; *of patient* visita *f*; **examine** esaminare; *patient* visitare

example [ɪgˈzɑːmpl] esempio *m*; **for ~** ad *or* per esempio

excavate [ˈekskəveɪt] (*dig*) scavare; *of archaeologist* riportare alla luce; **excavation** scavo *m*

exceed [ɪkˈsiːd] (*be more than*) eccedere; superare;

(*go beyond*) oltrepassare, superare; **exceedingly** estremamente

excel [ɪk'sel] **1** *v/i* eccellere; ~ **at** eccellere in **2** *v/t*: ~ **o.s.** superare se stesso; **excellence** eccellenza *f*; **excellent** eccellente

except [ɪk'sept] eccetto; ~ **for** fatta eccezione per; **exceptional** eccezionale; **exceptionally** (*extremely*) eccezionalmente; **exception** eccezione *f*

excerpt ['eksɜːpt] estratto *m*

excess [ɪk'ses] **1** *n* eccesso *m* **2** *adj* in eccesso; **excess baggage** eccedenza *f* di bagaglio; **excessive** eccessivo

exchange [ɪks'tʃeɪndʒ] **1** *n* scambio *m* **2** *v/t* cambiare (**for** con); **exchange rate** FIN tasso *m* di cambio

Exchequer [ɪks'tʃekə(r)] tesoro *m*

excite [ɪk'saɪt] (*make enthusiastic*) eccitare; **excited** eccitato; **get** ~ eccitarsi; **excitement** eccitazione *f*; **exciting** eccitante, emozionante

exclaim [ɪk'skleɪm] esclamare; **exclamation** esclamazione *f*; **exclamation mark**, *Am* **exclamation point** punto *m* esclamativo

exclude [ɪk'skluːd] escludere; **excluding** ad esclusione di; **exclusive** esclusivo

excuse 1 [ɪk'skjuːs] *n* scusa *f* **2** [ɪk'skjuːz] *v/t* scusare; ~ **me**

to get attention, interrupting scusami; *to get past* permesso

ex-di'rectory: **be** ~ non comparire sull'elenco telefonico

execute ['eksɪkjuːt] *criminal* giustiziare; *plan* attuare; **execution** *of criminal* esecuzione *f*; *of plan* attuazione *f*; **executive** dirigente *m/f*

exempt [ɪg'zempt]: **be** ~ **from** essere esente da

exercise ['eksəsaɪz] **1** *n* esercizio *m*; MIL esercitazione *f* **2** *v/t muscle* fare esercizio con; *dog* far fare esercizio a; *caution* adoperare **3** *v/i* fare esercizio; **exercise bike** cyclette *f inv*; **exercise book** EDU quaderno *m* di esercizi

exhale [eks'heɪl] esalare

exhaust [ɪg'zɔːst] **1** *n fumes* gas *mpl* di scarico; *pipe* tubo *m* di scappamento **2** *v/t* (*tire*) estenuare; (*use up*) esaurire; **exhausted** (*tired*) esausto; **exhausting** estenuante; **exhaustion** spossatezza *f*; **exhaustive** esauriente; **exhaust pipe** tubo *m* di scappamento

exhibit [ɪg'zɪbɪt] **1** *n in exhibition* oggetto *m* esposto; LAW prova *f* **2** *v/t of artist* esporre; (*give evidence of*) manifestare; **exhibition** esposizione *f*; *of bad behaviour* manifestazione *f*; *of skill* dimostrazione *f*

exhilarating [ɪg'zɪləreɪtɪŋ] emozionante

exile ['eksaɪl] **1** n esilio m; *person* esiliato m, -a f **2** v/t esiliare

exist [ɪg'zɪst] esistere; ~ **on** vivere di; existence esistenza f; **in** ~ esistente; existing attuale

exit ['eksɪt] **1** n uscita f **2** v/i COMPUT uscire

exonerate [ɪg'zɒnəreɪt] scagionare

exorbitant [ɪg'zɔːbɪtənt] esorbitante

exotic [ɪg'zɒtɪk] esotico

expand [ɪk'spænd] **1** v/t espandere **2** v/i espandersi; *of metal* dilatarsi; expanse distesa f; expansion espansione f; *of metal* dilatazione f

expect [ɪk'spekt] **1** v/t aspettare; *(suppose, demand)* aspettarsi **2** v/i: **be ~ing** aspettare un bambino; **I ~ so** immagino di sì; expectant mother donna f in stato interessante; expectation aspettativa f

expedition [ekspɪ'dɪʃn] spedizione f

expel [ɪk'spel] espellere

expendable [ɪk'spendəbl] *person* sacrificabile

expenditure [ɪk'spendɪtʃə(r)] spesa f

expense [ɪk'spens] spesa f; expenses spese fpl; expensive caro

experience [ɪk'spɪərɪəns] **1** n esperienza f **2** v/t *pain, pleasure* provare; *difficulty* incon-

trare; experienced con esperienza

experiment [ɪk'sperɪmənt] **1** n sperimento m **2** v/i fare esperimenti; experimental sperimentale

expert ['ekspɜːt] **1** adj esperto **2** n esperto m, -a f; expertise competenza f

expiration date [ɪkspɪ'reɪʃn] *Am* data f di scadenza; expire scadere; expiry scadenza f; expiry date data f di scadenza

explain [ɪk'spleɪn] spiegare; explanation spiegazione f; explanatory esplicativo

explicit [ɪk'splɪsɪt] *instructions* esplicito; explicitly *state, forbid* esplicitamente

explode [ɪk'spləʊd] **1** v/i *of bomb* esplodere **2** v/t *bomb* fare esplodere

exploit[1] ['eksplɔɪt] n exploit m inv

exploit[2] [ɪk'splɔɪt] v/t *person, resources* sfruttare

exploitation [eksplɔɪ'teɪʃn] sfruttamento m

exploration [eksplə'reɪʃn] esplorazione f; exploratory *surgery* esplorativo; explore *country, possibility etc* esplorare; explorer esploratore m, -trice f

explosion [ɪk'spləʊʒn] *also in population* esplosione f; explosive esplosivo m

export ['ekspɔːt] **1** n esportazione f; *item* prodotto m di esportazione **2** *v/t goods*, COMPUT esportare; **exporter** esportatore *m*, -trice *f*

expose [ɪkˈspəʊz] (*uncover*) scoprire; *scandal, person* denunciare; **exposure** esposizione *f*; *to cold weather* esposizione *f* prolungata al freddo; *of dishonest behaviour* denuncia *f*; PHOT posa *f*

express [ɪkˈspres] **1** *adj* (*fast, explicit*) espresso **2** *n* (*train*) espresso *m* **3** *v/t* esprimere; **expression** espressione *f*; **expressive** espressivo; **expressly** espressamente; **expressway** autostrada *f*

expulsion [ɪkˈspʌlʃn] espulsione *f*

extend [ɪkˈstend] **1** *v/t* estendere; *house, repertoire* ampliare; *runway* prolungare; *contract, visa* prorogare **2** *v/i of garden etc* estendersi; **extension** *to house* annesso *m*; *of contract, visa* proroga *f*; TELEC interno *m*; **extension cable** prolunga *f*; **extensive** ampio; **extent** ampiezza *f*; **to a certain ~** fino a un certo punto

exterior [ɪkˈstɪərɪə(r)] **1** *adj* esterno **2** *n of building* esterno *m*; *of person* aspetto *m* esteriore

exterminate [ɪkˈstɜːmɪneɪt] sterminare

external [ɪkˈstɜːnl] (*outside*) esterno

extinct [ɪkˈstɪŋkt] *species*

estinto; **extinction** *of species* estinzione *f*; **extinguish** spegnere; **extinguisher** estintore *m*

extortion [ɪkˈstɔːʃn] estorsione *f*

extra [ˈekstrə] **1** *n* extra *m inv* **2** *adj* in più; **be ~** (*cost more*) essere a parte **3** *adv* particolarmente

extract¹ [ˈekstrækt] *n* estratto *m*

extract² [ɪkˈstrækt] *v/t* estrarre; *information* estorcere

extraction [ɪkˈstrækʃn] estrazione *f*

extradite [ˈekstrədaɪt] estradare; **extradition** estradizione *f*

extramarital [ekstrəˈmærɪtl] extraconiugale

extraordinary [ɪkˈstrɔːdɪnərɪ] straordinario

extra 'time SP tempi *mpl* supplementari

extravagance [ɪkˈstrævəgəns] stravaganza *f*; **extravagant** *with money* stravagante

extreme [ɪkˈstriːm] **1** *n* estremo *m* **2** *adj* estremo; **extremely** estremamente; **extremist** estremista *m/f*

extrovert [ˈekstrəvɜːt] estroverso *m*, -a *f*

exuberant [ɪgˈzjuːbərənt] esuberante

eye [aɪ] **1** *n* occhio *m* **2** *v/t* scrutare; **eyeball** bulbo *m* oculare; **eyebrow** sopracciglio *m*; **eyecatching** appariscente; **eyeglasses** *Am* occhiali *mpl*; **eyelid** palpebra *f*; **eyeliner** eyeliner *m inv*; **eyeshadow** ombretto *m*;

eyesight vista *f*; **eyesore** pugno *m* in un occhio; **eyewitness** testimone *m/f* oculare

F

fabric ['fæbrık] tessuto *m*
fabulous ['fæbjʊləs] fantastico
façade [fə'sɑːd] facciata *f*
face [feıs] **1** *n* viso *m*, faccia *f*; ~ **to** ~ faccia a faccia; *lose* ~ perdere la faccia **2** *v/t person*, *sea etc* essere di fronte a; *facts* affrontare

◆ **face up to** affrontare
'**facecloth** guanto *m* di spugna; **facelift** lifting *m inv* del viso; **facial** pulizia *f* del viso
facilitate [fə'sılıteıt] facilitare; **facilities** strutture *fpl*
fact [fækt] fatto *m*; *in* ~, *as a matter of* ~ in realtà
faction ['fækʃn] fazione *f*
factor ['fæktə(r)] fattore *m*
factory ['fæktərı] fabbrica *f*
faculty ['fækəltı] facoltà *f inv*
fad [fæd] mania *f* passeggera
fade [feıd] *of colours* sbiadire; *of light* smorzarsi; *of memories* svanire; **faded** *colour*, *jeans* sbiadito
fag [fæg] F *Br* cigarette sigaretta *f*; *Am pej* homosexual finocchio *m*
fail [feıl] **1** *v/i* fallire **2** *v/t test* essere bocciato a; *he never*

~s to write non manca mai di scrivere **2** *n*: *without* ~ con certezza; **failing** difetto *m*; **failure** fallimento *m*
faint [feınt] **1** *adj* vago **2** *v/i* svenire; **faintly** vagamente
fair[1] [feə(r)] *(fun* ~*)* luna park *m inv*; COM fiera *f*
fair[2] [feə(r)] **1** *adj hair* biondo; *complexion* chiaro; *(just)* giusto **2** *adv*: ~ *enough* e va bene
fairly ['feəlı] *treat* giustamente; *(quite)* piuttosto; **fairness** *of treatment* giustizia *f*
fairy ['feərı] fata *f*; **fairy tale** fiaba *f*, favola *f*
faith [feıθ] fede *f*; **faithful** fedele
fake [feık] **1** *n* falso *m* **2** *adj* falso **3** *v/t (forge)* falsificare; *(feign)* simulare
fall[1] [fɔːl] *n Am* autunno *m*
fall[2] [fɔːl] **1** *v/i of person*, *night* cadere; *of prices*, *temperature* calare; ~ *ill* ammalarsi **2** *n of person*, *government* caduta *f*; *in price*, *temperature* calo *m*

◆ **fall back on** ricorrere a
◆ **fall behind** *with work* rimanere indietro
◆ **fall for** *(fall in love with)* in-

namorarsi di; (*be deceived by*) abboccare a

♦ **fall through** *of plans* andare a monte

fallible ['fæləbl] fallibile

falling star ['fɔːlɪŋ] stella *f* cadente

false [fɔːls] falso; **false start** *in race* falsa partenza *f*; **false teeth** dentiera *f*; **falsify** falsificare

fame [feɪm] fama *f*

familiar [fə'mɪljə(r)] familiare; (*intimate*) intimo; **be ~ with sth** conoscere bene qc; **familiarity** *with subject etc* buona conoscenza *f* (**with** di); **familiarize**: **~ o.s. with ...** familiarizzarsi con ...

family ['fæmlɪ] famiglia *f*; **family doctor** medico *m* di famiglia; **family name** cognome *m*; **family planning** pianificazione *f* familiare; **family planning clinic** consultorio *m* per la pianificazione familiare; **family tree** albero *m* genealogico

famine ['fæmɪn] fame *f*

famous ['feɪməs] famoso; **be ~ for ...** essere noto per ...

fan[1] [fæn] *n* (*supporter*) fan *m*/*f*

fan[2] [fæn] **1** *n for cooling: electric* ventilatore *m*; *handheld* ventaglio *m* **2** *v*/*t*: **~ o.s.** farsi aria

fanatical [fə'nætɪkl] fanatico; **fanaticism** fanatismo *m*

'fan belt MOT cinghia *f* della ventola

fancy ['fænsɪ] **1** *adj design* stravagante **2** *n*: **as the ~ takes you** quanto ti va; **take a ~ to s.o.** prendere a benvolere qu **3** *v*/*t* F avere voglia di; **he fancies you** gli piaci; **fancy dress** costume *m*

fantasize ['fæntəsaɪz] fantasticare; **fantastic** (*very good*) fantastico; (*very big*) enorme; **fantasy** fantasia *f*

far [fɑː(r)] lontano; (*much*) molto; **~ away** lontano; **how ~ is it to ...?** quanto dista ...?; **as ~ as the corner** fino all'angolo; **as ~ as I know** per quanto ne so; **you've gone too ~** *in behaviour* sei andato troppo oltre; **so ~ so good** fin qui tutto bene

farce [fɑːs] farsa *f*

fare [feə(r)] *n for travel* tariffa *f*

Far 'East Estremo Oriente *m*

farewell [feə'wel] addio *m*

farfetched [fɑː'fetʃt] inverosimile

farm [fɑːm] fattoria *f*

♦ **farm out** dare in appalto

farmer ['fɑːmə(r)] agricoltore *m*, -trice *f*; **farmhouse** cascina *f*; **farming** agricoltura *f*; **farmworker** bracciante *m*/*f*; **farmyard** cortile *m* di una cascina

far-'off lontano; **farsighted** previdente; *optically* presbite

fart [fɑːt] **1** *n* F scoreggia *f* F, peto *m* **2** *v/i* F scoreggiare F, petare

farther ['fɑːðə(r)] più lontano; **farthest** più lontano

fascinate ['fæsɪneɪt] affascinare; **fascinating** affascinante; **fascination** *with subject* fascino *m*

fascism ['fæʃɪzm] fascismo *m*; **fascist** *n* **1** fascista *m/f* **2** *adj* fascista

fashion ['fæʃn] moda *f*; (*manner*) maniera *f*, modo *m*; **in ~** alla moda; **out of ~** fuori moda; **fashionable** alla moda; **fashionably** alla moda; **fashion-conscious** fanatico della moda; **fashion designer** stilista *m/f*; **fashion show** sfilata *f* di moda

fast[1] [fɑːst] **1** *adj* veloce, rapido; **be ~** *of clock* essere avanti **2** *adv* velocemente; **~ asleep** profondamente addormentato

fast[2] [fɑːst] *n not eating* digiuno *m*

fasten ['fɑːsn] **1** *v/t* chiudere; *dress, seat-belt* allacciare; **~ sth onto sth** attaccare qc a qc **2** *v/i of dress etc* allacciarsi; **fastener** chiusura *f*

'fast food fast food *m*; **fast forward 1** *n on video etc* riavvolgimento *m* rapido **2** *v/i* riavvolgere rapidamente; **fast lane** *on road* corsia *f* di sorpasso; **in the ~** *fig: of life a*

cento all'ora; **fast train** rapido *m*

fat [fæt] **1** *adj* grasso **2** *n* grasso *m*

fatal ['feɪtl] fatale

fatality [fə'tælətɪ] vittima *f*; **fatally**: **~ injured** ferito a morte

fate [feɪt] fato *m*

'fat free privo di grassi

Father ['fɑːðə(r)] padre *m*; **Father Christmas** Babbo *m* Natale; **fatherhood** paternità *f*; **father-in-law** suocero *m*; **fatherly** paterno

fatigue [fə'tiːg] stanchezza *f*

fatten ['fætn] *animal* ingrassare; **fatty 1** *adj* grasso **2** *n* F *person* ciccione *m*, -a *f* F

faucet ['fɔːsɪt] *Am* rubinetto *m*

fault [fɔːlt] *n* (*defect*) difetto *m*; **it's your / my ~** è colpa tua / mia; **find ~ with** criticare; **faultless** impeccabile; **faulty** difettoso

favor *etc Am* ☞ **favour** *etc*

favour ['feɪvə(r)] **1** *n* favore *m*; **do s.o. a ~** fare un favore a qu; **in ~ of** ... a favore di ... **2** *v/t* (*prefer*) preferire, prediligere; **favourable** favorevole; **favourite 1** *n* prediletto *m*, -a *f*; *food* piatto *m* preferito; *in race, competition* favorito *m*, -a *f* **2** *adj* preferito; **favouritism** favoritismo *m*

fax [fæks] **1** *n* fax *m inv* **2** *v/t document* inviare per fax

fear [fɪə(r)] **1** *n* paura *f* **2** *v/t*

avere paura di; **fearless** intrepido; **fearlessly** intrepidamente

feasibility study [fiːzə'bɪlətɪ] studio *m* di fattibilità; **feasible** fattibile

feast [fiːst] banchetto *m*

feat [fiːt] prodezza *f*

feather ['feðə(r)] piuma *f*

feature ['fiːtʃə(r)] **1** *n* on face tratto *m*; of city, building, style caratteristica *f*; in newspaper servizio *m*; film lungometraggio *m*; **make a ~ of ...** mettere l'accento su ... **2** *v/t* of film avere come protagonista; **feature film** lungometraggio *m*

February ['februərɪ] febbraio *m*

federal ['fedərəl] federale; **federation** federazione *f*

fed 'up F: **be ~ with ...** essere stufo di ... F

fee [fiː] tariffa *f*; of lawyer, doctor etc onorario *m*

feeble ['fiːbl] debole

feed [fiːd] nutrire; family mantenere; baby dare da mangiare a; **feedback** riscontro *m*, feedback *m*

feel [fiːl] **1** *v/t* (touch) toccare; (sense) sentire; pain, pleasure sentire; (think) pensare **2** *v/i* sentirsi; **it ~s like silk** sembra seta; **I ~ tired** sono stanco; **how are you ~ing today?** come ti senti oggi?; **do you ~ like a drink?** hai voglia di bere qualcosa?; **I**

don't ~ like it non ne ho voglia

◆ **feel up to** sentirsi in grado di

feeler ['fiːlə(r)] of insect antenna *f*; **feeling** sentimento *m*; (emotion) sensazione *f*; (sensation) sensibilità *f*

feet [fiːt] pl → **foot**

fellow 'citizen concittadino *m*, -a *f*

felony ['felənɪ] delitto *m*

felt [felt] feltro *m*; **felt tip, felt-tip(ped) pen** pennarello *m*

female ['fiːmeɪl] **1** femmina; typical of women femminile **2** *n* femmina *f*; F (woman) donna *f*

feminine ['femɪnɪn] **1** adj femminile **2** *n* GRAM femminile *m*; **feminism** femminismo *m*; **feminist 1** *n* femminista *f* **2** adj femminista

fence [fens] *n* recinto *m*; **sit on the ~** non prendere partito

fender ['fendə(r)] Am parafango *m*

fermentation [fɜːmen'teɪʃn] fermentazione *f*

ferocious [fə'rəʊʃəs] feroce

ferry ['ferɪ] traghetto *m*

fertile ['fɜːtaɪl] fertile; **fertility** fertilità *f*; **fertilize** fecondare; **fertilizer** for soil fertilizzante *m*

fervent ['fɜːvənt] fervente

fester ['festə(r)] of wound fare infezione

festival ['festɪvl] festival *m*

inv; **festive** festivo; **the ~ season** le festività; **festivities** festeggiamenti *mpl*

fetal ['fi:tl] fetale

fetch [fetʃ] andare / venire a prendere; *thing* prendere; *price* rendere

fetus ['fi:təs] feto *m*

feud [fju:d] **1** *n* faida *f* **2** *v/i* litigare

fever ['fi:və(r)] febbre *f*; **feverish** *also fig* febbrile

few [fju:] **1** *adj* pochi; **a ~ people** alcune persone, qualche persona; **a ~ books** alcuni libri, qualche libro; **quite a ~**, **a good ~** (*a lot*) parecchi **2** *pron* (*not many*) pochi; **a ~** (*some*) alcuni; **quite a ~**, **a good ~** (*a lot*) parecchi; **fewer** meno (**than**) di

fiancé [fɪ'ɒnseɪ] fidanzato *m*; **fiancée** fidanzata *f*

fiasco [fɪ'æskəʊ] fiasco *m*

fiber *Am* **fibre**

fibre ['faɪbə(r)] fibra *f*; **fibre optics** tecnologia *f* delle fibre ottiche; **fibreglass** fibra *f* di vetro

fickle ['fɪkl] incostante

fiction ['fɪkʃn] narrativa *f*; (*made-up story*) storia *f*; **fictional** immaginario; **fictitious** fittizio

fiddle ['fɪdl] **1** *n* F (*violin*) violino *m*; **it's a ~** F (*cheat*) è una fregatura F **2** *v/i*: **~ with ...** giocherellare con ...; **~ around with ...** trafficare con ... **3** *v/t accounts* truccare

fidget ['fɪdʒɪt] agitarsi; **fidgety** in agitazione

field [fi:ld] campo *m*; (*competitors in race*) formazione *f*; **fielder** SP esterno *m*

fierce [fɪəs] *animal* feroce; *storm* violento; **fiercely** ferocemente

fiery ['faɪərɪ] focoso

fifteen [fɪf'ti:n] quindici; **fifteenth** quindicesimo; **fifth** quinto; **fiftieth** cinquantesimo; **fifty** cinquanta; **fifty-fifty** metà e metà

fig [fɪg] fico *m*

fight [faɪt] **1** *n* lotta *f*; *in war* combattimento *m*; (*argument*) litigio *m*; *in boxing* incontro *m* **2** *v/t* combattere; *injustice, fire* lottare contro; *in boxing* battersi contro **3** *v/i in war* combattere; *of drunks, schoolkids* azzuffarsi; (*argue*) litigare; **fighter** combattente *m/f*; *aeroplane* caccia *m inv*; (*boxer*) pugile *m*; **she's a ~** è combattiva; **fighting** risse *fpl*; MIL lotta *f*

figurative ['fɪgjərətɪv] *use of word* figurato; *art* figurativo

figure ['fɪgə(r)] *n* (*digit*) cifra *f*; *of person* linea *f*; (*form, shape*) figura *f*

♦ **figure on** F (*plan*) contare (di)

♦ **figure out** (*understand*) capire; *calculation* calcolare

file[1] [faɪl] **1** *n for papers* raccoglitore *m*; *contents* dossier *m inv*; COMPUT file *m inv*; **on ~**

in archivio **2** *v/t documents* schedare

file² [faɪl] *n for wood, fingernails* lima *f*

filing cabinet ['faɪlɪŋ, *Am* **file cabinet** schedario *m*

fill [fɪl] riempire; *tooth* otturare

♦ **fill in** *form* compilare; *hole* riempire; **fill s.o. in** mettere al corrente qu

♦ **fill out 1** *v/t form* compilare **2** *v/i (get fatter)* arrotondarsi

fillet ['fɪlɪt] filetto *m*

filling ['fɪlɪŋ] **1** *n in sandwich* ripieno *m; in tooth* otturazione *f* **2** *adj food* pesante; **filling station** stazione *f* di rifornimento

film [fɪlm] **1** *n for camera* pellicola *f; at cinema* film *m inv* **2** *v/t* filmare; *scene* girare; **film-maker** regista *m/f;* **film star** stella *f* del cinema

filter ['fɪltə(r)] **1** *n* filtro *m* **2** *v/t* filtrare

filth [fɪlθ] sporcizia *f; filthy* sporco; *language etc* volgare

final ['faɪnl] **1** *adj* finale **2** *n* SP finale *f; finale* finale *m; finalist* finalista *m/f; finalize* mettere a punto; *finally* infine; *(at last)* finalmente

finance ['faɪnæns] **1** *n* finanza *f* **2** *v/t* finanziare; *financial* finanziario; *financially* finanziariamente; *financial year* anno *m* fiscale; *financier* finanziatore *m,* -trice *f*

find [faɪnd] trovare

♦ **find out** scoprire

findings ['faɪndɪŋz] *of report* conclusioni *fpl*

fine¹ [faɪn] *day, weather, city* bello; *wine, performance* buono; *distinction, line* sottile; **how's that? – that's ~** com'è? – va benissimo; **that's ~ by me** a me sta bene

fine² [faɪn] **1** *n penalty* multa *f* **2** *v/t* multare

finger ['fɪŋgə(r)] **1** *n* dito *m* **2** *v/t* passare le dita su; **fingernail** unghia *f; fingerprint* impronta *f* digitale

finicky ['fɪnɪkɪ] *person* pignolo; *design* complicato

finish ['fɪnɪʃ] **1** *v/t finire;* **~ doing sth** finire di fare qc **2** *v/i* finire **3** *n of product* finitura *f*

♦ **finish up** *food* finire; **he finished up liking London** Londra ha finito per piacergli

♦ **finish with** *boyfriend etc* lasciare

'finishing line traguardo *m*

Finland ['fɪnlənd] Finlandia *f;* **Finn** finlandese *m/f;* **Finnish 1** *adj* finlandese, finnico **2** *n language* finlandese *m*

fir [fɜː(r)] abete *m*

fire ['faɪə(r)] **1** *n* fuoco *m; (blaze)* incendio *m; bonfire, campfire etc* falò *m inv;* **be on ~** essere in fiamme; **catch ~** prendere fuoco; **set sth on ~, set ~ to sth** dare fuoco a qc **2** *v/i (shoot)* sparare **3** *v/t* F *(dismiss)* licenziare; **fire alarm** allarme *m* antincendio; **firearm** arma *f* da fuoco; **fire brigade** vigili *mpl* del fuoco; **firecracker** petardo *m*; **fire department** *Am* vigili *mpl* del fuoco; **fire engine** autopompa *f*; **fire escape** scala *f* antincendio; **fire extinguisher** estintore *m*; **fire fighter** pompiere *m*; **fireman** pompiere *m*; **fireplace** camino *m*; **fire station** caserma *f* dei pompieri; **fire truck** autopompa *f*; **fireworks** fuochi *mpl* d'artificio

firm[1] [fɜːm] *adj* grip, handshake energico; *muscles* sodo; *voice, parents* deciso; *decision* risoluto; *date, offer* definitivo; *control* rigido; *foundations* solido; *believer* convinto

firm[2] [fɜːm] *n* COM azienda *f*

first [fɜːst] 1 *adj* primo 2 *n* primo *m*, -a *f* 3 *adv* arrive, finish per primo; *(beforehand)* prima; **~ of all** (for one reason) innanzitutto; **at ~** in un primo tempo, al principio; **first aid** pronto soccorso *m*; **first class** 1 *adj* di prima classe 2 *adv* travel in prima classe; **first floor** primo piano *m*; piano *m* terra; **First Lady** First Lady *f inv*; **firstly** in primo luogo; **first name** nome *m* di battesimo; **first night** prima serata *f*; **first-rate** di prima qualità

fiscal ['fɪskl] fiscale; `**fiscal year** *Am* anno *m* fiscale

fish [fɪʃ] 1 *n* pesce *m* 2 *v/i* pescare; **fisherman** pescatore *m*; **fish finger** bastoncino *m* di pesce; **fishing** pesca *f*; **fishing boat** peschereccio *m*; **fishing rod** canna *f* da pesca; **fishmonger** pescivendolo *m*; **fish stick** *Am* bastoncino *m* di pesce; **fishy** F *(suspicious)* sospetto

fist [fɪst] pugno *m*

fit[1] [fɪt] *n* MED attacco *m*; **a ~ of jealousy** un accesso di gelosia

fit[2] [fɪt] *adj* physically in forma; *morally* adatto; **keep ~** tenersi in forma

fit[3] [fɪt] 1 *v/t of clothes* andare bene a; *(attach)* installare 2 *v/i of clothes* andare bene; *of piece of furniture etc* starci

fitness ['fɪtnɪs] *physical* forma *f*; **fitting** appropriato; **fittings** equipaggiamento *msg*

five [faɪv] cinque

fix [fɪks] 1 *n (solution)* soluzione *f* 2 *v/t (attach, arrange)* fissare; *(repair)* aggiustare; *lunch* preparare; *dishonestly: match etc* manipolare; **fixed** *in position* fisso; *timescale, exchange rate* stabilito

fizzy ['fɪzɪ] *drink* gassato

flab [flæb] *on body* ciccia *f*; **flabby** *muscles* flaccido

flag[1] [flæg] *n* bandiera *f*

flag[2] [flæg] *v/i (tire)* soccombere

'**flagpole** asta f

flagrant ['fleɪgrənt] flagrante

flair [fleə(r)] (*talent*) talento m; (*style*) stile m

flake [fleɪk] of *snow* fiocco m; of *paint, plaster* scaglia f

flamboyant [flæm'bɔɪənt] *personality* esuberante; flamboyantly in modo vistoso

flame [fleɪm] n fiamma f; **go up in ~s** incendiarsi

flammable ['flæməbl] infiammabile

flank [flæŋk] 1 n fianco m 2 v/t: **be ~ed by** essere affiancato da

flannel ['flænl] guanto m di spugna

flap [flæp] 1 n of *envelope, pocket* falda f; of *table* ribalta f; **be in a ~** F essere in fibrillazione F 2 v/t *wings* sbattere 3 v/i of *flag etc* sventolare

◆ **flare up** [fler] of *violence, illness* esplodere; of *fire* divampare

flash [flæʃ] 1 n of *light* lampo m; PHOT flash m inv; **in a ~** F in un istante; **~ of lightning** lampo m 2 v/t of *light* lampeggiare 3 v/t: **~ one's headlights** lampeggiare; flashback in *film* flashback m inv; flashlight pila f; PHOT flash m inv; flashy *pej* appariscente

flask [flɑːsk] (*vacuum ~*) termos m inv

flat¹ [flæt] 1 adj piatto; *beer* sgassato; *battery, tyre* a terra;

shoes basso; **A / B ~** MUS la / si bemolle; **and that's ~** F punto e basta F 2 adv MUS sotto tonalità; **~ out** *work, run* a tutto gas 3 n gomma f a terra

flat² [flæt] n (*apartment*) appartamento m

flatly ['flætlɪ] *refuse, deny* risolutamente; flatmate compagno m, -a f di appartamento; flat rate tariffa f forfettaria; flat screen monitor schermo m piatto; flatten *land, road* livellare; *by bombing, demolition* radere al suolo

flatter ['flætə(r)] adulare; flatterer adulatore m, -trice f; flattering *comments* lusinghiero; **Jane's dress is very ~** il vestito di Jane le dona molto; flattery adulazione f

flavor Am → **flavour**

flavour ['fleɪvə(r)] 1 n gusto m 2 v/t of *food* insaporire; flavouring aroma m

flaw [flɔː] difetto m; flawless perfetto

flea [fliː] pulce f

flee [fliː] scappare

fleet [fliːt] NAUT flotta f; of *taxis, trucks* parco m macchine

fleeting ['fliːtɪŋ] *visit etc* di sfuggita

flesh [fleʃ] carne f; of *fruit* polpa f

flex [fleks] 1 v/t *muscles* flettere 2 n ELEC cavo m; flex(i)-time orario m flessibile;

flexibility flessibilità *f*; **flexible** flessibile

flicker ['flɪkə(r)] *of light* tremolare

flier ['flaɪə(r)] (*circular*) volantino *m*

flight [flaɪt] volo *m*; (*fleeing*) fuga *f*; **~ (of stairs)** rampa *f* (di scale); **flight attendant** assistente *m/f* di volo; **flight deck** *in plane* cabina *f* di pilotaggio; *of aircraft carrier* ponte *m* di decollo; **flight number** numero *m* di volo; **flight path** rotta *f* (di volo); **flight recorder** registratore *m* di volo; **flight time** *departure* orario *m* di volo; *duration* durata *f* di volo; **flighty** volubile

flimsy ['flɪmzɪ] *furniture* leggero; *dress, material* sottile; *excuse* debole

flinch [flɪntʃ] sobbalzare

flipper ['flɪpə(r)] *for swimming* pinna *f*

flirt [flɜːt] **1** *v/i* flirtare **2** *n* flirt *m inv*; **flirtatious** civettuolo

float [fləʊt] galleggiare; FIN fluttuare

flock [flɒk] **1** *n of sheep* gregge *m* **2** *v/i* accorrere in massa

flood [flʌd] **1** *n* inondazione *f* **2** *v/t of river* inondare; **flooding** inondazione *f*; **floodlight** riflettore *m*; **flood waters** acque *fpl* di inondazione

floor [flɔː(r)] pavimento *m*; (*story*) piano *m*; **floorboard**

asse *f* del pavimento; **floorlamp** *Am* lampada *f* a stelo

flop [flɒp] **1** *v/i* crollare; F (*fail*) fare fiasco **2** *n* F (*failure*) fiasco *m*; **floppy (disk)** floppy *m inv*, floppy disk *m inv*

Florence ['flɒrəns] Firenze *f*; **Florentine 1** *adj* fiorentino **2** *n* fiorentino *m*, -a *f*

florist ['flɒrɪst] fiorista *m/f*

flour ['flaʊə(r)] farina *f*

flourish ['flʌrɪʃ] fiorire; *of business, civilization* prosperare; **flourishing** *business, trade* prospero

flow [fləʊ] **1** *v/i of river, traffic, current* scorrere; *of work* procedere **2** *n of river, ideas* flusso *m*; **flowchart** diagramma *m* (di flusso)

flower ['flaʊə(r)] **1** *n* fiore *m* **2** *v/i* fiorire; **flowerpot** vaso *m* per fiori

flu [fluː] influenza *f*

fluctuate ['flʌktjʊeɪt] oscillare; **fluctuation** oscillazione *f*

fluency ['fluːənsɪ] *in a language* scioltezza *f*; **fluent** fluente; **he speaks ~ Spanish** parla correntemente lo spagnolo; **fluently** *speak, write* correntemente

fluid ['fluːɪd] fluido *m*

flunk [flʌŋk] *Am* F essere bocciato a

flush [flʌʃ] **1** *v/t toilet* tirare l'acqua di **2** *v/i (go red)* diventare rosso **3** *adj (level)* a filo; **~ with ...** a filo con ...

flute [fluːt] MUS flauto *m* traverso

flutter ['flʌtə(r)] *of wings* sbattere; *of flag* sventolare; *of heart* battere forte

fly[1] [flaɪ] *n insect* mosca *f*

fly[2] [flaɪ] *n on trousers* patta *f*

fly[3] [flaɪ] *v/i* volare; *of flag* sventolare; (*rush*) precipitarsi; ~ **into a rage** perdere le staffe **2** *v/t aeroplane* pilotare; *airline* volare con; (*transport by air*) spedire per via aerea

◆ **fly away** *of bird, plane* volare via

◆ **fly back** (*travel back*) ritornare (in aereo)

◆ **fly past** *of time* volare

flying ['flaɪɪŋ] volare *m*; **flyover** MOT cavalcavia *m inv*

foam [fəʊm] **1** *n on liquid* schiuma *f*; **foam rubber** gommapiuma® *f*

focus ['fəʊkəs] *of attention* centro *m*; PHOT fuoco *m*; **be in ~** / **be out of ~** PHOT essere a fuoco / non essere a fuoco

◆ **focus on** *issue* focalizzare l'attenzione su; PHOT mettere a fuoco

fodder ['fɒdə(r)] foraggio *m*

fog [fɒg] nebbia *f*; **foggy** nebbioso

foil[1] [fɔɪl] *n* carta *f* stagnola

foil[2] [fɔɪl] *v/t* (*thwart*) sventare

fold [fəʊld] **1** *v/t paper etc* piegare; ~ **one's arms** incrociare le braccia **2** *v/i of business*

chiudere i battenti **3** *n in cloth etc* piega *f*

◆ **fold up 1** *v/t chairs etc* chiudere; *clothes* piegare **2** *v/i of chair, table* chiudere

folder ['fəʊldə(r)] *for documents* cartellina *f*; COMPUT *directory f inv*; **folding** pieghevole

foliage ['fəʊlɪɪdʒ] fogliame *m*

folk [fəʊk] (*people*) gente *f*; **my ~** (*family*) i miei parenti; **come in, ~s** F entrate, gente F; **folk music** musica *f* folk; **folk singer** cantante *m/f* folk; **folk song** canzone *f* popolare

◆ **follow up** *inquiry* dare seguito a

follow ['fɒləʊ] **1** *v/t* (*also understand*) seguire **2** *v/i* seguire; *logically* quadrare; **as ~s** quanto segue

follower ['fɒləʊə(r)] *of politician etc* seguace *m/f*; *of football team* tifoso *m*, -a *f*; **following 1** *adj* seguente **2** *n people* seguito *m*; **the ~** quanto segue

fond [fɒnd] (*loving*) affezionato; *memory* caro; **he is ~ of travel** gli piace viaggiare; **I'm very ~ of him** gli voglio molto

fondle ['fɒndl] accarezzare

fondness ['fɒndnɪs] *for person* affetto *m*; *for wine, food* gusto *m*

font [fɒnt] *for printing* carattere *m*; *in church* fonte *f* battesimale

food [fuːd] cibo *m*; *Italian* ~ la cucina italiana; *there's no* ~ *in the house* non c'è niente da mangiare in casa; **foodie** buongustaio *m*, -a *f*; **food poisoning** intossicazione *f* alimentare

fool [fuːl] **1** *n* pazzo *m*, -a *f*; *make a* ~ *of o.s.* rendersi ridicolo **2** *v/t* ingannare; **foolhardy** temerario; **foolish** sciocco; **foolproof** a prova di idiota

foot [fʊt] (*pl feet* [fiːt]) *also measurement* piede *m*; *on* ~ a piedi; *at the* ~ *of the page* a piè di pagina; *put one's* ~ *in it* F fare una gaffe; **footage** pellicola *f* cinematografica; **football** (*soccer*) calcio *m*; *American football m* americano; (*ball*) pallone *m* da calcio; *for American football* pallone *m* da football americano; **footballer** calciatore *m*, -trice *f*; **football pitch** campo *m* da calcio; **football player** *soccer* calciatore *m*, -trice *f*; *American style* giocatore *m* di football americano; **foothills** colline *fpl* pedemontane; **footnote** nota *f* a piè di pagina; **footpath** sentiero *m*; **footprint** impronta *f* di piede; **footstep** passo *m*

for [fɔː(r)] per; *a train to* ~ ... un treno per ...; *what is this* ~? a cosa serve?; *what* ~? a che

scopo?, perché?; ~ *three days* per tre giorni; *I am* ~ *the idea* sono a favore dell'idea; *how much did you sell it* ~? a quanto l'hai venduto?

forbid [fəˈbɪd] vietare, proibire (*to do* di fare); **forbidden** vietato, proibito; **smoking** ~ vietato fumare; **parking** ~ divieto di sosta; **forbidding** ostile

force [fɔːs] **1** *n* forza *f*; *come into* ~ *of law etc* entrare in vigore; *the* ~*s* MIL le forze armate **2** *v/t door, lock* forzare; ~ *s.o. to do sth* forzare *or* costringere qu a fare qc; **forced entry** effrazione *f*; **forced landing** atterraggio *m* d'emergenza; **forceful** *argument*, *speaker* convincente; *character* energico

forceps [ˈfɔːseps] MED forcipe *f*

forcibly [ˈfɔːsəblɪ] *restrain* con la forza

foreboding [fəˈbəʊdɪŋ] presentimento *m*; **forecast 1** *n* previsione *f* **2** *v/t* prevedere; **forefathers** antenati *mpl*; **forefinger** indice *m*; **foregone**: *that's a* ~ *conclusion* è una conclusione scontata; **foreground** primo piano *m*; **forehand** *in tennis* diritto *m*; **forehead** fronte *f*

foreign [ˈfɒrən] straniero; *trade*, *policy* estero; **foreign affairs** affari *mpl* esteri; **foreign body** corpo *m* estraneo; **foreign currency** valuta *f* estera; **foreigner** straniero *m*, -a *f*; **foreign exchange** cambio *m* valutario; **Foreign Office** Ministero *m* degli esteri; **Foreign Secretary** *in UK* ministro *m* degli esteri

'**foreman** caposquadra *m*;

'**foremost 1** *adv* (*uppermost*) soprattutto **2** *adj* (*leading*) principale

forensic 'medicine [fə'rensık] medicina *f* legale; **forensic scientist** medico *m* legale

'**forerunner** precursore *m*;

foresee prevedere; **foresight** lungimiranza *f*

forest ['fɒrıst] foresta *f*; **forestry** scienze *fpl* forestali

fore'tell predire

forever [fə'revə(r)] per sempre

foreword ['fɔːwɜːd] prefazione *f*

forfeit ['fɔːfıt] *right*, *privilege etc* perdere

forge [fɔːdʒ] (*counterfeit*) contraffare; *signature* falsificare; **forgery** (*banknote*) falsificazione *f*; (*document*) falso *m*

forget [fə'get] dimenticare; **forgetful** smemorato

forgive [fə'gıv] perdonare; **forgiveness** perdono *m*

fork [fɔːk] *for eating* forchetta *f*; *for gardening* forca *f*; *in road* biforcazione *f*; **forklift truck** muletto *m*

form [fɔːm] **1** *n* (*shape*) forma

f; (*document*) modulo *m*; *in school class* classe *f*; **be on / off** ~ essere in / fuori forma **2** *v/t in clay etc* modellare; *friendship* creare; *opinion* formarsi; *past tense etc* formare; (*constitute*) costituire **3** *v/i* (*take shape*, *develop*) formarsi; **formal** formale; **formality** formalità *f inv*; **formally** formalmente

format ['fɔːmæt] **1** *v/t diskette* formattare; *document* impaginare **2** *n* (*size: of magazine etc*) formato *m*; (*makeup: of programme*) formula *f*

formation [fɔː'meıʃn] formazione *f*

former ['fɔːmə(r)] *wife*, *president* ex *inv*; *statement*, *arrangement* precedente; **the** ~ quest'ultimo; **formerly** precedentemente

formidable ['fɔːmıdəbl] imponente

formula ['fɔːmjʊlə] formula *f*

fort [fɔːt] MIL forte *m*

forthcoming [fɔː'kʌmıŋ] (*future*) prossimo; *personality* comunicativo

'**forthright** schietto

fortieth ['fɔːtııθ] quarantesimo, -a

fortnight ['fɔːtnaıt] due settimane

fortress ['fɔːtrıs] MIL fortezza *f*

fortunate ['fɔːʃʊnət] fortunato; **fortunately** fortunatamente; **fortune** sorte *f*; (*lot f* *of money*) fortuna *f*; **tell s.o.'s** ~ predire il futuro a qu; **fortune-teller** chiromante *m/f*

forty ['fɔːtɪ] quaranta

Forum ['fɔːrəm] *Roman* foro *m*

forward ['fɔːwəd] **1** *adv* avanti **2** *adj pej*: *diretto* **3** *n* SP attaccante *m* **4** *v/t letter* inoltrare; **forwarding agent** COM spedizioniere *m*; **forward-looking** progressista

fossil ['fɒsəl] fossile *m*

foster ['fɒstə(r)] *child* avere in affidamento; *attitude, belief* incoraggiare; **foster parents** genitori *mpl* con affidamento

foul [faul] **1** *n* SP fallo *m* **2** *adj smell* pessimo; *weather* orribile **3** *v/t* SP fare un fallo contro

found [faund] *school etc* fondare; **foundation** *of theory etc* fondamenta *fpl*; (*organization*) fondazione *f*; **make-up** fondotinta *m*; **foundations** *of building* fondamenta *fpl*; **founder** fondatore *m*, -trice *f*

fountain ['fauntɪn] fontana *f*; **four** [fɔː(r)] quattro; **four-star** *hotel etc* a quattro stelle; **fourteen** quattordici; **fourteenth** quattordicesimo; **fourth** quarto; **four-wheel drive** MOT quattro per quattro *m inv*

fox [fɒks] **1** *n* volpe *f* **2** *v/t* (*puz-*

zle) mettere in difficoltà

foyer ['fɔɪeɪ] atrio *m*

fraction ['frækʃn] frazione *f*; **fractionally** lievemente

fracture ['fræktʃə(r)] **1** *n* frattura *f* **2** *v/t* fratturare

fragile ['frædʒaɪl] fragile

fragment ['frægmənt] frammento *m*

fragrance ['freɪgrəns] fragranza *f*; **fragrant** profumato

frail [freɪl] gracile

frame [freɪm] **1** *n of picture, window* cornice *f*; *of glasses* montatura *f*; *of bicycle* telaio *m*; ~ **of mind** stato m d'animo **2** *v/t picture* incorniciare; F *person* incastrare F; **framework** struttura *f*

France [frɑːns] Francia *f*

franchise ['fræntʃaɪz] *for business* concessione *f*

frank [fræŋk] franco; **frankly** francamente; **frankness** franchezza *f*

frantic ['fræntɪk] *attempt* frenetico; (*worried*) agitatissimo

fraternal [frə'tɜːnl] fraterno

fraud [frɔːd] frode *f*; *person* impostore *m*, -trice *f*; **fraudulent** fraudolento

frayed [freɪd] *cuffs* liso

freak [friːk] **1** *n unusual event* fenomeno *m* anomalo; *two-headed person etc* scherzo *m* di natura; F *strange person* tipo *m*, -a *f* strambo, -a; **movie** ~ F (*fanatic*) fanatico

freckle

m, -a *f* del cinema **2** *adj* wind, storm violento

freckle ['frekl] lentiggine *f*

free [fri:] **1** *adj* libero; (*no cost*) gratuito; **for ~** travel, get sth gratis **2** *v/t* prisoners liberare; **freedom** libertà *f*; **free enterprise** liberalismo *m* economico; **freefone** numero *m* verde; **free kick** in soccer calcio *m* di punizione; **freelance** free lance *inv*; **freely** admit apertamente; **free sample** campione *m* gratuito; **free speech** libertà *f* di espressione; **freeway** Am autostrada *f*

freeze [fri:z] **1** *v/t* gelare; wages, account congelare; video bloccare **2** *v/i* of water gelare; **freeze-dried** liofilizzato; **freezer** freezer *m* inv, congelatore *m*; **freezing** ['fri:zıŋ] gelato; **it's ~ (cold)** of weather si gela; of water è gelata; **I'm ~** sono congelato **2** *n*: **10 below ~** 10 gradi sotto zero

freight [freit] carico *m*; costs trasporto *m*; **freighter** ship nave *f* da carico; plane aereo *m* da carico

French [frentʃ] **1** *adj* francese **2** *n* (*language*) francese *m*; **the ~** i francesi; **French fries** patate *fpl* fritte; **Frenchman** francese *m*; **French windows** vetrata *f*; **Frenchwoman** francese *f*

frenzied ['frenzıd] attack, activity frenetico; mob impaz-

zito; **frenzy** frenesia *f*

frequency ['fri:kwənsı] frequenza *f*

frequent[1] ['fri:kwənt] *adj* frequente

frequent[2] [frı'kwent] *v/t* bar etc frequentare

frequently ['fri:kwəntlı] frequentemente

fresh [freʃ] fresco; start nuovo; Am (*impertinent*) sfacciato; **fresh air** aria *f* fresca

◆ **freshen up** ['freʃn] **1** *v/i* rinfrescarsi **2** *v/t* room, paintwork rinfrescare

freshly ['freʃlı] appena; **freshman** studente *m* del primo anno, matricola *f*; **freshwater** d'acqua dolce

friction ['frıkʃn] PHYS frizione *f*; between people attrito *m*

Friday ['fraıdeı] venerdì *m* inv

fridge [frıdʒ] frigo *m*

fried egg [fraıd] uovo *m* fritto

friend [frend] amico *m*, -a *f*; **make ~s** fare amicizia; **friendliness** amichevolezza *f*; **friendly 1** *adj* amichevole; (*easy to use*) facile da usare; **be ~ with s.o.** (*be friends*) essere amico di qu **2** *n* SP amichevole *f*; **friendship** amicizia *f*

fries [fraız] patate *fpl* fritte

fright [fraıt] paura *f*; **frighten** spaventare; **be ~ed (of)** aver paura (di); **frightening** spaventoso

frill [frıl] on dress etc volant *m* inv; **~s** (*fancy extras*) fronzoli *mpl*

fringe [frɪndʒ] frangia *f*; *(edge)* margini *mpl*; **fringe benefits** benefici *mpl* accessori

frisk [frɪsk] frugare F

◆ **fritter away** ['frɪtə(r)] *time, fortune* sprecare

frivolity [frɪ'vɒlətɪ] frivolezza *f*; **frivolous** frivolo

frizzy ['frɪzɪ] *hair* crespo

frog [frɒg] rana *f*; **frogman** sommozzatore *m*

from [frɒm] ◊ *in time* da; **~ in time to** da; **~ 9 to 5 (o'clock)** dalle 9 alle 5; **~ today on** da oggi in poi ◊ *in space* da; **~ here to there** da qui a lì ◊ *origin* di; *a letter ~ Jo* una lettera di Jo; *I am ~ Liverpool* sono di Liverpool ◊ *(because of)* di; *tired ~ the journey* stanco del viaggio; *it's ~ overeating* è a causa del troppo mangiare

front [frʌnt] **1** *n of building* lato *m* principale; *of car, statue* davanti *m inv*; *of book* copertina *f*; *(cover organization)* facciata *f*; MIL, *of weather* fronte *m*; **in ~** davanti; **in ~ of** davanti a **2** *adj wheel, seat* anteriore **3** *v/t* TV *programme* presentare; **front door** porta *f* principale

frontier ['frʌntɪə(r)] *also fig* frontiera *f*

'front line MIL fronte *m*; **front page** *of newspaper* prima pagina *f*; **front-wheel drive** trazione *f* anteriore

frost [frɒst] brina *f*; **frostbite** congelamento *m*; **frosting** *Am on cake* glassatura *f*; **frosty** *also fig* gelido

froth [frɒθ] spuma *f*

frown [fraʊn] **1** *n* cipiglio *m* **2** *v/i* aggrottare le sopracciglia

frozen ['frəʊzn] gelato; *wastes* gelido; *food* surgelato; *I'm ~* F sono congelato F

fruit [fruːt] frutto *m*; *collective* frutta *f*; **fruitful** *discussions etc* fruttuoso; **fruit juice** succo *m* di frutta; **fruit machine** slot machine *f inv*; **fruit salad** macedonia *f*

frustrate [frʌ'streɪt] *person* frustrare; *plans* scombussolare; **frustrating** frustrante; **frustration** frustrazione *f*; **sexual ~** insoddisfazione *f* sessuale

fry [fraɪ] friggere; **frying pan** padella *f*

fuck [fʌk] V scopare V; **~ !** cazzo! V

fuel ['fjuːəl] **1** *n* carburante *m* **2** *v/t fig* alimentare

fugitive ['fjuːdʒətɪv] *n* fuggiasco *m*, -a *f*

fulfil, *Am* **fulfill** [fʊl'fɪl] *dreams* realizzare; *contract* eseguire; *requirements* corrispondere a; *feel ~led in job, life* sentirsi soddisfatto; **fulfilment**, *Am* **fulfillment** *of contract* esecuzione *f*; *of dreams* realizzazione *f*; *moral, spiritual* soddisfazione *f*

full [fʊl] pieno (**of** di); *account* esauriente; *life* intenso; **~ up**

hotel, *with food* pieno; *in ~ write* per intero; *pay in ~* saldare il conto; **full moon** luna *f* piena; **full stop** punto *m* fermo; **full-time** a tempo pieno; **fully booked**, *recovered* completamente; *understand*, *explain* perfettamente; *describe* ampiamente

fumble ['fʌmbl] *catch* farsi sfuggire

fumes [fju:mz] esalazioni *fpl*

fun [fʌn] **1** *n* divertimento *m*; **it was great ~** era molto divertente; **have ~!** divertiti!; **for ~** per divertirsi; *(joking)* per scherzo; **make ~ of** prendere in giro **2** *adj* F divertente

function ['fʌŋkʃn] **1** *n* *(purpose)* funzione *f*; *(reception etc)* cerimonia *f* **2** *v/i* funzionare; **~ as** servire da; **functional** funzionale

fund [fʌnd] **1** *n* fondo *m* **2** *v/t project etc* finanziare

fundamental [fʌndə'mentl] fondamentale; **fundamentalist** fondamentalista *m/f*; **fundamentally** fondamentalmente

funding ['fʌndɪŋ] *money* fondi *mpl*

funeral ['fju:nərəl] funerale *m*; **funeral home**, **funeral parlour** obitorio *m*

fungus ['fʌŋgəs] fungo *m*

funicular ('railway) [fju:'nɪkjʊlə(r)] funicolare *f*

funnily ['fʌnɪlɪ] *(oddly)* stra-

namente; *(comically)* in modo divertente; **~ enough** per quanto strano; **funny** *(comical)* divertente; *(odd)* strano

fur [fɜ:(r)] pelliccia *f*; *on animal* pelo *m*

furious ['fjʊərɪəs] *(angry)* furioso; *(intense)* spaventoso

furnace ['fɜ:nɪs] forno *m*

furnish ['fɜ:nɪʃ] *room* arredare; *(supply)* fornire; **furniture** mobili *mpl*; **a piece of ~** un mobile

further ['fɜ:ðə(r)] **1** *adj* *(additional)* ulteriore; *(more distant)* più lontano; **have you anything ~ to say?** ha qualcosa da aggiungere? **2** *adv walk*, *drive* oltre; **~, I want to say ...** inoltre, volevo dire ...; **two miles ~ (on)** due miglia più avanti **3** *v/t cause etc* favorire; **furthermore** inoltre; **furthest: furthest 1** *adj* più lontano **2** *adv*: **this is the ~ north** è il punto più a nord

furtive ['fɜ:tɪv] *glance* furtivo

fury ['fjʊərɪ] furore *m*

fuse [fju:z] ELEC **1** *n* fusibile *m* **2** *v/i* bruciarsi **3** *v/t* bruciare; **fusebox** scatola *f* dei fusibili

fusion ['fju:ʒn] fusione *f*

fuss [fʌs] agitazione *f*; *about film*, *event* scalpore *m*; **make a ~** complain fare storie; **make a ~ of** be very attentive to colmare qu di attenzioni; **fussy** *person* difficile; *design* *etc* complicato; **be a ~ eater** essere schizzinoso nel mangiare

futile ['fju:taɪl] futile; **futility** futilità *f*

future ['fju:tʃə(r)] **1** *n* futuro *m* **2** *adj* futuro; **futuristic** futuristico

fuzzy ['fʌzɪ] *hair* crespo; (*out of focus*) sfuocato

G

gadget ['gædʒɪt] congegno *m*

gag [gæg] **1** *n* bavaglio *m*; (*joke*) battuta *f* **2** *v/t person* imbavagliare; *the press* azzittire

gain [geɪn] (*acquire*) acquisire, acquistare; **~ 10 pounds** aumentare di 10 libbre

gala ['gɑːlə] *concert etc* serata *f* di gala

galaxy ['gæləksɪ] galassia *f*

gale [geɪl] bufera *f*

gallery ['gælərɪ] galleria *f*

gallon ['gælən] gallone *m*; *(0,546l, in USA 0,785l,)*

gallop ['gæləp] galoppare

gamble ['gæmbl] giocare (d'azzardo); **gambler** giocatore *m*, -trice *f* (d'azzardo); **gambling** gioco *m* (d'azzardo)

game [geɪm] gioco *m*; (*match, in tennis*) partita *f*

gang [gæŋ] banda *f*; **gangster** malvivente *m*, gangster *m inv*; **gangway** passaggio *m*; *for ship* passerella *f*

gap [gæp] *in wall, for parking* buco *m*; *in conversation* vuoto *m*; *in time* intervallo *m*; *in story, education* lacuna *f*; *between personalities* scarto *m*

gape [geɪp] *of person* rimanere a bocca aperta; **gaping** *hole* spalancato

'gap year *anno tra la fine del liceo e l'inizio dell'università dedicato ad altre attività*

garage ['gærɪdʒ] *for parking* garage *m inv*; *for repairs* officina *f*; *for petrol* stazione *f* di servizio

garbage ['gɑːbɪdʒ] rifiuti *mpl*; (*fig: nonsense*) idiozie *fpl*; **garbage can** *Am* bidone *m* della spazzatura; **garbage truck** *Am* camion *m* della nettezza urbana

garbled ['gɑːbld] *message* ingarbugliato

garden ['gɑːdn] giardino *m*; *for vegetables* orto *m*; **gardening** giardinaggio *m*

garish ['geərɪʃ] sgargiante

garlic ['gɑːlɪk] aglio *m*

garment ['gɑːmənt] *fml* capo *m* d'abbigliamento

garnish ['gɑːnɪʃ] guarnire

gas [gæs] gas *m inv*; *Am* (*gasoline*) benzina *f*

gash [gæʃ] taglio *m*

gasket ['gæskɪt] guarnizione f

gasoline ['gæsəliːn] *Am* benzina f

gasp [gɑːsp] **1** *n* sussulto *m* **2** *v/i* rimanere senza fiato; ~ **for breath** essere senza fiato

'gas pedal *Am* acceleratore *m*; **gas pump** *Am* pompa *f* della benzina; **gas station** *Am* stazione *f* di rifornimento; **gas stove** cucina *f* a gas

gate [geɪt] cancello *m*; *of city, castle, at airport* porta *f*; **gateway** ingresso *m*; *fig* via *f* d'accesso

gather ['gæðə(r)] **1** *v/t facts* raccogliere; ~ **speed** acquistare velocità **2** *v/i* (*understand*) dedurre; **gathering** (*group of people*) raduno *m*

gaudy ['gɔːdɪ] pacchiano

gauge [geɪdʒ] **1** *n* indicatore *m* **2** *v/t pressure* misurare; *opinion* valutare

gaunt [gɔːnt] smunto

gawky ['gɔːkɪ] impacciato

gawp [gɔːp] F fissare come un ebete F

gay [geɪ] gay *inv*; **gay marriage** matrimonio *m* gay

gaze [geɪz] **1** *n* sguardo *m* **2** *v/i* fissare

gear [gɪə(r)] (*equipment*) equipaggiamento *m*; *in vehicles* marcia *f*; **gearbox** MOT scatola *f* del cambio; **gear lever**, **gear shift** MOT leva *f* del cambio

geese [giːs] *pl* ☞ **goose**

gel [dʒel] *for hair, shower* gel *m inv*

gem [dʒem] gemma *f*; *fig: book etc* capolavoro *m*; *person* perla *f* rara

Gemini ['dʒeminaɪ] ASTR Gemelli *mpl*

gender ['dʒendə(r)] genere *m*

gene [dʒiːn] gene *m*

general ['dʒenrəl] **1** *n* MIL generale *m* **2** *adj* generale; **generalization** generalizzazione *f*; **generalize** generalizzare; **generally** generalmente; ~ **speaking** in generale

generate ['dʒenəreɪt] generare; *in linguistics* formare; **generation** generazione *f*; **generator** ELEC generatore *m*

generosity [dʒenə'rɒsɪtɪ] generosità *f*; **generous** generoso

genetic [dʒɪ'netɪk] genetico; **genetically** geneticamente; ~ **modified** transgenico; **genetic engineering** ingegneria *f* genetica; **genetic fingerprint** esame *m* del DNA; **genetics** genetica *f*

genial ['dʒiːnɪəl] gioviale

genitals ['dʒenɪtlz] genitali *mpl*

genius ['dʒiːnɪəs] genio *m*

Genoa ['dʒenəʊə] Genova *f*

genocide ['dʒenəsaɪd] genocidio *m*

gentle ['dʒentl] delicato; *breeze, slope* dolce; **gentle-**

man signore *m*; *he's a real ~* è un vero gentleman; **gentleness** delicatezza *f*; *~ of breeze*, *slope* dolcezza *f*; **gently** delicatamente; *blow*, *slope* dolcemente

gents [dʒents] *toilet* bagno *m* degli uomini

genuine ['dʒenjuɪn] autentico; (*sincere*) sincero; **genuinely** sinceramente

geographical [dʒɪə'græfɪkl] geografico; **geography** geografia *f*

geological [dʒɪə'lɒdʒɪkl] geologico; **geologist** geologo *m*, -a *f*; **geology** geologia *f*

geometric, **geometrical** [dʒɪə'metrɪk(l)] geometrico; **geometry** geometria *f*

geriatric [dʒerɪ'ætrɪk] **1** *adj* geriatrico **2** *n* anziano *m*, -a *f*

germ [dʒɜːm] *also fig* germe *m*

German ['dʒɜːmən] **1** *adj* tedesco **2** *n person* tedesco *m*, -a *f*; *language* tedesco *m*; **German measles** rosolia *f*; **German shepherd** pastore *m* tedesco; **Germany** Germania *f*

gesture ['dʒestʃə(r)] *also fig* gesto *m*

get [get] prendere; (*fetch*) andare a prendere; (*receive: letter*) ricevere; (*receive: knowledge*, *respect etc*) ottenere; (*become*) diventare; (*understand*) afferrare; *~ sth done causative* farsi fare qc; *~*

s.o. to do sth far fare qc a qu; *I'll ~ him to do it* glielo faccio fare; *~ to do sth have opportunity* avere di fare qc; *~ one's hair cut* tagliarsi i capelli; *~ sth ready* preparare qc; *~ going* (*leave*) andare via; *have got* avere; *I have got to study* devo studiare

◆ **get at** (*criticize*) prendersela con; (*imply*, *mean*) volere arrivare a

◆ **get back 1** *v/i* (*return*) ritornare; *I'll get back to you on that* ti faccio sapere **2** *v/t* (*obtain again*) recuperare

◆ **get by** (*pass*) passare; *financially* tirare avanti

◆ **get down 1** *v/i from ladder etc* scendere; (*duck etc*) abbassarsi **2** *v/t* (*depress*) buttare giù

◆ **get in 1** *v/i of train*, *plane* arrivare; (*come home*) arrivare a casa; *to car* salire; *how did they get in? of thieves*, *mice etc* come sono entrati? **2** *v/t to suitcase etc* far entrare

◆ **get into** *house* entrare in; *car* salire in

◆ **get off 1** *v/i from bus etc* scendere; (*finish work*) finire; (*not be punished*) cavarsela **2** *v/t* (*remove*) togliere; *clothes* togliersi

◆ **get off with** F *sexually* rimorchiare F; *get off with a small fine* cavarsela con una piccola multa

◆ **get on 1** *v/i of bike, bus, train* salire; *(be friendly)* andare d'accordo; *(of time)* farsi tardi; *(advance: make progress)* procedere; **he's getting on well at school** se la sta cavando bene a scuola **2** *v/t:* **get on the bus** salire sull'autobus

◆ **get out 1** *v/i of car etc* scendere; *of prison* uscire; **get out!** fuori!; **let's get out of here** usciamo da qui **2** *v/t nail, something jammed* tirare fuori; *stain* mandare via; *gun, pen* tirare fuori

◆ **get over** *fence, disappointment etc* superare; *lover etc* dimenticare

◆ **get through** *on telephone* prendere la linea; *(make self understood)* farsi capire

◆ **get up 1** *v/i of person, wind* alzarsi **2** *v/t (climb: hill)* salire su

'**getaway car** macchina *f* per la fuga; **get-together** ritrovo *m*

ghastly ['gɑːstlɪ] orrendo

ghetto ['getəʊ] ghetto *m*

ghost [gəʊst] fantasma *m*, spettro *m*; **ghostly** spettrale

ghoul [guːl] persona *f* morbosa

giant ['dʒaɪənt] **1** *n* gigante *m* **2** *adj* gigante

gibberish ['dʒɪbərɪʃ] F bestialità *fpl* F

gibe [dʒaɪb] frecciatina *f*

giddiness ['gɪdɪnɪs] giramenti *mpl* di testa; **giddy: I feel ~** mi gira la testa

gift [gɪft] regalo *m*; *(talent)* dono *m*; **gifted** dotato; **gift token**, **gift voucher** buono *m* d'acquisto; **giftwrap: ~ sth** fare un pacco regalo

gig [gɪg] F concerto *m*

gigabyte ['gɪgəbaɪt] COMPUT gigabyte *m* inv

gigantic [dʒaɪ'gæntɪk] gigante

giggle ['gɪgl] **1** *v/i* ridacchiare **2** *n* risatina *f*

gimmick ['gɪmɪk] trovata *f*

gin [dʒɪn] gin *m* inv; **~ and tonic** gin and tonic *m* inv

ginger ['dʒɪndʒə(r)] **1** *n* spice zenzero *m* **2** *adj hair* rosso carota; *cat* rosso

gipsy ['dʒɪpsɪ] zingaro *m*, -a *f*

giraffe [dʒɪ'rɑːf] giraffa *f*

girder ['gɜːdə(r)] *n* trave *f*

girl [gɜːl] ragazza *f*; **girlfriend** *of boy* ragazza *f*; *of girl* amica *f*; **girl guide** giovane esploratrice *f*; **girlish** tipicamente femminile

gist [dʒɪst] sostanza *f*

give [gɪv] dare; *present* fare; *(supply: electricity etc)* fornire; *talk, groan* fare; *party* dare; *pain, appetite* far venire

◆ **give away** *as present* regalare; *(betray)* tradire

◆ **give back** restituire

◆ **give in 1** *v/i (surrender)* arrendersi **2** *v/t (hand in)* consegnare

◆ **give onto** (*open onto*) dare su

◆ **give out 1** v/t *leaflets etc* distribuire **2** v/i *of supplies, strength* esaurirsi

◆ **give up 1** v/t *smoking etc* rinunciare a; **give o.s. up to the police** consegnarsi alla polizia **2** v/i (*cease habit*) smettere; (*stop making effort*) lasciar perdere

◆ **give way** *of bridge etc* cedere; MOT dare la precedenza

give-and-'take concessioni *fpl* reciproche

gizmo ['gɪzməʊ] *Am* aggeggio *m*

glad [glæd] contento; **gladly** volentieri

glamor ['glæmə(r)] *Am* ☞ **glamour**, **glamorize** esaltare; **glamorous** affascinante; **glamour** fascino *m*

glance [glɑːns] **1** *n* sguardo *m*; **at first** ~ a prima vista **2** v/i dare un'occhiata *or* uno sguardo

gland [glænd] ghiandola *f*

glare [gleə(r)] **1** *n of sun, lights* luce *f* abbagliante **2** v/i *of sun, lights* splendere di luce abbagliante

◆ **glare at** guardare di storto

glaring ['gleərɪŋ] *mistake* lampante

glass [glɑːs] *material* vetro *m*; *for drink* bicchiere *m*; **glasses** occhiali *mpl*

glazed [gleɪzd] *expression* assente

gleam [gliːm] **1** *n* luccichio *m* **2** v/i luccicare

glee [gliː] allegria *f*; **gleeful** allegro

glib [glɪb] poco convincente; **glibly** in modo poco convincente

glide [glaɪd] *of skier, boat* scivolare; *of bird, plane* planare; **glider** aliante *m*; **gliding** SP volo *m* planato

glimpse [glɪmps] **1** *n* occhiata *f*; **catch a ~ of** intravedere **2** v/t intravedere

glint [glɪnt] **1** *n* luccichio *m* **2** v/i *of light, eyes* luccicare

glisten ['glɪsn] scintillare

glitter ['glɪtə(r)] brillare

gloat [gləʊt] gongolare

◆ **gloat over** compiacersi di

global ['gləʊbl] (*worldwide*) mondiale; *without exceptions* globale; **globalization** globalizzazione *f*; **globalize** globalizzare; **global warming** effetto *m* serra; **globe** globo *m*; *model of earth* mappamondo *m*

gloom [gluːm] (*darkness*) penombra *f*; *mood* tristezza *f*; **gloomy** *room* buio; *mood, person* triste; *day* grigio

glorious ['glɔːrɪəs] *weather, day* splendido; *victory* glorioso; **glory** gloria *f*; (*beauty*) splendore *m*

gloss [glɒs] (*shine*) lucido *m*; **glossary** glossario *m*; **gloss paint** vernice *f* lucida;

glossy 1 adj paper patinato **2** n magazine rivista f su carta patinata

glove [glʌv] guanto m; **glove compartment** cruscotto m

glow [gləʊ] **1** n of light, fire bagliore m; in cheeks colorito m vivo; of candle luce f fioca **2** v/i of light brillare; **her cheeks ~ed** è diventata rossa; **glowing** description entusiastico

glucose ['gluːkəʊs] glucosio m

glue [gluː] **1** n colla f **2** v/t: **~ sth to sth** incollare qc a qc

glum [glʌm] triste

glut [glʌt] eccesso m

glutton ['glʌtən] ghiottone m, -a f

gnaw [nɔː] bone rosicchiare

go [gəʊ] **1** n (try) tentativo m; **it's my ~** tocca a me; **have a ~ at sth** (try) fare un tentativo in qc; **be on the ~** essere indaffarato; **in one ~** drink, write etc tutto in una volta **2** v/i andare; (leave: of train, plane) partire; (leave: of people) andare via; (work, function) funzionare; (become) diventare; (come out: of stain etc) andare via; (cease: of pain etc) sparire; (match: of colours etc) stare bene insieme; **let's ~!** andiamo!; **how's the work ~ing?** come va il lavoro?; **be all gone** (finished) essere finito; **to ~** Am food da asporto

♦ **go along with** suggestion concordare con

♦ **go away** of person, pain andare via; of rain smettere

♦ **go back** (return) ritornare; (date back) rimontare; **go back to sleep** tornare a dormire

♦ **go by** of car, people, time passare

♦ **go down** scendere; of sun, ship tramontare; of ship affondare; of swelling diminuire

♦ **go in** to room, house entrare; of sun andare via; (fit: of part etc) andare

♦ **go off 1** v/i (leave) andarsene; of bomb esplodere; of gun sparare; of alarm scattare; of light spegnersi; of milk etc andare a male **2** v/t (stop liking) stufarsi di

♦ **go on** (continue) andare avanti; (happen) succedere

♦ **go out** of person uscire; of light, fire spegnersi

♦ **go out with** romantically uscire con

♦ **go over** (check) esaminare

♦ **go through** hard times passare; (check) controllare; (read through) leggere

♦ **go under** (sink) affondare; of company fallire

♦ **go up** salire

♦ **go without 1** v/t food etc fare a meno di **2** v/i farne a meno

'go-ahead 1 n via libera m;

get the ~ avere il via libera **2** *adj (enterprising, dynamic)* intraprendente

goal [gəʊl] *(sport: target)* rete *f; (sport: points)* gol *m inv; (objective)* obiettivo *m;* **goalie** F portiere *m;* **goalkeeper** portiere *m;* **goal kick** rimessa *f;* **goalpost** palo *m*

goat [gəʊt] capra *f*

gobble [ˈgɒbl] tranguiare

gobbledygook [ˈgɒbldɪguːk] F linguaggio *m* incomprensibile

'go-between mediatore *m*, -trice *f*

god [gɒd] dio *m;* **thank God!** grazie a Dio!; **godchild** figlioccio *m*, -a *f;* **goddess** dea *f;* **godfather** *also in mafia* padrino *m;* **godmother** madrina *f*

gofer [ˈgəʊfə(r)] F galoppino *m*, -a *f*

goggles [ˈgɒglz] occhialini *mpl*

goings-on [gəʊɪŋzˈɒn] vicende *fpl*

gold [gəʊld] **1** *n* oro *m* **2** *adj* d'oro; **golden** dorato; **golden wedding** *(anniversary)* nozze *fpl* d'oro; **goldfish** pesce *m* rosso; **gold mine** *fig* miniera *f* d'oro

golf [gɒlf] golf *m;* **golf ball** palla *f* da golf; **golf club** *organization* club *m* di golf; **golf stick** mazza *f* da golf; **golf course** campo *m* di golf; **golfer** giocatore *m*, -trice

di golf

gondola [ˈgɒndələ] gondola *f;* **gondolier** gondoliere *m*

good [gʊd] **1** *adj* buono; *weather, film* bello; *actor, child* bravo; **be ~ many** un bel po (di); **be ~ at** essere bravo in; **be ~ for s.o.** fare bene a qu; **be ~ for sth** andare bene per qc; **~!** bene!; **it's ~ to see you** è bello vederti **2** *n* bene *m;* **it did him no ~** non gli ha fatto bene; **good-bye** arrivederci; **say ~ to s.o.** salutare qu; **good-for-nothing** buono *m*, -a *f* a nulla; **Good Friday** venerdì *m inv* santo; **good-humoured**, *Am* **good-humored** di buon umore; **good-looking** attraente; **good-natured** di buon cuore; **goodness** bontà *f;* **thank ~!** grazie al cielo!; **goods** COM merce *fsg;* **goodwill** buona volontà *f*

goof [guːf] F fare una gaffe

goose [guːs] *(pl geese* [giːs]*)* oca *f;* **gooseberry** uva *f* spina; **goose bumps** pelle *f* d'oca

gorgeous [ˈgɔːdʒəs] stupendo; *smell* ottimo

gorilla [gəˈrɪlə] gorilla *m*

Gospel [ˈgɒspl] vangelo *m*

gossip [ˈgɒsɪp] **1** *n* pettegolezzo *m; person* pettegolo *m*, -a *f* **2** *v/i* spettegolare; **gossip column** cronaca *f* rosa

gourmet [ˈgʊəmeɪ] *n* buongustaio *m*, -a *f*

govern [ˈɡʌvn] governare; **government** governo *m*; **governor** governatore *m*

gown [ɡaʊn] *long dress* abito *m* lungo; *wedding dress* abito *m* da sposa; *of academic, judge* toga *f*; *of surgeon* camice *m*

grab [ɡræb] afferrare; **~ some sleep** farsi una dormita

grace [ɡreɪs] *of dancer etc* grazia *f*; *before meals* preghiera *f* (prima di un pasto); **graceful** aggraziato; **gracious** *person* cortese; *style* elegante

grade [ɡreɪd] **1** *n* (*quality*) qualità *f inv*; EDU voto *m* **2** *v/t* classificare; **grade crossing** *Am* passaggio *m* a livello; **grade school** *Am* scuola *f* elementare

gradient [ˈɡreɪdɪənt] pendenza *f*

gradual [ˈɡrædʒʊəl] graduale; **gradually** gradualmente

graduate [ˈɡrædʒʊət] **1** *n* laureato *m*, -a *f* **2** *v/i from university* laurearsi; **graduation** laurea *f*; *ceremony* cerimonia *f* di laurea

graffiti [ɡrəˈfiːtiː] graffiti *mpl*

graft [ɡrɑːft] **1** *n* BOT innesto *m*; MED trapianto *m*; F (*hard work*) duro lavoro *m*; *Am* F corruzione *f* **2** *v/t* BOT innestare; MED trapiantare

grain [ɡreɪn] cereali *mpl*; *seed* granello *m*; *of rice, wheat* chicco *m*; *in wood* venatura *f*

gram [ɡræm] grammo *m*

grammar [ˈɡræmə(r)] grammatica *f*; **grammar school** liceo *m*; **grammatical** grammaticale

grand [ɡrænd] **1** *adj* grandioso; F (*very good*) eccezionale **2** *n* F (£1000) mille sterline *fpl*; **grandchild** nipote *m/f*; **granddaughter** nipote *f*; **grandeur** grandiosità *f*; **grandfather** nonno *m*; **grand jury** *Am* gran giurì *m*; **grandmother** nonna *f*; **grandparents** nonni *mpl*; **grand piano** pianoforte *m* a coda; **grandson** nipote *m*

granite [ˈɡrænɪt] granito *m*

granny [ˈɡrænɪ] F nonna *f*

grant [ɡrɑːnt] **1** *n money* sussidio *m*; *for university* borsa *f* di studio **2** *v/t visa* assegnare; *permission* concedere; *wish* esaudire; **take sth for ~ed** dare qc per scontato; **he takes his wife for ~ed** considera quello che fa sua moglie come dovuto

granule [ˈɡrænjuːl] granello *m*

grape [ɡreɪp] acino *m* d'uva; **~s** uva *fsg*; **grapefruit** pompelmo *m*; **grapefruit juice** succo *m* di pompelmo

graph [ɡrɑːf] grafico *m*; **graphic 1** *adj* grafico; (*vivid*) vivido **2** *n* COMPUT grafico *m*; **~s** grafica *f*

♦ **grapple with** [ˈɡræpl] *attacker* lottare con; *problem*

grill

etc essere alle prese con

grasp [grɑːsp] **1** *n physical* presa *f*; *mental* comprensione *f* **2** *v/t physically, mentally* afferrare

grass [grɑːs] erba *f*; **grasshopper** cavalletta *f*; **grass roots** *people* massa *f* popolare; **grassy** erboso

grate¹ [greɪt] *n metal* grata *f*

grate² [greɪt] **1** *v/t in cooking* grattugiare **2** *v/i of sounds* stridere

grateful ['greɪtfʊl] grato (**to** a); **gratefully** con gratitudine

gratify ['grætɪfaɪ] soddisfare

grating ['greɪtɪŋ] **1** *n* grata *f* **2** *adj sound, voice* stridente

gratitude ['grætɪtjuːd] gratitudine *f*

grave¹ [greɪv] *n* tomba *f*

grave² [greɪv] *adj* grave

gravel ['grævl] ghiaia *f*

'gravestone lapide *f*; **graveyard** cimitero *m*

gravity ['grævətɪ] PHYS forza *f* di gravità

gravy ['greɪvɪ] sugo *m* della carne

gray *Am* ☞ **grey**

graze¹ [greɪz] *v/i of cow, horse* brucare

graze² [greɪz] **1** *v/t arm etc* graffiare **2** *n* graffio *m*

grease [griːs] grasso *m*; **greasy** food, hair grasso; hands, plate unto

great [greɪt] grande; F (*very good*) fantastico; **Great Bri**-

tain Gran Bretagna *f*; **greatly** molto; **greatness** grandezza *f*

Greece [griːs] Grecia *f*

greed [griːd] avidità *f*; *for food* ingordigia *f*; **greedily** con avidità; *eat* con ingordigia; **greedy** avido; *for food* ingordo

Greek [griːk] **1** *n* greco *m*, -a *f*; *language* greco *m* **2** *adj* greco

green [griːn] verde; *environmentally* ecologico; **the Greens** POL i verdi; **green beans** *mpl*; **green belt** zona *f* verde tutt'intorno ad una città; **green card** *driving insurance* carta *f* verde; *Am* (*work permit*) permesso *m* di lavoro; **greenhouse** serra *f*; **greenhouse effect** effetto *m* serra; **greens** verdura *f*

greet [griːt] salutare; **greeting** saluto *m*

grenade [grɪ'neɪd] granata *f*

grey [greɪ] grigio; *hair* bianco; **grey-haired** con i capelli bianchi; **greyhound** levriero *m*

grid [grɪd] grata *f*; *on map* reticolato *m*; **gridiron** *Am* SP campo *m* da calcio; **gridlock** *in traffic* ingorgo *m*

grief [griːf] dolore *m*; **grief-stricken** addolorato; **grievance** rimostranza *f*; **grieve** essere addolorato (**for** per)

grill [grɪl] **1** *n for cooking* grill *m inv*; *metal frame* griglia *f*;

dish grigliata *f*; *on window* grata *f* **2** *v/t food* fare alla griglia; (*interrogate*) mettere sotto torchio

grille [grɪl] grata *f*

grim [grɪm] cupo; *determination* accanito

grimace ['grɪməs] smorfia *f*

grime [graɪm] sporcizia *f*; **grimy** sudicio

grin [grɪn] **1** *n* sorriso *m* **2** *v/i* sorridere

grind [graɪnd] *coffee, meat* macinare; **~ one's teeth** digrignare i denti

grip [grɪp] **1** *n on rope etc* presa *f* **2** *v/t* afferrare; *of brakes* fare presa su; **be ~ped by sth** *by panic* essere preso da qc; **gripping** avvincente

gristle ['grɪsl] cartilagine *f*

grit [grɪt] **1** *n* (*dirt*) granelli *mpl*; *for roads* sabbia *f* **2** *v/t*: **~ one's teeth** stringere i denti; **gritty** F *book, film etc* realistico

groan [grəʊn] **1** *n* gemito *m* **2** *v/i* gemere

grocer ['grəʊsə(r)] droghiere *m*; **at the ~'s** (*shop*) dal droghiere; **groceries** generi *mpl* alimentari; **grocery store** *Am* drogheria *f*

groggy ['grɒgɪ] F intontito

groin [grɔɪn] ANAT inguine *m*

groom [gru:m] **1** *n for bride* sposo *m*; *for horse* stalliere *m* **2** *v/t horse* strigliare; (*train, prepare*) preparare; **well ~ed** *in appearance* ben curato

groove [gru:v] scanalatura *f*

grope [grəʊp] **1** *v/i in the dark* brancolare **2** *v/t sexually* palpeggiare

gross [grəʊs] (*coarse, vulgar*) volgare; *exaggeration* madornale; FIN lordo

grotty ['grɒtɪ] F *street, flat* squallido; **I feel ~** sto da schifo F

ground [graʊnd] **1** *n* suolo *m*; (*area, for sport*) terreno *m*; (*reason*) motivo *m*, ragione *f*; *Am* ELEC terra *f*; **on the ~** per terra; **on the ~s of** a causa di **2** *v/t Am* ELEC mettere a terra; **ground floor** pianoterra *m inv*; **grounding** *in subject* basi *fpl*; **groundless** infondato; **ground meat** *Am* carne *f* tritata; **groundwork** lavoro *m* di preparazione

group [gru:p] **1** *n* gruppo *m* **2** *v/t* raggruppare; **groupie** *ragazza che segue un gruppo o cantante rock in tutti i concerti*

grouse [graʊs] F **1** *n* lamentela *f* **2** *v/i* brontolare

grovel ['grɒvl] *fig* umiliarsi

grow [grəʊ] **1** *v/i* crescere; *of number* aumentare; *of business* svilupparsi; **~ old / tired** invecchiare / stancarsi; **~ into sth** diventare qc **2** *v/t flowers* coltivare

◆ **grow up** *of person* crescere; *of city* svilupparsi

growl [graʊl] **1** *n* grugnito *m* **2** *v/i* ringhiare

gunman

'grown-up1 *n* adulto *m*, -a *f* 2
adj adulto

growth [grəʊθ] *of person* crescita *f*; *of company* sviluppo
m; (*increase*) aumento *m*;
MED tumore *m*

grudge [grʌdʒ] 1 *n* rancore *m*;
bear s.o. a ~ portare rancore
a qu 2 *v/t*: **~ s.o. sth** invidiare
qc a qu; **grudging** riluttante;
grudgingly a malincuore

gruelling, *Am* grueling
['gruːəlɪŋ] estenuante

gruff [grʌf] burbero

grumble ['grʌmbl] brontolare; **grumbler** brontolone *m*,
-a *f*

grunt [grʌnt] 1 *n* grugnito *m* 2
v/i grugnire

guarantee [gærən'tiː] 1 *n* garanzia *f*; **~ period** periodo *m*
di garanzia 2 *v/t* garantire;
guarantor garante *m*

guard [gɑːd] 1 *n* guardia *m*;
be on one's ~ against stare
in guardia contro 2 *v/t* fare la
guardia a; **guard dog** cane
m da guardia; **guarded** *reply*
cauto; **guardian** LAW tutore
m, -trice *f*

guerrilla [gəˈrɪlə] guerrigliero
m, -a *f*; **guerrilla warfare**
guerriglia *f*

guess [ges] 1 *n* supposizione
f 2 *v/t the answer* indovinare;
I ~ so suppongo di sì 3 *v/i* indovinare; **guesswork** congettura *f*

guest [gest] ospite *m/f*;
guesthouse pensione *f*;

guestroom camera *f* degli
ospiti

guidance ['gaɪdəns] consigli
mpl; **guide 1** *n person, book*
guida *f* 2 *v/t* guidare; **guidebook** guida *f* turistica; **guided missile** missile *m* guidato; **guide dog** cane *m* per
ciechi; **guided tour** visita *f*
guidata; **guidelines** direttive *fpl*

guilt [gɪlt] colpa *f*; LAW colpevolezza *f*; **guilty** *also* LAW
colpevole; **have a ~ conscience** avere la coscienza
sporca

guinea pig ['gɪnɪpɪg] porcellino *m* d'india; *for experiments, fig* cavia *f*

guitar [gɪˈtɑː(r)] chitarra *f*;
guitarist chitarrista *m/f*

gulf [gʌlf] golfo *m*; *fig* divario
m

gull [gʌl] *bird* gabbiano *m*

gullet ['gʌlɪt] ANAT esofago *m*

gullible ['gʌlɪbl] credulone

gulp [gʌlp] 1 *n of water* sorso
m; *of air* boccata *f* 2 *v/i in surprise* deglutire

♦ gulp down *drink* ingoiare;
food trangugiare

gum1 [gʌm] *in mouth* gengiva
f

gum2 [gʌm] (*glue*) colla *f*;
(*chewing gum*) gomma *f*

gun [gʌn] *pistol, revolver, rifle*
arma *f* da fuoco; (*cannon*)
cannone *m*

♦ gun down sparare a morte

'gunfire spari *mpl*; **gunman**

uomo *m* armato; *robber* rapinatore *m*; **gunshot** sparo *m*; **gunshot wound** ferita *f* da arma da fuoco

gurgle ['gɜːgl] *of baby, drain* gorgogliare

guru ['guru] *fig* guru *m inv*

gush [gʌʃ] *of liquid* sgorgare

gust [gʌst] raffica *f*

gusto ['gʌstəʊ]: **with ~** con slancio

gusty ['gʌstɪ] *of weather* ventoso; **~ wind** vento a raffiche

gut [gʌt] **1** *n* intestino *m*; F *(stomach)* pancia *f* **2** *v/t (destroy)* sventrare; **guts** *pl (courage)* fegato *m* F; **gutsy**

F *person* che ha fegato; F *thing to do* che richiede fegato

gutter ['gʌtə(r)] *on pavement* canaletto *m* di scolo; *on roof* grondaia *f*

guy [gaɪ] F tipo *m* F; **hey, you ~s** ei, gente

guzzle ['gʌzl] ingozzarsi di

gym [dʒɪm] palestra *f*; *activity* ginnastica *f*; **gymnast** ginnasta *m/f*; **gymnastics** ginnastica *f*

gynaecologist [gaɪnɪ'kɒlədʒɪst] ginecologo *m*, -a *f*; **gynaecology**, *Am* **gynecology** ginecologia *f*

gypsy ['dʒɪpsɪ] zingaro *m*, -a *f*

H

habit ['hæbɪt] abitudine *f*

habitable ['hæbɪtəbl] abitabile; **habitat** habitat *m inv*

habitual [hə'bɪtjʊəl] solito; *smoker, drinker* incallito

hacker ['hækə(r)] COMPUT hacker *m/f inv*

hackneyed ['hæknɪd] trito

haemorrhage ['hemərɪdʒ] **1** *n* emorragia *f* **2** *v/i* avere un'emorragia

haggard ['hægəd] tirato

haggle ['hægl] contrattare

hail [heɪl] grandine *f*

hair [heə(r)] capelli *mpl*; *single* capello *m*; *on body, of animal* pelo *m*; **hairbrush** spazzola *f* per capelli; **haircut** taglio *m*

di capelli; **hairdo** pettinatura *f*; **hairdresser** parrucchiere *m*, -a *f*; **at the ~'s** dal parrucchiere; **hairdryer** fon *m inv*; **hairpin** forcina *f*; **hairpin bend** tornante *m*; **hair-raising** terrificante; **hair remover** crema *f* depilatoria; **hair-splitting** pedanteria *f*; **hairstyle** acconciatura *f*; **hairstylist** parrucchiere *m*, -a *f*; **hairy** *arm, animal* peloso; F *(frightening)* preoccupante

half [hɑːf] **1** *n* metà *f inv*, mezzo *m*; **~ past ten** le dieci e mezza; **~ an hour** mezz'ora **2** *adj* mezzo **3** *adv* a metà;

half-hearted poco convinto;
half time SP intervallo m;
halfway **1** adj stage, point intermedio **2** adv also fig a metà strada; **~ finished** fatto a metà

hall [hɔːl] large room sala f; hallway in house ingresso m

Hallowe'en [hæləʊˈiːn] vigilia f d'Ognissanti

halo [ˈheɪləʊ] aureola f

halt [hɔːlt] **1** v/i fermarsi **2** v/t fermare

halve [hɑːv] dimezzare

ham [hæm] prosciutto m; hamburger hamburger m inv

hammer [ˈhæmə(r)] **1** n martello m **2** v/i martellare; ~ **at the door** picchiare alla porta

hammock [ˈhæmək] amaca f

hamper¹ [ˈhæmpə(r)] n for food cestino m

hamper² [ˈhæmpə(r)] v/t (obstruct) ostacolare

hamster [ˈhæmstə(r)] criceto m

hand [hænd] n mano m; of clock lancetta f; (worker) operaio m; **at ~**, **to ~** a portata di mano; **by ~** a mano; **on the one ~ ...**, **on the other ~ ...** da un lato ..., dall'altro ...; **in ~** (being done) in corso; **on your right** ~ sulla tua destra; **change ~s** cambiare di mano; **give s.o. a ~** dare una mano a qu

◆ hand down passare

◆ hand out distribuire
◆ hand over consegnare; child to parent etc dare

handbag borsetta f; hand baggage bagaglio m a mano; handbrake freno m a mano; handcuff ammanettare; handcuffs manette fpl; handheld COMPUT palmare m, PDA m inv

handicap [ˈhændɪkæp] handicap m inv; handicapped handicappato

handkerchief [ˈhæŋkətʃɪf] fazzoletto m

handle [ˈhændl] **1** n maniglia f **2** v/t goods maneggiare; case, deal trattare; difficult person prendere; **let me ~ this** lascia fare a me; handlebars manubrio msg

hand luggage bagaglio m a mano; handmade fatto a mano; hands-free vivavoce m inv; handshake stretta f di mano; hands-off approach teorico; **he has a ~ style of management** non partecipa direttamente agli aspetti pratici della gestione

handsome [ˈhænsəm] bello

hands-on experience pratico; **he has a ~ style of management** partecipa direttamente agli aspetti pratici della gestione

handwriting calligrafia f; handwritten scritto a mano; handy tool, device pratico; **it's ~ for the shops** è como-

hang

do per i negozi

hang [hæŋ] **1** v/t picture appendere; person impiccare **2** v/i of dress, hair cadere **3** n: **get the ~ of** F capire

♦ **hang on** (wait) aspettare

♦ **hang up** TELEC riattaccare

hangar ['hæŋə(r)] hangar m inv

hanger ['hæŋə(r)] for clothes gruccia f

hang glider ['hæŋglaɪdə(r)] deltaplano m; **hang gliding** deltaplano m; **hangover** postumi mpl della sbornia

hankie, hanky ['hæŋkɪ] F fazzoletto m

haphazard [hæp'hæzəd] a casaccio

happen ['hæpn] succedere

happily ['hæpɪlɪ] allegramente; (gladly) volentieri; (luckily) per fortuna; **happiness** felicità f; **happy** felice; **happy-go-lucky** spensierato

harass [hə'ræs] tormentare; sexually molestare; **harassed** stressato; **harassment** persecuzione f; **sexual ~ molestie** fpl sessuali

harbour, Am **harbor** ['hɑːbə(r)] **1** n porto m **2** v/t criminal dar rifugio a; grudge covare

hard [hɑːd] **1** adj duro; (difficult) difficile; facts, evidence concreto; drug pesante; **~ of hearing** duro d'orecchio **2** adv work con impegno; rain, pull, push forte; **try ~**

impegnarsi; **hardback** libro m con copertina rigida; **hard-boiled** egg sodo; **hard copy** copia f stampata; **hard core** pornography pornografia f hard-core; **hard currency** valuta f forte; **hard disk** disco m rigido, **hard disk** drive m inv; **harden 1** v/t indurire **2** v/i of glue indurirsi; of attitude irrigidirsi; **hard hat** casco m; (construction worker) muratore m; **hardheaded** pratico; **hardhearted** dal cuore duro; **hard line** linea f dura; **hardliner** sostenitore m, -trice f della linea dura

hardly ['hɑːdlɪ] a malapena; ~ ever quasi mai; **you can ~ expect him to ...** non puoi certo aspettarti che lui ...

hardness ['hɑːdnɪs] durezza f; (difficulty) difficoltà f; **hardship** difficoltà fpl economiche; **hard up** al verde; **hardware** ferramenta fpl; COMPUT hardware m; **hardware store** negozio m di ferramenta; **hard-working** che lavora duro; **hardy** resistente

harm [hɑːm] **1** n danno m **2** v/t danneggiare; **harmful** dannoso; **harmless** innocuo

harmonious [hɑːˈməʊnɪəs] armonioso; **harmonize** armonizzare; **harmony** armonia f

harp [hɑːp] arpa f

harsh [hɑːʃ] criticism, words

duro; *colour, light* troppo forte; harshly duramente

harvest ['hɑːvɪst] raccolto *m*

hash mark [hæʃ] cancelletto *m*

haste [heɪst] fretta *f*; *hastily* in fretta; **hasty** frettoloso

hat [hæt] cappello *m*

hatch [hætʃ] *for serving food* passavivande *m inv*; *on ship* boccaporto *m*

◆ **hatch out** *of eggs* schiudersi

hatchet ['hætʃɪt] ascia *f*; **bury the ~** seppellire l'ascia di guerra

hate [heɪt] **1** *n* odio *m* **2** *v/t* odiare; hatred odio *m*

haughty ['hɔːtɪ] altezzoso

haul [hɔːl] **1** *n of fish* pescata *f* **2** *v/t (pull)* trascinare; **haulage** autotrasporto *m*

haunch [hɔːntʃ] anca *f*

haunt [hɔːnt] *v/t*: **this place is ~ed** qui c'è un fantasma / ci sono i fantasmi *n* ritrovo *m*

have [hæv] **1** *v/t* ◇ avere; *breakfast, shower* fare; **I'll ~ a coffee** prendo un caffè; ◇ *must*: **~ (got) to** dovere; **I ~ (got) to go** devo andare ◇ *causative*: **I had the printer fixed** ho fatto riparare la stampante **2** *v/aux* avere; *with verbs of motion* essere; **~ you seen her?** l'hai vista?; **I ~ come** sono venuto

◆ **have on** *(wear)* portare, indossare; **do you have anything on tonight?** *(have planned)* hai programmi per stasera?

haven ['heɪvn] *fig* oasi *f inv*

hawk [hɔːk] *also fig* falco *m*

hay [heɪ] fieno *m*; **hay fever** raffreddore *m* da fieno

hazard ['hæzəd] *n* rischio *m*; **hazard lights** MOT luci *fpl* di emergenza; **hazardous** rischioso

haze [heɪz] foschia *f*

hazelnut ['heɪzlnʌt] nocciola *f*

hazy ['heɪzɪ] *view* indistinto; *memories* vago

he [hiː] lui; **~'s French** è francese; **there ~ is** eccolo

head [hed] **1** *n* testa *f*; *(boss, leader)* capo *m*; *of primary school* direttore *m*, -trice *f*; *of secondary school* preside *m/f*; *on beer* schiuma *f*; **~s or tails?** testa o croce?; **at the ~ of the list** in cima alla lista **2** *v/t (lead)* essere a capo di; *ball* colpire di testa

◆ **head for** *place* dirigersi verso; *(be destined for)* andare incontro a

'**headache** mal *m* di testa; **headband** fascia *f* per i capelli; **header** *in soccer* colpo *m* di testa; *in document* intestazione *f*; **headhunter** COM cacciatore *m* di teste; **heading** *in list* titolo *m*; **headlamp** fanale *m*; **headline** in *newspaper* titolo *m*; **make the ~s** fare titolo; **headmaster** *in primary school* direttore *m*; *in secondary school* preside *m*; **headmistress** *in primary school* direttrice *f*; *in secondary school* preside *f*; **head office** *of company* sede *f* centrale; **head-on 1** *adv crash* frontalmente **2** *adj crash* frontale; **headphones** cuffie *fpl*; **headquarters** sede *fsg*; MIL quartiere *msg* generale; **headrest** poggiatesta *m inv*; **headroom** *for vehicle under bridge* altezza *f* utile; *in car* altezza *f* dell'abitacolo; **headscarf** foulard *m inv*; **headstrong** testardo; **head waiter** capocameriere *m*; **heady** *wine etc* inebriante

heal [hiːl] guarire

health [helθ] salute *f*; *(public ~)* sanità *f*; **your ~!** (alla) salute!; **health care** assistenza *f* sanitaria; **health food** alimenti *mpl* naturali; **health food store** negozio *m* di alimenti naturali; **health insurance** assicurazione *f* contro le malattie; **health resort** stazione *f* termale; **healthy** *also fig* sano

heap [hiːp] *n* mucchio *m*

hear [hɪə(r)] sentire

◆ **hear from** *(have news from)* avere notizie di

hearing [ˈhɪərɪŋ] udito *m*; LAW udienza *f*; **be within / out of**

~ essere / non essere a portata di voce; **hearing aid** apparecchio *m* acustico

hearse [hɜːs] carro *m* funebre

heart [haːt] cuore *m*; *of problem etc* nocciolo *m*; **know sth by ~** sapere qc a memoria; **heart attack** infarto *m*; **heartbreaking** straziante; **heartbroken** affranto; **heartburn** bruciore *m* di stomaco; **heart failure** infarto *m*

hearth [haːθ] focolare *m*

heartless [ˈhaːtlɪs] spietato; **heart throb** F idolo *m*; **hearty** *appetite* robusto; *meal* sostanzioso; *person* gioviale

heat [hiːt] calore *m*; *(hot weather)* caldo *m*

◆ **heat up** riscaldare

heated [ˈhiːtɪd] *pool* riscaldato; *discussion* animato; **heater** *radiator* termosifone *m*; *electric, gas* stufa *f*; *in car* riscaldamento *m*; **heating** riscaldamento *m*; **heatproof**, **heat-resistant** termoresistente; **heatwave** ondata *f* di caldo

heave [hiːv] *(lift)* sollevare

heaven [ˈhevn] paradiso *m*; **good ~s!** santo cielo!; **heavenly** F divino

heavy [ˈhevɪ] pesante; *cold, rain, accent* forte; *traffic* intenso; *food* pesante; *smoker* accanito; *drinker* forte; *loss, casualties* ingente; **heavy-duty** resistente; **heavy-**

weight SP di pesi massimi

hectic ['hektɪk] frenetico

hedge [hedʒ] siepe f; **hedge-hog** riccio m

heel [hi:l] of foot tallone m, calcagno m; of shoe tacco m; **heel bar** calzoleria f istantanea

hefty ['heftɪ] massiccio

height [haɪt] altezza f; of aeroplane altitudine f; **at the ~ of summer** nel pieno dell'estate; **heighten** effect, tension aumentare

heir [eə(r)] erede m; **heiress** ereditiera f

helicopter ['helɪkɒptə(r)] elicottero m

hell [hel] inferno m; **what the ~ are you doing** F che diavolo fai? F; **go to ~!** F va' all'inferno! F

hello [hə'ləʊ] informal ciao; more formal buongiorno; buona sera; TELEC pronto; **say ~ to s.o.** salutare qu

helmet ['helmɪt] of motorcyclist casco m; of soldier elmetto m

help [help] **1** n aiuto m **2** v/t aiutare; **~ o.s.** to food servirsi; **I can't ~ it** non ci posso far niente; **helper** aiutante m/f; **helpful** person di aiuto; advice utile; **he was very ~** mi è stato di grande aiuto; **helping** of food porzione f; **helpless** (unable to cope) indifeso; (powerless) impotente; **helplessness** impotenza

f; **help menu** COMPUT menu m inv della guida in linea

hem [hem] of dress etc orlo m

hemisphere ['hemɪsfɪə(r)] emisfero m

'hemline orlo m

hemorrhage Am ☞ **haemorrhage**

hen [hen] gallina f

'hen party equivalente al femminile della festa d'addio al celibato

hepatitis [hepə'taɪtɪs] epatite f

her [hɜ:(r)] **1** adj il suo m, la sua f, i suoi mpl, le sue fpl; **~ sister / brother** sua sorella / suo fratello **2** pron direct object la; indirect object le; after prep lei; **I know ~** la conosco; **I gave ~ the keys** le ho dato le chiavi; **this is for ~** questo è per lei; **who? - ~** chi? - lei

herb [hɜ:b] for medicines erba f medicinale; for flavouring erba f aromatica; **herb(al) tea** tisana f

herd [hɜ:d] mandria f

here [hɪə(r)] qui, qua; **~'s to you!** as toast salute!; **~ you are** giving sth ecco qui

hereditary [hə'redɪtərɪ] ereditario; **heredity** ereditarietà f inv; **heritage** patrimonio m

hernia ['hɜ:nɪə] MED ernia f

hero ['hɪərəʊ] eroe m; **heroic** eroico; **heroically** eroicamente

heroin ['herəʊɪn] eroina f

heroine ['herəʊɪn] eroina f

heroism ['herəʊɪzm] eroismo m

herpes ['hɜːpiːz] MED herpes m

hers [hɜːz] il suo m, la sua f, i suoi mpl, le sue fpl; *a friend of* ~ un suo amico

herself [hɜː'self] *reflexive* si; *emphatic* se stessa; *after prep* sé, se stessa; *she hurt* ~ si è fatta male

hesitant ['hezɪtənt] esitante; hesitantly con esitazione; hesitate esitare; hesitation esitazione f

heterosexual [hetərəʊ'seksjʊəl] eterosessuale

hi [haɪ] ciao

hibernate ['haɪbəneɪt] andare in letargo

hiccup ['hɪkʌp] singhiozzo m; *(minor problem)* intoppo m

hidden ['hɪdn] nascosto

hide¹ [haɪd] 1 v/t nascondere 2 v/i nascondersi

hide² [haɪd] n *of animal* pelle f

hide-and-seek nascondino m; hideaway rifugio m

hideous ['hɪdɪəs] orrendo; *crime* atroce

hiding ['haɪdɪŋ] *(beating)* batosta f; hiding place nascondiglio m

hierarchy ['haɪərɑːkɪ] gerarchia f

high [haɪ] 1 adj alto; *wind, speed* forte; *quality, hopes* buono; *(on drugs)* fatto F 2 n *in statistics* livello m record

3 adv in alto; highbrow intellettuale; highchair seggiolone m; highclass di (prima) classe; High Court Corte f Suprema; high-frequency ad alta frequenza; high-grade di buona qualità; high-handed autoritario; high-heeled col tacco alto; high jump salto m in alto; high-level ad alto livello; highlight 1 n *(main event)* clou m inv; *in hair* colpo m di sole 2 v/t *with pen* evidenziare; COMPUT selezionare; highlighter evidenziatore m; highly *desirable, likely* molto; *paid* profumatamente; *think* ~ *of s.o.* stimare molto qu; highly strung nervoso; high performance *drill, battery* ad alto rendimento; high-pitched acuto; high point clou m inv; high-powered *engine* potente; *intellectual* di prestigio; high-pressure TECH ad alta pressione; *salesman* aggressivo; high pressure *weather* alta pressione f; high school scuola f superiore; high street via f principale; high tech 1 n high-tech m 2 adj high tech; highway Am autostrada f

hijack ['haɪdʒæk] 1 v/t dirottare 2 n dirottamento m; hijacker dirottatore m, -trice f

hike¹ [haɪk] 1 n camminata f 2 v/i fare camminate

hike² [haɪk] *n in prices* aumento *m*

hiker ['haɪkə(r)] escursionista *m/f*; **hiking** escursionismo *m*

hilarious [hɪ'leərɪəs] divertentissimo

hill [hɪl] collina *f*; (*slope*) altura *f*; **hillside** pendio *m*; **hilltop** cima *f* della collina; **hilly** collinoso

hilt [hɪlt] impugnatura *f*

him [hɪm] *direct object* lo; *indirect object* gli; *after prep* lui; *I know* ~ lo conosco; *I gave* ~ *the keys* gli ho dato le chiavi; *this is for* ~ questo è per lui; *who?* - ~ chi? - lui

himself [hɪm'self] se stesso; *after prep* sé, se stesso; *he hurt* ~ si è fatto male

hinder ['hɪndə(r)] intralciare; **hindrance** intralcio *m*

hinge [hɪndʒ] cardine *m*

hint [hɪnt] (*clue*) accenno *m*; (*piece of advice*) consiglio *m*; (*implied suggestion*) allusione *f*; *of red, sadness etc* punta *f*

hip [hɪp] fianco *m*; **hip pocket** tasca *f* posteriore

hippopotamus [hɪpə'pɒtəməs] ippopotamo *m*

hire ['haɪə(r)] *room, hall* affittare; *workers, staff* assumere; *conjuror etc* ingaggiare; **hire car** macchina *f* a noleggio; **hire purchase** acquisto *m* rateale

his [hɪz] **1** *adj* il suo *m*, la sua *f*, i suoi *mpl*, le sue *fpl*; ~ *sis-*

ter / brother sua sorella / suo fratello **2** *pron* il suo *m*, la sua *f*, i suoi *mpl*, le sue *fpl*; *a friend of* ~ un suo amico

hiss [hɪs] sibilare

historian [hɪ'stɔːrɪən] storico *m*, -a *f*; **historic** storico; **historical** storico; **history** storia *f*

hit [hɪt] **1** *v/t* colpire; (*collide with*) sbattere contro; *I* ~ *my knee* ho battuto il ginocchio; *it suddenly* ~ *me* (*I realized*) improvvisamente ho realizzato **2** *n* (*blow*) colpo *m*; (*success*) successo *m*; *on website* visita *f*

◆ **hit out at** (*criticize*) attaccare

hitch [hɪtʃ] **1** *n* (*problem*) contrattempo *m* **2** *v/t*: ~ *sth to sth* legare qc a qc; ~ *a lift* (*hitchhike*) chiedere un passaggio **3** *v/i* (*hitchhike*) fare l'autostop; **hitchhike** fare l'autostop; **hitchhiker** autostoppista *m/f*; **hitchhiking** autostop *m*

hi-tech **1** *n* high-tech **2** *adj* high tech

'hitlist libro *m* nero; **hitman** sicario *m*; **hit-or-miss**: *on a* ~ *basis* affidandosi al caso; **hit squad** commando *m*

HIV [eɪtʃaɪ'viː] *f* (= *human immunodeficiency virus*) HIV *m*

hive [haɪv] *for bees* alveare *m*

HIV-'positive sieropositivo

hoard [hɔːd] **1** *n* provvista *f*; ~

of money gruzzolo *m* **2** *v/t* accumulare; **hoarding** tabellone *m* per affissioni pubblicitarie

hoarse [hɔːs] rauco

hoax [həʊks] scherzo *m*; *malicious* falso allarme *m*

hobble ['hɒbl] zoppicare

hobby ['hɒbɪ] hobby *m inv*

hobo ['həʊbəʊ] *Am* barbone *m*, -a *f*

hockey ['hɒkɪ] hockey *m* (su prato); *Am* hockey *m* sul ghiaccio

hog [hɒg] *esp Am* maiale *m*

hoist [hɔɪst] **1** *n* montacarichi *m inv* **2** *v/t* (*lift*) sollevare; *flag* issare

hold [həʊld] **1** *v/t in hand* tenere; (*support, keep in place*) reggere; *passport* avere; *prisoner, suspect* trattenere; (*contain*) contenere; *job, post* occupare; ~ *hands* tenersi per mano; ~ *one's breath* trattenere il fiato; ~ *that ...* (*believe, maintain*) sostenere che ...; ~ *the line* TELEC resti in linea **2** *n in ship, plane* stiva *f*; *catch* ~ *of sth* afferrare qc; *lose one's* ~ *on sth on rope etc* perdere la presa su qc

◆ **hold back 1** *v/t crowds* contenere; *facts* nascondere **2** *v/i* (*hesitate*) esitare

◆ **hold on 1** *v/t in hand* tenere; *prospect* offrire **2** *v/i* (*of supplies*) durare; (*survive*) resistere

◆ **hold up** *hand* alzare; *bank etc* rapinare; (*make late*) trattenere

holder ['həʊldə(r)] (*container*) contenitore *m*; *of passport* titolare *m*; *of ticket* possessore *m*; *of record* detentore *m*, -trice *f*; **holding company** holding *f inv*; **holdup** (*robbery*) rapina *f*; (*delay*) ritardo *m*

hole [həʊl] buco *m*

holiday ['hɒlədeɪ] vacanza *f*; *public* giorno *m* festivo; (*day off*) giorno *m* di ferie; *go on* ~ andare in vacanza

Holland ['hɒlənd] Olanda *f*

hollow ['hɒləʊ] cavo, vuoto; *cheeks* infossato

holocaust ['hɒləkɔːst] olocausto *m*

hologram ['hɒləgræm] ologramma *m*

holster ['həʊlstə(r)] fondina *f*

holy ['həʊlɪ] santo; **Holy Spirit** Spirito *m* Santo; **Holy Week** settimana *f* santa

home [həʊm] **1** *n* casa *f*; (*native country*) patria *f*; *for old people* casa *f* di riposo; *for children* istituto *m*; *at* ~ a casa; SP in casa; *make yourself at* ~ fai come a casa tua; *work from* ~ lavorare da casa **2** *adv* andare a casa; *go* ~ andare a casa; *is she* ~ *yet?* è tornata?; **home address** indirizzo *m* di casa; **home banking** home-banking *m*; **homecoming** ritorno *m*; **home**

computer computer *m inv* (per casa); **home game** incontro *m*; **homeless** senza tetto; **the ~ i** senzacasa; **homeloving** casalingo; **homely** semplice; (*welcoming*) accogliente; **homemade** fatto in casa, casalingo; **home match** incontro *m* casalingo; **Home Office** Ministero *m* degli Interni; **home page** home page *f*; **Home Secretary** Ministro *m* degli Interni; **homesick**: **be ~** avere nostalgia di casa; **home town** città *f inv* natale; **homeward** verso casa; **homework** EDU compiti *mpl* a casa

homicide ['hɒmɪsaɪd] *crime* omicidio *m*; *Am*: *police department* (squadra *f*) omicidi *f*

homophobia [hɒmə'fəʊbɪə] omofobia *f*

homosexual [hɒmə'sekʃʊəl] **1** *adj* omosessuale **2** *n* omosessuale *m/f*

honest ['ɒnɪst] onesto; **honestly** onestamente; **~!** ma insomma!; **honesty** onestà *f*

honey ['hʌnɪ] miele *m*; F (*darling*) tesoro *m*; **honeymoon** luna *f* di miele

honk [hɒŋk] *horn* suonare

honor *Am* ☞ **honour**

honour ['ɒnə(r)] **1** *n* onore *m* **2** *v/t* onorare; **honourable** onorevole

hood [hʊd] *over head* cappuc-

cio *m*; *over cooker* cappa *f*; MOT *on convertible* capote *f inv*; *Am* MOT cofano *m*

hoodlum ['huːdləm] gangster *m inv*

hook [hʊk] gancio *m*; *for fishing* amo *m*; **off the ~** TELEC staccato; **hooked**: **be ~ on s.o. / sth** essere fanatico di qu / qc; **be ~ on sth** *on drugs* essere assuefatto a qc; **hooker** F prostituta *f*; *in rugby* tallonatore *m*

hooligan ['huːlɪgən] teppista *m/f*; **hooliganism** teppismo *m*

hoot [huːt] **1** *v/t horn* suonare **2** *v/i* of car suonare il clacson; *of owl* gufare

hop [hɒp] saltare

hope [həʊp] **1** *n* speranza *f* **2** *v/i* sperare; **~ for sth** augurarsi qc; **I ~ so** spero di sì **3** *v/t*: **~ that ...** sperare che; **hopeful** ottimista; (*promising*) promettente; **hopefully** *say, wait* con ottimismo; (*I / we hope*) si spera; **hopeless** *position, prospect* senza speranza; (*useless: person*) negato F

horizon [hə'raɪzn] orizzonte *m*; **horizontal** orizzontale

hormone ['hɔːməʊn] ormone *m*

horn [hɔːn] *of animal* corno *m*; MOT clacson *m inv*

hornet ['hɔːnɪt] calabrone *m*

horny ['hɔːnɪ] *Am* F *sexually* arrapato P

horrible ['hɒrɪbl] orribile; horrify inorridire; *I was horrified* ero scioccato; horrifying *experience* terrificante; *idea, prices* allucinante; horror orrore *m*; *the ~s of war* le atrocità della guerra

horse [hɔːs] cavallo *m*; horse race corsa *f* di cavalli; horseshoe ferro *m* di cavallo

horticulture ['hɔːtɪkʌltʃə(r)] orticoltura *f*

hose [həʊz] tubo *m* di gomma

hospitable [hɒ'spɪtəbl] ospitale

hospital ['hɒspɪtl] ospedale *m*; hospitality ospitalità *f*

host [həʊst] *at party, reception* padrone *m* di casa; *of TV programme* presentatore *m*, -trice *f*

hostage ['hɒstɪdʒ] ostaggio *m*; *be taken ~* essere preso in ostaggio; hostage taker sequestratore *m*

hostel ['hɒstl] *for students* pensionato *m*; (*youth ~*) ostello *m* (della gioventù)

hostess ['həʊstɪs] *at party, reception* padrona *f* di casa; *on aeroplane* hostess *f inv*

hostile ['hɒstaɪl] ostile; hostility ostilità *f inv*

hot [hɒt] *weather, water* caldo; (*spicy*) piccante; F (*good*) bravo (*at sth* in qc); *it's ~* fa caldo; *I'm ~* ho caldo; hot dog hot dog *m inv*

hotel [həʊ'tel] albergo *m*

hour ['aʊə(r)] ora *f*

house 1 [haʊs] *n* casa *f*; POL camera *f*; THEA sala *f*; *at your ~* a casa tua, da te 2 [haʊz] *v/t* alloggiare; housebreaking furto *m* con scasso; household famiglia *f*; household name nome *m* conosciuto; housekeeper governante *f*; House of Representatives la camera *f* dei rappresentanti; housewarming (party) *festa per inaugurare la nuova casa*; housewife casalinga *f*; housework lavori *mpl* domestici; housing alloggi *mpl*; TECH alloggiamento *m*

hovel ['hɒvl] tugurio *m*

hover ['hɒvə(r)] librarsi

how [haʊ] come; *~ are you?* come stai?; *~ about ...?* che ne dici di ...?; *~ much?* quanto?; *~ much is it?* di cost quant'è?; *~ many?* quanti?; *~ odd / lovely!* che strano / bello!; however comunque; *~ big they are* per quanto grandi siano

howl [haʊl] *of dog* ululare; *of person in pain* urlare; *~ with laughter* sbellicarsi dalle risate; howler *mistake* strafalcione *m*

hub [hʌb] *of wheel* mozzo *m*; hubcap coprimozzo *m*

◆ huddle together ['hʌdl] stringersi l'un l'altro

hug [hʌg] 1 *v/t* abbracciare 2 *n* abbraccio *m*

hydrant

huge [hju:dʒ] enorme

hull [hʌl] scafo *m*

hum [hʌm] canticchiare; *of machine* ronzare

human ['hju:mən] **1** *n* essere *m* umano **2** *adj* umano; human being essere *m* umano

humane [hju:'mein] umano

humanitarian [hju:mæni-'teəriən] umanitario

humanity [hju:'mænəti] umanità *f*; human race genere *m* umano; human resources risorse *fpl* umane

humble ['hʌmbl] umile; *house* modesto

humdrum ['hʌmdrʌm] monotono

humid ['hju:mid] umido; humidifier umidificatore *m*; humidity umidità *f*

humiliate [hju:'milieit] umiliare; humiliating umiliante; humiliation umiliazione *f*; humility umiltà *f*

humor *Am* ☞ **humour**

humorous ['hju:mərəs] *person* spiritoso; *story* umoristico; humour umorismo *m*; (*mood*) umore *m*; **sense of** ~ senso dell'umorismo

hunch [hʌntʃ] (*idea*) impressione *f*; *of detective* intuizione *f*

hundred ['hʌndrəd] cento *m*; **a** ~ ... cento ...; hundredth centesimo

Hungarian [hʌŋ'geəriən] **1** *adj* ungherese **2** *n person* ungherese *m/f*; *language* un-

gherese *m*; Hungary Ungheria *f*

hunger ['hʌŋgə(r)] fame *f*

hung-'over: *feel* ~ avere i postumi della sbornia

hungry ['hʌŋgri] affamato; **I'm** ~ ho fame

hunk [hʌŋk] *n* tocco *m*; F (*man*) fusto *m* F

hunt [hʌnt] **1** *n for animals* caccia *f*; *for job, house, missing child* ricerca *f* **2** *v/t animal* cacciare; hunter cacciatore *m*, -trice *f*; hunting caccia *f*

hurdle ['hɜ:dl] *also fig* ostacolo *m*

hurl [hɜ:l] scagliare

hurray [hu'rei] urrà!

hurricane ['hʌrikən] uragano *m*

hurried ['hʌrid] frettoloso; hurry **1** *n* fretta *f*; **be in a** ~ avere fretta **2** *v/i* sbrigarsi ♦ hurry up **1** *v/i* sbrigarsi; **hurry up!** sbrigati! **2** *v/t* fare fretta a

hurt [hɜ:t] **1** *v/i* far male; **does it** ~? ti fa male? **2** *v/t physically* far male a; *emotionally* ferire

husband ['hʌzbənd] marito *m*

hush [hʌʃ] silenzio *m* ♦ hush up *scandal etc* mettere a tacere

husky ['hʌski] *voice* roco

hut [hʌt] capanno *m*

hybrid ['haibrid] ibrido *m*

hydrant ['haidrənt] idrante *m*

hydraulic [haɪˈdrɔːlɪk] idraulico

hydroelectric [haɪdrəʊˈlektrɪk] idroelettrico

hydrogen [ˈhaɪdrədʒən] idrogeno *m*

hygiene [ˈhaɪdʒiːn] igiene *f*; **hygienic** igienico

hymn [hɪm] inno *m* (sacro)

hype [haɪp] pubblicità *f*

hyperactive [haɪpərˈæktɪv] iperattivo; **hypermarket** ipermercato *m*; **hypersensitive** ipersensibile; **hypertext** COMPUT ipertesto *m*

hyphen [ˈhaɪfn] trattino *m*

hypnosis [hɪpˈnəʊsɪs] ipnosi

f; **hypnotize** ipnotizzare

hypocrisy [hɪˈpɒkrəsɪ] ipocrisia *f*; **hypocrite** ipocrita *m/f*; **hypocritical** ipocrita

hypothermia [haɪpəʊˈθɜːmɪə] ipotermia *f*

hypothesis [haɪˈpɒθəsɪs] ipotesi *f inv*; **hypothetical** ipotetico

hysterectomy [hɪstəˈrektəmɪ] isterectomia *f*

hysteria [hɪˈstɪərɪə] isteria *f*; **hysterical** isterico; F (*very funny*) buffissimo; **become** ~ avere una crisi isterica; **hysterics** *laughter* attacco *m* di risa; MED crisi *f* isterica

I

I [aɪ] io; ~ **am** English sono inglese; **here** ~ **am** eccomi

ice [aɪs] ghiaccio *m*; **iceberg** iceberg *m inv*; **icebox** *Am* frigo *m*; **ice cream** gelato *m*; **ice cube** cubetto *m* di ghiaccio; **iced** *drink* ghiacciato; *cake* glassato; **ice hockey** hockey *m* sul ghiaccio; **ice lolly** ghiacciolo *m*; **ice rink** pista *f* di pattinaggio; **ice skate** pattinare (sul ghiaccio); **ice skating** pattinaggio *m* (sul ghiaccio)

icicle [ˈaɪsɪkl] ghiacciolo *m*

icing [ˈaɪsɪŋ] glassa *f*

icon [ˈaɪkɒn] *cultural* mito *m*; COMPUT icona *f*

icy [ˈaɪsɪ] *road, surface* ghiac-

ciato; *welcome* glaciale

ID [aɪˈdiː] (= *identity*): **have you got any** ~ **on you?** ha un documento d'identità?

idea [aɪˈdɪə] idea *f*; **good** ~**!** ottima idea!; **I have no** ~ non ne ho la minima idea; **ideal** ideale; **idealistic** *person* idealista; *views* idealistico

identical [aɪˈdentɪkl] identico; ~ **twins** gemelli *mpl* monozigotici; **identification** identificazione *f*, riconoscimento *m*; *papers etc* documento *m* di riconoscimento *or* d'identità; **identify** (*recognize*) identificare, riconoscere; (*point out*) individuare;

identity identità f inv; **~ card** carta f d'identità

ideological [aɪdɪə'lɒdʒɪkl] ideologico; **ideology** ideologia f

idiomatic [ɪdɪə'mætɪk] naturale

idiot ['ɪdɪət] idiota m/f; **idiotic** [ɪdɪ'ɒtɪk] idiota

idle ['aɪdl] **1** adj person disoccupato; threat vuoto; machinery inattivo **2** v/i of engine girare al minimo

idol ['aɪdl] idolo m; **idolize** ['aɪdəlaɪz] idolatrare

idyllic [ɪ'dɪlɪk] idilli(a)co

if [ɪf] se

ignite [ɪg'naɪt] dar fuoco a; **ignition** [ɪg'nɪʃn] in car accensione f; **~ key** chiave f dell'accensione

ignorance ['ɪgnərəns] ignoranza f; **ignorant** (rude) cafone; **be ~ of sth** ignorare qc; **ignore** ignorare

ill [ɪl] ammalato; **fall ~, be taken ~** ammalarsi; **feel ~** sentirsi male

illegal [ɪ'liːgl] illegale

illegible [ɪ'ledʒəbl] illeggibile

illegitimate [ɪlɪ'dʒɪtɪmət] child illegittimo

illicit [ɪ'lɪsɪt] copy, imports illegale; pleasure, relationship illecito

illiterate [ɪ'lɪtərət] analfabeta

illness ['ɪlnɪs] malattia f

illogical [ɪ'lɒdʒɪkl] illogico

ill'treat maltrattare

illuminating [ɪ'luːmɪneɪtɪŋ] remarks etc chiarificatore

illusion [ɪ'luːʒn] illusione f

illustrate ['ɪləstreɪt] illustrare; **illustration** illustrazione f; with examples esemplificazione f; **illustrator** illustratore m, -trice f

image ['ɪmɪdʒ] immagine f; (exact likeness) ritratto; **image-conscious** attento all'immagine

imaginary [ɪ'mædʒɪnərɪ] immaginario; **imagination** immaginazione f, fantasia f; **imaginative** fantasioso; **imagine** immaginare; **you're imagining things** è frutto della tua immaginazione

IMF [aɪem'ef] (= **International Monetary Fund**) FMI m (= Fondo m Monetario Internazionale)

imitate ['ɪmɪteɪt] imitare; **imitation** imitazione f

immaculate [ɪ'mækjʊlət] immacolato

immature [ɪmə'tʃʊə(r)] immaturo

immediate [ɪ'miːdɪət] immediato; **the ~ family** i familiari più stretti; **immediately** immediatamente; **~ after the bank** subito dopo la banca

immense [ɪ'mens] immenso

immerse [ɪ'mɜːs] immergere

immigrant ['ɪmɪgrənt] immigrato m, -a f; **immigrate** immigrare; **immigration** immigrazione f

imminent ['ɪmɪnənt] imminente

immobilize [ɪˈməʊbɪlaɪz] immobilizzare; immobilizer on car immobilizzatore m

immoderate [ɪˈmɒdərət] smodato

immoral [ɪˈmɒrəl] immorale; immorality immoralità f inv

immortal [ɪˈmɔːtl] immortale; immortality immortalità f

immune [ɪˈmjuːn] to illness, infection immune; from ruling, requirement esente; immune system MED sistema m immunitario; immunity immunità f inv; from ruling esenzione f

impact [ˈɪmpækt] of meteorite, vehicle urto m; of new manager etc impatto m; (effect) effetto m

impair [ɪmˈpeə(r)] danneggiare

impartial [ɪmˈpɑːʃl] imparziale

impassable [ɪmˈpɑːsəbl] road impraticabile

impassioned [ɪmˈpæʃnd] speech, plea appassionato

impatience [ɪmˈpeɪʃəns] impazienza f; impatient impaziente; impatiently con impazienza

impeach [ɪmˈpiːtʃ] President mettere in stato d'accusa

impeccable [ɪmˈpekəbl] impeccabile

impede [ɪmˈpiːd] ostacolare; impediment in speech difetto m

impending [ɪmˈpendɪŋ] imminente

imperative [ɪmˈperətɪv] 1 adj essenziale 2 n GRAM imperativo m

imperfect [ɪmˈpɜːfekt] 1 adj imperfetto 2 n GRAM imperfetto m

impersonal [ɪmˈpɜːsənl] impersonale; impersonate as a joke imitare; illegally fingersi

impertinence [ɪmˈpɜːtɪnəns] impertinenza f; impertinent impertinente

impervious [ɪmˈpɜːvɪəs]: ~ to indifferente a

impetuous [ɪmˈpetjʊəs] impetuoso

impetus [ˈɪmpɪtəs] of campaign etc impeto m

implement [ˈɪmplɪmənt] 1 n utensile m 2 v/t implementare

implicate [ˈɪmplɪkeɪt] implicare; implication conseguenza f possibile; by ~ implicitamente

implicit [ɪmˈplɪsɪt] implicito; trust assoluto

implore [ɪmˈplɔː(r)] implorare

imply [ɪmˈplaɪ] implicare; (suggest) insinuare

impolite [ˌɪmpəˈlaɪt] maleducato

import [ˈɪmpɔːt] 1 n importazione f; item articolo m d'importazione 2 v/t importare

importance [ɪmˈpɔːtəns] importanza f; important importante

importer [ɪmˈpɔːtə(r)] importatore *m*, -trice *f*

impose [ɪmˈpəʊz] *tax* imporre; **~ o.s. on s.o.** disturbare qu; **imposing** imponente

impossibility [ɪmpɒsɪˈbɪlɪtɪ] impossibilità *f inv*; **impossible** impossibile

impotence [ˈɪmpətəns] impotenza *f*; **impotent** impotente

impractical [ɪmˈpræktɪkəl] *person* senza senso pratico; *suggestion* poco pratico

impress [ɪmˈpres] fare colpo su; **be ~ed by s.o. / sth** essere colpito da qu / qc; **impression** impressione *f*; (*impersonation*) imitazione *f*; **impressionable** impressionabile; **impressive** notevole

imprint [ˈɪmprɪnt] *of credit card* impressione *f*

imprison [ɪmˈprɪzn] incarcerare; **imprisonment** carcerazione *f*

improbable [ɪmˈprɒbəbl] improbabile

improve [ɪmˈpruːv] migliorare; **improvement** miglioramento *m*

improvise [ˈɪmprəvaɪz] improvvisare

impudent [ˈɪmpjʊdənt] impudente

impulse [ˈɪmpʌls] impulso *m*; **do sth on an ~** fare qc d'impulso; **impulsive** impulsivo

in [ɪn] **1** *prep* ◇ *place*: **~ Milan** a Milano; **~ the street** per strada; **~ the box** nella scato-

la; **wounded ~ the leg** ferito alla gamba ◇ *time*: **~ 1999** nel 1999; **~ two hours** *from now* tra due ore; *over period of* in due ore; **~ the morning** la mattina; **~ the summer** d'estate; **~ September** a or in settembre ◇ *manner*: **~ English** in inglese; **~ a loud voice** a voce alta; **~ yellow** di giallo ◇ (*while*): **~ crossing the road** mentre attraversava la strada ◇: **one ~ ten** uno su dieci **2** *adv*: **be ~** *at home* essere a casa; *in the building etc* esserci; *arrived*: *of train* essere arrivato; *in its position* essere dentro; **is she ~?** c'è?; **~ here / there** qui / lì (dentro) **3** *adj* (*fashionable*, *popular*) in, di moda

inability [ɪnəˈbɪlɪtɪ] incapacità *f inv*

inaccurate [ɪnˈækjʊrət] inaccurato

inactive [ɪnˈæktɪv] inattivo

inadequate [ɪnˈædɪkwət] inadeguato

inadvisable [ɪnədˈvaɪzəbl] sconsigliabile

inanimate [ɪnˈænɪmət] inanimato

inappropriate [ɪnəˈprəʊprɪət] inappropriato

inaudible [ɪnˈɔːdɪbl] impercettibile

inaugural [ɪnˈɔːgjʊrəl] *speech* inaugurale; **inaugurate** inaugurare

inborn [ˈɪnbɔːn] innato

Inc. [ɪŋk] (= *incorporated*) Inc.

incalculable [ɪn'kælkjʊləbl] incalcolabile

incapable [ɪn'keɪpəbl] incapace (*of doing* di fare)

incense ['ɪnsens] *in church* incenso *m*

incentive [ɪn'sentɪv] incentivo *m*

incessant [ɪn'sesnt] incessante; **incessantly** incessantemente

incest ['ɪnsest] incesto *m*

inch [ɪntʃ] pollice *m*

incident ['ɪnsɪdənt] incidente *m*; **incidental** casuale; **~ expenses** spese accessorie; **incidentally** a proposito

incision [ɪn'sɪʒn] incisione *f*; **incisive** acuto

incite [ɪn'saɪt] incitare; **~ s.o. to do sth** istigare qu a fare qc

inclination [ɪnklɪ'neɪʃn] inclinazione *f*

inclose, inclosure ☞ **enclose, enclosure**

include [ɪn'kluːd] includere, comprendere; **including** compreso, incluso; **inclusive 1** *adj price* tutto compreso **2** *prep*: **~ of VAT** IVA compresa **3** *adv*: **from Monday to Thursday** ~ dal lunedì di giovedì compreso

incoherent [ɪnkəʊ'hɪrənt] incoerente

income ['ɪnkəm] reddito *m*; **income tax** imposta *f* sul

reddito

incoming ['ɪnkʌmɪŋ] *adj flight, phonecall, mail* in arrivo; *tide* montante; *president* entrante

incomparable [ɪn'kɒmprəbl] incomparabile

incompatibility [ɪnkəmpætɪ-'bɪlɪtɪ] incompatibilità *f inv*; **incompatible** incompatibile

incompetence [ɪn'kɒmpɪtəns] incompetenza *f*; **incompetent** incompetente

incomplete [ɪnkəm'pliːt] incompleto

incomprehensible [ɪnkɒm-prɪ'hensɪbl] incomprensibile

inconceivable [ɪnkən'siːvəbl] inconcepibile

inconsiderate [ɪnkən'sɪd-ərət] poco gentile

inconsistent [ɪnkən'sɪstənt] incoerente

inconsolable [ɪnkən'səʊləbl] *adj* inconsolabile

inconspicuous [ɪnkən'spɪk-jʊəs] poco visibile; **make o.s.** ~ passare inosservato

inconvenience [ɪnkən'viː-nɪəns] inconveniente *m*; **inconvenient** scomodo; *time* poco opportuno

incorporate [ɪn'kɔːpəreɪt] includere

incorrect [ɪnkə'rekt] *answer* errato; *behaviour* scorretto; **am I** ~ **in thinking …?** sbaglio a pensare che …?

increase 1 [ɪn'kriːs] *v/t & v/i* aumentare **2** ['ɪnkriːs] *n* aumento *m*; **on the ~** in aumento; **increasing** crescente; **increasingly** sempre più

incredible [ɪn'kredɪbl] incredibile

incur [ɪn'kɜː(r)] *costs* affrontare; *debts* contrarre; *s.o.'s anger* esporsi a

incurable [ɪn'kjʊərəbl] incurabile

indecent [ɪn'diːsnt] indecente

indecisive [ɪndɪ'saɪsɪv] indeciso; **indecisiveness** indecisione *f*

indeed [ɪn'diːd] *(in fact)* in effetti; *(yes, agreeing)* esatto; **very much ~** moltissimo

indefinable [ɪndɪ'faɪnəbl] indefinibile

indefinite [ɪn'defɪnɪt] indeterminato; **~ article** GRAM articolo *m* indeterminativo; **indefinitely** a tempo indeterminato

indelicate [ɪn'delɪkət] indelicato

independence [ɪndɪ'pendəns] indipendenza *f*; **Independence Day** in USA festa *f* dell'indipendenza americana *(4 luglio)*; **independent** indipendente; **independently** indipendentemente; **~ of** indipendentemente da

indescribable [ɪndɪ'skraɪbəbl] indescrivibile

index ['ɪndeks] indice *m*

India ['ɪndɪə] India *f*; **Indian 1** *adj* indiano **2** *n person* india-

no *m*, -a *f*; *American* indiano *m*, -a *f* d'america

indicate ['ɪndɪkeɪt] **1** *v/t* indicare **2** *v/i when driving* segnalare (il cambiamento di direzione); **indication** indicazione *f*; **indicator** MOT freccia *f*

indict [ɪn'daɪt] incriminare

indifference [ɪn'dɪfrəns] indifferenza *f*; **indifferent** indifferente; *(mediocre)* mediocre

indigestion [ɪndɪ'dʒestʃn] indigestione *f*

indignant [ɪn'dɪgnənt] indignato; **indignation** indignazione *f*

indirect [ɪndɪ'rekt] indiretto; **indirectly** indirettamente

indiscreet [ɪndɪ'skriːt] indiscreto

indiscriminate [ɪndɪ'skrɪmɪnət] indiscriminato

indispensable [ɪndɪ'spensəbl] indispensabile

indisposed [ɪndɪ'spəʊzd] *(not well)* indisposto

indisputable [ɪndɪ'spjuːtəbl] indiscutibile

indistinct [ɪndɪ'stɪŋkt] indistinto

indistinguishable [ɪndɪ'stɪŋgwɪʃəbl] indistinguibile

individual [ɪndɪ'vɪdʒʊəl] **1** *n* individuo *m* **2** *adj (separate)* singolo; *(personal)* individuale; **individually** individualmente

indoctrinate [ɪn'dɒktrɪneɪt]

indottrinare

Indonesia [ɪndə'niːʒə] Indonesia f; **Indonesian 1** adj indonesiano **2** n person indonesiano m, -a f

indoor ['ɪndɔː(r)] activities, games al coperto; arena, pool coperto; **indoors** in building all'interno m; at home in casa

indorse ☞ **endorse**

indulgent [ɪn'dʌldʒənt] indulgente

industrial [ɪn'dʌstrɪəl] industriale; industrial dispute vertenza f sindacale; industrialist industriale m; industrious diligente; industry industria f

ineffective [ɪnɪ'fektɪv] inefficace

inefficient [ɪnɪ'fɪʃənt] inefficiente

inept [ɪ'nept] inetto

inequality [ɪnɪ'kwɒlɪtɪ] disuguaglianza f

inescapable [ɪnɪ'skeɪpəbl] inevitabile

inevitable [ɪn'evɪtəbl] inevitabile; inevitably inevitabilmente

inexcusable [ɪnɪk'skjuːzəbl] imperdonabile

inexhaustible [ɪnɪg'zɔːstəbl] supply inesauribile

inexpensive [ɪnɪk'spensɪv] poco costoso, economico

inexperienced [ɪnɪk'spɪərɪənst] inesperto

inexplicable [ɪnɪk'splɪkəbl] inspiegabile

infallible [ɪn'fælɪbl] infallibile

infamous ['ɪnfəməs] famigerato

infancy ['ɪnfənsɪ] of person infanzia f; of state, institution stadio m iniziale; **infant** bambino m piccolo, bambina f piccola; **infantile** pej infantile

infantry ['ɪnfəntrɪ] fanteria f

infatuated [ɪn'fætʃueɪtɪd]: **be ~ with** s.o. essere infatuato di qu

infect [ɪn'fekt] of person contagiare; food, water contaminare; **become ~ed** of wound infettarsi; of person contagiarsi; **infection** infezione f; **infectious** disease infettivo, contagioso; laughter contagioso

infer [ɪn'fɜː(r)]: **~ sth from sth** dedurre qc da qc

inferior [ɪn'fɪərɪə(r)] inferiore; **inferiority** inferiorità f; **inferiority complex** complesso m d'inferiorità

infertile [ɪn'fɜːtaɪl] sterile; **infertility** sterilità f

infidelity [ɪnfɪ'delɪtɪ] infedeltà f inv

infinite ['ɪnfɪnət] infinito; **infinitive** infinito m

infinity [ɪn'fɪnɪtɪ] infinito m

inflammable [ɪn'flæməbl] infiammabile; **inflammation** MED infiammazione f

inflatable [ɪn'fleɪtəbl] dinghy gonfiabile; **inflate** tyre, dinghy gonfiare; economy infla-

zionare; **inflation** inflazione
f; **inflationary** inflazionisti-
co
inflexible [ɪnˈfleksɪbl] inefles-
sibile
inflict [ɪnˈflɪkt]: ~ **sth on s.o.**
punishment infliggere qc a
qu; *suffering* procurare qc a
qu
'in-flight: ~ *entertainment* intrattenimento a bordo
influence [ˈɪnfluəns] **1** *n* influenza f **2** *v/t* s.o.'s thinking
esercitare un'influenza su;
decision influenzare; **influ-**
ential *writer, film-maker* autorevole; **she knows ~ peo-**
ple conosce gente influente
inform [ɪnˈfɔːm] **1** *v/t* informare **2** *v/i:* ~ **on s.o.** denunciare
qu
informal [ɪnˈfɔːml] informale; **informality** informalità f
informant [ɪnˈfɔːmənt] informatore m, -trice f; **informa-**
tion informazione f; **a bit of**
~ un'informazione; **informa-**
tion science informatica f;
information technology informatica f; **informative** *arti-*
cle etc istruttivo; **he wasn't**
very ~ non è stato di grande
aiuto; **informer** informatore
m, -trice f
infra-red [ɪnfrəˈred] infrarosso
infrastructure [ˈɪnfrə-
strʌktʃə(r)] infrastruttura f
infrequent [ɪnˈfriːkwənt] raro
infuriate [ɪnˈfjʊərɪeɪt] far in-

furiare; **infuriating** esasperante
ingenious [ɪnˈdʒiːnɪəs] ingegnoso
ingot [ˈɪŋgət] lingotto m
ingratitude [ɪnˈgrætɪtjuːd] ingratitudine f
ingredient [ɪnˈgriːdɪənt] *for*
cooking ingrediente m; *for*
success elemento m
inhabit [ɪnˈhæbɪt] abitare; **in-**
habitant abitante m/f
inhale [ɪnˈheɪl] **1** *v/t* inalare **2**
v/i when smoking aspirare
inherit [ɪnˈherɪt] ereditare; **in-**
heritance eredità f *inv*
inhibited [ɪnˈhɪbɪtɪd] inibito;
inhibition inibizione f
inhospitable [ɪnhɒˈspɪtəbl]
inospitale
'in-house 1 *adj* aziendale **2**
adv work all'interno dell'a-
zienda
inhuman [ɪnˈhjuːmən] disumano
initial [ɪˈnɪʃl] **1** *adj* iniziale **2** *n*
iniziale f **3** *v/t (write initials*
on) siglare (con le iniziali);
initially inizialmente; **initi-**
ate avviare; **initiation** avviamento m; **initiative** iniziativa f; **do sth on one's own**
~ fare qc di propria iniziativa; **take the ~** prendere l'iniziativa
inject [ɪnˈdʒekt] iniettare;
capital investire; **injection**
iniezione f; *of capital* investimento m
injure [ˈɪndʒə(r)] ferire; **in-**

jured 1 adj leg ferito; feelings offeso **2** npl feriti mpl; **injury** ferita f

injustice [ɪn'dʒʌstɪs] ingiustizia f

ink [ɪŋk] inchiostro m; **inkjet (printer)** stampante f a getto d'inchiostro

inland ['ɪnlənd] areas dell'interno; mail nazionale; **Inland Revenue** fisco m

in-laws ['ɪnlɔːz] famiglia della moglie / del marito; (wife's / husband's parents) suoceri mpl

inmate ['ɪnmeɪt] of prison detenuto m, -a f; of mental hospital ricoverato m, -a f

inn [ɪn] locanda f

innate [ɪ'neɪt] innato

inner ['ɪnə(r)] interno; **inner city** centro in degrado di una zona urbana; ~ **decay** degrado del centro urbano

innocence ['ɪnəsns] innocenza f; **innocent** innocente

innocuous [ɪ'nɒkjʊəs] innocuo

innovation [ɪnə'veɪʃn] innovazione f; **innovative** innovativo; **innovator** innovatore m, -trice f

inoculate [ɪ'nɒkjʊleɪt] vaccinare; **inoculation** vaccinazione f

inoffensive [ɪnə'fensɪv] inoffensivo

'in-patient degente m/f

input ['ɪnpʊt] **1** n contributo m; COMPUT input m inv **2**

v/t into project contribuire con; COMPUT inserire

inquest ['ɪnkwest] inchiesta f giudiziaria

inquire [ɪn'kwaɪə(r)] domandare; ~ **into sth** svolgere indagini su qc; **inquiry** richiesta f di informazioni; (public ~) indagine f

inquisitive [ɪn'kwɪzətɪv] curioso

insane [ɪn'seɪn] pazzo

insanitary [ɪn'sænɪtrɪ] antigienico

insanity [ɪn'sænɪtɪ] infermità f mentale

inscription [ɪn'skrɪpʃn] iscrizione f

insect ['ɪnsekt] insetto m; **insecticide** insetticida m

insecure [ɪnsɪ'kjʊə(r)] insicuro; **insecurity** insicurezza f

insensitive [ɪn'sensɪtɪv] insensibile

insert 1 ['ɪnsɜːt] n in magazine etc inserto m **2** [ɪn'sɜːt] v/t inserire

inside [ɪn'saɪd] **1** n interno m; of road destra f; sinistra f; ~ **out** a rovescio; **turn sth ~ out** rivoltare qc; **know sth ~ out** sapere qc a menadito **2** prep dentro; ~ **of 2 hours** in meno di due ore **3** adv stay, go dentro **4** adj interno; ~ **information** informazioni riservate; ~ **lane** SP corsia f interna; on road corsia f di marcia

inside 'pocket tasca f interna; **insider**: *an ~ from the Department* un impiegato del Ministero; **insider trading** FIN insider trading *m*; **insides** pancia *fsg*; *intestines* budella *fpl*

insignificant [ɪnsɪɡ'nɪfɪkənt] insignificante

insincere [ɪnsɪn'sɪə(r)] falso; **insincerity** falsità *f*

insinuate [ɪn'sɪnjʊeɪt] *(imply)* insinuare

insist [ɪn'sɪst] insistere; *please keep it, I ~* tienilo, ci tengo!

◆ **insist on** esigere; *insist on doing sth* insistere per fare qc

insistent [ɪn'sɪstənt] insistente

insolent ['ɪnsələnt] insolente

insoluble [ɪn'sɒljʊbl] *problem* insolubile; *substance* insolubile

insolvent [ɪn'sɒlvənt] insolvente

insomnia [ɪn'sɒmnɪə] insonnia *f*

inspect [ɪn'spekt] *work, tickets, baggage* controllare; *factory, school* ispezionare; **inspection** *of work, tickets, baggage* controllo *m*; *of factory, school* ispezione *f*; **inspector** *in factory* ispettore *m*, -trice *f*; *on buses* controllore *m*; *of police* ispettore *m*

inspiration [ɪnspə'reɪʃn] ispirazione *f*; *(very good idea)* lampo *m* di genio; **inspire**

respect etc suscitare; *be ~d by s.o. / sth* essere ispirato da qu / qc

instability [ɪnstə'bɪlɪtɪ] instabilità *f inv*

install [ɪn'stɔːl] installare; **installation** installazione *f*; *military ~* struttura *f* militare; **instalment**, *Am* **installment** *of story, TV drama etc* puntata *f*; *(payment)* rata *f*; **installment plan** *Am* acquisto *m* rateale

instance ['ɪnstəns] *(example)* esempio *m*; *for ~* per esempio

instant ['ɪnstənt] **1** *adj* immediato **2** *n* istante *m*; *in an ~* in un attimo; **instantaneous** immediato; **instant coffee** caffè *m inv* istantaneo *or* solubile; **instantly** istantaneamente

instead [ɪn'sted] invece; *~ of* invece di

instinct ['ɪnstɪŋkt] istinto *m*; **instinctive** istintivo

institute ['ɪnstɪtjuːt] **1** *n* istituto *m* **2** *v/t new law* introdurre; *enquiry* avviare; **institution** istituto *m*; *sth traditional* istituzione *f*; *(setting up)* avviamento *m*

instruct [ɪn'strʌkt] *(order)* dare istruzioni a; *(teach)* istruire; **instruction** istruzione *f*; *~s for use* istruzioni per l'uso; **instructive** istruttivo; **instructor** istruttore *m*, -trice *f* instrument ['ɪnstrʊmənt] strumento *m*

insubordinate [ɪnsə'bɔ:dɪnət] insubordinato

insufficient [ɪnsə'fɪʃnt] insufficiente

insulate ['ɪnsjʊleɪt] ELEC isolare; *against cold* isolare termicamente; insulation ELEC isolamento *m*; *against cold* isolamento *m* termico

insulin ['ɪnsjʊlɪn] insulina *f*

insult 1 ['ɪnsʌlt] *n* insulto *m* 2 [ɪn'sʌlt] *v/t* insultare

insurance [ɪn'ʃʊərəns] assicurazione *f*; insurance company compagnia *f* di assicurazioni; insurance policy polizza *f* di assicurazione; insurance premium premio *m* assicurativo; insure assicurare

insurmountable [ɪnsə'maʊntəbl] insormontabile

intact [ɪn'tækt] intatto

integrate ['ɪntɪgreɪt] integrare; integrity integrità *f*

intellect ['ɪntəlekt] intelletto *m*; intellectual 1 *adj* intellettuale 2 *n* intellettuale *m/f*

intelligence [ɪn'telɪdʒəns] intelligenza *f*; (*information*) informazioni *fpl*; intelligent intelligente

intelligible [ɪn'telɪdʒəbl] intelligibile

intend [ɪn'tend]: ~ *to do sth* (*do on purpose*) volere fare qc; (*plan to do*) avere intenzione di fare qc

intense [ɪn'tens] intenso; *concentration* profondo; *personality* serio; intensify 1 *v/t effect, pressure* intensificare 2 *v/i of pain* acuirsi; *of fighting* intensificarsi; intensity intensità *f inv*; intensive intensivo; intensive care (unit) MED (reparto *m* di) terapia *f* intensiva

intention [ɪn'tenʃn] intenzione *f*; intentional intenzionale; intentionally intenzionalmente

interaction [ɪntər'ækʃn] interazione *f*; interactive interattivo

intercept [ɪntə'sept] intercettare

interchange ['ɪntətʃeɪndʒ] MOT interscambio *m*; interchangeable interscambiabile

intercom ['ɪntəkɒm] citofono *m*

intercourse ['ɪntəkɔ:s] *sexual* rapporto *m* sessuale

interdependent [ɪntədɪ'pendənt] interdipendente

interest ['ɪntrəst] 1 *n* interesse *m*; *money paid / received* interessi *mpl*; **take an ~ in sth** interessarsi di qc 2 *v/t* interessare; interested interessato; **be ~ in sth** interessarsi di qc; interesting interessante; interest rate FIN tasso *m* d'interesse

interface ['ɪntəfeɪs] 1 *n* interfaccia *f* 2 *v/i* interfacciarsi

interfere [ɪntəˈfɪə(r)] interferire; interference interferenza f; on radio interferenze fpl

interior [ɪnˈtɪərɪə(r)] 1 adj interno 2 n of house interno m; of country entroterra m; interior decorator arredatore m, -trice f; interior design architettura f d'interni; interior designer architetto m d'interni

interlude [ˈɪntəluːd] at theatre, concert intervallo m; (period) parentesi f inv

intermediary [ɪntəˈmiːdɪərɪ] intermediario m, -a f; intermediate intermedio

intermission [ɪntəˈmɪʃn] in theatre, cinema intervallo m

internal [ɪnˈtɜːnl] interno; internally: he's bleeding ~ ha un'emorragia interna; not to be taken ~ per uso esterno; Internal Revenue (Service) Am fisco m

international [ɪntəˈnæʃnl] 1 adj internazionale 2 n match partita f internazionale; player giocatore m, -trice f della nazionale; internationally a livello internazionale

Internet [ˈɪntənet] Internet m; on the ~ su Internet; ~ service provider provider m inv di servizi Internet

interpret [ɪnˈtɜːprɪt] 1 v/t tradurre; piece of music, comment etc interpretare 2 v/i fa-

re da interprete; interpretation traduzione f; of piece of music, meaning interpretazione f; interpreter interprete m/f

interrogate [ɪnˈterəgeɪt] interrogare; interrogation interrogatorio m; interrogator interrogante m/f

interrupt [ɪntəˈrʌpt] interrompere; interruption interruzione f

intersect [ɪntəˈsekt] 1 v/t intersecare 2 v/i intersecarsi; intersection of roads incrocio m

interstate [ˈɪntəsteɪt] Am autostrada f interstatale

interval [ˈɪntəvl] intervallo m; sunny ~ schiarite

intervene [ɪntəˈviːn] of person, police etc intervenire; of time trascorrere; intervention intervento m

interview [ˈɪntəvjuː] 1 on TV, in paper intervista f; for job intervista f d'assunzione, colloquio m di lavoro 2 v/t on TV, for paper intervistare; for job sottoporre a intervista; interviewer on TV, for paper intervistatore m, -trice f; (for job) persona che conduce un'intervista d'assunzione

intimate [ˈɪntɪmət] intimo; be ~ with s.o. sexually avere rapporti intimi con qu

intimidate [ɪnˈtɪmɪdeɪt] intimidire; intimidation intimidazione f

into ['ɪntʊ] in; **be ~ sth** F (*like*) amare qc; (*be involved with*) interessarsi di qc; **be ~ drugs** fare uso di droga; **when you're ~ the job** quando sei pratico del lavoro

intolerable [ɪn'tɒlərəbl] intollerabile; **intolerant** intollerante

intoxicated [ɪn'tɒksɪkeɪtɪd] ubriaco

intravenous [ɪntrə'viːnəs] endovenoso

intricate ['ɪntrɪkət] complicato

intrigue 1 ['ɪntriːg] n intrigo m **2** [ɪn'triːg] v/t intrigare; **I would be ~d to know ...** m'interesserebbe molto sapere ...; **intriguing** intrigante

introduce [ɪntrə'djuːs] *person* presentare; *new technique etc* introdurre; **may I ~ ...?** permette che le presenti ...?; **introduction** *to person* presentazione f; *to new food, sport etc* approccio m; *in book, of new technique* introduzione f

introvert ['ɪntrəvɜːt] introverso m, -a f

intrude [ɪn'truːd] importunare; **intruder** intruso m, -a f; **intrusion** intrusione f

intuition [ɪntjuː'ɪʃn] intuito m

invade [ɪn'veɪd] invadere

invalid¹ ['ɪnvælɪd] *adj* non valido

invalid² ['ɪnvəlɪd] n MED invalido m, -a f

invalidate [ɪn'vælɪdeɪt] invalidare

invaluable [ɪn'væljʊbl] prezioso

invariably [ɪn'veɪrɪəblɪ] (*always*) invariabilmente

invasion [ɪn'veɪʒn] invasione f

invent [ɪn'vent] inventare; **invention** invenzione f; **inventive** fantasioso; **inventor** inventore m, -trice f

inventory ['ɪnvəntrɪ] inventario m

invert [ɪn'vɜːt] invertire; **inverted commas** virgolette fpl

invest [ɪn'vest] investire

investigate [ɪn'vestɪgeɪt] indagare su; **investigation** indagine f; **investigative journalism** giornalismo m investigativo

investment [ɪn'vestmənt] investimento m; **investor** investitore m, -trice

invigorating [ɪn'vɪgəreɪtɪŋ] *climate* tonificante

invincible [ɪn'vɪnsəbl] invincibile

invisible [ɪn'vɪzɪbl] invisibile

invitation [ɪnvɪ'teɪʃn] invito m; **invite** invitare

invoice ['ɪnvɔɪs] **1** n fattura f **2** v/t *customer* fatturare

involuntary [ɪn'vɒləntrɪ] involontario

involve [ɪn'vɒlv] *hard work, expense* comportare; (*con-*

cern) riguardare; *what does it ~?* che cosa comporta?; *get ~d with sth* entrare a far parte di qc; *get ~d with s.o.* emotionally, romantically legarsi a qu; *involved* (complex) complesso; *involvement in a project etc* partecipazione *f*; *in crime, accident* coinvolgimento *m*

invulnerable [ɪn'vʌlnərəbl] invulnerabile

inward ['ɪnwəd] **1** *adj feeling, thoughts* intimo **2** *adv* verso l'interno; **inwardly** dentro di sé

IQ [aɪ'kjuː] (= *intelligence quotient*) quoziente *m* d'intelligenza

Iran [ɪ'rɑːn] Iran *m*; **Iranian 1** *adj* iraniano **2** *n* iraniano *m*, -a *f*

Iraq [ɪ'ræk] Iraq *m*; **Iraqi 1** *adj* iracheno **2** *n* iracheno *m*, -a *f*

Ireland ['aɪələnd] Irlanda *f*; **Irish** irlandese; **Irishman** irlandese *m*; **Irishwoman** irlandese *f*

iron ['aɪən] **1** *n* ferro *m*; *for clothes* ferro *m* da stiro **2** *v/t shirts etc* stirare

ironic(al) [aɪ'rɒnɪk(l)] ironico
'ironing board asse *m* da stiro

irony ['aɪərənɪ] ironia *f*

irrational [ɪ'ræʃənl] irrazionale

irreconcilable [ɪrekən'saɪləbl] inconciliabile

irregular [ɪ'regjʊlə(r)] irrego-

lare

irrelevant [ɪ'reləvənt] non pertinente

irreplaceable [ɪrɪ'pleɪsəbl] insostituibile

irrepressible [ɪrɪ'presbl] *sense of humour* incontenibile; *person* che non si lascia abbattere

irresistible [ɪrɪ'zɪstəbl] irresistibile

irresponsible [ɪrɪ'spɒnsəbl] irresponsabile

irreverent [ɪ'revərənt] irriverente

irrevocable [ɪ'revəkəbl] irrevocabile

irrigate ['ɪrɪgeɪt] irrigare; **irrigation** irrigazione *f*

irritable ['ɪrɪtəbl] irritabile; **irritate** irritare; **irritating** irritante; **irritation** irritazione *f*

Islam ['ɪzlɑːm] Islam *m*; **Islamic** islamico

island ['aɪlənd] isola *f*; **islander** isolano *m*, -a *f*

isolate ['aɪsəleɪt] isolare; **isolated** isolato; **isolation** isolamento *m*; *in ~ taken etc* da solo

ISP [aɪes'piː] (= *Internet service provider*) provider *m inv* di servizi Internet

Israel ['ɪzreɪl] Israele *m*; **Israeli 1** *adj* israeliano **2** *n person* israeliano *m*, -a *f*

issue ['ɪʃuː] **1** *n* (*matter*) questione *f*; (*result*) risultato *m*; *of magazine* numero *m*; *take ~ with s.o. / sth* prendere posizione contro qu / qc **2** v/t *passports* rilasciare; *supplies* distribuire; *coins* emettere; *warning* dare

IT [aɪ'tiː] (= *information technology*) IT *f*

it [ɪt] ◇ *as subject:* **what colour is ~?** – **~ is red** di che colore è? – è rosso; **~'s raining** piove; **~'s me / him** sono io / è lui; **~'s Charlie here** TELEC sono Charlie; **that's ~!** (*that's right*) proprio così!; (*finished*) finito! ◇ *as object* lo *m*, la *f*; **I broke ~** l'ho rotto, -a

Italian [ɪ'tæljən] **1** *adj* italiano **2** *n person* italiano *m*, -a *f*; *language* italiano *m*

italic [ɪ'tælɪk] in corsivo

Italy ['ɪtəlɪ] Italia *f*

itch [ɪtʃ] **1** *n* prurito *m* **2** *v/i* prudere

item ['aɪtəm] *on agenda* punto *m* (all'ordine del giorno); *on shopping list* articolo *m*; *in accounts* voce *f*; *news* ~ notizia *f*; itemize *invoice* dettagliare

itinerary [aɪ'tɪnərərɪ] itinerario *m*

its [ɪts] il suo *m*, la sua *f*, i suoi *mpl*, le sue *fpl*

it's [ɪts] ☞ *it is, it has*

itself [ɪt'self] *reflexive* si; *emphatic* di per sé; **by ~** (*alone*) da solo; (*automatically*) da sé

J

jab [dʒæb] conficcare

jack [dʒæk] MOT cric *m inv*; *in cards* fante *m*

jacket ['dʒækɪt] *n* giacca *f*; *of book* copertina *f*

jackpot primo premio *m*; **hit the ~** vincere il primo premio; *fig* fare un terno al lotto

jagged ['dʒægɪd] frastagliato

jail [dʒeɪl] prigione *f*

jam¹ [dʒæm] *for bread* marmellata *f*

jam² [dʒæm] **1** *n* MOT ingorgo *m*; **be in a ~** F (*difficulty*) essere in difficoltà **2** *v/t* (*ram*) ficcare; (*cause to stick*) bloc-

care; **be ~med** *of roads* essere congestionato; *of door, window* essere bloccato **3** *v/i* (*stick*) bloccarsi

janitor ['dʒænɪtə(r)] custode *m*

January ['dʒænjʊərɪ] gennaio *m*

Japan [dʒə'pæn] Giappone *m*; **Japanese 1** *adj* giapponese **2** *n person* giapponese *m*/*f*; *language* giapponese *m*

jar¹ [dʒɑː(r)] *container* barattolo *m*

jargon ['dʒɑːgən] gergo *m*

javelin ['dʒævlɪn] giavellotto *m*

jaw [dʒɔː] mascella *m*

jaywalker ['dʒeɪwɔːkə(r)] pedone *m* indisciplinato

jazz [dʒæz] jazz *m*

jealous ['dʒeləs] geloso; **jealousy** gelosia *f*

jeans [dʒiːnz] jeans *mpl*

jeep [dʒiːp] jeep *f inv*

jeer [dʒɪə(r)] **1** *n* scherno *m* **2** *v/i* schernire; **~ at** schernire

Jello® ['dʒeləʊ] *Am* gelatina *f*

jelly ['dʒelɪ] *Br* gelatina *f*; *Am* marmellata *f*; **jellyfish** medusa *f*

jeopardize ['dʒepədaɪz] mettere in pericolo

jerk[1] [dʒɜːk] **1** *n* scossone *m* **2** *v/t* dare uno strattone

jerk[2] [dʒɜːk] *n* F idiota *m/f*

jerky ['dʒɜːkɪ] *movement* a scatti

Jesus ['dʒiːzəs] Gesù *m*

jet [dʒet] **1** *n* of *water* zampillo *m*; (*nozzle*) becco *m*; *airplane* jet *m inv* **2** *v/i travel* volare; **jetlag** jet-lag *m*

jettison ['dʒetɪsn] gettare; *fig* abbandonare

jetty ['dʒetɪ] molo *m*

Jew [dʒuː] ebreo *m*, -a *f*

jewel ['dʒuːəl] gioiello *m*; *fig: person* perla *f*; **jeweller**, *Am* **jeweler** gioielliere *m*

Jewish ['dʒuːɪʃ] ebraico; *people* ebreo

jigsaw (puzzle) ['dʒɪgsɔː] puzzle *m inv*

jilt [dʒɪlt] piantare F

jingle ['dʒɪŋgl] **1** *n song* jingle *m inv* **2** *v/i* of *keys, coins* tin-

---

tinnare

jinx [dʒɪŋks] *person* iettatore *m*, -trice *f*; **there's a ~ on this project** questo progetto è iellato

jittery ['dʒɪtərɪ] F nervoso

job [dʒob] (*employment*) lavoro *m*; (*task*) compito *m*; **it's a good ~ you ...** meno male che tu ...; **job description** elenco *m* delle mansioni; **jobless** disoccupato

jockey ['dʒokɪ] fantino *m*

jog [dʒog] **1** *n* corsa *f*; **go for a ~** andare a fare footing **2** *v/i* as *exercise* fare footing **3** *v/t elbow etc* urtare; **~ s.o.'s memory** rinfrescare la memoria a qu; **jogger** *person* persona *f* che fa footing; *Am shoe* scarpa *f* da ginnastica; **jogging** footing *m*; **go ~** fare footing

john [dʒon] *Am* F gabinetto *m*

join [dʒoɪn] **1** *n* giuntura *f* **2** *v/i* of *roads, rivers* unirsi; (*become a member*) iscriversi **3** *v/t* (*connect*) unire; *person* unirsi a; *club* iscriversi a; (*go to work for*) entrare in; *of road* congiungersi a

♦ **join in** partecipare

joint [dʒoɪnt] **1** *n* ANAT articolazione *f*; *in woodwork* giunto *m*; of *meat* arrosto *m*; of *cannabis* spinello *m* **2** *adj* (*shared*) comune; **joint account** conto *m* comune; **joint venture** joint venture *f inv*

joke [dʒəʊk] **1** *n story* barzelletta *f*; (*practical ~*) scherzo *m* **2** *v/i* (*pretend*) scherzare; **joker** *in cards* jolly *m inv*; F burlone *m*, -a *f*; **jokingly** scherzosamente

jostle [ˈdʒɒsl] spintonare

journal [ˈdʒɜːnl] *magazine* rivista *f*; *diary* diario *m*; **journalism** giornalismo *m*; **journalist** giornalista *m/f*

journey [ˈdʒɜːnɪ] viaggio *m*

joy [dʒɔɪ] gioia *f*

jubilant [ˈdʒuːbɪlənt] esultante; **jubilation** giubilo *m*

judge [dʒʌdʒ] **1** *n* giudice *m* **2** *v/t* giudicare; *competition* fare da giudice a **3** *v/i* giudicare; **judg(e)ment** giudizio *m*; ***an error of ~*** un errore di valutazione; **Judg(e)ment Day** il giorno *m* del giudizio

judicial [dʒuːˈdɪʃl] giudiziario

jug [dʒʌg] brocca *f*

juggle [dʒʌgl] fare giochi di destrezza con; *fig: conflicting demands* destreggiarsi fra; *figures* manipolare; **juggler** giocoliere *m*

juice [dʒuːs] succo *m*; **juicy** succoso; *news, gossip* piccante

July [dʒʊˈlaɪ] luglio *m*

jumbo (jet) [ˈdʒʌmbəʊ] jumbo *m* (jet); **jumbo-sized** gigante

jump [dʒʌmp] **1** *n* salto *m*; (*increase*) impennata *f* **2** *v/i* saltare; (*increase*) aumentare rapidamente, avere un'impennata; *in surprise* sobbalzare; **~ to conclusions** arrivare a conclusioni affrettate **3** *v/t fence etc* saltare; F (*attack*) aggredire; **~ the queue** non rispettare la fila; **~ the lights** passare col rosso

◆ **jump at** *opportunity* prendere al balzo

jumper [ˈdʒʌmpə(r)] *Br* golf *m inv*; *Am dress* scamiciato *m*; **jumpy** nervoso

junction [ˈdʒʌŋkʃn] *of roads* incrocio *m*

June [dʒuːn] giugno *m*

jungle [ˈdʒʌŋgl] giungla *f*

junior [ˈdʒuːnɪə(r)] **1** *adj* (*subordinate*) subalterno; (*younger*) giovane **2** *n in rank* subalterno *m*, -a *f*; ***she is ten years my ~*** ha dieci anni meno di me; **junior high** *Am* scuola *f* per ragazzi dai *12 ai 15 anni*

junk [dʒʌŋk] robaccia *f*; **junk food** alimenti *mpl* poco sani, porcherie *fpl*; **junkie** F tossico *m*, -a *f* F; **junk mail** posta *f* spazzatura

jurisdiction [dʒʊərɪsˈdɪkʃn] LAW giurisdizione *f*

juror [ˈdʒʊərə(r)] giurato *m*, -a *f*; **jury** giuria *f*

just [dʒʌst] **1** *adj* giusto **2** *adv* (*barely*) appena; (*exactly*) proprio; (*only*) solo; ***I've seen her*** l'ho appena vista; **~** (*almost*) quasi; ***I was ~ about to leave when ...*** stavo proprio per andarmene quando ...; ~ *now* (*a few moments ago*) proprio ora; (*at the moment*) al momento; ~ *you wait!* aspetta un po'!; ~ *be quiet!* fai silenzio!; ~ *as rich* altrettanto ricco

justice ['dʒʌstɪs] giustizia *f*

justifiable [dʒʌstɪ'faɪəbl] giustificabile; **justifiably** a ra-

gione; **justification** giustificazione *f*; **justify** also text giustificare

justly ['dʒʌstlɪ] giustamente

◆ **jut out** [dʒʌt] sporgere

juvenile ['dʒuːvənaɪl] 1 *adj* minorile; *pej* puerile 2 *n* *fml* minore *m/f*; **juvenile delinquent** delinquente *m/f* minorile

K

k [keɪ] (= *kilobyte*) k (= kilobyte *m inv*); (= *thousand*) mille

kangaroo [kæŋgə'ruː] canguro *m*

keel [kiːl] NAUT chiglia *f*

keen [kiːn] *person* entusiasta; *interest*, *competition* vivo; *be ~ on* sth essere appassionato di qc; *be ~ to do sth* aver molta voglia di fare qc

keep [kiːp] 1 *v/t* tenere; (*not lose*) mantenere; (*detain*) trattenere; *family* mantenere; *animals* allevare; ~ *a promise* mantenere una promessa; ~ *s.o. company* tenere compagnia a qu; ~ *s.o. waiting* far aspettare qu; ~ *sth to o.s.* (*not tell*) tenere qc per sé; ~ *sth from s.o.* nascondere qc a qu; ~ *s.o. from doing sth* impedire a qu di fare qc; ~ *trying!* continua a provare! 2 *v/i* (*remain*) rimanere; *of food, milk*

conservarsi; ~ *left* tenere la sinistra; ~ *straight on* vai sempre dritto; ~ *still* stare fermo

◆ **keep away 1** *v/i* stare alla larga; *keep away from ...* stai alla larga da ... 2 *v/t* tenere lontano; *keep s.o. away from sth* tenere qu lontano da qc

◆ **keep back** (*hold in check*) trattenere; *information* nascondere

◆ **keep down** *voice* abbassare; *costs, inflation* contenere; *food* trattenere

◆ **keep off 1** *v/t* (*avoid*) evitare; *keep off the grass* non calpestare l'erba 2 *v/i: if the rain keeps off* se non piove

◆ **keep on 1** *v/i* continuare; *keep on doing sth* continuare a fare qc 2 *v/t employee, coat* tenere

◆ **keep out** *v/t the cold* pro-

teggere da; *person* escludere
2 *v/i of room* non entrare (*of*
in); *of argument etc* non immischiarsi (*of* in); **keep out**
as sign vietato l'ingresso

◆ **keep to** *path, rules* seguire;
keep to the point non divagare

◆ **keep up 1** *v/i when running
etc* tener dietro **2** *v/t pace,
payments* stare dietro a;
bridge, pants tenere

◆ **keep up with** stare al passo con; (*stay in touch with*)
mantenere i rapporti con

keeping ['ki:pɪŋ]: **be in ~ with**
essere in armonia con;
keepsake ricordo *m*

kennel ['kenl] canile *m*; **kennels** canile *m*

kerb [kɜ:b] orlo *m* del marciapiede

ketchup ['ketʃʌp] ketchup *m inv*

kettle ['ketl] bollitore *m*

key [ki:] **1** *n to door, drawer*,
MUS chiave *f*; *on keyboard*
tasto *m* **2** *adj* (*vital*) chiave
3 *v/t* COMPUT battere

◆ **key in** *data* immettere

keyboard COMPUT, MUS tastiera *f*; **keyboarder** COMPUT, MUS tastierista *m/f*;
keycard tessera *f* magnetica;
keyed-up agitato; **keyhole**
buco *m* della serratura;
keyring portachiavi *m inv*;
keyword parola *f* chiave

khaki ['kɑ:kɪ] cachi *inv*

kick [kɪk] **1** *n* calcio *m*; (*just*)

for~s F (solo) per il gusto di
farlo **2** *v/t* dare un calcio *a*; F
habit liberarsi *da* **3** *v/i* dare
calci; SP calciare; *of horse*
scalciare

◆ **kick around** (*treat harshly*)
maltrattare; F (*discuss*) discutere *di*; **kick a ball
around** giocare a pallone

◆ **kick off** *of player* dare il
calcio d'inizio; F (*start*) iniziare;

◆ **kick out** buttar fuori

'**kickback** F (*bribe*) tangente
f; **kickoff** SP calcio *m* d'inizio

kid [kɪd] **1** *n* F (*child*) bambino
m, -a *f*; F (*young person*)
ragazzo *m*, -a *f*; **~ brother**
fratello minore **2** *v/t* F prendere in giro **3** *v/i* F scherzare

kidnap ['kɪdnæp] rapire, sequestrare; **kidnapper** rapitore *m*, -trice *f*; **kidnapping** rapimento *m*, sequestro *m* (di
persona)

kidney ['kɪdnɪ] ANAT rene *m*;
in cooking rognone *m*

kill [kɪl] uccidere; *plant, time*
ammazzare; **be ~ed in an
accident** morire in un incidente; **~ o.s.** suicidarsi; **killer**
(*murderer*) assassino *m*, -a *f*;
(*hired ~*) killer *m/f inv*; **killing** omicidio *m*; **make a ~**
F (*lots of money*) fare un pacco di soldi

kiln [kɪln] fornace *f*

kilo ['ki:ləʊ] chilo *m*; **kilobyte**

kilobyte *m inv*; **kilogram** chilogrammo *m*; **kilometre**, *Am* **kilometer** chilometro *m*

kind¹ [kaɪnd] *adj* gentile

kind² [kaɪnd] *n* (*sort*) tipo *m*; (*make, brand*) marca *f*; **nothing of the ~!** niente affatto!; **~ of sad / strange** F un po' triste / strano

kind-hearted [kaɪnd'hɑːtɪd] di buon cuore; **kindly** gentile; **kindness** gentilezza *f*

king [kɪŋ] *m inv*; **kingdom** regno *m*

kinky ['kɪŋkɪ] F particolare F

kiosk ['kiːɒsk] edicola *f*

kiss [kɪs] **1** *n* bacio *m* **2** *v/t* baciare **3** *v/i* baciarsi

kit [kɪt] *kit m inv*; (*equipment*) attrezzatura *f*

kitchen ['kɪtʃɪn] cucina *f*

kite [kaɪt] aquilone *m*

kitten ['kɪtn] gattino *m*

kitty ['kɪtɪ] *money* cassa *f* comune

knack [næk] capacità *f*; **there's a ~ to it** bisogna saperlo fare

knee [niː] ginocchio *m*; **kneecap** rotula *f*

kneel [niːl] inginocchiarsi

'knee-length al ginocchio

knife [naɪf] **1** *n* coltello *m* **2** *v/t* accoltellare

knight [naɪt] *n* cavaliere *m*

knit [nɪt] **1** *v/t* fare a maglia **2** *v/i* lavorare a maglia; **knitwear** maglieria *f*

knob [nɒb] *on door* pomello *m*; *of butter* noce *f*

knock [nɒk] **1** *n on door* colpo *m*; (*blow*) botta *f* **2** *v/t* (*hit*) colpire; *head, knee* battere; F (*criticize*) criticare **3** *v/i at the door* bussare (*at* a); **I ~ed my head** ho battuto la testa

♦ **knock down** *of car* investire; *object, building* butar giù; F (*reduce the price of*) scontare

♦ **knock out** (*make unconscious*) mettere K.O. F; *power lines etc* mettere fuori uso; (*eliminate*) eliminare

♦ **knock over** far cadere; *of car* investire

'knockout *in boxing* K.O. *m inv*

knot [nɒt] **1** *n* nodo *m* **2** *v/t* annodare

know [nəʊ] **1** *v/t* sapere; *person, place* conoscere; (*recognize*) riconoscere; **2** *v/i* sapere; **I don't ~** non so **3** *n*: **be in the ~** F essere beninformato; **know-all** F sapientone *m*, *-a f*; **knowhow** F know-how *m*; **knowing** d'intesa; **knowingly** (*wittingly*) deliberatamente; *smile etc* con aria d'intesa; **know-it-all** *Am* F sapientone *m*, *-a f*; **knowledge** conoscenza *f*; **to the best of my ~** per quanto ne sappia

knuckle ['nʌkl] nocca *f*

Koran [kəˈrɑːn] Corano *m*

Korea [kə'ri:ə] Corea f; **Korean 1** adj coreano **2** n coreano m, -a f; language coreano m

kosher ['kəʊʃə(r)] REL kasher; F a posto
kudos ['kju:dɒs] gloria f

L

lab [læb] laboratorio m
label ['leɪbl] **1** n etichetta f **2** v/t baggage mettere l'etichetta su
labor Am ☞ **labour**
laboratory [lə'bɒrətrɪ] laboratorio m
laborious [lə'bɔ:rɪəs] laborioso
'**labor union** Am sindacato m
labour ['leɪbə(r)] lavoro m; in pregnancy travaglio m; **be in ~** avere le doglie fpl; **laboured** style, speech pesante; **labourer** manovale m
lace [leɪs] material pizzo m; for shoe laccio m
lack [læk] **1** n mancanza f **2** v/t mancare di **3** v/i: **be ~ing** mancare
lacquer ['lækə(r)] lacca f
ladder ['lædə(r)] scala f (a pioli); in tights sfilatura f
laden ['leɪdn] carico
ladies room ['leɪdɪːz] bagno m per donne
lady ['leɪdɪ] signora f; **ladybird**, Am **ladybug** coccinella f; **ladylike** da signora; **she's not very ~** non è certo una signora
lager ['lɑ:gə(r)] birra f (bionda)

laidback [leɪd'bæk] rilassato
lake [leɪk] lago m
lamb [læm] agnello m
lame [leɪm] person zoppo; excuse zoppicante
laminated ['læmɪneɪtɪd] surface laminato; paper plastificato
lamp [læmp] lampada f; **lamppost** lampione m; **lampshade** paralume m
land [lænd] **1** n terreno m; (shore) terra f; (country) paese m; **by~** per via di terra; **on ~** sulla terraferma **2** v/t aeroplane far atterrare; job accaparrarsi **3** v/i of aeroplane atterrare; of ball, sth thrown cadere; **landing** of aeroplane atterraggio m; top of staircase pianerottolo m; **landing strip** pista f d'atterraggio; **landlady** of bar proprietaria f; of rented room padrona f di casa; **landlord** of bar proprietario m; of rented room padrone m di casa; **landmark** punto m di riferimento; fig pietra f miliare; **landowner** proprietario m, -a f terriero, -a; **landscape 1** n paesaggio m **2** adv print landscape, orizzontale;

landslide frana *f*; **landslide victory** vittoria *f* schiacciante

lane [leɪn] *in country* viottolo *m*; *(alley)* vicolo *m*; MOT corsia *f*

language ['læŋgwɪdʒ] lingua *f*; *(speech, style)* linguaggio *m*; **language lab** laboratorio *m* linguistico

lap[1] [læp] *of track* giro *m* (di pista)

lap[2] [læp] *of water* sciabordio *m*

lap[3] [læp] *of person* grembo *m*

lapel [lə'pel] bavero *m*

lapse [læps] **1** *n (mistake, slip)* mancanza *f*; *of time* intervallo *m*; ~ **of memory** vuoto *m* di memoria **2** *v/i* scadere; ~ **into** cadere in

laptop COMPUT laptop *m inv*

larceny ['lɑːsənɪ] furto *m*

larder ['lɑːdə(r)] dispensa *f*

large [lɑːdʒ] grande; **at** ~ *in* libertà; **largely** *(mainly)* in gran parte

laryngitis [lærɪn'dʒaɪtɪs] laringite *f*

laser ['leɪzə(r)] laser *m inv*; **laser printer** stampante *f* laser

lash[1] [læʃ] *with whip* frustare

lash[2] [læʃ] *(eyelash)* ciglio *m*

last[1] [lɑːst] **1** *adj in series* ultimo; *(preceding)* precedente; ~ **night** ieri sera; ~ **year** l'anno scorso **2** *adv* ~ l'ha finito per ultimo; *in race* è arrivato ultimo; **when I** ~ **saw him** l'ultima volta che

l'ho visto; **at** ~ finalmente

last[2] [lɑːst] *v/i* durare

lasting ['lɑːstɪŋ] duraturo; **lastly** per finire

late [leɪt] **1** *adj (behind time)* in ritardo; *in day* tardi; **it's getting** ~ si sta facendo tardi; **the** ~ **19th century** il tardo XIX secolo **2** *adv* tardi; **lately** recentemente; **later** più tardi; **see you** ~! a più tardi; ~ **on** più tardi; **latest** *adj* ultimo, più recente **2** *n*: **at the** ~ al più tardi

Latin ['lætɪn] **1** *adj* latino **2** *n* latino *m*; **Latin America** America *f* Latina; **Latin American 1** *n* latino-americano *m*, -a *f* **2** *adj* latino-americano

latitude ['lætɪtjuːd] latitudine *f*; *(freedom to act)* libertà *f* d'azione

latter ['lætə(r)]: **the** ~ quest'ultimo

laugh [lɑːf] **1** *n* risata *f*; **it was a** ~ F ci siamo divertiti **2** *v/i* ridere

♦ **laugh at** ridere di

laughter ['lɑːftə(r)] risata *f*, ridere

launch [lɔːntʃ] **1** *n boat* lancia *f*; *of rocket, product* lancio *m*; *of ship* varo *m* **2** *v/t rocket, product* lanciare; *ship* varare

launder ['lɔːndə(r)] lavare e stirare; ~ **money** riciclare denaro sporco; **laundrette** lavanderia *f* automatica; **laundromat**® *Am* lavanderia *f* automatica; **laundry**

place lavanderia *f; clothes* bucato *m*

lavatory ['lævətrɪ] gabinetto *m*

lavish ['lævɪʃ] *meal* lauto; *reception, lifestyle* sontuoso

law [lɔː] legge *f; criminal / civil ~* diritto *m* penale / civile; *against the ~* contro la legge; *forbidden by ~* vietato dalla legge; **law-abiding** che rispetta la legge; **law court** tribunale *m;* **lawful** legale; **lawless** senza legge

lawn [lɔːn] prato *m* (all'inglese); **lawn mower** tagliaerba *m inv*

lawsuit azione *f* legale; **lawyer** avvocato *m*

lax [læks] permissivo

laxative ['læksətɪv] lassativo *m*

lay [leɪ] *(put down)* posare; *eggs* deporre; V *(sexually)* scopare V

♦ **lay off** *workers* licenziare; *temporarily* mettere in cassa integrazione

♦ **lay out** *objects* disporre; *page* impaginare

layer ['leɪə(r)] strato *m*

layman laico *m*

lay-out *of page* impaginazione *f; of garden, room* disposizione *f*

lazy ['leɪzɪ] *person* pigro; *day* passato a oziare

lb (= *pound*) libbra *f*

lead[1] [liːd] **1** *v/t procession, race* essere in testa a; *compa-* ny, team essere a capo di; *(guide, take)* condurre **2** *v/i in race, competition* essere in testa; *(provide leadership)* dirigere; *a street ~ing off the square* una strada che parte dalla piazza; *a street ~ing into the square* una strada che sbocca sulla piazza **3** *n in race* posizione *f* di testa; *be in the ~* essere in testa; *take the ~* passare in testa

lead[2] [liːd] *for dog* guinzaglio *m*

lead[3] [led] *substance* piombo *m*

leaded ['ledɪd] *petrol* con piombo

leader ['liːdə(r)] capo *m; in race, on market* leader *m/f inv; in newspaper* editoriale *m;* **leadership** *of party etc* direzione *f,* leadership *f; ~ contest* lotta *f* per la direzione

lead-free ['ledfriː] *petrol* senza piombo

leading ['liːdɪŋ] *runner* in testa; *company, product* leader *inv;* **leading-edge** *company, technology* all'avanguardia

leaf [liːf] foglia *f*

♦ **leaf through** sfogliare

leaflet ['liːflət] dépliant *m inv*

league [liːg] lega *f;* SP campionato *m*

leak [liːk] **1** *n of water* perdita *f; of gas* fuga *f; there's been a ~ of information* c'è stata una

una fuga di notizie **2** v/i of pipe perdere; of boat far acqua

lean[1] [li:n] **1** v/i be at an angle pendere; **~ against sth** appoggiarsi a qc **2** v/t appoggiare

lean[2] [li:n] adj meat magro

leap [li:p] **1** n salto m **2** v/i saltare; **leap year** anno m bisestile

learn [lɜːn] imparare; (hear) apprendere; **learner** principiante m/f; **learning** (knowledge) sapere m; act apprendimento m

lease [li:s] **1** n (contratto m di) affitto m **2** v/t flat, equipment affittare

♦ **lease out** dare in affitto

leash [li:ʃ] for dog guinzaglio m

least [li:st] **1** adj (slightest) minimo **2** adv meno **3** n minimo m; **not in the ~** suprised per niente sorpreso; **at ~** almeno

leather ['leðə(r)] **1** n pelle f, cuoio m **2** adj di pelle, di cuoio

leave [li:v] **1** n (holiday) congedo m; MIL licenza f **2** v/t lasciare; room, house, office uscire da; station, airport partire da; (forget) dimenticare; **~ school** finire gli studi; **~ s.o. / sth alone** lasciare stare qu / qc; **be left** rimanere **3** v/i of person, plane, bus partire

♦ **leave behind** intentionally lasciare; (forget) dimenticare

♦ **leave out** omettere; (not put away) lasciare in giro; **leave me out of this** non mi immischiare in questa faccenda

'leaving party festa f d'addio

lecture ['lektʃə(r)] **1** n lezione f **2** v/i at university insegnare; **lecture hall** aula f magna; **lecturer** professore m, -essa universitaria, m

ledge [ledʒ] of window davanzale m; on rock face sporgenza f; **ledger** COM libro m mastro

left[1] [left] **1** adj sinistro; POL di sinistra **2** n sinistra f; **on / to the ~** a sinistra **3** adv a sinistra; **left-hand** sinistro; **left-handed** mancino; **left luggage** (office) deposito m bagagli; **left-overs** food avanzi mpl; **left-wing** POL di sinistra

leg [leg] of person, table gamba f; of animal zampa f; of turkey, chicken coscia f; of lamb cosciotto m; **pull s.o.'s ~** prendere in giro qu

legacy ['legəsɪ] eredità f inv

legal ['liːgl] legale; **legal adviser** consulente m/f legale; **legality** legalità f inv; **legalize** legalizzare

legend ['ledʒənd] leggenda f; **legendary** leggendario

legible ['ledʒəbl] leggibile

legislate ['ledʒɪsleɪt] legiferare; **legislation** legislazione f;

legislative legislativo; **legislature** POL legislatura *f*

legitimate [lɪˈdʒɪtɪmət] legittimo

'leg room spazio *m* per le gambe

leisure [ˈleʒə(r)] svago *m*; **at your~** con comodo; **leisurely** tranquillo

lemon [ˈlemən] limone *m*; **lemonade** fizzy gazzosa *f*; *made from lemon juice* limonata *f*

lend [lend] prestare; **~ s.o. sth** prestare qc a qu

length [leŋθ] lunghezza *f*; *piece: of material* taglio *m*; **at ~** explain a lungo; (*eventually*) alla fine; **lengthen** allungare; **lengthy** lungo

lenient [ˈliːnɪənt] indulgente

lens [lenz] *of camera* obiettivo *m*; *of spectacles* lente *f*; *of eye* cristallino *m*

Lent [lent] REL Quaresima *f*

Leo [ˈliːəʊ] ASTR Leone *m*

leopard [ˈlepəd] leopardo *m*

leotard [ˈliːətɑːd] body *m inv*

lesbian [ˈlezbɪən] **1** *n* lesbica *f* **2** *adj* di ~ per lesbiche

less [les] (di) meno; **~ interesting** meno interessante; **~ than £200** meno di £200; **lessen** diminuire

lesson [ˈlesn] lezione *f*

let [let] (*allow*) lasciare; (*rent*) affittare; **~ s.o. do sth** lasciar fare qc a qu; **~ me go!** lasciami andare!; **~'s go / stay** andiamo / restia-

mo; **~ alone** tanto meno; **~ go of sth** *of rope, handle* mollare qc
♦ **let down** *hair* sciogliersi; *blinds* abbassare; (*disappoint*) deludere; *dress, trousers* allungare
♦ **let in** *to house* far entrare
♦ **let out** *from room* far uscire; *jacket etc* allargare; *groan, yell* emettere
♦ **let up** (*stop*) smettere

lethal [ˈliːθl] mortale

lethargic [lɪˈθɑːdʒɪk] fiacco; **lethargy** fiacchezza *f*

letter [ˈletə(r)] lettera *f*; **letterbox** *on street* buca *f* delle lettere; *in door* cassetta *f* della posta; **letterhead** *heading* intestazione *f*; (*headed paper*) carta *f* intestata

lettuce [ˈletɪs] lattuga *f*

leukemia [luːˈkiːmɪə] leucemia *f*

level [ˈlevl] **1** *adj surface* piano; *in competition, scores* pari; **draw ~ with s.o.** *in match* pareggiare **2** *n* livello *m*; **on the ~** F (*honest*) onesto; **level crossing** passaggio *m* a livello; **level-headed** posato

lever [ˈliːvə(r), *Am* ˈlevər] **1** *n* leva *f* **2** *v/t*: **~ sth open** aprire qc facendo leva; **leverage** forza *f*; (*influence*) influenza *f*

levy [ˈlevi] *taxes* imporre

liability [laɪəˈbɪlətɪ] (*responsibility*) responsabilità *f inv*; **liable** responsabile; **it's ~ to**

break (*likely*) è probabile che si rompa

◆ **liaise with** [lɪ'eɪz] tenere i contatti con

liaison [lɪ'eɪzɒn] (*contacts*) contatti *mpl*

liar ['laɪə(r)] bugiardo *m*, -a *f*

libel ['laɪbl] **1** *n* diffamazione *f* **2** *v/t* diffamare

liberal ['lɪbrəl] (*broad-minded*), POL liberale; *portion etc* abbondante

liberate ['lɪbəreɪt] liberare; **liberated** emancipato; **liberation** liberazione *f*; **liberty** libertà *f inv*; **at ~** *of prisoner etc* in libertà; **be at ~ to do sth** poter fare qc

Libra ['liːbrə] ASTR Bilancia *f*

librarian [laɪ'breərɪən] bibliotecario *m*, -a *f*; **library** biblioteca *f*

Libya ['lɪbɪə] Libia *f*; **Libyan 1** *adj* libico **2** *n person* libico *m*, -a *f*

lice [laɪs] *pl* ☞ **louse**

licence ['laɪsns] (*driving ~*) patente *f*; (*road tax ~*) bollo *m* (auto); *for TV* canone *m* (televisivo); *for imports / exports* licenza *f*; *for dog* tassa *f*

license ['laɪsns] **1** *v/t* (*issue ~ to*) rilasciare la licenza a; **the car isn't ~d** la macchina non ha il bollo **2** *n Am* ☞ **licence**; **license number** *Am* numero *m* di targa; **license plate** *Am* targa *f*

lick [lɪk] **1** *n* leccata *f* **2** *v/t* leccare; **~ one's lips** leccarsi i

baffi

lid [lɪd] coperchio *m*

lie[1] [laɪ] **1** *n* bugia *f*; **tell ~s** dire bugie **2** *v/i* mentire

lie[2] [laɪ] *v/i of person* sdraiarsi; *of object* stare; (*be situated*) trovarsi

◆ **lie down** sdraiarsi

lieutenant [lef'tenənt, *Am* luː'tenənt] tenente *m*

life [laɪf] vita *f*; *of machine* durata *f*; *of battery* autonomia *f*; **that's ~!** così è la vita!; **life belt** salvagente *m inv*; **lifeboat** lancia *f* di salvataggio; **life expectancy** aspettativa *f* di vita; **lifeguard** bagnino *m*, -a *f*; **life imprisonment** ergastolo *m*; **life insurance** assicurazione *f* sulla vita; **life jacket** giubbotto *m* di salvataggio; **lifeless** senza vita; **lifelike** fedele; **lifelong** di vecchia data; **lifesized** a grandezza naturale; **life-threatening** mortale; **lifetime**: **in my ~** in vita mia

lift [lɪft] **1** *v/t* sollevare **2** *v/i of fog* diradarsi **3** *n in building* ascensore *m*; *in car* passaggio *m*; **give s.o. a ~** dare un passaggio a qu; **lift-off** *of rocket* decollo *m*

ligament ['lɪgəmənt] legamento *m*

light[1] [laɪt] **1** *n* luce *f*; **have you got a ~?** hai da accendere? **2** *v/t* accendere; (*illuminate*) illuminare **3** *adj not dark* chiaro

♦ **light up 1** v/t (*illuminate*) illuminare **2** v/i (*start to smoke*) accendersi una sigaretta

light[2] [laɪt] **1** *adj not heavy* leggero **2** *adv*: *travel* ~ viaggiare leggero

'**light bulb** lampadina *f*

lighten[1] ['laɪtn] *colour* schiarire

lighten[2] ['laɪtn] *load* alleggerire

lighter ['laɪtə(r)] *for cigarettes* accendino *m*; **light-headed** stordito; **lighting** illuminazione *f*; **lightness** leggerezza *f*; **lightning** fulmine *m*; **lightweight** *in boxing* peso *m* leggero; **light year** anno *m* luce

like[1] [laɪk] **1** *prep* come; ~ *this* / *that* così; *what is she* ~? *in looks, character* com'è?; *it's not* ~ *him not his character* non è da lui; *look* ~ *s.o.* assomigliare a qu **2** *conj* (*as*) come; ~ *I said* come ho già detto

like[2] [laɪk] v/t: *I* ~ *it* / *her* mi piace; *I would* ~ *...* vorrei ...; *I would* ~ *to* ... vorrei ...; *would you* ~ *...?* ti va ...?; *would you* ~ *to* ...?* ti va di ...?; *he* ~*s swimming* gli piace nuotare; *if you* ~ se vuoi

likeable ['laɪkəbl] simpatico; **likelihood** probabilità *f*; **likely** probabile; *not* ~*!* difficile!; **likeness** (*resemblance*) somiglianza *f*; **likewise** altrettanto; **liking** predilizione *f*; *take a* ~ *to s.o.* prendere qu in simpatia

lily ['lɪlɪ] giglio *m*

limb [lɪm] arto *m*

lime[1] [laɪm] *fruit* limetta *f*

lime[2] [laɪm] *substance* calce *f*

limit ['lɪmɪt] **1** *n* limite *m*; *that's the* ~*!* è il colmo! **2** v/t limitare; **limitation** limite *m*; **limited company** società *f inv* a responsabilità limitata

limousine ['lɪməziːn] limousine *f inv*

limp[1] [lɪmp] *adj* floscio

limp[2] [lɪmp] **1** *n*: *he has a* ~ zoppica **2** v/i zoppicare

line[1] [laɪn] *n* linea *f*; *of people, trees* fila *f*; *of text* riga *f*; *of business* settore *m*; *the* ~ *is busy* è occupato; *hold the* ~ rimanga in linea; *draw the* ~ *at sth* non tollerare qc; ~ *of inquiry* pista *f*; ~ *of reasoning* filo *m* del ragionamento; *stand in* ~ *Am* fare la fila; *in* ~ *with* ... (*conforming with*) in linea con ...

line[2] [laɪn] v/t foderare

linear ['lɪnɪə(r)] lineare

linen ['lɪnɪn] *material* lino *m*; *sheets etc* biancheria *f*

liner ['laɪnə(r)] *ship* transatlantico *m*

linesman ['laɪnzmən] SP guardalinee *m inv*

linger ['lɪŋɡə(r)] *of person* attardarsi; *of smell, pain* persistere

lingerie ['lænʒərɪ] lingerie f

linguist ['lɪŋgwɪst] linguista m/f; person good at languages poliglotta m/f; linguistic linguistico

lining ['laɪnɪŋ] of clothes fodera f; of brakes guarnizione f

link [lɪŋk] 1 n legame m; in chain anello m 2 v/t collegare

lion ['laɪən] leone m

lip [lɪp] labbro m; ~s labbra

liposuction ['lɪpəʊsʌkʃən] liposuzione f

'lipread leggere le labbra; lipstick rossetto m

liqueur [lɪ'kjʊə(r)] liquore m

liquid ['lɪkwɪd] 1 n liquido m 2 adj liquido; liquidate liquidare; liquidation liquidazione f; go into ~ andare in liquidazione; liquidity FIN liquidità f; liquidize frullare; liquidizer frullatore m

liquor ['lɪkə(r)] superalcolici mpl; liquor store Am negozio m di alcolici

lisp [lɪsp] 1 n lisca f 2 v/i parlare con la lisca

list [lɪst] 1 n elenco m, lista f 2 v/t elencare

◆ listen to ascoltare

listener ['lɪsnə(r)] to radio ascoltatore m, -trice f; he's a good ~ sa ascoltare

listings magazine ['lɪstɪŋz] guida f dei programmi radio / TV

listless ['lɪstlɪs] apatico

liter Am ☞ litre

literal ['lɪtərəl] letterale; literally letteralmente

literary ['lɪtərərɪ] letterario; literature letteratura f; (leaflets) opuscoli mpl

litre ['liːtə(r)] litro m

litter ['lɪtə(r)] rifiuti mpl; of animal cucciolata f; litter bin bidone m dei rifiuti

little ['lɪtl] 1 adj piccolo 2 n: the ~ I know il poco che so; a ~ un po'; a ~ wine un po' di vino 3 adv: ~ by ~ (a) poco a poco; a ~ bigger un po' più grande

live¹ [lɪv] v/i (reside) abitare; (be alive) vivere

◆ live up: live it up fare la bella vita

◆ live up to essere all'altezza di

live² [laɪv] 1 adj broadcast dal vivo; ammunition carico 2 adv broadcast in diretta; record dal vivo

livelihood ['laɪvlɪhʊd] mezzi mpl di sostentamento; earn one's ~ guadagnarsi da vivere; liveliness vivacità f; lively vivace

liver ['lɪvə(r)] fegato m

livestock ['laɪvstɒk] bestiame m

livid ['lɪvɪd] (angry) furibondo

living ['lɪvɪŋ] 1 adj in vita 2 n: earn one's ~ guadagnarsi da vivere; what do you do for a ~? che lavoro fai?; living room salotto m, soggiorno *m*

lizard [ˈlɪzəd] lucertola *f*

load [ləʊd] **1** *n* carico *m*; **~s of** F un sacco di **2** *v/t* caricare

loaf [ləʊf]: **a ~ of bread** una pagnotta

◆ **loaf around** F oziare

loafer [ˈləʊfə(r)] *shoe* mocassino *m*

loan [ləʊn] **1** *n* prestito *m*; **on ~** in prestito **2** *v/t*: **~ s.o. sth** prestare qc a qu

loathe [ləʊð] detestare; **loathing** disgusto *m*

lobby [ˈlɒbɪ] *in hotel, theatre* atrio *m*; POL lobby *f inv*

lobe [ləʊb] *of ear* lobo *m*

lobster [ˈlɒbstə(r)] aragosta *f*

local [ˈləʊkl] **1** *adj people, bar* del posto; *produce* locale **2** *n* persona *f* del posto; locale *m*; **local call** TELEC telefonata *f* urbana; **local elections** elezioni *fpl* amministrative; **local government** amministrazione *f* locale; **locality** località *f inv*; **localize** localizzare; **locally** *live, work* nella zona; **local time** ora *f* locale

locate [ləʊˈkeɪt] *new factory etc* situare; *identify position of* localizzare; **be ~d** essere situato; **location** *(siting)* ubicazione *f*; *identifying position of* localizzazione *f*; **on ~** *film* in esterni

lock¹ [lɒk] *of hair* ciocca *f*

lock² [lɒk] **1** *n on door* serratura *f* **2** *v/t door* chiudere a chiave

◆ **lock up** *in prison* mettere dentro

locker [ˈlɒkə(r)] armadietto *m*; **locker room** spogliatoio *m*

locust [ˈləʊkəst] locusta *f*

lodge [lɒdʒ] **1** *v/t complaint* presentare **2** *v/i of bullet* conficcarsi

lofty [ˈlɒftɪ] *peak* alto; *ideals* nobile

log [lɒg] *wood* ceppo *m*; *written record* giornale *m*

◆ **log in** fare il log in

◆ **log off** disconnettersi (**from** da)

◆ **log on** fare il log on, connettersi (**to** a)

◆ **log out** fare il log out

log 'cabin casetta *f* di legno

logic [ˈlɒdʒɪk] logica *f*; **logical** logico; **logically** a rigor di logica; *arrange* in modo logico

logistics [ləˈdʒɪstɪks] *npl* logistica *f*

logo [ˈləʊgəʊ] logo *m inv*

loiter [ˈlɔɪtə(r)] gironzolare

lollipop [ˈlɒlɪpɒp] lecca lecca *m inv*

London [ˈlʌndən] Londra *f*

loneliness [ˈləʊnlɪnɪs] solitudine *f*; **lonely** *person* solo; *place* isolato; **loner** persona *f* solitaria

long¹ [lɒŋ] **1** *adj* lungo; **it's a ~ way** è lontano **2** *adv*: **don't be ~** torna fra **5 weeks is too ~** 5 settimane è troppo; **will it take ~?** ci vorrà tanto?; *that was ~ ago* è stato tanto tempo fa; *~ before then* molto prima di allora; *before ~* poco tempo dopo; *we can't wait any ~er* non possiamo attendere oltre; *he no ~er works here* non lavora più qui; *so ~ as (provided)* sempre che; *so ~!* arrivederci!

long² [lɒŋ] *v/i*: *~ for sth* desiderare ardentemente qc; *be ~ing to do sth* desiderare ardentemente fare qc; *long-distance phonecall* interurbano; *race* di fondo; *flight* intercontinentale; **longevity** longevità *f*; **longing** desiderio *m*; **longitude** longitudine *f*; **long jump** salto *m* in lungo; **long-range** *missile* a lunga gittata; *forecast* a lungo termine; **long-sleeved** a maniche lunghe; **long-standing** di vecchia data; **long-term** *plans, investment* a lunga scadenza; *relationship* stabile; **long wave** RAD onde *fpl* lunghe

loo [luː] F gabinetto *m*

look [lʊk] **1** *n (appearance)* aspetto *m*; *(glance)* sguardo *m*; **have a ~** *at* sth *examine* dare un'occhiata a qc; *can I have a ~ around?* *in shop etc* posso dare un'occhiata?; *~s (beauty)* bellezza *f* **2** *v/i* guardare; *(search)* cercare; *(seem)* sembrare

◆ **look after** badare a

◆ **look ahead** *fig* pensare al futuro

◆ **look around** *in shop etc* dare un'occhiata in giro; *(look back)* guardarsi indietro

◆ **look at** guardare; *(consider)* considerare

◆ **look back** guardare indietro

◆ **look down on** disprezzare

◆ **look for** cercare

◆ **look forward to**: *I'm looking forward to the holidays* non vedo l'ora che arrivino le vacanze

◆ **look into** *(investigate)* esaminare

◆ **look onto** *garden, street* dare su

◆ **look out** *of window etc* guardare fuori; *(pay attention)* fare attenzione; *look out!* attento!

◆ **look over** *house, translation* esaminare

◆ **look through** *magazine, notes* scorrere

◆ **look to** *(rely on)* contare su

◆ **look up 1** *v/i from paper etc* sollevare lo sguardo; *(improve)* migliorare **2** *v/t word, phone number* cercare; *(visit)* andare a trovare

◆ **look up to** *(respect)* avere rispetto per

'lookout *person* sentinella *f*; *be on the ~ for accommodation etc* cercare di trovare; *new staff etc* essere alla ricerca di

loop [luːp] cappio m; **loophole** in law etc scappatoia f

loose [luːs] wire, button allentato; clothes ampio; tooth che tentenna; morals dissoluto; wording vago; **~ change** spiccioli mpl; **loosely** tied senza stringere; **worded** vagamente; **loosen** allentare

loot [luːt] **1** n bottino m **2** v/t & v/i saccheggiare; **looter** saccheggiatore m, -trice f

lop-sided [lɒpˈsaɪdɪd] sbilenco

Lord [lɔːd] (God) Signore m; **the (House of) ~s** la camera dei Lord

lorry [ˈlɒrɪ] camion m inv; **lorry driver** camionista m

lose [luːz] **1** v/t object perdere **2** v/i SP perdere; of clock andare indietro; **I'm lost** mi sono perso; **get lost!** F sparisci!; loser in contest perdente m/f; F in life sfigato m, -a f F

loss [lɒs] perdita f; **make a ~** subire una perdita; **be at a ~** essere perplesso

lost [lɒst] perso; **lost property office**, Am **lost and found** ufficio m oggetti smarriti

lot [lɒt]: **a ~ (of)**, **~s (of)** molto; **~s of ice creams** molti gelati; **the ~** tutto

lotion [ˈləʊʃn] lozione f

lottery [ˈlɒtərɪ] lotteria f

loud [laʊd] music, voice, noise forte; colour sgargiante; **loudspeaker** altoparlante m; for stereo cassa f dello stereo

lounge [laʊndʒ] in house soggiorno m; in hotel salone m; at airport sala f partenze

louse [laʊs] (pl **lice** [laɪs]) pidocchio m; **lousy** F schifoso F

lout [laʊt] teppista m/f

lovable [ˈlʌvəbl] adorabile; **love 1** n amore m; in tennis zero m; **be in ~** essere innamorato; **fall in ~** innamorarsi; **make ~** fare l'amore (**to** con) **2** v/t amare; **~ doing sth** amare fare qc; **love affair** relazione f; **lovely** face, colour, holiday bello; meal, smell buono; **we had a ~ time** siamo stati benissimo; **lover** amante m/f; **loving** affettuoso; **lovingly** amorosamente

low [ləʊ] **1** adj basso; quality scarso; **be feeling ~** sentirsi giù; **be on petrol** avere poca benzina **2** n in weather depressione f; in sales, statistics minimo m; **lowbrow** di scarso spessore culturale; **low-calorie** ipocalorico; **low-cut dress** scollato; **lower** boat, sth to the ground calare; flag, hemline ammainare; pressure, price abbassare; **low-fat** a basso contenuto lipidico; **lowkey** discreto

loyal [ˈlɔɪəl] leale; **loyally** lealmente; loyalty lealtà *f inv*

lozenge ['lɒzɪndʒ] rombo *m*; *tablet* pastiglia *f*

Ltd (= *limited*) s.r.l. (= società a responsabilità limitata)

lubricant ['lu:brɪkənt] lubrificante *m*; lubricate lubrificare; lubrication lubrificazione *f*

lucid ['lu:sɪd] (*clear*) chiaro; (*sane*) lucido

luck [lʌk] fortuna *f*; *bad ~* sfortuna; *hard ~! che* sfortuna!; *good ~* fortuna *f*; *good ~!* buona fortuna!; luckily fortunatamente; lucky fortunato; *you were~* hai avuto fortuna; *that's ~!* che fortuna!

lucrative ['lu:krətɪv] redditizio

ludicrous ['lu:dɪkrəs] ridicolo

lug [lʌg] F trascinare

luggage ['lʌgɪdʒ] bagagli *mpl*

lukewarm ['lu:kwɔ:m] tiepido

lull [lʌl] *in fighting* momento *m* di calma; *in conversation* pausa *f*

lumber ['lʌmbə(r)] (*timber*) legname *m*

luminous ['lu:mɪnəs] luminoso

lump [lʌmp] *of sugar* zolletta *f*; (*swelling*) nodulo *m*; lump sum pagamento *m* unico; lumpy *sauce* grumoso; *mattress* pieno di buchi

lunacy ['lu:nəsɪ] pazzia *f*

lunar ['lu:nə(r)] lunare

lunatic ['lu:nətɪk] pazzo *m*, -a *f*

lunch [lʌntʃ] pranzo *m*; *have ~* pranzare; lunch box cestino *m* del pranzo; lunch break pausa *f* pranzo; lunch hour pausa *f* pranzo; lunchtime ora *f* di pranzo

lung [lʌŋ] polmone *m*

lurch [lɜ:tʃ] barcollare

lure [luə(r)] 1 *n* attrattiva *f* 2 *v/t* attirare

lurid ['luərɪd] *colour* sgargiante; *details* scandaloso

lurk [lɜ:k] *of person* appostarsi; *of doubt* persistere

lush [lʌʃ] *vegetation* lussureggiante

lust [lʌst] libidine *f*

luxurious [lʌg'ʒuərɪəs] lussuoso; luxuriously lussuosamente; luxury 1 *n* lusso *m* 2 *adj* di lusso

lynch [lɪntʃ] linciare

lyrics ['lɪrɪks] parole *fpl*, testi *mpl*

M

MA [emˈeɪ] (= *Master of Arts*) master *m* *in univ*

ma'am [mæm] *Am* signora *f*

machine [məˈʃiːn] macchina *f*; **machine gun** mitragliatrice *f*; **machinery** macchinario *m*

machismo [məˈkɪzməʊ] machismo *m*

macho [ˈmætʃəʊ] macho *m*

macro [ˈmækrəʊ] COMPUT macro *f*

mad [mæd] pazzo *m*; F (*angry*) furioso; **be ~ about** F (*keen on*) andar matto per; **drive s.o. ~** far impazzire qu; **~ about** F impazzire

madden [mædn] (*infuriate*) esasperare; **maddening** esasperante

made-to-measure su misura

'madhouse *fig* manicomio *m*; **madly** come un matto; **~ in love** pazzamente innamorato; **madman** pazzo *m*; **madness** pazzia *f*

Madonna [məˈdɒnə] Madonna *f*

Mafia [ˈmæfɪə] Mafia *f*

magazine [mægəˈziːn] *printed* rivista *f*

Magi [ˈmeɪdʒaɪ] REL Re Magi *mpl*

magic [ˈmædʒɪk] **1** *n* magia *f*; *tricks* giochi *mpl* di prestigio **2** *adj* magico; **magical** magico; **magician** *performer* mago *m*, -a *f*; **magic spell** in-

cantesimo *m*

magnanimous [mægˈnænɪməs] magnanimo

magnet [ˈmægnɪt] calamita *f*, magnete *m*; **magnetic** calamitato; *also fig* magnetico; **magnetism** *of person* magnetismo *m*

magnificence [mægˈnɪfɪsəns] magnificenza *f*; **magnificent** magnifico

magnify [ˈmægnɪfaɪ] ingrandire; *difficulties* ingigantire; **magnifying glass** lente *f* d'ingrandimento

magnitude [ˈmægnɪtjuːd] *of problem* portata *f*

maid [meɪd] *servant* domestica *f*; *in hotel* cameriera *f*

maiden name [ˈmeɪdn] nome *m* da ragazza; **maiden voyage** viaggio *m* inaugurale

mail [meɪl] **1** *n* posta *f* **2** *v/t letter* spedire; *person* spedire a; **mailbox** *Am* buca *f* delle lettere; *of house* cassetta *f* delle lettere; COMPUT (*not Am*) casella *f* postale; **mailing list** mailing list *m inv*; **mailman** *Am* postino *m*; **mail-order firm** ditta *f* di vendita per corrispondenza; **mailshot** mailing *m inv*

maim [meɪm] mutilare

main [meɪn] principale; **main course** piatto *m* principale;

mainframe mainframe *m inv*; mainland terraferma *f*, continente *m*; **on the ~** sul continente; **mainly** principalmente; **main road** strada *f* principale; **main street** corso *m*

maintain [meɪnˈteɪn] *pace, speed, relationship* mantenere; *innocence, guilt* sostenere; **~ that** sostenere che; **~ tenance** *of machine, house* manutenzione *f*; *money* alimenti *mpl*; *of law and order* mantenimento *m*

majestic [məˈdʒestɪk] maestoso

major [ˈmeɪdʒə(r)] **1** *adj (significant)* importante, principale; **in C ~** MUS in Do maggiore **2** *n* MIL maggiore *m*

◆ **major in** *Am* specializzarsi in

majority [məˈdʒɒrətɪ] *also* POL maggioranza *f*; **be in the ~** essere in maggioranza

make [meɪk] **1** *n (brand)* marca *f* **2** *v/t face; decision* prendere; *(earn)* guadagnare; MATH fare; **~ it** *catch bus, train, come, succeed* farcela; *what time do you* **~** *it?* che ore fai?; **~ believe** far finta; **~ do with** arrangiarsi con; *what do you* **~** *of it?* cosa ne pensi?; **~ s.o. do sth** *(force to)* far fare qc a qu; *(cause to)* spingere qu a fare qc; **~ s.o. happy** far felice qu, rendere felice qu

◆ **make off with** *(steal)* svignarsela con

◆ **make out** *list* fare; *cheque* compilare; *(see)* distinguere; *(imply)* far capire

◆ **make up 1** *v/i of woman, actor* truccarsi; *after quarrel* fare la pace **2** *v/t story, excuse* inventare; *face* truccare; *(constitute)* costituire; **be made up of** essere composto da; **make it up** *after quarrel* fare la pace

◆ **make up for** compensare **make-believe** finta *f*

maker [ˈmeɪkə(r)] *manufacturer* fabbricante *m/f*; **make-shift** improvvisato; **make-up** *(cosmetics)* trucco *m*

maladjusted [mælədˈdʒʌstɪd] disadattato

male [meɪl] **1** *adj* maschile; *animal* maschio **2** *n man* uomo *m*; *animal, bird* maschio *m*; **male chauvinism** maschilismo *m*; **male chauvinist pig** maschilista *m*

malevolent [məˈlevələnt] malevolo

malfunction [mælˈfʌŋkʃn] **1** *n* cattivo *m* funzionamento **2** *v/i* funzionare male

malice [ˈmælɪs] cattiveria *f*, malvagità *f*; **malicious** cattivo, malvagio

malignant [məˈlɪgnənt] *tumour* maligno

mall [mæl] *(shopping ~)* centro *m* commerciale

malnutrition [mælnjuːˈtrɪʃn]

denutrizione f

maltreat [mæl'triːt] maltrattare; **maltreatment** maltrattamento m

mammal ['mæml] mammifero m

man [mæn] **1** n (pl **men** [men]) uomo m; humanity umanità f; in draughts pedina f **2** v/t telephones, front desk essere di servizio a; **it was ~ed by a crew of three** aveva un equipaggio di tre persone

manage ['mænɪdʒ] v/t business, money gestire; **can you ~ the suitcase?** ce la fai a portare la valigia?; **to ...** riuscire a ...**2** v/i cope, financially tirare avanti; (financially); **can you ~?** ce la fai?; **manageable** suitcase etc maneggevole; hair docile; able to be done fattibile; **management** (managing) gestione f, (managers) direzione f; **management consultant** consulente m/f di gestione aziendale; **manager** manager m/f inv, direttore m, -trice f; **managerial** manageriale; **managing director** direttore m generale

mandate ['mændeɪt] (authority, task) mandato m; **mandatory** obbligatorio

maneuver Am → **manoeuvre**

mangle ['mæŋgl] (crush) stritolare

manhandle ['mænhændl] person malmenare; object caricare

manhood ['mænhʊd] maturity età f adulta; (virility) virilità f; **manhunt** caccia f all'uomo

mania ['meɪnɪə] (craze) mania f; **maniac** F pazzo m, -a f

manicure ['mænɪkjʊə(r)] manicure f inv

manifest ['mænɪfest] **1** adj palese **2** v/t manifestare

manipulate [mə'nɪpjʊleɪt] manipolare; **manipulation** manipolazione f; **manipulative** manipolatore

man'kind umanità f; **manly** virile; **man-made** sintetico

manner ['mænə(r)] of doing sth maniera f, modo m; (attitude) modo m di fare; **manners: good / bad ~** buone / cattive maniere fpl; **have no ~** essere maleducato

manoeuvre [mə'nuːvə(r)] **1** n manovra f **2** v/t manovrare

'manpower manodopera f, personale m; **manslaughter** omicidio m colposo

manual ['mænjʊəl] **1** adj manuale **2** n manuale m; **manually** manualmente

manufacture [mænju-'fæktʃə(r)] **1** n manifattura f **2** v/t equipment fabbricare; **manufacturer** fabbricante m/f; **manufacturing** industry manifatturiero

manure [mə'njʊə(r)] letame

m

manuscript ['mænjʊskrɪpt] manoscritto *m; typed* dattiloscritto *m*

many ['menɪ] **1** *adj* molti; ~ *times* molte volte; *not* ~ *people / taxis* poche persone / pochi taxi; *too* ~ *problems / beers* troppi problemi / troppe birre **2** *pron* molti *m*, molte *f*; *a great* ~, *a good* ~ moltissimi; *how* ~ *do you need?* quanti ve ne servono? *as* ~ *as 200* ben 200

map [mæp] cartina *f*; (*street* ~) pianta *f*, piantina *f*

maple ['meɪpl] acero *m*

mar [mɑː(r)] guastare

marathon ['mærəθən] *race* maratona *f*

marble ['mɑːbl] *material* marmo *m*

March [mɑːtʃ] marzo *m*

march [mɑːtʃ] **1** *n* marcia *f*; (*demonstration*) dimostrazione *f*, manifestazione *f* **2** *v/i* marciare; *in protest* dimostrare, manifestare; **march**er dimostrante *m/f*, manifestante *m/f*

Mardi Gras ['mɑːdɪgrɑː] *Am* martedì *m* grasso

margin ['mɑːdʒɪn] *of page* margine *m*; COM margine *m* di guadagno; *by a narrow* ~ di stretta misura; **marginal** (*slight*) leggero; **marginally** (*slightly*) leggermente

marihuana [ˌmærɪhuˈɑːnə] marijuana *f*

marina [məˈriːnə] porticciolo *m*

marine [məˈriːn] **1** *adj* marino **2** *n* MIL marina *f* militare

marital ['mærɪtl] coniugale; **marital status** stato *m* civile

maritime ['mærɪtaɪm] marittimo

mark [mɑːk] **1** *n* (*stain*) macchia *f*; (*sign, token*) segno *m*; (*trace*) EDU voto *m* **2** *v/t* (*stain*) macchiare; EDU correggere; (*indicate*) indicare; (*commemorate*) celebrare **3** *v/i* (*of fabric*) macchiarsi; **marked** (*definite*) spiccato; **marker** (*highlighter*) evidenziatore *m*

market ['mɑːkɪt] **1** *n* mercato *m* **2** *v/t* vendere; **marketable** commercializzabile; **market economy** economia *f* di mercato; **marketing** marketing *m*; **market leader** leader *m inv* del mercato; **market-place** *in town* piazza *f* del mercato; *for commodities* piazza *f*, mercato *m*; **market research** ricerca *f* di mercato; **market share** quota *f* di mercato

'mark-up ricarico *m*

marmalade [ˈmɑːməleɪd] marmellata *f* d'arance

marriage ['mærɪdʒ] matrimonio *m*; *event* nozze *fpl*; **marriage certificate** certificato *m* di matrimonio; **married** sposato; *be* ~ *to ...* essere sposato con ...; **married life** vita *f* coniugale; **marry** sposare; *of priest* unire in matrimonio; **get married** sposarsi

marsh [mɑːʃ] palude *f*

marshal [ˈmɑːʃl] *official* membro *m* del servizio d'ordine

martial arts [mɑːʃlˈɑːts] arti *fpl* marziali; **martial law** legge *f* marziale

martyr [ˈmɑːtə(r)] martire *m/f*

marvel [ˈmɑːvl] meraviglia *f*; **marvellous,** *Am* **marvelous** meraviglioso

Marxism [ˈmɑːksɪzm] marxismo *m*; **Marxist 1** *adj* marxista **2** *n* marxista *m/f*

mascara [mæˈskɑːrə] mascara *m inv*

mascot [ˈmæskət] mascotte *f inv*

masculine [ˈmæskjʊlɪn] maschile; **masculinity** (*virility*) virilità *f*

mash [mæʃ] passare, schiacciare; **mashed potatoes** purè *m* di patate

mask [mɑːsk] **1** *n* maschera *f* **2** *v/t feelings* mascherare

masochism [ˈmæsəkɪzm] masochismo *m*; **masochist** masochista *m/f*

mass¹ [mæs] **1** *n great amount* massa *f*; **~es of** F un sacco di F **2** *v/i* radunarsi

mass² [mæs] REL messa *f*

massacre [ˈmæsəkə(r)] **1** *n also fig* massacro *m* **2** *v/t also fig* massacrare

massage [ˈmæsɑːʒ] **1** *n* massaggio *m* **2** *v/t* massaggiare; *figures* manipolare

massive [ˈmæsɪv] enorme; *heart attack* grave

mass 'media mass media *mpl*; **mass-produce** produrre in serie; **mass production** produzione *f* in serie; **mass transit** *Am* i trasporti pubblici

mast [mɑːst] *of ship* albero *m*; *for radio signal* palo *m* dell'antenna

master [ˈmɑːstə(r)] **1** *n of dog* padrone *m*; *of ship* capitano *m* **2** *v/t skill, language* avere completa padronanza di; *situation* dominare; **master bedroom** camera *f* da letto principale; **master key** passe-partout *m inv*; **masterly** magistrale; **mastermind 1** *n fig* cervello *m* **2** *v/t* ideare; **masterpiece** capolavoro *m*; **master's (degree)** master *m inv*; **mastery** padronanza *f*

mat [mæt] *for floor* tappetino *m*; *for table* tovaglietta *f* all'americana

match¹ [mætʃ] *n for cigarette* fiammifero *m*; *made of wax* cerino *m*

match² [mætʃ] *n (competition)* partita *f*; **be no ~ for s.o.** non poter competere con qu **2** *v/t* (*be the same as*) abbinare; (*equal*) uguagliare **3** *v/i of colours, pat-

meager

terns intonarsi

matching ['mætʃɪŋ] abbinato

mate [meɪt] **1** *n of animal* compagno *m*, -a *f*; NAUT secondo *m*; F *friend* amico *m*, -a *f* **2** *v/i* accoppiarsi

material [mə'tɪərɪəl] **1** *n fabric* stoffa *f*, tessuto *m*; *substance* materia *f*; **~s** occorrente *m* **2** *adj* materiale; **materialism** materialismo *m*; **materialist** materialista *m/f*; **materialistic** materialistico; **materialize** materializzarsi

maternal [mə'tɜːnl] materno; **maternity** maternità *f*; **maternity leave** congedo *m* per maternità; **maternity ward** reparto *m* maternità

math [mæθ] *Am* ☞ **maths**; **mathematical** matematico; **mathematician** matematico *m*, -a *f*; **mathematics** matematica *f*; **maths** matematica *f*

matinée ['mætɪneɪ] matinée *f inv*

matriarch ['meɪtrɪɑːk] matriarca *f*

matrimony ['mætrɪmənɪ] matrimonio *m*

matt [mæt] opaco

matter ['mætə(r)] **1** *n (affair)* questione *f*, faccenda *f*; PHYS materia *f*; **as a ~ of fact** a dir la verità; **what's the ~?** cosa c'è?; **no ~ what she says** qualsiasi cosa dica **2** *v/i* importare; **it doesn't ~** non importa; **matter-of-fact**

distaccato

mattress ['mætrɪs] materasso *m*

mature [mə'tjʊə(r)] **1** *adj* maturo **2** *v/i of person, insurance policy etc* maturare; *of wine* invecchiare; **maturity** maturità *f*

maximize ['mæksɪmaɪz] massimizzare; **maximum 1** *adj* massimo **2** *n* massimo *m*

May [meɪ] maggio *m*

may [meɪ] ◇ *(possibility)*: **it ~ rain** potrebbe piovere, può darsi che piova; **it ~ not happen** può darsi che non succeda ◇ *(permission)*: **~ I help?** posso aiutare?

maybe ['meɪbiː] forse

mayonnaise [meɪə'neɪz] maionese *f*

mayor ['meə(r)] sindaco *m*

maze [meɪz] *also fig* dedalo *m*, labirinto *m*

MB (= **megabyte**) MB *m* (= megabyte *m inv*)

MBA [embiː'eɪ] (= **master of business administration**) master in amministrazione aziendale

MD [em'diː] (= **Doctor of Medicine**) dottore in medicina

me [miː] mi; *after prep, stressed* me; **she knows ~** mi conosce; **she spoke to ~** mi ha parlato; **it's ~** sono io; **who? – ~?** chi? – io?

meadow ['medəʊ] prato *m*

meagre, *Am* **meager** ['miːgə(r)] scarso

meal [miːl] pranzo *m*, pasto *m*;
enjoy your ~! buon appetito!

mean¹ [miːn] *adj with money* avaro; *(nasty)* cattivo

mean² [miːn] 1 *v/t (signify)* significare, voler dire; **do you ~ it?** dici sul serio?; **to do sth** avere l'intenzione di fare qc; **be ~t for** essere destinato a; *of remark* essere diretto a 2 *v/i*: **~ well** avere buone intenzioni

meaning [ˈmiːnɪŋ] *of word* significato *m*; **meaningful** *(comprehensible)* comprensibile; *(constructive)* costruttivo; *glance* eloquente; **meaningless** *sentence etc* senza senso; *gesture* vuoto

means [miːnz] *financial* mezzi *mpl*; *(nsg: way)* modo *m*; **~ of transport** mezzo *m* di trasporto; **by all ~** *(certainly)* certamente; **by no ~** *rich* lungi dall'essere ricco; **by ~ of** per mezzo di

meantime [ˈmiːntaɪm] intanto

measles [ˈmiːzlz] morbillo *m*

measure [ˈmeʒə(r)] 1 *n (step)* misura *f* 2 *v/t* prendere le misure di 3 *v/i* misurare

♦ **measure up to** dimostrarsi all'altezza di

measurement [ˈmeʒəmənt] *action* misurazione *f*; *(dimension)* misura *f*; **measuring tape** metro *m* a nastro

meat [miːt] carne *f*; **meatball**

polpetta *f*

mechanic [mɪˈkænɪk] meccanico *m*; **mechanical** *also fig* meccanico; **mechanical engineer** ingegnere *m* meccanico; **mechanically** *also fig* meccanicamente; **mechanism** meccanismo *m*; **mechanize** meccanizzare

medal [ˈmedl] medaglia *f*; **medallist**, *Am* **medalist** vincitore *m*, -trice *f* di una medaglia

meddle [ˈmedl] *(interfere)* immischiarsi; **~ with** *(tinker)* mettere le mani in

media [ˈmiːdɪə]: **the ~** i mass media *mpl*; **media coverage**: **it was given a lot of ~** gli è stato dato molto spazio in TV e sui giornali

mediaeval ☞ **medieval**

median strip [miːdɪənˈstrɪp] *Am* banchina *f* spartitraffico

'media studies scienze *fpl* delle comunicazioni

mediate [ˈmiːdɪeɪt] fare da mediatore a, -trice *f*; **mediation** mediazione *f*; **mediator** mediatore *m*, -trice *f*

medical [ˈmedɪkl] 1 *adj* medico 2 *n* visita *f* medica; **medicated** medicato; **medication** medicina *f*; **medicinal** medicinale; **medicine** medicina *f*

medieval [medɪˈiːvl] medievale

mediocre [miːdɪˈəʊkə(r)] mediocre; **mediocrity** mediocrità f

meditate ['mediteit] meditare; **meditation** meditazione f

Mediterranean [meditə'reiniən] **1** adj mediterraneo **2** n: **the ~** il Mar Mediterraneo; area i paesi mediterranei

medium ['mi:diəm] **1** adj (average) medio; steak cotto al punto giusto **2** n in size media f; (vehicle) strumento m; (spiritualist) medium m/f inv; **medium-sized** di grandezza media; **medium wave** RAD onde fpl medie

medley ['medli] (assortment) misto m

meet [mi:t] **1** v/t incontrare; (get to know) conoscere; (collect) andare or venire a prendere; in competition affrontare; of eyes incrociare; (satisfy) soddisfare; **I'll ~ you there** ci vediamo lì **2** v/i incontrarsi; in competition affrontarsi; of eyes incrociarsi; of committee etc riunirsi; **have you two met?** (do you know each other?) vi conoscete? **3** n SP raduno m sportivo

♦ **meet with** person avere un incontro con; opposition, approval etc incontrare; **it met with success / failure** ha avuto successo / è fallito

meeting ['mi:tiŋ] incontro m; of committee, in business riunione f; **he's in a ~** è in riunione

megabyte ['megəbait] COMPUT megabyte m inv

mellow ['meləu] **1** adj maturo **2** v/i of person addolcirsi

melodious [mi'ləudiəs] melodioso

melodramatic [melədrə'mætik] melodrammatico

melody ['melədi] melodia f

melon ['melən] melone m

melt [melt] **1** v/i sciogliersi **2** v/t sciogliere; **melting pot** fig crogliolo m di culture

member ['membə(r)] of family componente m/f; of club socio m; of organization membro m; **Member of Congress** membro m del Congresso; **Member of Parliament** membro m del Parlamento, deputato m; **membership** iscrizione f; number of members numero m dei soci

membrane ['membrein] membrana f

memento [me'mentəu] souvenir m inv

memo ['meməu] circolare f

memoirs ['memwɑːz] memorie fpl

memorable ['memərəbl] memorabile

memorial [mɪ'mɔːriəl] **1** adj commemorativo **2** n also fig memorial m inv

memorize ['meməraiz] memorizzare; **memory** (recollection) ricordo *m*; *power of recollection* memoria *f*; COMPUT memoria *f*; **memory stick** memory stick *f inv*

men [men] *pl* ☞ **man**

menace ['menis] **1** *n* (*threat*) minaccia *f*; *person* pericolo *m* pubblico; (*nuisance*) peste *f* **2** *v/t* minacciare; **menacing** minaccioso

mend [mend] riparare

menial ['mi:nɪəl] umile

menopause ['menəpɔ:z] menopausa *f*

'men's room bagno *m* (degli uomini)

menstruate ['menstrʊeɪt] avere le mestruazioni; **menstruation** mestruazione *f*

mental ['mentl] mentale; F (*crazy*) pazzo; **mental hospital** ospedale *m* psichiatrico; **mental illness** malattia *f* mentale; **mentality** mentalità *f inv*; **mentally** inwardly mentalmente; *calculate etc* a mente; **mentally ill** malato di mente

mention ['menʃn] **1** *n* cenno *m* **2** *v/t* accennare a; *don't ~ it* (*you're welcome*) non c'è di che

mentor ['mentɔ:(r)] guida *f* spirituale

menu ['menju:] *also* COMPUT menu *m inv*

mercenary ['mɜ:sɪnərɪ] **1** *adj* mercenario **2** *n* MIL mercenario *m*

merchandise ['mɜ:tʃəndaɪz] merce *f*

merchant ['mɜ:tʃənt] commerciante *m/f*; **merchant bank** banca *f* d'affari

merciful ['mɜ:sɪfʊl] misericordioso; **mercifully** (*thankfully*) per fortuna; **merciless** spietato; **mercy** misericordia *f*; **be at s.o.'s ~** essere alla mercé di qu

mere [mɪə(r)] semplice; **merely** soltanto

merge [mɜ:dʒ] *of two lines etc* unirsi; *of companies* fondersi; **merger** COM fusione *f*

merit ['merɪt] **1** *n* (*worth*) merito *m*; (*advantage*) vantaggio *m* **2** *v/t* meritare

mesh [meʃ] *in net* maglia *f*

mess [mes] (*untidiness*) disordine *m*; (*trouble*) pasticcio *m*; **be a ~** *of room, desk, hair* essere in disordine; *of situation, s.o.'s life* essere un pasticcio

message ['mesɪdʒ] *also fig* messaggio *m*

messenger ['mesɪndʒə(r)] (*courier*) fattorino *m*, -a *f*

messy ['mesɪ] *room* in disordine; *person* disordinato; *job* sporco; *divorce, situation* antipatico

metabolism [mətæ'bəlɪzm] metabolismo *m*

metal ['metl] **1** *adj in or* di metallo **2** *n* metallo *m*; **metallic** metallico

metaphor ['metəfə(r)] metafora *f*

meteor ['mi:tɪə(r)] meteora f; meteoric fig fulmineo; meteorite meteorite m or f

meteorological [mi:tɪərə'lɒdʒɪkl] meteorologico; meteorologist meteorologo m, -a f; meteorology meteorologia f

meter¹ ['mi:tə(r)] for gas etc contatore m; (parking ~) parchimetro m

meter² Am ☞ metre

method ['meθəd] metodo m; methodical metodico

meticulous [mɪ'tɪkjʊləs] meticoloso

metre ['mi:tə(r)] metro m

metropolis [mɪ'trɒpəlɪs] metropoli f inv; metropolitan metropolitano

mew [mju:] ☞ miaow

Mexican ['meksɪkən] 1 adj messicano 2 n messicano m, -a f; Mexico Messico m

miaow [mɪaʊ] 1 n miao m 2 v/i miagolare

mice [maɪs] pl ☞ mouse

'microchip microchip m inv; microclimate microclima m; microcosm microcosmo m; microorganism microrganismo m; microphone microfono m; microprocessor microprocessore m; microscope microscopio m; microscopic microscopico; microwave oven forno m a microonde

midday [mɪd'deɪ] mezzogiorno m

middle ['mɪdl] 1 adj di mezzo 2 n mezzo m; in the ~ of floor, room nel centro di, in mezzo a; of period of time a metà di; be in the ~ of doing sth stare facendo qc; middle-aged di mezz'età; Middle Ages Medioevo m; middle class borghese; middle class(es) la borghesia f; Middle East Medio Oriente m; middleman intermediario m; middle name secondo nome m; middleweight boxer peso m medio

midfielder [mɪd'fi:ldə(r)] centrocampista m

midnight ['mɪdnaɪt] mezzanotte f; midsummer piena estate f; midweek a metà settimana; Midwest regione f medio-occidentale degli USA; midwife ostetrica f; midwinter pieno inverno m

might¹ [maɪt]: I ~ be late potrei far tardi; it ~ rain magari piove; you ~ have told me! potevi dirmelo!

might² [maɪt] (power) forze fpl

mighty ['maɪtɪ] 1 adj potente 2 adv F (extremely) molto

migraine ['mi:greɪn] emicrania f

migrant worker ['maɪgrənt] emigrante m/f; migrate emigrare; of birds migrare; migration emigrazione f; of birds migrazione f

mike [maɪk] F microfono m

Milan [mɪ'læn] Milano f

mild [maɪld] *weather* mite; *cheese, person* dolce; *curry* poco piccante; *punishment, sedative* leggero; **mildness** *of weather* mitezza f; *of person, voice* dolcezza f

mile [maɪl] miglio m; **~s better** F molto meglio; **mileage** chilometraggio m; **mileometer** contachilometri m; **milestone** *also fig* pietra f miliare

militant ['mɪlɪtənt] **1** *adj* militante **2** n militante m f

military ['mɪlɪtrɪ] **1** *adj* militare **2** n: **the ~** l'esercito m; **military service** servizio m militare

militia [mɪ'lɪʃə] milizia f

milk [mɪlk] **1** n latte m **2** v/t mungere; **milk chocolate** cioccolato m al latte; **milkman** lattaio m; **milkshake** frappé m inv

mill [mɪl] *for grain* mulino m; *for textiles* fabbrica f

millennium [mɪ'lenɪəm] millennio m

milligram ['mɪlɪgræm] milligrammo m

millimetre, *Am* **millimeter** ['mɪlɪmɪːtə(r)] millimetro m

million ['mɪljən] milione m; **millionaire** miliardario m, -a f

mime [maɪm] mimare

mimic ['mɪmɪk] **1** n imitatore m, -trice f **2** v/t imitare

mince [mɪns] *meat* carne f tritata

mind [maɪnd] **1** n mente f; **it's all in your ~** è solo la tua immaginazione; **be out of one's ~** essere matto; **keep sth in ~** tenere presente qc; **change one's ~** cambiare idea; **it didn't enter my ~** non mi è passato per la testa; **make up one's ~** decidersi; **have sth on one's ~** essere preoccupato per qc; **keep one's ~ on sth** concentrarsi su qc; **speak one's ~** dire quello che si pensa **2** v/t (*look after*) tenere d'occhio; *children* badare a; (*heed*) fare attenzione a; **I don't ~ what we do** non importa cosa facciamo; **do you ~ if I smoke?** le dispiace se fumo?; **~ the step!** attento al gradino!; **~ your own business!** fatti gli affari tuoi! **3** v/i: **~!** (*be careful*) attenzione!; **never ~!** non farci caso!; **I don't ~** è uguale or indifferente; **mind-boggling** incredibile; **mindless** *violence* insensato

mine¹ [maɪn] *pron* il mio m, la mia f, i miei mpl, le mie fpl; **a cousin of ~** un mio cugino

mine² [maɪn] n *for coal etc* miniera f

mine³ [maɪn] **1** n *explosive* mina f **2** v/t minare 'minefield *also fig* campo *m* minato; miner minatore *m*

mineral ['mɪnərəl] minerale *m*; mineral water acqua *f* minerale

'minesweeper NAUT dragamine *m inv*

mingle ['mɪŋgl] *of sounds* mischiarsi; *at party* mescolarsi

mini ['mɪnɪ] *skirt* mini *f inv*

miniature ['mɪnɪtʃə(r)] in miniatura

minimal ['mɪnɪməl] minimo; minimalism minimalismo *m*; minimize minimizzare *v/t*; minimum **1** *adj* minimo **2** *n* minimo *m*; minimum wage salario *m* minimo garantito

mining ['maɪnɪŋ] industria *f* mineraria

'miniskirt minigonna *f*

minister ['mɪnɪstə(r)] POL ministro *m*; REL pastore *m*; ministerial ministeriale; Minister of Defence ministro *m* della difesa; ministry POL ministero *m*

mink [mɪŋk] visone *m*

minor ['maɪnə(r)] **1** *adj* piccolo; *in D~* MUS in Re minore **2** *n* LAW minorenne *m/f*; minority minoranza *f*

mint [mɪnt] *herb* menta *f*; *chocolate* cioccolato *m* alla menta; *sweet* mentina *f*

minus ['maɪnəs] **1** *n* (*~ sign*) meno *m* **2** *prep* meno; *~ 10 degrees* 10 gradi sotto zero

minuscule ['mɪnəskjuːl] minuscolo

minute¹ ['mɪnɪt] *n of time* minuto *m*; *in a ~* (*soon*) in un attimo; *just a ~* un attimo

minute² [maɪ'njuːt] *adj* (*tiny*) piccolissimo; (*detailed*) minuzioso; *in ~ detail* minuziosamente

minute hand ['mɪnɪt] lancetta *f* dei minuti

minutely [maɪ'njuːtlɪ] (*in detail*) minuziosamente; (*very slightly*) appena

minutes ['mɪnɪts] *of meeting* verbale *m*

miracle ['mɪrəkl] miracolo *m*; miraculous miracoloso; miraculously miracolosamente

mirror ['mɪrə(r)] **1** *n* specchio *m*; MOT specchietto *m* **2** *v/t* riflettere

misanthropist [mɪ'zænθrəpɪst] misantropo *m*

misbehave [mɪsbə'heɪv] comportarsi male; misbehaviour, *Am* misbehavior comportamento *m* scorretto

miscalculate [mɪs'kælkjuleɪt] calcolare male; miscalculation errore *m* di calcolo

miscarriage [mɪs'kærɪdʒ] MED aborto *m* spontaneo; *~ of justice* errore *m* giudiziario

miscellaneous [mɪsə'leɪnɪəs] eterogeneo

mischief ['mɪstʃɪf] (*naughtiness*) birichinate *fpl*; mischievous (*naughty*) birichino; (*malicious*) perfido

misconception [mɪskən-ˈsepʃn] idea *f* sbagliata

misconduct [mɪsˈkɒndʌkt] reato *m* professionale

misconstrue [mɪskənˈstruː] interpretare male

misdemeanour, *Am* **misdemeanor** [mɪsdəˈmiːnə(r)] infrazione *f*

miser [ˈmaɪzə(r)] avaro *m*, -a *f*

miserable [ˈmɪzrəbl] (*unhappy*) infelice; *weather, performance* deprimente

miserly [ˈmaɪzəli] *person* avaro; *amount* misero

misery [ˈmɪzəri] (*unhappiness*) tristezza *f*; (*wretchedness*) miseria *f*

misfire [mɪsˈfaɪə(r)] *of scheme* far cilecca; *of engine* perdere colpi

misfit [ˈmɪsfɪt] *in society* disadattato *m*, -a *f*

misfortune [mɪsˈfɔːtʃən] sfortuna *f*

misgivings [mɪsˈgɪvɪŋz] dubbi *mpl*

misguided [mɪsˈgaɪdɪd] *attempts, theory* sbagliato

mishandle [mɪsˈhændl] *situation* gestire male

misinform [mɪsɪnˈfɔːm] informare male

misinterpret [mɪsɪnˈtɜːprɪt] interpretare male; **misinterpretation** interpretazione *f* errata

misjudge [mɪsˈdʒʌdʒ] giudicare male

mislay [mɪsˈleɪ] smarrire

mislead [mɪsˈliːd] trarre in inganno; **misleading** fuorviante

mismanage [mɪsˈmænɪdʒ] gestire male; **mismanagement** cattiva gestione *f*

misprint [ˈmɪsprɪnt] refuso *m*

mispronounce [mɪsprəˈnaʊns] pronunciare male; **mispronunciation** errore *m* di pronuncia

misread [mɪsˈriːd] *word, figures* leggere male; *situation* interpretare male

misrepresent [mɪsreprɪˈzent] *facts, truth* travisare

miss[1] [mɪs]: **Miss Smith** signorina Smith; **~!** signorina!

miss[2] [mɪs] **1** *n:* **give the meeting a ~** non andare alla riunione **2** *v/t* (*not hit*) mancare; *emotionally* sentire la mancanza di; *bus, train, plane* perdere; (*not be present at*) mancare a; **I ~ you** mi manchi **3** *v/i* fallire

misshapen [mɪsˈʃeɪpən] deforme

missile [ˈmɪsaɪl] (*rocket*) missile *m*

missing [ˈmɪsɪŋ] scomparso; **be ~** *of person, plane* essere disperso; **there's a piece ~** manca un pezzo

mission [ˈmɪʃn] (*task, people*) missione *f*

misspell [mɪsˈspel] scrivere male

mist [mɪst] foschia *f*

mistake [mɪˈsteɪk] **1** *n* errore *m*, sbaglio *m*; **make a ~** fare un errore, sbagliarsi; **by ~** per errore **2** *v/t* sbagliare; **~ sth for sth** scambiare qc per qc; **mistaken** sbagliato; **be ~** sbagliarsi

mister [ˈmɪstə(r)] → **Mr**

mistress [ˈmɪstrɪs] *lover* amante *f*; *of dog* padrona *f*

mistrust [mɪsˈtrʌst] **1** *n* diffidenza *f* **2** *v/t* diffidare di

misty [ˈmɪstɪ] *weather* nebbioso; *eyes* velato

misunderstand [mɪsʌndəˈstænd] fraintendere; **misunderstanding** *mistake* malinteso *m*, equivoco *m*; *argument* dissapore *m*

misuse **1** [mɪsˈjuːs] *n* uso *m* improprio **2** [mɪsˈjuːz] *v/t* usare impropriamente

mitigating circumstances [ˈmɪtɪɡeɪtɪŋ] circostanze *fpl* attenuanti

mitt [mɪt] *in baseball* guantone *m*; **mitten** muffola *f*

mix [mɪks] **1** *n* (*mixture*) mescolanza *f*; *in cooking: ready to use* preparato *m* **2** *v/t* mescolare **3** *v/i socially* socializzare

♦ mix up confondere; **mix sth up with sth** scambiare qc per qc; **mix-up** *emotionally* avere disturbi emotivi; *of figures, papers* essere in disordine; **be mixed up in** essere coinvolto in

mixed [mɪkst] misto; *reac-* *tions, reviews* contrastante; **I've got ~ feelings** sono combattuto; **mixer** *for food* mixer *m inv*; *drink* bibita da mischiare a un superalcolico; **mixture** miscuglio *m*; *medicine* sciroppo *m*; **mix-up** confusione *f*

moan [məʊn] **1** *n of pain* lamento *m*, gemito *m*; (*complaint*) lamentela *f* **2** *v/i in pain* lamentarsi, gemere; (*complain*) lamentarsi

mob [mɒb] **1** *n* folla *f* **2** *v/t* prendere d'assalto

mobile [ˈməʊbaɪl] **1** *adj that can be moved* mobile; **she's less ~ now** non si può muovere tanto, ora **2** *n for decoration* mobile *m inv*; *phone* telefonino *m*; **mobile home** casamobile *f*; **mobile phone** telefono *m* cellulare; **mobility** mobilità *f*

mobster [ˈmɒbstə(r)] gangster *m inv*

mock [mɒk] **1** *adj exam, election* simulato **2** *v/t* deridere; **mockery** (*derision*) scherno *m*; (*travesty*) farsa *f*

mode [məʊd] *form* mezzo *m*; COMPUT modalità *f inv*

model [ˈmɒdl] **1** *adj employee, husband* modello; *boat, plane in miniatura* **2** *n* (*miniature*) modellino *m*; (*pattern*) modello *m*; (*fashion* ~) indossatrice *f*; **male ~** indossatore *m* **3** *v/t* indossare **4** *v/i for designer* fare l'indossatore /

-trice; *for artist* posare

modem ['məʊdem] modem *m inv*

moderate 1 ['mɒdərət] *adj* moderato **2** ['mɒdərət] *n* POL moderato *m*, -a *f* **3** ['mɒdəreɪt] *v/t* moderare; **moderately** abbastanza; **moderation** (*restraint*) moderazione *f*

modern ['mɒdn] moderno; **modernization** modernizzazione *f*; **modernize 1** *v/t* modernizzare **2** *v/i* modernizzarsi

modest ['mɒdɪst] modesto; **modesty** modestia *f*

modification [mɒdɪfɪ'keɪʃn] modifica *f*; **modify** modificare

module ['mɒdjuːl] modulo *m*

moist [mɔɪst] umido; **moisten** inumidire; **moisture** umidità *f*; **moisturizer** *for skin* idratante *m*

molasses [mə'læsɪz] melassa *f*

mold *etc Am* ☞ **mould** *etc*

molecule ['mɒlɪkjuːl(r)] molecola *f*

molest [mə'lest] *child, woman* molestare

mollycoddle ['mɒlɪkɒdl] F coccolare

molten ['məʊltən] fuso

mom [mɒm] F mamma *f*

moment ['məʊmənt] attimo *m*, istante *m*; **at the ~** al momento; **for the ~** per il momento; **momentarily** (*for a moment*) per un momento; *Am* (*in a moment*) da un momento all'altro; **momentary** momentaneo; **momentous** importante

momentum [mə'mentəm] impeto *m*

monarch ['mɒnək] monarca *m*

monastery ['mɒnəstrɪ] monastero *m*; **monastic** monastico

Monday ['mʌndeɪ] lunedì *m inv*

monetary ['mʌnɪtrɪ] monetario

money ['mʌnɪ] denaro *m*, soldi *mpl*; **money belt** marsupio *m*; **money market** mercato *m* monetario; **money order** vaglia *m*

mongrel ['mʌŋɡrəl] cane *m* bastardo

monitor ['mɒnɪtə(r)] **1** *n* COMPUT monitor *m inv* **2** *v/t* osservare

monk [mʌŋk] frate *m*, monaco *m*

monkey ['mʌŋkɪ] scimmia *f*; F (*child*) diavoletto *m*; **monkey wrench** chiave *f* a rullino

monologue, *Am* **monolog** ['mɒnəlɒɡ] monologo *m*

monopolize [mə'nɒpəlaɪz] *also fig* monopolizzare; **monopoly** monopolio *m*

monotonous [mə'nɒtənəs] monotono; **monotony** monotonia *f*

monster ['mɒnstə(r)] mostro m; **monstrosity** obbrobrio m

month [mʌnθ] mese m; **monthly 1** adj mensile **2** adv mensilmente **3** n magazine mensile m

monument ['mɒnjʊmənt] monumento m

mood [muːd] (frame of mind) umore m; (bad ~) malumore m; of meeting, country clima m; **be in a good / bad ~** essere di cattivo / buon umore; **moody** lunatico; (bad-tempered) di cattivo umore

moon [muːn] luna f; **moonlight 1** n chiaro m di luna **2** v/i F lavorare in nero; **moonlit** night di luna piena

moor [mʊə(r)] boat ormeggiare

moose [muːs] alce m

mop [mɒp] **1** n for floor mocio® m; for dishes spazzolino per i piatti **2** v/t floor lavare; eyes, face asciugare

◆ **mop up** raccogliere; MIL eliminare

moped ['məʊped] motorino m

moral ['mɒrəl] **1** adj morale; person di saldi principi morali **2** n of story morale f; **~s** principi mpl morali

morale [mə'rɑːl] morale m

morality [mə'rælətɪ] moralità f inv

morbid ['mɔːbɪd] morboso

more [mɔː(r)] **1** adj più, altro; **some ~ tea?** dell'altro tè?; **a few ~ sandwiches** qualche

altro tramezzino; **for ~ information** per maggiori informazioni; **~ and ~ students / time** sempre più studenti / tempo; **there's no ~ ...** non c'è più ... **2** adv più; with verbs di più; **~ important** più importante; **~ and ~** sempre di più; **~ or less** più o meno; **once ~** ancora una volta; **~ than 100** oltre 100; **I don't live there any~** non abito più lì **3** pron: **do you want some ~?** ne vuoi ancora?, ne vuoi dell'altro; **a little ~** un altro po'; **moreover** inoltre

morgue [mɔːg] obitorio m

morning ['mɔːnɪŋ] mattino m, mattina f; **in the ~** di mattina; (tomorrow) domattina; **this ~** stamattina; **tomorrow ~** domani mattina; **good ~** buongiorno

moron ['mɔːrɒn] F idiota m/f

morphine ['mɔːfiːn] morfina f

mortal ['mɔːtl] **1** adj mortale **2** n mortale m/f; **mortality** mortalità f

mortar ['mɔːtə(r)] MIL mortaio m cement malta f

mortgage ['mɔːgɪdʒ] **1** n mutuo m ipotecario **2** v/t ipotecare

mortuary ['mɔːtjʊərɪ] camera f mortuaria

mosaic [məʊ'zeɪɪk] mosaico m

Moscow ['mɒskəʊ] Mosca f

Moslem ☞ **Muslim**

mosque [mɒsk] moschea f

mosquito [mɒsˈkiːtəʊ] zanzara f

moss [mɒs] muschio m

most [məʊst] **1** *adj* la maggior parte di; **~ Saturdays** quasi tutti i sabati **2** *adv* (*very*) estremamente; **the ~ beautiful** il più bello; **the one I like ~** quello che mi piace di più; **~ of all** soprattutto **3** *pron* la maggior parte (**of** di); **at (the) ~** al massimo; **make the ~ of** approfittare (al massimo) di; **mostly** per lo più

MOT [eməʊˈtiː] *revisione annuale obbligatoria dei veicoli*

motel [məʊˈtel] motel *m inv*

moth [mɒθ] falena f; (*clothes ~*) tarma f

mother [ˈmʌðə(r)] **1** *n* madre f **2** *v/t* fare da mamma a; **motherhood** maternità f; **Mothering Sunday** ☞ **Mother's Day**; **mother-in-law** suocera f; **motherly** materno; **Mother's Day** Festa f della mamma; **mother tongue** madrelingua f

motif [məʊˈtiːf] motivo m

motion [ˈməʊʃn] *n* (*movement*) moto m; (*proposal*) mozione f; **motionless** immobile

motivate [ˈməʊtɪveɪt] *person* motivare; **motivation** motivazione f; **motive** motivo m

motor [ˈməʊtə(r)] motore m; F *car* macchina f; **motorbike** moto f; **motorboat** motoscafo m; **motorcycle** motoci-

cletta f; **motorcyclist** motociclista *m/f*; **motor home** casamobile f; **motorist** automobilista *m/f*; **motor mechanic** meccanico m; **motor racing** automobilismo m; **motor vehicle** autoveicolo m; **motorway** autostrada f

motto [ˈmɒtəʊ] motto m

mould¹ [məʊld] n *on food* muffa f

mould² [məʊld] **1** n stampo m **2** *v/t also fig* plasmare

mouldy [ˈməʊldɪ] *food* ammuffito

mound [maʊnd] (*hillock*) collinetta f; (*pile*) mucchio m; *Am: in baseball* pedana f del lanciatore

mount [maʊnt] **1** n (*horse*) cavalcatura f; **Mount McKinlay** il Monte McKinlay **2** *v/t steps* salire; *horse* montare a; *bicycle* montare in; *campaign* organizzare; *jewel* montare **3** *v/i* (*increase*) aumentare

◆ **mount up** accumularsi

mountain [ˈmaʊntɪn] montagna f; **mountain bike** mountain bike f *inv*; **mountaineer** alpinista *m/f*; **mountaineering** alpinismo m; **mountainous** montuoso

mourn [mɔːn] **1** *v/t* piangere **2** *v/i*: **~ for** piangere la morte di; **mourner** persona che partecipa a un corteo funebre; **mournful** triste; **mourning** lutto m; **be in ~** essere in lutto; **wear** ~ portare il lutto

mouse [maʊs] (*pl* **mice** [maɪs]) topo *m*; COMPUT mouse *m inv*; **mouse mat** COMPUT tappetino *m* del mouse

moustache [mə'stɑːʃ] baffi *mpl*

mouth [maʊθ] bocca *f*; *of river* foce *f*; **mouthful** *of food* boccone *m*; *of drink* sorsata *f*; **mouthorgan** armonica *f* a bocca; **mouthpiece** *of instrument* bocchino *m*; *(spokesperson)* portavoce *m/f*; **mouthwash** collutorio *m*; **mouthwatering** che fa venire l'acquolina

move [muːv] **1** *n* (*step, action, in game*) mossa *f*; *change of house* trasloco *m*; **get a** ~ **on!** F spicciati! **2** *v/t object* spostare, muovere; *(transfer)* trasferire; *emotionally* commuovere; ~ **house** traslocare **3** *v/i* muoversi, spostarsi; *(transfer)* trasferirsi

◆ **move around** *in room* muoversi; *from place to place* spostarsi

◆ **move in** trasferirsi

movement *m*; **movers** *Am firm* ditta *f* di traslochi

movie ['muːvɪ] film *m inv*; **go to a** ~ / **the** ~**s** andare al cinema; **moviegoer** frequentatore *m*, -trice *f* di cinema; **movie theater** *Am* cinema *m inv*

moving ['muːvɪŋ] *which can move* mobile; *emotionally* commovente

mow [məʊ] *grass* tagliare, falciare; **mower** tosaerba *m inv*

MP [em'piː] (= *Member of Parliament*) deputato *m*; (= *Military Policeman*) polizia *f* militare

mph [empiː'eɪtʃ] (= *miles per hour*) miglia orarie

Mr ['mɪstə(r)] signor

Mrs ['mɪsɪz] signora

Ms [mɪz] signora *appellativo usato sia per donne sposate che nubili*

much [mʌtʃ] **1** *adj* molto; **so** ~ **money** tanti soldi; **how** ~ **sugar?** quanto zucchero?; **as** ~ ... **as** ... tanto ... quanto ... **2** *adv* molto; **very** ~ moltissimo; **too** ~ troppo; **as** ~ **as** ... tanto quanto ... **3** *pron* molto; **nothing** ~ niente di particolare

mud [mʌd] fango *m*

muddle ['mʌdl] **1** *n* disordine *m*; **I'm in a** ~ sono confuso **2** *v/t* confondere

muddy ['mʌdɪ] *hands, boots* sporco di fango

muesli ['muːzlɪ] müsli *m*

muffin ['mʌfɪn] pasticcino *m*

muffle ['mʌfl] *sound* attutire; *voice* camuffare; **muffler** *Am* MOT marmitta *f*

mug[1] [mʌg] *n for tea, coffee* tazzone *m*; F *(face)* faccia *f*

mug[2] [mʌg] *v/t attack* aggredire

mugger ['mʌgə(r)] aggressore *m*; **mugging** aggressione *f*; **muggy** afoso

mule [mju:l] *animal* mulo *m*; *Am (slipper)* mule *f inv*

multicultural [mʌltɪ'kʌltʃərəl] multiculturale

multilateral [mʌltɪ'lætərəl] POL multilaterale

multimedia [mʌltɪ'mi:dɪə] 1 *adj* multimediale 2 *n* multimedialità *f*

multinational [mʌltɪ'næʃnl] 1 *adj* multinazionale 2 *n* COM multinazionale *f*

multiple ['mʌltɪpl] multiplo; **multiple sclerosis** sclerosi *f* multipla

multiplex (cinema) ['mʌltɪpleks] cinema *m inv* multisale

multiplication [mʌltɪplɪ'keɪʃn] moltiplicazione *f*; **multiply** 1 *v/t* moltiplicare 2 *v/i* moltiplicarsi

multi-storey (car park) [mʌltɪ'stɔːrɪ] parcheggio *m* a più piani

mum [mʌm] mamma *f*

mumble ['mʌmbl] 1 *n* borbottio *m* 2 *v/t & v/i* borbottare

mummy ['mʌmɪ] mamma *f*

mumps [mʌmps] orecchioni *mpl*

munch [mʌntʃ] sgranocchiare

municipal [mjuː'nɪsɪpl] municipale

mural ['mjʊərəl] murale *m*

murder ['mɜːdə(r)] 1 *n* omicidio *m* 2 *v/t* uccidere; *song* rovinare; **murderer** omicida *m/f*

murky ['mɜːkɪ] *also fig* torbido

murmur ['mɜːmə(r)] 1 *n* mormorio *m* 2 *v/t* mormorare

muscle ['mʌsl] muscolo *m*; **muscular** *pain, strain* muscolare; *person* muscoloso

museum [mjuː'zɪəm] museo *m*

mushroom ['mʌʃrʊm] 1 *n* fungo *m* 2 *v/i* crescere rapidamente

music ['mjuːzɪk] musica *f*; *in written form* spartito *m*; **musical** 1 *adj* musicale; *person* portato per la musica; *voice* melodioso 2 *n* musical *m inv*; **musical instrument** strumento *m* musicale; **musician** musicista *m/f*

Muslim ['mʊzlɪm] 1 *adj* islamico 2 *n* musulmano *m*, -a *f*

mussel ['mʌsl] cozza *f*

must [mʌst] ◇ *(necessity)*: **be on time** devo arrivare in orario; **I ~n't be late** non devo far tardi ◇ *(probability)*: **it ~ be about 6 o'clock** devono essere circa le sei

mustache *Am* ➞ **moustache**

mustard ['mʌstəd] senape *f*

musty ['mʌstɪ] *smell* di stantio; *room* che sa di stantio

mutilate ['mjuːtɪleɪt] mutilare

mutiny ['mjuːtɪnɪ] 1 *n* ammutinamento *m* 2 *v/i* ammutinarsi

mutter ['mʌtə(r)] farfugliare

nationalism

mutual ['mjuːtjʊəl] *admiration* reciproco; *friend* in comune

muzzle ['mʌzl] 1 *n of animal* muso *m; for dog* museruola *f* 2 *v/t:* ~ *the press* imbavagliare la stampa

my [maɪ] il mio *m,* la mia *f,* i miei *mpl,* le mie *fpl;* ~ *sister / brother* mia sorella / mio fratello

myself [maɪ'self] mi; *emphatic* io stesso; *after prep* me stesso; *I've hurt* ~ mi sono fatto male

mysterious [mɪ'stɪərɪəs] misterioso; mysteriously misteriosamente; mystery mistero *m;* mystify lasciare perplesso

myth [mɪθ] *also fig* mito *m;* mythical mitico

N

nag [næg] 1 *v/i of person* brontolare di continuo 2 *v/t* assillare; nagging *person* brontolone; *doubt, pain* assillante

nail [neɪl] *for wood* chiodo *m; on finger, toe* unghia *f;* nail clippers *npl* tagliaunghie *m inv;* nail file limetta *f* per unghie; nail polish smalto *m* per unghie; nail polish remover solvente *m* per unghie

naive [naɪ'iːv] ingenuo

naked ['neɪkɪd] nudo

name [neɪm] 1 *n* nome *m; what's your* ~? come ti chiami? 2 *v/t* chiamare; namely cioè; namesake omonimo *m,* -a *f*

nanny ['nænɪ] bambinaia *f*

nap [næp] sonnellino *m; have a* ~ farsi un sonnellino

napkin ['næpkɪn] *(table* ~) tovagliolo *m; (sanitary* ~) assorbente *m*

Naples ['neɪpəlz] Napoli *f*

nappy ['næpɪ] pannolino *m*

narcotic [naː'kɒtɪk] narcotico *m*

narrate [nə'reɪt] raccontare, narrare; narrative 1 *n story* racconto 2 *adj poem, style* narrativo; narrator narratore *m,* -trice *f*

narrow ['nærəʊ] stretto; *views, mind* ristretto; *victory* di stretta misura; narrowly *win* di stretta misura; ~ *escape sth* scampare a qc per un pelo F; narrow-minded di idee ristrette

nasty ['naːstɪ] *person, remark, smell, weather* cattivo; *cut, wound, disease* brutto

nation ['neɪʃn] nazione *f;* national 1 *adj* nazionale 2 *n* cittadino *m,* -a *f;* national anthem inno *m* nazionale; national debt debito *m* pubblico; nationalism nazionalismo *m*; **nationality** nazionalità *f inv*; **nationalize** *industry etc* nazionalizzare

native ['neɪtɪv] **1** *adj* indigeno; **~ language** madrelingua *f* **2** *n* (*tribesman*) indigeno *m*, -a *f*; **she's a ~ of New York** è originaria di New York; **Native American** indiano *m*, -a *f* d'america; **native speaker: English ~** English *m*, persona *f* di madrelingua inglese

NATO ['neɪtəʊ] (= **North Atlantic Treaty Organization**) NATO *f*

natural ['nætʃrəl] naturale; **naturalist** naturalista *m/f*; **naturalize: become ~d** naturalizzarsi; **naturally** (*of course*) naturalmente; (*behave, speak* con naturalezza; (*by nature*) per natura; **nature** natura *f*; **nature reserve** riserva *f* naturale

naughty ['nɔːtɪ] cattivo; *photograph, word etc* spinto

nausea ['nɔːzɪə] nausea *f*; **nauseate** (*fig: disgust*) disgustare; **nauseating** *smell, taste* nauseante; *person* disgustoso; **nauseous: feel ~** avere la nausea

nautical ['nɔːtɪkl] nautico

naval ['neɪvl] navale; *officer, uniform* della marina

navel ['neɪvl] ombelico *m*

navigate ['nævɪgeɪt] *also* COMPUT navigare; *in car* fare da navigatore / -trice; **navigation** navigazione *f*; **navigator** *on ship, in aeroplane* ufficiale *m* di rotta; *in car* navigatore *m*, -trice *f*

navy ['neɪvɪ] marina *f* militare; **navy blue 1** *n* blu *m inv* scuro **2** *adj* blu scuro

near [nɪə(r)] **1** *adv* vicino **2** *prep* vicino a; **do you go ~ the bank?** vai dalle parti della banca? **3** *adj* vicino; **in the ~ future** nel prossimo futuro; **nearby** *live* vicino; **nearly** quasi; **near-sighted** miope

neat [niːt] *room, desk, person* ordinato; *whisky* liscio; *solution* efficace; F (*terrific*) fantastico

necessarily ['nesəsərɪlɪ] necessariamente; **necessary** necessario; **it is ~ to …** è necessario …, bisogna …; **necessity** necessità *f inv*

neck [nek] collo *m*; **necklace** collana *f*; **neckline** *of dress* scollo *m*; **necktie** cravatta *f*

née [neɪ] nata

need [niːd] **1** *n* bisogno *m*; **if ~ be** se necessario; **be in ~** (*be needy*) essere bisognoso; **be in ~ of sth** aver bisogno di qc; **you don't ~ to wait** non c'è bisogno che aspetti; **I ~ to talk to you** ti devo parlare

needle ['niːdl] *for sewing, on dial* ago *m*; **needlework** cucito *m*

needy ['niːdɪ] bisognoso

negative ['negətɪv] negativo

neglect [nɪ'glekt] **1** *n* trascuratezza *f* **2** *v/t* trascurare; neglected *gardens, author* trascurato

negligence ['neglɪdʒəns] negligenza *f*; **negligent** negligente; **negligible** *quantity* trascurabile

negotiable [nɪ'gəʊʃəbl] negoziabile; **negotiate 1** *v/i* trattare **2** *v/t deal, settlement* negoziare; *obstacles* superare; *bend in road* affrontare; **negotiation** negoziato *m*; **negotiator** negoziatore *m*, -trice *f*

neighbor *etc Am* ☞ **neighbour** *etc*

neighbour ['neɪbə(r)] vicino *m*, -a *f*; *neighbourhood in town* quartiere *m*; **in the ~ of** *fig* intorno a; **neighbouring** *house, state* confinante; **neighbourly** amichevole

neither ['naɪðə(r)] **1** *adj*: ~ *player* nessuno dei due giocatori **2** *pron* nessuno *m* dei due, nessuna *f* delle due **3** *adv*: ~ *... nor ...* né ... né ... **4** *conj* neanche; ~ *do I* neanch'io

neon light ['niːɒn] luce *f* al neon

nephew ['nevjuː] nipote *m* (di zii)

nerve [nɜːv] nervo *m*; (*courage*) coraggio *m*; (*impudence*) faccia *f* tosta; **get on s.o.'s ~s** dare sui nervi a qu; **nerve-racking** snervante; **nervous** nervoso; **be ~ about doing sth** essere an-

sioso all'idea di fare qc; **nervous breakdown** esaurimento *m* nervoso; **nervousness** nervosismo *m*; **nervous wreck**: **be a ~** avere i nervi a pezzi; **nervy** *Am* (*cheeky*) sfacciato

nest [nest] nido *m*

net[1] [net] *n for fishing* retino *m*; *for tennis* rete *f*; COMPUT Internet *f*; **on the ~** su Internet

net[2] [net] *adj* COM netto

nettle ['netl] ortica *f*

'network *of contacts, cells* rete *f*; COMPUT network *m inv*; **networking** *presa di contatti professionali in situazioni informali*

neurologist [njʊə'rɒlədʒɪst] neurologo *m*, -a *f*

neurosis [njʊə'rəʊsɪs] nevrosi *f inv*; **neurotic** nevrotico

neuter ['njuːtə(r)] *animal* sterilizzare

neutral ['njuːtrəl] **1** *adj country* neutrale; *colour* neutro **2** *n gear* folle *m*; **neutrality** neutralità *f*; **neutralize** neutralizzare

never ['nevə(r)] mai; ~*! in disbelief* ma va'!; **you're ~ going to believe this** non ci crederesti mai; **nevertheless** comunque, tuttavia

new [njuː] nuovo; **that's nothing ~** non è una novità; **newborn** neonato; **newcomer** nuovo arrivato *m*, nuova arrivata *f*; **newly** (*recently*) re-

centemente; **newly weds**
sposini *mpl*

news [nju:z] notizia *f*; *on TV,
radio* notiziario *m*; novità *f
inv*; **any ~?** ci sono novità?;
that's ~ to me mi giunge
nuovo; **newsagent** giornalaio *m*; **newscast** telegiornale
m; **newscaster** giornalista
m/f televisivo, -a; **news
flash** notizia *f* flash; **newspaper** giornale *m*; **news-
reader** giornalista *m/f* radiotelevisivo, -a; **news report**
notiziario *m*; **newsstand**
edicola *f*; **newsvendor** edi-
colante *m/f*

New 'Year anno *m* nuovo;
Happy New Year! buon anno!; **New Year's Day** capodanno *m*; **New Year's Eve**
San Silvestro *m*

next [nekst] **1** *adj in time* prossimo; *in space* vicino; **the ~
month** il mese dopo; **who's
~?** a chi tocca? **2** *adv* dopo; **~
to** (*beside*) accanto a; (*in
comparison with*) a paragone
di; **next door 1** *adj:* ~ **neighbour** vicino *m*, -a *f* di casa **2**
adv live nella casa accanto;
next of kin parente *m/f* prossimo

nibble ['nɪbl] mordicchiare

nice [naɪs] *person* carino, -a,
gentile; *day, weather, party* bello;
meal, food buono; **that's
very ~ of you** molto gentile
da parte tua!; **nicely** *written,
presented* bene

niche [niːʃ] nicchia *f*

nick [nɪk] *cut* taglietto *m*; **in
the ~ of time** appena in tem-
po

nickel ['nɪkl] *material* nichel
m; *Am coin* moneta *f* da 5
centesimi di dollaro

'nickname soprannome *m*

niece [niːs] nipote *f* (di zii)

night [naɪt] notte *f*; (*evening*)
sera *f*; **at ~** di notte / di sera;
last ~ ieri notte / ieri sera;
stay the ~ rimanere a dormire; **work ~s** fare il turno di
notte; **good ~** buona notte;
nightcap (*drink*) bicchierino
bevuto prima di andare a letto; **nightclub** night(-club) *m
inv*; **nightdress** camicia *f* da
notte; **night flight** volo *m*
notturno; **nightlife** vita *f*
notturna; **nightly** ogni notte;
late at night ogni notte;
nightmare *also fig* incubo
m; **night porter** portiere *m*
notturno; **night school**
scuola *f* serale; **night shift**
turno *m* di notte; **nightshirt**
camicia *f* da notte (*da
uomo*); **nightspot** locale *m*
notturno; **nighttime: at ~**
di notte, la notte

nimble ['nɪmbl] agile

nine [naɪn] nove; **nineteen** diciannove; **nineteenth** diciannovesimo; **ninetieth** novantesimo; **ninety** novanta;
ninth nono

nip [nɪp] (*pinch*) pizzico *m*;
(*bite*) morso *m*

nipple ['nɪpl] capezzolo m

nitrogen ['naɪtrədʒn] azoto m

no [nəʊ] **1** adv no **2** adj nessuno; **there's ~ coffee left** non c'è più caffè; **I have ~ money** non ho soldi; **~ smoking** vietato fumare

noble ['nəʊbl] nobile

nobody ['nəʊbədɪ] nessuno; **~ knows** nessuno lo sa; **there was ~ at home** non c'era nessuno in casa

no-brainer [nəʊ'breɪnə(r)] F cretinata f; **a real ~ of a decision** una decisione semplicissima

nod [nɒd] **1** n cenno m del capo **2** v/i fare un cenno col capo; **~ in agreement** annuire ♦ nod off (fall asleep) appisolarsi

noise [nɔɪz] (sound) rumore m; loud, unpleasant chiasso m; noisy rumoroso; children, party chiassoso; **don't be so ~** non fate tanto rumore

nominal ['nɒmɪnl] amount simbolico

nominate ['nɒmɪneɪt] (appoint) designare; nomination (appointing) nomina f; person proposed candidato m, -a f; nominee candidato m, -a f

nonalco'holic analcolico

nonchalant ['nɒnʃələnt] noncurante

noncommissioned 'officer ['nɒnkəmɪʃnd] sottufficiale m

noncommittal [nɒnkə'mɪtl] person, response evasivo

nondescript ['nɒndɪskrɪpt] ordinario

none [nʌn] nessuno m, -a f; **there are ~ left** non ne sono rimasti; **there is ~ left** non ne è rimasto, non è rimasto niente

nonentity [nɒn'entətɪ] nullità f inv

nonetheless [nʌnðə'les] nondimeno

none'xistent inesistente

non'fiction opere fpl non di narrativa

noninter'ference, noninter'vention non intervento m

no-'nonsense approach pragmatico

non'payment mancato pagamento m

nonpol'luting non inquinante

non'resident in country non residente m/f; (in hotel) persona chi non è cliente di un albergo

nonre'turnable a fondo perduto

nonsense ['nɒnsəns] sciocchezze fpl; **don't talk ~** non dire sciocchezze

non'smoker non fumatore m, -trice f

non'standard fuori standard, non di serie; use of a word che fa eccezione

non'stick pans antiaderente

non'stop **1** adj flight, train di-

retto; *chatter* continuo **2** *adv*
fly, *travel* senza scalo; *chatter*,
argue di continuo

non'union non appartenente
al sindacato

non'violence non violenza *f*;
nonviolent non violento

noodles ['nuːdlz] spaghetti
mpl cinesi

noon [nuːn] mezzogiorno *m*

'no-one [nuː] → nobody

noose [nuːs] cappio *m*

nor [nɔː(r)] né; ~ do I neanch'io, neanche a me

norm [nɔːm] norma *f*; normal
normale; normality normalità *f*; normally (*usually*) di
solito; *in a normal way* normalmente

north [nɔːθ] **1** *n* nord **m 2** *adj*
settentrionale, nord *inv* **3**
adv travel verso nord; ~ of
a nord di; North America
America *f* del Nord; North
American **1** *n* nordamericano *m*, -a *f* **2** *adj* nordamericano; northeast nordest;
northerly *wind* settentrionale; *direction* nord *inv*; northern settentrionale; northerner settentrionale *m/f*;
North Korea Corea *f* del
Nord; North Korean **1** *adj*
nordcoreano **2** *n* nordcoreano *m*, -a *f*; North Pole polo
m nord; northward *travel*
verso nord; northwest nordovest *m*

Norway ['nɔːweɪ] Norvegia *f*;
Norwegian **1** *adj* norvegese

2 *n person* norvegese *m/f*;
language norvegese *m*

nose [nəuz] naso *m*; *right under my ~!* proprio sotto il naso!

◆ nose around F curiosare

nostalgia [nɒ'stældʒɪə] nostalgia *f*; nostalgic nostalgico

nostril ['nɒstrəl] narice *f*

nosy ['nəuzɪ] F curioso

not [nɒt] non; *I hope ~* spero
di no; *I don't know* non so;
he didn't help non ha aiutato; ~ *me* io no

notable ['nəutəbl] notevole

notch [nɒtʃ] tacca *f*

note [nəut] MUS, *comment on
text* nota *f*; *short letter* biglietto *m*; *memo to self* appunto
m; *money* banconota *f*; *take
~s* prendere appunti; *take ~
of sth* prendere nota di qc;
notebook taccuino *m*; COMPUT notebook *m inv*; noted
noto; notepad bloc-notes
m inv; notepaper carta *f*
da lettere

nothing ['nʌθɪŋ] niente; ~ *but*
nient'altro che; ~ *much*
niente di speciale; *for* ~
(*for free*) gratis; (*for no reason*) per una nonnulla

notice ['nəutɪs] **1** *n on notice
board, in street* avviso *m*; (*advance warning*) preavviso *m*;
in newspaper annuncio *m*; *to
leave job* preavviso *m*; *to
leave house* disdetta *f*; *at
short* ~ con un breve preav-

viso; *until further* ~ fino a nuovo avviso; *hand in one's* ~ *to employer* presentare le dimissioni; *take no* ~ *of s.o.* / *sth* non fare caso a qu / qc **2** *v/t* notare; *notice board* bacheca *f*; *noticeable* sensibile

notify ['nǝʊtɪfaɪ] informare

notion ['nǝʊʃn] idea *f*

notorious [nǝʊ'tɔːrɪǝs] famigerato

nought [nɔːt] zero *m*

noun [naʊn] nome *m*, sostantivo *m*

nourishing ['nʌrɪʃɪŋ] nutriente; **nourishment** nutrimento *m*

novel [nɒvl] romanzo *m*; **novelist** romanziere *m*, -a *f*

novelty ['nɒvltɪ] novità *f inv*

November [nǝʊ'vembǝ(r)] novembre *m*

novice ['nɒvɪs] principiante *m/f*

now [naʊ] ora, adesso; ~ *and again*, ~ *and then* ogni tanto; *by* ~ ormai; *from* ~ *on* d'ora in poi; *right* ~ subito; *just* ~ (proprio) adesso; ~, ~! su, su!; nowadays oggigiorno

nowhere ['nǝʊweǝ(r)] da nessuna parte; *it's* ~ *near finished* è ben lontano dall'essere terminato

nuclear ['njuːklɪǝ(r)] nucleare; **nuclear energy** energia *f* nucleare; **nuclear physics** fisica *f* nucleare; **nuclear**

power energia *f* nucleare; POL potenza *f* nucleare; **nuclear power station** centrale *f* nucleare; **nuclear reactor** reattore *m* nucleare; **nuclear waste** scorie *fpl* radioattive; **nuclear weapon** arma *f* nucleare

nude [njuːd] **1** *adj* nudo **2** *n painting* nudo *m*; *in the* ~ nudo

nudge [nʌdʒ] dare un colpetto di gomito a; *parked car* spostare leggermente

nudist ['njuːdɪst] nudista *m/f*

nuisance ['njuːsns] seccatura *f*; *make a* ~ *of o.s.* dare fastidio

null and 'void [nʌl] nullo

numb [nʌm] intirizzito; *emotionally* impietrito

number ['nʌmbǝ(r)] **1** *n* numero *m*; (*quantity*) quantità *f inv* **2** *v/t* put a number on numerare; **number plate** *of vehicle* targa *f*

numeral ['njuːmǝrǝl] numero *m*

numerate ['njuːmǝrǝt] *adj*: *be* ~ avere buone basi in matematica; *of children* saper contare

numerous ['njuːmǝrǝs] numeroso

nun [nʌn] suora *f*

nurse [nɜːs] infermiere *m*, -a *f*; **nursery** *school* asilo *m*; *in house* stanza *f* dei bambini; *for plants* vivaio *m*; **nursery rhyme** filastrocca *f*;

nursery school scuola *f* materna; **nursing** professione *f* d'infermiere; **nursing home** *for old people* casa *f* di riposo

nut [nʌt] noce *f*; *for bolt* dado *m*; **nutcrackers** schiaccianoci *m* inv

nutrient ['nju:trɪənt] sostanza *f* nutritiva; **nutrition** alimen-

tazione *f*; **nutritious** nutriente *f*

nuts [nʌts] F (*crazy*) svitato; **be ~ about s.o.** essere pazzo di qu

'nutshell: in a ~ in poche parole

nutty ['nʌtɪ] *taste* di noce; F (*crazy*) pazzo

O

oak [əʊk] *tree* quercia *f*; *wood* rovere *m*

oar [ɔ:(r)] remo *m*

oasis [əʊ'eɪsɪs] *also fig* oasi *f* inv

oath [əʊθ] LAW giuramento *m*; (*swearword*) imprecazione *f*

'oatmeal farina *f* d'avena

obedience [ə'bi:dɪəns] ubbidienza *f*; **obedient** ubbidiente; **obediently** docilmente

obese [əʊ'bi:s] obeso; **obesity** obesità *f*

obey [ə'beɪ] *parents* ubbidire a; *law* osservare

obituary [ə'bɪtjʊərɪ] necrologio *m*

object[1] ['ɒbdʒɪkt] *n* (*thing*) oggetto *m*; (*aim*) scopo *m*; GRAM complemento *m*

object[2] [əb'dʒekt] *v/i* avere da obiettare

objection [əb'dʒekʃn] obiezione *f*; **objectionable** (*unpleasant*) antipatico; **objective 1** *adj* obiettivo **2** *n* obiet-

tivo *m*; **objectively** obiettivamente; **objectivity** obiettività *f*

obligation [ɒblɪ'geɪʃn] obbligo *m*; **obligatory** obbligatorio; **obliging** servizievole

oblique [ə'bli:k] **1** *adj* *reference* indiretto **2** *n* *in punctuation* barra *f*

obliterate [ə'blɪtəreɪt] *city* annientare; *memory* cancellare

oblivion [ə'blɪvɪən] oblio *m*; **fall into ~** cadere in oblio

oblong ['ɒblɒŋ] **1** *adj* rettangolare **2** *n* rettangolo *m*

obnoxious [əb'nɒkʃəs] offensivo; *smell* sgradevole; *person* odioso; *dog, child* insopportabile

obscene [əb'si:n] osceno; *salary, poverty* vergognoso; **obscenity** oscenità *f* inv

obscure [əb'skjʊə(r)] oscuro; **obscurity** oscurità *f* inv

observant [əb'zɜ:vnt] osservante; **observation** osservazione *f*; **observatory** osservatorio *m*; **observe** osservare; **observer** osservatore *m*, -trice *f*

obsess [əb'ses]: **be ~ed with** essere fissato con; **obsession** fissazione *f*; **obsessive** ossessivo

obsolete ['ɒbsəli:t] *model* obsoleto; *word* disusato

obstacle ['ɒbstəkl] *also fig* ostacolo

obstetrician [ɒbstə'trɪʃn] ostetrico *m*, -a *f*; **obstetrics** ostetricia *f*

obstinacy ['ɒbstɪnəsɪ] ostinazione *f*; **obstinate** ostinato

obstruct [əb'strʌkt] *road* ostruire; *investigation, police* ostacolare; **obstruction** *on road etc* ostruzione *f*; **obstructive** *behaviour, tactics* ostruzionista

obtain [əb'teɪn] ottenere; **obtainable** *products* reperibile

obtuse [əb'tju:s] *fig* ottuso

obvious ['ɒbvɪəs] ovvio, evidente; **obviously** ovviamente, evidentemente

occasion [ə'keɪʒn] occasione *f*; **occasional** sporadico; **I like the ~ whisky** bevo un whisky ogni tanto; **occasionally** ogni tanto

occupant ['ɒkjupənt] *of vehicle* occupante *m*/*f*; *of building* abitante *m*/*f*; **occupation** (*job*) professione *f*; *of country* occupazione *f*; **occupy** occupare

occur [ə'kɜ:(r)] accadere; **it**

~red to me that ... mi è venuto in mente che ...; **occurrence** evento *m*

ocean ['əʊʃn] oceano *m*

o'clock [ə'klɒk]: **at five ~** alle cinque; **it's one ~** è l'una; **it's three ~** sono le tre

October [ɒk'təʊbə(r)] ottobre *m*

octopus ['ɒktəpəs] polpo *m*

odd [ɒd] (*strange*) strano; (*not even*) dispari; **the ~ one out** l'eccezione *f*; **50 ~** 50 e rotti; **oddball** F persona *f* stramba; **odds and ends** *objects* cianfrusaglie *fpl*; *things to do* cose *fpl*; **odds-on: the ~ favourite** il favorito; **it's ~ that ...** è praticamente scontato che ...

odometer [əʊ'dɒmətə(r)] *Am* contachilometri *m*

odour, *Am* **odor** ['əʊdə(r)] odore *m*

of [ɒv] **the name ~ the street / hotel** il nome della strada / dell'albergo; **it's made ~ steel** è di acciaio; **die ~ cancer** morire di cancro; **a friend ~ mine** un mio amico; **very nice ~ him** molto gentile da parte sua

off [ɒf] **1** *prep*: **a lane ~ the main road** not far from un sentiero poco lontano dalla strada principale; *leading off* un sentiero che parte dalla strada principale; **£20 ~ the price** 20 sterline di sconto **2** *adv*: **be ~ of light,**

TV etc essere spento; of gas, tap essere chiuso; (cancelled) essere annullato; of food essere finito; **she was ~ today** not at work oggi non era al lavoro; **we're ~ tomorrow** leaving partiamo domani; **take a day ~** prendere un giorno libero; **it's 3 miles ~** dista 3 miglia; **it's a long way ~** è molto lontano 3 adj food andato a male; **~ switch** interruttore m di spegnimento

offence [ə'fens] LAW reato m; **take ~ at sth** offendersi per qc; offend (insult) offendere; offender LAW delinquente m/f; offense Am ☞ offence; offensive 1 adj behaviour, remark, offensivo; smell sgradevole 2 n (MIL: attack) offensiva f

offer ['ɒfə(r)] 1 n offerta f 2 v/t offrire; **~ s.o. sth** offrire qc a qu

offhand attitude disinvolto

office ['ɒfɪs] ufficio m; (position) carica f; office hours orario m d'ufficio; officer MIL ufficiale m; in police agente m/f; official 1 adj ufficiale 2 n funzionario m, -a f; officially ufficialmente; officious invadente

'off-licence negozio m di alcolici

'off-line disconnesso, off-line inv; **go ~** disconnettersi

'off-peak rates ridotto; **~ elec-**tricity elettricità f a tariffa ridotta

'off-season bassa stagione f

'offset losses compensare

'offshore drilling rig, investment off-shore inv

'offside 1 adj wheel etc destro; on the left sinistro 2 adv SP in fuorigioco

'offspring figli mpl; of animal piccoli mpl

off-the-'record ufficioso

often ['ɒfn] spesso; **how ~ do you go there?** ogni quanto tempo ci vai?

oil [ɔɪl] 1 n olio m; petroleum petrolio m; for central heating nafta f 2 v/t oliare; oil change cambio m dell'olio; oil company compagnia f petrolifera; oilfield giacimento m petrolifero; oil painting quadro m a olio; oil refinery raffineria f di petrolio; oil rig piattaforma f petrolifera; oil slick chiazza f di petrolio; oil tanker petroliera f; oil well pozzo m petrolifero; oily unto

ointment ['ɔɪntmənt] pomata f

ok [əʊ'keɪ] can I? - ~ posso? - va bene!; **is it ~ with you if ...?** ti va bene se ...?; **does that look ~?** ti sembra che vada bene?; **that's ~ by me** per me va bene; **are you ~?** well, not hurt stai bene?; **he's ~** (is a good guy) è in gamba

old [əʊld] vecchio; (*previous*) precedente; **how ~ is he?** quanti anni ha?; **old age** vecchiaia *f*; **old-age pensioner** pensionato *m*, -a *f*; **old-fashioned** antiquato

olive ['ɒlɪv] oliva *f*; **olive oil** olio *m* d'oliva

Olympic 'Games [əˈlɪmpɪk] Olimpiadi *fpl*, giochi *mpl* olimpici

omelette *Am* **omelet** ['ɒmlɪt] frittata *f*

ominous ['ɒmɪnəs] sinistro

omission [əˈmɪʃn] omissione *f*; *on purpose* esclusione *f*; **omit** omettere; *on purpose* escludere; **~ to do sth** tralasciare di fare qc

on [ɒn] **1** *prep* su; **~ the table** sul tavolo; **~ the bus** in autobus; **~ TV** alla TV; **~ Sunday** domenica; **~ Sundays** di domenica; **~ the 1st of June** il primo (di) giugno; **I'm ~ antibiotics** sto prendendo antibiotici; **this is ~ me** (*I'm paying*) offro io; **have you any money ~ you?** hai dei soldi con te?; **~ his arrival** al suo arrivo; **~ hearing this** al sentire queste parole **2** *adv*: **be ~** *of light, TV etc* essere acceso; *of gas, tap* essere aperto; *of machine* essere in funzione; *of handbrake* essere inserito; **it's ~ after the news** *of programme* è dopo il notiziario; **the meeting is ~ scheduled**

to happen la riunione si fa; **with his jacket ~** con la giacca; **what's ~ tonight?** *on TV etc* cosa c'è stasera?; **I've got something ~ tonight** *planned* stasera ho un impegno; **you're ~** I accept your offer *etc* d'accordo; **that's ~ not** (*not allowed, not fair*) non è giusto; **~ you go** (*go ahead*) fai pure; **talk ~** continuare a parlare; **and so ~** e così via; **talk etc ~** senza sosta **3** *adj*: **the ~ switch** l'interruttore *m* d'accensione

once [wʌns] **1** *adv* (*one time*) una volta; (*formerly*) un tempo; **~ again, ~ more** ancora una volta; **at ~** (*immediately*) subito; **all at ~** (*suddenly*) improvvisamente; (*all*) **at ~** (*together*) contemporaneamente; **~ upon a time there was ...** c'era una volta ... **2** *conj* non appena; **~ you have finished** non appena hai finito

one [wʌn] **1** *n number* uno *m* **2** *adj* uno, -a; **~ day** un giorno *m* **3** *pron* uno *m*, -a *f*; **which ~?** quale?; **that ~** quello *m*, -a *f*; **this ~** questo *m*, -a *f*; **~ by ~** *enter, deal with* uno alla volta; **~ another** l'un l'altro, a vicenda; **what can ~ say?** cosa si può dire?; **the little ~s** i piccoli; **one-off** *n* fatto *m* eccezionale; *person* persona *f* eccezionale **2** *adj* unico; **one-parent family** famiglia

f monogenitore; **oneself** si;
after prep se stesso *m*, -a *f*,
sé; *cut ~* tagliarsi; *do sth ~*
fare *o* da sé; **one-way
street** strada *f* a senso unico;
one-way ticket biglietto *m*
di sola andata

onion ['ʌnjən] cipolla *f*

'on-line connesso, on-line
inv; *go ~* connettersi; **on-line
banking** telebanking *m*; **on-line shopping** shopping *m*
in Rete

onlooker ['ɒnlʊkə(r)] astante
m

only ['əʊnlɪ] **1** *adv* solo; *not ~
X but also Y* non solo X ma
anche Y; *~ just* a malapena **2**
adj unico; *~ son* unico figlio
maschio

'onset inizio *m*

'onside SP non in fuorigioco

on-the-job 'training training
m inv sul lavoro

onto ['ɒntu]: *put sth ~ sth*
mettere qc sopra qc

onwards ['ɒnwədz] in avanti;
from ... ~ da ... in poi

opaque [əʊ'peɪk] *glass* opaco

open ['əʊpən] **1** *adj* aperto; *in
the ~ air* all'aria aperta **2** *v/t*
aprire **3** *v/i* of door, shop
aprirsi; *of flower* sbocciare;
open-air *meeting, concert* all'aperto; *pool* scoperto;
open day giornata *f* di apertura al pubblico; **open-ended**
contract etc aperto; **opening**
in wall etc apertura *f*; *of
film, novel etc* inizio *m*; *(job*

going) posto *m* vacante;
openly *(honestly, frankly)*
apertamente; **open-minded**
aperto; **open ticket** biglietto
m aperto

opera ['ɒpərə] lirica *f*, opera *f*;
opera house teatro *m* dell'opera; **opera singer** cantante lirico *m*, -a *f*

operate ['ɒpəreɪt] **1** *v/i* of
company operare; *of airline,
bus service* essere in servizio;
of machine funzionare; MED
operare, intervenire **2** *v/t*
machine far funzionare

◆ **operate on** MED operare

'operating room Am MED sala *f* operatoria; **operating
system** COMPUT sistema *m*
operativo; **operation** operazione *f*; MED intervento *m*
(chirurgico), operazione *f*;
of machine funzionamento
m; *have an ~* MED subire
un intervento (chirurgico);
operator TELEC centralinista *m/f*; *of machine* operatore
m, -trice *f*; *(tour ~)* operatore
m turistico

opinion [ə'pɪnjən] opinione *f*,
parere *m*; *in my ~* a mio parere; **opinion poll** sondaggio
m d'opinione

opponent [ə'pəʊnənt] avversario *m*, -a *f*

opportunist [ɒpə'tjuːnɪst]
opportunista *m/f*; **opportunity** opportunità *f inv*

oppose [ə'pəʊz] opporsi a; *be
~d to ...* essere contrario a

...; **as ~d to** ... piuttosto che ...

opposite ['ɒpəzit] **1** *adj direction* opposto; *meaning, views* contrario; *house* di fronte; **the ~ side of the road** l'altro lato della strada **2** *n* contrario *m*; **opposite number** omologo *m*

opposition [ɒpə'ziʃn] opposizione *f*

oppress [ə'pres] *people* opprimere; **oppressive** *rule* oppressivo; *weather* opprimente

optical illusion ['ɒptikl] illusione *f* ottica

optician [ɒp'tiʃn] *dispensing* ottico *m*, -a *f*; **ophthalmic** optometrista *m/f*

optimism ['ɒptimizm] ottimismo *m*; **optimist** ottimista *m/f*; **optimistic** *view* ottimistico; *person* ottimista; **optimistically** ottimisticamente

optimum ['ɒptiməm] **1** *adj* ottimale **2** *n* optimum *m inv*

option ['ɒpʃn] possibilità *f inv*, opzione *f*; **he had no other ~** non ha avuto scelta; **optional** facoltativo

or [ɔː(r)] o; **he can't hear ~ see** non può né sentire né vedere; **~ else!** o guai a te!

oral ['ɔːrəl] orale

orange ['ɒrindʒ] **1** *adj colour* arancione **2** *n fruit* arancia *f*; *colour* arancione *m*; **orange juice** succo *m* d'arancia

orator ['ɒrətə(r)] oratore *m*, -trice *f*

orbit ['ɔːbit] **1** *n of earth* orbita *f* **2** *v/t the earth* orbitare intorno a

orchard ['ɔːtʃəd] frutteto *m*

orchestra ['ɔːkistrə] orchestra *f*

orchid ['ɔːkid] orchidea *f*

ordain [ɔː'dein] *priest* ordinare

ordeal [ɔː'diːl] esperienza *f* traumatizzante

order ['ɔːdə(r)] **1** *n* ordine *m*; *for goods, in restaurant* ordinazione *f*; **in ~ to do sth** così da fare qc; **out of ~** *(not functioning)* fuori servizio; *(not in sequence)* fuori posto **2** *v/t* ordinare; **~ s.o. to do sth** ordinare a qu di fare qc **3** *v/i* ordinare

orderly ['ɔːdəli] **1** *adj room, mind* ordinato; *crowd* disciplinato **2** *n in hospital* inserviente *m/f*

ordinarily [ɔːdi'neərili] *(as a rule)* normalmente; *ordinary* normale; *pej* ordinario

ore [ɔː(r)] minerale *m* grezzo

organ ['ɔːgən] ANAT, MUS organo *m*; **organic** *food, fertilizer* biologico; **organically** *grown* biologicamente; **organism** organismo *m*

organization [ɔːgənai'zeiʃn] organizzazione *f*; **organize** organizzare; **organizer** *person* organizzatore *m*, -trice *f*

orgasm ['ɔːgæzm] orgasmo *m*

orient ['ɔːriənt] *Am* orientare; **Oriental 1** orientale **2** *n* orientale *m/f*; **orientate** orientare

origin ['ɒrɪdʒɪn] origine *f*; **original 1** *adj* originale **2** *n painting etc* originale *m*; **originality** originalità *f*; **originally** (*at first*) in origine; **~ he comes from France** è di origini francesi; **originate 1** *v/t scheme, idea* dare origine a **2** *v/i of idea, belief* avere origine

ornamental [ɔːnə'mentl] ornamentale

ornate [ɔː'neɪt] *style* ornato

orphan ['ɔːfn] orfano *m*, -a *f*

orthodox ['ɔːθədɒks] *also fig* ortodosso

orthopedic [ɔːθə'piːdɪk] ortopedico

ostensibly [ɒ'stensəblɪ] apparentemente

ostentatious [ɒsten'teɪʃəs] ostentato

ostracize ['ɒstrəsaɪz] ostracizzare

other ['ʌðə(r)] **1** *adj* altro; **the ~ day** l'altro giorno; **every ~ day** a giorni alterni; **every ~ person** una persona su due **2** *n* altro *m*, -a *f*; **the ~s** gli altri; **otherwise** altrimenti; (*differently*) diversamente

ought [ɔːt] *I / you* **~ to know** dovrei / dovresti saperlo; **you ~ to have done it** avresti dovuto farlo

ounce [aʊns] oncia *f*

our ['aʊə(r)] il nostro *m*, la nostra *f*, i nostri *mpl*, le nostre *fpl*; **~ brother / sister** nostro fratello / nostra sorella; **ours** il nostro *m*, la nostra *f*, i nostri *mpl*, le nostre *fpl*; **ourselves** ci; *emphatic* noi stessi / noi stesse; *after prep* noi

oust [aʊst] *from office* esautorare

out [aʊt]: **be ~** *of light, fire* essere spento; *of flower* essere sbocciato; *of sun* splendere; *not at home, not in building* essere fuori; *of calculations* essere sbagliato; (*be published*) essere uscito; *of secret* essere svelato; *no longer in competition* essere eliminato; (*no longer in fashion*) essere out; **he's ~ in the garden** è in giardino; (*get*) fuori!; **that's ~!** (*out of the question*) è fuori discussione!; **he's ~ to win** fully intends to è deciso a vincere

outboard 'motor motore *m* fuoribordo

'outbreak scoppio *m*

'outcast emarginato *m*, -a *f*

'outcome risultato *m*

'outcry protesta *f*

out'dated sorpassato

out'do superare

out'door *toilet, activities, life* all'aperto; *pool* scoperto; **outdoors** all'aperto

outer ['aʊtə(r)] *wall etc*

esterno

'**outfit** (*clothes*) completo *m*; (*company, organization*) organizzazione *f*

'**outgoing** *flight, mail* in partenza; *personality* estroverso

out'**grow** *habits, interests* perdere

'**outing** ('autıŋ) (*trip*) gita *f*

out'**last** durare più di

'**outlet** *of pipe* scarico *m*; *for sales* punto *m* di vendita; *Am* ELEC presa *f* (di corrente)

'**outline 1** *n of person, building etc* profilo *m*; *of plan, novel* abbozzo *m* **2** *v/t plans etc* abbozzare

out'**live** sopravvivere a

'**outlook** (*prospects*) prospettiva *f*

'**outnumber** superare numericamente

out of ◇ *motion* fuori; *fall* ~ *the window* cadere fuori dalla finestra ◇ *position* da **20 miles** ~ **Newcastle** 20 miglia da Newcastle ◇ *cause* per; ~ *jealousy* per gelosia ◇ (*without*) senza; *we're* ~ *petrol* siamo senza benzina ◇ *from a group* su **5** – **10** 5 su 10

out-of-date *passport* scaduto; *values* superato

'**output 1** *n of factory* produzione *f*; COMPUT output *m inv* **2** *v/t* (*produce*) produrre

'**outrage 1** *n in feeling* sdegno *m*; *act* atrocità *f inv* **2** *v/t* indi-

gnare; **outrageous** *acts* scioccante; *prices* scandaloso

'**outright 1** *adj winner* assoluto **2** *adv win* nettamente; *kill* sul colpo

'**outset**: *at* / *from the* ~ all' / - dall'inizio

out'**shine** eclissare

'**outside 1** *adj* esterno **2** *adv sit, go* fuori **3** *prep* fuori di; (*apart from*) al di fuori di **4** *n of building, case* esterno *m*; **at the** ~ al massimo; out-**sider** estraneo *m*, -a *f*; *in election, race* outsider *m inv*

'**outsize** *clothing* di taglia forte

'**outskirts** periferia *f*

out'**smart** ☞ **outwit**

'**outsource** dare in appalto a terzi

out'**standing** eccezionale; FIN da saldare

outstretched ('autstretʃt) *hands* teso

outward ('autwəd) *appearance* esteriore; ~ *journey* viaggio *m* d'andata; out-**wardly** esteriormente

out'**weigh** contare più di

out'**wit** riuscire a gabbare

oval ('əʊvl) ovale

oven ('ʌvn) forno *m*

over ('əʊvə(r)) **1** *prep* (*above*) sopra, su; (*across*) dall'altra parte di; (*more than*) oltre; (*during*) nel corso di; *travel all* ~ *Brazil* girare tutto il Brasile; *you find them* *all ~ Brazil* si trovano dappertutto in Brasile; *we're the worst* il peggio è passato; *~ and above* oltre a **2** *adv*: *be ~ (finished)* essere finito; *(left)* essere rimasto; *~ to you (your turn)* tocca a te; *~here / there* qui / lì; *it hurts all ~* mi fa male dappertutto; *painted white all ~* tutto dipinto di bianco; *I've told you ~ and ~ again* te l'ho detto mille volte; *do sth ~ again* rifare qc

'overall *length* totale; *overalls* tuta *f* da lavoro

over'awe intimidire

over'balance perdere l'equilibrio

over'bearing autoritario

'overcast *sky* nuvoloso

over'charge *customer* far pagare più del dovuto a

'overcoat cappotto *m*

over'come *difficulties* superare; *be ~ by emotion* essere sopraffatto dall'emozione

over'crowded sovraffollato

over'do *(exaggerate)* esagerare; *in cooking* stracuocere; *overdone meat* stracotto

'overdose overdose *f inv*

'overdraft *of* (di conto); *have an ~* avere il conto scoperto; *overdraw*: *be £800 ~n* essere (allo) scoperto di 800 sterline

over'dressed troppo elegante

'overdrive MOT overdrive *m inv*

over'estimate sovrastimare

over'expose sovraesporre

'overflow¹ *n pipe* troppopieno *m*

over'flow² *v/i of water* traboccare; *of river* straripare

over'haul *engine* revisionare; *plans* rivedere

'overhead *lights, cables* in alto, aereo; *railway* sopraelevato; *overheads* FIN costi *mpl* di gestione

over'hear sentire per caso

over'heated *room, engine* surriscaldato

overjoyed [əʊvəˈdʒɔɪd] felicissimo

'overland via terra

over'lap *(partly cover)* sovrapporsi; *(partly coincide)* coincidere

over'load sovraccaricare

over'look *of tall building etc* dominare, dare su; *deliberately* chiudere un occhio su; *accidentally* non notare

overly [ˈəʊvəlɪ] troppo; *not ~ ...* non particolarmente ...

'overnight *travel* di notte; *stay* per la notte; *fig change etc* da un giorno all'altro

'overpass cavalcavia *m inv*

over'power *physically* sopraffare

overpriced [əʊvəˈpraɪst] troppo caro

overrated [əʊvəˈreɪtɪd] sopravvalutato

over'ride *decision etc* annulla-

re; (*be more important than*)
prevalere su; **overriding**
decision principale

over'rule *decision* annullare
over'seas all'estero
over'see sorvegliare
over'shadow *fig* eclissare
'oversight svista *f*
oversimpli'fication semplificazione *f* eccessiva
over'sleep non svegliarsi in tempo
over'state esagerare; **overstatement** esagerazione *f*
over'take *in work, development* superare; MOT sorpassare
over'throw[1] *v/t government* rovesciare
'overthrow[2] *n of government* rovesciamento *m*
'overtime 1 *n* straordinario *m* **2** *adv:* **work ~** fare lo straordinario
over'turn 1 *v/t vehicle, object* ribaltare; *government* rovesciare **2** *v/i of vehicle* ribaltarsi

'overview visione *f* d'insieme
overwhelming [əʊvə'welmɪŋ] *feeling* profondo; *majority* schiacciante
over'work 1 *n* lavoro *m* eccessivo **2** *v/i* lavorare troppo
owe [əʊ] *v/t* dovere (**s.o.** a qu); *owing to* a causa di
owl [aʊl] gufo *m*
own[1] [əʊn] *v/t* possedere
own[2] [əʊn] **1** *adj* proprio; **my ~ car** la mia macchina; **my very ~ mother** proprio mia madre **2** *pron:* **a car of my ~** un'auto tutta mia; **on my / his ~** da solo
♦ **own up** confessare
owner ['əʊnə(r)] proprietario *m*, -a *f*; **ownership** proprietà *f*
oxygen ['ɒksɪdʒən] ossigeno *m*
oyster ['ɔɪstə(r)] ostrica *f*
ozone ['əʊzəʊn] ozono *m*; **ozone layer** fascia *f* or strato *m* d'ozono

PA [piː'eɪ] (= **personal assistant**) assistente personale
pace [peɪs] (*step*) passo *m*; (*speed*) ritmo *m*; **pacemaker** MED pacemaker *m inv*; SP battistrada *m inv*
Pacific [pə'sɪfɪk]: **the ~ (Ocean)** il Pacifico
pacifier ['pæsɪfaɪə(r)] *Am for*

baby succhiotto *m*; **pacifism** pacifismo *m*; **pacifist** pacifista *m/f*; **pacify** placare
pack [pæk] **1** *n* (*back~*) zaino *m*; *of cereal, food* confezione *f*; *of cigarettes* pacchetto *m*; *of peas etc* confezione *f*; *of cards* mazzo *m* **2** *v/t bag* fare; *item of clothing etc* mettere in

valigia; *goods* imballare; *groceries* imbustare **3** *v/i* fare la valigia / le valigie; **package 1** *n* (*parcel*) pacco *m*; *of offers etc* pacchetto *m* **2** *v/t* confezionare; **packaging** *also fig* confezione *f*; **packed** (*crowded*) affollato; **packet** confezione *f*; *of cigarettes, crisps* pacchetto *m*

pact [pækt] patto *m*

pad[1] [pæd] **1** *n piece of cloth etc* tampone *m*; *for writing* blocchetto *m* **2** *v/t with material* imbottire; *speech, report* farcire

pad[2] [pæd] *v/i* (*move quietly*) camminare a passi felpati

padding ['pædɪŋ] *material* imbottitura *f*; *in speech etc* riempitivo *m*

paddle ['pædl] **1** *n for canoe* pagaia *f* **2** *v/i in canoe* pagaiare

paddock ['pædək] paddock *m inv*

padlock ['pædlɒk] lucchetto *m*

page[1] [peɪdʒ] *n of book etc* pagina *f*

page[2] [peɪdʒ] *v/t* (*call*) chiamare con l'altoparlante

pager ['peɪdʒə(r)] cercapersone *m inv*

paid em'ployment occupazione *f* rimunerata

pain [peɪn] dolore *m*; **be in ~** soffrire; **a ~ in the neck** F una rottura *f* di scatole; **painful** (*distressing*) doloro-

so; (*laborious*) difficile; **painfully** (*extremely*, *acutely*) estremamente; **painkiller** analgesico *m*; **painstaking** accurato

paint [peɪnt] **1** *n for wall, car* vernice *f*; *for artist* colore *m* **2** *v/t wall etc* pitturare; *picture* dipingere; **paintbrush** pennello *m*; **painter** *decorator* imbianchino *m*; *artist* pittore *m*, -trice *f*; **painting** *activity* pittura *f*; (*picture*) quadro *m*; **paintwork** vernice *f*

pair [peə(r)] *of objects* paio *m*; *of animals, people* coppia *f*; **a ~ of shoes** un paio di scarpe

pajamas *Am* ☞ **pyjamas**

Pakistan [pɑːkɪ'stɑːn] Pakistan *m*; **Pakistani 1** *n* pakistano *m*, -a *f* **2** *adj* pakistano

pal [pæl] F (*friend*) amico *m*, -a *f*

palace ['pælɪs] palazzo *m* signorile

palate ['pælət] palato *m*

palatial [pə'leɪʃl] sfarzoso

pale [peɪl] pallido

Palestine ['pæləstaɪn] Palestina *f*; **Palestinian 1** *n* palestinese *m/f* **2** *adj* palestinese

pallet ['pælɪt] pallet *m inv*

pallor ['pælə(r)] pallore *m*

palm [pɑːm] *of hand* palma *f*; **palm tree** palma *f*

paltry ['pɔːltrɪ] irrisorio

pamper ['pæmpə(r)] viziare

pamphlet ['pæmflɪt] volantino *m*

pan [pæn] *for cooking* pentola

f; *for frying* padella *f*; **pancake** crêpe *f inv*

pandemonium [pændɪ'məʊnɪəm] pandemonio *m*

pane [peɪn]: **~ (of glass)** vetro *m*

panel ['pænl] pannello *m*; *of experts* gruppo *m*; *of judges* giuria *f*; **panelling**, *Am* **paneling** rivestimento *m* a pannelli

panic ['pænɪk] **1** *n* panico *m* **2** *v/i*: **don't ~** non farti prendere dal panico; **panic-stricken** in preda al panico

panorama [pænə'rɑ:mə] panorama *m*; **panoramic** panoramico

pant [pænt] ansimare

panties ['pæntɪz] mutandine *fpl*

pantihose ☞ **pantyhose**

pants [pænts] pantaloni *mpl*

pantyhose ['pæntɪhəʊz] collant *mpl*

papal ['peɪpəl] pontificio

paper ['peɪpə(r)] **1** *n material* carta *f*; *(news~)* giornale *m*; *(wall~)* carta *f* da parati; *academic relazione *f*; *(examination ~)* esame *m*; **~s** *(identity ~s, documents)* documenti *mpl* **2** *adj* di carta **3** *v/t room, walls* tappezzare; **paperback** tascabile *m*; **paper clip** graffetta *f*; **paperwork** disbrigo delle pratiche

parachute ['pærəʃu:t] **1** *n* paracadute *m inv* **2** *v/i* paracadutarsi **3** *v/t troops, supplies*

paracadutare

parade [pə'reɪd] **1** *n (procession)* sfilata *f* **2** *v/i* sfilare

paradise ['pærədaɪs] paradiso *m*

paradox ['pærədɒks] paradosso *m*; **paradoxical** paradossale; **paradoxically** paradossalmente

paragraph ['pærəgrɑ:f] paragrafo *m*

parallel ['pærəlel] **1** *n (in geometry)* parallela *f*; GEOG, *fig* parallelo *m*; **do two things in ~** fare due cose in parallelo **2** *adj also fig* parallelo **3** *v/t (match)* uguagliare

paralysis [pə'ræləsɪs] *also fig* paralisi *f inv*; **paralyze** *also fig* paralizzare

paramedic [pærə'medɪk] paramedico *m*, *-a f*

parameter [pə'ræmɪtə(r)] parametro *m*

paramilitary [pærə'mɪlɪtrɪ] **1** *adj* paramilitare **2** *n* appartenente ad un'organizzazione paramilitare

paranoia [pærə'nɔɪə] paranoia *f*; **paranoid** paranoico

paraphrase ['pærəfreɪz] parafrasare

parasite ['pærəsaɪt] *also fig* parassita *m*

parasol ['pærəsɒl] parasole *m*

paratrooper ['pærətru:pə(r)] MIL paracadutista *m*

parcel ['pɑ:sl] pacco *m*

pardon ['pɑ:dn] **1** *n* LAW gra-

zia f; **I beg your ~?** (what did
you say) prego?; **I beg your ~**
(I'm sorry) scusi 2 v/t scusare;
LAW graziare

parent ['peərənt] genitore m;
parental dei genitori; **parent
company** società f inv
madre; **parent-teacher association** organizzazione
composta da genitori e insegn-
anti

parish ['pærɪʃ] parrocchia f

park¹ [pɑːk] n parco m

park² [pɑːk] v/t & v/i MOT parcheggiare

parking ['pɑːkɪŋ] MOT parcheggio m; **no ~** sosta f vietata; **parking brake** Am freno m a mano; **parking garage** Am parcheggio co-
perto; **parking lot** Am parcheggio m; **parking meter**
parchimetro m; **parking
ticket** multa f per sosta vietata

parliament ['pɑːləmənt] parlamento m

parole [pə'rəʊl] 1 n libertà f
vigilata 2 v/t concedere la libertà vigilata a

parrot ['pærət] pappagallo m

part [pɑːt] 1 n parte f; of machine pezzo m; Am: in hair riga f; **take ~ in** prendere parte
in 2 adv (partly) in parte 3 v/i
separarsi 4 v/t: **~ one's hair**
farsi la riga; **partial** (incomplete) parziale; **be ~ to** avere
un debole per; **partially** parzialmente

participant [pɑː'tɪsɪpənt] partecipante m/f; **participate**
partecipare (**in** a); **participation** partecipazione f

particular [pə'tɪkjʊlə(r)] (specific) particolare; (fussy) pignolo; **in ~** in particolare;
particularly particolarmente

parting ['pɑːtɪŋ] of people separazione f; in hair riga f

partition [pɑː'tɪʃn] (screen)
tramezzo m; (of country)
suddivisione f

partly ['pɑːtlɪ] in parte

partner ['pɑːtnə(r)] COM socio
m, -a f; in relationship partner m/f inv; in particular activity compagno m, -a f; **partnership** COM società f inv; in
particular activity sodalizio m

'part-time part-time

party ['pɑːtɪ] 1 n (celebration)
festa f; POL partito m;
(group) gruppo m 2 v/i F
far baldoria; **party-pooper**
F guastafeste m/f inv

pass [pɑːs] 1 n for entry passi
m inv; SP passaggio m; in
mountains passo m; **make a
~ at** fare avances a 2 v/t
(hand) passare; (go past) passare davanti a; (overtake) sorpassare; (go beyond) superare; (approve) approvare; SP
passare; **~ an exam** superare
un esame; **~ sentence** LAW
emanare la sentenza; **~ the
time** passare il tempo 3 v/i
passare; in exam essere pro-

mosso

♦ **pass away** euph spegnersi

♦ **pass on 1** v/t information, book, savings passare (**to** a) **2** v/i (euph.: die) mancare

♦ **pass out** (faint) svenire

♦ **pass up** opportunity lasciarsi sfuggire

passable ['pɑːsəbl] road transitabile; (acceptable) passabile

passage ['pæsɪdʒ] (corridor) passaggio m; from book passo m; **the ~ of time** il passare del tempo

passenger ['pæsɪndʒə(r)] passeggero m, -a f

passer-by [pɑːsə'baɪ] passante m/f

passion ['pæʃn] passione f; **passionate** appassionato

passive ['pæsɪv] **1** adj passivo **2** n GRAM passivo m; **passive smoking** fumo m passivo

'**passport** passaporto m; **passport control** controllo m passaporti; **password** parola f d'ordine; COMPUT password f inv

past [pɑːst] **1** adj (former) precedente; **in the ~ few days** nei giorni scorsi **2** n passato m; **in the ~** nel passato **3** prep in position oltre; **it's ~ half ~ two** sono le due e mezza; **it's ~ seven o'clock** sono le sette passate **4** adv: **run ~** passare di corsa

pasta ['pæstə] pasta f

paste [peɪst] **1** n (adhesive) colla f **2** v/t (stick) incollare

pastime ['pɑːstaɪm] passatempo m

pastry ['peɪstrɪ] for pie pasta f (sfoglia); (small cake) pasticcino m

'**past tense** GRAM passato m

pasty ['peɪstɪ] complexion smorto

pat [pæt] **1** n colpetto m; affectionate buffetto m **2** v/t dare un colpetto a; affectionately dare un buffetto a

patch [pætʃ] **1** n on clothing pezza f; (period of time) periodo m; (area) zona f; **go through a bad ~** attraversare un brutto periodo; **be not a ~ on** fig non essere niente a paragone di **2** v/t clothing rattoppare

♦ **patch up** (repair) riparare alla meglio; quarrel risolvere

patchy ['pætʃɪ] quality irregolare; work discontinuo, disuguale

patent ['peɪtnt] **1** adj palese **2** n for invention brevetto m **3** v/t invention brevettare

paternal [pə'tɜːnl] paterno; **paternalism** paternalismo m; **paternalistic** paternalistico; **paternity** paternità f inv; **paternity leave** congedo m di paternità

path [pɑːθ] sentiero m; fig strada f

pathetic [pə'θetɪk] patetico; F (very bad) penoso

pathological [pæθəˈlɒdʒɪkl] patologico

patience [ˈpeɪʃns] pazienza *f*; *card game* solitario *m*; **patient 1** *n* paziente *m/f* **2** *adj* paziente; *be ~!* abbi pazienza!; **patiently** pazientemente

patio [ˈpætɪəʊ] terrazza *f*

patriot [ˈpeɪtrɪət] patriota *m/f*; **patriotic** patriottico; **patriotism** patriottismo *m*

patrol [pəˈtrəʊl] **1** *n* pattuglia *f* **2** *v/t* border pattugliare; **patrol car** autopattuglia *f*; **patrolman** agente *m/f* di pattuglia; **patrol wagon** *Am* furgone *m* cellulare

patron [ˈpeɪtrən] *of artist* patrocinatore *m*, -trice *f*; *of charity* patrono *m*, -essa *f*; *of shop, cinema* cliente *m/f*; **patronize** *person* trattare con condiscendenza; **patronizing** condiscendente; **patron saint** patrono *m*, -a *f*

pattern [ˈpætn] *on fabric* motivo *m*, disegno *m*; *for sewing* (carta) modello *m*; *in behaviour, events* schema *m*

paunch [pɔːntʃ] pancia *f*

pause [pɔːz] **1** *n* pausa *f* **2** *v/i* fermarsi **3** *v/t tape* fermare

pave [peɪv] pavimentare; *~ the way for* fig aprire la strada a; **pavement** *Br* marciapiede *m*; *Am* manto *m* stradale

paw [pɔː] **1** *n* of animal, F (hand) zampa *f* **2** *v/t* F palpare

pawn [pɔːn] *in chess* pedone *m*; *fig* pedina *f*

pay [peɪ] **1** *n* paga *f* **2** *v/t* pagare; *~ s.o. a compliment* fare un complimento a qu **3** *v/i* pagare; (*be profitable*) rendere; *it doesn't ~ to ...* non conviene ...; *~ for purchase* pagare

◆ **pay back** *person* restituire i soldi a; *loan* restituire; (*get revenge on*) farla pagare a

◆ **pay off 1** *v/t debt* estinguere; *workers* liquidare; *corrupt official* comprare **2** *v/i* (*be profitable*) dare frutti

◆ **pay up** pagare

payable [ˈpeɪəbl] pagabile; **pay cheque**, *Am* **pay check** assegno *m* paga; **payday** giorno *m* di paga; **payee** beneficiario *m*, -a *f*; **payment** pagamento *m*; **pay phone** telefono *m* pubblico

PC [piːˈsiː] (= *personal computer*) PC *m inv*; (= *politically correct*) politicamente corretto; (= *police constable*) agente *m/f* di polizia

PDA [piːdiːˈeɪ] (= *personal digital assistant*) PDA *m inv*

pea [piː] pisello *m*

peace [piːs] pace *f*; **peaceful** tranquillo; *demonstration* pacifico; **peacefully** tranquillamente; *demonstrate* pacificamente

peach [piːtʃ] pesca *f*; *tree* pesco *m*

peak [pi:k] **1** *n* vetta *f; fig* apice *m* **2** *v/i* raggiungere il livello massimo; peak hours ore *fpl* di punta

peanut ['pi:nʌt] arachide *f*; **get paid ~s** F essere pagati una miseria F; peanut butter burro *m* d'arachidi

pear [peə(r)] pera *f; tree* pero *m*

pearl [pɜːl] perla *f*

pebble ['pebl] ciottolo *m*

pecan ['pi:kæn] noce *f* pecan

peck [pek] **1** *n (bite)* beccata *f*; *(kiss)* bacetto *m* **2** *v/t (bite)* beccare; *(kiss)* dare un bacetto a

peculiar [pɪ'kju:lɪə(r)] *(strange)* strano; **~ to** *(special)* caratteristico di; peculiarity *(strangeness)* stranezza *f*; *(special feature)* caratteristica *f*

pedal ['pedl] **1** *n of bike* pedale *m* **2** *v/i* pedalare; *(cycle)* andare in bicicletta

pedantic [pɪ'dæntɪk] pedante

peddle ['pedl] *drugs* spacciare

pedestrian [pɪ'destrɪən] pedone *m*; pedestrian crossing passaggio *m* pedonale; pedestrian precinct zona *f* pedonale

pediatric [pi:dɪ'ætrɪk] pediatrico; pediatrician pediatra *m/f*; pediatrics pediatria *f*

pedicure ['pedɪkjuə(r)] pedicure *f inv*

pedigree ['pedɪgri:] **1** *n* pedi-

gree *m inv* **2** *adj* di razza pura

pee [pi:] F fare pipì *m*

peek [pi:k] **1** *n* sbirciata *f* **2** *v/i* sbirciare F

peel [pi:l] **1** *n* buccia *f; of citrus fruit* scorza *f* **2** *v/t fruit, vegetables* sbucciare **3** *v/i of nose, shoulders* spellarsi; *of paint* scrostarsi

peep [pi:p] ☞ **peek**; peephole spioncino *m*

peer¹ [pɪə(r)] *n (equal)* pari *m/f inv*

peer² [pɪə(r)] *v/i* guardare; **~ at** scrutare

peg [peg] *for coat* attaccapanni *m inv; for tent* picchetto *m*; **off the ~** prêt-à-porter

pejorative [pɪ'dʒɒrətɪv] peggiorativo

pellet ['pelɪt] pallina *f*; *(bullet)* pallino *m*

pen¹ [pen] penna *f*

pen² [pen] *(enclosure)* recinto *m*

pen³ [pen] *Am* ☞ **penitentiary**

penalize ['pi:nəlaɪz] penalizzare

penalty ['penltɪ] ammenda *f; in soccer* rigore *m; in rugby* punizione *f*; **take the ~** battere il rigore / la punizione; penalty area SP area *f* di rigore; penalty clause LAW penale *f*; penalty kick *in soccer* calcio *m* di rigore; *in rugby* calcio *m* di punizione; penalty shoot-out rigori *mpl*; **penalty spot** dischetto *m* di rigore

pencil ['pensɪl] matita *f*; **pencil sharpener** temperamatite *m inv*

pendant ['pendənt] *necklace* pendaglio *m*

penetrate ['penɪtreɪt] penetrare in; **penetration** penetrazione *f*

penguin ['peŋgwɪn] pinguino *m*

penicillin [penɪ'sɪlɪn] penicillina *f*

peninsula [pə'nɪnsjolə] penisola *f*

penis ['piːnɪs] pene *m*

penitence ['penɪtəns] penitenza *f*; **penitentiary** *Am* prigione *f*

'pen name pseudonimo *m*

pennant ['penənt] gagliardetto *m*

penniless ['penɪlɪs] al verde

'pen pal amico *m*, -a *f* di penna

pension ['penʃn] pensione *f*
◆ **pension off** mandare in pensione

'pension scheme schema *m* pensionistico

pensive ['pensɪv] pensieroso

Pentagon ['pentəgɒn]: **the ~** il Pentagono

pentathlon [pen'tæθlən] pentathlon *m inv*

penthouse ['penthaʊs] attico *m*

pent-up ['pentʌp] represso

penultimate [pe'nʌltɪmət] penultimo

people [piːpl] gente *f*, persone *fpl*; (*nsg: race, tribe*) popolazione *f*; **the ~** (*the citizens*) il popolo; **the American ~** gli americani; **~ say ...** si dice che ...

pepper ['pepə(r)] *spice* pepe *m*; *vegetable* peperone *m*; **peppermint** *sweet* mentina *f*, *flavouring* menta *f*

per [pɜː(r)] *a* **100 km ~ hour** 100 km all'ora; **£50 ~ night** 50 sterline a notte; **~ annum** all'anno

perceive [pə'siːv] percepire; (*view, interpret*) interpretare

percent [pə'sent] per cento; **percentage** percentuale *f*

perceptible [pə'septəbl] percettibile; **perceptibly** percettibilmente; **perception** percezione *f*, (*insightfulness*) sensibilità *f*; (*of person*) perspicace

percolate ['pɜːkəleɪt] *of coffee* filtrare; **percolator** caffettiera *f* a filtro

perfect 1 ['pɜːfɪkt] *adj* perfetto **2** ['pɜːfɪkt] *n* GRAM passato *m* prossimo **3** [pə'fekt] *v/t* perfezionare; **perfection** perfezione *f*; **perfectionist** perfezionista *m/f*; **perfectly** perfettamente

perforated ['pɜːfəreɪtɪd] *line* perforato

perform [pə'fɔːm] **1** *v/t* (*carry out*) eseguire; *of actors* interpretare **2** *v/i of actor, musi-*

cian, dancer esibirsi; **the car ~s well** la macchina dà ottime prestazioni; performance *by actor* interpretazione *f; by musician* esecuzione *f; (show)* spettacolo *m; of employee, company etc* rendimento *m; of machine* prestazioni *fpl;* performer artista *m/f*

perfume ['pɜːfjuːm] profumo *m*

perfunctory [pə'fʌŋktəri] superficiale

perhaps [pə'hæps] forse

peril ['perəl] pericolo *m*

perimeter [pə'rɪmɪtə(r)] perimetro *m*

period ['pɪərɪəd] *time* periodo *m; (menstruation)* mestruazioni *fpl; Am punctuation mark* punto *m* fermo; **I don't want to, ~!** *Am* non voglio, punto e basta!; **periodic** periodico; **periodical** periodico *m*

peripheral [pə'rɪfərəl] **1** *adj not crucial* marginale **2** *n* COMPUT periferica *f;* periphery periferia *f*

perish ['perɪʃ] *of rubber* deteriorarsi; *of person* perire; perishable *food* deteriorabile

perjure ['pɜːdʒə(r)]: **~ o.s.** spergiurare; perjury falso giuramento *m*

perk [pɜːk] *of job* vantaggio *m*

perm [pɜːm] **1** *n* permanente *f* **2** *v/t:* **have one's hair ~ed** farsi fare la permanente;

permanent permanente; *job, address* fisso; permanently permanentemente

permeate ['pɜːmɪeɪt] permeare

permissible [pə'mɪsəbl] permesso, ammissibile; permission permesso *m;* permissive permissivo

permit **1** [pɜːmɪt] *n* permesso *m* **2** [pə'mɪt] *v/t* permettere (**s.o. to do** a qu di fare)

perpendicular [pɜːpən'dɪkjulə(r)] perpendicolare

perpetual [pə'petʃuəl] perenne; perpetually perennemente

perplex [pə'pleks] lasciare perplesso; perplexity perplessità *f inv*

persecute ['pɜːsɪkjuːt] perseguitare; persecution persecuzione *f;* persecutor persecutore *m,* -trice *f*

perseverance [pɜːsɪ'vɪərəns] perseveranza *f;* persevere perseverare

persist [pə'sɪst] persistere; persistent *person, questions* insistente; *rain, unemployment etc* continuo; persistently *(continually)* continuamente

person ['pɜːsn] persona *f;* **in ~** di persona; personal personale; personal computer personal computer *m inv;* personality personalità *f inv;* personally personalmente; **don't take it** ~ non offenderti; **personal organizer** agenda *f* elettronica; **personal stereo Walkman®** *m inv*; **personify** *of person* personificare

personnel [pɜːsə'nel] *employees* personale *m*; *department* ufficio *m* del personale

perspective [pə'spektɪv] *in art* prospettiva *f*; **get sth into** ~ vedere qc nella giusta prospettiva

perspiration [pɜːspɪ'reɪʃn] traspirazione *f*; **perspire** sudare

persuade [pə'sweɪd] persuadere; ~ **s.o. to do sth** persuadere qu a fare qc; **persuasion** persuasione *f*; **persuasive** persuasivo

perturb [pə'tɜːb] inquietare; **perturbing** inquietante

pervasive [pə'veɪsɪv] *influence, ideas* diffuso

perversion [pə'vɜːʃn] *sexual* perversione *f*; **pervert** *sexual* pervertito *m*, -a *f*

pessimism ['pesɪmɪzm] pessimismo *m*; **pessimist** pessimista *m/f*; **pessimistic** *view* pessimistico; *person* pessimista

pest [pest] animale / insetto *m* nocivo; F *person* peste *f*

pester ['pestə(r)] assillare; ~ **s.o. to do sth** assillare qu perché faccia qc

pesticide ['pestɪsaɪd] pesticida *m*

pet [pet] **1** *n animal* animale *m* domestico; *(favourite)* favorito *m*, -a *f* **2** *adj* preferito **3** *v/t animal* accarezzare **4** *v/i of couple* pomiciare F

petite [pə'tiːt] minuta

petition [pə'tɪʃn] petizione *f*

petrify ['petrɪfaɪ] terrorizzare

petrochemical [petrəʊ'kemɪkl] petrolchimico

petrol ['petrl] benzina *f*

petroleum [pɪ'trəʊliəm] petrolio *m*

'petrol pump pompa *f* della benzina; **petrol station** stazione *f* di rifornimento

petting ['petɪŋ] petting *m*

petty ['petɪ] *person, behaviour* meschino; *details* insignificante; **petty cash** piccola cassa *f*

pew [pjuː] banco *m* (di chiesa)

pharmaceutical [fɑːmə'sjuːtɪkl] farmaceutico; **pharmaceuticals** farmaceutici *mpl*

pharmacist ['fɑːməsɪst] farmacista *m/f*; **pharmacy** *shop* farmacia *f*

phase [feɪz] fase *f*

◆ **phase in** introdurre gradualmente

◆ **phase out** eliminare gradualmente

PhD [piːeɪtʃ'diː] (= *Doctor of Philosophy*) dottorato *m* di ricerca

phenomenal [fɪ'nɒmɪnl] fenomenale; **phenomenon** fenomeno *m*

philanthropic [fɪlən'θrɒpɪk] filantropico; **philanthropist** filantropo *m*, -a *f*; **philanthropy** filantropia *f*

Philippines ['fɪlɪpi:nz]: **the ~** le Filippine *fpl*

philosopher [fɪ'lɒsəfə(r)] filosofo *m*, -a *f*; **philosophical** filosofico; **philosophy** filosofia *f*

phobia ['fəʊbɪə] fobia *f*

phon(e)y ['fəʊnɪ] F falso

phone [fəʊn] **1** *n* telefono *m*; **be on the ~** be talking essere al telefono **2** *v/t* telefonare a **3** *v/i* telefonare; **phone book** guida *f* telefonica, elenco telefonico *m*; **phone booth** cabina *f* telefonica; **phone call** telefonata *f*; **phone card** scheda *f* telefonica; **phone number** numero *m* di telefono

photo ['fəʊtəʊ] foto *f*; **photocopier** fotocopiatrice *f*; **photocopy 1** *n* fotocopia *f* **2** *v/t* fotocopiare; **photogenic** fotogenico; **photograph 1** *n* fotografia *f* **2** *v/t* fotografare; **photographer** fotografo *m*, -a *f*; **photography** fotografia *f*

phrase [freɪz] **1** *n* frase *f* **2** *v/t* esprimere

physical ['fɪzɪkl] **1** *adj* fisico **2** *n* MED visita *f* medica; **physically** fisicamente

physician [fɪ'zɪʃn] medico *m*

physicist ['fɪzɪsɪst] fisico *m*, -a *f*; **physics** fisica *f*

physiotherapist [fɪzɪəʊ'θerəpɪst] fisioterapeuta *m/f*; **physiotherapy** fisioterapia *f*

physique [fɪ'zi:k] fisico *m*

pianist ['pɪənɪst] pianista *m/f*; **piano** piano *m*

pick [pɪk] (*choose*) scegliere; *flowers, fruit* raccogliere; **~ one's nose** mettersi le dita nel naso

♦ **pick up 1** *v/t* prendere; *phone* sollevare; *baby* prendere in braccio; *from ground* raccogliere; (*collect*) andare / venire a prendere; *information* raccogliere; *in car* far salire; *man, woman* rimorchiare F; *language, skill* imparare; *habit, illness* prendere; (*buy*) trovare **2** *v/i* (*improve*) migliorare

picket ['pɪkɪt] **1** *n* of strikers picchetto *m* **2** *v/t* picchettare

'pickpocket borseggiatore *m*, -trice *f*; **pick-up** (*truck*) Am furgone *m* (aperto), pick up *m inv*; **picky** F difficile (da accontentare)

picnic ['pɪknɪk] **1** *n* picnic *m inv* **2** *v/i* fare un picnic

picture ['pɪktʃə(r)] **1** *n* photo foto *f*; *painting* quadro *m*; *illustration* figura *f*; *film* film *m inv*; **put / keep s.o. in the ~** mettere / tenere al corrente qu **2** *v/t* immaginare; **pictures** cinema *m*; **picturesque** pittoresco

pie [paɪ] *sweet* torta *f*; *savoury* pasticcio *m*

piece [piːs] pezzo *m*; **a ~ of pie / bread** una fetta di torta / pane; **a ~ of advice** un consiglio; **take to ~s** smontare

♦ **piece together** *broken plate* rimettere insieme; *evidence* ricostruire

piecemeal ['piːsmiːl] poco alla volta

pier [pɪə(r)] *at seaside* pontile *m*

pierce [pɪəs] (*penetrate*) trapassare; *ears* farsi i buchi in; **piercing** *noise* lacerante; *eyes* penetranti; *wind* pungente

pig [pɪg] *also fig* maiale *m*

pigeon ['pɪdʒɪn] piccione *m*; **pigeonhole** casella *f*

pigheaded [pɪg'hedɪd] testardo; **pigsty** *also fig* porcile *m*

pile [paɪl] mucchio *m*; **F a ~ of work** un sacco di lavoro F

♦ **pile up** *v/i of work, bills* accumularsi **2** *v/t* ammucchiare

pile-up ['paɪlʌp] MOT tamponamento *m* a catena

pilfering ['pɪlfərɪŋ] piccoli furti *mpl*

pilgrim ['pɪlgrɪm] pellegrino *m*, -a *f*

pill [pɪl] pastiglia *f*; **be on the ~** prendere la pillola

pillar ['pɪlə(r)] colonna *f*; **pillarbox** *f* delle lettere

pillow ['pɪləʊ] guanciale *m*; **pillowcase, pillowslip** federa *f*

pilot ['paɪlət] **1** *n of plane* pilota *m/f* **2** *v/t plane* pilotare

pimp [pɪmp] ruffiano *m*

pimple ['pɪmpl] brufolo *m*

PIN [pɪn] (= **personal identification number**) numero *m* di codice segreto

pin [pɪn] **1** *n for sewing* spillo *m*; *in bowling* birillo *m*; (*badge*) spilla *f*; ELEC spinotto *m* **2** *v/t* (*hold down*) immobilizzare; (*attach*) attaccare; *on lapel* appuntare

♦ **pin up** *notice* appuntare

pinafore dress ['pɪnəfɔːr] scamiciato *m*

pincers ['pɪnsəz] *tool* tenaglie *fpl*; *of crab* chele *fpl*

pinch [pɪntʃ] **1** *n* pizzico *m* **2** *v/t* pizzicare **3** *v/i of shoes* stringere

pine [paɪn] pino *m*; **~ furniture** mobili *mpl* di pino; **pineapple** ananas *m inv*

pink [pɪŋk] rosa *inv*

pinnacle ['pɪnəkl] *fig* apice *m*

pinpoint indicare con esattezza; **pins and needles** formicolio *m*

pint [paɪnt] pinta *f*

pin-up (girl) pin-up *f inv*

pioneer [paɪə'nɪə(r)] **1** *n fig* pioniere *m*, -a *f* **2** *v/t* essere il / la pioniere di; **pioneering** *work* pionieristico

pious ['paɪəs] pio

pip [pɪp] *of fruit* seme *m*

pipe [paɪp] **1** *n* tubo *m*; *for smoking* pipa *f* **2** *v/t* trasportare con condutture; **pipe-**

line conduttura *f*; **in the ~** *fig* in arrivo

pirate ['paɪərət] **1** *n* pirata *m* **2** *v/t software* piratare

Pisces ['paɪsiːz] ASTR Pesci *m/f inv*

piss [pɪs] **1** *v/i* P (*urinate*) pisciare P **2** *n* (*urine*) piscio *m* P; **take the ~out of s.o.** P prendere qu per il culo P ◆ **piss off** P **1** *v/i* sparire; **piss off!** levati dalle palle! P **2** *v/t*: **it pisses me off** mi fa incazzare

pissed [pɪst] P (*drunk*) sbronzo F; *Am* (*annoyed*) seccato

pistol ['pɪstl] pistola *f*

piston ['pɪstən] pistone *m*

pit [pɪt] *n* (*hole*) buca *f*; (*coal mine*) miniera *f*

pitch[1] [pɪtʃ] *n* MUS intonazione *f*

pitch[2] [pɪtʃ] *v/t tent* piantare; *ball* lanciare

pitcher[1] ['pɪtʃə(r)] *in baseball* lanciatore *m*

pitcher[2] ['pɪtʃə(r)] *container* brocca *f*

pitfall ['pɪtfɔːl] tranello *m*

pitiful ['pɪtɪful] *sight* pietoso; *excuse, attempt* penoso; **pitiless** spietato

pittance ['pɪtns] miseria *f*

pity ['pɪtɪ] **1** *n* pietà *f*; *it's a ~ that* è un peccato che; *what a ~!* che peccato!; *take ~ on* avere pietà di **2** *v/t person* avere pietà di

pizza ['piːtsə] pizza *f*

placard ['plækɑːd] cartello *m*

place [pleɪs] **1** *n* posto *m*; *flat, house* casa *f*; *at my / his ~* a casa mia / sua; *in ~ of* invece di; *feel out of ~* sentirsi fuori posto; *take ~* aver luogo; *in the first ~* (*firstly*) in primo luogo **2** *v/t* (*put*) piazzare; *I can't quite ~ you* non mi ricordo dove ci siamo conosciuti; *~ an order* fare un'ordinazione

placid ['plæsɪd] placido

plagiarism ['pleɪdʒərɪzm] plagio *m*; **plagiarize** plagiare

plague [pleɪg] **1** *n* peste *f* **2** *v/t* (*bother*) tormentare

plain[1] [pleɪn] *n* pianura *f*

plain[2] [pleɪn] **1** *adj* (*clear, obvious*) chiaro; *not fancy* semplice; *not pretty* scialbo; *not patterned* in tinta unita; (*blunt*) franco; **~ chocolate** cioccolato *m* fondente **2** *adv* semplicemente; **plainly** (*clearly*) chiaramente; (*bluntly*) francamente; (*simply*) semplicemente; **plain-spoken** franco

plaintive ['pleɪntɪv] lamentoso

plait [plæt] treccia *f*

plan [plæn] **1** *n* (*project, intention*) piano *m*; (*drawing*) progetto *m* **2** *v/t* (*prepare*) organizzare; (*design*) progettare; *~ to do* avere in programma di **3** *v/i* pianificare

plane[1] [pleɪn] (*aeroplane*) aereo *m*

plane² [pleɪn] *tool* pialla f

planet ['plænɪt] pianeta m

plank [plæŋk] *of wood* asse f; *fig: of policy* punto m

planning ['plænɪŋ] pianificazione f

plant¹ [plɑ:nt] **1** *n* pianta f **2** *v/t* piantare

plant² [plɑ:nt] *(factory)* stabilimento m; *(equipment)* impianto m

plantation [plæn'teɪʃn] piantagione f

plaque [plæk] *on wall, teeth* placca f

plaster ['plɑ:stə(r)] **1** *n on wall* intonaco m; *sticking* cerotto m **2** *v/t wall* intonacare

plastic ['plæstɪk] **1** *n* plastica f **2** *adj* di plastica; **plastic money** carte fpl di credito; **plastic surgeon** chirurgo m plastico; **plastic surgery** chirurgia f plastica

plate [pleɪt] *for food* piatto m; *sheet of metal* lastra f

plateau ['plætəʊ] altopiano m

platform ['plætfɔ:m] *(stage)* palco m; *of railway station* binario m; *fig: political* piattaforma f

platinum ['plætɪnəm] **1** *n* platino m **2** *adj* di platino

platonic [plə'tɒnɪk] platonico

platoon [plə'tu:n] *of soldiers* plotone m

plausible ['plɔ:zəbl] plausibile

of children, SP giocare; *of musician* suonare **3** *v/t MUS* suonare; *game* giocare a; *opponent* giocare contro; *(perform: Macbeth etc)* rappresentare; *particular role* interpretare; **~ a joke on** fare uno scherzo a

◆ **play around** F *(be unfaithful)*: **his wife's been playing around** sua moglie lo ha tradito

◆ **play down** minimizzare

◆ **play up** *of machine* dare noie; *of child* fare i capricci; *of tooth, bad back etc* fare male

player ['pleɪə(r)] SP giocatore m, -trice f; *musician* musicista m/f; *actor* attore m, -trice f; **playful** *punch, mood* scherzoso; *puppy* giocherellone; **playground** *in school* cortile m per la ricreazione; *in park* parco m giochi; **playing card** carta f da gioco; **playwright** commediografo m, -a f

plaza ['plɑ:zə] *for shopping* centro m commerciale

plc [pi:el'si:] (= **public limited company**) società f inv a responsabilità limitata quotata in borsa

plea [pli:] appello m

plead [pli:d]: **~ guilty / not guilty** dichiararsi colpevole / innocente; **~ with** supplicare

pleasant ['pleznt] piacevole

please [pli:z] **1** *adv* per favore; **more tea? – yes,** ~ ancora tè? – sì, grazie; ~ **do** fai pure, prego **2** *v/t* far piacere a; ~ **yourself** fai come ti pare; **pleased** contento; ~ **to meet you** piacere!; **pleasing** piacevole; **pleasure** (*happiness, satisfaction*) contentezza *f*; (*as opposed to work*) piacere *m*; (*delight*) gioia *f*; **it's a** ~ (*you're welcome*) è un piacere; **with** ~ con vero piacere

pleat [pli:t] *in skirt* piega *f*

pledge [pledʒ] **1** *n* (*promise*) promessa *f* **2** *v/t* (*promise*) promettere

plentiful ['plentifol] abbondante; **plenty** abbondanza *f*; ~ **of** molto; **that's** ~ basta così; **there's** ~ **for everyone** ce n'è per tutti

pliable ['plaɪəbl] flessibile

pliers ['plaɪəz] pinze *fpl*

plight [plaɪt] situazione *f* critica

plod [plɒd] *walk* trascinarsi

plook [plu:k] brufolo *m*

plot[1] [plɒt] *n land* appezzamento *m*

plot[2] [plɒt] **1** *n* (*conspiracy*) complotto *m*; *of novel* trama *f* **2** *v/t & v/i* complottare

plotter ['plɒtə(r)] cospiratore *m*, -trice *f*; COMPUT plotter *m inv*

plough, *Am* **plow** [plaʊ] **1** *n* aratro *m* **2** *v/t & v/i* arare

◆ **plough back** *profits* reinvestire

pluck [plʌk] *eyebrows* pinzare; *chicken* spennare

plug [plʌg] **1** *n for sink, bath* tappo *m*; *electrical* spina *f*; (*spark* ~) candela *f*; *for new book etc* pubblicità *f* **2** *v/t hole* tappare; *new book etc* fare pubblicità a

◆ **plug in** attaccare (alla presa)

plumage ['plu:mɪdʒ] piumaggio *m*

plumber ['plʌmə(r)] idraulico *m*; **plumbing** *pipes* impianto *m* idraulico

plummet ['plʌmɪt] *of aeroplane* precipitare; *of share prices* crollare

plump [plʌmp] *person, chicken* in carne; *hands, feet, face* paffuto

plunge [plʌndʒ] **1** *n* caduta *f*; *in prices* crollo *m*; **take the** ~ fare il gran passo **2** *v/i* precipitare; *of prices* crollare **3** *v/t knife* conficcare; **plunging** *neckline* profondo

plural ['plʊərəl] plurale *m*

plus [plʌs] **1** *prep* più **2** *adj*: **£500** ~ oltre 500 sterline **3** *n symbol* più *m inv*; (*advantage*) vantaggio *m* **4** *conj* (*moreover, and then*) per di più

plush [plʌʃ] di lusso

plywood ['plaɪwʊd] compensato *m*

PM [pi:'em] (= *Prime Minister*) primo ministro *m*

p.m. [pi:'em] (= *post meridi-*

em): **at 2 ~** alle 2 del pomeriggio; **at 10.30 ~** alle 10.30 di sera

pneumonia [nju:'məʊnɪə] polmonite f

poach[1] [pəʊtʃ] *cook* bollire; *egg* fare in camicia

poach[2] [pəʊtʃ] *game* cacciare di frodo; *fish* pescare di frodo

poached egg [pəʊtʃ'eg] uovo m in camicia

P.O. Box [pi:'əʊbɒks] casella f postale

pocket ['pɒkɪt] **1** n tasca f **2** adj (*miniature*) in miniatura **3** v/t intascare; **pocket book** Am (*wallet*) portafoglio m; (*purse*) borsetta f; **pocket calculator** calcolatrice f tascabile

podium ['pəʊdɪəm] podio m

poem ['pəʊɪm] poesia f; **poet** poeta m, -essa f; **poetic** poetico; **poetic justice** giustizia f divina; **poetry** poesia f

poignant ['pɔɪnjənt] commovente

point [pɔɪnt] **1** n *of pencil, knife* punta f; *in competition* punto m; (*purpose*) senso m; (*moment*) punto m; *in argument, discussion* punto m; *in decimals* virgola f; **that's beside the ~** non c'entra; **be on the ~ of** stare giusto per; **get to the ~** venire al dunque; **what's the ~?** a questo, in effetti, è vero; **the ~ is ...** il fatto è che ...; **there's**

no ~ in waiting non ha senso aspettare **2** v/i indicare **3** v/t *gun* puntare (**at** contro)

♦ **point out** *sights, advantages* indicare

♦ **point to** *with finger* additare; (*fig: indicate*) far presupporre

pointed ['pɔɪntɪd] *remark* significativo; **pointer** *for teacher* bacchetta f; (*hint*) consiglio m; (*sign, indication*) indizio m; **pointless** inutile; **point of view** punto m di vista

poise [pɔɪz] padronanza f di sé; **poised** *person* posato

poison ['pɔɪzn] **1** n veleno m **2** v/t avvelenare; **poisonous** velenoso

poke [pəʊk] **1** n colpetto m **2** v/t (*prod*) dare un colpetto a; (*stick*) ficcare

♦ **poke around** F curiosare

poker ['pəʊkə(r)] *card game* poker m

Poland ['pəʊlənd] Polonia f

polar ['pəʊlə(r)] polare

Pole [pəʊl] polacco m, -a f

pole[1] [pəʊl] *of wood, metal* paletto m

pole[2] [pəʊl] *of earth* polo m

'polevault salto m con l'asta

police [pə'li:s] polizia f; **police car** auto f della polizia; **policeman** poliziotto m; **police state** stato m di polizia; **police station** commissariato m di polizia; **policewoman** donna f poliziotto policy¹ ['pɒlɪsɪ] politica f

policy² ['pɒlɪsɪ] (insurance ~) polizza f

polio ['pəʊlɪəʊ] polio f

Polish ['pəʊlɪʃ] **1** adj polacco **2** n language polacco m

polish ['pɒlɪʃ] **1** n product lucido m; (nail ~) smalto m **2** v/t lucidare; speech rifinire; polished performance impeccabile

polite [pə'laɪt] cortese; politely cortesemente; politeness cortesia f

political [pə'lɪtɪkl] politico; politically correct politicamente corretto; politician uomo m politico, donna f politica; politics politica f

poll [pəʊl] **1** n (survey) sondaggio m; go to the ~s (vote) andare alle urne **2** v/t people fare un sondaggio tra; votes guadagnare

pollen ['pɒlən] polline m

'polling station seggio m elettorale

pollster ['pəʊlstə(r)] esperto m, -a f di sondaggi

pollutant [pə'luːtənt] sostanza f inquinante; pollute inquinare; pollution inquinamento m

'polo shirt polo f inv

polyester [pɒlɪ'estə(r)] poliestere m

polystyrene [pɒlɪ'staɪriːn] polistirolo m

polyunsaturated [pɒlɪʌn'sætʃəreɪtɪd] polinsa-

turo

pompous ['pɒmpəs] pomposo

pond [pɒnd] stagno m

pontiff ['pɒntɪf] pontefice m

pony ['pəʊnɪ] pony m inv; ponytail coda f (di cavallo)

poo(h) [puː] F (faeces) popò f inv

poodle ['puːdl] barboncino m

pool¹ [puːl] n (swimming ~) piscina f; of water, blood pozza f

pool² [puːl] n game biliardo m

pool³ [puːl] **1** n common fund cassa f comune **2** v/t resources mettere insieme

'pool hall sala f da biliardo; pool table tavolo m da biliardo

poop [puːp] Am F (faeces) popò f inv

pooped [puːpt] F stanco morto

poor [pʊə(r)] **1** adj povero; not good misero; be in ~ health essere in cattiva salute **2** n: the ~ i poveri; poorly **1** adv male **2** adj (unwell) indisposto

pop¹ [pɒp] **1** n noise schiocco m **2** v/i of balloon etc scoppiare **3** v/t cork stappare; balloon far scoppiare

pop² [pɒp] **1** n MUS pop m **2** adj pop inv

pop³ [pɒp] Am F papà m inv

◆ pop out F (go out for a short time) fare un salto fuori

◆ pop up F (appear suddenly)

saltare fuori

'popcorn popcorn *m*

pope [pəup] papa *m*

Popsicle® ['pɒpsɪkl] *Am* ghiacciolo *m*

popular ['pɒpjulə(r)] popolare; *belief, support* diffuso; **popularity** popolarità *f*

populate ['pɒpjuleɪt] popolare; **population** popolazione *f*

porch [pɔːtʃ] portico *m; Am: outside house* veranda *f*

◆ pore over studiare attentamente

pork [pɔːk] maiale *m*

porn [pɔːn] F porno *m* F; **pornographic** pornografico; **pornography** pornografia *f*

port¹ [pɔːt] *n (harbour, drink)* porto *m*

port² [pɔːt] *adj (left-hand)* babordo

portable ['pɔːtəbl] **1** *adj* portatile **2** *n* portatile *m*

porter ['pɔːtə(r)] portiere *m*

porthole ['pɔːthəul] NAUT oblò *m inv*

portion ['pɔːʃn] parte *f; of food* porzione *f*

portrait ['pɔːtreɪt] **1** *n* ritratto *m* **2** *adv print* verticale; **portray** *of artist* ritrarre; *of actor* interpretare; *of author* descrivere

Portugal ['pɔːtjugl] Portogallo *m;* **Portuguese 1** *adj* portoghese **2** *n person* portoghese *m/f; language* portoghese *m*

pose [pəuz] **1** *n (pretence)* posa *f* **2** *v/i for artist* posare; **~ as** farsi passare per **3** *v/t problem, threat* creare

posh [pɒʃ] F elegante; *pej* snob

position [pə'zɪʃn] **1** *n* posizione *f;* **what would you do in my ~?** cosa faresti al mio posto? **2** *v/t* sistemare, piazzare

positive ['pɒzɪtɪv] *positive:* **be ~** *(sure)* essere certo; **positively** *(downright)* decisamente; *(definitely)* assolutamente; *think* in modo positivo

possess [pə'zes] possedere; **possession** *(ownership)* possesso *m; thing owned* bene *m;* **~s** averi *mpl;* **possessive** *also* GRAM possessivo

possibility [pɒsə'bɪlətɪ] possibilità *f inv;* **possible** possibile; **the best ~ ...** la miglior ... possibile; **possibly** *(perhaps)* forse; **that can't ~ be right** non è possibile che sia giusto

post¹ [pəust] **1** *n of wood, metal* palo *m* **2** *v/t notice* affiggere; *profits* annunciare; **keep s.o. ~ed** tenere informato qu

post² [pəust] **1** *n (place of duty)* posto *m* **2** *v/t soldier, employee* assegnare; *guards* piazzare

post³ [pəust] **1** *n (mail)* posta *f* **2** *v/t letter* spedire (per posta); *(put in the mail)* imbucare

postage ['pəʊstɪdʒ] affranca-tura *f*; **postage stamp** *fml* francobollo *m*; **postal** postale; **postbox** buca *f* delle lettere; **postcard** cartolina *f*; **postcode** codice *m* di avviamento postale; **postdate** postdatare

poster ['pəʊstə(r)] manifesto *m*; *for decoration* poster *m inv*

postgraduate ['pəʊstgrædjuːt] **1** *n* studente *m* / studentessa *f* di un corso post-universitario **2** *adj* post-universitario

posthumous ['pɒstjʊməs] postumo

posting ['pəʊstɪŋ] (*assignment*) incarico *m*

'postman postino *m*; **postmark** timbro *m* postale

postmortem [pəʊst'mɔːtəm] autopsia *f*

'post office ufficio *m* postale

postpone [pəʊst'pəʊn] rinviare; **postponement** rinvio *m*

pot¹ [pɒt] *for cooking* pentola *f*; *for coffee* caffettiera *f*; *for tea* teiera *f*; *for plant* vaso *m*

pot² [pɒt] F (*marijuana*) erba *f* F

potato [pə'teɪtəʊ] patata *f*; **potato crisps**, *Am* **potato chips** patatine *fpl*

potent ['pəʊtənt] potente

potential [pə'tenʃl] **1** *adj* potenziale **2** *n* potenziale *m*;

potentially *adv* potenzialmente

pothole ['pɒthəʊl] *in road* buca *f*

potter ['pɒtə(r)] vasaio *m*, -a *f*; **pottery** ceramica *f*; *items* vasellame *m*; *place* laboratorio *m* di ceramica

potty ['pɒtɪ] *for baby* vasino *m*

pouch [paʊtʃ] (*bag*) borsa *f*

poultry ['pəʊltrɪ] *birds* volatili *mpl*; *meat* pollame *m*

pound¹ [paʊnd] *n weight* libbra *f*; FIN sterlina *f*

pound² [paʊnd] *n for strays* canile *m* municipale; *for cars* deposito *m* auto

pound³ [paʊnd] *v/i of heart* battere forte; **~ on** (*hammer on*) picchiare su

pour [pɔː(r)] **1** *v/t liquid* versare **2** *v/i*: **it's ~ing** (**with rain**) sta diluviando

◆ **pour out** *liquid* versare; *troubles* sfogarsi raccontando

pout [paʊt] fare il broncio

poverty ['pɒvətɪ] povertà *f*

powder ['paʊdə(r)] **1** *n* polvere *f*; *for face* cipria *f* **2** *v/t*: **~ one's face** mettersi la cipria

power ['paʊə(r)] **1** *n* (*strength*) forza *f*; *of engine* potenza *f*; (*authority*) potere *m*; (*energy*) energia *f*; (*electricity*) elettricità *f*; **in ~** POL al potere **2** *v/t*: **~ed by atomic energy** a propulsione atomica; **power cut** interruzione *f* di corrente; **power failure** guasto *m* alla linea elettrica; **powerful** potente; **powerless** impotente; *be ~ to ...* non poter far niente per ...; **power line** linea f elettrica; **power outage** *Am* interruzione f di corrente; **power station** centrale f elettrica; **power steering** servosterzo m

PR [piː'ɑː(r)] (= *public relations*) relazioni fpl pubbliche

practical ['præktɪkl] pratico; **practically** *behave, think* in modo pratico; (*almost*) praticamente

practice ['præktɪs] **1** n pratica f; (*training*) esercizio m; (*rehearsal*) prove fpl; (*custom*) consuetudine f; *in ~* (*in reality*) in pratica; *be out of ~* essere fuori allenamento **2** v/t & v/i Am → **practise**

practise ['præktɪs] **1** v/t esercitarsi in; *law, medicine* esercitare **2** v/i esercitarsi

pragmatic [præg'mætɪk] pragmatico

prairie ['preərɪ] prateria f

praise [preɪz] **1** n lode f **2** v/t lodare; **praiseworthy** lodevole

prawn [prɔːn] gamberetto m

pray [preɪ] pregare; **prayer** preghiera f

preach [priːtʃ] predicare; **preacher** predicatore m, -trice f

precarious [prɪ'keərɪəs] precario

precaution [prɪ'kɔːʃn] precauzione f; **precautionary** *measure* di precauzione

precede [prɪ'siːd] precedere; **precedent** precedente m; **preceding** precedente

precious ['preʃəs] prezioso

precise [prɪ'saɪs] preciso; **precisely** precisamente; **precision** precisione f

precocious [prɪ'kəʊʃəs] *child* precoce

preconceived [priːkən'siːvd] *idea* preconcetto

precondition [priːkən'dɪʃn] condizione f indispensabile

predator ['predətə(r)] *animal* predatore m, -trice f; **predatory** rapace

predecessor ['priːdɪsesə(r)] predecessore m

predicament [prɪ'dɪkəmənt] situazione f difficile

predict [prɪ'dɪkt] predire; **predictable** prevedibile; **prediction** predizione f

predominant [prɪ'dɒmɪnənt] predominante; **predominantly** prevalentemente

prefabricated [priː'fæbrɪkeɪtɪd] prefabbricato

preface ['prefɪs] prefazione f

prefer [prɪ'fɜː(r)] preferire (*to* a); **preferable** preferibile; **preferably** preferibilmente; **preference** preferenza f; **preferential** preferenziale

pregnancy ['pregnənsɪ] gravidanza f; **pregnant** incinta; *get ~* restare incinta prehistoric [pri:hɪsˈtɒrɪk] preistorico

prejudice [ˈpredʒʊdɪs] 1 n pregiudizio m 2 v/t person influenzare; chances pregiudicare; prejudiced pregiudicato

preliminary [prɪˈlɪmɪnərɪ] preliminare

premarital [pri:ˈmærɪtl] prematrimoniale

premature [ˈpremətjʊə(r)] prematuro

premeditated [pri:ˈmedɪteɪtɪd] premeditato

premier [ˈpremɪə(r)] (Prime Minister) premier m inv

première [ˈpremɪeə(r)] premiere f inv, prima f

premises [ˈpremɪsɪz] locali mpl

premium [ˈpri:mɪəm] in insurance premio m

prenatal [pri:ˈneɪtl] prenatale

preoccupied [prɪˈɒkjʊpaɪd] preoccupato

preparation [prepəˈreɪʃn] preparazione f; in ~ for in vista di; ~s preparativi mpl; prepare 1 v/t preparare; be ~d to do sth (willing) essere preparato a fare qc; be ~d for sth (be expecting) essere preparato per qc 2 v/i prepararsi

preposition [prepəˈzɪʃn] preposizione f

preposterous [prɪˈpɒstərəs] ridicolo

prerequisite [pri:ˈrekwɪzɪt] condizione f indispensabile

prescribe [prɪˈskraɪb] of doctor prescrivere; prescription MED ricetta f medica

presence [ˈprezns] presenza f; in the ~ of in presenza di

present¹ [ˈpreznt] 1 adj (current) attuale; be ~ essere presente 2 n: the ~ also GRAM il presente; at ~ al momento

present² [ˈpreznt] n (gift) regalo m

present³ [prɪˈzent] v/t award consegnare; bouquet offrire; programme presentare; ~ s.o. with sth, ~ sth to s.o. offrire qc a qu

presentation [preznˈteɪʃn] presentazione f; present-day di oggi; presenter presentatore m, -trice f; presently (at the moment) attualmente; (soon) tra breve

preservative [prɪˈzɜ:vətɪv] conservante m; preserve 1 n (domain) dominio m 2 v/t standards, peace etc mantenere; wood etc proteggere; food conservare

preside [prɪˈzaɪd] at meeting presiedere; presidency presidenza f; president presidente m; presidential presidenziale

press [pres] 1 n: the ~ la stampa 2 v/t button premere; (urge) far pressione su; (squeeze) stringere; clothes stirare; grapes, olives spremere 3 v/i: ~ for fare pressioni per ottenere; press conference conferenza *f* stampa; **pressing** urgente; **press-up** flessione *f* sulle braccia

pressure ['preʃə(r)] **1** *n* pressione *f* **2** *v/t* fare delle pressioni su

prestige [pre'sti:ʒ] prestigio *m*; **prestigious** prestigioso

presumably [prɪ'zju:məblɪ] presumibilmente; **presume** presumere; **presumption** *of innocence, guilt* presunzione *f*

presuppose [pri:sə'pəʊz] presupporre

pre-tax ['pri:tæks] al lordo d'imposta

pretence [prɪ'tens] finta *f*; **pretend 1** *v/t* fingere **2** *v/i* fare finta; **pretense** *Am* → **pretence**; **pretentious** pretenzioso

pretext ['pri:tekst] pretesto *m*

pretty ['prɪtɪ] **1** *adj* carino **2** *adv* (*quite*) piuttosto

prevail [prɪ'veɪl] (*triumph*) prevalere; **prevailing** prevalente

prevent [prɪ'vent] prevenire; **~ s.o.** (*from*) *doing sth* impedire a qu di fare qc; **prevention** prevenzione *f*; **preventive** preventivo

preview ['pri:vju:] **1** *n* of film, exhibition anteprima *f*

previous ['pri:vɪəs] precedente; **~ to** prima di; **previously** precedentemente

prey [preɪ] preda *f*

price [praɪs] **1** *n* prezzo *m* **2** *v/t* COM fissare il prezzo di; **priceless** di valore inestimabile; **price war** guerra *f* dei prezzi; **pricey** F caro

prick[1] [prɪk] **1** *n* pain puntura *f* **2** *v/t* (*jab*) pungere

prick[2] [prɪk] *n* V (*penis*) cazzo *m* V; *person* testa *f* di cazzo V

prickle ['prɪkl] *on plant* spina *f*; **prickly** *plant* spinoso; *beard* ispido; (*irritable*) permaloso

pride [praɪd] **1** *n* in person, achievement orgoglio *m*; (*self-respect*) amor *m* proprio **2** *v/t*: **~ o.s. on** vantarsi di

priest [pri:st] prete *m*

primarily [praɪ'meərɪlɪ] principalmente; **primary 1** *adj* principale **2** *n* Am POL (elezione *f*) primaria *f*; **primary school** scuola *f* elementare

prime 'minister primo ministro *m*

primitive ['prɪmɪtɪv] primitivo

prince [prɪns] principe *m*; **princess** principessa *f*

principal ['prɪnsəpl] **1** *adj* principale **2** *n* of school preside *m/f*; **principally** principalmente

principle ['prɪnsəpl] principio *m*; **on ~** per principio; **in ~** in linea di principio

print [prɪnt] **1** *n* in book etc caratteri *mpl*; *photograph* stampa *f*; *mark* impronta *f*; **out of ~** esaurito **2** *v/t* stampare; (*use block capitals*) scrivere in stampatello; **printer** tipografo *m*; **machine** stampante *f*; **printout** stampato *m*

prior ['praɪə(r)] **1** *adj* precedente **2** *prep*: **~ to** prima di

prioritize [praɪ'ɒrətaɪz] (*put in order of priority*) classificare in ordine d'importanza; (*give priority to*) dare precedenza a; **priority** priorità *f inv*; **have ~** avere la precedenza

prison ['prɪzn] prigione *f*; **prisoner** prigioniero *m*, -a *f*; **take s.o. ~** fare prigioniero qu; **prisoner of war** prigioniero *m* di guerra

privacy ['prɪvəsɪ] privacy *f*; **private 1** *adj* privato **2** *n* MIL soldato *m* semplice; **in ~** in privato; **privately** (*in private*) in privato; (*inwardly*) dentro di sé; **~ owned** privato; **private sector** settore *m* privato; **privatize** privatizzare

privilege ['prɪvɪlɪdʒ] privilegio *m*; (*honour*) onore *m*; **privileged** privilegiato; (*honoured*) onorato

prize [praɪz] **1** *n* premio *m* **2** *v/t* dare molto valore a; **prizewinner** vincitore *m*, -trice *f*; **prizewinning** vincente

pro[1] [prəʊ] *n*: **the ~s and cons** i pro e i contro

pro[2] [prəʊ] ☞ **professional**

pro[3] [prəʊ] *prep*: **be ~ ...** (*in favour of*) essere a favore di ...

probability [prɒbə'bɪlətɪ] probabilità *f inv*; **probable** probabile; **probably** probabilmente

probation [prə'beɪʃn] *in job* periodo *m* di prova; LAW libertà *f* vigilata; **on ~** in job in prova

probe [prəʊb] **1** *n* (*investigation*) indagine *f*; *scientific* sonda *f* **2** *v/t* esplorare; (*investigate*) investigare

problem ['prɒbləm] problema *m*; **no ~** non c'è problema

procedure [prə'siːdʒə(r)] procedura *f*

proceed [prə'siːd] *of people* proseguire; *of work etc* procedere; **proceedings** (*events*) avvenimenti *mpl*; **proceeds** ricavato *m*

process ['prəʊses] **1** *n* processo *m* **2** *v/t food, raw materials* trattare; *data* elaborare; *application etc* sbrigare; **~ed cheese** formaggio *m* fuso; **procession** processione *f*; **processor** processore *m*

prod [prɒd] **1** *n* colpetto *m* **2** *v/t* dare un colpetto a

prodigy ['prɒdɪdʒɪ]: (*infant*) **~** bambino *m*, -a *f* prodigio

produce[1] ['prɒdjuːs] *n* prodotti *mpl*

produce[2] [prə'djuːs] *v/t* produrre; (*bring about*) dare origine a; (*bring out*) tirar fuori; *play* mettere in scena

producer 510

producer [prə'dju:sə(r)] produttore *m*, -trice *f*; *of play* regista *m/f*; **product** prodotto *m*; (*result*) risultato *m*; **production** produzione *f*; *of play* regia *f*; **a new ~ of ...** una nuova messa in scena di ...; **productive** produttivo; **productivity** produttività *f*

profess [prə'fes] dichiarare; **profession** professione *f*; **professional 1** *adj* professionale; *advice, help* di un esperto; *piece of work* da professionista; **turn ~** passare al professionismo **2** *n* professionista *m/f*; **professionally** *play sport* a livello professionistico; (*well, skilfully*) in modo professionale

professor [prə'fesə(r)] professore *m* (universitario)

proficiency [prə'fɪʃnsɪ] competenza *f*; **proficient** competente

profile ['prəʊfaɪl] profilo *m*

profit ['prɒfɪt] **1** *n* profitto *m* **2** *v/i*: **~ from** trarre profitto da; **profitability** redditività *f*; **profitable** redditizio

profound [prə'faʊnd] profondo

prognosis [prɒg'nəʊsɪs] prognosi *f inv*

programme, *Am and Br* COMPUT **program** ['prəʊgræm] **1** *n* programma *m* **2** *v/t* programmare; **programmer** COMPUT programmatore *m*, -trice *f*

progress 1 ['prəʊgres] *n* progresso *m*; **in ~** in corso **2** [prə'gres] *v/i* (*advance in time*) procedere; (*move on*) avanzare; (*make progress*) fare progressi; **progressive** (*enlightened*) progressista; *which progresses* progressivo; **progressively** progressivamente

prohibit [prə'hɪbɪt] proibire; **prohibitive** *prices* proibitivo

project[1] ['prɒdʒekt] *n* (*plan*) piano *m*; (*undertaking*) progetto *m*; EDU ricerca *f*

project[2] [prə'dʒekt] **1** *v/t* fig*ures, sales* fare una proiezione di; *film* proiettare **2** *v/i* (*stick out*) sporgere in fuori

projection [prə'dʒekʃn] (*forecast*) proiezione *f*; **projector** *for slides* proiettore *m*

prologue, *Am* **prolog** ['prəʊlɒg] prologo *m*

prolong [prə'lɒŋ] prolungare

prominent ['prɒmɪnənt] *nose, chin* sporgente; (*significant*) prominente

promiscuity [prɒmɪ'skju:ətɪ] promiscuità *f*; **promiscuous** promiscuo

promise ['prɒmɪs] **1** *n* promessa *f* **2** *v/t & v/i* promettere; **promising** promettente

promote [prə'məʊt] promuovere; **promoter** *of event* promoter *m/f inv*; **promotion** promozione *f*; **get ~ in job** essere promosso

prompt [prɒmpt] **1** *adj* (*on time*) puntuale; (*speedy*) tempestivo **2** *adv*: **at two o'clock ~** alle due in punto **3** *v/t* (*cause*) causare; *actor* dare l'imbeccata a; **promptly** (*on time*) puntualmente; (*immediately*) prontamente

prone [prəʊn]: **be ~ to** essere soggetto a

pronoun ['prəʊnaʊn] pronome *m*

pronounce [prə'naʊns] pronunciare; (*declare*) dichiarare

pronto ['prɒntəʊ] F immediatamente

pronunciation [prənʌn-sɪ'eɪʃn] pronuncia *f*

proof [pru:f] prova *f*; *of book* bozza *f*

prop [prɒp] **1** *v/t* appoggiare **2** *n* THEA materiale *m* di scena

♦ **prop up** *also fig* sostenere

propaganda [prɒpə'gændə] propaganda *f*

propel [prə'pel] spingere; *of engine, fuel* azionare; **propeller** elica *f*

proper ['prɒpə(r)] (*real*) vero e proprio; (*correct*) giusto; (*fitting*) appropriato; **properly** (*correctly*) correttamente; (*fittingly*) in modo appropriato

property ['prɒpətɪ] proprietà *f inv*; **property developer** impresario *m* edile

proportion [prə'pɔːʃn] proporzione *f*; **proportional**

proporzionale; **proportional representation** POL rappresentanza *f* proporzionale

proposal [prə'pəʊzl] proposta *f*; **propose 1** *v/t* (*suggest*) proporre; **~ to do sth** (*plan*) proporsi di fare qc **2** *v/i* *make offer of marriage* fare una proposta di matrimonio; **proposition 1** *n* proposta *f* **2** *v/t woman* fare proposte sessuali a

proprietor [prə'praɪətə(r)] proprietario *m*, -a *f*

prose [prəʊz] prosa *f*

prosecute ['prɒsɪkjuːt] LAW intentare azione legale contro; *of lawyer* sostenere l'accusa contro; **prosecution** LAW azione *f* giudiziaria; (*lawyers*) accusa *f*

prospect ['prɒspekt] (*chance, likelihood*) probabilità *f inv*; *thought of something in the future* prospettiva *f*; **~s** prospettive *fpl*; **prospective** potenziale

prosper ['prɒspə(r)] prosperare; **prosperity** prosperità *f*; **prosperous** prospero

prostitute ['prɒstɪtjuːt] prostituta *f*; **male ~** prostituto *m*; **prostitution** prostituzione *f*

protect [prə'tekt] proteggere; **protection** protezione *f*; **protective** protettivo; **protector** protettore *m*, -trice *f*

protein ['prəʊtiːn] proteina *f*

protest **1** ['prəʊtest] *n* protesta *f* **2** [prə'test] *v/t* protestare **3** [prə'test] *v/i* protestare; POL manifestare, protestare

Protestant ['prɒtɪstənt] **1** *n* protestante *m/f* **2** *adj* protestante

protester [prə'testə(r)] dimostrante *m/f*, manifestante *m/f*

prototype ['prəʊtətaɪp] prototipo *m*

protrude [prə'truːd] sporgere; **protruding** sporgente

proud [praʊd] orgoglioso, fiero; **be ~ of** essere fiero di; **proudly** con orgoglio

prove [pruːv] dimostrare

proverb ['prɒvɜːb] proverbio *m*

provide [prə'vaɪd] *money, food* fornire; *opportunity* offrire; **~ s.o. with sth** fornire qu di qc; **~d that** *(on condition that)* a condizione that

province ['prɒvɪns] provincia *f*; **provincial** *also pej* provinciale

provision [prə'vɪʒn] *(supply)* fornitura *f*; *of law, contract* disposizione *f*; **provisional** provvisorio

provocation [prɒvə'keɪʃn] provocazione *f*; **provocative** provocatorio; *sexually* provocante; **provoke** *(cause)* causare; *(annoy)* provocare

prowl [praʊl] aggirarsi; **prowler** tipo *m* sospetto

proximity [prɒk'sɪmətɪ] prossimità *f*

proxy ['prɒksɪ] *(authority)* procura *f*; *person* procuratore *m*, -trice *f*, mandatario *m*, -a *f*

prudence ['pruːdns] prudenza *f*; **prudent** prudente

prudish ['pruːdɪʃ] che si scandalizza facilmente

pry [praɪ] essere indiscreto

PS ['piːes] (= **postscript**) P.S. (= post scriptum *m*)

pseudonym ['sjuːdənɪm] pseudonimo *m*

psychiatric [saɪkɪ'ætrɪk] psichiatrico; **psychiatrist** psichiatra *m/f*; **psychiatry** psichiatria *f*

psychoanalysis [saɪkəʊə'næləsɪs] psicanalisi *f*; **psychoanalyst** psicanalista *m/f*; **psychoanalyze** psicanalizzare

psychological [saɪkə'lɒdʒɪkl] psicologico; **psychologically** psicologicamente; **psychologist** psicologo *m*, -a *f*; **psychology** psicologia *f*

psychopath ['saɪkəpæθ] psicopatico *m*, -a *f*

psychosomatic [saɪkəʊsə'mætɪk] psicosomatico

pub [pʌb] *pub m inv*

pubic hair [pjuː'bɪk'heə(r)] peli *mpl* del pube

public ['pʌblɪk] **1** *adj* pubblico **2** *n:* **the ~** il pubblico; **in ~** in pubblico; **public transport** mezzi *mpl* pubblici

publication [pʌblɪ'keɪʃn]

pubblicazione *f*

public 'holiday giorno *m* festivo

publicity [pʌb'lɪsətɪ] pubblicità *f*; publicize make known far sapere in giro; COM reclamizzare

publicly ['pʌblɪklɪ] pubblicamente

'public school *Br* scuola *f* privata; *Am* scuola pubblica

publish ['pʌblɪʃ] pubblicare; publisher editore *m*; publishing editoria *f*; publishing company casa *f* editrice

pudding ['pudɪŋ] *dish* budino *m*; *part of meal* dolce *m*

puddle ['pʌdl] *n* pozzanghera *f*

puff [pʌf] 1 *n* of wind, smoke soffio *m* 2 *v/i* (pant) ansimare; puffy eyes, face gonfio

puke [pju:k] F vomitare

pull [pul] 1 *n* on rope tirata *f*; F (appeal) attrattiva *f*; F (influence) influenza *f* 2 *v/t* (drag) tirare; *tooth* togliere; ~ *a muscle* farsi uno strappo muscolare 3 *v/i* tirare

◆ pull ahead *in race, competition* portarsi in testa

◆ pull down (lower) tirar giù; (demolish) demolire

◆ pull in *of bus, train* arrivare

◆ pull out 1 *v/t* tirar fuori; *troops* (far) ritirare 2 *v/i* of agreement, competition, MIL ritirarsi; *of ship* partire

◆ pull over *of driver* accostarsi

◆ pull through *from an illness* farcela F

◆ pull up 1 *v/t* (raise) tirar su; *plant, weeds* strappare 2 *v/i* of car etc fermarsi

pulley ['pulɪ] puleggia *f*

pulsate [pʌl'seɪt] *of heart, blood* pulsare; *of rhythm* vibrare

pulse [pʌls] polso *m*

pulverize ['pʌlvəraɪz] polverizzare

pump [pʌmp] 1 *n* pompa *f* 2 *v/t* pompare

pumpkin ['pʌmpkɪn] zucca *f*

pun [pʌn] gioco *m* di parole

punch [pʌntʃ] 1 *n blow* pugno *m*; *implement* punzonatrice *f* 2 *v/t* with fist dare un pugno a; *hole* perforare; *ticket* forare

punctual ['pʌŋktjuəl] puntuale; punctuality puntualità *f*

punctuation ['pʌŋktjuˈeɪʃn] punteggiatura *f*

puncture ['pʌŋktʃə(r)] 1 *n* foratura *f* 2 *v/t* forare

punish ['pʌnɪʃ] punire; punishing *pace, schedule* estenuante; punishment punizione *f*

puny ['pju:nɪ] *person* gracile

pup [pʌp] cucciolo *m*

pupil¹ ['pju:pl] *of eye* pupilla *f*

pupil² ['pju:pl] (student) allievo *m*, -a *f*

puppet ['pʌpɪt] burattino *m*; *with strings* marionetta *f*

puppy ['pʌpɪ] cucciolo *m*

purchase[1] ['pɜːtʃəs] **1** *n* acquisto *m* **2** *v/t* acquistare

purchase[2] ['pɜːtʃəs] *n* (*grip*) presa *f*

purchaser ['pɜːtʃəsə(r)] acquirente *m/f*

pure [pjʊə(r)] puro; ~ **new wool** pura lana *f* vergine; *purely* puramente

purge [pɜːdʒ] **1** *n of political party* epurazione *f* **2** *v/t* epurare

purify ['pjʊərɪfaɪ] purificare

puritan ['pjʊərɪtən] puritano *m*, -a *f*

purity ['pjʊərɪtɪ] purezza *f*

purple ['pɜːpl] viola *inv*

purpose ['pɜːpəs] (*aim*, *object*) scopo *m*; **on** ~ di proposito; *purposely* di proposito

purr [pɜː(r)] *of cat* fare le fusa

purse [pɜːs] *for money* borsellino *m*; *Am handbag* borsetta *f*

pursue [pə'sjuː] *person* inseguire; *career* intraprendere; *course of action* proseguire; *pursuer* inseguitore *m*, -trice *f*; *pursuit* (*chase*) inseguimento *m*; *of happiness etc* ricerca *f*; *activity* occupazione *f*

push [pʊʃ] **1** *n* (*shove*) spinta *f* **2** *v/t* (*shove*) spingere; *button* premere; (*pressurize*) fare pressioni su; F *drugs* spacciare; **be ~ed for** F essere a corto di **3** *v/i* spingere

◆ **push on** (*continue*) continuare

'pushchair passeggino *m*; **pusher** F *of drugs* spacciatore *m*, -trice *f*; **push-up** flessione *f* sulle braccia; **pushy** F troppo intraprendente

puss, pussy (*cat*) [pʊs, 'pʊsɪ (kæt)] F micio *m*, -a *f*

put [pʊt] mettere; *question* porre; ~ **the cost at** stimare il costo intorno a

◆ **put across** *ideas etc* trasmettere

◆ **put aside** mettere da parte

◆ **put away** *in cupboard etc* mettere via; *in institution* rinchiudere; (*consume*) far fuori; *money* mettere da parte; *Am animal* abbattere

◆ **put back** (*replace*) rimettere a posto

◆ **put down** mettere giù; *deposit* versare; *rebellion* reprimere; *animal* abbattere; (*belittle*) sminuire; *in writing* scrivere; **put X down to Y** (*attribute*) attribuire X a Y

◆ **put forward** *idea etc* avanzare

◆ **put in** inserire; *overtime* fare; *time*, *effort* dedicare; *request*, *claim* presentare

◆ **put off** *light*, *TV* spegnere; (*postpone*) rimandare; (*deter*) scoraggiare; (*repel*) disgustare

◆ **put on** *light*, *TV* accendere; *music* mettere su; *jacket*, *shoes*, *glasses* mettersi; *make-up* mettere; (*perform*) mettere in scena; (*assume*) affettare; *she's just putting it on* sta solo fingendo

◆ **put out** *hand* allungare; *fire light* spegnere

◆ **put together** (*assemble*) montare; (*organize*) organizzare

◆ **put up** *hand* alzare; *person* ospitare; (*erect*) costruire; *prices* aumentare; *poster* affiggere; *money* fornire; *put up for sale* mettere in vendita

◆ **put up with** sopportare
putty ['pʌtɪ] mastice *m*
puzzle ['pʌzl] **1** *n* (*mystery*) mistero *m*; *game* rebus *m inv*; *jigsaw* puzzle *m inv* **2** *v/t* lasciar perplesso; *puzzling* inspiegabile
PVC [piːviː'siː] (= *polyvinyl chloride*) PVC *m* (= polivinilcloruro *m*)
pyjamas [pə'dʒɑːməz] pigiama *m*
pylon ['paɪlən] pilone *m*

Q

quack [kwæk] *of duck* fare qua qua
quadrangle ['kwɒdræŋgl] *figure* quadrilatero *m*; *courtyard* cortile *m*
quadruped ['kwɒdruped] quadrupede *m*
quail [kweɪl] perdersi d'animo
quaint [kweɪnt] *pretty* pittoresco; *eccentric*: *ideas* etc curioso
quake [kweɪk] **1** *n* (*earthquake*) terremoto *m* **2** *v/i also fig* tremare
qualification [kwɒlɪfɪ'keɪʃn] *from university* etc titolo *m* di studio; *qualified doctor, engineer* etc abilitato; (*restricted*) con riserva; **qualify** **1** *v/t of degree, course* etc abilitare; *remark* etc precisare **2** *v/i* (*get certificate* etc) ottene-

re la qualifica (*as* di); *in competition* qualificarsi
quality ['kwɒlətɪ] qualità *f inv*; **quality control** controllo *m* (di) qualità; **quality time** tempo *m* di qualità
qualm [kwɑːm]: **have no ∼s about** ... non aver scrupoli a ...
quandary ['kwɒndərɪ] dilemma *m*; **be in a ∼** avere un dilemma
quantify ['kwɒntɪfaɪ] quantificare
quantity ['kwɒntətɪ] quantità *f inv*
quarantine ['kwɒrəntiːn] quarantena *f*
quarrel ['kwɒrəl] **1** *n* litigio *m* **2** *v/i* litigare
quarry[1] ['kwɒrɪ] *in hunt* preda *f*
quarry[2] ['kwɒrɪ] *for mining*

quart 516

cava f

quart [kwɔːt] quarto m di gallone (Br 1,136 l, Am 0,946 l)

quarter ['kwɔːtə(r)] quarto m; part of town quartiere m; **a ~ of an hour** un quarto d'ora; (**a**) **~ to 5** le cinque meno un quarto; (**a**) **~ past 5** le cinque e un quarto; **quarter-final** partita f dei quarti mpl di finale; **quarter-finalist** concorrente m/f dei quarti di finale; **quarterly 1** adj trimestrale **2** adv trimestralmente; **quarters** MIL quartieri mpl; **quartet** MUS quartetto m

quartz [kwɔːts] quarzo m

quash [kwɒʃ] rebellion reprimere; court decision annullare

quaver ['kweɪvə(r)] **1** n in voice tremolio m; MUS croma f **2** v/i voice tremolare

quay [kiː] banchina f

queasy ['kwiːzɪ] nauseato

queen [kwiːn] regina f

queer [kwɪə(r)] (peculiar) strano

quell [kwel] soffocare

quench [kwentʃ] also fig spegnere

query ['kwɪərɪ] **1** n interrogativo m **2** v/t express doubt about contestare; check controllare

quest [kwest] ricerca f

question ['kwestʃn] **1** n domanda f; matter questione f; **it's a ~ of money** è questione di soldi; **that's out of the ~** è fuori discussione **2** v/t person interrogare; (doubt) dubitare di; **questionable** discutibile; (dubious) dubbio; **questioning 1** adj look, tone interrogativo **2** n interrogatorio m; **question mark** punto m interrogativo; **questionnaire** questionario m

queue [kjuː] **1** n coda f, fila f **2** v/i fare la fila or la coda

quibble ['kwɪbl] cavillare

quick [kwɪk] person svelto; reply, change veloce; **be ~!** fai presto!, fai in fretta!; **let's have a ~ drink** beviamo qualcosina?; **quickly** rapidamente, in fretta; **quickwitted** sveglio

quid [kwɪd] F sterlina f; **50 ~** 50 sterline

quiet ['kwaɪət] voice, music basso; engine silenzioso; street, life, town tranquillo; **keep ~ about sth** tenere segreto qc; **~!** silenzio!; **quietly** not loudly silenziosamente; (without fuss) semplicemente; (peacefully) tranquillamente; **quietness** of night, street tranquillità f, calma f; of voice dolcezza f

quilt [kwɪlt] on bed piumino m

quinine ['kwɪniːn] chinino m

quip [kwɪp] **1** n battuta f (di spirito) **2** v/i scherzare

quirk [kwɜːk] bizzarria f; **quirky** bizzarro

quit [kwɪt] **1** *v/t job* mollare F **2** *v/i* (*leave job*) licenziarsi; COMPUT uscire

quite [kwaɪt] (*fairly*) abbastanza; (*completely*) completamente; *is that right? – not ~* giusto? – non esattamente; *~!* esatto!; *~ a lot drink, change* parecchio; *~ a lot better* molto meglio; *~ a few* un bel po'; *it was ~ a surprise* è stata una bella sorpresa

quiver ['kwɪvə(r)] tremare

quiz [kwɪz] **1** *n* quiz *m inv* **2** *v/t* interrogare

quota ['kwəʊtə] quota *f*

quotation [kwəʊ'teɪʃn] *from author* citazione *f*; *price* preventivo *m*; **quotation marks** virgolette *fpl*; **quote 1** *n from author* citazione *f*; *price* preventivo *m*; (*quotation mark*) virgoletta *f*; *in ~s* tra virgolette **2** *v/t text* citare; *price* stimare

R

rabbit ['ræbɪt] coniglio *m*

rabble ['ræbl] marmaglia *f*; **rabble-rouser** agitatore *m*, -trice *f*

rabies ['reɪbiːz] rabbia *f*, idrofobia *f*

raccoon [rə'kuːn] procione *m*

race[1] [reɪs] *n of people* razza *f*

race[2] [reɪs] **1** *n* SP gara *f*; *the ~s* (*horse races*) le corse **2** *v/i* (*run fast*) correre **3** *v/t*: *I'll ~ you* facciamo una gara

'racecourse ippodromo *m*; **racehorse** cavallo *m* da corsa; **race riot** scontri *mpl* razziali; **racetrack** pista *f*; *for horses* ippodromo *m*

racial ['reɪʃl] razziale

racing ['reɪsɪŋ] corse *fpl*; **racing car** auto *f inv* da corsa; **racing driver** pilota *m* automobilistico

racism ['reɪsɪzm] razzismo *m*;

racist **1** *n* razzista *m/f* **2** *adj* razzista

rack [ræk] **1** *n for parking bikes* rastrelliera *f*; *for bags on train* portabagagli *m inv*; *for CDs* porta-CD *m inv* **2** *v/t*: *~ one's brains* scervellarsi

racket[1] ['rækɪt] SP racchetta *f*

racket[2] ['rækɪt] (*noise*) baccano *m*; *criminal activity* racket *m inv*

radar ['reɪdɑː(r)] radar *m inv*

radiance ['reɪdɪəns] splendore *m*; **radiant** *smile* splendente; *appearance* raggiante; **radiate** *of heat, light* diffondersi; *of heat, light* diffondersi; **radiation** PHYS radiazione *f*; **radiator** *in room* termosifone *m*; *in car* radiatore *m*

radical ['rædɪkl] **1** *adj* radicale **2** *n* radicale *m/f*; **radicalism**

POL radicalismo *m*; radically radicalmente
radio ['reɪdɪəʊ] radio *f inv*; **on
the** ~ alla radio; radioactive
radioattivo; radioactivity
radioattività *f*; radio alarm
radiosveglia *f*; radiographer
radiologo *m*, -a *f*; radiogra-
phy radiografia *f*; radio station stazione *f* radiofonica,
radio *f inv*
radius ['reɪdɪəs] raggio *m*
raft [rɑːft] zattera *f*
rafter ['rɑːftə(r)] travicello *f*, trave
cio *m*
rag [ræg] *for cleaning etc* straccio *m*
rage [reɪdʒ] **1** *n* rabbia *f*, collera *f*; **be all the** ~ essere di
moda **2** *v/i of person* infierire; *of storm* infuriare
ragged ['rægɪd] stracciato
raid [reɪd] **1** *n* raid *m inv* **2** *v/t
of police, robbers* fare un
raid in; *fridge, orchard* fare razzia
in; raider *on bank etc* rapinatore *m*, -trice *f*
rail [reɪl] *on track* rotaia *f*;
(*hand-*) corrimano *m*; (*barrier*) parapetto *m*; **towel** ~
portasciugamano *m inv*; **by**
~ in treno; railings *around
park etc* inferriata *f*; railroad
Am ferrovia *f*; railway ferrovia *f*; railway station stazione *f* ferroviaria
rain [reɪn] **1** *n* pioggia *f*; **in the**
~ sotto la pioggia **2** *v/i* piovere; **it's ~ing** sta piovendo;
rainbow arcobaleno *m*;
raincheck: **can I take a** ~

on that? *Am* F posso riser-
varmi di farlo in seguito?;
raincoat impermeabile *m*;
raindrop goccia *f* di pioggia;
rainfall piovosità *f*; rain forest foresta *f* pluviale; rain-
proof *fabric* impermeabile;
rainstorm temporale *m*;
rainy *day* di pioggia; *weather*
piovoso; **it's** ~ piove molto
raise [reɪz] **1** *n in salary* aumento *m* **2** *v/t shelf, question*
sollevare; *offer* aumentare;
children allevare; *money* raccogliere
raisin ['reɪzn] uva *f* passa
rake [reɪk] *for garden* rastrello
m
rally ['rælɪ] *meeting* raduno *m*;
MOT rally *m inv*; *in tennis*
scambio *m*
RAM [ræm] COMPUT (= **random access memory**)
RAM *f inv*
ram [ræm] **1** *n* montone *m* **2**
v/t ship, car sbattere contro
ramble ['ræmbl] **1** *n walk*
escursione *f* **2** *v/i walk* fare
passeggiate; *in speaking* divagare; *talk incoherently* va-
neggiare; rambling *speech*
sconnesso
ramp [ræmp] rampa *f*; *for rais-
ing vehicle* ponte *m* idraulico
rampant ['ræmpənt] *inflation*
dilagante
rampart ['ræmpɑːt] bastione
m
ramshackle ['ræmʃækl] sgan-
gherato

rationally

ranch [rɑ:ntʃ] ranch *m inv*;
rancher (*owner*) proprietario *m* di un ranch; **ranchhand** lavoratore *m*, -trice *f*
di un ranch

rancid ['rænsɪd] rancido

rancour, *Am* **rancor**
['ræŋkə(r)] rancore *m*

R&D [ɑ:rən'di:] (= *research
and development*) ricerca
f e sviluppo *m*

random ['rændəm] **1** *adj* casuale; **~ sample** campione
m casuale **2** *n*: **at ~** a caso

randy ['rændɪ] F arrapato P

range [reɪndʒ] **1** *n of products*
gamma *f*; *of missile, gun* gittata *f*; *of salary* scala *f*; *of
voice* estensione *f*; *of mountains* catena *f*; **at close ~** a distanza ravvicinata **2** *v/i*: **~
from X to Y** variare da X a
Y; **ranger** *Am* guardia *f* forestale

rank [ræŋk] **1** *n* MIL grado *m*;
in society rango *m*; **the ~s**
MIL la truppa **2** *v/t* classificare

♦ **rank among** classificarsi
tra

ransack ['rænsæk] saccheggiare

ransom ['rænsəm] riscatto *m*;
ransom money ((soldi *mpl*
del) riscatto *m*

rap [ræp] **1** *n at door etc* colpo
m; MUS rap *m* **2** *v/t table etc*
battere

rape[1] [reɪp] **1** *n* stupro *m* **2** *v/t*
violentare

rape[2] [reɪp] *n* BOT colza *f*

rapid ['ræpɪd] rapido; **rapidity**
rapidità *f*; **rapidly** rapidamente; **rapids** rapide *fpl*

rapist ['reɪpɪst] violentatore
m

rare [reə(r)] raro; *steak* al sangue; **rarely** raramente; **rarity**
rarità *f inv*

rascal ['rɑ:skl] birbante *m/f*

rash[1] [ræʃ] *n* MED orticaria *f*

rash[2] [ræʃ] *adj action* avventato

rashly ['ræʃlɪ] avventatamente

raspberry ['rɑ:zbərɪ] lampone *m*

rat [ræt] ratto *m*

rate [reɪt] *of exchange* tasso *m*;
of pay, pricing tariffa *f*;
(speed) ritmo *m*; **at this ~**
*(at this speed, carrying on like
this)*di questo passo; **at any ~**
in ogni modo

rather ['rɑ:ðə(r)] piuttosto; **I
would ~ stay here** preferirei
stare qui

ratification [rætɪfɪ'keɪʃn] ratifica *f*; **ratify** ratificare

ratings ['reɪtɪŋz] indice *m*
d'ascolto

ratio ['reɪʃɪəʊ] proporzione *f*

ration ['ræʃn] **1** *n* razione *f* **2**
v/t supplies razionare

rational ['ræʃənl] razionale;
rationality razionalità *f*; **rationalization** razionalizzazione *f*; **rationalize** razionalizzare; **rationally** razionalmente

rattle ['rætl] **1** n noise rumore m; toy sonaglio m **2** v/t scuotere **3** v/i far rumore; **rattlesnake** serpente m a sonagli

raucous ['rɔːkəs] sguaiato

rave [reɪv] **1** v/i delirare; ~ **about sth** be very enthusiastic entusiasmarsi per qc **2** n party rave m inv

ravenous ['rævənəs] famelico

'**rave review** recensione f entusiastica

ravine [rə'viːn] burrone m

ravishing ['rævɪʃɪŋ] incantevole

raw [rɔː] meat, vegetable crudo; sugar, iron grezzo; **raw materials** materia f prima

ray [reɪ] raggio m

razor ['reɪzə(r)] rasoio m; **razor blade** lametta f da barba

re [riː] COM con riferimento a

reach [riːtʃ] **1** n: **within** ~ vicino (of a); **within arm's reach** a portata (of di); **out of** ~ non a portata (of di); **keep out of** ~ **of children** tenere lontano dalla portata dei bambini **2** v/t city arrivare a; decision, agreement raggiungere; **can you** ~ **it?** ci arrivi?

react [rɪ'ækt] reagire; **reaction** reazione f; **reactionary 1** n POL reazionario m, -a f **2** adj POL reazionario; **reactor** nuclear reattore m

read [riːd] leggere

◆ **read out** aloud leggere a voce alta

◆ **read up on** documentarsi su

readable ['riːdəbl] leggibile; **reader** person lettore m, -trice f

readily ['redɪlɪ] (willingly) volentieri; (easily) facilmente

reading ['riːdɪŋ] also from meter lettura f

readjust [riːə'dʒʌst] **1** v/t regolare **2** v/i to conditions riadattarsi

ready ['redɪ] pronto; **get** (o.s.) ~ prepararsi; **get sth** ~ preparare qc; **ready cash** contanti mpl; **ready-made** stew etc precotto; solution bell'e pronto; **ready-to-wear** confezionato

real [rɪːl] vero; **real estate** proprietà fpl immobiliari; **real estate agent** agente m/f immobiliare; **realism** realismo m; **realist** realista m/f; **realistic** realistico; **realistically** realisticamente; **reality** realtà f inv; **reality show** TV reality show m inv; **realize** rendersi conto di, realizzare; **I** ~ **now that ...** ora capisco che ...; really veramente; ~? davvero?; **not** ~ (not much) non proprio; **real-time** COMPUT in tempo reale; **real time** COMPUT tempo m reale

realtor ['rɪːltə(r)] Am agente m/f immobiliare; **realty** Am

reciprocal

proprietà *fpl* immobiliari

reappear [riːəˈpɪə(r)] riapparire; **reappearance** ricomparsa *f*

rear [rɪə(r)] **1** *n* of building retro *m*; of train parte *f* posteriore **2** *adj* posteriore

rearm [riːˈɑːm] **1** *v/t* riarmare **2** *v/i* riarmarsi

rearrange [riːəˈreɪndʒ] *furniture* spostare; *schedule, meetings* cambiare

rear-view 'mirror specchietto *m* retrovisore

reason [ˈriːzn] **1** *n* faculty ragione *f*; (*cause*) motivo *m*; **listen to ~** ascoltare ragione **2** *v/i*: **~ with s.o.** far ragionare con qu; **reasonable** *person, price* ragionevole; *weather, health* discreto; **a ~ number of people** un discreto numero di persone; **reasonably** *act, behave* ragionevolmente; (*quite*) abbastanza; **reasoning** ragionamento *m*

reassure [riːəˈʃʊə(r)] rassicurare; **reassuring** rassicurante

rebate [ˈriːbeɪt] *money back* rimborso *m*

rebel 1 [ˈrebl] *n* ribelle *m/f* **2** [rɪˈbel] *v/i* ribellarsi; **rebellion** ribellione *f*; **rebellious** ribelle; **rebelliousness** spirito *m* di ribellione

rebound [rɪˈbaʊnd] *of ball etc* rimbalzare

rebuild [ˈriːbɪld] ricostruire

recall [rɪˈkɔːl] richiamare; (*remember*) ricordare

recap [ˈriːkæp] F ricapitolare

recapture [riːˈkæptʃə(r)] *criminal* ricatturare; *town* riconquistare

recede [rɪˈsiːd] *of flood waters* abbassarsi; **receding** *forehead, chin* sfuggente; **have a ~ hairline** essere stempiato

receipt [rɪˈsiːt] *for purchase* ricevuta *f*, scontrino *m*; **~s** FIN introiti *mpl*; **receive** ricevere; **receiver** TELEC ricevitore *m*; *for radio* apparecchio *m* ricevente; **receivership**: **be in~** essere in amministrazione controllata

recent [ˈriːsnt] recente; **recently** recentemente

reception [rɪˈsepʃn] *reception* f inv; *formal party* ricevimento *m*; (*welcome*) accoglienza *f*; *on radio, mobile* ricezione *f*; **reception desk** banco *m* della reception; **receptionist** receptionist *m/f* inv; **receptive**: **be ~ to sth** essere ricettivo verso qc

recess [rɪˈses] *in wall etc* rientranza *f*; *of parliament* vacanza *f*; *Am* EDU intervallo *m*; **recession** *economic* recessione *f*

recharge [riːˈtʃɑːdʒ] *battery* ricaricare

recipe [ˈresəpɪ] ricetta *f*

recipient [rɪˈsɪpɪənt] destinatario *m*, -a *f*

reciprocal [rɪˈsɪprəkl] reciproco

recite [rɪ'saɪt] *poem* recitare; *details, facts* enumerare

reckless ['reklɪs] spericolato; **recklessly** in modo spericolato; *spend* avventatamente

reckon ['rekən] (*think, consider*) pensare

◆ **reckon on** contare su

reclaim [rɪ'kleɪm] *land* bonificare; *lost property* recuperare

recline [rɪ'klaɪn] sdraiarsi; **recliner** *chair* poltrona *f* reclinabile

recluse [rɪ'kluːs] eremita *m/f*

recognition [rekəg'nɪʃn] *of state, s.o.'s achievements* riconoscimento *m*; **recognizable** riconoscibile; **recognize** riconoscere

recoil [rɪ'kɔɪl] indietreggiare

recollect [rekə'lekt] rammentare; **recollection** ricordo *m*

recommend [rekə'mend] consigliare; **recommendation** consiglio *m*

recompense ['rekəmpens] ricompensa *f*; LAW risarcimento *m*

reconcile ['rekənsaɪl] *people, differences* riconciliare; *facts* conciliare; **~ o.s. to ...** rassegnarsi a ...; **reconciliation** *of people, differences* riconciliazione *f*; *of facts* conciliazione *f*

recondition [riːkən'dɪʃn] ricondizionare

reconnaissance [rɪ'kɒnɪsns] MIL ricognizione *f*

reconsider [riːkən'sɪdə(r)] **1** *v/t offer* riconsiderare **2** *v/i* ripensare

reconstruct [riːkən'strʌkt] *city, crime, life* ricostruire

record[1] ['rekɔːd] *n* MUS disco *m*; SP etc record *m inv*, primato *m*; *written document etc* documento *m*, nota *f*; *in database* record *m inv*; **~s** archivio *m*; **say sth off the ~** dire qc ufficiosamente; **have a criminal ~** avere precedenti penali

record[2] [rɪ'kɔːd] *v/t electronically* registrare; *in writing* annotare

'record-breaking da record;

recorder [rɪ'kɔːdə(r)] MUS flauto *m* dolce

'record holder primatista *m/f*

recording [rɪ'kɔːdɪŋ] registrazione *f*; **recording studio** sala *f* di registrazione

'record player giradischi *m inv*

re-count ['riːkaʊnt] **1** *n of votes* nuovo conteggio *m* **2** *v/t* (*count again*) ricontare

recount [rɪ'kaʊnt] (*tell*) raccontare

recoup [rɪ'kuːp] *financial losses* rifarsi di

recover [rɪ'kʌvə(r)] **1** *v/t stolen goods* recuperare **2** *v/i from illness* rimettersi; *of business* riprendersi; **~ery of stolen goods** recupero *m*; *from illness* guarigione *f*

recreation [rekrɪ'eɪʃn] ricreazione *f*; **recreational** *done* *for pleasure* ricreativo

recruit [rɪ'kruːt] **1** *n* MIL recluta *f*; *to company* neoassunto *m*, -a *f* **2** *v/t new staff* assumere; *members* arruolare; re**cruitment** assunzione *f*; MIL, POL reclutamento *m*

rectangle ['rektæŋgl] rettangolo *m*; **rectangular** rettangolare

rectify ['rektɪfaɪ] rettificare

recuperate [rɪ'kjuːpəreɪt] recuperare

recur [rɪ'kɜː(r)] *of error, event* ripetersi; *of symptoms* ripresentarsi; **recurrent** ricorrente

recyclable [riː'saɪkləbl] riciclabile; **recycle** riciclare; re**cycling** riciclo *m*

red [red] rosso; **in the ~** FIN in rosso; **Red Cross** Croce *f* Rossa

redecorate [riː'dekəreɪt] ritinteggiare; *change wallpaper* ritappezzare

redeem [rɪ'diːm] *debt* estinguere; *sinners* redimere; re**deeming feature** aspetto *m* positivo

redevelop [riːdɪ'veləp] *part of town* risanare

red-handed [red'hændɪd]: **catch s.o. ~** cogliere qu in flagrante; **redhead** rosso *m*, -a *f*; **red light** *at traffic lights* rosso *m*; **red light district** quartiere *m* a luci rosse; **red meat** carni *fpl* rosse; **redneck** *Am* F reazionario

m, -a *f*; **red tape** F burocrazia *f*

reduce [rɪ'djuːs] ridurre; re**duction** riduzione *f*

redundancy [rɪ'dʌndənsɪ] *at work* licenziamento *m*; re**dundant** (*unnecessary*) superfluo; **be made ~** *at work* essere licenziato

reef [riːf] *in sea* scogliera *f*; **reef knot** nodo *m* piano

reek [riːk] puzzare (**of** di)

reel [riːl] *of film* rullino *m*; *of thread* rocchetto *m*; *of tape* bobina *f*; *of fishing line* mulinello *m*

re-e-lect rieleggere; **re-election** rielezione *f*

re-entry *of spacecraft* rientro *m*

ref [ref] F arbitro *m*

♦ **refer to** [rɪ'fɜː(r)] riferirsi a; *dictionary etc* consultare

referee [refə'riː] SP arbitro *m*; *for job* referenza *f*; re**ference** (*allusion*) allusione *f*; *for job* referenza *f*; (**~ number**) (numero *m* di) riferimento *m*; **reference book** opera *f* di consultazione; **reference number** numero *m* di riferimento

referendum [refə'rendəm] referendum *m inv*

refill ['riːfɪl] riempire

refine [rɪ'faɪn] raffinare; re**finement** *to process, machine* miglioramento *m*; **refinery** raffineria *f*

reflect [rɪ'flekt] **1** *v/t light* riflettere; **be ~ed in** riflettersi in 2 *v/i* (*think*) riflettere; **reflection** *in water, glass etc* riflesso *m*; (*consideration*) riflessione *f*; **on ~** dopo aver ci riflettuto

reflex ['ri:fleks] *in body* riflesso *m*

reform [rɪ'fɔ:m] **1** *n* riforma *f* **2** *v/t* riformare; **reformer** riformatore *m*, -trice *f*

refrain [rɪ'freɪn] *fml:* **please ~ from smoking** si prega di non fumare

refresh [rɪ'freʃ] *person* ristorare; **feel ~ed** sentirsi ristorato; **refreshing** *drink* rinfrescante; *experience* piacevole; **refreshments** rinfreschi *mpl*

refrigerate [rɪ'frɪdʒəreɪt]: **keep ~d** conservare in frigo; **refrigerator** frigorifero *m*

refuel [riː'fjuːəl] **1** *v/t aeroplane* rifornire di carburante **2** *v/i* of *aeroplane, car* fare rifornimento

refuge ['refjuːdʒ] rifugio *m*; **take ~ from** *storm etc* ripararsi; **refugee** rifugiato *m*, -a *f*, profugo *m*, -a *f*

refund 1 ['riːfʌnd] *n* rimborso *m* **2** [rɪ'fʌnd] *v/t* rimborsare

refusal [rɪ'fjuːzl] rifiuto *m*

refuse¹ ['refjuːs] *n* rifiuti *mpl*

refuse² [rɪ'fjuːz] rifiutare; **~ to do sth** rifiutare di fare qc

regain [rɪ'geɪn] *control, lost territory, the lead* riconquistare

regard [rɪ'gɑːd] **1** *n:* **have great ~ for s.o.** avere molta stima di qu; **with ~ to** riguardo a; (**kind**) **~s** cordiali saluti; **with no ~ for** senza alcun riguardo per **2** *v/t:* **~ as** considerare come qc; **regarding** riguardo a; **regardless** lo stesso; **~ of** senza tener conto di

regime [reɪ'ʒiːm] (*government*) regime *m*

regiment ['redʒɪmənt] reggimento *m*

region ['riːdʒən] regione *f*; **in the ~ of** intorno a; **regional** regionale

register ['redʒɪstə(r)] **1** *n* registro *m* **2** *v/t birth, death: by individual* denunciare; *by authorities* registrare; *vehicle* iscrivere; *letter* assicurare; *emotion* mostrare **3** *v/i at university* iscriversi; **registered letter** (lettera *f*) assicurata *f*; **registration** *f*; **registration number** MOT numero *m* di targa; **registry office** ufficio *m* di stato civile

regret [rɪ'gret] **1** *v/t* rammaricarsi di; *missed opportunity* rimpiangere **2** *n* rammarico *m*; **regretful** di rammarico; **regrettable** deplorevole; **regrettably** purtroppo

regular ['regjʊlə(r)] **1** *adj* regolare; (*ordinary*) normale **2** *n at bar etc* cliente *m/f* abituale; **regularity** regolarità *f* *inv*; **regularly** regolarmente

regulate ['regjʊleɪt] regolare; **regulation** (*rule*) regolamento *m*; *control* controllo *m*

rehabilitate [riːhə'bɪlɪteɪt] *ex-criminal* riabilitare; *disabled person* rieducare

rehearsal [rɪ'hɜːsl] prova *f*; **rehearse** provare

reign [reɪn] **1** *n* regno *m* **2** *v/i* regnare

reimburse [riːɪm'bɜːs] rimborsare

reinforce [riːɪn'fɔːs] rinforzare; **reinforced concrete** cemento *m* armato; **reinforcements** MIL rinforzi *mpl*

reinstate [riːɪn'steɪt] reintegrare

reiterate [riː'ɪtəreɪt] *fml* ripetere

reject [rɪ'dʒekt] respingere; **rejection** rifiuto *m*

relapse ['riːlæps] MED ricaduta *f*

relate [rɪ'leɪt] **1** *v/t story* raccontare **2** *v/i*: **~ to ...** *be connected with* riferirsi a ...; **he doesn't ~ to people** non sa stabilire un rapporto con gli altri; **related** *by family* imparentato; *events, ideas etc* collegato; **relation** *in family* parente *m/f*; (*connection*) rapporto *m*; **business ~s** rapporti d'affari; **relationship** rapporto *m*; **relative 1** *n* parente *m/f* **2** *adj* relativo; **relatively** relativa-

mente

relax [rɪ'læks] **1** *v/i* rilassarsi; **~!** rilassati! **2** *v/t* rilassare; **relaxation** relax *m inv*; *of rules etc* rilassamento *m*; **relaxed** rilassato; **relaxing** rilassante

relay [riː'leɪ] **1** *v/t* trasmettere **2** *n*: **~** (**race**) (corsa *f* a) staffetta *f*

release [rɪ'liːs] **1** *n from prison* rilascio *m*; *of CD etc* uscita *f*; *of software* versione *f* **2** *v/t prisoner* rilasciare; *handbrake* togliere; *film, record* far uscire; *information* rendere noto

relegate ['relɪgeɪt] relegare; **be ~d** SP essere retrocesso; **relegation** SP retrocessione *f*

relent [rɪ'lent] cedere; **relentless** incessante, implacabile

relevance ['reləvəns] pertinenza *f*

relevant ['reləvənt] pertinente

reliability [rɪlaɪə'bɪlətɪ] affidabilità *f*; **reliable** affidabile; **reliance** dipendenza *f* (**on** da); **reliant**: **be ~ on** dipendere da

relic ['relɪk] reliquia *f*

relief [rɪ'liːf] sollievo *m*; *relieve pressure, pain* alleviare; (*take over from*) dare il cambio a; **be ~d** *at news etc* essere sollevato

religion [rɪ'lɪdʒən] religione *f*; **religious** religioso; **religiously** religiosamente

relinquish [rɪ'lɪŋkwɪʃ] rinunciare a

relish ['relɪʃ] **1** *n sauce* salsa *f*; *(enjoyment)* gusto *m* **2** *v/t idea, prospect* gradire

relive [riː'lɪv] rivivere

relocate [riːlə'keɪt] *of business, employee* trasferirsi

reluctance [rɪ'lʌktəns] riluttanza *f*; **reluctant** riluttante; **be ~ to do sth** essere restio a fare qc; **reluctantly** a malincuore

♦ **rely on** [rɪ'laɪ] contare su; **rely on s.o. to do sth** contare su qu perché faccia qc

remain [rɪ'meɪn] rimanere; **remainder** *also* MATH resto *m*; **remaining** restante; **remains** *of body* resti *mpl*

remake ['riːmeɪk] *of film* remake *m inv*

remand [rɪ'mɑːnd] **1** *v/t*: **~ s.o. in custody** ordinare la custodia cautelare di qu **2** *n*: **be on ~** essere in attesa di giudizio

remark [rɪ'mɑːk] **1** *n* commento *m* **2** *v/t* osservare; **remarkable** notevole; **remarkably** notevolmente

remarry [riː'mærɪ] risposarsi

remedy ['remədɪ] rimedio *m*

remember [rɪ'membə(r)] **1** *v/t* ricordare **2** *v/i* ricordare, ricordarsi

remind [rɪ'maɪnd]: **~ s.o. of s.o. / sth** ricordare qu / qc a qu; **~ s.o. to do sth** ricordare a qu di fare qc; **reminder** promemoria *m*; COM *for*

payment sollecito *m*

reminisce [remɪ'nɪs] rievocare il passato

remission [rɪ'mɪʃn] REL MED remissione *f*

remnant ['remnənt] resto *m*; *of fabric* scampolo *m*

remorse [rɪ'mɔːs] rimorso *m*; **remorseless** spietato

remote [rɪ'məʊt] *village* isolato; *possibility* remoto; *(aloof)* distante; *ancestor* lontano; **remote control** *for TV* telecomando *m*; **remotely** *related, connected* lontanamente; **just ~ possible** vagamente possibile

removable [rɪ'muːvəbl] staccabile; **removal** rimozione *f*; *from home* trasloco; **removal firm** ditta *f* di traslochi; **remove** togliere; MED asportare; *doubt, suspicion* eliminare

remuneration [rɪmjuːnə-'reɪʃn] rimunerazione *f*

Renaissance [rɪ'neɪsəns] Rinascimento *m*

rename [riː'neɪm] ribattezzare; *file* rinominare

rendez-vous ['rɒndeɪvuː] *(meeting)* incontro *m*

renew [rɪ'njuː] *contract* rinnovare; **feel ~ed** sentirsi rinato; **renewal** *of contract etc* rinnovo *m*

renounce [rɪ'naʊns] rinunciare a

renovate ['renəveɪt] ristrutturare; **renovation** ristrutturazione f

rent [rent] **1** n affitto m; **for ~** affittasi **2** v/t apartment affittare; car, equipment, noleggiare; (~ out) affittare; **rental** for apartment affitto m; for car noleggio m; for TV, phone canone m; **rental car** macchina f a noleggio; **rent-free** gratis

reopen [riːˈəʊpn] riaprire

reorganization [riːɔːɡənaɪˈzeɪʃn] riorganizzazione f; **reorganize** riorganizzare

repaint [riːˈpeɪnt] ridipingere

repair [rɪˈpeə(r)] **1** v/t riparare **2** n: **in a bad state of ~** in cattivo stato; **~s** riparazioni fpl; **repairman** tecnico m

repatriate [riːˈpætrɪeɪt] rimpatriare; **repatriation** rimpatrio m

repay [riːˈpeɪ] money restituire; person ripagare; **repayment** pagamento m

repeal [rɪˈpiːl] law abrogare

repeat [rɪˈpiːt] **1** v/t ripetere **2** n programme replica f; **repeatedly** ripetutamente

repel [rɪˈpel] invaders, attack respingere; (disgust) ripugnare; **repellent 1** n (insect ~) insettifugo m **2** adj ripugnante

repercussions [riːpəˈkʌʃnz] ripercussioni fpl

repertoire [ˈrepətwɑː(r)] repertorio m

repetition [repɪˈtɪʃn] ripetizione f; **repetitive** ripetitivo

replace [rɪˈpleɪs] (put back) mettere a posto; (take the place of) sostituire; **replacement** person sostituto m, -a f; act sostituzione f; **replacement part** pezzo m di ricambio

replay [ˈriːpleɪ] **1** n recording replay m inv; match spareggio m **2** v/t match rigiocare

replenish [rɪˈplenɪʃ] container riempire; supplies rifornire

replica [ˈreplɪkə] copia f

reply [rɪˈplaɪ] **1** n risposta f **2** v/t & v/i rispondere

report [rɪˈpɔːt] **1** n (account) resoconto m; by journalist servizio m; EDU pagella f **2** v/t facts fare un servizio su; to authorities denunciare **3** v/i of journalist fare un reportage; (present o.s.) presentarsi

◆ **report to** in business rendere conto a

reporter [rɪˈpɔːtə(r)] giornalista m/f

repossess [riːpəˈzes] COM riprendere possesso di

represent [reprɪˈzent] rappresentare; **representative 1** n rappresentante m/f **2** adj (typical) rappresentativo

repress [rɪˈpres] reprimere; **repression** POL repressione f; **repressive** POL repressivo

reprieve [rɪˈpriːv] **1** n LAW sospensione f della pena capitale; fig proroga f **2** v/t prisoner sospendere l'esecuzione di

reprimand ['reprimɑːnd] ammonire

reprint ['riːprɪnt] 1 *n* ristampa *f* 2 *v/t* ristampare

reprisal [rɪ'praɪzl] rappresaglia *f*; **take ~s** fare delle rappresaglie

reproach [rɪ'prəʊtʃ] 1 *n* rimprovero *m*; **be beyond ~** essere irreprensibile 2 *v/t* rimproverare; **reproachful** di rimprovero

reproduce [riːprə'djuːs] 1 *v/t* riprodurre 2 *v/i* riprodursi; **reproduction** riproduzione *f*; **reproductive** riproduttivo

reptile ['reptaɪl] rettile *m*

republic [rɪ'pʌblɪk] repubblica *f*; **republican** 1 *n* repubblicano *m*, -a *f* 2 *adj* repubblicano

repulsive [rɪ'pʌlsɪv] ripugnante

reputable ['repjʊtəbl] rispettabile; **reputation** reputazione *f*; **reputedly** a quanto si dice

request [rɪ'kwest] 1 *n* richiesta *f*; **on ~** su richiesta *f* 2 *v/t* richiedere

require [rɪ'kwaɪə(r)] (*need*) aver bisogno di; **it ~s great care** richiede molta cura; **as ~d by law** come prescritto dalla legge; **required** (*necessary*) necessario; **requirement** (*need*) esigenza *f*; (*condition*) requisito *m*

requisition [rekwɪ'zɪʃn] re-

quisire

reroute [riː'ruːt] *aeroplane etc* deviare

rerun ['riːrʌn] 1 *n of programme* replica *f* 2 *v/t programme* replicare

reschedule [riː'ʃedjuːl] stabilire di nuovo

rescue ['reskjuː] 1 *n* salvataggio *m*; **come to s.o.'s ~** andare in aiuto a qu 2 *v/t* salvare

research [rɪ'sɜːtʃ] ricerca *f*; **research and development** ricerca *f* e sviluppo *m*; **research assistant** assistente ricercatore *m*, -trice *f*; **researcher** ricercatore *m*, -trice *f*

resemblance [rɪ'zembləns] somiglianza *f*; **resemble** (as)somigliare a

resent [rɪ'zent] risentirsi per; **resentful** pieno di risentimento; **resentfully** con risentimento; **resentment** risentimento *m*

reservation [rezə'veɪʃn] *of room, table* prenotazione *f*; *mental, special area* riserva *f*; **I have a ~** *in hotel, restaurant* ho prenotato; **reserve** 1 *n* (*store*) riserva *f*; (*aloofness*) riserbo *m*; *SP* riserva *f*; **~s** *FIN* riserve *fpl*; **keep sth in ~** tenere qc di riserva 2 *v/t seat, table* prenotare; *judgment* riservarsi; **reserved** *person, manner* riservato; *table, seat* prenotato

reservoir ['rezəvwɑː(r)] *for water* bacino *m* idrico

residence ['rezɪdəns] *fml: house etc* residenza *f*; *(stay)* permanenza *f*; **residence permit** permesso *m* di residenza; **resident** residente *m/f*; **residential** residenziale

residue ['rezɪdjuː] residuo *m*

resign [rɪ'zaɪn] **1** *v/t position* dimettersi da; **o.s. to** rassegnarsi a **2** *v/i from job* dimettersi; **resignation** *from job* dimissioni *fpl*; *mental* rassegnazione *f*

resilient [rɪ'zɪlɪənt] *personality* che ha molte risorse; *material* resistente

resist [rɪ'zɪst] **1** *v/t* resistere a **2** *v/i* resistere; **resistance** resistenza *f*; **resistant** *material* resistente

resolute ['rezəluːt] risoluto; **resolution** *(decision)* risoluzione *f*; *made at New Year etc* proposito *m*; *(determination)* risolutezza *f*; *of problem* soluzione *f*; *of image* risoluzione *f*

resort [rɪ'zɔːt] *place* località *f inv*; *holiday* ~ luogo *m* di villeggiatura; **ski** ~ stazione *f* sciistica; **as a last** ~ come ultima risorsa

◆ **resort to** far ricorso a

◆ **resound with** [rɪ'zaʊnd] risuonare di

resounding [rɪ'zaʊndɪŋ] *success, victory* clamoroso

resource [rɪ'sɔːs] risorsa *f*; **financial** ~**s** mezzi *mpl* economici; **leave s.o. to his own** ~ lasciare qu in balia di se stesso; **resourceful** pieno di risorse

respect [rɪ'spekt] **1** *n* rispetto *m*; **with** ~ **to** riguardo a; **in this / that** ~ quanto a questo; **in many** ~**s** sotto molti aspetti; **pay one's last** ~**s to s.o.** rendere omaggio a qu **2** *v/t* rispettare; **respectability** rispettabilità *f*; **respectable** rispettabile; **respectful** rispettoso; **respective** rispettivo; **respectively** rispettivamente

respiration [respɪ'reɪʃn] respirazione *f*; **respirator** MED respiratore *m*

respite ['respaɪt] tregua *f*; **without** ~ senza tregua

respond [rɪ'spɒnd] rispondere; **response** risposta *f*

responsibility [rɪspɒnsɪ'bɪlətɪ] responsabilità *f inv*; **responsible** responsabile **(for** di); *job, position* di responsabilità

rest[1] [rest] **1** *n* riposo *m*; **set s.o.'s mind at** ~ tranquillizzare qu **2** *v/i* riposare; ~ **on** … *(be based on)* basarsi su …; *(lean against)* poggiare su … **3** *v/t (lean, balance)* poggiare

rest[2] [rest]: **the** ~ il resto *m*

restaurant ['restrɒnt] ristorante *m*

restful ['restfʊl] riposante;

rest home casa *f* di riposo;
restless irrequieto; *have a
~ night* passare una notte
agitata; **restlessly** nervosamente

restoration [restə'reɪʃn] restauro *m*; *restore building
etc* restaurare; *(bring back)*
restituire

restrain [rɪ'streɪn] *dog, troops*
frenare; *emotions* reprimere;
~ o.s. trattenersi; **restraint**
(self-control) autocontrollo
m

restrict [rɪ'strɪkt] limitare; **restricted** *view* limitato; **restriction** restrizione *f*

'rest room *Am* gabinetto *m*

result [rɪ'zʌlt] risultato *m*; *as
a ~ of this* in conseguenza a
ciò

♦ **result from** risultare da,
derivare da

♦ **result in** dare luogo a

résumé ['rezʊmeɪ] *Am* curriculum vitae *m inv*

resume [rɪ'zju:m] riprendere

resumption [rɪ'zʌmpʃn] ripresa *f*

resurface [ri:'sɜ:fɪs] **1** *v/t
roads* asfaltare **2** *v/i (reappear)* riaffiorare

Resurrection [rezə'rekʃn]
REL resurrezione *f*

retail ['ri:teɪl] **1** *adv* al dettaglio **2** *v/i: ~ at* essere in vendita a; **retailer** dettagliante
m/f; **retail price** prezzo *m*
al dettaglio

retain [rɪ'teɪn] conservare; retainer FIN onorario *m*

retaliate [rɪ'tælɪeɪt] vendicarsi; **retaliation** rappresaglia *f*

rethink [ri:'θɪŋk] riconsiderare

reticence ['retɪsns] riservatezza *f*; **reticent** riservato

retire [rɪ'taɪə(r)] *from work*
andare in pensione; **retired**
in pensione; **retirement** pensione *f*; *act* pensionamento
m; **retirement age** età *f inv*
pensionabile; **retiring** riservato

retort [rɪ'tɔ:t] **1** *n* replica *f* **2** *v/t*
replicare

retract [rɪ'trækt] *claws* ritrarre; *undercarriage* far rientrare; *statement* ritrattare

re-'train riqualificarsi

retreat [rɪ'tri:t] **1** *v/i* ritirarsi **2**
n MIL ritirata *f*; *place* rifugio
m

retrieve [rɪ'tri:v] recuperare;
retriever *dog* cane *m* da riporto

retroactive [retrəʊ'æktɪv] retroattivo; **retroactively** far retroattivamente

retrograde ['retrəgreɪd] retrogrado

retrospective [retrə'spekt ɪv]
retrospettiva *f*

return [rɪ'tɜːn] **1** *n* ritorno *m*;
(giving back) restituzione *f*;
COMPUT (tasto *m*) invio *m*;
in tennis risposta *f* al servizio; *(~ ticket)* andata e ritorno *m inv*; *by ~ (of post)* a
stretto giro di posta; *~s*

reward

(*profit*) rendimento *m*; **many happy ~s (of the day)** cento di questi giorni; **in ~ for** in cambio di **2** *v/t* (*give back*) restituire; (*put back*) rimettere; (*favour, invitation*) ricambiare **3** *v/i* (*go back, come back*) ritornare; *of symptoms, doubts etc* ricomparire; **return flight** volo *m* di ritorno; **return ticket** biglietto *m* (di) andata e ritorno

reunification [riːjuːnɪfɪ'keɪʃn] riunificazione *f*

reunion [riː'juːnɪən] riunione *f*; **reunite** riunire

reusable [riː'juːzəbl] riutilizzabile; **reuse** riutilizzare

♦ **rev up** [rev] *engine* far andare su di giri

revaluation [riːvæljuː'eɪʃn] rivalutazione *f*

reveal [rɪ'viːl] (*make visible*) mostrare; (*make known*) rivelare; **revealing** *remark* rivelatore; *dress* scollato; **revelation** rivelazione *f*

revenge [rɪ'vendʒ] vendetta *f*; **take one's ~** vendicarsi

revenue ['revənjuː] reddito *m*

reverberate [rɪ'vɜːbəreɪt] *of sound* rimbombare

revere [rɪ'vɪə(r)] riverire; **reverence** rispetto *m*; **Reverend** REL reverendo *m*; **reverent** riverente

reverse [rɪ'vɜːs] **1** *adj* *sequence* opposto; **in ~ order** in ordine inverso **2** *n* (*opposite*) contrario *m*; (*back*) ro-

vescio *m*; MOT retromarcia *f* **3** *v/t* *sequence* invertire; **~ the charges** TELEC telefonare a carico del destinatario **4** *v/i* MOT fare marcia indietro

review [rɪ'vjuː] **1** *n of book, film* recensione *f*; *of troops* rivista *f* *of situation etc* revisione *f* **2** *v/t* *book* recensire; *troops* passare in rivista; *situation etc* riesaminare; **reviewer** *of book, film* critico *m*, -a *f*

revise [rɪ'vaɪz] **1** *v/t* *opinion, text* rivedere; EDU ripassare **2** *v/i* EDU ripassare; **revision** *of opinion, text* revisione *f*; *for exam* ripasso *m*

revival [rɪ'vaɪvl] *of custom, style etc* revival *m inv*; *of patient* ripresa *f*; **revive 1** *v/t* *custom, style etc* riportare alla moda; *patient* rianimare **2** *v/i of business etc* riprendersi

revoke [rɪ'vəʊk] *licence* revocare

revolt [rɪ'vəʊlt] **1** *n* rivolta *f* **2** *v/i* ribellarsi; **revolting** schifoso; **revolution** rivoluzione *f*; **revolutionary 1** *n* POL rivoluzionario *m*, -a *f* **2** *adj* rivoluzionario; **revolutionize** rivoluzionare

revolve [rɪ'vɒlv] ruotare; **revolver** revolver *m inv*

revulsion [rɪ'vʌlʃn] ribrezzo *m*

reward [rɪ'wɔːd] **1** *n* *financial* ricompensa *f*; *benefit derived* vantaggio *m* 2 *v/t financially* ricompensare; **rewarding** *experience* gratificante

rewind [riːˈwaɪnd] *film, tape* riavvolgere

rewrite [riːˈraɪt] riscrivere

rhetoric [ˈretərɪk] retorica *f*

rheumatism [ˈruːmətɪzm] reumatismo *m*

rhinoceros [raɪˈnɒsərəs] rinoceronte *m*

rhubarb [ˈruːbɑːb] rabarbaro *m*

rhyme [raɪm] **1** *n* rima *f* **2** *v/i* rimare; **~ with** fare rima con

rhythm [ˈrɪðm] ritmo *m*

rib [rɪb] ANAT costola *f*

ribbon [ˈrɪbən] nastro *m*

rice [raɪs] riso *m*

rich [rɪtʃ] **1** *adj* ricco; *food* pesante **2** *n*: **the ~** i ricchi *mpl*; **richly** *deserved* pienamente

ricochet [ˈrɪkəʃeɪ] rimbalzare

rid [rɪd]: **get ~ of** sbarazzarsi di; **riddance**: **good ~!** che liberazione!

ride [raɪd] **1** *n on horse* cavalcata *f*; *in vehicle* giro *m*; *(journey)* viaggio *m*; **do you want a ~ into town?** vuoi uno strappo in città? **2** *v/t*: **~ a horse** andare a cavallo; **~ a bike** andare in bicicletta **3** *v/i on horse* andare a cavallo; *on bike* andare in *vehicle* viaggiare; **rider** *on horse* cavallerizzo *m*, -a *f*; *on bike* ciclista *m/f*

ridge [rɪdʒ] *raised strip* sporgenza *f*; *of mountain* cresta

f; *of roof* punta *f*

ridicule [ˈrɪdɪkjuːl] **1** *n* ridicolo *m* **2** *v/t* ridicolizzare; **ridiculous** ridicolo; **ridiculously** incredibilmente

riding [ˈraɪdɪŋ] *on horseback* equitazione *f*

rifle [ˈraɪfl] fucile *m*

rift [rɪft] *in earth* crepa *f*; *in party etc* spaccatura *f*

rig [rɪg] **1** *n (oil ~)* piattaforma *f* petrolifera **2** *v/t elections* manipolare

right [raɪt] **1** *adj (correct)* esatto; *(proper, just)* giusto; *(suitable)* adatto; *not left* destro; **be ~** *of answer* essere esatto; *of person* avere ragione; *of clock* essere giusto; **put things ~** sistemare le cose **2** *adv (directly)* proprio; *(correctly)* bene; *(completely)* completamente; *not left* a destra; **~ now** *(immediately)* subito; *(at the moment)* adesso **3** *n civil, legal etc* diritto *m*; *not left*, POL destra *f*; **on the ~** a destra; **turn to the ~** take a **~** girare a destra; **be in the ~** avere ragione; **know ~ from wrong** saper distinguere il bene dal male; **right-angle** angolo *m* retto; **rightful** *owner etc* legittimo; **right-hand drive** MOT guida *f* a destra; *car* auto *f* inv con guida a destra; **righthanded**: **be ~** usare la (mano) destra; **righthand man** braccio *m* destro; **right of way** *in traffic* (diritto *m* di) precedenza *f*; *across land* diritto *m* di accesso; **right wing** POL destra *f*; SP esterno *m* destro; **right-wing** POL di destra; **right winger** POL persona *f* di destra; **right-wing extremism** POL estremismo *m* di destra

rigid ['rɪdʒɪd] *material, principles* rigido; *attitude* inflessibile

rigor *Am* ☞ **rigour**

rigorous ['rɪgərəs] rigoroso; **rigorously** *check* rigorosamente; **rigour** rigore *m*

rile [raɪl] F irritare

rim [rɪm] *of wheel* cerchione *m*; *of cup* orlo *m*; *of spectacles* montatura *f*

ring[1] [rɪŋ] (*circle*) cerchio *m*; *on finger* anello *m*; *in boxing* ring *m inv*, quadrato *m*; *at circus* pista *f*

ring[2] [rɪŋ] **1** *n of bell* trillo *m*; *of voice* suono *m* **2** *v/t bell* suonare; TELEC chiamare **3** *v/i of bell* suonare; **ringleader** capobanda *m inv*; **ring-pull** linguetta *f*

rink [rɪŋk] pista *f* di pattinaggio su ghiaccio

rinse [rɪns] **1** *n for hair colour* cachet *m inv* **2** *v/t* sciacquare

riot ['raɪət] **1** *n* sommossa *f* **2** *v/i* causare disordini; **rioter** dimostrante *m/f*; **riot police** reparti *mpl* (di polizia) antisommossa

rip [rɪp] **1** *n in cloth etc* strappo

m **2** *v/t cloth etc* strappare
◆ **rip off** F *customers* fregare F

ripe [raɪp] *fruit* maturo; **ripen** *of fruit* maturare; **ripeness** *of fruit* maturazione *f*

'rip-off F fregatura *f* F

ripple ['rɪpl] *on water* increspatura *f*

rise [raɪz] **1** *v/i from chair etc* alzarsi; *of sun* sorgere; *of price, temperature* aumentare; *of water level* salire **2** *n* aumento *m*; **give ~ to** dare origine a; **riser: be an early / be a late ~** essere mattiniero / alzarsi sempre tardi

risk [rɪsk] **1** *n* rischio *m*; **take a ~** correre un rischio **2** *v/t* rischiare; **risky** rischioso

ritual ['rɪtjʊəl] **1** *n* rituale *m* **2** *adj* rituale

rival ['raɪvl] **1** *n* rivale *m/f*; *in business* concorrente *m/f* **2** *v/t* competere con; **rivalry** rivalità *f inv*

river ['rɪvə(r)] fiume *m*; **riverbank** sponda *f* del fiume; **riverbed** letto *m* del fiume; **riverside 1** *adj* sul fiume **2** *n* riva *f* del fiume

riveting ['rɪvɪtɪŋ] avvincente

Riviera [rɪvɪ'eərə]: **the Italian ~** la riviera (ligure)

road [rəʊd] strada *f*; **it's just down the ~** è qui vicino; **roadblock** posto *m* di blocco; **road hog** pirata *m* della strada; **road holding** *of vehicle* tenuta *f* di strada; **road**

map carta *f* automobilistica; **road rage** comportamento di estrema aggressività da parte di automobilisti; **road safety** sicurezza *f* sulle strade; **roadsign** cartello *m* stradale; **roadway** carreggiata *f*; **road works** *npl* lavori *mpl* stradali; **roadworthy** in buono stato di marcia

roam [rəʊm] vagabondare

roar [rɔː(r)] **1** *n* of engine rombo *m*; of lion ruggito *m*; of traffic fragore *m* **2** *v/i* of engine rombare; of lion ruggire; of person gridare; **~ with laughter** ridere fragorosamente

roast [rəʊst] **1** *n* in beef etc arrosto *m* **2** *v/t* arrostire; coffee beans, peanuts tostare **3** *v/i* of food arrostire; in hot room, climate scoppiare di caldo; **roast beef** arrosto *m* di manzo; **roast pork** arrosto *m* di maiale

rob [rɒb] person, bank rapinare; **robber** rapinatore *m*, -trice *f*; **robbery** rapina *f*

robe [rəʊb] of judge toga *f*; of priest tonaca *f*; Am (dressing gown) vestaglia *f*

robin ['rɒbɪn] pettirosso *m*

robot ['rəʊbɒt] robot *m inv*

robust [rəʊ'bʌst] robusto

rock [rɒk] **1** *n* roccia *f*; MUS rock *m*; **on the ~s** drink con ghiaccio; marriage in crisi **2** *v/t* baby cullare; cradle far dondolare; (surprise) scon-

volgere **3** *v/i* on chair dondolarsi; **rock and roll** rock and roll *m*; **rock band** gruppo *m* rock; **rock-bottom** prices bassissimo; **rock bottom**: **reach ~** toccare il fondo; **rock climber** rocciatore *m*, -trice *f*; **rock climbing** roccia *f*

rocket ['rɒkɪt] **1** *n* razzo *m* **2** *v/i* of prices etc salire alle stelle

rocking chair ['rɒkɪŋ] sedia *f* a dondolo; **rocking horse** cavallo *m* a dondolo

'rock star rockstar *f inv*

rocky ['rɒkɪ] shore roccioso; (shaky) instabile

rod [rɒd] sbarra *f*; for fishing canna *f*

rodent ['rəʊdnt] roditore *m*

rogue [rəʊg] briccone *m*, -a *f*

role [rəʊl] ruolo *m*; **role model** modello *m* di comportamento

roll [rəʊl] **1** *n* of bread panino *m*; of film rullino *m*; (list, register) lista *f* **2** *v/i* of ball etc rotolare; of boat dondolare

◆ **roll over 1** *v/i* rigirarsi **2** *v/t* person, object girare; loan, agreement rinnovare

'roll call appello *m*; **roller** for hair bigodino *m*; **roller blade**® roller blade *m inv*; **roller coaster** montagne *fpl* russe; **roller skate** pattino *m* a rotelle

ROM [rɒm] COMPUT (= **read only memory**) ROM *f inv*

Roman ['rəumən] **1** adj romano **2** n Romano m, -a f; **Roman Catholic 1** n REL cattolico m, -a f **2** adj cattolico

romance [rə'mæns] (affair) storia f d'amore; novel romanzo m rosa; film film m inv d'amore; **romantic** romantico

Rome [rəum] Roma f

roof [ru:f] tetto m; **roof box** MOT box portabagagli m inv; **roof rack** MOT portabagagli m inv

rookie ['ruki] Am F pivello m

room [ru:m] stanza f; (bedroom) camera f (da letto); (space) posto m; **room clerk** Am receptionist m/f inv; **room mate** Am compagno m, -a f di stanza; in apartment compagno m, -a f di appartamento; **room service** servizio m in camera; **room temperature** temperatura f ambiente; **roomy** house, car etc spazioso; clothes ampio

root [ru:t] radice f

rope [rəup] corda f, fune f

rosary ['rəuzəri] REL rosario m

rose [rəuz] BOT rosa f

roster ['rɒstə(r)] turni mpl; actual document tabella f dei turni

rostrum ['rɒstrəm] podio m

rosy ['rəuzi] roseo

rot [rɒt] **1** n marciume m **2** v/i marcire

rotate [rəu'teɪt] **1** v/i of blades, earth ruotare **2** v/t girare; crops avvicendare; **rotation** rotazione f; in ~ a turno

rotten ['rɒtn] food, wood etc marcio; F (very bad) schifoso F

rough [rʌf] **1** adj hands, skin, surface ruvido; ground accidentato; (coarse) rozzo; (violent) violento; crossing movimentato; seas grosso; (approximate) approssimativo; ~ **draft** abbozzo m **2** adv: **sleep** ~ dormire all'addiaccio **3** n in golf erba f alta; **roughage** in food fibre fpl; **roughly** (approximately) circa; (harshly) bruscamente; ~ **speaking** grosso modo

roulette [ru:'let] roulette f inv

round [raund] **1** adj rotondo **2** n of postman, doctor giro m; of toast fetta f; of drinks giro m; of competition girone m; in boxing match round m inv **3** v/t corner girare **4** adv & prep ☞ **around**

◆ **round up** figure arrotondare; suspects, criminals radunare

roundabout ['raundəbaut] **1** adj indiretto **2** n on road rotatoria f; **round-the-world** intorno al mondo; **round trip ticket** Am biglietto m (di) andata e ritorno; **round-up of cattle** raduno m; of suspects, criminals retata f; of news riepilogo m

rouse [rauz] from sleep svegliare; *emotions* risvegliare; **rousing** entusiasmante

route [ru:t] *of car* itinerario *m*; *of plane, ship* rotta *f*; *of bus* percorso *m*

routine [ru:'ti:n] **1** *adj* abituale **2** *n* routine *f*; **as a matter of ~** d'abitudine

row[1] [rəʊ] *n* (*line*) fila *f*; **5 days in a ~** 5 giorni di fila

row[2] [rəʊ] *v/t boat* remare

row[3] [raʊ] *n* (*quarrel*) litigio *m*; (*noise*) baccano *m*

'rowboat *Am* barca *f* a remi

rowdy ['raʊdɪ] turbolento

'rowing boat barca *f* a remi

royal ['rɔɪəl] reale; **royalty** (*royal persons*) reali *mpl*; *on book, recording* royalty *f inv*

rub [rʌb] sfregare, strofinare

rubber ['rʌbə(r)] **1** *n* gomma *f* **2** *adj* di gomma; **rubber band** elastico *m*

rubbish ['rʌbɪʃ] immondizia *f*; (*poor quality*) porcheria *f*; (*nonsense*) sciocchezza *f*; **rubbish bin** pattumiera *f*

rubble ['rʌbl] macerie *fpl*

ruby ['ru:bɪ] *jewel* rubino *m*

rucksack ['rʌksæk] zaino *m*

rudder ['rʌdə(r)] timone *m*

ruddy ['rʌdɪ] *complexion* rubicondo

rude [ru:d] maleducato; *language* volgare; **it's ~ to ... è** cattiva educazione ...; **rudely** (*impolitely*) scortesemente; **rudeness** maleducazione *f*

rudimentary [ru:dɪ'mentərɪ]

rudimentale; **rudiments** rudimenti *mpl*

rueful ['ru:fʊl] rassegnato; **ruefully** con aria rassegnata

ruffian ['rʌfɪən] delinquente *m/f*

ruffle ['rʌfl] **1** *n* (*on dress*) gala *f* **2** *v/t hair* scompigliare; *person* turbare; **get ~d** agitarsi

rug [rʌg] tappeto *m*; (*blanket*) coperta *f* (*da viaggio*)

rugby ['rʌgbɪ] rugby *m*; **rugby league** rugby *m* a tredici; **rugby player** giocatore *m* di rugby; **rugby union** rugby *m* a quindici

rugged ['rʌgɪd] *coastline* frastagliato; *face, features* marcato

ruin ['ru:ɪn] **1** *n* rovina *f* **2** *v/t* rovinare

rule [ru:l] **1** *n of club, game* regola *f*; (*authority*) dominio *m*; *for measuring* metro *m* (a stecche); **as a ~** generalmente **2** *v/t country* governare; **the judge ~d that ...** il giudice ha stabilito che ... **3** *v/i of monarch* regnare
◆ **rule out** escludere

ruler ['ru:lə(r)] *for measuring* righello *m*; *of state* capo *m*; **ruling 1** *n* decisione *f* **2** *adj party* di governo

rum [rʌm] *drink* rum *m inv*

rumble ['rʌmbl] *of stomach* brontolare; *of thunder* rimbombare

rumour, *Am* **rumor** ['ru:-

mə(r)] 1 *n* voce *f* 2 *v/t*: **it is
~ed that ...** corre voce che
...

rump [rʌmp] *of animal* groppa *f*

rumple ['rʌmpl] *clothes, paper*
spiegazzare

'rumpsteak bistecca *f* di girello

run [rʌn] 1 *n* on foot corsa *f*;
Am in tights sfilatura *f*; **go
for a ~** andare a correre;
go for a ~ in the car andare
a fare un giro in macchina;
make a ~ for it scappare; **a
criminal on the ~** un evaso,
un'evasa; **in the short ~ / in
the long ~** sulle prime / alla
lunga; **a ~ on the dollar** una
forte richiesta di dollari 2 *v/i
of person, animal* correre; *of
river* scorrere; *of trains, buses*
viaggiare; *of paint, makeup*
sbavare; *of nose* colare; *of
play* tenere il cartellone; *of
software* girare; *of engine,
machine* funzionare; **~ for
President** *in election* candidarsi alla presidenza 3 *v/t*
correre; (*take part in: race*)
partecipare a; *business, hotel,
project etc* gestire; *software*
lanciare; *car* usare; *risk* correre; **can I ~ you to the station?** ti porto alla stazione?
♦ **run across** (*meet*) imbattersi in
♦ **run away** scappare
♦ **run down** 1 *v/t* (*knock
down*) investire; (*criticize*)

parlare male di; *stocks* ridurre 2 *v/i of battery* scaricarsi
♦ **run into** (*meet*) imbattersi
in; *difficulties* trovare
♦ **run off** 1 *v/i* scappare 2 *v/t*
(*print off*) stampare
♦ **run out** *of contract, time*
scadere; *of supplies* esaurirsi
♦ **run out of** *patience* perdere; *supplies* rimanere senza;
I ran out of petrol ho finito
la benzina
♦ **run over** 1 *v/t* (*knock down*)
investire; *details* rivedere 2
v/i of water etc traboccare
♦ **run up** *debts, bill* accumulare

'runaway ragazzo *m*, -a *f*
scappato di casa; **run-down**
person debilitato; *area, building* fatiscente

rung [rʌŋ] *of ladder* piolo *m*

runner ['rʌnə(r)] *athlete* velocista *m/f*; **runner beans** fagiolini *mpl*; **runner-up** secondo *m*, -a *f* classificato
(-a); **running 1** *n* SP corsa
f; *of business* gestione *f* 2
adj: **for two days ~** per due
giorni di seguito; **running
water** acqua *f* corrente; **run-
ny** *substance* liquido; *nose*
che cola; **run-up** rincorsa
f; **in the ~ to** nel periodo che
precede; **runway** pista *f*

rupture ['rʌptʃə(r)] 1 *n* rottura
f; MED lacerazione *f*; (*hernia*)
ernia *f* 2 *v/i of pipe etc* scoppiare

rural ['rʊərəl] rurale

ruse [ru:z] stratagemma m

rush [rʌʃ] 1 n corsa f; do sth in a ~ fare qc di corsa; be in a ~ andare di fretta 2 v/t person mettere fretta a; meal mangiare in fretta; ~ s.o. to hospital portare qu di corsa all'ospedale 3 v/i affrettarsi; rush hour ora f di punta

Russia ['rʌʃə] Russia f; Russian 1 adj russo 2 n russo m, -a f; language russo m

rust [rʌst] 1 n ruggine f 2 v/i arrugginirsi; rust-proof a prova di ruggine

rusty ['rʌstɪ] also fig arrugginito

rut [rʌt] in road solco m; be in a ~ fig essersi fossilizzato

ruthless ['ru:θlɪs] spietato; ruthlessly spietatamente; ruthlessness spietatezza f

rye [raɪ] segale f; rye bread pane m di segale

S

sabotage ['sæbətɑːʒ] 1 n sabotaggio m 2 v/t sabotare; saboteur sabotatore m, -trice f

sachet ['sæʃeɪ] bustina f

sack [sæk] 1 n bag sacco m 2 v/t F licenziare

sacred ['seɪkrɪd] sacro

sacrifice ['sækrɪfaɪs] 1 n also fig sacrificio m 2 v/t sacrificare

sacrilege ['sækrɪlɪdʒ] sacrilegio m

sad [sæd] triste; state of affairs deplorevole

saddle ['sædl] 1 n sella f 2 v/t horse sellare; ~ s.o. with sth fig affibbiare qc a qu

sadism ['seɪdɪzm] sadismo m; sadist sadista m/f; sadistic sadistico

sadly ['sædlɪ] tristemente; (regrettably) purtroppo; sadness tristezza f

safe [seɪf] 1 adj not dangerous sicuro; not in danger al sicuro; driver prudente 2 n cassaforte f; safeguard 1 n protezione f, salvaguardia f; as a ~ against per proteggersi contro 2 v/t proteggere; safely arrive, complete test etc senza problemi; drive prudentemente; assume tranquillamente; safety sicurezza f; safety pin spilla f di sicurezza

sag [sæg] of ceiling incurvarsi; of rope allentarsi

saga ['sɑːgə] saga f

sage [seɪdʒ] herb salvia f

Sagittarius [sædʒɪ'teərɪəs] ASTR Sagittario m

sail [seɪl] 1 n of boat vela f; trip veleggiata f; go for a ~ fare un giro in barca (a vela) 2 v/t yacht pilotare 3 v/i fare vela; (depart) salpare; sailboard **1** *n* windsurf *m inv* **2** *v/i* fare windsurf; **sailboarding** windsurf *m*; **sailboat** *Am* barca *f* a vela; **sailing** SP vela *f*; **sailing boat** barca *f* a vela; **sailor** marinaio *m*

saint [seint] santo *m*, -a *f*

sake [seik]: **for my ~** per il mio bene; **for the ~ of** per

salad ['sæləd] insalata *f*; **salad dressing** condimento *m* per l'insalata

salary ['sæləri] stipendio *m*

sale [seil] vendita *f*; *at reduced prices* svendita *f*, saldi *mpl*; **for ~** *sign* in vendita; **be on ~** essere in vendita; **sales department** reparto *m* vendite; **sales clerk** *Am in store* commesso *m*, -a *f*; **sales figures** fatturato *m*; **salesman** venditore *m*; **sales manager** direttore *m*, -trice *f* delle vendite; **saleswoman** venditrice *f*

salient ['seiliənt] saliente

saliva [sə'laivə] saliva *f*

salmon ['sæmən] salmone *m*

saloon [sə'lu:n] (*bar*) bar *m inv*; MOT berlina *f*

salt [sɒlt] sale *m*; **salty** salato

salute [sə'lu:t] **1** *n* MIL saluto *m* **2** *v/t & v/i* salutare

salvage ['sælvidʒ] *from wreck* ricuperare

salvation [sæl'veiʃn] salvezza *f*

same [seim] **1** *adj* stesso **2** *pron* stesso; **the ~** lo stesso, la stessa; **Happy New Year**

– the ~ to you Buon anno! **– grazie e altrettanto!**; **it's all the ~ to me** per me è uguale **3** *adv*: **the ~** allo stesso modo; **look / sound the ~** sembrare uguale

sample ['sɑ:mpl] campione *m*

sanction ['sæŋkʃn] **1** *n* (*approval*) approvazione *f*; (*penalty*) sanzione *f* **2** *v/t* (*approve*) sancire

sanctity ['sæŋktəti] santità *f*

sand [sænd] **1** *n* sabbia *f*; **2** *v/t with sandpaper* smerigliare

sandal ['sændl] sandalo *m*

sandbag sacchetto *m* di sabbia; **sand dune** duna *f*; **sander** *tool* smerigliatrice *f*; **sandpaper 1** *n* carta *f* smerigliata **2** *v/t* smerigliare

sandwich ['sænwidʒ] tramezzino *m*

sandy ['sændi] *beach* sabbioso; *full of sand* pieno di sabbia; *hair* rossiccio

sane [sein] sano di mente

sanitarium [sæni'teriəm] casa *f* di cura

sanitary ['sænitəri] *conditions* igienico; *installations* sanitario; **sanitary towel** assorbente *m* (igienico); **sanitation** impianti *mpl* igienici; (*removal of waste*) fognature *fpl*

sanity ['sænəti] sanità *f* mentale

Santa Claus ['sæntəklɔ:z] Babbo *m* Natale

sap [sæp] **1** *n in tree* linfa *f* **2** *v/t*

s.o.'s energy indebolire

sapphire ['sæfaɪə(r)] zaffiro *m*

sarcasm ['sɑːkæzm] sarcasmo *m*; **sarcastic** sarcastico; **sarcastically** sarcasticamente

sardine [sɑːˈdiːn] sardina *f*

Sardinia [sɑːˈdɪnɪə] Sardegna *f*; **Sardinian 1** *adj* sardo **2** *n* sardo *m*, -a *f*

sardonic [sɑːˈdɒnɪk] sardonico

Satan ['seɪtn] Satana *m*

satellite ['sætəlaɪt] satellite *m*; **satellite dish** antenna *f* parabolica; **satellite TV** TV *f inv* satellitare

satin ['sætɪn] satin *m*

satire ['sætaɪə(r)] satira *f*; **satirical** satirico; **satirize** satireggiare

satisfaction [sætɪsˈfækʃn] soddisfazione *f*; **satisfactory** soddisfacente; *just good enough* sufficiente; **satisfy** soddisfare; *requirement* rispondere a; *I am satisfied that ...* (*convinced*) sono convinto che ...

Saturday ['sætədeɪ] sabato *m*

sauce [sɔːs] salsa *f*, sugo *m*; **saucepan** pentola *f*; **saucer** piattino *m*

Saudi Arabia [saʊdɪəˈreɪbɪə] Arabia *f* Saudita; **Saudi Arabian 1** *adj* saudita **2** *n person* saudita *m/f*

sauna ['sɔːnə] sauna *f*

sausage ['sɒsɪdʒ] salsiccia *f*

savage ['sævɪdʒ] **1** *adj animal* selvaggio; *criticism* feroce **2** *n* selvaggio *m*, -a *f*; **savagery** ferocia *f*

save [seɪv] **1** *v/t* (*rescue*) salvare; *money, time, effort* risparmiare; (*collect*) raccogliere; COMPUT salvare; *goal* parare **2** *v/i* (*put money aside*) risparmiare; SP parare **3** *n* SP parata *f*; **saver** *person* risparmiatore *m*, -trice *f*; **savings** risparmi *mpl*; **savings account** libretto *m* di risparmio; **savings and loan** *Am* istituto *m* di credito immobiliare; **savings bank** cassa *f* di risparmio

saviour, *Am* **savior** ['seɪvjə(r)] REL salvatore *m*

savor *etc Am* ☞ **savour** *etc*

savour ['seɪvə(r)] assaporare; **savoury** *not sweet* salato (*non dolce*)

saw [sɔː] **1** *n tool* sega *f* **2** *v/t* segare; **sawdust** segatura *f*

saxophone ['sæksəfəʊn] sassofono *m*

say [seɪ] dire; *that is to* ~ sarebbe a dire; *saying* detto *m*

scab [skæb] *on skin* crosta *f*

scaffolding ['skæfəldɪŋ] impalcature *fpl*

scald [skɔːld] scottare; ~ *o.s.* scottarsi

scale¹ [skeɪl] *on fish* scaglia *f*

scale² [skeɪl] **1** *n of map,* MUS scala *f*; *of project* portata *f* **2** *v/t cliffs etc* scalare

scales [skeɪlz] *for weighing*

bilancia *fsg*

scallop ['skɒləp] capasanta *f*

scalp [skælp] cuoio *m* capelluto

scalpel ['skælpl] bisturi *m*

scam [skæm] F truffa *f*

scampi ['skæmpɪ] gamberoni *mpl* in pastella fritti

scan [skæn] **1** *v/t* horizon scrutare; page scorrere; foetus fare l'ecografia di; brain fare la TAC di; COMPUT scannerizzare **2** *n* (brain ∼) TAC *f inv*; of foetus ecografia *f*

♦ **scan in** COMPUT scannerizzare

scandal ['skændl] scandalo *m*; **scandalize** scandalizzare; **scandalous** scandaloso

scanner ['skænə(r)] scanner *m inv*

scanty ['skæntɪ] clothes succinto

scapegoat ['skeɪpgəut] capro *m* espiatorio

scar [skɑ:(r)] **1** *n* cicatrice *f* **2** *v/t* lasciare cicatrici su; fig segnare

scarce [skeəs] in short supply scarso; **scarcely** appena; **there was ∼ anything left** non rimaneva quasi più niente; **scarcity** scarsità *f inv*

scare [skeə(r)] **1** *v/t* spaventare; **be ∼d of** avere paura di **2** *n* (panic, alarm) panico *m*; **scaremonger** allarmista *m/f*

scarf [skɑ:f] around neck

sciarpa *f*; over head foulard *m inv*

scarlet ['skɑ:lət] scarlatto

scary ['skeərɪ] che fa paura

scathing ['skeɪðɪŋ] caustico

scatter ['skætə(r)] **1** *v/t* leaflets, seeds spargere; crowd disperdere **2** *v/i* of people disperdersi; **scatterbrained** sventato; **scattered** family, villages sparpagliato; **showers** precipitazioni sparse

scavenge ['skævɪndʒ] frugare tra i rifiuti; **scavenger** animale *m* necrofago; person persona che fruga tra i rifiuti

scenario [sɪ'nɑ:rɪəʊ] scenario *m*

scene [si:n] scena *f*; (argument) scenata *f*; **make a ∼** fare una scenata; **∼s** THEA scenografia *f*; **behind the ∼s** dietro le quinte; **scenery** paesaggio *m*; THEA scenario *m*

scent [sent] profumo *m*; of animal odore *m*

sceptic ['skeptɪk] scettico *m*, -a *f*; **sceptical** scettico; **scepticism** scetticismo *m*

schedule ['ʃedju:l] **1** *n* of events, work programma *m*; for trains orario *m*; **be on ∼** of work, of train etc essere in orario; **be behind ∼** of work, of train etc essere in ritardo **2** *v/t* put on schedule programmare; **scheduled flight** volo *m* di linea

scheme [ski:m] **1** *n* (plan) pia-

no m; (plot) complotto m **2**
v/i (plot) complottare, tramare; **scheming** intrigante

schizophrenia [skɪtsəˈfriː-
nɪə] schizofrenia f; **schizo-
phrenic 1** n schizofrenico
m, -a f **2** adj schizofrenico

scholar [ˈskɒlə(r)] studioso
m, -a f; **scholarly** Dotto;
scholarship (scholarly
work) erudizione f; (financial award) borsa f di studio

school [skuːl] scuola f; Am
(university) università f inv;
school bag cartella f;
schoolboy scolaro m;
schoolchildren scolari
mpl; **school days** tempi
mpl della scuola; **schoolgirl**
scolara f; **schoolteacher** insegnante m/f

science [ˈsaɪəns] scienza f;
science fiction fantascienza
f; **scientific** scientifico; **scientist** scienziato m, -a f

scissors [ˈsɪzəz] forbici fpl

scoff[1] [skɒf] v/t food sbafare

scoff[2] [skɒf] v/i (mock) canzonare

scold [skəʊld] sgridare

scoop [skuːp] for grain, flour
paletta f; for ice cream cucchiaio m dosatore; of ice
cream pallina f; (story) scoop
m inv

scooter [ˈskuːtə(r)] with motor scooter m inv; child's monopattino m

scope [skəʊp] portata f; (freedom, opportunity) possibilità
f

scorch [skɔːtʃ] bruciare;
scorching torrido

score [skɔː(r)] **1** n SP punteggio m; (written music) spartito m; of film etc colonna f so-
nora; **what's the ~?** SP a
quanto sono / siamo? **2** v/t
goal, point segnare; (cut) incidere **3** v/i segnare; (keep
the score) tenere il punteggio; **scoreboard** segnapunti
m inv; **scorer** of goal, point
marcatore m, -trice f

scorn [skɔːn] **1** n disprezzo m
2 v/t idea disprezzare; **scornful** sprezzante; **scornfully**
sprezzantemente

Scorpio [ˈskɔːpɪəʊ] ASTR
Scorpione m

Scot [skɒt] scozzese m/f;
Scotch (whisky) scotch m
inv; **Scotch tape**® Am
scotch® m; **Scotland** Scozia
f; **Scotsman** scozzese m;
Scotswoman scozzese f;
Scottish scozzese

scoundrel [ˈskaʊndrəl] birbante m/f

scour [ˈskaʊə(r)] (search) setacciare

scowl [skaʊl] **1** n sguardo m
torvo **2** v/i guardare storto

scramble [ˈskræmbl] **1** n
(rush) corsa f **2** v/t message
rendere indecifrabile **3** v/i:
he ~d to his feet si rialzò
in fretta; **scrambled eggs**
uova fpl strapazzate

scrap [skræp] **1** n metal rottame *m*; (*fight*) zuffa *f*; (*little bit*) briciolo *m* **2** *v/t* plan, project abbandonare

scrape [skreɪp] **1** *n* on paintwork graffio *m* **2** *v/t* paintwork, arm *etc* graffiare; **~ a living** sbarcare il lunario

'scrap metal rottami *mpl*

scrappy ['skræpɪ] *work, writing* senza capo né coda

scratch [skrætʃ] **1** *n* mark graffio *m*; **start from ~** ricominciare da zero; **not up to ~** non all'altezza **2** *v/t* (*mark*) graffiare; *because of itch* grattare **3** *v/i* *of cat, nails* graffiare

scrawl [skrɔːl] **1** *n* scarabocchio *m* **2** *v/t* scarabocchiare

scrawny ['skrɔːnɪ] scheletrico

scream [skriːm] **1** *n* urlo *m* **2** *v/i* urlare

screech [skriːtʃ] **1** *n* of tyres stridio *m*; (*scream*) strillo *m* **2** *v/i* of tyres stridere; (*scream*) strillare

screen [skriːn] **1** *n* in room, hospital paravento *m*; of smoke cortina *f*; cinema, COMPUT, of television schermo *m* **2** *v/t* (*protect, hide*) riparare; *film* proiettare; *for security reasons* vagliare; **screenplay** sceneggiatura *f*; **screen saver** COMPUT salvaschermo *m inv*; **screen test** *for movie* provino *m*

screw [skruː] **1** *n* vite *f* (metallica) **2** *v/t* avvitare (**to** a); V scopare V; F (*cheat*) fregare

F; **screwdriver** cacciavite *m*; **screwed up** F *psychologically* complessato; **screw top** *on bottle* tappo *m* a vite; **screwy** F svitato

scribble ['skrɪbl] **1** *n* scarabocchio *m* **2** *v/t & v/i* (*write quickly*) scarabocchiare

script [skrɪpt] *for film, play* copione *m*; (*form of writing*) scrittura *f*; scripture: **the (Holy) Scriptures** le Sacre Scritture *fpl*; **scriptwriter** sceneggiatore *m*, -trice *f*

◆ **scroll down** [skrəul] COMPUT far scorrere il testo in avanti

◆ **scroll up** COMPUT far scorrere il testo indietro

scrounge [skraundʒ] scroccare; **scrounger** scroccone *m*, -a *f*

scrub [skrʌb] *floors, hands* sfregare (con spazzola)

scrum [skrʌm] *in rugby* mischia *f*

scruples ['skruːplz] scrupoli *mpl*; **scrupulous** scrupoloso; **scrupulously** (*meticulously*) scrupolosamente

scrutinize ['skruːtɪnaɪz] *text* esaminare attentamente; *face* scrutare; **scrutiny** attento esame *m*

scuba diving ['skuːbə] immersione *f* subacquea

scuffle ['skʌfl] tafferuglio *m*

sculptor ['skʌlptə(r)] scultore *m*, -trice *f*; **sculpture** scultura *f* scum [skʌm] on liquid schiuma f; (pej: people) feccia f

sea [siː] mare m; **by the ~** al mare; seabird uccello m marino; seafood frutti mpl di mare; seafront lungomare m inv; seagull gabbiano m

seal[1] [siːl] n animal foca f

seal[2] [siːl] 1 n on document sigillo m; TECH chiusura f ermetica 2 v/t container chiudere ermeticamente

'sea level: above / below ~ sopra / sotto il livello del mare

seam [siːm] on garment cucitura f; of ore filone m

'seaman marinaio m; seaport porto m marittimo

search [sɜːtʃ] 1 n for s.o. / sth ricerca f; of person, building perquisizione f 2 v/t person, building, baggage perquisire; area perlustrare

◆ search for cercare

searching ['sɜːtʃɪŋ] look penetrante; searchlight riflettore m

'seashore riva f (del mare); seasick: be ~ avere il mal di mare; get ~ soffrire il mal di mare; seaside: at the ~ al mare; ~ resort località f inv balneare

season ['siːzn] stagione f; in / out of ~ in / fuori stagione; seasonal stagionale; seasoned wood stagionato; traveller, campaigner etc

esperto; seasoning condimento m; season ticket abbonamento m

seat [siːt] 1 n posto m; of trousers fondo m; POL seggio m; **please take a ~** si accomodi 2 v/t (have seating for) avere posti a sedere per; seat belt cintura f di sicurezza

'sea urchin riccio m di mare; seaweed alga f

secluded [sɪ'kluːdɪd] appartato

second ['sekənd] 1 n of time secondo m; just a ~ un attimo 2 adj secondo 3 adv come in secondo 4 v/t motion appoggiare; secondary secondario; second floor secondo piano; Am primo piano m; second hand on clock lancetta f dei secondi; second-hand di seconda mano; secondly in secondo luogo; second-rate di second'ordine; second thoughts: **I've had ~ thoughts** ci ho ripensato

secrecy ['siːkrəsɪ] segretezza f; secret 1 n segreto m 2 adj segreto; secret agent agente m segreto

secretarial [sekrə'teərɪəl] tasks, job di segretaria; secretary segretario m, -a f; POL ministro m; Secretary of State in USA Segretario m di Stato

secretive ['siːkrətɪv] riservato; secretly segretamente;

secret service servizio *m* segreto

sect [sekt] setta *f*

section ['sekʃn] sezione *f*

sector ['sektə(r)] settore *m*

secular ['sekjʊlə(r)] laico

secure [sɪ'kjʊə(r)] **1** *adj shelf etc* saldo *feeling* sicuro; *job* stabile **2** *v/t shelf etc* assicurare; *s.o.'s help, finances* assicurarsi; **securities market** FIN mercato *m* dei titoli; **security** sicurezza *f*; *in relationship* stabilità *f*; *for investment* garanzia *f*; **security alert** stato *m* di allarme; **security-conscious** attento alla sicurezza; **security forces** forze *fpl* di sicurezza; **security guard** guardia *f* giurata; **security risk** minaccia *f* per la sicurezza

sedan [sɪ'dæn] *Am* MOT berlina *f*

sedate [sɪ'deɪt] *patient* somministrare sedativi a; **sedation: be under ~** essere sotto l'effetto di sedativi; **sedative** sedativo *m*

sedentary ['sedəntərɪ] *job* sedentario

sediment ['sedɪmənt] sedimento *m*

seduce [sɪ'djuːs] sedurre; **seduction** seduzione *f*; **seductive** *smile, look* seducente; *offer* allettante

see [siː] vedere; *(understand)* capire; **I'll ~ you to the door** t'accompagno alla porta; **~**

you! F ciao! F

◆ **see off** *at airport etc* salutare; *(chase away)* scacciare

seed [siːd] *single* seme *m*; *collective* semi *mpl*; *in tennis* testa *f* di serie; **seedy** *bar, district* squallido

seeing (that) ['siːɪŋ] visto che

'seeing eye dog® *Am* cane *m* per ciechi

seek [siːk] cercare

seem [siːm] sembrare; **seemingly** apparentemente

seesaw ['siːsɔː] altalena *f* (a bilico)

'see-through trasparente

segment ['segmənt] segmento *m*; *of orange* spicchio *m*; **segregate** ['segrɪgeɪt] separare; **segregation** segregazione *f*

seismology [saɪz'mɒlədʒɪ] sismologia *f*

seize [siːz] *s.o., s.o.'s arm* afferrare; *power* prendere; *opportunity* cogliere; *of police etc* sequestrare

◆ **seize up** *of engine* grippare

seizure ['siːʒə(r)] MED attacco *m*; *of drugs etc* sequestro *m*

seldom ['seldəm] raramente

select [sɪ'lekt] **1** *v/t* selezionare **2** *adj (exclusive)* scelto; **selection** scelta *f*; *that / those chosen* selezione *f*; **selective** selettivo

self [self] io *m*; **self-assurance** sicurezza *f* di sé; **self--assured** sicuro di sé; **self-**

-catering apartment appartamento *m* indipendente con cucina; **self-centred,** *Am* **self-centered** egocentrico; **self-confessed** dichiarato; **self-confidence** fiducia *f* in se stessi; **self-confident** sicuro di sé; **self-conscious** insicuro; *smile* imbarazzato; *feel ~* sentirsi a disagio; **self-consciousness** disagio *m*; **self-control** autocontrollo *m*; **self-defence,** *Am* **self-defense** *personal* legittima difesa *f; of state* autodifesa *f;* **self-doubt** dubbi *mpl* personali; **self-employed** autonomo; **self-evident** evidente; **self-expression** espressione *f* di sé; **self-government** autogoverno *m;* **self-interest** interesse *m* personale; **selfish** egoista; **selfless** *person* altruista; *attitude* altruistico; **self-made man** self-made man *m inv;* **self-pity** autocommiserazione *f;* **self-portrait** autoritratto *m;* **self-reliant** indipendente; **self-respect** dignità *f;* **self-satisfied** *pej* soddisfatto di sé; **self-service** self-service; **self-service restaurant** self-service *m inv;* **self-taught** autodidatta

sell [sel] **1** *v/t* vendere **2** *v/i of products* vendere; **sell-by date** data *f* di scadenza; *be past its ~* essere scaduto;

seller venditore *m,* -trice *f;* **selling** COM vendita *f;* **selling point** COM punto *m* forte (che fa vendere il prodotto)

Sellotape® ['seləteip] scotch® *m*

semester [sɪ'mestə(r)] semestre *m*

semi ['semɪ, *Am* 'semaɪ] *Br* villa *f* bifamiliare; *Am truck* autoarticolato *m;* **semicircle** semicerchio *m;* **semi-colon** punto e virgola *m;* **semiconductor** ELEC semiconduttore *m;* **semidetached (house)** villa *f* bifamiliare; **semifinal** semifinale *f;* **semifinalist** semifinalista *m/f*

seminar ['semɪnɑː(r)] seminario *m*

semi-skilled parzialmente qualificato

senate ['senət] senato *m;* **senator** senatore *m,* -trice *f*

send [send] mandare (*to* a)

◆ **send back** mandare indietro

◆ **send for** *doctor, help* (mandare a) chiamare

◆ **send off** *letter, fax etc* spedire; *footballer* espellere

◆ **send up** (*mock*) prendere in giro

sender ['sendə(r)] *of letter* mittente *m/f*

senile ['siːnaɪl] *pej* rimbambito; **senility** *pej* rimbambimento *m*

senior ['siːnɪə(r)] (*older*) più

servant

anziano; *in rank* di grado superiore; **senior citizen** anziano *m*, -a *f*; **seniority** *in job* anzianità *f*

sensation [sen'seɪʃn] *(feeling)* sensazione *f*; *(surprise event)* scalpore *m*; **be a ~** essere sensazionale; **sensational** sensazionale

sense [sens] **1** *n (meaning)* significato *m*; *(purpose, point, sight, smell etc)* senso *m*; *(common sense)* buonsenso *m*; *(feeling)* sensazione *f*; **come to one's ~s** tornare in sé; **it doesn't make ~** non ha senso; **there's no ~ in trying** non ha senso provare **2** *v/t* sentire; **senseless** *(pointless)* assurdo

sensible ['sensəbl] *person, decision* assennato; *advice* sensato; *clothes, shoes* pratico; **sensibly** assennatamente

sensitive ['sensətɪv] sensibile; **sensitivity** sensibilità *f inv*

sensor ['sensə(r)] sensore *m*

sensual ['sensjʊəl] sensuale; **sensuality** sensualità *f*

sensuous ['sensjʊəs] sensuale

sentence ['sentəns] **1** *n* GRAM frase *m*; LAW condanna *f* **2** *v/t* LAW condannare

sentiment ['sentɪmənt] *(sentimentality)* sentimentalismo *m*; *(opinion)* opinione *f*; **sentimental** sentimentale; **sentimentality** sentimentalismo

m

sentry ['sentrɪ] sentinella *f*

separate 1 ['sepərət] *adj* separato **2** ['sepəreɪt] *v/t* separare (**from** da) **3** ['sepəreɪt] *v/i* of couple separarsi; **separated** *couple* separato; **separately** separatamente; **separation** separazione *f*

September [sep'tembə(r)] settembre *m*

septic ['septɪk] infetto; **go ~** of wound infettarsi

sequel ['si:kwəl] seguito *m*

sequence ['si:kwəns] sequenza *f*; **in ~** di seguito

Serbia ['sɜːbɪə] Serbia *f*; **Serbian 1** *adj* serbo **2** *n* serbo *m*, -a *f*; *language* serbo *m*

serene [sɪ'ri:n] sereno

sergeant ['sɑːdʒənt] sergente *m*

serial ['sɪərɪəl] serial *m inv*; **serialize** novel on TV trasmettere a puntate; **serial killer** serial killer *m/f inv*; **serial number** of product numero *m* di serie

series ['sɪəri:z] serie *f inv*

serious ['sɪərɪəs] illness, situation grave; person, company serio; **I'm ~** dico sul serio; **seriously** injured gravemente; *(extremely)* estremamente; **take s.o. ~** prendere sul serio qu; **seriousness** of situation, illness etc gravità *f*; of person serietà *f*

sermon ['sɜːmən] predica *f*

servant ['sɜːvənt] domestico

m, -a f

serve [sɜːv] **1** n in tennis servizio m **2** v/t food, customer, one's country servire; **it ~s you right** ti sta bene **3** v/i servire; as politician etc prestare servizio; **server** COMPUT server m inv; **service 1** n also in tennis servizio m; for machine manutenzione f; for vehicle revisione f; **~s** servizi; **the ~s** MIL le forze armate **2** v/t vehicle revisionare; machine fare la manutenzione di; **service charge** servizio m; **serviceman** MIL militare m; **service provider** COMPUT fornitore m di servizi; **service sector** settore m terziario; **service station** stazione f di servizio; **serving** of food porzione f

session ['seʃn] of parliament sessione f; with consultant etc seduta f

set [set] **1** n of tools set m inv; of dishes, knives servizio m; of books raccolta f; group of people cerchia f; MATH insieme m; (THEA: scenery) scenografia f; where a film is made, in tennis set m inv **2** v/t (place) mettere; film, novel etc ambientare; date, time, limit fissare; alarm clock mettere; broken limb ingessare; jewel montare; **~ the table** apparecchiare (la tavola); **~ a task for s.o.** assegnare un compito a qu **3** v/i of sun tramontare; of glue indurirsi **4** adj ideas rigido; (ready) pronto; **be very ~ in one's ways** essere abitudinario; **~ meal** menù m inv fisso

◆ **set off 1** v/i on journey partire **2** v/t explosion causare; alarm far scattare

◆ **set out 1** v/i on journey partire **2** v/t ideas esporre; **set out to do sth** (intend) proporsi di fare qc

◆ **set up 1** v/t company fondare; system mettere in opera; equipment, machine piazzare; F (frame) incastrare F **2** v/i in business mettersi in affari

◆ **setback** contrattempo m

settee [se'tiː] divano m

setting ['setɪŋ] of novel etc ambientazione f; of house posizione f

settle ['setl] **1** v/i of bird, dust, beer posarsi; of building assestarsi; to live stabilirsi **2** v/t dispute comporre; issue, uncertainty risolvere; debts, bill saldare; nerves, stomach calmare; **that ~s it!** è deciso!

◆ **settle down** (stop being noisy) calmarsi; (stop wild living) mettere la testa a posto; in an area stabilirsi

◆ **settle for** (accept) accontentarsi di

◆ **settle up** (pay) regolare i conti; in hotel etc pagare il conto

settled ['setld] *weather* stabile; **settlement** *of dispute* composizione *f*; *(payment)* pagamento *m*; **settler** *in new country* colonizzatore *m*, -trice *f*

'set-up *(structure)* organizzazione *f*; *(relationship)* relazione *f*; F *(frameup)* montatura *f*

seven ['sevn] sette; **seventeen** diciassette; **seventeenth** diciassettesimo; **seventh** settimo; **seventieth** settantesimo; **seventy** settanta

sever ['sevə(r)] *arm, cable etc* recidere; *relations* troncare

several ['sevrl] **1** *adj* parecchi **2** *pron* parecchi *m*, -ie *f*

severe [sɪ'vɪə(r)] *illness* grave; *penalty, teacher, face* severo; *winter, weather* rigido; **severely** *punish* severamente; *speak* duramente; *injured, disrupted* gravemente; **severity** *of illness* gravità *f*; *of look etc* durezza *f*; *of penalty* severità *f*; *of winter* rigidità *f*

sew [səʊ] cucire

sewage ['suːɪdʒ] acque *fpl* di scolo; **sewer** fogna *f*

sewing ['səʊɪŋ] cucito *m*

sex [seks] sesso *m*; **have ~ with** avere rapporti sessuali con; **sexist 1** *adj* sessista **2** *n* sessista *m/f*; **sexual** sessuale; **sexual intercourse** rapporti *mpl* sessuali; **sexuality** sessualità *f*; **sexually ses-**

sualmente; **sexually transmitted disease** malattia *f* venerea; **sexy** sexy *inv*

shabbily ['ʃæbɪli] *dressed* in modo trasandato; *treat* in modo meschino; **shabby** *coat etc* trasandato; *treatment* meschino

shack [ʃæk] baracca *f*

shade [ʃeɪd] **1** *n for lamp* paralume *m*; *of colour* tonalità *f inv*; **in the ~** all'ombra **2** *v/t from sun, light* riparare

shadow ['ʃædəʊ] ombra *f*

shady ['ʃeɪdi] *spot* all'ombra; *character* losco

shaft [ʃɑːft] *of axle* albero *m*; *of mine* pozzo *m*

shake [ʃeɪk] **1** *n*: **give sth a good ~** dare una scrollata a qc **2** *v/t* scuotere; *emotionally* sconvolgere; **~ one's head** *in refusal* scuotere la testa; **~ hands with s.o.** stringere la mano a qu **3** *v/i of hands, voice, building* tremare; **shaken** *emotionally* scosso; **shake-up** rimpasto *m*; **shaky** *table etc* traballante; *after illness, shock* debole; *grasp of sth, grammar etc* incerto; *voice, hand* tremante

shall [ʃæl] ◊ *future*: **I ~ do my best** farò del mio meglio ◊ *suggesting*: **~ we go now?** andiamo?

shallow ['ʃæləʊ] *water* poco profondo; *person* superficiale

shambles ['ʃæmblz] casino *m* F

shame [ʃeɪm] **1** *n* vergogna *f*; **what a ~!** che peccato!; **~ on you!** vergognati! **2** *v/t family etc* svergognare; **shameful** vergognoso; **shameless** svergognato

shampoo [ʃæm'puː] shampoo *m inv*

shape [ʃeɪp] **1** *n* forma *f* **2** *v/t clay* dar forma a; *character* forgiare; *the future* determinare; **shapeless** *dress etc* informe; **shapely** *figure* ben fatto

share [ʃeə(r)] **1** *n* parte *f*; FIN azione *f* **2** *v/t* dividere; *s.o.'s feelings* condividere **3** *v/i* dividere; **shareholder** azionista *m/f*

shark [ʃɑːk] squalo *m*

sharp [ʃɑːp] **1** *adj knife* affilato; *mind, pain* acuto; *taste* aspro **2** *adv* MUS in diesis; **at 3 o'clock ~** alle 3 precise; **sharpen** *knife* affilare; *skills* raffinare; **sharp practice** pratiche *fpl* poco oneste

shatter ['ʃætə(r)] **1** *v/t glass* frantumare; *illusions* distruggere **2** *v/i of glass* frantumarsi; **shattered** F (*exhausted*) esausto; (*very upset*) sconvolto; **shattering** *news, experience* sconvolgente

shave [ʃeɪv] **1** *v/t* radere **2** *v/i* farsi la barba **3** *n*: **have a ~** farsi la barba; **that was a close ~** ce l'abbiamo fatta

per un pelo; **shaven** *head* rasato; **shaver** *electric* rasoio *m*

shawl [ʃɔːl] scialle *m*

she [ʃiː] lei; **~ has three children** ha tre figli; **there ~ is** eccola

shears [ʃɪəz] *for gardening* cesoie *fpl; for sewing* forbici *fpl*

sheath [ʃiːθ] *for knife* guaina *f; contraceptive* preservativo *m*

shed[1] [ʃed] *v/t blood* spargere; *tears* versare; *leaves* perdere

shed[2] [ʃed] *n* baracca *f*

sheep [ʃiːp] pecora *f*; **sheepdog** cane *m* pastore; **sheepish** imbarazzato

sheer [ʃɪə(r)] *madness, luxury* puro; *cliffs* ripido

sheet [ʃiːt] *for bed* lenzuolo *m; of paper* foglio *m; of metal, glass* lastra *f*

shelf [ʃelf] mensola *f*; **shelves** scaffale *msg*, ripiani *mpl*

shell [ʃel] **1** *n of mussel etc* conchiglia *f; of egg* guscio *m; of tortoise* corazza *f*; MIL granata *f* **2** *v/t peas* sbucciare; MIL bombardare; **shellfire** bombardamento *m*; **shellfish** crostacei *mpl*

shelter ['ʃeltə(r)] **1** *n* (*refuge*) riparo *m; construction* rifugio *m* **2** *v/i* ripararsi **3** *v/t* (*protect*) proteggere; **sheltered** *place* riparato; **lead a ~ life** vivere nella bambagia

shelve [ʃelv] *fig plans* accantonare

shepherd ['ʃepəd] pastore m

sherry ['ʃerɪ] sherry m inv

shield [ʃiːld] **1** n scudo m; sports trophy scudetto m; TECH schermo m di protezione f; Am badge of policeman distintivo m **2** v/t (protect) proteggere

shift [ʃɪft] **1** n (change) cambiamento m; period of work turno m **2** v/t (move) spostare; stains etc togliere **3** v/i (move) spostarsi; of wind cambiare direzione; **shift key** COMPUT tasto m shift; **shifty** pej losco

shimmer ['ʃɪmə(r)] luccicare

shin [ʃɪn] stinco m

shine [ʃaɪn] **1** v/i splendere; fig: of student etc brillare **2** n on shoes etc lucentezza f

shingle ['ʃɪŋgl] on beach ciottoli mpl

shiny ['ʃaɪnɪ] lucido

ship [ʃɪp] **1** n nave f **2** v/t (send) spedire; (send by sea) spedire via mare **3** v/i of new product essere spedito; **shipment** carico m; **shipowner** armatore m; **shipping** (sea traffic) navigazione f; (sending) trasporto m; **shipping company** compagnia f di navigazione; **shipshape** in perfetto ordine; **shipwreck 1** n naufragio m **2** v/t: **be ~ed** naufragare; **shipyard** cantiere m navale

shirker ['ʃɜːkə(r)] scansafati-

che m/f inv

shirt [ʃɜːt] camicia f

shit [ʃɪt] **1** n P merda f P; bad quality goods, work stronzata f P **2** v/i cagare P **3** int merda P; **shitty** F di merda P

shiver ['ʃɪvə(r)] rabbrividire

shock [ʃɒk] **1** n shock m inv; ELEC scossa f; **be in ~** MED essere in stato di shock **2** v/t scioccare; **shock absorber** MOT ammortizzatore m; **shocking** scandaloso; F (very bad) allucinante F

shoddy ['ʃɒdɪ] goods scadente; behaviour meschino

shoe [ʃuː] scarpa f; **shoe-lace** laccio m di scarpa; **shoemaker** calzolaio m; **shoe mender** calzolaio m; **shoeshop**, Am **shoestore** negozio m di scarpe

shoot [ʃuːt] **1** n BOT germoglio m **2** v/t sparare; film girare; **~ s.o. in the leg** colpire qu alla gamba

◆ **shoot down** plane abbattere

◆ **shoot up** of prices salire alle stelle; of children crescere molto; of new buildings etc spuntare

shooting star ['ʃuːtɪŋ] stella f cadente

shop [ʃɒp] **1** n negozio m; **talk ~** parlare di lavoro **2** v/i fare acquisti; **go ~ping** andare a fare spese; **shop assistant** commesso m, -a f; **shopkeeper** negoziante m/f;

shoplifter taccheggiatore *m*, -trice *f*; **shoplifting** taccheggio *m*; **shopper** acquirente *m/f*; **shopping** *items* spesa *f*; **go ~** andare a fare spese; **do one's ~** fare la spesa; **shopping bag** borsa *f* per la spesa; **shopping list** lista *f* della spesa; **shopping mall** centro *m* commerciale; **shop window** vetrina *f*

shore [ʃɔː(r)] riva *f*; **on ~** *not at sea* a terra

short [ʃɔːt] **1** *adj* corto; *in height* basso; *in time* breve; **be ~ of** essere a corto di **2** *adv*: **cut ~** interrompere; **go ~ of** fare a meno di; *in* **~** in breve; **shortage** mancanza *f*; **shortcoming** difetto *m*; **shortcut** scorciatoia *f*; **shorten 1** *v/t* accorciare **2** *v/i* accorciarsi; **shortfall** deficit *m inv*; *in hours etc* mancanza *f*; **shortlist** *of candidates* rosa *f* dei candidati; **short-lived** di breve durata; **shortly** (*soon*) tra breve; **~ before / after** poco prima / dopo; **shortness** *of visit* brevità *f*; *in height* bassa statura *f*; **shorts** calzoncini *mpl*; **shortsighted** *also fig* miope; **short-sleeved** a maniche corte; **short-staffed** a corto di personale; **short-tempered** irascibile; **short-term** a breve termine; **short wave** RAD onde *fpl* corte; **shot** [ʃɒt] *from gun* sparo *m*;

(*photograph*) foto *f*; (*injection*) puntura *f*; **like a ~** *accept, run off* come un razzo; **shotgun** fucile *m* da caccia

should [ʃʊd]: **what ~ I do?** cosa devo fare?; **you ~n't do that** non dovresti farlo; **you ~ have heard him!** avresti dovuto sentirlo!

shoulder [ˈʃəʊldə(r)] ANAT spalla *f*

shout [ʃaʊt] **1** *n* grido *m*, urlo *m* **2** *v/t & v/i* gridare, urlare; **shouting** urla *fpl*

shove [ʃʌv] **1** *n* spinta *f* **2** *v/t & v/i* spingere

shovel [ˈʃʌvl] **1** *n* pala *f* **2** *v/t* spalare

show [ʃəʊ] **1** *n* THEA, TV spettacolo *m*; (*display*) manifestazione *f*; **on ~** *at exhibition* esposto; **it's all done for ~** *pej* è tutta una scena **2** *v/t passport etc* mostrare; *interest, emotion* dimostrare; *at exhibition* esporre; *film* proiettare **3** *v/i* (*be visible*) vedersi; **does it ~?** si vede?; **what's ~ing at the cinema?** cosa danno al cinema?

◆ **show in** far entrare

◆ **show off 1** *v/t skills* mettere in risalto **2** *v/i pej* mettersi in mostra

◆ **show up 1** *v/t shortcomings etc* far risaltare **2** *v/i* F (*arrive, turn up*) farsi vedere F; (*be visible*) notarsi

ˈshow business il mondo dello spettacolo; **showcase**

vetrinetta f; fig vetrina f;
showdown regolamento *m*
di conti

shower ['ʃauə(r)] **1** *n* of rain
acquazzone *m*; to wash doccia *f*; **take a ~** fare una doccia
2 *v/i* fare la doccia; **shower-proof** impermeabile

'**showjumping** concorso *m*
ippico; **show-off** *pej* esibizionista *m/f*; **showroom**
show-room *m inv*; **showy**
appariscente

shred [ʃred] **1** *n* of paper striscolina *f*; of cloth brandello
m; of evidence etc briciolo *m*
2 *v/t* paper stracciare; *in
cooking* sminuzzare; **shredder** *for documents* distruttore *m* di documenti

shrewd [ʃruːd] scaltro; *investment* oculato; **shrewdness**
oculatezza f

shriek [ʃriːk] **1** *n* strillo *m* **2** *v/i*
strillare

shrill [ʃrɪl] stridulo

shrimp [ʃrɪmp] gamberetto *m*

shrine [ʃraɪn] santuario *m*

shrink[1] [ʃrɪŋk] *v/i* of material
restringersi; of support etc diminuire

shrink[2] [ʃrɪŋk] *n* F (psychiatrist) strizzacervelli *m/f inv*

'**shrink-wrapping** process
cellofanatura f; material cellophane® *m*

shrivel ['ʃrɪvl] avvizzire

Shrove 'Tuesday [ʃrəʊv]
martedì *m* grasso

shrub [ʃrʌb] arbusto *m*;

shrubbery arboreto *m*

shrug [ʃrʌg]: **~ one's
shoulders** alzare le spalle

shudder ['ʃʌdə(r)] **1** *n* of fear,
disgust brivido *m*; of earth etc
tremore *m* **2** *v/i* with fear, disgust rabbrividire; of earth,
building tremere; **I ~ to think**
non oso immaginare

shuffle ['ʃʌfl] **1** *v/t cards* mescolare **2** *v/i in walking* strascicare i piedi

shun [ʃʌn] evitare

shut [ʃʌt] **1** *v/t* chiudere **2** *v/i*
of door, box chiudersi; of
shop, bank chiudere; **they
were ~** era chiuso

◆ **shut down 1** *v/t business*
chiudere; *computer* spegnere
2 *v/i* of business chiudere i
battenti; of computer spegnersi

◆ **shut up** F (be quiet) star
zitto; **shut up!** zitto!

shutter ['ʃʌtə(r)] on window
battente *m*; PHOT otturatore
m

'**shuttlebus** bus *m inv* navetta

shy [ʃaɪ] timido; **shyness** timidezza f

Sicilian [sɪ'sɪljən] **1** adj siciliano **2** *n* siciliano *m*, -a f; **Sicily**
Sicilia f

sick [sɪk] sense of humour crudele; **I feel ~ about
to vomit** ho la nausea; **be ~**
(vomit) vomitare; **be ~ of**
(fed up with) essere stufo di

sicken ['sɪkn] **1** *v/t* (disgust) disgustare; Am (make ill) fare ammalare **2** v/i: **be ~ing for sth** covare qc; **sickening** disgustoso; **sick leave: be on ~** essere in (congedo per) malattia; **sickness** malattia f; (vomiting) nausea f

side [saɪd] of box, house lato m; of person, mountain fianco m; of page, record facciata f; SP squadra f; **take ~s** (favour one side) prendere posizione; **I'm on your ~** sono dalla tua (parte); **~ by ~** fianco a fianco; **at the ~ of the road** sul ciglio della strada; **on the small ~** piuttosto piccolo; **sideboard** furniture credenza f; **side effect** effetto m collaterale; **sideline 1** n attività f inv collaterale **2** v/t: **feel ~d** sentirsi sminuito; **sidestep** scansare; fig schivare; **side street** via f laterale; **sidewalk** Am marciapiede m; **sideways** di lato

siege [siːdʒ] assedio m; **lay ~ to** assediare

sieve [sɪv] setaccio m

sift [sɪft] setacciare

sigh [saɪ] **1** n sospiro m **2** v/i sospirare

sight [saɪt] vista f; **~s** of city luoghi mpl da visitare; **catch ~ of** intravedere; **know by ~** conoscere di vista; **in ~ of** essere visibile da; **out of ~** non visibile; **lose ~ of** main objective etc perdere di vista; **sightseeing** visita f turistica; **go ~** fare un giro turisti-

co; **sightseer** turista m/f

sign [saɪn] **1** n (indication) segno m; (road ~) segnale m; outside shop insegna f **2** v/t & v/i document firmare

signal ['sɪgnl] **1** n segnale m **2** v/i of driver segnalare

signatory ['sɪgnətri] firmatario m, -a f

signature ['sɪgnətʃə(r)] firma f

significance [sɪg'nɪfɪkəns] importanza f; (meaning) significato m; **significant** event etc significativo; (quite large) notevole; **significantly** larger, more expensive notevolmente

signify ['sɪgnɪfaɪ] significare; **'sign language** linguaggio m dei segni; **signpost** cartello m stradale

silence ['saɪləns] **1** n silenzio m **2** v/t mettere a tacere; **silencer** MOT marmitta f; silent silenzioso; film muto; **stay ~ not** comment tacere

silhouette [sɪluː'et] sagoma f

silicon ['sɪlɪkən] silicio m

silicone ['sɪlɪkəʊn] silicone m

silk [sɪlk] **1** n seta f **2** adj shirt etc di seta; **silky** setoso

silliness ['sɪlɪnɪs] stupidità f; **silly** stupido

silo ['saɪləʊ] silo m

silver ['sɪlvə(r)] **1** n argento m; objects argenteria f **2** adj ring d'argento; colour argentato; **silverware** argenteria f

similar ['sɪmɪlə(r)] simile (**to**

a); **similarity** rassomiglianza f; **similarly** allo stesso modo

simple ['sɪmpl] semplice; **person** sempliciotto; **simple-minded** pej sempliciotto; **simplicity** semplicità f; **simplify** semplificare; **simplistic** semplicistico; **simply** (absolutely) assolutamente; in a simple way semplicemente

simultaneous [sɪml'teɪnɪəs] simultaneo; **simultaneously** simultaneamente

sin [sɪn] **1** n peccato m **2** v/i peccare

since [sɪns] **1** prep da; ~ **last week** dalla scorsa settimana **2** adv da allora; **I haven't seen him** ~ non lo vedo da allora **3** conj in expressions of time da quando; (seeing that) visto che

sincere [sɪn'sɪə(r)] sincero; **sincerely** con sincerità; **hope** sinceramente; **Yours** ~ Distinti saluti; **sincerity** sincerità f

sinful ['sɪnful] peccaminoso

sing [sɪŋ] cantare

singe [sɪndʒ] bruciacchiare

singer ['sɪŋə(r)] cantante m/f

single ['sɪŋgl] **1** adj (sole) solo; (not double) singolo; bed, sheet a una piazza; (not married) single; with reference to Europe unico; **there wasn't a** ~ ... non c'era nemmeno un ...; **in** ~ **file** in fila indiana **2** n MUS singolo m; (~ room) (camera f) singola f; ticket

biglietto m di sola andata; person single m/f inv; ~**s** in tennis singolo; **single-handed** da solo; **single-minded** determinato; **single mother** ragazza f madre; **single parent** genitore m single; **single parent family** famiglia f monoparentale; **single room** (camera f) singola f

singular ['sɪŋgjʊlə(r)] GRAM **1** adj singolare **2** n singolare m

sinister ['sɪnɪstə(r)] sinistro

sink [sɪŋk] **1** n lavandino m **2** v/i of ship affondare; of object andare a fondo; of sun calare; of interest rates etc scendere **3** v/t ship (far) affondare; funds investire

◆ **sink in** of liquid penetrare; **it still hasn't really sunk in** of realization ancora non mi rendo conto

sinner ['sɪnə(r)] peccatore m, -trice f

sinusitis [saɪnə'saɪtɪs] MED sinusite f

sip [sɪp] **1** n sorso m **2** v/t sorseggiare

sir [sɜː(r)] signore m; **Sir Charles** Sir Charles

siren ['saɪrən] sirena f

sirloin ['sɜːlɔɪn] controfiletto m

sister ['sɪstə(r)] sorella f; in hospital (infermiera f) caposala f; **sister-in-law** cognata f

sit [sɪt] **1** v/i sedere; (sit down)

sedersi **2** *v/t exam* dare
◆ **sit down** sedersi

sitcom ['sɪtkɒm] sitcom *f inv*

site [saɪt] **1** *n* luogo *m* **2** *v/t new offices etc* situare

sitting ['sɪtɪŋ] *of committee, court* sessione *f; for artist* seduta *f; for meals* turno *m;* **sitting room** salotto *m*

situated ['sɪtjʊeɪtɪd] situato; **be ~** trovarsi; **situation** situazione *f; of building etc* posizione *f*

six [sɪks] sei; **sixteen** sedici; **sixteenth**: sedicesimo; **sixth** sesto; **sixtieth** sessantesimo; **sixty** sessanta

size [saɪz] dimensioni *fpl; of clothes* taglia *f*, misura *f; of shoes* numero *m;* **sizeable** considerevole

skate [skeɪt] **1** *n* pattino *m* **2** *v/i* pattinare; **skateboard** skateboard *m inv;* **skateboarding** skateboard *m;* **skater** pattinatore *m*, -trice *f;* **skating** pattinaggio *m;* **skating rink** pista *f* di pattinaggio

skeleton ['skelɪtn] scheletro *m*

skeptic *Am* ☞ **sceptic**

sketch [sketʃ] **1** *n* abbozzo *m;* THEA sketch *m inv* **2** *v/t* abbozzare; **sketchy** *knowledge etc* lacunoso

ski [skiː] **1** *n* sci *m inv* **2** *v/i* sciare

skid [skɪd] **1** *n* sbandata *f* **2** *v/i* sbandare

skier ['skiːə(r)] sciatore *m*, -trice *f;* **skiing** sci *m;* **go ~** andare a sciare; **ski instructor** maestro *m*, -a *f* di sci

skilful, *Am* **skillful** ['skɪlful] abile; **skilfully**, *Am* **skillfully** abilmente

'ski lift impianto *m* di risalita

skill [skɪl] abilità *f inv; what ~s do you have?* quali capacità possiede?; **skilled** abile; **skillful** *Am* ☞ **skilful**

skim [skɪm] *surface* sfiorare; *milk* scremare

skimpy ['skɪmpɪ] *account etc* scarso; *dress* succinto

skin [skɪn] **1** *n of* pelle *f; of fruit* buccia *f* **2** *v/t* scoiare; **skin diving** immersioni *fpl* subacquee

skinny ['skɪnɪ] magro; **skin-tight** aderente

skip [skɪp] **1** *n little jump* salto *m* **2** *v/i* saltellare; *with skipping rope* saltare **3** *v/t* (omit) saltare

'ski pole racchetta *f* da sci

skipper ['skɪpə(r)] NAUT skipper *m inv; of team* capitano *m*

'ski resort stazione *f* sciistica

skirt [skɜːt] gonna *f;* **skirting board** battiscopa *m*

'ski run pista *f* da sci; **ski tow** sciovia *f*

skull [skʌl] cranio *m*

skunk [skʌŋk] moffetta *f*

sky [skaɪ] cielo *m;* **skylight** lucernario *m;* **skyline** profilo *m* (contro il cielo); **sky-**

scraper grattacielo *m*

slab [slæb] *of stone* lastra *f*; *of cake etc* fetta *f*

slack [slæk] *rope* allentato; *person, work* negligente; *period* lento; slacken *rope* allentare; *pace* rallentare; slacks pantaloni *mpl* casual

♦ slag off [slæg] P parlare male di

slam [slæm] *door* sbattere

slander ['slɑːndə(r)] 1 *n* diffamazione *f* 2 *v/t* diffamare; slanderous diffamatorio

slang [slæŋ] slang *m inv*; *of a specific group* gergo *m*

slant [slɑːnt] 1 *v/i* pendere 2 *n* pendenza *f*; *given to a story* angolazione *f*; slanting *roof* spiovente

slap [slæp] 1 *n blow* schiaffo *m* 2 *v/t* schiaffeggiare; slapdash *person* frettoloso; pressapochista; slap-up *meal* F pranzo *m* coi fiocchi

slash [slæʃ] 1 *n cut* taglio *m*; *in punctuation* barra *f* 2 *v/t skin, painting* squarciare; *prices* abbattere

slaughter ['slɔːtə(r)] 1 *n of animals* macellazione *f*; *of people, troops* massacro *m* 2 *v/t animals* macellare; *people, troops* massacrare; slaughterhouse macello *m*

slave [sleɪv] schiavo *m*, -a *f*

slay [sleɪ] ammazzare; slaying Am (*murder*) omicidio *m*

sleaze [sliːz] POL corruzione *f*; sleazy *bar, characters* sor-

---

slide

dido

sleep [sliːp] 1 *n* sonno *m*; go to ~ addormentarsi; I couldn't get to ~ non sono riuscito a dormire 2 *v/i* dormire

♦ sleep in (*have a long lie*) dormire fino a tardi

♦ sleep on *proposal, decision* dormire su; sleep on it dormirci su

♦ sleep with (*have sex with*) andare a letto con

sleeping bag ['sliːpɪŋ] sacco *m* a pelo; sleeping car RAIL vagone *m* letto; sleeping pill sonnifero *m*; sleepless *night* in bianco; sleep walker sonnambulo *m*, -a *f*; sleep walking sonnambulismo *m*; sleepy *child* assonnato; *town* addormentato; I'm ~ ho sonno

sleet [sliːt] nevischio *m*

sleeve [sliːv] *of jacket etc* manica *f*; sleeveless senza maniche

sleight of 'hand [slaɪt] gioco *m* di prestigio

slender ['slendə(r)] *adj* snello; *chance, margin* piccolo

slice [slaɪs] 1 *n also fig* fetta *f* 2 *v/t loaf etc* affettare

slick [slɪk] 1 *adj performance* brillante; (*pej: cunning*) scaltro 2 *n of oil* chiazza *f* di petrolio

slide [slaɪd] 1 *n for kids* scivolo *m*; PHOT diapositiva *f* 2 *v/i* scivolare; *of exchange rate etc*

calare 3 v/t far scivolare
slight [slaɪt] **1** adj person, figure gracile; (small) leggero; **no, not in the ~est** no, per nulla **2** n (insult) offesa f; slightly leggermente
slim [slɪm] **1** adj slanciato; chance scarso 2 v/i dimagrire; **I'm ~ming** sono a dieta
slime [slaɪm] melma f; **slimy** liquid melmoso; person viscido
sling [slɪŋ] **1** n for arm fascia f a tracolla **2** v/t (throw) lanciare
slip [slɪp] **1** n (mistake) errore m **2** v/i on ice etc scivolare; of quality etc peggiorare; **he ~ped out of the room** è sgattaiolato fuori dalla stanza **3** v/t (put) far scivolare; **it ~ped my mind** mi è passato di mente
♦ **slip up** (make a mistake) sbagliarsi
slipped 'disc [slɪpt] ernia f del disco
slipper ['slɪpə(r)] pantofola f
slippery ['slɪpərɪ] scivoloso
'slip road rampa f di accesso; **slip-up** (mistake) errore m
slit [slɪt] **1** n (tear) strappo m; (hole) fessura f; in skirt spacco m **2** v/t envelope, packet aprire (tagliando); throat tagliare
sliver ['slɪvə(r)] scheggia f
slob [slɒb] pej sudicione m, -a f
slog [slɒɡ] faticata f

slogan ['sləʊɡən] slogan m inv
slop [slɒp] rovesciare, versare
slope [sləʊp] **1** n pendenza f; of mountain pendio m **2** v/i essere inclinato; **the road ~s down to the sea** la strada scende fino al mare
sloppy ['slɒpɪ] work, editing trascurato; in dressing sciatto; (too sentimental) sdolcinato
slot [slɒt] fessura f; in schedule spazio m; **slot machine** for vending distributore m automatico; for gambling slot-machine f inv
Slovak ['sləʊvæk] **1** adj slovacco **2** n slovacco m, -a f; language slovacco m; Slovakia Slovacchia f
Slovene ['sləʊviːn] **1** adj sloveno **2** n sloveno m, -a f; language sloveno m; Slovenia Slovenia f
slovenly ['slʌvnlɪ] sciatto
slow [sləʊ] lento; **be ~** of clock essere indietro
♦ **slow down** rallentare
'slowcoach F lumaca f F; **slowdown** in production rallentamento m; **slowly** lentamente; **slow motion: in ~** al rallentatore; **slowness** lentezza f; **slowpoke** Am F lumaca f F
sluggish ['slʌɡɪʃ] lento
slum [slʌm] slum m inv
slump [slʌmp] **1** n in trade crollo m **2** v/i economically

crollare; *of person* accasciarsi

slur [slɜː(r)] **1** *n* calunnia *f* **2** *v/t words* biascicare

slush [slʌʃ] fanghiglia *f*; (*pej: sentimental stuff*) smancerie *fpl*; **slush fund** fondi *mpl* neri

slut [slʌt] *pej* sgualdrina *f*

sly [slaɪ] scaltro

smack [smæk] **1** *n on the bottom* sculacciata *f*; *in the face* schiaffo *m* **2** *v/t child* picchiare; *bottom* sculacciare

small [smɔːl] **1** *adj* piccolo **2** *n*: **the ~ of the back** le reni; **small change** spiccioli *mpl*; **small hours**: **the ~** le ore *fpl* piccole; **small talk** conversazione *f* di circostanza

smart[1] [smɑːt]*adj* (*elegant*) elegante; (*intelligent*) intelligente; *pace* svelto; **get ~ with** fare il furbo con F

smart[2] [smɑːt] *v/i* (*hurt*) bruciare

'smart card smart card *f inv*; **smartly** *dressed* elegantemente

smash [smæʃ] **1** *n noise* fracasso *m*; (*car crash*) scontro *m*; *in tennis* schiacciata *f* **2** *v/t break* spaccare; *hit hard* sbattere; **~ sth to pieces** mandare in frantumi qc **3** *v/i break* frantumarsi

smattering ['smætərɪŋ] *of a language* infarinatura *f*

smear [smɪə(r)] **1** *n of ink etc*

macchia *f*; MED striscio *m*; *on character* calunnia *f* **2** *v/t character* calunniare

smell [smel] **1** *n* odore *m*; **sense of ~** olfatto *m*, odorato *m* **2** *v/t* sentire odore di; *test by smelling* sentire **3** *v/i unpleasantly* puzzare; (*sniff*) odorare; **what does it ~ of?** che odore ha?; **you ~ of beer** puzzi di birra; **smelly** puzzolente

smile [smaɪl] **1** *n* sorriso *m* **2** *v/i* sorridere

smirk [smɜːk] sorriso *m* compiaciuto

smoke [sməʊk] **1** *n* fumo *m*; **have a ~** fumare **2** *v/t cigarettes etc* fumare; *bacon* affumicare **3** *v/i* fumare; **smoke-free** totalmente non smoking; **smoker** fumatore *m*, -trice *f*; **smoking** fumo *m*; **no ~** vietato fumare; **smoky** *room, air* pieno di fumo

smolder *Am* → **smoulder**

smooth [smuːð] **1** *adj surface, skin, sea* liscio; *sea* calmo; *transition* senza problemi; *pej: person* mellifluo **2** *v/t hair* lisciare; **smoothly** *without problems* senza problemi

smother ['smʌðə(r)] *flames, person* soffocare

smoulder ['sməʊldə(r)] covare sotto la cenere

smudge [smʌdʒ] **1** *n* sbavatura *f* **2** *v/t* sbavare

smug [smʌg] compiaciuto

smuggle ['smʌgl] contrabbandare; **smuggler** contrabbandiere *m*, -a *f*; **smuggling** contrabbando *m*

smutty ['smʌtɪ] *joke* sconcio

snack [snæk] spuntino *m*

snag [snæg] (*problem*) problema *m*

snail [sneɪl] chiocciola *f*, *in cooking* lumaca *f*; **snail mail** F posta *f* lumaca

snake [sneɪk] serpente *m*

snap [snæp] **1** *n sound* botto *m*; PHOT foto *f* **2** *v/t break* spezzare; (*say sharply*) dire bruscamente **3** *v/i break* spezzarsi **4** *adj decision* immediato; *temper, mood* irritabile; F (*quick*) rapido; (*elegant*) elegante; **snapshot** istantanea *f*

snarl [snɑːl] **1** *n of dog* ringhio *m* **2** *v/i* ringhiare

snatch [snætʃ] afferrare; (*steal*) scippare; (*kidnap*) rapire

snazzy ['snæzɪ] F chic *inv*

sneakers ['sniːkəz] *Am* scarpe *fpl* da ginnastica

sneaky ['sniːkɪ] F (*crafty*) scaltro

sneer [snɪə(r)] **1** *n* sogghigno *m* **2** *v/i* sogghignare

sneeze [sniːz] **1** *n* starnuto *m* **2** *v/i* starnutire

snicker ['snɪkə(r)] ridacchiare

sniff [snɪf] **1** *v/i to clear nose* tirare su col naso; *of dog* fiutare **2** *v/t smell* annusare

sniper ['snaɪpə(r)] cecchino *m*

snivel ['snɪvl] *pej* frignare

snob [snɒb] snob *m/f inv*; **snobbery** snobismo *m*; **snobbish** snob *inv*

◆ **snoop around** [snuːp] ficcanasare

snooty ['snuːtɪ] snob *inv*

snooze [snuːz] **1** *n* sonnellino *m*; **have a ~** fare un sonnellino **2** *v/i* sonnecchiare

snore [snɔː(r)] russare; **snoring** russare *m*

snorkel ['snɔːkl] boccaglio *m*

snort [snɔːt] sbuffare

snow [snəʊ] **1** *n* neve *f* **2** *v/i* nevicare

◆ **snow under**: **be snowed under with ...** essere sommerso di ...

'snowball palla *f* di neve; **snow chains** *npl* MOT catene *fpl* da neve; **snowdrift** cumulo *m* di neve; **snowflake** fiocco *m* di neve; **snowman** pupazzo *m* di neve; **snowplough**, *Am* **snowplow** spazzaneve *m inv*; **snowstorm** tormenta *f*; **snowy** *weather* nevoso; *roofs, hills* innevato

snub [snʌb] **1** *n* affronto *m* **2** *v/t* snobbare; **snub-nosed** col naso all'insù

snug [snʌg] al calduccio; (*tight-fitting*) attillato

so [səʊ] **1** *adv* così; **~ hot** così caldo; **not ~ much** non così tanto; **~ much easier** molto più facile; **I miss you ~**

manchi tanto; **~ am / do I** anch'io; **and ~ on** e così via **2** *pron*: **I hope ~** spero di sì; **I don't think ~** non credo, credo di no **50 or ~** circa 50 **3** *conj* (*for that reason*) così; (*in order that*) così che; **(that) I could come too** così che potessi venire anch'io; **~ what?** E allora?

soak [səʊk] (*steep*) mettere a bagno; (*of water*) inzuppare; **soaked** fradicio; **soaking (wet)** bagnato fradicio

soap [səʊp] *for washing* sapone *m*; **soap (opera)** soap (opera) *f inv*, telenovela *f*; **soapy** *water* saponato

soar [sɔː(r)] *of rocket etc* innalzarsi; *of prices* aumentare vertiginosamente

sob [sɒb] **1** *n* singhiozzo *m* **2** *v/i* singhiozzare

sober ['səʊbə(r)] sobrio; (*serious*) serio

◆ **sober up** smaltire la sbornia

so-'called cosiddetto

soccer ['sɒkə(r)] calcio *m*

sociable ['səʊʃəbl] socievole

social ['səʊʃl] sociale; **social democrat** socialdemocratico *m*, -a *f*; **socialism** socialismo *m*; **socialist 1** *adj* socialista **2** *n* socialista *m/f*; **socialize** socializzare; **social life** vita *f* sociale; **social science** scienza *f* sociale; **social security** sussidio *m* della previdenza sociale; **social**

work assistenza *f* sociale; **social worker** assistente *m/f* sociale

society [sə'saɪətɪ] società *f inv*; (*organization*) associazione *f*

sociologist [səʊsɪ'ɒlədʒɪst] sociologo *m*, -a *f*; **sociology** sociologia *f*

sock[1] [sɒk] *n* calzino *m*

sock[2] [sɒk] *v/t* F (*punch*) dare un pugno a

socket ['sɒkɪt] *for light bulb* portalampada *m inv*; *in wall* presa *f* (di corrente); *of eye* orbita *f*

soda ['səʊdə] (**~ water**) seltz *m inv*; *Am* bibita *f* analcolica

sofa ['səʊfə] divano *m*

soft [sɒft] *pillow* soffice; *chair, skin* morbido; *light, colour* tenue; *music* soft *inv*; *voice* sommesso; (*lenient*) indulgente; **soft drink** bibita *f*; **soft drug** droga *f* leggera; **soften** *butter etc* ammorbidire; *position* attenuare; *impact, blow* attutire; **softly** *speak* sommessamente; **software** software *m*

soggy ['sɒgɪ] molle e pesante

soil [sɔɪl] **1** *n* (*earth*) terra *f* **2** *v/t* sporcare

solar 'energy ['səʊlə(r)] energia *f* solare; **solar panel** pannello *m* solare

soldier ['səʊldʒə(r)] soldato *m*

sole[1] [səʊl] *n of foot* pianta *f* (del piede); *of shoe* suola *f*

sole² [səʊl] *adj* unico; (*exclusive*) esclusivo

solely ['səʊlɪ] solamente

solemn ['sɒləm] solenne; **solemnity** solennità *f inv*; **solemnly** solennemente

solicit [sə'lɪsɪt] *of prostitute* adescare; **solicitor** avvocato *m*

solid ['sɒlɪd] (*hard*) solido; (*without holes*) compatto; *gold, silver* massiccio; (*sturdy*) robusto; *evidence* concreto; *support* forte; **solidarity** solidarietà *f*; **solidify** solidificarsi; **solidly** *built* solidamente; *in favour of sth* all'unanimità

solitaire ['sɒlɪteə(r)] *card game* solitario *m*

solitary ['sɒlɪtərɪ] *life, activity* solitario; (*single*) solo; **solitude** solitudine *f*

solo ['səʊləʊ] **1** *n* MUS assolo *m* **2** *adj performance* solista; **soloist** solista *m/f*

soluble ['sɒljʊbl] *substance* solubile; *problem* risolvibile; **solution** soluzione *f*

solve [sɒlv] risolvere; **solvent** *financially* solvibile

sombre, *Am* **somber** ['sɒmbə(r)] (*dark*) scuro; (*serious*) tetro

some [sʌm] **1** *adj* (*amount*) un po' di, del; (*number*) qualche, dei *m*, delle *f*; **~ people say that ...** alcuni dicono che ... **2** *pron* (*amount*) un po'; (*number*) alcuni *m*, -e

f; **would you like ~?** ne vuoi un po'?; **~ of the students** alcuni studenti; **somebody** qualcuno; **someday** un giorno; **somehow** (*by one means or another*) in qualche modo; (*for some unknown reason*) per qualche motivo; **someone** ☞ **somebody** **someplace** ☞ **somewhere**

somersault ['sʌməsɔːlt] **1** *n* capriola *f* **2** *v/i* fare una capriola

'something qualcosa; **sometime** (*one of these days*) uno di questi giorni; **~ last year** l'anno scorso; **sometimes** a volte; **somewhat** piuttosto; **somewhere 1** *adv* da qualche parte **2** *pron* un posto; **let's go ~ quiet** andiamo in un posto tranquillo

son [sʌn] figlio *m*

song [sɒŋ] canzone *f*; *of birds* canto *m*

'son-in-law genero *m*; **son of a bitch** V figlio *m* di puttana P

soon [suːn] presto; **as ~ as** non appena; **as ~ as possible** prima possibile; **~er or later** presto o tardi; **the ~er the better** prima è, meglio è; **how ~ can you be ready?** fra quanto sei pronto?

soothe [suːð] calmare

sophisticated [sə'fɪstɪkeɪtɪd] sofisticato; **sophistication** *of person* raffinatezza *f*; *of machine* complessità *f* sophomore ['sɒfəmɔːr] *Am* studente *m/f* del secondo anno

soprano [sə'prɑːnəʊ] soprano *m/f*

sordid ['sɔːdɪd] sordido

sore [sɔːr] 1 *adj* (*painful*) dolorante; **is it ~?** fa male? 2 *n* piaga *f*; **sore throat** mal *m* di gola

sorrow ['sɒrəʊ] dispiacere *m*, dolore *m*

sorry ['sɒrɪ] *day, sight* triste; (*I'm*) ~! *apologizing* scusa!; *polite form* scusi!; **I'm ~** *regretting* mi dispiace; **I feel ~ for her** mi dispiace per lei

sort [sɔːt] 1 *n* tipo *m*; **~ of** ... F un po' ...; **is it finished? – ~ of** F è terminato? – quasi 2 *v/t* separare; COMPUT ordinare

SOS [esəʊes] SOS *m inv*

so-'so F così così

soul [səʊl] anima *f*; **the poor ~** il poverino, la poverina

sound¹ [saʊnd] 1 *adj* (*sensible*) valido; (*healthy*) sano; *sleep* profondo; *structure* solido 2 *adv*: **be ~ asleep** dormire profondamente

sound² [saʊnd] 1 *n* suono *m*, (*noise*) rumore *m* 2 *v/i*: **that ~s interesting** sembra interessante

'soundbite slogan *m inv*; soundly *sleep* profondamente; *beaten* duramente; soundproof insonorizzato; soundtrack colonna *f* sono-

ra

soup [suːp] minestra *f*

sour ['saʊər] *apple, orange* aspro; *milk, expression, comment* acido

source [sɔːs] fonte *f*; *of river* sorgente *f*

south [saʊθ] 1 *adj* meridionale, del sud 2 *n* sud *m* 3 *adv travel* verso sud; **~ of** a sud di; **South Africa** Repubblica *f* Sudafricana; **South African** 1 *adj* sudafricano 2 *n* sudafricano *m*, -a *f*; **South America** Sudamerica *m*; **South American** 1 *adj* sudamericano 2 *n* sudamericano *m*, -a *f*; **southeast** 1 *n* sud-est *m* 2 *adj* sud-orientale 3 *adv* verso sud-est; **southeastern** sud-orientale; **southerly** meridionale; **southern** del sud; **southerner** abitante *m/f* del sud; **southernmost** più a sud; **South Pole** polo *m* sud; **southwards** verso sud; **southwest** 1 *n* sud-ovest *m* 2 *adj* sud-occidentale 3 *adv* verso sud-ovest; **southwestern** sud-occidentale

souvenir [suːvə'nɪər] souvenir *m inv*

sovereign ['sɒvrɪn] *state* sovrano; **sovereignty** *of state* sovranità *f*

sow¹ [saʊ] *n* (*female pig*) scrofa *f*

sow² [səʊ] *v/t seeds* seminare

soya sauce ['sɔɪə] salsa *f* di

soia

space [speɪs] spazio *m*; *in car park* posto *m*; **space-bar** COMPUT barra *f* spaziatrice; **spacecraft** veicolo *m* spaziale; **spaceship** astronave *f*; **space shuttle** shuttle *m inv*; **space station** stazione *f* spaziale; **spacious** spazioso

spade [speɪd] *for digging* vanga *f*; **~s** *in card game* picche *mpl*

spaghetti [spəˈgeti] spaghetti *mpl*

Spain [speɪn] Spagna *f*

spam [spæm] spam *f*

span [spæn] coprire; *of bridge* attraversare

Spaniard [ˈspænjəd] spagnolo *m*, -a *f*; **Spanish 1** *adj* spagnolo **2** *n language* spagnolo *m*

spanner [ˈspænə(r)] chiave *f* inglese

spare [speə(r)] **1** *v/t (do without)* fare a meno di; *can you ~ £50?* mi puoi prestare 50 sterline?; *can you ~ the time?* hai tempo?; *have money / time to ~* avere soldi / tempo d'avanzo **2** *adj* in più **3** *n* ricambio *m*; **spare part** pezzo *m* di ricambio; **spare ribs** costine *fpl* di maiale; **spare room** stanza *f* degli ospiti; **spare time** tempo *m* libero; **spare wheel** MOT ruota *f* di scorta; **sparing**: *be ~ with* andarci piano con; **sparingly** con modera-

zione

spark [spɑːk] scintilla *f*

sparkle [ˈspɑːkl] brillare; **sparkling wine** vino *m* frizzante

'spark plug candela *f*

sparrow [ˈspærəʊ] passero *m*

sparse [spɑːs] *vegetation* rado; **sparsely**: *~ populated* scarsamente popolato

spartan [ˈspɑːtn] spartano

spasmodic [spæzˈmɒdɪk] irregolare

spate [speɪt] *fig* ondata *f*

spatial [ˈspeɪʃl] spaziale

speak [spiːk] **1** *v/i* parlare; **~ing** TELEC sono io **2** *v/t for eign language* parlare; *the truth* dire

♦ **speak up** (*speak louder*) parlare ad alta voce

speaker [ˈspiːkə(r)] oratore *m*, -trice *f*; *of sound system* cassa *f*; **Italian ~** italofono *m*, -a *f*; **speaker phone** telefono *m* con vivavoce

spear [spɪə(r)] lancia *f*

special [ˈspeʃl] speciale; (*particular*) particolare; **special effects** effetti *mpl* speciali; **specialist** specialista *m/f*; **speciality** specialità *f inv*; **specialize** specializzarsi (*in* in); **specially** *➙* **especially**; **specialty** specialità *f inv*

species [ˈspiːʃiːz] specie *f inv*

specific [spəˈsɪfɪk] specifico; **specifically** specificamente; **specifications** *of machine etc* caratteristiche *fpl* tecniche; **specify** specificare

specimen ['spesimən] campione *m*

spectacle ['spektəkl] (*impressive sight*) spettacolo *m*; (*a pair of*) **~s** (un paio di) occhiali *mpl*; **spectacular** spettacolare

spectator [spek'teitə(r)] spettatore *m*, -trice *f*

spectrum ['spektrəm] *fig* gamma *f*

speculate ['spekjulert] (*on sth*) fare congetture (**on** su); FIN speculare; **speculation** congetture *fpl*; FIN speculazione *f*; **speculator** FIN speculatore *m*, -trice *f*

speech [spi:tʃ] *n* discorso *m*; *in play* monologo *m*; (*ability to speak*) parola *f*; (*way of speaking*) linguaggio *m*; **speechless** *with shock, surprise* senza parole

speed [spi:d] **1** *n* velocità *f inv*; (*quickness*) rapidità *f inv* **2** *v/i* (*go quickly*) andare a tutta velocità; (*drive too quickly*) superare il limite di velocità

◆ **speed up 1** *v/i* andare più veloce **2** *v/t* accelerare

'speedboat motoscafo *m*; **speed bump** dosso *m* di rallentamento; **speedily** rapidamente; **speeding** *when driving* eccesso *m* di velocità; **speed limit** limite *m* di velocità; **speedometer** tachimetro *m*; **speedy** rapido

spell¹ [spel] **1** *v/t*: *how do you ~ ...?* come si scrive ...?; *could you ~ that please?* me lo può dettare lettera per lettera? **2** *v/i* sapere come si scrivono le parole

spell² [spel] *n* (*period of time*) periodo *m*

'spellchecker COMPUT correttore *m* ortografico; **spelling** ortografia *f*

spend [spend] *money* spendere; *time* passare; **spendthrift** *pej* spendaccione *m*, -a *f*

sperm [spɜ:m] spermatozoo *m*; (*semen*) sperma *m*

sphere [sfiə(r)] *also fig* sfera *f*

spice [spais] (*seasoning*) spezia *f*; **spicy** *food* piccante

spider ['spaidə(r)] ragno *m*; **spider's web** ragnatela *f*

spike [spaik] *on railings* spuntone *m*; *on plant* spina *f*; *on animal* aculeo *m*; *on running shoes* chiodo *m*

spill [spil] **1** *v/t* versare **2** *v/i* versarsi **3** *n* of oil etc fuoriuscita *f*

spin¹ [spin] **1** *n* giro *m*; *on ball* effetto *m* **2** *v/t* far girare; *ball* imprimere l'effetto a **3** *v/i* of wheel girare

spin² [spin] *v/t wool, cotton* filare; *web* tessere

spinach ['spinidʒ] spinaci *mpl*

spinal ['spainl] spinale; **spinal column** colonna *f* vertebrale, spina *f* dorsale; **spinal cord** midollo *m* spinale

'spin doctor *esperto che ha il compito di presentare ai media le decisioni di un partito o personaggio politico sotto la luce migliore*

spine [spaɪn] *of person, animal* spina *f* dorsale; *of book* dorso *m*; *on plant, hedgehog* spina *f*; spineless (*cowardly*) smidollato

'spin-off applicazione *f* secondaria

spinster ['spɪnstə(r)] zitella *f*

spiny ['spaɪnɪ] spinoso

spiral ['spaɪrəl] 1 *n* spirale *f* 2 *v/i* (*rise quickly*) salire vertiginosamente; spiral staircase scala *f* a chiocciola

spire ['spaɪə(r)] spira *f*, guglia *f*

spirit ['spɪrɪt] spirito *m*; spirited *debate* animato; *defence* energico; *performance* brioso; spirits (*morale*) morale *msg*; be in good / poor ~ essere su / giù di morale; spiritual spirituale

spit [spɪt] *of person* sputare

spite [spaɪt] dispetto *m*; in ~ of malgrado; spiteful dispettoso; spitefully dispettosamente

spitting image ['spɪtɪŋ]: be the ~ of s.o. essere il ritratto sputato di s.o.

splash [splæʃ] 1 *n* (*noise*) tonfo *m*; (*small amount of liquid*) schizzo *m*; (*of colour*) macchia *f* 2 *v/t person* schizzare; *water, mud* spruzzare 3 *v/i* schizzare; *of waves* infrangersi

'splashdown ammaraggio *m*

splendid ['splendɪd] magnifico; splendour, *Am* splendor magnificenza *f*

splint [splɪnt] MED stecca *f*

splinter ['splɪntə(r)] 1 *n* scheggia *f* 2 *v/i* scheggiarsi

split [splɪt] 1 *n in leather* strappo *m*; *in wood* crepa *f*; (*disagreement*) spaccatura *f*; (*division, share*) divisione *f* 2 *v/t leather* strappare; *wood, logs* spaccare; (*cause disagreement in*) spaccare; (*divide*) dividere 3 *v/i of leather* strapparsi; *of wood* spaccarsi; (*disagree*) spaccarsi

◆ split up *of couple* separarsi

splitting ['splɪtɪŋ]: ~ headache feroce mal *m inv* di testa

spoil [spɔɪl] *child* viziare; *surprise, party* rovinare; spoilsport F guastafeste *m/f*; spoilt *child* viziato; be ~ for choice avere (solo) l'imbarazzo della scelta

spoke [spəʊk] *of wheel* raggio *m*

spokesperson ['spəʊkspɜːsən] portavoce *m/f*

sponge [spʌndʒ] spugna *f*; sponger F scroccone *m*, -a *f*

sponsor ['spɒnsə(r)] 1 *n for immigration etc* garante *m/f inv*; *of TV programme, sports event, for fundraising* sponsor *m inv* 2 *v/t for immigra-*

sprint

tion, *membership* garantire per; *TV programme*, *sports event* sponsorizzare; **sponsorship** sponsorizzazione *f*

spontaneous [spɒn'teɪnɪəs] spontaneo; **spontaneously** spontaneamente

spool [spuːl] bobina *f*

spoon [spuːn] cucchiaio *m*; **spoonful** cucchiaio *f*

sporadic [spə'rædɪk] sporadico

sport [spɔːt] sport *m inv*; **sporting** sportivo; **sports jacket** giacca *f* sportiva; **sports car** auto *f inv* sportiva; **sportsman** sportivo *m*; **sportswear** abbigliamento *m* sportivo; **sportswoman** sportiva *f*; **sporty** sportivo

spot[1] [spɒt] *n* (*pimple*) brufolo *m*; *caused by measles etc* foruncolo *m*; *part of pattern* pois *m inv*

spot[2] [spɒt] *n* (*place*) posticino *m*; **on the ~** (*in the place in question*) sul posto; (*immediately*) immediatamente

spot[3] [spɒt] *v/t* (*notice*) notare; (*identify*) trovare

'spot check controllo *m* casuale; **spotless** pulitissimo; **spotlight** faretto *m*; **spotty** *with pimples* brufoloso

spouse [spaʊs] *fml* coniuge *m/f*

spout [spaʊt] **1** *n* beccuccio *m* **2** *v/i of liquid* sgorgare **3** *v/t* F: **~ nonsense** ciarlare

sprain [spreɪn] **1** *n* slogatura *f* **2** *v/t* slogarsi

sprawl [sprɔːl] stravaccarsi; *of city* estendersi; **send s.o. ~ing** *of punch* mandare qu a gambe all'aria; **sprawling** *city* tentacolare

spray [spreɪ] **1** *n of sea water* spruzzi *mpl*; *for hair* lacca *f*; (*container*) spray *m inv* **2** *v/t* spruzzare; **spraygun** pistola *f* a spruzzo

spread [spred] **1** *n of disease*, *religion etc* diffusione *f*; F *big meal* banchetto *m* **2** *v/t* (*lay*) stendere; *butter*, *jam* spalmare; *news*, *rumour*, *disease* diffondere; *arms*, *legs* allargare **3** *v/i* diffondersi; **spreadsheet** COMPUT spreadsheet *m inv*

sprightly ['spraɪtlɪ] arzillo

spring[1] *n* [sprɪŋ] *season* primavera *f*

spring[2] [sprɪŋ] *n device* molla *f*

spring[3] [sprɪŋ] **1** *n* (*jump*) balzo *m*; (*stream*) sorgente *f* **2** *v/i* (*jump*) balzare; **~ from** derivare da

'springboard trampolino *m*; **spring onion** cipollotto *m*; **springtime** primavera *f*

sprinkle ['sprɪŋkl] spruzzare; **~ sth with** cospargere qc di; **sprinkler** *for garden* irrigatore *m*; *in ceiling* sprinkler *m inv*

sprint [sprɪnt] **1** *n*: scatto *m*; **the 100 metres ~** i cento metri piani **2** *v/i* fare uno scatto;

sprinter SP velocista *m/f*

spud [spʌd] F patata *f*

spy [spaɪ] **1** *n* spia *f* **2** *v/i* fare la spia **3** *v/t* (*see*) scorgere

♦ **spy on** spiare

squabble ['skwɒbl] **1** *n* bisticcio *m* **2** *v/i* bisticciare

squalid ['skwɒlɪd] squallido; **squalor** squallore *m*

squander ['skwɒndə(r)] *money* dilapidare

square [skweə(r)] **1** *adj in shape* quadrato; *~ mile* miglio quadrato **2** *n shape* quadrato *m*; *in town* piazza *f*; *in board game* casella *f*; MATH quadrato *m*; *we're back to ~ one* siamo punto e a capo; **square root** radice *f* quadrata

squash[1] [skwɒʃ] *n vegetable* zucca *f*

squash[2] [skwɒʃ] *n game* squash *m*

squash[3] [skwɒʃ] *v/t* (*crush*) schiacciare

squat [skwɒt] **1** *adj in shape* tozzo **2** *v/i* (*sit*) accovacciarsi; *illegally* occupare abusivamente

squeak [skwiːk] **1** *n of mouse* squittio *m*; *of hinge* cigolio *m* **2** *v/i of mouse* squittire; *of hinge* cigolare; *of shoes* scricchiolare; **squeaky** *hinge* cigolante; *shoes* scricchiolante; *voice* stridulo; **squeaky clean** F pulito

squeal [skwiːl] **1** *n of pain, laughter* strillo *m*; *of brakes*

stridore *m* **2** *v/i* strillare; *of brakes* stridere

squeamish ['skwiːmɪʃ]: *be ~* avere lo stomaco delicato

squeeze [skwiːz] **1** *n of hand, shoulder* stretta *f* **2** *v/t hand* stringere; *orange, lemon* spremere; *sponge* strizzare

squid [skwɪd] calamaro *m*

squint [skwɪnt] strabismo *m*

squirm [skwɜːm] (*wriggle*) contorcersi; *~ (with embarrassment)* morire di vergogna

squirrel ['skwɪrəl] scoiattolo *m*

squirt [skwɜːt] **1** *v/t* spruzzare **2** *n* F *pej* microbo *m* F

St *abbr* (= *saint*) S. (= santo *m*, santa *f*); (= *street*) v. (= via *f*)

stab [stæb] accoltellare

stability [stə'bɪlətɪ] stabilità *f*; **stabilize 1** *v/t* stabilizzare **2** *v/i* stabilizzarsi; **stable 1** *adj* stabile; **2** *n for horses* stalla *f*; *establishment* scuderia *f*

stack [stæk] **1** *n* (*pile*) pila *f*; *~s of* F un sacco di F **2** *v/t* mettere in pila

stadium ['steɪdɪəm] stadio *m*

staff [stɑːf] (*employees*) personale *msg*; (*teachers*) corpo *m* insegnante; **staffroom** *in school* sala *f* professori

stage[1] [steɪdʒ] *n in life, project etc* fase *f*; *of journey* tappa *f*

stage[2] [steɪdʒ] **1** *n* (*pile*) THEA palcoscenico *m* **2** *v/t play* mettere in scena; *demonstration* organizzare

stagger ['stægə(r)] **1** v/i barcollare **2** v/t (amaze) sbalordire; holidays, breaks etc scaglionare; **staggering** sbalorditivo

stagnant ['stægnənt] also fig stagnante; **stagnate** of person, mind vegetare

'**stag party** (festa f di) addio m al celibato

stain [steɪn] **1** n (dirty mark) macchia f; for wood mordente m **2** v/t (dirty) macchiare; wood dare il mordente a **3** v/i of wine etc macchiare; of fabric macchiarsi; **stained-glass window** vetrata f colorata; **stainless steel** acciaio m inossidabile

stair [steə(r)] scalino m; **the ~s** le scale; **staircase** scala f

stake [steɪk] **1** n of wood paletto m; when gambling puntata f; (investment) partecipazione f; **be at ~** essere in gioco **2** v/t tree puntellare; money puntare

stale [steɪl] bread raffermo; air viziato; fig: news vecchio; **stalemate** in chess stallo m; fig punto m morto

stalk[1] [stɔːk] n of fruit picciolo m; of plant gambo m

stalk[2] [stɔːk] v/t animal seguire; person perseguitare (con telefonate, lettere ecc)

stall[1] [stɔːl] n at market bancarella f; for cow, horse box m inv

stall[2] [stɔːl] **1** v/i of vehicle fermarsi; (play for time) temporeggiare **2** v/t engine far spegnere; people trattenere

stalls [stɔːlz] platea f

stalwart ['stɔːlwət] supporter fedele

stamina ['stæmɪnə] resistenza f

stammer ['stæmə(r)] **1** n balbuzie f **2** v/i balbettare

stamp[1] [stæmp] **1** n for letter francobollo m; (date ~ etc) timbro m **2** v/t letter affrancare; document, passport timbrare; **~ed addressed envelope** busta f affrancata per la risposta

stamp[2] [stæmp] v/t: **~ one's feet** pestare i piedi

stance [stæns] (position) presa f di posizione

stand [stænd] **1** n at exhibition stand m inv; (witness ~) banco m dei testimoni; (support, base) base f; LAW **take the ~** testimoniare **2** v/i (be situated: of person) stare; of object, building trovarsi; as opposed to sit stare in piedi; (rise) alzarsi in piedi **3** v/t (tolerate) sopportare; (put) mettere; **you don't ~ a chance** non hai alcuna probabilità; **~ s.o. a drink** offrire da bere a qu

◆ **stand by 1** v/i (not take action) stare a guardare; (be ready) tenersi pronto **2** v/t person stare al fianco di; de-

cision mantenere

◆ **stand down** (*withdraw*) ritirarsi

◆ **stand for** (*tolerate*) tollerare; (*mean*) significare; *freedom etc* rappresentare

◆ **stand out** spiccare; *of person, building* distinguersi

◆ **stand up 1** *v/i* alzarsi in piedi **2** *v/t* F *on date* dare buca a F

◆ **stand up for** difendere

◆ **stand up to** far fronte a

standard ['stændəd] **1** *adj* (*usual*) comune; *model* standard *inv* **2** *n* (*level*) livello *m*; (*expectation*) aspettativa *f*; TECH standard *m inv*; **be up to ~** essere di buona qualità; **standardize** standardizzare; **standard of living** tenore *m* di vita

'**standby** *ticket* biglietto *m* stand-by; **on ~** *at airport* in lista d'attesa; **on ~** *of troops etc* pronto; **standing** *in society etc* posizione *f*; (*repute*) reputazione *f*; **of long ~** di lunga durata; **standoffish** scostante; **standpoint** punto *m* di vista; **standstill**: **be at a ~** essere fermo; **bring to a ~** fermare

staple¹ ['steɪpl] *n* (*foodstuff*) alimento *m* base

staple² ['steɪpl] **1** *n* (*fastener*) graffa *f* **2** *v/t* pinzare

stapler ['steɪplə(r)] pinzatrice *f*

~**ar** [stɑː(r)] **1** *n in sky* stella *f*;

fig star f inv **2** *v/t*: *a film ~ring Julia Roberts* un film interpretato da Julia Roberts; **starboard** *an* film tribordo

stare [steə(r)] fissare; **~ at** fissare

stark [stɑːk] **1** *adj landscape* desolato; *colour scheme* austero; *reminder, contrast* brusco **2** *adv*: **~ naked** completamente nudo

starling ['stɑːlɪŋ] storno *m*

starry ['stɑːrɪ] *night* stellato

start [stɑːt] **1** *n* inizio *m*; **get off to a good ~** cominciare bene **2** *v/i* iniziare, cominciare; *of engine, car* partire; **~ing from tomorrow** a partire da domani **3** *v/t* cominciare; *engine, car* mettere in moto; *business* mettere su; **~ to do sth, ~ doing sth** cominciare a fare qc; **starter** *of meal* antipasto *m*; *of car* motorino *m* d'avviamento; *in race* starter *m inv*; **starting point** punto *m* di partenza; **starting salary** stipendio *m* iniziale

startle ['stɑːtl] far trasalire; **startling** sorprendente

'**start-up** COM nuova azienda *f*

starvation [stɑː'veɪʃn] fame *f*; **starve** soffrire la fame; *I'm starving* F sto morendo di fame

state¹ [steɪt] **1** *n of car, house, part of country* stato *m*; **the States** gli Stati Uniti **2** *adj* di stato; *school* statale; *banquet etc* ufficiale

state² [steɪt] *v/t* dichiarare

'State Department Ministero *m* degli Esteri; **statement** *to police* deposizione *f*; *(announcement)* dichiarazione *f*; *(bank* ~) estratto *m* conto; **state of emergency** stato *m* d'emergenza; **state-of-the-art** allo stato dell'arte; **statesman** statista *m*

static (elec'tricity) ['stætɪk] elettricità *f* statica

station ['steɪʃn] **1** *n* stazione *f* **2** *v/t guard etc* disporre; **stationary** fermo

stationery ['steɪʃənərɪ] articoli *mpl* di cancelleria

'station wagon giardiniera *f*

statistical [stə'tɪstɪkl] statistico; **statistically** statisticamente; **statistician** esperto *m*, -a *f* di statistica; **statistics** *science* statistica *f*; *npl figures* statistiche *fpl*

statue ['stætjuː] statua *f*

status ['steɪtəs] posizione *f*; **status symbol** status symbol *m inv*

statute ['stætjuːt] statuto *m*

staunch [stɔːntʃ] leale

stay [steɪ] **1** *n* soggiorno *m* **2** *v/i in a place* stare; *in a condition* restare; ~ *in a hotel* stare in albergo; ~ *right there!* non ti muovere

◆ **stay behind** rimanere

◆ **stay up** *(not go to bed)* rimanere alzato

steadily ['stedɪlɪ] *improve etc* costantemente; *look* fisso

steady 1 *adj voice, hands* fermo; *job, boyfriend* fisso; *beat* regolare; *improvement, decline* costante **2** *adv*: **be going** ~ fare coppia fissa; ~ **on!** calma! **3** *v/t bookcase etc* rendere saldo

steak [steɪk] bistecca *f*, carne *f* (di manzo)

steal [stiːl] **1** *v/t* rubare **2** *v/i (be a thief)* rubare; ~ **in / out** entrare / uscire furtivamente

stealthy ['stelθɪ] furtivo

steam [stiːm] **1** *n* vapore *m* **2** *v/t food* cuocere al vapore; **steamed up** F *angry* furibondo; **steamer** *for cooking* vaporiera *f*

steel [stiːl] **1** *n* acciaio *m* **2** *adj* d'acciaio; **steelworker** operaio *m* di acciaieria

steep¹ [stiːp] *adj hill etc* ripido; F *prices* alto

steep² [stiːp] *v/t (soak)* lasciare a bagno

steer¹ [stɪr] *n animal* manzo *m*

steer² [stɪə(r)] *v/t* manovrare; *person* guidare; *conversation* spostare; **steering** MOT sterzo *m*; **steering wheel** volante *m*

stem¹ [stem] *n of plant, glass* stelo *m*; *of word* radice *f*

stem² [stem] *v/t (block)* arginare

'stem cell cellula *f* staminale

stench [stentʃ] puzzo *m*

stencil ['stensil] **1** *n* stencil *m inv* **2** *v/t pattern* disegnare con lo stencil

step [step] **1** *n* (*pace*) passo *m*; (*stair*) gradino *m*; (*measure*) provvedimento *m*; **~ by ~** poco a poco **2** *v/i*: **~ into / out of** salire in / scendere da

◆ **step down** *from post etc* dimettersi

◆ **step up** (*increase*) aumentare

'**stepbrother** fratellastro *m*; **stepdaughter** figliastra *f*; **stepfather** patrigno *m*; **stepladder** scala *f* a libretto; **stepmother** matrigna *f*; **stepsister** sorellastra *f*; **stepson** figliastro *m*

stereo ['steriəʊ] (*sound system*) stereo *m inv*; **stereotype** stereotipo *m*

sterile ['sterail] sterile; **sterilize** sterilizzare

sterling ['stɜːlɪŋ] FIN sterlina *f*

stern[1] [stɜːn] *adj* severo

stern[2] [stɜːn] *n* NAUT poppa *f*

sternly ['stɜːnlɪ] severamente

steroids ['sterɔɪdz] anabolizzanti *mpl*

stethoscope ['steθəskəʊp] fonendoscopio *m*

stew [stjuː] *n* spezzatino *m*

steward ['stjuːəd] *on plane, ship* steward *m inv*; *at demonstration, meeting* membro *m* del servizio d'ordine; **stewardess** *on plane, ship* hostess *f inv*

stick[1] [stɪk] *n wood* rametto *m*; (*walking ~*) bastone *m*; **out in the ~s** F a casa del diavolo F

stick[2] [stɪk] **1** *v/t with adhesive* attaccare; *needle, knife* conficcare; F (*put*) mettere **2** *v/i* (*jam*) bloccarsi; (*adhere*) attaccarsi

◆ **stick by** F *person* rimanere al fianco di

◆ **stick to** F (*keep to*) attenersi a; F (*follow*) seguire

◆ **stick up for** F difendere

sticker ['stɪkə(r)] adesivo *m*; **sticking plaster** cerotto *m*; **stick-in-the-mud** F abitudinario *m*, -a *f*; **sticky** appiccicoso; *label* adesivo

stiff [stɪf] **1** *adj brush, cardboard, leather* rigido; *muscle, body* anchilosato; *paste* sodo; *in manner* freddo; *drink, competition* forte; *fine* salato **2** *adv*: **be bored ~** F essere annoiato a morte F; **stiffness** *of muscles* indoenimento *m*; *of material* rigidità *f*; *of manner* freddezza *f*

stifle ['staɪfl] *also fig* soffocare; **stifling** soffocante

stigma ['stɪgmə] vergogna *f*

stilettos [stɪ'letəʊz] *npl* (*shoes*) scarpe *fpl* con tacco a spillo

still[1] [stɪl] **1** *adj* (*motionless*) immobile; *without wind* senza vento; *drink* non gas(s)ato **2** *adv*: **keep / stand ~!** stai fermo!

still² [stɪl] adv (yet) ancora; (nevertheless) comunque; **she ~ hasn't finished** non ha ancora finito; **~ more** ancora più

'stillborn nato morto; **still life** natura f morta

stilted ['stɪltɪd] poco naturale

stimulant ['stɪmjʊlənt] stimolante m; **stimulate** stimolare; **stimulating** stimolante; **stimulation** stimolazione f; **stimulus** (incentive) stimolo m

sting [stɪŋ] **1** n from bee puntura f; from jellyfish pizzico m **2** v/t of bee pungere; of jellyfish pizzicare **3** v/i of eyes, scratch bruciare; **stinging criticism** pungente

stingy ['stɪndʒɪ] F tirchio F

stink [stɪŋk] **1** n (bad smell) puzza f; F (fuss) putiferio m F; **kick up a ~** F fare un casino F **2** v/i (smell bad) puzzare; F (be very bad) fare schifo F

stipulate ['stɪpjʊleɪt] stabilire; **stipulation** condizione f

stir [stɜː(r)] **1** v/t mescolare **2** v/i of sleeping person muoversi; **stirring** music, speech commovente

stitch [stɪtʃ] **1** n in sewing punto m; in knitting maglia f; **~es** MED punti mpl (di sutura); **be in ~es** ridere a crepapelle **2** v/t sew cucire; **stitching** (stitches) cucitura f

stock [stɒk] **1** n (reserves)

provvista f; COM of store stock m inv; animals bestiame m; FIN titoli mpl; for soup etc brodo m; **in ~ / out of ~** disponibile / esaurito; **take ~** fare il punto **2** v/t vendere; **stockbroker** agente m/f di cambio; **stock exchange** borsa f valori; **stockholder** azionista m/f; **stockist** rivenditore m; **stock market** mercato m azionario; **stockpile 1** n of food, weapons scorta f **2** v/t fare scorta di

stocky ['stɒkɪ] tarchiato

stodgy ['stɒdʒɪ] food pesante

stoical ['stəʊɪkl] stoico; **stoicism** stoicismo m

stomach ['stʌmək] **1** n stomaco m; (abdomen) pancia f **2** v/t (tolerate) sopportare; **stomach-ache** mal m di stomaco

stone [stəʊn] pietra f; (pebble) sasso m; in fruit nocciolo m; **stoned** on drugs fatto F; **stone-deaf** sordo (come una campana)

stool [stuːl] seat sgabello m

stoop¹ [stuːp] v/i (bend down) chinarsi; (have bent back) essere curvo

stoop² [stuːp] n Am (porch) porticato m

stop [stɒp] **1** n for train, bus fermata f **2** v/t (put an end to) mettere fine a; (prevent) fermare; (cease) smettere; person, car, bus fermare; *cheque* bloccare; **~ doing sth** smettere di fare qc **3** *v/i* (*come to a halt*) fermarsi; *of rain, noise* smettere

◆ **stop over** fare sosta

'**stopgap** *person* tappabuchi *m/f inv; thing* soluzione *f* temporanea; (*traffic light*) rosso *m*; (*brake light*) fanalino *m* d'arresto; **stopover** sosta *f; in air travel* scalo *m* intermedio; **stopper** tappo *m*; **stop sign** (segnale *m* di) stop *m inv;* **stopwatch** cronometro *m*

storage ['stɔːrɪdʒ]: **put sth in ~** mettere qc in magazzino, in deposito; **store 1** *n large shop* negozio *m*; (*stock*) riserva *f*; (*storehouse*) deposito *m* **2** *v/t* tenere; COMPUT memorizzare; **storekeeper** *Am* negoziante *m/f*; **store window** *Am* vetrina *f*

storey ['stɔːrɪ] *of building* piano *m*

storm [stɔːm] tempesta *f*; **stormy** tempestoso

story[1] ['stɔːrɪ] (*tale*) racconto *m*; (*account*) storia *f*; (*newspaper article*) articolo *m*; F (*lie*) bugia *f*

story[2] ['stɔːrɪ] *of building* piano *m*

stout [staʊt] *person* robusto

stove [stəʊv] *for cooking* cucina *f; for heating* stufa *f*

stow [stəʊ] riporre

◆ **stow away** imbarcarsi clandestinamente

'**stowaway** passeggero *m*, -a *f* clandestino, -a

straight [streɪt] **1** *adj line* retto; *hair, whisky* liscio; *back, knees* dritto; (*honest, direct*) onesto; (*tidy*) in ordine; (*conservative*) convenzionale; (*not homosexual*) etero; **keep a ~ face** non ridere **2** *adv* dritto; *think* con chiarezza; **go ~** F *of criminal* rigare dritto; **give it to me ~** F dimmi francamente; **~ ahead** avanti dritto; **carry~ on** proseguire dritto; **~away, ~ out** immediatamente; **~ out** *say sth* chiaro e tondo; **straighten** raddrizzare; **straightforward** (*honest, direct*) franco; (*simple*) semplice

strain[1] [streɪn] **1** *n physical* sforzo *m; mental* tensione *f* **2** *v/t* (*injure*) affaticare; *finances*, gravare su

strain[2] [streɪn] *v/t vegetables* scolare; *oil, fat etc* filtrare

strained [streɪnd] teso; **strainer** *for vegetables etc* colino *m*

strait [streɪt] GEOG stretto *m*; **straitlaced** puritano

strand [strænd] piantare in asso F; **be~ed** essere bloccato

strange [streɪndʒ] (*odd, curious*) strano; (*unknown, foreign*) sconosciuto; **strangely** (*oddly*) stranamente; **~ enough** strano ma vero;

stranger *person you don't know* sconosciuto *m*, -a *f*; **I'm a ~ here myself** non sono di queste parti

strangle ['stræŋgl] strangolare

strap [stræp] *of bag* tracolla *f*; *of bra, dress* bretellina *f*, spallina *f*; *of watch* cinturino *m*; *of shoe* listino *m*; **strapless** senza spalline

strategic [strə'ti:dʒɪk] strategico; **strategy** strategia *f*

straw [strɔː] paglia *f*; *for drink* cannuccia *f*; **strawberry** fragola *f*

stray [streɪ] **1** *adj animal* randagio; *bullet* vagante **2** *n dog, cat* randagio *m* **3** *v/i of animal* smarrirsi; *of child* allontanarsi; *fig: of eyes, thoughts* vagare

streak [striːk] **1** *n of dirt, paint* striscia *f*; *in hair* mèche *f inv*; *fig: of nastiness etc* vena *f* **2** *v/i move quickly* sfrecciare

stream [striːm] **1** *n* ruscello *m*; *fig: of people, complaints* fiume *m*; **come on ~** *of plant* entrare in attività; *of oil* arrivare **2** *v/i* riversarsi; **streamline** *fig* snellire; **streamlined** *car, plane* aerodinamico; *organization* snellito

street [striːt] strada *f*; *in address* via *f*; **streetcar** *Am* tram *m inv*; **streetlight** lampione *m*; **street value** *of drugs* valore *m* di mercato; **streetwise** scafato F

strength [streŋθ] forza *f*; *(strong point)* punto *m* forte; **strengthen** **1** *v/t* rinforzare **2** *v/i* consolidarsi

strenuous ['strenjʊəs] faticoso; **strenuously** *deny* recisamente

stress [stres] **1** *n (emphasis)* accento *m*; *(tension)* stress *m inv* **2** *v/t syllable* accentare; *importance etc* sottolineare; **stressed out** stressato; **stressful** stressante

stretch [stretʃ] **1** *n of land, water* tratto *m*; **at a ~** *(non-stop)* di fila **2** *adj fabric* elasticizzato **3** *v/t material* tendere; *small income* far bastare; **~ the rules** F fare uno strappo (alla regola); **he ~ed out his hand** allungò la mano **4** *v/i to relax muscles* stirarsi; *to reach sth* allungarsi; *(spread)* estendersi; **stretcher** barella *f*

strict [strɪkt] *person* severo; *instructions* tassativo; **strictly**: **be brought up ~** ricevere un'educazione rigida; **it is ~ forbidden** è severamente proibito

stride [straɪd] **1** *n* falcata *f*; **take sth in one's ~** affrontare qc senza drammi; **make great ~s** *fig* far passi da gigante **2** *v/i* procedere a grandi passi; **he strode up to me** avanzò verso di me

strident ['straɪdnt] stridulo; *demands* veemente

strike [straɪk] **1** *n of workers* sciopero *m*; *of oil* scoperta *f*; **be on ~** essere in sciopero **2** *v/i of workers* scioperare; *(attack)* aggredire; *of disaster* colpire; *of clock* suonare **3** *v/t (hit)* colpire; *match* accendere (sfregando); *of idea, thought* venire in mente a; *of oil* trovare; **she struck me as being** ... mi ha dato l'impressione di essere ...

◆ **strike out** *(delete)* depennare

'strikebreaker crumiro *m*, -a *f*; **striker** *person on strike* scioperante *m/f*; *in football* bomber *m* inv, cannoniere *m*; **striking** *(marked)* marcato; *(eye-catching)* impressionante; *(attractive)* attraente; *colour* forte

string [strɪŋ] *(cord)* spago *m*; *of violin, tennis racket* corda *f*; **the ~s** MUS gli archi; **a ~ of** *(series)* una serie di; **stringed instrument** strumento *m* ad arco

stringent ['strɪndʒnt] rigoroso

strip [strɪp] **1** *n* striscia *f*; *(comic ~)* fumetto *m*; *of soccer player* divisa *f* **2** *v/t (remove)* staccare; *bed* disfare; *(undress)* spogliare; **~ s.o. of sth** spogliare qu di qc **3** *v/i (undress)* spogliarsi; *of stripper* fare lo spogliarello; **strip club** locale *m* di spogliarelli

stripe [straɪp] striscia *f*; MIL gallone *m*; **striped** a strisce

stripper ['strɪpə(r)] spogliarellista *f*; **male ~** spogliarellista *m*; **striptease** spogliarello *m*

strive [straɪv]: **~ to do sth** sforzarsi di fare qc; **~ for sth** lottare per (ottenere) qc

stroke [strəʊk] **1** *n* MED ictus *m* inv; *when painting* pennellata *f*; *style of swimming* stile *m* di nuoto; **~ of luck** colpo *m* di fortuna **2** *v/t* accarezzare

stroll [strəʊl] **1** *n* passeggiata *f*; **go for a ~** fare una passeggiata **2** *v/i* fare due passi; **she ~ed back to the office** tornò in ufficio in tutta calma; **stroller** *Am for baby* passeggino *m*

strong [strɒŋ] forte; *structure* resistente; *candidate* valido; *taste, smell* intenso; *views, beliefs* fermo; *arguments* convincente; *objections* energico; **~ support** largo consenso; **strongly** *believe, object* fermamente; *built* solidamente; **feel ~ about sth** avere molto a cuore qc; **strong-minded** risoluto; **strong point** (punto *m*) forte *m*; **strongroom** camera *f* blindata; **strong-willed** deciso

structural ['strʌktʃərəl] strutturale; **structure 1** *n something built* costruzione *f*; *of novel, society etc* struttura *f* **2** *v/t* strutturare

struggle ['strʌgl] **1** n (fight) colluttazione f; fig lotta f; (hard time) fatica f **2** v/i with a person lottare; (have a hard time) faticare; **~ to do sth** faticare a fare qc

strut [strʌt] camminare impettito

stub [stʌb] **1** n of cigarette mozzicone m; of cheque, ticket matrice f **2** v/t: **~ one's toe** urtare il dito del piede ♦ **stub out** spegnere

stubble ['stʌbl] on man's face barba f ispida

stubborn ['stʌbən] person testardo; defence, refusal ostinato

stubby ['stʌbɪ] tozzo

stuck [stʌk] F: **be ~ on s.o.** essere cotto di qu F; **stuck-up** F presuntuoso

student ['stjuːdnt] studente m, -essa f

studio ['stjuːdɪəʊ] studio m; (recording **~**) sala f di registrazione

studious ['stjuːdɪəs] studioso; **study 1** n studio m **2** v/t & v/i studiare

stuff [stʌf] **1** n roba f **2** v/t turkey farcire; **~ sth into sth** ficcare qc in qc; **stuffing** for turkey farcia f; in chair, teddy bear imbottitura f; **stuffy** room mal ventilato; person inquadrato

stumble ['stʌmbl] inciampare; **stumbling-block** fig scoglio m

stump [stʌmp] **1** n of tree ceppo m **2** v/t of question, questioner sconcertare

stun [stʌn] of blow stordire; of news sbalordire; **stunning** (amazing) sbalorditivo; (very beautiful) splendido

stunt [stʌnt] for publicity trovata f pubblicitaria; in film acrobazia f; **stuntman** in movie cascatore m

stupefy ['stjuːpɪfaɪ] sbalordire

stupendous [stjuː'pendəs] (marvellous) fantastico; mistake enorme

stupid ['stjuːpɪd] stupido; **stupidity** stupidità f

sturdy ['stɜːdɪ] robusto

stutter ['stʌtə(r)] balbettare

style [staɪl] stile m; (fashion) moda f; (fashionable elegance) classe f; (hair~) pettinatura f; **stylish** elegante; **stylist** (hair ~) parrucchiere m, -a f

subcommittee ['sʌbkəmɪtɪ] sottocommissione f

subconscious [sʌb'kɒnʃəs] subconscio; **the ~ (mind)** il subconscio; **subconsciously** inconsciamente

subcontract [sʌbkən'trækt] subappaltare; **subcontractor** subappaltatore m, -trice f

subdivide [sʌbdɪ'vaɪd] suddividere

subdue [səb'djuː] sottomettere

subheading ['sʌbhedɪŋ] sottotitolo *m*

subhuman [sʌb'hju:mən] subumano

subject 1 ['sʌbdʒɪkt] *n of monarch* suddito *m*, -a *f*; (*topic*) argomento *m*; EDU materia *f*; GRAM soggetto *m*; **change the ~** cambiare argomento **2** ['sʌbdʒɪkt] *adj*: **be ~ to** essere soggetto a; **~ to availability** nei limiti della disponibilità **3** [səb'dʒekt] *v/t* sottoporre; **subjective** soggettivo

sublet ['sʌblet] subaffittare

subma'chine gun mitra *m*

submarine ['sʌbməri:n] sottomarino *m*, sommergibile *m*

submerge [səb'mɜ:dʒ] **1** *v/t* sommergere **2** *v/i of submarine* immergersi

submission [səb'mɪʃn] (*surrender*) sottomissione *f*; *request to committee etc* richiesta *f*; **submissive** sottomesso; **submit 1** *v/t plan, proposal* presentare **2** *v/i* sottomettersi

subordinate [sə'bɔ:dɪnət] **1** *adj employee, position* subalterno **2** *n* subalterno *m*, -a *f*

subpoena [sə'pi:nə] **1** *n* citazione *f* **2** *v/t person* citare in giudizio

◆ **subscribe to** [səb'skraɪb] *magazine etc* abbonarsi a; *theory* condividere

subscriber [səb'skraɪbə(r)] *to*

magazine abbonato *m*, -a *f*; **subscription** abbonamento *m*

subsequent ['sʌbsɪkwənt] successivo; **subsequently** successivamente

subside [səb'saɪd] *of waters, winds* calare; *of building* sprofondare; *of fears* calmarsi

subsidiary [səb'sɪdɪərɪ] filiale *f*

subsidize ['sʌbsɪdaɪz] sovvenzionare; **subsidy** sovvenzione *f*

substance ['sʌbstəns] sostanza *f*

substandard [sʌb'stændəd] scadente

substantial [səb'stænʃl] considerevole; *meal* sostanzioso; **substantially** (*considerably*) considerevolmente; (*in essence*) sostanzialmente

substantive [səb'stæntɪv] sostanziale

substitute ['sʌbstɪtju:t] **1** *n for person* sostituto *m*, -a *f*; *for commodity* alternativa *f*; SP riserva *f* **2** *v/t*: **~ X for Y** sostituire Y con X **3** *v/i*: **~ for s.o.** sostituire qu; **substitution** (*act*) sostituzione *f*

subtitle ['sʌbtaɪtl] sottotitolo *m*

subtle ['sʌtl] sottile; *flavour* delicato

subtract [səb'trækt] sottrarre

suburb ['sʌbɜ:b] sobborgo *m*; **the ~s** la periferia; **subur-**

ban di periferia

subversive [səb'vɜ:sɪv] **1** *adj* sovversivo **2** *n* sovversivo *m*, -a *f*

subway ['sʌbweɪ] *Br* sottopassaggio *m*; *Am* metropolitana *f*

sub'zero: ~ *temperatures* temperature sottozero

succeed [sək'si:d] **1** *v/i* avere successo; *to throne* succedere; ~ *in doing sth* riuscire a fare qc **2** *v/t* (*come after*) succedere a; **success** [sək'ses] successo *m*; **be a** ~ avere successo; **successful** *person* affermato; *marriage, party* riuscito; **be** ~ riuscire; **he's very** ~ è arrivato; **successfully** con successo; **we** ~ **completed** ... siamo riusciti a portare a termine ...; **successive** successivo; **three** ~ **days** tre giorni di seguito; **successor** successore *m*

succinct [sək'sɪŋkt] succinto

succumb [sə'kʌm] (*give in*) cedere

such [sʌtʃ] **1** *adj* (*of that kind*) del genere; ~ **a** (*so much of a*) un / una tale; ~ **as** come; **he made** ~ **a fuss** ha fatto una tale scenata; **there is no** ~ **word as ...** la parola ... non esiste **2** *adv* così; ~ **nice people** gente così simpatica

suck [sʌk] **1** *v/t lollipop etc* succhiare **2** *v/i*: **it** ~**s** P fa schifo P

♦ **suck up to** F leccare i pie-

di a F

sucker ['sʌkə(r)] F *person* pollo F; **suction** aspirazione *f*

sudden ['sʌdn] improvviso; **all of a** ~ all'improvviso; **suddenly** improvvisamente

sue [su:] **1** *v/t* fare causa a **2** *v/i* fare causa

suede [sweɪd] pelle *f* scamosciata

suffer ['sʌfə(r)] **1** *v/i* (*be in pain*) soffrire; **be** ~**ing from** avere; ~ **from** soffrire di **2** *v/t loss, setback* subire; **suffering** sofferenza *f*

sufficient [sə'fɪʃnt] sufficiente; **sufficiently** abbastanza

suffocate ['sʌfəkeɪt] soffocare; **suffocation** soffocamento *m*

sugar ['ʃʊɡə(r)] **1** *n* zucchero *m* **2** *v/t* zuccherare

suggest [sə'dʒest] proporre, suggerire; **suggestion** proposta *f*, suggerimento *m*

suicide ['su:ɪsaɪd] suicidio *m*; **commit** ~ suicidarsi; **suicide bomber** kamikaze *m inv*

suit [su:t] **1** *n for man* vestito *m*, completo *m*; *for woman* tailleur *m inv*; *in cards* seme *m* **2** *v/t of clothes, colour* stare bene a; ~ **yourself!** F fai come ti pare!; **be** ~**ed for sth** essere fatto per qc; **suitable** adatto; **suitably** adeguatamente; **suitcase** valigia *f*

suite [swi:t] *of rooms* suite *f inv*; *of furniture* divano *m* e poltrone *fpl* coordinati; MUS suite *f inv*

sulk [sʌlk] fare il broncio; **sulky** imbronciato

sullen ['sʌlən] crucciato

sultry ['sʌltrɪ] *climate* afoso; *sexually* sensuale

sum [sʌm] somma *f*; *in arithmetic* addizione *f*

◆ **sum up 1** *v/t (summarize)* riassumere; *(assess)* valutare **2** *v/i* LAW riepilogare

summarize ['sʌməraɪz] riassumere; **summary** riassunto *m*

summer ['sʌmə(r)] estate *f*

summit ['sʌmɪt] *of mountain* vetta *f*; POL summit *m inv*

summon ['sʌmən] convocare; **summons** LAW citazione *f*

sun [sʌn] sole *m*; **in the ~** al sole; **out of the ~** all'ombra; **sunbathe** prendere il sole; **sunbed** lettino *m* solare; **sunblock** protezione *f* solare totale; **sunburn** scottatura *f*; **sunburnt** scottato; **Sunday** domenica *f*; **sunglasses** occhiali *mpl* da sole; **sunny** *day* di sole; *spot* soleggiato; *disposition* allegro; **it's ~** c'è il sole; **sunrise** alba *f*; **sunset** tramonto *m*; **sunshade** ombrellone *m*; **sunshine** (luce *f* del) sole *m*; **sunstroke** colpo *m* di sole; **suntan** abbronzatura *f*; **get a ~** abbronzarsi

super ['suːpə(r)] F fantastico

superb [su'pɜːb] magnifico

superficial [suːpə'fɪʃl] superficiale

superfluous [su'pɜːfluəs] superfluo

super'human sovrumano

superintendent [suːpərɪn'tendənt] *Br of police* commissario *m*; *Am of apartment block* custode *m/f*

superior [su'pɪərɪə(r)] **1** *adj (better)* superiore **2** *n in organization* superiore *m*

superlative [su'pɜːlətɪv] **1** *adj (superb)* eccellente **2** *n* GRAM superlativo *m*

'supermarket supermercato *m inv*

super'natural 1 *adj powers* soprannaturale **2** *n:* **the ~** il soprannaturale

'superpower POL superpotenza *f*

supersonic [suːpə'sɒnɪk] supersonico

superstition [suːpə'stɪʃn] superstizione *f*; **superstitious** superstizioso

supervise ['suːpəvaɪz] supervisionare; **supervisor** *at work* supervisore *m*

supper ['sʌpə(r)] cena *f*

supple ['sʌpl] *person, limbs* snodato; *material* flessibile

supplement ['sʌplɪmənt] supplemento *m*

supplier [sə'plaɪə(r)] COM fornitore *m*; **supply 1** *n* fornitura *f*; **~ and demand** domanda *e* offerta; **supplies** rifornimenti **2** *v/t goods* fornire; **~**

s.o. **with** *sth* fornire qc a qu

support [sə'pɔːt] **1** *n for structure* supporto *m*; *(backing)* sostegno *m* **2** *v/t structure*, *(back)* sostenere; *financially* mantenere; *football team* fare il tifo per; **supporter** sostenitore *m*, -trice *f*; *of football team etc* tifoso *m*, -a *f*; **supportive**: **be ~ towards** *s.o.* dare il proprio appoggio a qu

suppose [sə'pəʊz] *(imagine)* supporre; *it is ~d to ... (is meant to)* dovrebbe ...; *(is said to)* dicono che ...; *you are not ~d to ... (not allowed to)* non dovresti ...; **supposedly** presumibilmente

suppress [sə'pres] reprimere; **suppression** repressione *f*

supremacy [suː'preməsɪ] supremazia *f*; **supreme** supremo *m*; **Supreme Court** Corte *f* Suprema

surcharge ['sɜːtʃɑːdʒ] *for travel* sovrapprezzo *m*; *for mail* soprattassa *f*

sure [ʃʊə(r)] **1** *adj* sicuro; **make ~ that ...** assicurarsi che ... **2** *adv* certamente; **~ enough** infatti; **~!** F certo!; **surely** certamente; *(gladly)* volentieri; **that's not right!** non può essere!; **surety** *for loan* cauzione *f*

surf [sɜːf] **1** *n on sea* spuma *f* **2** *v/t the Net* navigare in

surface ['sɜːfɪs] **1** *n* superficie

f; **on the ~** *fig* superficialmente **2** *v/i from water* risalire in superficie; *(appear)* farsi vivo; **surface mail** posta *f* ordinaria

'surfboard tavola *f* da surf; **surfer** surfista *m/f*; **surfing** surf *m*; **go ~** fare surf

surge [sɜːdʒ] *in electric current* sovratensione *f* transitoria; *in demand* impennata *f*

surgeon ['sɜːdʒən] chirurgo *m*; **surgery** intervento *m* chirurgico; *place of work* ambulatorio *m*; **~ hours** orario *m* d'ambulatorio; **surgical** chirurgico; **surgically** chirurgicamente

surly ['sɜːlɪ] scontroso

surmount [sə'maʊnt] *difficulties* sormontare

surname ['sɜːneɪm] cognome *m*

surpass [sə'pɑːs] superare

surplus ['sɜːpləs] **1** *n* surplus *m inv* **2** *adj* eccedente

surprise [sə'praɪz] **1** *n* sorpresa *f* **2** *v/t* sorprendere; **be ~d** essere sorpreso; **look ~d** avere l'aria sorpresa; **surprising** sorprendente; **surprisingly** sorprendentemente

surrender [sə'rendə(r)] **1** *v/i of army* arrendersi **2** *v/t weapons etc* consegnare **3** *n* resa *f*

surrogate 'mother ['sʌrəgət] madre *f* biologica

surround [sə'raʊnd] **1** *v/t* circondare **2** *n of picture etc* bordo *m*; **surrounding** circostante; **surroundings** dintorni *mpl*; *fig* ambiente *m*

survey 1 ['sɜːveɪ] *n of modern literature etc* quadro *m* generale; *of building* perizia *f*; *poll* indagine *f* **2** [sə'veɪ] *v/t* (*look at*) osservare; *building* periziare; **surveyor** perito *m*

survival [sə'vaɪvl] sopravvivenza *f*; **survive** *v/i* sopravvivere; *his two surviving daughters* le due figlie ancora in vita **2** *v/t* sopravvivere a; **survivor** superstite *m/f*; *he's a* ~ *fig* se la cava sempre

suspect 1 ['sʌspekt] *n* indiziato *m*, -a *f* **2** [sə'spekt] *v/t person* sospettare; (*suppose*) supporre; **suspected** *murderer* presunto; *cause, heart attack etc* sospetto

suspend [sə'spend] (*hang*), *from office* sospendere; **suspenders** *Br* giarrettiere *fpl*; *Am for pants* bretelle *fpl*

suspense [sə'spens] suspense *f*; **suspension** MOT, *from duty* sospensione *f*

suspicion [sə'spɪʃn] sospetto *m*; **suspicious** *causing suspicion* sospetto; *feeling suspicion* sospettoso; *be ~ of* sospettare di; **suspiciously** *behave* in modo sospetto; *examine* sospettosamente

sustain [sə'steɪn] sostenere; **sustainable** sostenibile

SUV [esjuː'viː] (= *sports utility vehicle*) Suv *m inv*, gip-

pone *m*

swab [swɒb] tampone *m*

swallow¹ ['swɒləʊ] *v/t & v/i* inghiottire

swallow² ['swɒləʊ] *n bird* rondine *f*

swamp [swɒmp] **1** *n* palude *f* **2** *v/t*: *be ~ped with* essere sommerso da; **swampy** paludoso

swan [swɒn] cigno *m*

swap [swɒp] **1** *v/t*: ~ *sth for sth* scambiare qc con qc **2** *v/i* fare scambio

swarm [swɔːm] **1** *n of bees* sciame *m* **2** *v/i*: *the town was ~ing with ...* la città brulicava di ...

swarthy ['swɔːðɪ] scuro

swat [swɒt] *fly* schiacciare

sway [sweɪ] **1** *n* (*power*) influenza *f* **2** *v/i* barcollare

swear [sweə(r)] **1** *v/i* (*use swearword*) imprecare; ~ *at s.o.* dire parolacce a qu **2** *v/t* (*promise*) giurare; LAW, *on oath* giurare

◆ **swear in**: *the witness was sworn in* il testimone ha prestato giuramento

'**swearword** parolaccia *f*

sweat [swet] **1** *n* sudore *m* **2** *v/i* sudare; **sweat band** fascia *f* asciugasudore; **sweater** maglione *m*; **sweats** *Am* tuta *f* (*da ginnastica*); **sweatshirt** felpa *f*; **sweaty** *hands* sudato; *smell* di sudore

Swede [swiːd] svedese *m/f*; **Sweden** Svezia *f*; **Swedish**

1 adj svedese **2** n svedese m

sweep [swi:p] **1** v/t floor, leaves spazzare **2** n (long curve) curva f; sweeping changes radicale; **a ~ state-ment** una generalizzazione

sweet [swi:t] **1** adj dolce; F (kind) gentile; F (cute) carino **2** n caramella f; (dessert) dolce m; sweet and sour agrodolce; sweetcorn mais m; sweeten zuccherare; sweetheart innamorato m, -a f

swell [swel] **1** v/i of wound, limb gonfiarsi **2** n of the sea mare m lungo; swelling MED gonfiore m

sweltering ['sweltərɪŋ] heat afoso, soffocante

swerve [swɜːv] of driver, car sterzare (bruscamente)

swift [swɪft] rapido

swim [swɪm] **1** v/i nuotare **2** n nuotata f; **go for a ~** andare a nuotare; swimmer nuotatore m, -trice f; swimming nuoto m; swimming costume m da bagno; swimming pool piscina f; swimsuit esp Am costume m da bagno

swindle ['swɪndl] **1** n truffa f **2** v/t truffare; **~ s.o. out of sth** estorcere qc a qu (con l'inganno)

swing [swɪŋ] **1** n of pendulum etc oscillazione f; for child altalena f; **a ~ to the left** una svolta verso la sinistra **2** v/t far dondolare **3** v/i dondola-

re; (turn) girare; of public opinion etc indirizzarsi

Swiss [swɪs] **1** adj svizzero **2** n person svizzero m, -a f; **the ~** gli svizzeri

switch [swɪtʃ] **1** n for light interruttore m; (change) cambiamento m **2** v/t (change) cambiare **3** v/i (change) cambiare; **~ to** passare a

♦ switch off spegnere

♦ switch on accendere

Switzerland ['swɪtsələnd] Svizzera f

swivel ['swɪvl] girarsi

swollen ['swəʊlən] gonfio

sword [sɔːd] spada f; swordfish pesce m spada inv

syllable ['sɪləbl] sillaba f

syllabus ['sɪləbəs] programma m

symbol ['sɪmbəl] simbolo m; symbolic simbolico; symbolism simbolismo m; symbolist simbolista m/f; symbolize simboleggiare

symmetrical [sɪ'metrɪkl] simmetrico; symmetry simmetria f

sympathetic [sɪmpə'θetɪk] (showing pity) compassionevole; (understanding) comprensivo; **be ~ towards an idea** simpatizzare per un'idea

♦ sympathize with ['sɪmpəθaɪz] person, views capire

sympathizer ['sɪmpəθaɪzə(r)] POL simpatizzante m/f; sympathy (pity) compassione f;

(understanding) comprensione *f*

symphony ['sɪmfənɪ] sinfonia *f*

symptom ['sɪmptəm] *also fig* sintomo *m*; **symptomatic:** *be ~ of* essere sintomatico di

synchronize ['sɪŋkrənaɪz] sincronizzare

synonym ['sɪnənɪm] sinonimo *m*; **synonymous** sinonimo

synthesizer ['sɪnθəsaɪzə(r)] MUS sintetizzatore *m*; syn-

thetic sintetico

syphilis ['sɪfɪlɪs] sifilide *f*

Syria ['sɪrɪə] Siria *f*; **Syrian 1** *adj* siriano **2** *n* siriano *m*, -a *f*

syringe [sɪ'rɪndʒ] siringa *f*

syrup ['sɪrəp] sciroppo *m*

system ['sɪstəm] *also computer* sistema *m*; *(orderliness)* ordine *m*; **systematic** sistematico; **systematically** sistematicamente; **systems analyst** COMPUT analista *m/f* di sistemi

T

table ['teɪbl] tavolo *m*; *of figures* tabella *f*, tavola *f*; **tablecloth** tovaglia *f*; **table lamp** lampada *f* da tavolo; **table of contents** indice *m*; **tablespoon** cucchiaio *m* da tavola

tablet ['tæblɪt] MED compressa *f*

'table tennis tennis *m* da tavolo, ping pong *m*

tabloid ['tæblɔɪd] *newspaper* quotidiano *m* formato tabloid; *pej* quotidiano *m* scandalistico

taboo [tə'buː] tabù *m inv*

tacit ['tæsɪt] tacito

tack [tæk] **1** *n (nail)* chiodino *m* **2** *v/t (sew)* imbastire **3** *v/i of yacht* virare di bordo

tackle ['tækl] **1** *n (equipment)* attrezzatura *f*; SP *in football*,

hockey contrasto *m*; *in rugby* placcaggio *m* **2** *v/t in football*, *hockey* contrastare; *in rugby* placcare; *problem, intruder* affrontare

tacky ['tækɪ] *paint* fresco; *glue* appiccicoso; F *(cheap, poor quality)* di cattivo gusto

tact [tækt] tatto *m*; **tactful** pieno di tatto; **tactfully** con grande tatto

tactical ['tæktɪkl] tattico; **tactics** tattica *f*

tactless ['tæktlɪs] privo di tatto

tadpole ['tædpəʊl] girino *m*

tag [tæg] *(label)* etichetta *f*

tail [teɪl] coda *f*; **tailback** coda *f*; **tail light** luce *f* posteriore

tailor ['teɪlə(r)] sarto *m*, -a *f*; **tailor-made** *also fig* (fatto) su misura

'tailpipe tubo *m* di scappamento

take [teɪk] prendere; (*transport*) portare; (*accompany*) accompagnare; (*accept: money, gift*) accettare; *maths, French, photograph, exam, shower, stroll* fare; (*endure*) sopportare; (*require*) richiedere; *how long does it ~?* quanto ci vuole?

◆ **take after** aver preso da

◆ **take away** *pain* far sparire; *object* togliere; MATH sottrarre; *take sth away from s.o.* togliere qc a qu; *to take away* food da asporto

◆ **take back** (*return: object*) riportare; (*receive back*) riprendere; *person* riaccompagnare; (*accept back: husband etc*) rimettersi insieme a; *sth said* ritirare; *that takes me back* mi riporta al passato

◆ **take down** *from shelf* tirare giù; *scaffolding* smontare; (*write down*) annotare

◆ **take in** (*take indoors*) portare dentro; (*give accommodation*) ospitare; (*make narrower*) stringere; (*deceive*) imbrogliare; (*include*) includere

◆ **take off 1** *v/t clothes, 10%* togliere; (*mimic*) imitare; *take a day off* prendere un giorno di ferie **2** *v/i of aeroplane* decollare; (*become popular*) far presa

◆ **take on** *job* intraprendere;

staff assumere

◆ **take out** *from bag, pocket* tirare fuori; *stain, appendix, tooth, word* togliere; *money from bank* prelevare; *to dinner etc* portar fuori; *insurance policy* stipulare, fare; *take it out on s.o.* prendersela con qu

◆ **take over 1** *v/t company etc* assumere il controllo di **2** *v/i of new management etc* assumere il controllo; (*do sth in s.o.'s place*) dare il cambio

◆ **take to** (*like*) prendere in simpatia; (*form habit of*) prendere l'abitudine di; *he immediately took to the new idea* la nuova idea gli è piaciuta subito

◆ **take up** *carpet etc* togliere; (*carry up*) portare sopra; *dress etc* accorciare; *judo, Spanish, new job* incominciare; *offer* accettare; *space, time* occupare; *I'll take you up on your offer* accetto la tua offerta

'takeoff *of airplane* decollo *m*; (*impersonation*) imitazione *f*; **takeover** COM rilevamento *m*; **takeover bid** offerta *f* pubblica di acquisto, OPA *f*; **takings** incassi *mpl*

tale [teɪl] storia *f*

talent ['tælənt] talento *m*; **talented** pieno di talento; **talent scout** talent scout *m/f inv*

talk [tɔːk] **1** *v/i* parlare **2** *v/t*

English etc parlare; business, politics parlare di; ~ s.o. into doing sth convincere qu a fare qc **3** n (conversation) conversazione f; (lecture) conferenza f; ~s (negotiations) trattative fpl
◆ talk back ribattere

talkative ['tɔːkətɪv] loquace; talk show talk show m inv

tall [tɔːl] alto; tall story bagianata f

tally ['tælɪ] **1** n conto m **2** v/i quadrare

tame [teɪm] animal addomesticato; joke etc blando
◆ tamper with ['tæmpə(r)] manomettere

tampon ['tæmpɒn] tampone m

tan [tæn] **1** n from sun abbronzatura f; colour marrone m rossiccio **2** v/i in sun abbronzarsi **3** v/t leather conciare

tangent ['tændʒənt] MATH tangente f

tangerine [tændʒə'riːn] tangerino m

tangible ['tændʒɪbl] tangibile f

tangle ['tæŋgl] nodo m

tango ['tæŋgəʊ] tango m

tank [tæŋk] recipiente m; MOT serbatoio m; MIL carro m armato; for skin diver bombola f (d'ossigeno); tanker ship nave f cisterna; truck autocisterna f

tanned [tænd] abbronzato

tantalizing ['tæntəlaɪzɪŋ] allettante; smell stuzzicante

tantamount ['tæntəmaʊnt]: be ~ to essere equivalente a

tantrum ['tæntrəm] capricci mpl; throw a ~ fare (i) capricci

tap [tæp] **1** n rubinetto m **2** v/t (hit) dare un colpetto a; phone mettere sotto controllo; tap dance n tip tap m

tape [teɪp] **1** n magnetic nastro m magnetico; recorded cassetta f; (sticky) nastro m adesivo; on ~ registrato **2** v/t conversation etc registrare; ~ sth to sth attaccare qc a qc col nastro adesivo; tape deck registratore m; tape drive COMPUT unità f inv di backup a nastro; tape measure metro m a nastro

taper ['teɪpə(r)] assottigliarsi

'tape recorder registratore m a cassette; tape recording registrazione f su cassetta

tar [tɑː(r)] catrame m

tardy ['tɑːdɪ] Am tardivo; arrival in ritardo

target ['tɑːgɪt] **1** n bersaglio m; for sales etc obiettivo m **2** v/t market rivolgersi a; target audience target m inv di pubblico; target date data f fissata; target group COM gruppo m target; target market mercato m target

tariff ['tærɪf] (price) tariffa f; (tax) tassa f

tarmac ['tɑːmæk] at airport pista f

tarnish ['tɑːnɪʃ] metal ossidare; *reputation* macchiare

tarpaulin [tɑːˈpɔːlɪn] tela *f* cerata

tart [tɑːt] torta *f*

task [tɑːsk] compito *m*; **task force** task force *f inv*

taste [teɪst] **1** *n* gusto *m* **2** *v/t food* assaggiare; (*experience: freedom etc*) provare **3** *v/i*: **it ~s like ...** ha sapore di ...; **it ~s very nice** è molto buono; **tasteful** di gusto; **tastefully** con gusto; **tasteless** *food* insaporo; *remark, person* privo di gusto; **tasting** *of wine* degustazione *f*; **tasty** gustoso

tattered [ˈtætəd] malridotto

tattoo [təˈtuː] tatuaggio *m*

taunt [tɔːnt] **1** *n* scherno *m* **2** *v/t* schernire

Taurus [ˈtɔːrəs] ASTR Toro *m*

taut [tɔːt] teso

tax [tæks] **1** *n* tassa *f*; **before / after** ~ al lordo / al netto di imposte **2** *v/t* tassare; **taxable income** reddito *m* imponibile; **taxation** tassazione *f*; **tax bracket** fascia *f* di reddito; **tax-deductible** deducibile dalle imposte; **tax disc** *for car* bollo *m* (di circolazione); **tax evasion** evasione *f* fiscale; **tax-free** esentasse *inv*; **tax haven** paradiso *m* fiscale

taxi [ˈtæksi] taxi *m inv*; **taxi driver** tassista *m/f*

taxing [ˈtæksɪŋ] estenuante

'taxi rank stazione *f* dei taxi

'taxpayer contribuente *m/f*; **tax return** *form* dichiarazione *f* dei redditi; **tax year** anno *m* fiscale

TB [tiːˈbiː] (= *tuberculosis*) tbc *f* (= tuberculosi *f*)

tea [tiː] *drink* tè *m inv*; *meal* cena *f*; **teabag** bustina *f* di tè

teach [tiːtʃ] *subject* insegnare; *person* insegnare a; **~ s.o. to do sth** insegnare a qu a fare qc; **teacher** insegnante *m/f*; **teaching** *profession* insegnamento *m*

'tea-cup tazza *f* da tè

teak [tiːk] teak *m*

team [tiːm] *in sport* squadra *f*; *at work* équipe *f inv*; **team mate** compagno *m*, -a *f* di squadra; **team spirit** spirito *m* d'équipe; **teamster** *Am* camionista *m*; **teamwork** lavoro *m* d'équipe

teapot [ˈtiːpɒt] teiera *f*

tear¹ [ter] *n in cloth etc* strappo *m* **2** *v/t paper, cloth* strappare; **be torn between two alternatives** essere combattuto tra due alternative **3** *v/i* (*run fast, drive fast*) sfrecciare

◆ **tear down** *poster* strappare; *building* buttar giù

◆ **tear out** *page* strappare; *hair* strapparsi

◆ **tear up** *paper* distruggere; *agreement* rompere

tear² [tɪr] *n in eye* lacrima *f*; **burst into ~s** scoppiare a piangere; **be in ~s** essere in lacrime

tearful ['tɪrfʊl] *look*, *voice* piangente; **tear gas** gas *m* lacrimogeno

tease [tiːz] *person* prendere in giro; *animal* stuzzicare

'teaspoon cucchiaino *m* da caffè

technical ['teknɪkl] tecnico; **technically** tecnicamente; **technician** tecnico *m*; **technique** tecnica *f*

technological [teknə'lɒdʒɪkl] tecnologico; **technology** tecnologia *f*; **technophobia** tecnofobia *f*

teddy bear ['tedɪbeə(r)] orsacchiotto *m*

tedious ['tiːdɪəs] noioso

tee [tiː] *in golf* tee *m inv*

teenage ['tiːneɪdʒ] *problems* degli adolescenti; **~ fashions** moda giovane; **teenager** adolescente *m/f*

teens [tiːnz] adolescenza *f*; **be in one's ~** essere adolescente

teeny ['tiːnɪ] F piccolissimo

teeth [tiːθ] *pl* ☞ **tooth**

teethe [tiːð] mettere i denti; **teething problems** difficoltà *fpl* iniziali

teetotal [tiː'təʊtl] *person* astemio; *party* senza alcolici

telecommunications [telɪkəmjuːnɪ'keɪʃnz] telecomunicazioni *fpl*

telegraph pole ['telɪɡrɑːfpəʊl] palo *m* del telegrafo

telepathic [telɪ'pæθɪk] telepa-

tico; **telepathy** telepatia *f*

telephone ['telɪfəʊn] **1** *n* telefono *m* **2** *v/t person* telefonare a **3** *v/i* telefonare; **telephone book** guida *f* telefonica; **telephone booth** cabina *f* telefonica; **telephone call** telefonata *f*; **telephone conversation** conversazione *f* telefonica; **telephone directory** elenco *m* telefonico; **telephone number** numero *m* telefonico

telephoto lens [telɪfəʊtəʊ'lenz] teleobiettivo *m*

telesales ['telɪseɪlz] vendita *f* telefonica

telescope ['telɪskəʊp] telescopio *m*

televise ['telɪvaɪz] trasmettere in televisione

television ['telɪvɪʒn] *also set* televisione *f*; *on* ~ alla televisione; **television programme**, *Am* **television program** programma *m* televisivo; **television studio** studio *m* televisivo

tell [tel] **1** *v/t* dire; *story* raccontare; **~ s.o. sth** dire qc a qu; **~ s.o. to do sth** dire a qu di fare qc; **it's hard to ~** è difficile a dirsi; **you never can ~** non si può mai dire; **~ X from Y** distinguere X da Y; **I can't ~ the difference between ...** non vedo nessuna differenza tra ... **2** *v/i* (*have effect*) farsi sentire; **time will ~** il tempo lo dirà;

tel**ler** *in bank* cassiere *m*, -a *f*; **telling off** rimprovero *m*;
give s.o. a ~ rimproverare qu; **telltale 1** *adj signs* rivelatore **2** *n* spione *m*, spiona *f*

temp [temp] **1** *n employee* impiegato *m*, -a interinale **2** *v/i* fare lavori interinali

temper ['tempə(r)] (*bad* ~): **have a terrible ~** essere irascibile; **be in a ~** essere arrabbiato; **keep one's ~** mantenere la calma; **lose one's ~** perdere le staffe

temperament ['tempərəmənt] temperamento *m*; **temperamental** (*moody*) lunatico; *machine* imprevedibile

temperate ['tempərət] temperato

temperature ['temprətʃə(r)] temperatura *f*; (*fever*) febbre *f*

temple¹ ['templ] REL tempio *m*

temple² ['templ] ANAT tempia *f*

tempo ['tempəʊ] ritmo *m*; MUS tempo *m*

temporarily [tempə'reərɪlɪ] temporaneamente; **temporary** ['tempərərɪ] temporaneo, provvisorio

tempt [tempt] tentare; **temptation** tentazione *f*; **tempting** allettante; *meal* appetitoso

ten [ten] dieci

tenacious [tɪ'neɪʃəs] tenace; **tenacity** tenacità *f*

tenant ['tenənt] inquilino *m*, -a *f*, locatario *m*, -a *f*

tend¹ [tend] *v/t* (*look after*) prendersi cura di

tend² [tend] *v/i*: **~ to do sth** tendere a fare qc

tendency ['tendənsɪ] tendenza *f*

tender¹ ['tendə(r)] *adj* (*sore*) sensibile; (*affectionate*) tenero; *steak* tenero

tender² ['tendə(r)] *n* COM offerta *f* ufficiale

tenderness ['tendənɪs] (*soreness*) sensibilità *f*; *of kiss, steak* tenerezza *f*

tendon ['tendən] tendine *m*

tennis ['tenɪs] tennis *m*; **tennis ball** palla *f* da tennis; **tennis court** campo *m* da tennis; **tennis player** tennista *m/f*

tenor ['tenə(r)] MUS tenore *m*

tense¹ [tens] *n* GRAM tempo *m*

tense² [tens] *adj voice, person* teso; *atmosphere* carico di tensione

tension ['tenʃn] tensione *f*

tent [tent] tenda *f*

tentative ['tentətɪv] esitante

tenterhooks ['tentəhʊks]: **be on ~** essere sulle spine

tenth [tenθ] decimo

tepid ['tepɪd] tiepido

term [tɜːm] periodo *m*; *of office* durata *f* in carica; EDU *three months* trimestre *m*; *two months* bimestre *m*; (*condition, word*) termine

m; **be on good / bad ~s
with s.o.** essere in buoni /
cattivi rapporti con qu; **in
the long / short ~** a lungo / breve termine; **come
to ~s with sth** venire a patti
con qc

terminal ['tɜːmɪnl] **1** *n at airport, for containers*, COMPUT
terminale *m*; *for buses* capolinea *m inv*; ELEC morsetto
m **2** *adj illness* in fase terminale; **terminally:~ ill** malato
(in fase) terminale; **terminate 1** *v/t contract, pregnancy*
interrompere **2** *v/i* terminare; **termination** *of contract,
pregnancy* interruzione *f*
terminology [tɜːmɪ'nɒlədʒɪ]
terminologia *f*
terminus ['tɜːmɪnəs] *for buses*
capolinea *m inv*; *for trains*
stazione *f* di testa
terrace ['terəs] *on hillside, at
hotel* terrazza *f*; *of houses* fila
f di case a schiera
terracotta [terə'kɒtə] di terracotta
terrain [tə'reɪn] terreno *m*
terrestrial [tə'restrɪəl] **1** *n* terrestre *m/f* **2** *adj television* di
terra
terrible ['terəbl] terribile; **ter-
ribly** *play* malissimo; *(very)*
molto
terrific [tə'rɪfɪk] eccezionale;
~! bene!; **terrifically** *(very)*
eccezionalmente
terrify ['terɪfaɪ] terrificare;
terrifying terrificante

territorial [terɪ'tɔːrɪəl] territo-
riale; **territory** *also fig* territorio *m*
terror ['terə(r)] terrore *m*; **terrorism** terrorismo *m*; **terrorist** terrorista *m/f*; **terrorist
attack** attentato *m* terrori-
stico; **terrorize** terrorizzare
terse [tɜːs] brusco
test [test] **1** *n* prova *f*, test *m
inv*; *for driving, medical* esa-
me *m*; **blood ~** analisi *f inv*
del sangue **2** *v/t soup, bath-
water* provare; *machine, theory* testare; *person, friendship*
mettere alla prova
testament ['testəmənt]:
Old / New Testament REL
Vecchio / Nuovo Testamen-
to
'**test-drive:** **go for a ~** fare un
giro di prova
testicle ['testɪkl] testicolo *m*
testify ['testɪfaɪ] LAW testimoniare
testimony ['testɪmənɪ] LAW
testimonianza *f*
'**test tube** provetta *f*
testy ['testɪ] suscettibile
tetanus ['tetənəs] tetano *m*
text [tekst] **1** *n* testo *m*; *(message)* SMS *m inv*, messaggino
m **2** *v/t* mandare un SMS a;
textbook libro *m* di testo
textile ['tekstaɪl] tessuto *m*
'**text-message** SMS *m inv*,
messaggino *m*
texture ['tekstʃə(r)] consistenza *f*
Thai [taɪ] **1** *adj* tailandese **2** *n*

person tailandese *m/f*; *language* tailandese *m*; Thailand Tailandia *f*

than [ðæn] *che*; *with numbers, pronouns, names* di; *older ~ me* più vecchio di me; *more French ~ Italian* più francese che italiana

thank [θæŋk] ringraziare; *~ you* grazie; *no ~ you* no, grazie; *thankful* riconoscente; *thankfully* con riconoscenza; *(luckily)* fortunatamente; *thankless* ingrato; *thanks* ringraziamenti *mpl*; *~!* grazie!; *~ to* grazie a; Thanksgiving (Day) *in USA* giorno *m* del ringraziamento

that [ðæt] **1** *adj* quel; *with masculine nouns before s+consonant, gn, ps and z* quello; *~ one* quello **2** *pron* quello *m*, -a *f*; *what is ~?* cos'è?; *who is ~?* chi è?; *~'s mine* è mio; *~'s tea* quello è tè; *~'s very kind* è molto gentile **3** *relative pron* che; *the car ~ you saw* la macchina che hai visto; *the day ~ he was born* il giorno in cui è nato **4** *adv* *(so)* così; *~ expensive* così caro **5** *conj* che; *I think ~ ... credo che ...*

thaw [θɔː] *of snow* sciogliersi; *of frozen food* scongelare

the [ðə] il *m*, la *f*; i *mpl*, le *fpl*; *with masculine nouns before s+consonant, gn, ps and z* lo *m*, gli *mpl*; *before vowel* l' *m/f*, gli *mpl*; *to ~ bathroom*

al bagno; *~ sooner ~ better* prima è, meglio è

theatre, *Am* **theater** ['θɪətə(r)] teatro *m*; MED sala *f* operatoria

theatrical [θɪ'ætrɪkl] *also fig* teatrale

theft [θeft] furto *m*

their [ðeə(r)] il loro *m*, la loro *f*; i loro *mpl*, le loro *fpl*; *(his or her)* il suo *m*, la sua *f*; i suoi *mpl*, le sue *fpl*; **theirs** il loro *m*, la loro *f*; i loro *mpl*, le loro *fpl*; *it was an idea of ~* è stata una loro idea

them [ðem] *direct object* li *m*, le *f*; *referring to things* essi *m*, esse *f*; *indirect object* loro, gli; *after preposition* loro; *referring to things* essi *m*, esse *f*; *(him or her)* lo *m*, la *f*; *I know ~* li / le conosco; *I sold it to ~* gliel'ho venduto, l'ho venduto a loro

theme [θiːm] tema *m*; **theme park** parco *m* a tema

themselves [ðem'selvz] si; *emphatic* loro stessi *mpl*, loro stesse *fpl*; *after prep* se stessi / se stesse; *they enjoyed ~* si sono divertiti

then [ðen] *(at that time, deducing)* allora; *(after that)* poi; *by ~* allora

theology [θɪ'ɒlədʒɪ] teologia *f*

theoretical [θɪə'retɪkl] teorico; **theoretically** teoricamente; **theory** teoria *f*

therapeutic [θerə'pjuːtɪk] terapeutico; **therapist** terapista *m/f*, terapeuta *m/f*; **therapy** terapia *f*

there [ðeə(r)] lì, là; **over ~** là; **down ~** laggiù; **~ is ...** c'è; **are ...** ci sono ...?; **~ is** c'è ...?; **are ~ ...?** ci sono ...?; **isn't ~?** non c'è ...?; **aren't ~?** non ci sono ...?; **~ you are** giving sth ecco qui; *finding sth; completing sth* ecco fatto; **~ and back** andata e ritorno; **~ he is!** eccolo!; **~, ~!** comforting su, dai!; **thereabouts** giù di lì; **therefore** quindi, pertanto

thermometer [θə'mɒmɪtə(r)] termometro *m*

thermos flask ['θɜ:məsflɑ:sk] termos *m inv*

thermostat ['θɜ:məstæt] termostato *m*

these [ði:z] **1** *adj* questi **2** *pron* questi, -e *f*

thesis ['θi:sɪs] tesi *f inv*

they [ðeɪ] ◇ loro; **~'re going to the theatre** vanno a teatro; **there ~ are** eccoli *mpl*, eccole *fpl* ◇ **if anyone looks at this, ~ will see that ...** se qualcuno lo guarda, vedrà che ...; **~ say that ...** si dice che ...; **~ are going to change the law** cambieranno la legge

thick [θɪk] spesso; *hair* folto; *fog, forest* fitto; *liquid* denso; F *(stupid)* ottuso; **thicken** *sauce* ispessire; **thick-skinned** fig insensibile

thief [θi:f] ladro *m*, -a *f*

thigh [θaɪ] coscia *f*

thin [θɪn] sottile; *person* magro; *hair* rado; *liquid* fluido

thing [θɪŋ] cosa *f*; **~s** *(belongings)* cose *fpl*; **it's a good ~ you told me** è un bene che tu me l'abbia detto

thingumajig ['θɪŋəmədʒɪɡ] F coso *m*, cosa *f*

think [θɪŋk] pensare; **I ~ so** penso *or* credo di sì; **I don't ~ so** non credo; **I'm ~ing about emigrating** sto pensando di emigrare

♦ **think over** riflettere su

♦ **think through** analizzare a fondo

♦ **think up** *plan* escogitare

'think tank comitato *m* di esperti

thin-skinned [θɪn'skɪnd] fig sensibile

third [θɜ:d] **1** *adj* terzo **2** *n* terzo *m*; **thirdly** in terzo luogo; **third-party** terzi *mpl*; **third-party insurance** assicurazione *f* sulla responsabilità civile; **Third World** Terzo Mondo *m*

thirst [θɜ:st] sete *f*; **thirsty** assetato; **be ~** avere sete

thirteen [θɜ:'ti:n] tredici; **thirteenth** tredicesimo; **thirtieth** trentesimo; **thirty** trenta

this [ðɪs] **1** *adj* questo; **~ one** questo (qui) **2** *pron* questo *m*, -a *f*; **~ is easy** è facile; **~ is ... introducing s.o.** questo / questa è ...; **3** *adv*: **~**

high alto così

thorn [θɔ:n] spina *f*; **thorny** *also fig* spinoso

thorough ['θʌrə] *search, knowledge* approfondito; *person* scrupoloso; **thoroughbred** *horse* purosangue *inv*; **thoroughly** *search for* accuratamente; *know, understand, clean* perfettamente; *agree, spoil completamente*; *stupid, rude* extremamente

those [ðəʊz] **1** *adj* quelli; *with masculine nouns before s+consonant, gn, ps and z* quegli **2** *pron* quelli *m*, -e *f*; *with masculine nouns before s+consonant, gn, ps and z* quegli

though [ðəʊ] **1** *conj* (*although*) benché (+*subj*); **as** ~ come se **2** *adv* però

thought [θɔ:t] pensiero *m*; **thoughtful** pensieroso; *reply* meditato; (*considerate*) gentile; **thoughtless** sconsiderato

thousand ['θaʊznd] mille; ~**s of** migliaia di; **thousandth** millesimo

thrash [θræʃ] picchiare; SP battere

◆ **thrash out** *solution* mettere a punto

thrashing ['θræʃɪŋ] botte *fpl*; SP batosta *f*

thread [θred] **1** *n* filo *m*; *of screw* filettatura *f* **2** *v/t needle* infilare il filo in; *beads* infila-

re; **threadbare** liso

threat [θret] minaccia *f*; **threaten** minacciare; **threatening** minaccioso; ~ **letter** lettera *f* minatoria

three [θri:] tre; **three quarters** tre quarti *mpl*

threshold ['θreʃhəʊld] *of house, new era* soglia *f*

thrifty ['θrɪftɪ] parsimonioso

thrill [θrɪl] **1** *n* emozione *f*; *physical feeling* brivido *m* **2** *v/t*: **be** ~**ed** essere emozionato; **thriller** giallo *m*; **thrilling** emozionante

thrive [θraɪv] *of plant* crescere rigoglioso; *of business* prosperare

throat [θrəʊt] gola *f*; **have a sore** ~ avere mal di gola; **throat lozenge** pastiglia *f* per la gola

throb [θrɒb] pulsare; *of heart* battere; *of music* rimbombare

throne [θrəʊn] trono *m*

throttle ['θrɒtl] **1** *n on motorbike* manetta *f* di accelerazione; *on boat* leva *f* di accelerazione **2** *v/t* (*strangle*) strozzare

through [θru:] **1** *prep* (*across*) attraverso; (*during*) durante; (*by means of*) tramite; **go** ~ **the city** attraversare la città; ~ **the winter** per tutto l'inverno; **arranged** ~ **him** organizzato tramite lui **2** *adv*: **wet** ~ completamente bagnato **3** *adj*: **be** ~ *of couple* essersi lasciati; *have arrived: of news etc* essere arrivato; **I'm~ with ...** *(finished with)* ho finito con ...; **I'm~ with him** ho chiuso con lui; **throughout 1** *prep:* **~ the night** per tutta la notte **2** *adv (in all parts)* completamente

throw [θrəʊ] **1** *v/t* lanciare; *into bin etc* gettare; *of horse* disarcinare; *(disconcert)* sconcertare; *party* **2** *n* lancio *m*

♦ **throw away** buttare via, gettare

♦ **throw out** *old things* buttare via; *from bar, house etc* buttare fuori; *plan* scartare

♦ **throw up 1** *v/t: of ball* lanciare **2** *v/i (vomit)* vomitare

'throw-away *remark* buttato lì; *(disposable)* usa e getta *inv*; **throw-in** SP rimessa *f*

thru [θruː] *Am* → **through**

thrust [θrʌst] *v/t (push hard)* spingere; *knife* conficcare; **~ one's way through the crowd** farsi largo tra la folla

thud [θʌd] *n* tonfo *m*

thug [θʌg] *hooligan* teppista *m*; *tough guy* bullo *m*

thumb [θʌm] **1** *n* pollice *m* **2** *v/t:* **~ a lift** fare l'autostop; **thumbtack** *Am* puntina *f*

thunder [θʌndə(r)] *n* tuono *m*; **thunderous** *applause* fragoroso; **thunderstorm** temporale *m*; **thunderstruck** allibito; **thundery** *weather* temporalesco

Thursday [θɜːzdeɪ] giovedì *m inv*

thus [ðʌs] *(in this way)* così

thwart [θwɔːt] *person, plans* ostacolare

Tiber [taɪbə(r)] Tevere *m*

tick [tɪk] **1** *n of clock* ticchettio *m*; *in text* segno *m* **2** *v/i of clock* ticchettare **3** *v/t with a ~* segnare

ticket [tɪkɪt] biglietto *m*; *in cloakroom* scontrino *m*; **ticket machine** distributore *m* di biglietti; **ticket office** biglietteria *f*

ticking [tɪkɪŋ] *noise* ticchettio *m*

tickle [tɪkl] **1** *v/t person* fare il solletico a **2** *v/i of material* dare prurito; *of person* fare il solletico

tidal wave [taɪdlweɪv] onda *f* di marea

tide [taɪd] marea *f*; **the ~ is in / out** c'è l'alta / la bassa marea

tidiness [taɪdɪnɪs] ordine *m*; **tidy** ordinato

♦ **tidy up 1** *v/t room, shelves* mettere in ordine; **tidy o.s. up** darsi una sistemata **2** *v/i* mettere in ordine

tie [taɪ] **1** *n (necktie)* cravatta *f*; (SP: *even result)* pareggio *m*; **he doesn't have any ~s** non ha legami **2** *v/t knot, hands* legare **3** *v/i* SP pareggiare

♦ **tie down** *with rope* legare; *(restrict)* vincolare

◆ **tie up** *person, laces, hair* legare; *boat* ormeggiare; **I'm tied up tomorrow** sono impegnato domani

tier [tɪə(r)] *of hierarchy* livello *m*; *in stadium* anello *m*

tiger ['taɪgə(r)] tigre *f*

tight [taɪt] **1** *adj clothes* stretto; *security* rigido; *rope* teso; *not leaving much time* giusto; *schedule* serrato; F *(drunk)* sbronzo F **2** *adv*: **hold s.o. / sth ~** tenere qu / qc stretto; **shut sth ~** chiudere bene qc; **tighten** *screw* serrare; *belt* stringere; *rope* tendere; *security* intensificare; **tight-fisted** taccagno; **tightly** → *tight adv*; **tightrope** fune *f* (per funamboli); **tights** collant *mpl*

tile [taɪl] *on floor* mattonella *f*; *on wall* piastrella *f*; *on roof* tegola *f*

till¹ [tɪl] → *until*

till² [tɪl] *(cash register)* cassa *f*

tilt [tɪlt] **1** *v/t* inclinare **2** *v/i* inclinarsi

timber ['tɪmbə(r)] legname *m*

time [taɪm] tempo *m*; *by the clock* ora *f*; *(occasion)* volta *f*; **for the ~ being** al momento; **have a good ~!** divertiti!; **what's the ~?** che ora è?, che ore sono?; **the first ~** la prima volta; **take your ~** fai con calma; **for a ~** per un po' (di tempo); **at any ~** in qualsiasi momento; **(and) about ~!** era ora!;

two at a ~ due alla volta; **at the same ~** *speak, reply etc* contemporaneamente; *(however)* nel contempo; **in ~** in tempo; *(eventually)* col tempo; **on ~** in orario; **in no ~** in un attimo; **time bomb** bomba *f* a orologeria; **time difference** fuso *m* orario; **time-lag** scarto *m* di tempo; **time limit** limite *m* temporale; **timely** tempestivo; **time out** SP time-out *m inv*; **timer** cronometro *m*; *on oven* timer *m inv*; **time-saving** risparmio *m* di tempo; **timescale** *of project* cronologia *f*; **time share** *(house, apartment)* multiproprietà *f inv*; **time switch** interruttore *m* a tempo; **timetable** orario *m*; **timewarp** trasposizione *f* temporale; **time zone** zona *f* di fuso orario

timid ['tɪmɪd] timido

tin [tɪn] *metal* stagno *m*; *container* barattolo *m*; **tinfoil** carta *f* stagnola

tinge [tɪndʒ] sfumatura *f*

tingle ['tɪŋgl] pizzicare

tinkle ['tɪŋkl] *of bell* tintinnio *m*

tin opener apriscatole *m inv*

tinsel ['tɪnsl] fili *mpl* d'argento

tint [tɪnt] **1** *n of colour* sfumatura *f*; *in hair* riflessante *m* **2** *v/t* hair fare dei riflessi a; **tinted** *glasses* fumé *inv*

tiny ['taɪnɪ] piccolissimo

tip¹ [tɪp] *n of stick, finger* punta *f; of cigarette* filtro *m*

tip² [tɪp] **1** *n advice* consiglio *m; money* mancia *f* **2** *v/t waiter etc* dare la mancia a

◆ **tip off** fare una soffiata a

'tip-off soffiata *f*

tipped [tɪpt] *cigarettes* col filtro

Tipp-Ex® ['tɪpeks] bianchetto *m*

tippy-toe ['tɪpɪtəʊ] *Am:* **on ~** sulla punta dei piedi

tipsy ['tɪpsɪ] alticcio

'tip-toe: on ~ sulla punta dei piedi

tire¹ [taɪr] *n Am* gomma *f*, pneumatico *m*

tire² [taɪr] **1** *v/t* stancare **2** *v/i* stancarsi

tired [taɪəd] stanco; **be ~ of s.o. / sth** essere stanco di qu / qc; **tiredness** stanchezza *f*; **tireless** instancabile; **tiresome** (*annoying*) fastidioso; **tiring** stancante

tissue ['tɪʃuː] ANAT tessuto *m*; (*handkerchief*) fazzolettino *m* (di carta); **tissue paper** carta *f* velina

title ['taɪtl] titolo *m*; LAW diritto *m*; **titleholder** SP detentore *m*, -trice *f* del titolo

to [tuː] **1** *prep* a; **~ Italy** in Italia; **~ Rome** a Roma; **let's go ~ my place** andiamo a casa mia; **~ the north of ...** a nord di ...; **give sth ~ s.o.** dare qc a qu; **from 10 ~ 15 people** tra 10 e 15 persone; **it's 5 ~ 11**

sono le undici meno cinque **2** *with verbs:* **~ speak, ~ see** parlare, vedere; **learn ~ drive** imparare a guidare; **nice ~ eat** buono da mangiare; **~ learn Italian** *in order to* per imparare l'italiano **3** *adv:* **~ and fro** avanti e indietro

toast [təʊst] **1** *n* pane *m* tostato; (*drinking*) brindisi *m inv* **2** *v/t bread* tostare; *drinking* fare un brindisi a; **toaster** tostapane *m inv*

tobacco [tə'bækəʊ] tabacco *m*

today [tə'deɪ] oggi

toddler ['tɒdlə(r)] bambino *m*, -a *f* ai primi passi

to-'do F casino *m* F

toe [təʊ] dito *m* del piede; *of shoes, socks* punta *f*; **big ~** alluce *m*; **toenail** unghia *f* del piede

toffee ['tɒfɪ] caramella *f* al mou

together [tə'geðə(r)] insieme

toilet ['tɔɪlɪt] gabinetto *m*; **go to the ~** andare in bagno; **toilet paper** carta *f* igienica; **toiletries** prodotti *mpl* da toilette

token ['təʊkən] (*sign*) pegno *m*; *for gambling* gettone *m*; (*gift* ~) buono *m*

tolerable ['tɒlərəbl] *pain etc* tollerabile; (*quite good*) accettabile; **tolerance** tolleranza *f*; **tolerant** tollerante; **tolerate** tollerare

toll[1] [təʊl] v/i of bell suonare

toll[2] [təʊl] n (deaths) bilancio m delle vittime

toll[3] [təʊl] n for bridge, road pedaggio m

'**toll booth** casello m; **toll-free number** Am TELEC numero m verde; **toll road** strada f a pedaggio

tomato [tə'mɑːtəʊ] pomodoro m; **tomato ketchup** ketchup m inv; **tomato sauce** for pasta etc salsa f or sugo m di pomodoro; (ketchup) ketchup m inv

tomb [tuːm] tomba f; **tombstone** lapide f

tomcat ['tɒmkæt] gatto m (maschio)

tomorrow [tə'mɒrəʊ] domani; **the day after** ~ dopodomani; ~ **morning** domattina, domani mattina

ton [tʌn] tonnellata f (Br 1016kg, Am 907kg)

tone [təʊn] of colour, musical instrument tonalità f inv; of conversation etc tono m; of neighbourhood livello m sociale; ~ **of voice** tono di voce; **toner** toner m inv

tongue [tʌŋ] lingua f

tonic ['tɒnɪk] MED ricostituente m; **tonic (water)** acqua f tonica

tonight [tə'naɪt] stanotte; (this evening) stasera

tonsillitis [tɒnsə'laɪtɪs] tonsillite f

too [tuː] (also) anche; (excessively) troppo; **me** ~ anch'io; ~ **much rice** troppo riso; ~ **many mistakes** troppi errori; **eat** ~ **much** mangiare troppo

tool [tuːl] attrezzo m; fig strumento m

tooth [tuːθ] (pl **teeth** [tiːθ]) dente m; **toothache** mal m di denti; **toothbrush** spazzolino m da denti; **toothpaste** dentifricio m; **toothpick** stuzzicadenti m

top [tɒp] **1** n of mountain, tree cima f; of wall, screen parte f alta; of page, list, street inizio m; (lid: of bottle etc, pen) tappo m; of the class, league testa f; (clothing) maglia f; (MOT: gear) marcia f più alta; **on** ~ of in cima a; **at the** ~ of list, tree, mountain in cima a; league in testa a; page, street all'inizio di; **get to the** ~ of company etc arrivare in cima; **get to the** ~ of mountain arrivare alla vetta; **be over the** ~ (exaggerated) essere esagerato **2** adj branches più alto; floor ultimo; management di alto livello; official di alto rango; player migliore; speed, note massimo

topic ['tɒpɪk] argomento m; **topical** attuale

topless ['tɒplɪs] topless inv; **topmost** branches, floor più alto; **topping** on pizza guarnizione f

topple ['tɒpl] **1** v/i crollare **2**

v/t government far cadere

top 'secret top secret *inv*

topsy-turvy [tɒpsɪ'tɜ:vɪ] sottosopra *inv*

torch [tɔ:tʃ] pila *f*; *with flame* torcia *f*

torment 1 ['tɔ:mənt] *n* tormento *m* **2** [tɔ:'ment] *v/t* tormentare

tornado [tɔ:'neɪdəʊ] tornado *m*

torpedo [tɔ:'pi:dəʊ] **1** *n* siluro *m* **2** *v/t* silurare; *fig* far saltare

torrent ['tɒrənt] torrente *m*; *of lava* fiume *m*; *of abuse, words* valanga *f*; **torrential** *rain* torrenziale

tortoise ['tɔ:təs] tartaruga *f*

torture ['tɔ:tʃə(r)] **1** *n* tortura *f* **2** *v/t* torturare

toss [tɒs] **1** *v/t ball* lanciare; *rider* disarcionare; *salad* mescolare; *~ a coin* fare testa o croce **2** *v/i:* **~ and turn** rigirarsi

total ['təʊtl] **1** *n* totale *m* **2** *adj amount, disaster* totale; *stranger* perfetto; **totalitarian** totalitario; **totally** totalmente, completamente

totter ['tɒtə(r)] barcollare

touch [tʌtʃ] **1** *n* tocco *m*; *sense* tatto *m*; *in rugby* touche *f*; **lose one's ~** perdere la mano; **kick the ball into ~** cacciare la palla fuoricampo; **lose ~ with s.o.** perdere i contatti con qu; **keep in ~ with s.o.** rimanere in contatto con qu; **be out of ~ with**

news non essere al corrente; *with people* non avere contatti **2** *v/t* toccare; *emotionally* commuovere **3** *v/i* toccare; *of two lines etc* toccarsi

◆ **touch down** *of plane* atterrare; SP fare meta

'touchdown *of plane* atterraggio *m*; *touching* commovente; **touchline** SP linea *f* laterale; **touch screen** schermo *m* tattile; **touchy** *person* suscettibile

tough [tʌf] *person* forte; *question, exam, meat, punishment* duro; *material* resistente

tour [tʊə(r)] **1** *n* giro *m*; *of tourist* giro *m* turistico; *of band* tournée *f inv* **2** *v/t area* girare **3** *v/i of tourist* andare in giro; *of band* andare in tournée; **tour guide** guida *f* turistica; **tourism** turismo *m*; **tourist** turista *m/f*; **tourist industry** industria *f* del turismo; **tourist (information) office** ufficio *m* informazioni turistiche

tournament ['tʊənəmənt] torneo *m*

'tour operator operatore *m* turistico

tow [təʊ] rimorchiare

◆ **tow away** *car* portare via col carro attrezzi

toward(s) [tə'wɔ:d(z)] verso; *rude* ~ maleducato nei confronti di; *work ~ (achieving) sth* lavorare per (raggiungere) qc

towel ['tauəl] asciugamano *m*

tower ['tauə(r)] torre *f*; **tower block** condominio *m* a torre

town [taun] città *f inv*; *opposed to city* cittadina *f*; **town centre**, *Am* **town center** centro *m*; **town council** consiglio *m* comunale; **town hall** municipio *m*

toxic ['tɒksɪk] tossico *m*; **toxin** tossina *f*

toy [tɔɪ] giocattolo *m*

trace [treɪs] **1** *n of substance* traccia *f* **2** *v/t* (*find*) rintracciare; (*draw*) tracciare

track [træk] (*path*) sentiero *m*; *on race course* pista *f*; (*race course*) circuito *m*; RAIL binario *m*; *on CD* brano *m*; **keep ~ of sth** tenersi al passo con qc

♦ **track down** rintracciare

'tracksuit tuta *f* (da ginnastica)

tractor ['træktə(r)] trattore *m*

trade [treɪd] **1** *n* commercio *m*; (*profession, craft*) mestiere *m* **2** *v/i* (*do business*) essere in attività; **~ in sth** commerciare in qc **3** *v/t* (*exchange*) scambiare (**for** con); **trade fair** fiera *f* campionaria; **trademark** marchio *m* registrato; **trader** commerciante *m/f*; **trade union** sindacato *m*

tradition [trə'dɪʃn] tradizione *f*; **traditional** tradizionale; **traditionally** tradizionalmente

traffic ['træfɪk] *on roads, in drugs* traffico *m*

♦ **traffic in** *drugs* trafficare

'traffic circle *Am* rotatoria *f*; **traffic cop** F vigile *m* (urbano); **traffic jam** ingorgo *m*; **traffic island** isola *f* spartitraffico; **traffic light(s)** semaforo *m*; **traffic police** polizia *f* stradale; **traffic sign** segnale *m* stradale; **traffic warden** ausiliario *m* (del traffico)

tragedy ['trædʒədɪ] tragedia *f*; **tragic** tragico

trail [treɪl] **1** *n* (*path*) sentiero *m*; *of person, animal* tracce *fpl*; *of blood* scia *f* **2** *v/t* (*follow*) seguire; (*drag*) trascinare; *caravan etc* trainare **3** *v/i* (*lag behind*) trascinarsi; **they're ~ing 3-1** stanno perdendo 3 a 1; **trailer** *pulled by vehicle* rimorchio *m*; *of film* trailer *m inv*; (*mobile home*) roulotte *f inv*

train¹ [treɪn] *n* treno *m*; **go by ~** andare in treno

train² [treɪn] **1** *v/t team, athlete* allenare; *employee* formare; *dog* addestrare **2** *v/i of team, athlete* allenarsi; *of teacher etc* fare il tirocinio

trainee [treɪ'niː] apprendista *m/f*; **trainer** SP allenatore *m*, -trice *f*; *of dog* addestratore *m*, -trice *f*; **~s** *shoes* scarpe *fpl* da ginnastica; **trainers** *shoes* scarpe *fpl* da ginnastica; **training** *of new staff* formazione f; SP allenamento m; **be in** ~ SP allenarsi; **be out of** ~ SP essere fuori allenamento

'train station stazione f ferroviaria

traitor ['treitǝ(r)] traditore m, -trice f

tram [træm] tram m inv

tramp [træmp] barbone m, -a f

◆ **trample on** calpestare

trampoline ['træmpǝli:n] trampolino m

tranquil ['træŋkwɪl] tranquillo; **tranquillity** ~ tranquillity tranquillità f; tranquillizer, Am **tranquilizer** tranquillante m

transaction [træn'zækʃn] transazione f

transatlantic [trænzǝt'læntɪk] transatlantico

transcript ['trænskrɪpt] trascrizione f

transfer 1 [træns'fɜ:(r)] v/t trasferire; LAW cedere **2** [træns'fɜ:(r)] v/i cambiare **3** ['trænsfɜ:(r)] n trasferimento m; LAW cessione f; of money bonifico m bancario; **transferable** ticket trasferibile; **transfer fee** for football player prezzo m d'acquisto

transform [træns'fɔ:m] trasformare; **transformation** trasformazione f; **transformer** ELEC trasformatore m

transfusion [træns'fju:ʒn] trasfusione f

transit ['trænzɪt]: **in** ~ in transito; **transition** transizione f; **transitional** di transizione; **transit lounge** at airport sala f passeggeri in transito; **transit passenger** passeggero m, -a f in transito

translate [træns'leɪt] tradurre; **translation** traduzione f; **translator** traduttore m, -trice f

transmission [trænz'mɪʃn] trasmissione f; **transmit** news, programme, disease trasmettere; **transmitter** RAD, TV trasmettitore m

transparency [træns'pærǝnsɪ] PHOT diapositiva f; **transparent** trasparente

transplant 1 [træns'plɑ:nt] v/t MED trapiantare **2** ['trænsplɑ:nt] n MED trapianto m

transport 1 [træn'spɔ:t] v/t trasportare **2** ['trænspɔ:t] n of trasporto m; means of transport mezzo m di trasporto; **public** ~ i trasporti pubblici; **transportation** trasporto m

transvestite [træns'vestaɪt] travestito m

trap [træp] **1** n trappola f; question tranello m **2** v/t intrappolare; **trappings** of power segni mpl esteriori

trash [træʃ] poor product robaccia *f*; *despicable person* fetente *m/f*; *Am* (*garbage*) spazzatura *f*; **trashcan** *Am* bidone *m* della spazzatura; **trashy** *goods, novel* scadente

trauma ['trɔːmə] *trauma m*; **traumatic** traumatico; **traumatize** traumatizzare

travel ['trævl] **1** *n* viaggiare *m*; **~s** viaggi *mpl* **2** *v/i* viaggiare; *I ~ to work by train* vado a lavorare in treno **3** *v/t miles* percorrere; **travel agency** agenzia *f* di viaggio; **travel agent** agente *m/f* di viaggio; **traveller**, *Am* **traveler** viaggiatore *m*, -trice *f*; **traveller's cheque**, *Am* **traveler's check** traveller's cheque *m inv*; **travel expenses** spese *fpl* di viaggio; **travel insurance** assicurazione *f* di viaggio

trawler ['trɔːlə(r)] peschereccio *m*

tray [treɪ] *for food, photocopier* vassoio *m*; *to go in oven* teglia *f*

treacherous ['tretʃərəs] traditore; **treachery** tradimento *m*

tread [tred] **1** *n* passo *m*; *of staircase* gradino *m*; *of tyre* battistrada *m inv* **2** *v/i* camminare

treason ['triːzn] tradimento *m*

treasure ['treʒə(r)] **1** *n also person* tesoro *m* **2** *v/t gift etc* custodire gelosamente;

treasurer tesoriere *m*, -a *f*; **Treasury Department** *Am* tesoro *m*

treat [triːt] **1** *n* trattamento *m* speciale; *it's my ~* (*I'm paying*) offro io **2** *v/t* trattare; *illness* curare; *~ s.o. to sth* offrire qc a qu; **treatment** trattamento *m*; *of illness* cura *f*

treaty ['triːti] trattato *m*

treble ['trebl] **1** *adv:* *~ the price* il triplo del prezzo **2** *v/i* triplicarsi

tree [triː] albero *m*

tremble ['trembl] tremare

tremendous [trɪ'mendəs] (*very good*) fantastico; (*enormous*) enorme; **tremendously** (*very*) incredibilmente; (*a lot*) moltissimo

tremor ['tremə(r)] *of earth* scossa *f*

trench [trentʃ] trincea *f*

trend [trend] tendenza *f*; **trendy** alla moda

trespass ['trespəs] invadere una proprietà privata; *no ~ing* divieto d'accesso; **trespasser** intruso *m*, -a *f*

trial ['traɪəl] LAW processo *m*; *of equipment* prova *f*; *on ~* LAW sotto processo; *stand ~ for sth* essere processato per qc; *have sth on ~ equipment* avere qc in prova; **trial period** periodo *m* di prova

triangle ['traɪæŋgl] triangolo *m*; **triangular** triangolare

tribe [traɪb] tribù *f inv*

tribunal [traɪ'bjuːnl] tribunale *m*

tributary ['trɪbjʊtərɪ] *of river* affluente *m*

trick [trɪk] **1** *n to deceive* stratagemma *m*; (*knack*) trucco *m*; *play a ~ on s.o.* fare uno scherzo a qu **2** *v/t* ingannare; **trickery** truffa *f*

trickle ['trɪkl] **1** *n* filo *m*; *a ~ of replies* poche risposte sporadiche **2** *v/i* gocciolare

tricky ['trɪkɪ] (*difficult*) complicato

trifle ['traɪfl] *n* (*triviality*) inezia *f*; *pudding* zuppa *f* inglese; **trifling** insignificante

trigger ['trɪgə(r)] *on gun* grilletto *m*

♦ **trigger off** scatenare

trim [trɪm] **1** *adj* (*neat*) ordinato; *figure* snello **2** *v/t hair, hedge* spuntare; *costs* tagliare; (*decorate*: *dress*) ornare **3** *n* (*light cut*) spuntata *f; in good ~* in buone condizioni

trinket ['trɪŋkɪt] ninnolo *m*

trio ['triːəʊ] MUS trio *m*

trip [trɪp] **1** *n* (*journey*) viaggio *m*, gita *f* **2** *v/i* (*stumble*) inciampare (*over* in) **3** *v/t* (*make fall*) fare inciampare

♦ **trip up** *v/t* (*make fall*) fare inciampare; (*cause to make a mistake*) confondere **2** *v/i* (*stumble*) inciampare; (*make a mistake*) sbagliarsi

triple ['trɪpl] → **treble**

trite [traɪt] trito

triumph ['traɪʌmf] trionfo *m*

trivial ['trɪvɪəl] banale; trivial-ity banalità *f inv*

trolley ['trɒlɪ] *in supermarket, at airport* carrello *m*

trombone [trɒm'bəʊn] trombone *m*

troops [truːps] truppe *fpl*

trophy ['trəʊfɪ] trofeo *m*

tropic ['trɒpɪk] tropico *m*; **tropical** tropicale; **tropics** tropici *mpl*

trot [trɒt] trottare

trouble ['trʌbl] **1** *n* (*difficulties*) problemi *mpl*; (*inconvenience*) fastidio *m*; (*disturbance*) disordini *mpl*; *the ~ with you is …* il tuo problema è …; *get into ~* mettersi nei guai **2** *v/t* (*worry*) preoccupare; (*bother, disturb*) disturbare; *of back, liver etc* dare dei fastidi a; **troublemaker** attaccabrighe *m/f inv*; **troubleshooting** mediazione *f; in software manual* ricerca *f* problemi e soluzioni; **troublesome** fastidioso

trousers ['traʊzəz] pantaloni *mpl*; *a pair of ~* un paio di pantaloni

trout [traʊt] trota *f*

truant ['truːənt]: *play ~* marinare la scuola

truce [truːs] tregua *f*

truck [trʌk] camion *m inv*; **truck driver** camionista *m*; **truck stop** *Am* posto *m* di ristoro per camionisti

trudge [trʌdʒ] **1** *v/i* arrancare; *~ around the shops* trascinarsi per i negozi **2** *n* camminata *f* stancante

true [truː] vero; **come ~ of** *hopes, dream* realizzarsi; **truly** davvero; **Yours ~** distinti saluti

trumpet ['trʌmpɪt] tromba *f*

trunk [trʌŋk] *of tree, body* tronco *m*; *of elephant* proboscide *f*; (*large case*) baule *m*; MOT bagagliaio *m inv*

trust [trʌst] **1** *n* fiducia *f*; FIN fondo *m* fiduciario **2** *v/t* fidarsi di; *trusted* fidato; **trustee** amministratore *m*, -trice *f* fiduciario, -a; **trustful, trusting** fiducioso; **trustworthy** affidabile

truth [truːθ] verità *f inv*; **truthful** *account* veritiero; *person* sincero

try [traɪ] **1** *v/t* provare; LAW processare; **~ to do sth** provare a fare qc, cercare di fare qc **2** *v/i* provare, tentare; **you must ~ harder** devi provare con più impegno **3** *n* tentativo *m*; *in rugby* meta *f*; **trying** (*annoying*) difficile

T-shirt ['tiːʃɜːt] maglietta *f*

tub [tʌb] (*bath*) vasca *f* da bagno; *of liquid* tinozza *f*; *for yoghurt* barattolo *m*; **tubby** tozzo

tube [tjuːb] tubo *m*; *of toothpaste* tubetto *m*; **tubeless** *tyre* senza camera d'aria

Tuesday ['tjuːzdeɪ] martedì *m inv*

tuft [tʌft] ciuffo *m*

tug [tʌg] **1** *n* NAUT rimorchia-

tore *m* **2** *v/t* (*pull*) tirare

tuition [tjuːˈɪʃn] lezioni *fpl*

tulip ['tjuːlɪp] tulipano *m*

tumble ['tʌmbl] ruzzolare; *of wall, prices* crollare; **tumbledown** in rovina, fatiscente; **tumbler** *for drink* bicchiere *m* (senza stelo); *in circus* acrobata *m/f*

tummy ['tʌmɪ] F pancia *f*; **tummy ache** mal *m* di pancia

tumour, *Am* **tumor** ['tuːmə(r)] tumore *m*

tumult ['tjuːmʌlt] tumulto *m*; **tumultuous** tumultuoso

tuna ['tjuːnə] tonno *m*

tune [tjuːn] **1** *n* motivo *m*; **in ~** *instrument* accordato **2** *v/t* *instrument* accordare; *engine* mettere a punto

◆ **tune up 1** *v/i of orchestra* accordare gli strumenti **2** *v/t engine* mettere a punto

tuneful ['tjuːnfʊl] melodioso; **tuner** (*hi-fi*) sintonizzatore *m*, tuner *m inv*; **tune-up of** *engine* messa fa punto

tunnel ['tʌnl] galleria *f*, tunnel *m inv*

turbine ['tɜːbaɪn] turbina *f*

turbulence ['tɜːbjʊləns] *in air travel* turbolenza *f*; **turbulent** turbolento

turf [tɜːf] tappeto *m* erboso; (*piece*) zolla *f*

Turin [tjʊˈrɪn] Torino *f*

Turk [tɜːk] turco *m*, -a *f*; **Turkey** Turchia *f*

turkey ['tɜːkɪ] tacchino *m*

Turkish ['tɜːkɪʃ] **1** *adj* turco **2** *n language* turco *m*

turmoil ['tɜːmɔɪl] agitazione *f*

turn [tɜːn] **1** *n* (*rotation*) giro *m*; *in road* curva *f*; *in variety show* numero *m*; **take ~s in doing sth** fare a turno a fare qc; **it's my ~** è il mio turno, tocca a me; **do s.o. a good ~** fare un favore a qu **2** *v/t wheel, corner* girare **3** *v/t of driver, car, wheel* girare; (*become*) diventare; **it has ~ed cold** è diventato freddo; **he has ~ed 40** ha compiuto 40 anni

◆ **turn around 1** *v/t object* girare; *company* dare una svolta positiva a; (COM *deal with*) eseguire; *order* evadere **2** *v/i of person* girarsi; *of driver* girare

◆ **turn away 1** *v/t* (*send away*) mandare via **2** *v/i* (*walk away*) andare via; (*look away*) girarsi dall'altra parte

◆ **turn back 1** *v/t edges, sheets* ripiegare **2** *v/i of walkers etc* tornare indietro; *in course of action* tirarsi indietro

◆ **turn down** *offer, invitation* rifiutare; *volume, heating* abbassare; *edge* ripiegare

◆ **turn in 1** *v/i* (*go to bed*) andare a letto **2** *v/t to police* denunciare

◆ **turn off 1** *v/t TV, engine* spegnere; *tap* chiudere; F (*sexually*) far passare la voglia a **2** *v/i of driver* svoltare

◆ **turn on 1** *v/t TV, engine* accendere; *tap* aprire; F (*sexually*) eccitare **2** *v/i of machine* accendersi

◆ **turn over 1** *v/i in bed* girarsi; *of vehicle* capottare **2** *v/t object, page* girare; FIN fatturare

◆ **turn up 1** *v/t collar, volume, heating* alzare **2** *v/i* (*arrive*) arrivare

turning ['tɜːnɪŋ] svolta *f*; **turning point** svolta *f* decisiva; **turnout** *of spectators* affluenza *f*; **turnover** FIN fatturato *m*; *of staff* ricambio *m*; **turnpike** *Am* strada *f* a pedaggio; **turn signal** *Am* MOT freccia *f*; **turn-up** *of trousers* risvolto *m*

turquoise ['tɜːkwɔɪz] turchese

turtle ['tɜːtl] tartaruga *f* marina; **turtleneck sweater** maglia *f* a lupetto

Tuscany ['tʌskənɪ] Toscana *f*

tusk [tʌsk] zanna *f*

tutor ['tjuːtə(r)] EDU *insegnante universitario che segue un piccolo gruppo di studenti*; (**private**) *n* insegnante *m/f* privato, -a

tuxedo [tʌk'siːdəʊ] *Am* smoking *m inv*

TV [tiː'viː] *TV f inv*; **on ~** alla TV; **TV dinner** piatto *m* pronto; **TV guide** guida *f* dei programmi TV; **TV programme**, *Am* **TV program** programma *m* televisivo

twang [twæŋ] **1** *n in voice* suono *m* nasale **2** *v/t guitar string* vibrare

tweezers ['twiːzəz] pinzette *fpl*

twelfth [twelfθ] dodicesimo; **twelve** dodici

twentieth ['twentɪɪθ] ventesimo; **twenty** venti; **twenty-four-seven** ventiquattr'ore su ventiquattro, sette giorni su sette

twice [twaɪs] due volte; **~ as much** il doppio; **~ as fast** veloce due volte tanto

twig [twɪg] ramoscello *m*

twilight ['twaɪlaɪt] crepuscolo *m*

twin [twɪn] gemello *m*; **twin beds** due lettini *mpl*

twinge [twɪndʒ] *of pain* fitta *f*

twinkle ['twɪŋkl] *of stars, eyes* scintillare

'twin room camera *f* da due letti; **twin town** città *f inv* gemellata

twirl [twɜːl] **1** *v/t* fare roteare **2** *n of cream etc* ricciolo *m*

twist [twɪst] **1** *v/t* attorcigliare; **~ one's ankle** prendere una storta **2** *v/i of road* snodarsi;

of river serpeggiare **3** *n in rope* attorcigliata *f*; *in road* curva *f*; *in plot* svolta *f*; **twisty** *road* contorto

twit [twɪt] F scemo *m*, -a *f*

twitch [twɪtʃ] **1** *n nervous* spasmo *m* **2** *v/i (jerk)* contrarsi

twitter ['twɪtə(r)] cinguettare

two [tuː] due; **the ~ of them** loro due

tycoon [taɪ'kuːn] magnate *m*

type [taɪp] **1** *n (sort)* tipo *m* **2** *v/t & v/i (use a keyboard)* battere (a macchina)

typhoon [taɪ'fuːn] tifone *m*

typhus ['taɪfəs] tifo *m*

typical ['tɪpɪkl] tipico; **that's ~ of you / him!** tipico!; **typically** tipicamente

typist ['taɪpɪst] dattilografo *m*, -a *f*

tyrannical [tɪ'rænɪkl] tirannico; **tyrannize** tiranneggiare; **tyranny** tirannia *f*; **tyrant** tiranno *m*, -a *f*

tyre [taɪr] gomma *f*, pneumatico *m*

Tyrol [tɪ'rəl] Tirolo *m*; **Tyrolean** tirolese

Tyrrhenian Sea [taɪ'riːnɪən] mar *m* Tirreno

U

ugly ['ʌglɪ] brutto

UK [juː'keɪ] (= *United Kingdom*) Regno *m* Unito

ulcer ['ʌlsə(r)] ulcera *f*

ultimate ['ʌltɪmət] *(best, de-*finitive)* definitivo; *(final)* ultimo; *(basic)* fondamentale; **ultimately** *(in the end)* in definitiva

ultimatum [ʌltɪ'meɪtəm] ultimatum *m inv*

ultrasound ['ʌltrəsaund]
MED ecografia *f*

ultraviolet [ʌltrə'vaɪələt] ultravioletto

umbrella [ʌm'brelə] ombrello *m*

umpire ['ʌmpaɪə(r)] arbitro *m*

umpteenth [ʌmp'tiːnθ] F ennesimo

UN [juː'en] (= *United Nations*) ONU *f* (= Organizzazione *f* delle Nazioni Unite)

unable [ʌn'eɪbl]: *be ~ to do sth* not know how to non saper fare qc; *not be in a position to* non poter fare qc

unacceptable [ʌnək'septəbl] inaccettabile

unaccountable [ʌnə-'kauntəbl] inspiegabile

unanimous [juː'nænɪməs] *verdict* unanime; *unanimously* all'unanimità

unapproachable [ʌnə-'prəutʃəbl] *person* inavvicinabile

unarmed [ʌn'ɑːmd] *person* disarmato; *~ combat* combattimento senz'armi

unassuming [ʌnə'sjuːmɪŋ] senza pretese

unattached [ʌnə'tætʃt] (*without a partner*) libero

unattended [ʌnə'tendɪd] incustodito

unauthorized [ʌn'ɔːθəraɪzd] non autorizzato

unavoidable [ʌnə'vɔɪdəbl]

inevitabile

unbalanced [ʌn'bælənst] non equilibrato; PSYCH squilibrato

unbearable [ʌn'beərəbl] insopportabile

unbeatable [ʌn'biːtəbl] *team, quality* imbattibile

unbeaten [ʌn'biːtn] *team* imbattuto

unbelievable [ʌnbɪ'liːvəbl] incredibile

unbias(s)ed [ʌn'baɪəst] imparziale

unblock [ʌn'blɒk] sbloccare

unbreakable [ʌn'breɪkəbl] *plates* infrangibile; *world record* imbattibile

unbutton [ʌn'bʌtn] sbottonare

uncanny [ʌn'kænɪ] *resemblance, skill* sorprendente; (*worrying: feeling*) inquietante

unceasing [ʌn'siːsɪŋ] incessante

uncertain [ʌn'sɜːtn] incerto; *origins* dubbio; *be ~ about sth* non essere certo su qc; *uncertainty* f *of the future* incertezza *f*; *there is still ~ about ...* ci sono ancora dubbi su ...

uncle ['ʌŋkl] zio *m*

uncomfortable [ʌn'kʌmftəbl] scomodo; *I feel ~ with him* mi sento a disagio con lui

uncommon [ʌn'kɒmən] raro

uncompromising [ʌn'kɒmprəmaızıŋ] fermo; *in a nega-tive way* intransigente

unconditional [ʌnkən'dıʃnl] incondizionato

unconscious [ʌn'kɒnʃəs] MED svenuto; PSYCH inconscio; **knock s.o. ~** stordire qu con un colpo; **be ~ of sth** (*not aware*) non rendersi conto di qc

uncontrollable [ʌnkən-'trəʊləbl] incontrollabile

unconventional [ʌnkən-'venʃnl] poco convenzionale

uncooperative [ʌnkəʊ'ɒprə-tıv] poco cooperativo

uncover [ʌn'kʌvə(r)] scoprire

undamaged [ʌn'dæmıdʒd] intatto

undecided [ʌndı'saıdıd] *question* irrisolto; **be ~ about sth** essere indeciso su qc

undeniable [ʌndı'naıəbl] innegabile

under ['ʌndə(r)] *prp* sotto; (*less than*) meno di; *it is ~ inves-tigation* viene indagato

'undercarriage carrello *m* d'atterraggio

'undercover *agent* segreto

under'cut COM vendere a minor prezzo di

under'done *meat* al sangue; (*not cooked enough*) non cotto abbastanza

under'estimate, sottovalutare

under'fed malnutrito

under'go *treatment* sottoporsi a; *experiences* vivere

under'graduate studente *m*, -essa *f* universitario, -a

'underground 1 *adj passages etc* sotterraneo; POL clandestino **2** *adv work* sottoterra; **go ~** POL entrare in clandestinità **3** *n* RAIL metropolitana *f*

'undergrowth sottobosco *m*

under'hand (*devious*) subdolo

under'line *text* sottolineare

under'lying di fondo

under'mine *s.o.'s position* minare

underneath [ʌndə'ni:θ] sotto

'underpants mutande *fpl* da uomo

'underpass *for pedestrians* sottopassaggio *m*

underprivileged [ʌndə'prıvı-lıdʒd] svantaggiato

under'rate sottovalutare

'undershirt *Am* canottiera *f*

understaffed [ʌndə'stɑ:ft] a corto di personale

under'stand capire; *I ~ that you ...* mi risulta che tu ...; **understandable** comprensibile; **understandably** comprensibilmente; **understanding 1** *adj person* comprensivo **2** *n* comprensione *f*; (*agreement*) intesa *f*

under'take *task* intraprendere; **~ to do sth** impegnarsi a fare qc; **undertaking** (*enterprise*) impresa *f*; (*promise*) promessa *f*

under'value sottovalutare

'**underwear** biancheria *f* intima

'**underworld** *criminal* malavita *f; in mythology* inferi *mpl*

under'**write** FIN sottoscrivere

un**deserved** [ʌndɪˈzɜːvd] immeritato

un**desirable** [ʌndɪˈzaɪərəbl] **1** *adj* indesiderabile **2** *n* persona *f* indesiderata

un**disputed** [ʌndɪˈspjuːtɪd] *champion* indiscusso

un**do** [ʌnˈduː] *parcel* disfare; *shirt* sbottonare; *shoes* slacciare; *s.o.'s work* annullare

un**doubtedly** [ʌnˈdaʊtɪdlɪ] indubbiamente

un**dress** [ʌnˈdres] **1** *v/t* spogliare; **get ~ed** spogliarsi **2** *v/i* spogliarsi

un**due** [ʌnˈdjuː] (*excessive*) eccessivo; **unduly** (*excessively*) eccessivamente

un**earth** [ʌnˈɜːθ] *remains* portare alla luce; (*fig: find*) scovare

un**easy** [ʌnˈiːzɪ] *relationship, peace* precario; **feel ~ about** non sentirsela di

un**eatable** [ʌnˈiːtəbl] immangiabile

un**economic** [ʌniːkəˈnɒmɪk] poco redditizio

un**educated** [ʌnˈedjʊkeɪtɪd] senza istruzione

un**employed** [ʌnɪmˈplɔɪd] **1** *adj* disoccupato **2** *npl:* **the ~** i disoccupati; **unemployment** disoccupazione *f;* **~ benefit** sussidio *m* di disoc-

cupazione

un**ending** [ʌnˈendɪŋ] interminabile

un**equal** [ʌnˈiːkwəl] disuguale

un**erring** [ʌnˈerɪŋ] *judgement, instinct* infallibile

un**even** [ʌnˈiːvn] *quality* irregolare; *ground* accidentato

un**eventful** [ʌnɪˈventful] *day, journey* tranquillo

un**expected** [ʌnɪkˈspektɪd] inatteso; **unexpectedly** inaspettatamente

un**fair** [ʌnˈfeə(r)] ingiusto

un**faithful** [ʌnˈfeɪθfʊl] *husband, wife* infedele; **be ~ to s.o.** essere infedele a qu

un**familiar** [ʌnfəˈmɪljə(r)] sconosciuto; **be ~ with sth** non conoscere qc

un**fasten** [ʌnˈfɑːsn] *belt* slacciare

un**favourable**, *Am* **unfavorable** [ʌnˈfeɪvərəbl] *report, review* negativo; *weather conditions* sfavorevole

un**finished** [ʌnˈfɪnɪʃt] non terminato; **leave sth ~** non terminare qc

un**fit** [ʌnˈfɪt] *adj physically* fuori forma; **be ~ to ...** *morally* non essere degno di ...; **~ to eat / drink** non commestibile / non potabile

un**fold** [ʌnˈfəʊld] **1** *v/t letter* spiegare; *arms* aprire **2** *v/i of story etc* svolgersi; *of view* spiegarsi

un**foreseen** [ʌnfɔːˈsiːn] imprevisto

unforgettable [ʌnfəˈgetəbl] indimenticabile

unforgivable [ʌnfəˈgɪvəbl] imperdonabile

unfortunate [ʌnˈfɔːtʃənət] *people* sfortunato; *event, choice of words* infelice; *that's ~ for you* è spiacevole per lei; **unfortunately** sfortunatamente

unfounded [ʌnˈfaʊndɪd] infondato

unfriendly [ʌnˈfrendlɪ] poco amichevole

ungrateful [ʌnˈgreɪtfʊl] ingrato

unhappiness [ʌnˈhæpɪnɪs] infelicità f; **unhappy** infelice; *customers etc* non soddisfatto (**with** di)

unharmed [ʌnˈhɑːmd] illeso

unhealthy [ʌnˈhelθɪ] *person* malaticcio; *conditions* malsano; *food, atmosphere* poco sano; *economy* traballante

unheard-of [ʌnˈhɜːdɒv] inaudito

unhygienic [ʌnhaɪˈdʒiːnɪk] non igienico

unification [juːnɪfɪˈkeɪʃn] unificazione f

uniform [ˈjuːnɪfɔːm] **1** n divisa f; MIL *also* uniforme f **2** adj uniforme

unify [ˈjuːnɪfaɪ] unificare

unilateral [juːnɪˈlætrəl] unilaterale

unimaginable [ʌnɪˈmædʒɪnəbl] inimmaginabile

unimaginative [ʌnɪˈmædʒɪnətɪv] senza fantasia

unimportant [ʌnɪmˈpɔːtənt] senza importanza

uninhabitable [ʌnɪnˈhæbɪtəbl] inabitabile; **uninhabited** *building* disabitato; *region* deserto

unintentional [ʌnɪnˈtenʃnl] involontario; **unintentionally** involontariamente

uninteresting [ʌnˈɪntrəstɪŋ] poco interessante

uninterrupted [ʌnɪntəˈrʌptɪd] ininterrotto

union [ˈjuːnɪən] POL unione f; (*trade ~*) sindacato m

unique [juːˈniːk] unico

unit [ˈjuːnɪt] unità f inv; (*department*) reparto m

unit 'cost COM costo m unitario

unite [juːˈnaɪt] **1** v/t unire **2** v/i unirsi; **united** unito; **United Kingdom** Regno m Unito; **United Nations** Nazioni fpl Unite; **United States (of America)** Stati mpl Uniti (d'America); **unity** unità f inv

universal [juːnɪˈvɜːsl] universale; **universe** universo m

university [juːnɪˈvɜːsətɪ] università f inv

unjust [ʌnˈdʒʌst] ingiusto

unkind [ʌnˈkaɪnd] cattivo

unknown [ʌnˈnəʊn] **1** adj sconosciuto **2** n: *a journey into the ~* un viaggio nell'ignoto

unleaded [ʌnˈledɪd] senza

piombo

unless [ən'les] a meno che; **~ he pays us tomorrow** a meno che non ci paghi domani; **~ I am mistaken** se non mi sbaglio

unlikely [ʌn'laɪklɪ] improbabile

unlimited [ʌn'lɪmɪtɪd] illimitato

unload [ʌn'ləʊd] scaricare

unlock [ʌn'lɒk] aprire (con la chiave)

unluckily [ʌn'lʌkɪlɪ] sfortunatamente; **unlucky** day, choice, person sfortunato; **that was so ~ for you!** che sfortuna hai avuto!

unmanned [ʌn'mænd] spacecraft senza equipaggio

unmarried [ʌn'mærɪd] non sposato

unmistakable [ʌnmɪ'steɪkəbl] inconfondibile

unnatural [ʌn'næʧrəl] non normale

unnecessary [ʌn'nesəsrɪ] non necessario; comment, violence gratuito

unnerving [ʌn'nɜːvɪŋ] inquietante

unobtainable [ʌnəb'teɪnəbl] goods introvabile; TELEC non ottenibile

unobtrusive [ʌnəb'truːsɪv] discreto

unoccupied [ʌn'ɒkjʊpaɪd] building, house vuoto; post vacante; room libero

unofficial [ʌnə'fɪʃl] non uffi-

ciale; announcement ufficioso; **unofficially** non ufficialmente

unorthodox [ʌn'ɔːθədɒks] poco ortodosso

unpack [ʌn'pæk] **1** v/t disfare **2** v/i disfare le valige

unpaid [ʌn'peɪd] work non retribuito

unpleasant [ʌn'pleznt] person, thing to say antipatico; smell, taste sgradevole

unplug [ʌn'plʌg] TV, computer staccare (la spina di)

unpopular [ʌn'pɒpjʊlə(r)] person mal visto; decision impopolare

unprecedented [ʌn'presɪdentɪd] senza precedenti

unpredictable [ʌnprɪ'dɪktəbl] imprevedibile

unpretentious [ʌnprɪ'tenʃəs] senza pretese

unproductive [ʌnprə'dʌktɪv] meeting sterile; soil improduttivo

unprofessional [ʌnprə'feʃnl] workmanship poco professionale

unprofitable [ʌn'prɒfɪtəbl] non redditizio

unprovoked [ʌnprə'vəʊkt] attack non provocato

unqualified [ʌn'kwɒlɪfaɪd] worker non qualificato; doctor, teacher non abilitato

unquestionably [ʌn'kwesʧnəblɪ] indiscutibilmente; **unquestioning** attitude assoluto

unreadable [ʌn'ri:dəbl] *book* illeggibile

unrealistic [ʌnrɪə'lɪstɪk] *person* poco realista; *expectations* poco realistico

unreasonable [ʌn'ri:znəbl] *person* irragionevole; *demand* eccessivo

unrelated [ʌnrɪ'leɪtɪd] *issues* senza (alcuna) attinenza; *people* non imparentato

unrelenting [ʌnrɪ'lentɪŋ] incessante

unreliable [ʌnrɪ'laɪəbl] poco affidabile

unrest [ʌn'rest] agitazione *f*

unrestrained [ʌnrɪ'streɪnd] *emotions* incontrollato, sfrenato

unroll [ʌn'rəʊl] srotolare

unruly [ʌn'ru:lɪ] indisciplinato

unsafe [ʌn'seɪf] pericoloso; ~ **to drink / eat** non potabile / non commestibile; **it is** ~ **to ...** è rischioso ...

unsanitary [ʌn'sænɪtrɪ] antigienico

unsatisfactory [ʌnsætɪs'fæktrɪ] poco soddisfacente

unscathed [ʌn'skeɪðd] (*not injured*) incolume; (*not damaged*) intatto

unscrew [ʌn'skru:] svitare

unscrupulous [ʌn'skru:pjələs] senza scrupoli

unselfish [ʌn'selfɪʃ] *person* altruista; *act* altruistico

unsettled [ʌn'setld] *issue* irrisolto; *weather* instabile; *life-*

style irrequieto; *bills* non pagato

unshaven [ʌn'ʃeɪvn] non rasato

unskilled [ʌn'skɪld] non specializzato

unsophisticated [ʌnsə'fɪstɪkeɪtɪd] *person, beliefs* semplice; *equipment* rudimentale

unstable [ʌn'steɪbl] instabile; *person* squilibrato

unsteady [ʌn'stedɪ] *ladder* malsicuro; **be** ~ **on one's feet** non reggersi bene sulle gambe

unsuccessful [ʌnsək'sesfʊl] *writer etc* di scarso successo; *candidate, party* sconfitto; *attempt* fallito; **he tried but was** ~ ha provato ma non ha avuto fortuna; **unsuccessfully** senza successo

unsuitable [ʌn'su:təbl] *partner, clothing* inadatto; *thing to say* inappropriato

unswerving [ʌn'swɜ:vɪŋ] *loyalty* incrollabile

unthinkable [ʌn'θɪŋkəbl] impensabile

untidy [ʌn'taɪdɪ] in disordine

untie [ʌn'taɪ] *knot* disfare; *laces* slacciare; *prisoner* slegare

until [ən'tɪl] **1** *prep* fino a; **from Monday** ~ **Friday** da lunedì a venerdì; **not** ~ **Friday** non prima di venerdì **2** *conj* finché (non); **can you wait** ~ **I'm ready?** puoi aspettare che sia pronta?

untiring [ʌn'taɪrɪŋ] *efforts* instancabile

untold [ʌn'təʊld] *riches* incalcolabile; *suffering* indescrivibile; *story* inedito

untrue [ʌn'truː] falso

unused [ʌn'juːzd] mai usato

unusual [ʌn'juːʒʊəl] insolito; *it's ~ for them not to write* non è da loro non scrivere; *unusually* insolitamente

unveil [ʌn'veɪl] *statue etc* scoprire

unwell [ʌn'wel]: *be / feel ~* stare / sentirsi male

unwilling [ʌn'wɪlɪŋ]: *be ~ to do* non essere disposto a fare; *unwillingly* malvolentieri

unwind [ʌn'waɪnd] **1** *v/t tape* svolgere **2** *v/i of tape* svolgersi; *of story* dipanarsi; *(relax)* rilassarsi

unwise [ʌn'waɪz] avventato, imprudente

unwrap [ʌn'ræp] aprire, scartare

unzip [ʌn'zɪp] *dress etc* aprire (la chiusura lampo di); COMPUT espandere

up [ʌp] **1** *adv*: *~ in the sky / ~ on the roof* in alto nel cielo / sul tetto; *~ here / there* quassù / lassù; *be ~ (out of bed)* essere in piedi; *of sun* essere sorto; *of temperature* essere aumentato; *(have expired)* essere scaduto; *what's ~?* F che c'è?; *~ to the year 1989* fino al 1989;

he came ~ to me mi si è avvicinato; *what are you ~ to these days?* cosa fai di bello?; *what are those kids ~ to?* cosa stanno combinando i bambini?; *be ~ to something (bad)* stare architettando qualcosa; *I don't feel ~ to it* non me la sento; *it's ~ to you* dipende da te; *it is ~ to them to solve it* their duty sta a loro risolverlo; *be ~ and about* after illness essersi ristabilito **2** *prep*: *further ~ the mountain* più in alto sulla montagna; *they ran ~ the street* corsero per strada; *we travelled ~ to Milan* siamo andati a Milano **3** *n*: *~s and downs* alti e bassi *mpl*

'upbringing educazione *f*

'upcoming *(forthcoming)* prossimo

up'date *file, records* aggiornare; *s.o. on sth* mettere qu al corrente di qc

up'grade *equipment etc* aggiornare; *memory* potenziare; *passenger* promuovere a una classe superiore; *product* migliorare

upheaval [ʌp'hiːvl] *emotional* sconvolgimento *m*; *physical* scombussolamento *m*; *political, social* sconvolgimento *m*

uphill ['ʌphɪl] **1** *adv*: *go / walk ~* salire **2** *adj climb* in salita; *struggle* arduo

up'hold *traditions, rights* sostenere; (*vindicate*) confermare

'upkeep manutenzione *f*

'upload COMPUT caricare, fare l'upload di

up'market *restaurant, hotel* elegante; *product* di qualità

upon [ə'pɒn] → **on**

upper ['ʌpə(r)] superiore; *deck, rooms* di sopra

upper 'class *adj* aristocratico; *family* dell'alta borghesia

'upright 1 *adj citizen* onesto **2** *adv sit* (ben) dritto; **upright** (**piano**) pianoforte *m* verticale

'uprising insurrezione *f*

'uproar trambusto *m*; (*protest*) protesta *f*

'upscale *Am restaurant, hotel* elegante; *product* di qualità

up'set 1 *v/t drink, glass* rovesciare; (*make sad*) fare stare male; (*distress*) sconvolgere; (*annoy*) seccare **2** *adj* (*sad*) triste; (*distressed*) sconvolto; (*annoyed*) seccato; **be / get ~** prendersela (**about** per); **have an ~ stomach** avere l'intestino in disordine; **up-setting**: **it's so ~** (**for me**) mi fa stare male, mi turba

up'side 'down capovolto; **turn sth ~** capovolgere qc

up'stairs 1 *adv* di sopra **2** *adj room* al piano di sopra

'upstream a monte

up'tight F (*nervous*) nervoso; (*inhibited*) inibito

up-to-'date *information* aggiornato; *fashions* più attuale

'up turn *in economy* ripresa *f*

upward ['ʌpwəd] in su; **~ of 10,000** oltre 10.000

uranium [jʊ'reɪnɪəm] uranio *m*

urban ['ɜːbən] *areas, population* urbano; *redevelopment* urbanistico

urchin ['ɜːtʃɪn] monello *m*, -a *f*

urge [ɜːdʒ] **1** *n* (forte) desiderio *m* **2** *v/t*: **~ s.o. to do sth** raccomandare (caldamente) a qu di fare qc; **urgency** urgenza *f*; **the ~ of the situation** la gravità della situazione; **urgent** urgente

urinate ['jʊərɪneɪt] orinare; **urine** urina *f*

US [juː'es] (= *United States*) USA *mpl*

us [ʌs] ci; *when two pronouns are used* ce; *after prep* noi; **don't leave ~** non ci lasciare, non lasciarci; **she gave them to ~** ce le ha date; **that's for ~** quello è per noi; **who's that? – it's ~** chi è? – siamo noi

USA [juːes'eɪ] (= *United States of America*) USA *mpl*

usage ['juːzɪdʒ] uso *m*

use 1 [juːz] *v/t tool, skills, knowledge* usare, utilizzare; *word, s.o.'s car* usare; *a lot of petrol* consumare; *pej: person* usare **2** [juːs] *n* uso *m*; **be**

of no ~ *to s.o.* non essere d'aiuto a qu; *it's no* ~ *waiting* non serve a niente aspettare

◆ **use up** finire

used¹ [ju:zd] *adj car etc* usato

used² [ju:st]: *be* ~ *to* essere abituato a; *get* ~ *to* abituarsi a

used³ [ju:st]: *I* ~ *to know him* lo conoscevo; *I* ~ *to like him un tempo mi piaceva*

useful ['ju:sfʊl] utile; *person* di grande aiuto; **usefulness** utilità *f*; **useless** *information, advice* inutile; *F person* incapace; *machine* inservibile; *feel* ~ sentirsi inutile; **us-er** *of product* utente *m/f*; **userfriendly** di facile uso

usual ['ju:ʒʊal] solito; *it's not* ~ *for this to happen* non succede quasi mai; *as* ~ come al solito; **usually** di solito

utensil [ju:'tensl] utensile *m*

utility [ju:'tɪlɪtɪ] (*usefulness*) utilità *f*; **utility pole** *Am* palo *m* del telegrafo; **utilize** utilizzare

utmost ['ʌtməʊst] **1** *adj* massimo **2** *n*: *do one's* ~ fare (tutto) il possibile

utter ['ʌtə(r)] **1** *adj* totale **2** *v/t sound* emettere; *word* proferire; **utterly** totalmente

V

vacancy ['veɪkənsɪ] *at work* posto *m* vacante; *in hotel* camera *f* libera; ~ *for a driver as advert* autista cercasi; *"no vacancies"* "completo"; **vacant** *building* vuoto; *room* libero; *look, expression* assente; *position* vacante; **vacantly** con sguardo assente; **vacate** *room* lasciar libero; **vacation** vacanza *f*; *be on* ~ essere in vacanza

vaccinate ['væksɪneɪt] vaccinare; **vaccination** vaccinazione *f*; **vaccine** vaccino *m*

vacuum ['vækjʊəm] **1** *n also fig* vuoto *m* **2** *v/t floors* passare l'aspirapolvere su

vagina [və'dʒaɪnə] vagina *f*

vagrant ['veɪgrənt] vagabondo *m*, -a *f*

vague [veɪg] vago; *I'm still* ~ *about it* non ho ancora le idee chiare al riguardo; **vaguely** vagamente

vain [veɪn] **1** *adj person* vanitoso; *hope* vano **2** *n*: *in* ~ invano

valiant ['væljənt] valoroso

valid ['vælɪd] valido; **validate** *with official stamp* convalidare; *alibi* confermare; **validity** *of reason, argument* validità *f*

valley ['vælɪ] valle *f*

valuable ['væljʊəbl] **1** *adj* prezioso **2** *n*: ~*s* oggetti *mpl* di

venerable

valore; **valuation** valutazione *f*; **value 1** *n* valore *m* **2** *v/t friendship, freedom* tenere a; **have an object ~d** far valutare un oggetto

valve [vælv] valvola *f*

van [væn] furgone *m*

vandal ['vændl] vandalo *m*; **vandalism** vandalismo *m*; **vandalize** vandalizzare

vanilla [vəˈnɪlə] **1** *n* vaniglia *f* **2** *adj ice cream* alla vaniglia; *flavour* di vaniglia

vanish ['vænɪʃ] sparire

vanity ['vænətɪ] *of person* vanità *f inv*

vapor ['veɪpə(r)] *Am →* **vapour**, **vaporize** vaporizzare; **vapour** vapore *m*

variable ['veərɪəbl] **1** *adj* variabile **2** *n* MATH, COMPUT variabile *f*; **variant** variante *f*; **variation** variazione *f*; **varied** *range, diet* vario; *life* movimentato; **variety** varietà *f inv*; *(type)* tipo *m*; **a ~ of things to do** varie cose da fare; **various** *(several)* vario; *(different)* diverso

varnish ['vɑːnɪʃ] **1** *n* for wood vernice *f*; *(nail ~)* smalto *m* **2** *v/t wood* verniciare; *nails* smaltare

vary ['veərɪ] variare

vase [vɑːz] vaso *m*

vast [vɑːst] vasto; *improvement* immenso; **vastly** immensamente

VAT [viːeɪˈtiː, væt] *abbr (= value added tax)* IVA *f* (= im-

posta *f* sul valore aggiunto)

Vatican ['vætɪkən]: **the ~** il Vaticano

vault[1] [vɔːlt] *n* in roof volta *f*; *cellar* cantina *f*; **~s** of bank caveau *m inv*

vault[2] [vɔːlt] **1** *n* SP volteggio *m* **2** *v/t* saltare

VCR [viːsiːˈɑː(r)] (= **video cassette recorder**) videoregistratore *m*

veal [viːl] (carne *f* di) vitello *m*

veer [vɪə(r)] *of car* sterzare; *of wind, party* cambiare direzione

vegetable ['vedʒtəbl] verdura *f*; **vegetarian 1** *n* vegetariano *m*, -a *f* **2** *adj* vegetariano; **vegetation** vegetazione *f*

vehement ['viːəmənt] veemente

vehicle ['viːɪkl] veicolo *m*; *for information etc* mezzo *m*

veil [veɪl] velo *m*

vein [veɪn] ANAT vena *f*; *in this ~ fig* su questo tono

Velcro® ['velkrəʊ] velcro *m*

velocity [vɪˈlɒsətɪ] velocità *f inv*

velvet ['velvɪt] velluto *m*

vendetta [venˈdetə] vendetta *f*

vending machine ['vendɪŋ] distributore *m* automatico; **vendor** LAW venditore *m*, -trice *f*

veneer [vəˈnɪə(r)] impiallacciatura *f*; *of politeness etc* parvenza *f*

venerable ['venərəbl] venerabile; **veneration** venerazione f

venereal disease [vɪˈnɪərɪəl] malattia f venerea

Venetian [vəˈniːʃn] *adj* veneziano **2** n veneziano m, -a f; **venetian blind** veneziana f; **Venice** Venezia f

venom [ˈvenəm] veleno m

ventilate [ˈventɪleɪt] ventilare; **ventilation** ventilazione f; **ventilator** ventilatore m; MED respiratore m

venture [ˈventʃə(r)] **1** n impresa f **2** v/i avventurarsi

venue [ˈvenjuː] *for meeting, concert etc* luogo m

veranda [vəˈrændə] veranda f

verb [vɜːb] verbo m; **verbal** (*spoken*) verbale; **verbally** verbalmente

verdict [ˈvɜːdɪkt] LAW verdetto m; (*opinion, judgment*) giudizio m

verge [vɜːdʒ] *of road* bordo m; **be on the ~ of ...** *ruin, collapse* essere sull'orlo di ...; **on the ~ of tears** sul punto di piangere

verification [verɪfɪˈkeɪʃn] verifica f; **verify** verificare

vermin [ˈvɜːmɪn] animali *mpl* nocivi

vermouth [ˈvɜːməθ] vermut m

versatile [ˈvɜːsətaɪl] versatile; **versatility** versatilità f

verse [vɜːs] *poetry* poesia f; *part of poem, song* strofa f

version [ˈvɜːʃn] versione f

versus [ˈvɜːsəs] contro

vertical [ˈvɜːtɪkl] verticale

vertigo [ˈvɜːtɪgəʊ] vertigini *fpl*

very [ˈveri] **1** *adv* molto; **~ fast** molto veloce, velocissimo; **the ~ best** il meglio **2** *adj*: **at that ~ moment** in quel preciso momento; **that's the ~ thing I need** è proprio quello che mi serve

vessel [ˈvesl] NAUT natante m

vest [vest] *Br undershirt* canottiera f; *Am* gilè m *inv*

vestige [ˈvestɪdʒ] vestigio m; **not a ~ of truth** neanche un'ombra di verità

vet¹ [vet] n (*veterinary surgeon*) veterinario m, -a f

vet² [vet] v/t *applicants etc* passare al vaglio

vet³ [vet] n MIL reduce m/f

veteran [ˈvetərən] **1** n veterano m, -a f; MIL reduce m/f **2** *adj* veterano

veto [ˈviːtəʊ] **1** n veto m **2** v/t mettere il veto a

via [ˈvaɪə] attraverso

viable [ˈvaɪəbl] in grado di sopravvivere; *alternative, plan* fattibile

vibrate [vaɪˈbreɪt] vibrare; **vibration** vibrazione f

vicar [ˈvɪkə(r)] parroco m anglicano

vice¹ [vaɪs] vizio m

vice² [vaɪs] *tool* morsa f

vice ˈpresident vice-presidente m

vice versa [vaɪsˈvɜːsə] viceversa

vicious ['vɪʃəs] *dog* feroce; *attack, criticism* brutale; **viciously** brutalmente

victim ['vɪktɪm] vittima *f*; **victimize** perseguitare

victorious [vɪk'tɔːrɪəs] *army* vittorioso; *team* vincente; **victory** vittoria *f*

video ['vɪdɪəʊ] **1** *n* video *m inv*; *tape* videocassetta *f*; *(VCR)* videoregistratore *m* **2** *v/t* registrare; **video camera** videocamera *f*; **video cassette** videocassetta *f*; **video conference** videoconferenza *f*; **video game** videogame *m inv*; **video recorder** videoregistratore *m*; **videotape** videocassetta *f*

vie [vaɪ] competere

Vietnam [viet'næm] Vietnam *m*; **Vietnamese 1** *adj* vietnamita **2** *n* vietnamita *m/f*; *language* vietnamita *m*

view [vjuː] **1** *n* veduta *f*; *of situation* parere *m*; **in ~ of** considerato; **be on ~** *of paintings* essere esposto; **with a ~ to** con l'intenzione di **2** *v/t* vedere; *TV programme* guardare **3** *v/i* *(watch TV)* guardare la TV; **viewer** *TV* telespettatore *m*, -trice *f*; **viewpoint** punto *m* di vista

vigor ['vɪgə(r)] *Am* ☞ **vigour**; **vigorous** vigoroso; **vigorously** vigorosamente; **vigour** vigore *m*

village ['vɪlɪdʒ] paese *m*; **vil-**

lager abitante *m/f* (del paese)

villain ['vɪlən] cattivo *m*, -a *f*; *F criminal* delinquente *m/f*

vindicate ['vɪndɪkeɪt] *(prove correct)* confermare; *(prove innocent)* scagionare; **I feel ~d by the report** il resoconto mi dà ragione

vindictive [vɪn'dɪktɪv] vendicativo

vine [vaɪn] *(grape~)* vite *f*; *climber* rampicante *m*

vinegar ['vɪnɪgə(r)] aceto *m*

vineyard ['vɪnjɑːd] vigneto *m*

vintage ['vɪntɪdʒ] **1** *n* *of wine* annata *f* **2** *adj* *(classic)* d'annata

viola [vɪ'əʊlə] MUS viola *f*

violate ['vaɪəleɪt] violare; **violation** violazione *f*; *Am (traffic ~)* infrazione *f*

violence ['vaɪələns] violenza *f*; **violent** violento

violin [vaɪə'lɪn] violino *m*; **violinist** violinista *m/f*

VIP [viːaɪ'piː] (= **very important person**) VIP *m/f*

viral ['vaɪrəl] virale

virgin ['vɜːdʒɪn] vergine *m/f*; **virginity** verginità *f*

Virgo ['vɜːgəʊ] ASTR Vergine *f*

virile ['vɪraɪl] virile; **virility** virilità *f*

virtual ['vɜːtjʊəl] effettivo; COMPUT virtuale; **virtually** *(almost)* praticamente

virtue ['vɜːtjuː] virtù *f inv*

virtuoso [vɜːtʊ'əʊzəʊ] MUS virtuoso *m*, -a *f*

virtuous ['vɜːtʃʊəs] virtuoso

virus ['vaɪərəs] MED, COMPUT virus *m inv*

visa ['viːzə] visto *m*

vise *Am* ☞ **vice²**

visibility [vɪzə'bɪlətɪ] visibilità *f*; **visible** visibile; *anger etc* evidente

vision ['vɪʒn] (*eyesight*) vista *f*; REL *etc* visione *f*

visit ['vɪzɪt] **1** *n* visita *f*; **pay s.o. a ~** fare una visita a qu **2** *v/t person* andare a trovare; *place, country, city, website* visitare; *doctor, dentist* andare da; **visitor** (*guest*) ospite *m*; *to museum etc* visitatore *m*, -trice *f*; (*tourist*) turista *m/f*

visor ['vaɪzə(r)] visiera *f*

visual ['vɪzjʊəl] *organs, memory* visivo; *arts* figurativo; **visualize** immaginare, (*foresee*) prevedere; **visually** visivamente

vital ['vaɪtl] (*essential*) essenziale; **vitality** vitalità *f*; **vitally**: **~ important** di vitale importanza

vitamin ['vɪtəmɪn] vitamina *f*; **vitamin pill** (confetto *m* di) vitamina *f*

vivacious [vɪ'veɪʃəs] vivace; **vivacity** vivacità *f*

vivid ['vɪvɪd] vivido; **vividly** in modo vivido

V-neck ['viːnek] maglione *m* con scollo a V

vocabulary [və'kæbjʊlərɪ] vocabolario *m*; *list of words* glossario *m*

vocal ['vəʊkl] *to do with the voice* vocale; *expressing opinions* eloquente; **become ~** cominciare a farsi sentire; **vocal group** MUS gruppo *m* vocale; **vocalist** MUS cantante *m/f*

vocation [və'keɪʃn] (*calling*) vocazione *f* (**for** a); (*profession*) professione *f*; **vocational guidance** professionale

vodka ['vɒdkə] vodka *f inv*

vogue [vəʊg] moda *f*; **be in ~** essere in voga

voice [vɔɪs] **1** *n* voce *f* **2** *v/t opinions* esprimere; **voice-activated** attivato dalla voce; **voice mail** segreteria *f* telefonica; *message* messagio *m* in segreteria

volatile ['vɒlətaɪl] *personality* volubile

volcano [vɒl'keɪnəʊ] vulcano *m*

volley ['vɒlɪ] *of shots* raffica *f*; *in tennis* volée *f* ou

volt [vəʊlt] volt *m inv*; **voltage** voltaggio *m*; **high ~** alta tensione *f*

volume ['vɒljuːm] volume *m*

voluntarily [vɒlən'teərɪlɪ] spontaneamente; **voluntary** volontario; **~ work** volontariato; **volunteer 1** *n* volontario *m*, -a *f* **2** *v/i* offrirsi volontario

vomit ['vɒmɪt] **1** *n* vomito *m* **2** *v/i* vomitare

voracious [vəˈreɪʃəs] vorace

vote [vəʊt] 1 n voto m; *right to vote* diritto m di voto 2 v/i POL votare (*for* a favore di, *against* contro); *voter* POL elettore m, -trice f; *voting* POL votazione f

♦ **vouch for** [vaʊtʃ] *truth* garantire; *person* garantire per

vow [vaʊ] 1 n voto m 2 v/t: ~ *to do* giurare di fare

vowel [vaʊl] vocale f

voyage [ˈvɔɪɪdʒ] viaggio m

vulgar [ˈvʌlgə(r)] volgare

vulnerable [ˈvʌlnərəbl] vulnerabile

vulture [ˈvʌltʃə(r)] avvoltoio m

W

waddle [ˈwɒdl] camminare ondeggiando

wade [weɪd] guadare

wafer [ˈweɪfə(r)] *cookie* cialda f; REL ostia f

waffle [ˈwɒfl] (*to eat*) tipo di cialda

wag [wæg] *finger* scuotere; *the dog ~ged its tail* il cane scodinzolò

wages [ˈweɪdʒɪz] paga f

waggle [ˈwægl] far muovere

wail [weɪl] *of person* gemere; *of siren* ululare

waist [weɪst] vita f; *waistcoat* gilè m inv; *waistline* vita f

wait [weɪt] 1 n attesa f 2 v/i aspettare; *I can't ~ to ...* non vedo l'ora di ... 3 v/t *meal* ritardare

♦ **wait for** aspettare

♦ **wait on** (*serve*) servire

♦ **wait up** restare alzato ad aspettare

waiter [ˈweɪtə(r)] cameriere m; *waiting list* lista f d'attesa; *waiting room* sala f d'at-

tesa; *waitress* cameriera f

waive [weɪv] (*renounce*) rinunciare a; (*dispense with*) fare al meno di

wake [weɪk] 1 v/i: ~ (*up*) svegliarsi 2 v/t svegliare; *wake-up call* sveglia f (telefonica)

Wales [weɪlz] Galles m

walk [wɔːk] 1 n camminata f; *go for a ~* fare due passi 2 v/i camminare; *as opposed to driving* andare a piedi; (*hike*) passeggiare 3 v/t *dog* portare fuori; ~ *the streets* (*walk around*) girare in lungo e in largo

♦ **walk out** *of spouse etc, from theatre* andarsene; (*go on strike*) scendere in sciopero

♦ **walk out on** *spouse, family* abbandonare

walker [ˈwɔːkə(r)] (*hiker*) escursionista m/f; *for baby* girello m; *for old person* deambulatore m; *be a slow / fast ~* avere il passo lento / spedito; *walking as opposed to driving* camminare *m*; (*hiking*) escursionismo *m*; **it's within ~ distance** ci si arriva a piedi; **Walkman** walkman *m inv*; **walkout** *strike* sciopero *m* selvaggio; **walkover** (*easy win*) vittoria *f* facile

wall [wɔːl] *also fig* muro *m*; *internal* parete *f*; **~s** *of a city* mura *fpl*; **drive s.o. up the ~** F far diventare matto qu

wallet ['wɒlɪt] portafoglio *m*

wallpaper 1 *n* tappezzeria *f*, carta *f* da parati **2** *v/t* tappezzare; **wall-to-wall carpet** moquette *f*

waltz [wɔːls] valzer *m inv*

wan [wɒn] *face* pallido

wander ['wɒndə(r)] (*roam*) gironzolare; (*stray*) allontanarsi

wangle ['wæŋgl] F rimediare F

want [wɒnt] **1** *n*: **for ~ of** per mancanza di **2** *v/t* volere; (*need*) avere bisogno di; **~ to do sth** volere fare qc; **she ~s you to go back** vuole che torni indietro **2** *v/i*: **~ for nothing** non mancare di niente; **wanted** *by police* ricercato

war [wɔː(r)] guerra *f*; *fig* lotta *f*

ward [wɔːd] *in hospital* corsia *f*; *child* minore *m* sotto tutela

♦ **ward off** *blow* parare; *attacker* respingere; *cold* combattere

warden ['wɔːdn] (*traffic* ~) vigile *m* urbano; *of hostel* direttore *m*, -trice *f*; *of nature reserve* guardiano *m*, -a *f*; *of prison* agente *m/f* di custodia; *Am* direttore *m*, -trice *f*

wardrobe *for clothes* armadio *m*; *clothes* guardaroba *m*

warehouse ['weəhaus] magazzino *m*

warfare guerra *f*; **warhead** testata *f*

warily ['weərɪlɪ] con aria guardinga

warm [wɔːm] caldo; *welcome, smile* caloroso; **it's ~** *of weather* fa caldo

♦ **warm up 1** *v/t* scaldare **2** *v/i* scaldarsi; *of athlete etc* fare riscaldamento

warmly ['wɔːmlɪ] *dressed* con abiti pesanti; *welcome, smile* calorosamente; **warmth** calore *m*; *of welcome, smile* calorosità *f*; **warm-up** SP riscaldamento *m*

warn [wɔːn] avvertire; **warning** avvertimento *m*; **without ~** senza preavviso

warp [wɔːp] *of wood* deformarsi; **warped** *fig* contorto

warplane aereo *m* militare

warrant ['wɒrənt] **1** *n* mandato *m* **2** *v/t* giustificare; **warranty** (*guarantee*) garanzia *f*

warrior ['wɒrɪə(r)] guerriero *m*, -a *f*

warship nave *f* da guerra

wart [wɔːt] verruca *f*

wary ['weərɪ] guardingo; **be ~ of** diffidare di

wash [wɒʃ] **1** *n*: *have a ~* darsi una lavata **2** *v/t* lavare; *~ one's hair* lavarsi i capelli **3** *v/i* lavarsi

◆ **wash up** *Br* lavare i piatti; *Am* (*wash one's hands and face*) lavarsi

washable ['wɒʃəbl] lavabile; washbasin, washbowl lavandino *m*; washcloth *Am* guanto *m* di spugna; washed out sfinito; washer *for tap etc* guarnizione *f*; washing washed clothes bucato *m*; clothes to be washed biancheria *f* da lavare; *do the ~* fare il bucato; washing machine lavatrice *f*; washing-up liquid detersivo *m* per i piatti; washroom *Am* servizi *mpl*

wasp [wɒsp] vespa *f*

waste [weɪst] **1** *n* spreco *m*; *from industrial process* rifiuti *mpl*; *it's a ~ of time / money* è tempo sprecato / sono soldi sprecati **2** *adj material* di scarto **3** *v/t* sprecare; waste disposal (unit) tritarifiuti *m inv*; wasteful *person* spercone; *methods* dispendioso; wasteland distesa *f* desolata; wastepaper cartaccia *f*; wastepaper basket, *Am* waste basket cestino *m* della cartaccia

watch [wɒtʃ] **1** *n timepiece* orologio *m*; MIL guardia *f*; *keep ~* stare all'erta **2** *v/t* guardare; (*spy on*) sorveglia-

re; (*look after*) tenere d'occhio **3** *v/i* guardare; watchful vigile

water ['wɔːtə(r)] **1** *n* acqua *f* **2** *v/t plant* annaffiare **3** *v/i of eyes* lacrimare; *my mouth is ~ing* ho l'acquolina in bocca; watercolour, *Am* watercolor acquerello *m*; watered down *fig* edulcorato; waterfall cascata *f*; waterline linea *f* di galleggiamento; waterlogged allagato; watermelon anguria *f*, cocomero *m*; waterproof impermeabile; waterside: *at the ~* sulla riva; waterskiing sci *m* nautico; watertight *compartment* stagno; *fig* inattaccabile; waterway corso *m* d'acqua navigabile; watery acquoso

watt [wɒt] watt *m inv*

wave[1] [weɪv] *n in sea* onda *f*

wave[2] [weɪv] **1** *n of hand* saluto *m* (con la mano) **2** *v/i with hand* salutare (con la mano) **3** *v/t flag etc* sventolare

'wavelength RAD lunghezza *f* d'onda; *be on the same ~ fig* essere sulla stessa lunghezza d'onda

waver ['weɪvə(r)] vacillare

wavy ['weɪvɪ] ondulato

wax [wæks] *n for furniture* cera *f*; *in ear* cerume *m*

way [weɪ] **1** *n* (*method, manner*) modo *m*; (*manner*) maniera *f*; (*route*) strada *f*; *this ~* (*like this*) così; (*in this direc-*

tion) da questa parte; **by the ~** (*incidentally*) a proposito; **in a ~** (*in certain respects*) in un certo senso; **be under ~** essere in corso; **give ~** MOT dare la precedenza; (*collapse*) crollare; (*have*) **one's (own) ~** averla vinta; **lead the ~** *also fig* fare strada; **lose one's ~** smarrirsi; **be in the ~** (*be an obstruction*) essere d'intralcio; **it's on the ~ to the station** è sulla strada della stazione; **I was on my ~ to the station** stavo andando alla stazione; **no ~!** neanche per sogno!; **there's no ~ he can do it** è impossibile che ce la faccia **2** *adv* F (*much*): **it's ~ too soon** è veramente troppo presto; **they are ~ behind with their work** sono molto indietro con il lavoro; **way in** entrata *f*; **way of life** stile *m* di vita; **way out** uscita *f*; *fig: from situation* via *f* d'uscita

we [wiː] *noi*; **~'re the best** siamo i migliori

weak [wiːk] debole; *tea, coffee* leggero; **weaken 1** *v/t* indebolire; **2** *v/i* indebolirsi; **weakness** debolezza *f*; **have a ~ for sth** (*liking*) avere un debole per qc

wealth [welθ] ricchezza *f*; **a ~ of** una grande abbondanza di; **wealthy** ricco

weapon ['wepən] arma *f*

wear [weə(r)] **1** *n*: **~ (and tear)** usura *f* **2** *v/t* (*have on*) indossare; (*damage*) logorare **3** *v/i* (*wear out*) logorarsi; (*last*) durare

♦ **wear down** fiaccare

♦ **wear off** *of effect* svanire

♦ **wear out 1** *v/t* (*tire*) estenuare; *shoes* consumare **2** *v/i of shoes, carpet* consumarsi

wearily ['wɪərɪlɪ] stancamente; **weary** stanco

weather ['weðə(r)] **1** *n* tempo *m*; **be feeling under the ~** sentirsi poco bene **2** *v/t crisis* superare; **weather-beaten** segnato; **weather forecast** previsioni *fpl* del tempo; **weatherman** meteorologo *m*

weave [wiːv] **1** *v/t cloth* tessere; *basket* intrecciare **2** *v/i* (*move*) zigzagare

web [web] *of spider* ragnatela *f*; **the Web** COMPUT il web *m*; **web page** pagina *f* web; **web site** sito *m* web

wedding ['wedɪŋ] matrimonio *m*; **wedding anniversary** anniversario *m* di matrimonio; **wedding day** giorno *m* del matrimonio; **wedding dress** abito *m* or vestito *m* da sposa; **wedding ring** fede *f*

wedge [wedʒ] to hold sth in place zeppa *f*; *of cheese etc* fetta *f*

Wednesday ['wenzdeɪ] mercoledì *m inv*

weed [wi:d] **1** *n* erbaccia *f* **2** *v/t* diserbare; **weed-killer** diserbante *m*; **weedy** F mingherlino

week [wi:k] settimana *f*; **~ tomorrow** una settimana a domani; **weekday** giorno *m* feriale; **weekend** fine *m* settimana, weekend *m inv*; **on the ~** durante il fine settimana; **weekly 1** *adj* settimanale **2** *n magazine* settimanale *m* **3** *adv* settimanalmente

weep [wi:p] piangere

'wee-wee F pipì *f inv* F; **do a ~** fare la pipì

weigh [weɪ] pesare

◆ weigh up (*assess*) valutare

weight [weɪt] peso *m*; **put on / lose ~** ingrassare / dimagrire; **weightlessness** assenza *f* di peso; **weightlifter** pesista *m/f*; **weightlifting** sollevamento *m* pesi; **weighty** *fig: important* importante

weir [wɪə(r)] chiusa *f*

weird [wɪəd] strano; **weirdo** F pazzoide *m/f*

welcome ['welkəm] **1** *adj* benvenuto; **make s.o. ~** accogliere bene qu; **you're ~!** prego!; **you're ~ to try some** serviti pure **2** *n also fig* accoglienza *f* **3** *v/t guests etc* accogliere; *fig: decision etc* rallegrarsi di; **she ~s a challenge** apprezza le sfide

weld [weld] saldare

welfare ['welfeə(r)] bene *m*; **welfare check** *Am* sussidio *m* di disoccupazione; **welfare state** stato *m* sociale; **welfare worker** assistente *m/f* sociale

well¹ [wel] *n for water, oil* pozzo *m*

well² [wel] **1** *adv* bene; **~ done!** bravo!; **as ~** (*too*) anche; **as ~ as** *in addition to* oltre a; **it's just as ~ you told me** hai fatto bene a dirmelo; **very ~** *acknowledging order* benissimo; *reluctantly agreeing* va bene; **~, ~!** *surprise* bene, bene!; **~ ...** *uncertainty, thinking* beh ... **2** *adj*: **be ~** stare bene; **feel ~** sentirsi bene; **get ~ soon!** guarisci presto!

well-'balanced equilibrato; well-behaved educato; well-being benessere *m*; well-done *meat* ben cotto; well-dressed ben vestito; well-earned meritato; well-heeled F danaroso; well-informed ben informato; well-known famoso; well-meaning spinto da buone intenzioni; well-off benestante; well-timed tempestivo; well-to-do abbiente

Welsh [welʃ] **1** *adj* gallese **2** *n language* gallese *m*; **the ~** i gallesi

west [west] **1** *n* ovest *m*, occidente *m*; **the West** POL l'Occidente 2 *adj* occidentale 3 *adv travel* verso ovest; ~ **of** a ovest di; **westerly** occidentale; **western 1** *adj* occidentale; **Western** occidentale 2 *n (film)* western *m inv*; **Westerner** occidentale *m/f*; **westernized** occidentalizzato; **West Indian 1** *adj* delle Indie Occidentali 2 *n* nativo *m* delle Indie Occidentali; **West Indies: the** ~ le Indie Occidentali; **westward** verso ovest

wet [wet] bagnato; *(rainy)* piovoso; ~ **paint** as sign vernice fresca; **wet suit** *for diving* muta *f*

whack [wæk] **1** *n* F *(blow)* colpo *m* **2** *v/t* F colpire; **whacked** F stanco morto

whale [weɪl] balena *f*

wharf [wɔːf] *n* banchina *f*

what [wɒt] **1** *pron* (che) cosa; ~ **is that?** (che) cos'è?; ~ **is it?** *(what do you want)* (che) cosa c'è?; ~? cosa?; **it's not** ~ **I meant** non è ciò che volevo dire; ~ **about some dinner?** e se mangiassimo qualcosa?; ~ **for?** *(why)* perché? **2** *adj* che inv, quale; ~ **colour is the car?** di che colore è la macchina? **3** *adv*: ~ **a brilliant idea!** che bella idea!; **whatever: I'll do** ~ **you want** farò (tutto) quello che vuoi; ~ **you do, it'll be a probem** qualsiasi cosa faccia, ci saranno problemi;

~ **people say** qualunque cosa dica la gente; ~ **gave you that idea?** cosa mai te lo ha fatto pensare?; **ok,** ~ F va bene, come vuoi / volete

wheat [wiːt] grano *m*, frumento *m*

wheel [wiːl] ruota *f*; *(steering* ~*)* volante *m*

'**wheelchair** sedia *f* a rotelle; **wheel clamp** ceppo *m* bloccaruote

wheeze [wiːz] ansimare

when [wen] *quando; (rainy)* **whenever** *(each time)* ogni volta che; *regardless of when* in qualunque momento

where [weə(r)] dove; **this is** ~ **I used to live** io abitavo qui; **whereabouts 1** *adv* dove **2** *npl*: **know s.o.'s** ~ sapere dove si trova qui; **whereas** mentre; **wherever 1** *conj* dovunque; ~ **you go** dovunque tu vada **2** *adv* dove; ~ **can he be?** dove sarà mai?

whet [wet] *appetite* stuzzicare

whether [ˈweðə(r)] se

which [wɪtʃ] **1** *adj* quale; ~ **one is yours?** qual è il tuo? **2** *pron interrogative* quale; *relative* che; **the car** ~ ... la macchina che ...; **on / in** ~ su / in cui; **whichever 1** *adj* qualunque **2** *pron* quello che *m*, quella che *f*; ~ **of the methods** qualunque metodo

whiff [wɪf]: **catch a** ~ **of** sentire

while [waɪl] **1** *conj* mentre; (*although*) benché (+ *subj*) **2** *n*: **a long ~ ago** molto tempo fa; **wait a long ~** aspettare molto *or* lungo; **for a ~** per un po'; **in a ~** fra poco

whim [wɪm] capriccio *m*

whimper ['wɪmpə(r)] gemere; *of animal* mugolare

whine [waɪn] *of dog* guaire; F (*complain*) piagnucolare

whip [wɪp] **1** *n* frusta *f* **2** *v/t* (*beat*) sbattere; *cream* montare; F (*defeat*) stracciare

'**whirlpool** *in river* mulinello *m*; *for relaxation* vasca *f* per idromassaggio

whisk [wɪsk] **1** *n* frusta *f*, *mechanical* frullino *m* **2** *v/t* *eggs* frullare

whisky, *Am* **whiskey** ['wɪskɪ] whisky *m inv*

whisper ['wɪspə(r)] bisbigliare

whistle ['wɪsl] **1** *n* *sound* fischio *m*; *device* fischietto *m* **2** *v/i* fischiare **3** *v/t* fischiettare

white [waɪt] **1** *n* bianco *m*; *person* bianco *m*, -a *f* **2** *adj* bianco; **go ~** sbiancare (in viso); **white coffee** caffè *m inv* con latte *or* panna; **white-collar worker** impiegato *m*, -a *f*; **White House** Casa *f* Bianca; **white lie** bugia *f* innocente; **whitewash 1** *n* calce *f*; *fig* copertura *f* **2** *v/t* imbiancare (con calce); **white wine** vino *m* bianco

whittle ['wɪtl] *wood* intagliare
◆ **whittle down** ridurre

whizzkid ['wɪzkɪd] F mago *m*, -a *f*

who [huː] *interrogative* chi; *relative* che; **the man ~ I was talking to** l'uomo con cui parlavo; **whoever** chiunque; (*interrogative*) chi mai; **~ can that be?** chi sarà mai?

whole [həʊl] **1** *adj* intero; **the ~ town** tutta la città; **two ~ hours / days** ben due ore / giorni; **it's a ~ lot easier** è molto più facile **2** *n* tutto *m*; **the ~ of the United States** tutti gli Stati Uniti; **on the ~** nel complesso; **whole-hearted** senza riserve; **wholemeal bread** pane *m* integrale; **wholesale** all'ingrosso; *fig* in massa; **wholesaler** grossista *m/f*; **wholesome** sano; **wholly** completamente

whom [huːm] *fml* chi; **to / for ~** a cui

whore [hɔː(r)] puttana *f*

whose [huːz] *interrogative* di chi; *relative* il / la cui; **~ is this?** di chi è questo?; **a man ~ wife ...** un uomo la cui moglie ...

why [waɪ] perché; **the reason ~** il motivo per cui

wicked ['wɪkɪd] (*evil*) malvagio; (*mischievous*) malizioso; P (*great*) grande

wicker ['wɪkə(r)] di vimini

wicket ['wɪkɪt] *Br* SP porta *f*;

Am in station, bank etc porta f

wide [waɪd] largo; *experience* vasto; *range* ampio; **be 12 metres ~** essere largo 12 metri; widely used, known largamente, largamente; **widen 1** v/t allargare **2** v/i allargarsi; **wide-open** spalancato; **wide-ranging** di largo respiro; **widespread** diffuso

widow [ˈwɪdəʊ] vedova f; **widower** vedovo m

width [wɪdθ] larghezza f; *of fabric* altezza f

wield [wiːld] *weapon* brandire; *power* esercitare

wife [waɪf] moglie f

wig [wɪɡ] parrucca f

wiggle [ˈwɪɡl] *loose screw etc* muovere; **~ one's hips** ancheggiare

wild [waɪld] *adj animal, flowers* selvatico; *teenager, party* scatenato; *scheme* folle; *applause* fragoroso; **be ~ about ...** (*keen on*) andare pazzo per ...; **go ~** impazzire; (*become angry*) andare su tutte le furie **2** n: **the ~s** le zone sperdute

wilderness [ˈwɪldənɪs] deserto m; *fig: garden etc* giungla f

'wildlife fauna f

wilful [ˈwɪlfəl] *person* ostinato; *action* intenzionale

will¹ [wɪl] n LAW testamento m

will² [wɪl] n (*willpower*) volontà f inv

will³ [wɪl] v/aux: **I ~ let you know tomorrow** ti farò sapere entro domani; **the car won't start** la macchina non parte; **~ you tell her that ... ?** dille che ...; **~ you have some more tea?** vuoi dell'altro tè?; **~ you stop that!** smettila!

wilful *Am* ☞ **wilful**

willing [ˈwɪlɪŋ] disponibile; **are you ~ to pay more?** sei disposto a pagare di più?; **willingly** volentieri; **willingness** disponibilità f; **willpower** forza f di volontà

willy-nilly [ˈwɪlɪˈnɪlɪ] (*at random*) a casaccio

wilt [wɪlt] *of plant* appassire

wily [ˈwaɪlɪ] astuto

wimp [wɪmp] F pappamolle m/f

win [wɪn] n vittoria f **2** v/t & v/i vincere

wince [wɪns] fare una smorfia

wind¹ [wɪnd] n vento m; (*flatulence*) aria f

wind² [waɪnd] **1** v/i *of path, stream* snodarsi; *of plant* avvolgersi **2** v/t avvolgere

◆ **wind up 1** v/t *clock* caricare; *car window* tirar su; *speech* concludere; *affairs, company* chiudere **2** v/i: **wind up in hospital** finire in ospedale

'wind-bag F trombone m; **windfall** *fig* colpo m di fortuna

winding [ˈwaɪndɪŋ] tortuoso

window ['wɪndəʊ] *also* COMPUT finestra *f*; *of shop* vetrina *f*; *of car, train* finestrino *m*; **in the ~** *of shop* in vetrina; **window box** fioriera *f*; **window seat** *on plane, train* posto *m* di finestrino; **window-shop**: **go ~ping** guardare le vetrine; **windowsill** davanzale *m*; **windscreen wiper** tergicristallo *m*; **windscreen**, *Am* **windshield** parabrezza *m inv*; **windsurfer** windsurfista *m/f*; *board* windsurf *m inv*; **windsurfing** windsurf *m*; **windy** ventoso; *it's getting ~* si sta alzando il vento

wine [waɪn] vino *m*; **wine glass** bicchiere *m* da vino; **wine merchant** *company* azienda *f* vinicola; *individual* vinaio *m*, *-a f*; **wine cellar** cantina *f*; **wine list** lista *f* dei vini; **winery** *Am* vigneto *m*

wing [wɪŋ] *also* SP ala *f*; *of car* parafango *m*; **wingspan** apertura *f* alare

wink [wɪŋk] *of person* strizzare gli occhi; **~ at s.o.** fare l'occhiolino a qu

winner ['wɪnə(r)] vincitore *m*, *-trice f*; **winning** vincente; **winning post** traguardo *m*; **winnings** vincita *fsg*

winter ['wɪntə(r)] inverno *m*; **winter sports** sport *m* invernali; **wintry** invernale

wipe [waɪp] *(dry)* asciugare; *(clean)* pulire; *tape* cancellare; **wiper** MOT tergicristallo *m*

wire ['waɪə(r)] filo *m* di ferro; ELEC filo *m* elettrico; **wiring** ELEC impianto *m* elettrico; **wiry** *person* dal fisico asciutto

wisdom ['wɪzdəm] saggezza *f*; **wisdom tooth** dente *m* del giudizio

wise [waɪz] saggio; **wisecrack** F spiritosaggine *f*; **wisely** *act* saggiamente

wish [wɪʃ] **1** *n* desiderio *m*; **best ~es** *for birthday etc* tanti auguri; *as greetings* cordiali saluti **2** *v/t* volere; **~ s.o. well** fare tanti auguri a qu
♦ **wish for** desiderare

wisp [wɪsp] *of hair* ciocca *f*; *of smoke* filo *m*

wistful ['wɪstfʊl] malinconico; **wistfully** malinconicamente

witch [wɪtʃ] strega *f*; **witch-hunt** *fig* caccia *f* alle streghe

with [wɪð] *prep* di; *(cause)* di; *shiver ~ fear* tremare di paura; *a girl ~ blue eyes* una ragazza dagli *or* con gli occhi azzurri; *I'm staying with my uncle* sto da mio zio; *are*

you ~ me? (*do you understand*) mi segui?; **~ no money** senza soldi

with'draw 1 *v/t* ritirare; *money from bank* prelevare **2** *v/i* ritirarsi; **withdrawal** ritiro *m*; *of money* prelievo *m*; **withdrawal symptoms** sindrome *f* da astinenza; **withdrawn** *person* chiuso

wither ['wiðə(r)] seccare

with'hold *information* nascondere; *consent* rifiutare; *payment* trattenere

with'in (*inside*) dentro; *in expressions of time* nel giro di, entro; *in expressions of distance* a meno di

with'out senza; **~ you / him** senza (di) te / lui; **~ looking** senza guardare

with'stand resistere a

witness ['wɪtnɪs] **1** *n* testimone *m*/*f* **2** *v/t* essere testimone di; *signature* attestare l'autenticità di

witticism ['wɪtɪsɪzm] arguzia *f*; **witty** arguto

wobble ['wɒbl] *of person* vacillare; *of object* traballare; **wobbly** *person* vacillante; *object* traballante; *voice, hand* tremante

wolf [wʊlf] **1** *n animal* lupo *m* **2** *v/t*: **~ (down)** divorare

woman ['wʊmən] donna *f*; **womanizer** donnaiolo *m*; **womanly** femminile

womb [wuːm] utero *m*

women ['wɪmɪn] *pl* ☞ **woman**;

women's lib movimento *m* di liberazione della donna

wonder ['wʌndə(r)] **1** *n* (*amazement*) *of science etc* meraviglia *f*; **no ~!** non mi stupisce!; **it's a ~ that ...** è incredibile che ... **2** *v/i* domandarsi; **I ~ if you could help** mi chiedevo se potessi aiutarmi; **wonderful** stupendo; **wonderfully** (*extremely*) estremamente

won't [wəʊnt] ☞ **will not**

wood [wʊd] legno *m*; *for fire* legna *f*; (*forest*) bosco *m*; **wooded** boscoso; **wooden** *made of wood* di legno; **woodpecker** picchio *m*; **woodwork** *parts made of wood* strutture *fpl* in legno; *activity* lavorazione *f* del legno

wool [wʊl] lana *f*; **woollen**, *Am* **woolen 1** *adj* di lana **2** *n* indumento *m* di lana

word [wɜːd] **1** *n* parola *f*; (*news*) notizie *fpl*; **have ~s** (*argue*) litigare; **have a ~ with s.o.** parlare con qu **2** *v/t* *article, letter* formulare; **word processor** word processor *m inv*

work [wɜːk] **1** *n* lavoro *m*; **out of ~** disoccupato **2** *v/i of person* lavorare; *study* studiare; *of machine*, (*succeed*) funzionare

◆ **work out 1** *v/t* *problem* capire; *solution* trovare **2** *v/i at gym* fare ginnastica; *of rela-*

tionship etc funzionare

workable ['wɜːkəbl] *solution* realizzabile; **workaholic** F stacanovista *m/f;* **workday** *hours of work* giornata *f* lavorativa; *not a holiday giorno m* feriale; **worker** lavoratore *m,* -trice *f;* **work force** forza *f* lavoro; **work hours** orario *m* di lavoro; **working class** classe *f* operaia; **working-class** operaio *m;* **working hours** ☞ **workhours**; **workload** carico *m* di lavoro; **workman** operaio *m;* **workmanlike** professionale; **workmanship** fattura *f;* **work of art** opera *f* d'arte; **workout** allenamento *m;* **work permit** permesso *m* di lavoro; **workshop** laboratorio *m; for mechanic* officina *f; (seminar)* workshop *m inv*

world mondo *m; out of this ~* F fantastico; **world-class** di livello internazionale; **World Cup** mondiali *mpl* (di calcio); **world-famous** di fama mondiale; **worldly** *goods* materiale; *not spiritual* terreno; *power* temporale; *person* mondano; **world record** record *m inv* mondiale; **world war** guerra *f* mondiale; **worldwide 1** *adj* mondiale **2** *adv* a livello mondiale

worn-'out *shoes, carpet* logoro; *person* esausto

worried ['wʌrɪd] preoccupato; **worry 1** *n* preoccupazione *f* **2** *v/t* preoccupare; *(upset)* turbare **3** *v/i* preoccuparsi; **worrying** preoccupante

worse [wɜːs] **1** *adj* peggiore; *things will get ~* le cose peggioreranno **2** *adv* peggio; **worsen** peggiorare

worship ['wɜːʃɪp] **1** *n* culto *m* **2** *v/t* venerare; *fig* adorare

worst [wɜːst] **1** *adj* peggiore **2** *adv* peggio **3** *n: the ~* il peggio; *if the ~ comes to the ~* nel peggiore dei casi; **worst-case scenario:** *the ~* la peggiore delle ipotesi

worth [wɜːθ] **1** *adj: be ~* valere; *it's ~ reading* vale la pena leggerlo; *be ~ it* valerne la pena **2** *n* valore *m;* **worthwhile** *cause* lodevole; *be ~* (*worth the effort, worth doing*) valere la pena

worthy ['wɜːðɪ] degno; *cause* lodevole; *be ~ of (deserve)* meritare

would [wʊd] *I ~ help if I could* ti aiuterei se potessi; *~ you like to go to the cinema?;* *~ you tell her that ...?* le dica che ...; *~ you close the door?* le dispiace chiudere la porta?

wound [wuːnd] **1** *n* ferita *f* **2** *v/t* ferire

wow [waʊ] wow

wrap [ræp] *gift* incartare; *(wind, cover)* avvolgere;

wrapper incarto m; **wrapping** involucro m; **wrapping paper** carta f da regalo

wrath [rɒθ] ira f

wreath [riːθ] corona f

wreck [rek] **1** n of ship relitto m; of car carcassa f; **be a nervous ~** sentirsi un rottame **2** v/t ship far naufragare; car demolire; plans, marriage distruggere; **wreckage** of car, plane rottami mpl; of marriage, career brandelli mpl; **wrecker** Am truck carro m attrezzi

wrench [renʃ] **1** n tool chiave f inglese **2** v/t (pull) strappare

wrestle ['resl] fare la lotta; **wrestler** lottatore m, -trice f; **wrestling** lotta f libera

wriggle ['rɪgl] (squirm) dimenarsi; along the ground strisciare

wrinkle ['rɪŋkl] in skin ruga f; in clothes grinza f

wrist [rɪst] polso m; **wristwatch** orologio m da polso

write [raɪt] scrivere; cheque fare

◆ **write down** annotare, scrivere

◆ **write off** debt cancellare; car distruggere

writer ['raɪtə(r)] autore m, -trice f; professional scrittore m, -trice f; **write-up** F recensione f

writhe [raɪð] contorcersi

writing ['raɪtɪŋ] as career scrivere m; (hand-writing) scrittura f; (words) scritta f; (script) scritto m; in ~ per iscritto; **writing paper** carta f da lettere

wrong [rɒŋ] **1** adj sbagliato; **be ~** of person sbagliare, avere torto; of answer, morally essere sbagliato; **get the ~ train** sbagliare treno; **what's ~?** cosa c'è?; **there is something ~ with the car** la macchina ha qualcosa che non va **2** adv in modo sbagliato; **go ~** of person sbagliare; of marriage, plan etc fallire **3** n immoral action torto m; immorality male m; **be in the ~** avere torto; **wrongful** illegale; **wrongly** erroneamente; **wrong number** numero m sbagliato

wry [raɪ] beffardo

X

xenophobia [zenəʊˈfəʊbɪə] xenofobia f

X-ray ['eksreɪ] **1** n radiografia f **2** v/t radiografare

Y

yacht [jɒt] *for pleasure* yacht *m inv*; *for racing* imbarcazione *f* da diporto; **yachting** navigazione *f* da diporto

Yank [jæŋk] F yankee *m inv*

yank [jæŋk] dare uno strattone a

yard¹ [jɑːd] *of prison, institution etc* cortile *m*; *for storage* deposito *m* all'aperto; *Am behind house* giardino *m*

yard² [jɑːd] *measurement* iarda *f*

'yardstick *fig* metro *m*

yarn [jɑːn] *(thread)* filato *m*; F *story* racconto *m*

yawn [jɔːn] **1** *n* sbadiglio *m* **2** *v/i* sbadigliare

year [jɪə(r)] anno *m*; **be six ~s old** avere sei anni; **yearly 1** *adj* annuale **2** *adv* annualmente; **twice ~** due volte (al)l'anno

yeast [jiːst] lievito *m*

yell [jel] **1** *n* urlo *m* **2** *v/t & v/i* urlare

yellow ['jeləʊ] giallo; **yellow pages**® pagine *fpl* gialle

yelp [jelp] **1** *n* guaito *m* **2** *v/i* guaire

yes [jes] sì; **say ~** dire di sì; **yes-man** *pej* yes man *m inv*

yesterday ['jestədeɪ] ieri; **the day before ~** l'altro ieri

yet [jet] **1** *adv* finora; **the fast-** est ~ il più veloce finora; **as ~** up to now per ora; **have you finished ~?** (non) hai (ancora) finito?; **he hasn't arrived ~** non è ancora arrivato; **~ bigger** ancora più grande **2** *conj* eppure

yield [jiːld] **1** *n* *from fields etc* raccolto *m*; *from investment* rendita *f* **2** *v/t fruit, harvest* dare, produrre; *interest* fruttare **3** *v/i (give way)* cedere

yob [jɒb] P teppista *m/f*

yoga ['jəʊgə] yoga *m*

yoghurt ['jɒgət] yogurt *m inv*

yolk [jəʊk] tuorlo *m*

you [juː] ◇ *subject: familiar singular* tu; *familiar polite plural* voi; *polite singular* lei; **do ~ know him?** lo conosci / conosce / conoscete? ◇ *direct object: familiar singular* ti; *familiar polite plural* vi; *polite singular* la; **he knows ~** ti / vi / la conosce ◇ *indirect object: familiar singular* ti; *when two pronouns are used* te; *familiar polite plural* vi; *when two pronouns are used* ve; *polite singular* le; **did he talk to ~?** ti / vi / le ha parlato?; **I told ~** te / ve l'ho detto, glielo ho detto ◇ *after prep: familiar singular* te; *familiar polite plural* voi; *polite singular* lei;

luti

this is for ~ questo è per te / voi / lei ◇ *impersonal:* **~ have to pay** si deve pagare; **fruit is good for ~** la frutta fa bene

young [jʌŋ] giovane; **youngster** ragazzo *m*, -a *f*

your [jɔː(r)], **yours** [jɔːz] *familiar singular* il tuo *m*, la tua *f*, i tuoi *mpl*, le tue *fpl*; *polite singular* il suo *m*, la sua *f*, i suoi *mpl*, le sue *fpl*; *familiar & polite plural* il vostro *m*, la vostra *f*, i vostri *mpl*, le vostre *fpl*; **your brother** tuo / suo / vostro fratello; **a friend of yours** un tuo / suo / vostro amico; **yours ... at end of letter** saluti ...; **yours sincerely** distinti saluti

your'self ti; *reflexive polite* si; *emphatic* tu stesso *m*, tu stessa *f*; *emphatic polite* lei stesso *m*, lei stessa *f*; **did you hurt ~?** ti sei / si è fatto male?

your'selves vi; *emphatic* voi stessi *mpl*, voi stesse *fpl*; **did you hurt ~?** vi siete fatti male?

youth [juːθ] gioventù *f*; (*young man*) ragazzo *m*; (*young people*) giovani *mpl*; **youth club** circolo *m* giovanile; **youthful** giovanile; *ideas* giovane

yo-yo ['jəʊjəʊ] yo-yo *m inv*; **yo-yo dieting** dieta *f* yo-yo

yuppie ['jʌpɪ] F yuppie *m/f inv*

Z

zap [zæp] F COMPUT (*delete*) cancellare; (*kill*) annientare; (*hit*) colpire; (*send*) mandare

zeal [ziːl] zelo *m*

zebra ['zebra] zebra *f*; **zebra crossing** strisce *fpl* pedonali

zero ['zɪərəʊ] zero *m*

zest [zest] (*enthusiasm*) gusto *m*; (*peel*) scorza *f*

zigzag ['zɪgzæg] **1** *n* zigzag *m inv* **2** *v/i* zigzagare

zilch [zɪltʃ] F un bel niente

zip [zɪp] (*cerniera f*) lampo *f*

◆ **zip up** *dress, jacket* allacciare; COMPUT zippare

'zip code *Am* codice *m* di avviamento postale; **zipper** *Am* (cerniera *f*) lampo *f*

zit [zɪt] *Am* brufolo *m*

zone [zəʊn] zona *f*

zonked [zɒŋkt] P (*exhausted*) stanco morto

zoo [zuː] zoo *m inv*

zoology [zuː'ɒlədʒɪ] zoologia *f*

zoom lens [zuːm] zoom *m inv*

zucchini [zuː'kiːnɪ] *Am* zucchino *m*

Verbi irregolari inglesi

Si riportano le tre forme principali di ciascun verbo: infinito, passato, participio passato.

arise - arose - arisen

awake - awoke - awoken, awaked

be (am, is, are) - was (were) - been

bear - bore - borne

beat - beat - beaten

become - became - become

begin - began - begun

bend - bent - bent

bet - bet, betted - bet, betted

bid - bid - bid

bind - bound - bound

bite - bit - bitten

bleed - bled - bled

blow - blew - blown

break - broke - broken

breed - bred - bred

bring - brought - brought

broadcast - broadcast - broadcast

build - built - built

burn - burnt, burned - burnt, burned

burst - burst - burst

buy - bought - bought

cast - cast - cast

catch - caught - caught

choose - chose - chosen

cling - clung - clung

come - came - come

cost (v/i) - cost - cost

creep - crept - crept

cut - cut - cut

deal - dealt - dealt

dig - dug - dug

dive - dived, dove [dəʊv] (1) - dived

do - did - done

draw - drew - drawn

dream - dreamt, dreamed - dreamt, dreamed

drink - drank - drunk

drive - drove - driven

eat - ate - eaten

fall - fell - fallen

feed - fed - fed

feel - felt - felt

fight - fought - fought

find - found - found

flee – fled – fled
fling – flung – flung
fly – flew – flown
forbid – forbad(e) – forbidden
forecast – forecast(ed) – forecast(ed)
forget – forgot – forgotten
forgive – forgave – forgiven
freeze – froze – frozen
get – got – got, gotten (2)
give – gave – given
go – went – gone
grind – ground – ground
grow – grew – grown
hang – hung, hanged – hung, hanged (3)
have – had – had
hear – heard – heard
hide – hid – hidden
hit – hit – hit
hold – held – held
hurt – hurt – hurt
keep – kept – kept
kneel – knelt, kneeled – knelt, kneeled
know – knew – known
lay – laid – laid
lead – led – led

lean – leaned, leant – leaned, leant (4)
leap – leaped, leapt – leaped, leapt (4)
learn – learned, learnt – learned, learnt (4)
leave – left – left
lend – lent – lent
let – let – let
lie – lay – lain
light – lighted, lit – lighted, lit
lose – lost – lost
make – made – made
mean – meant – meant
meet – met – met
mow – mowed – mowed, mown
pay – paid – paid
plead – pleaded, pled – pleaded, pled (5)
prove – proved – proved, proven
put – put – put
quit – quit(ted) – quit(ted)
read – read [red] – read [red]
ride – rode – ridden
ring – rang – rung
rise – rose – risen
run – ran – run

saw – sawed – sawn, sawed

say – said – said

see – saw – seen

seek – sought – sought

sell – sold – sold

send – sent – sent

set – set – set

sew – sewed – sewed, sewn

shake – shook – shaken

shed – shed – shed

shine – shone – shone

shit – shit(ted), shat – shit(ted), shat

shoot – shot – shot

show – showed – shown

shrink – shrank – shrunk

shut – shut – shut

sing – sang – sung

sink – sank – sunk

sit – sat – sat

slay – slew – slain

sleep – slept – slept

slide – slid – slid

sling – slung – slung

slit – slit – slit

smell – smelt, smelled – smelt, smelled (4)

sow – sowed – sown, sowed

speak – spoke – spoken

speed – sped, speeded – sped, speeded

spell – spelt, spelled – spelt, spelled (4)

spend – spent – spent

spill – spilt, spilled – spilt, spilled (4)

spin – spun – spun

spit – spat – spat

split – split – split

spoil – spoiled, spoilt – spoiled, spoilt (4)

spread – spread – spread

spring – sprang, sprung – sprung

stand – stood – stood

steal – stole – stolen

stick – stuck – stuck

sting – stung – stung

stink – stunk, stank – stunk

stride – strode – stridden

strike – struck – struck

swear – swore – sworn

sweep – swept – swept

swell – swelled – swollen

swim – swam – swum

swing – swung – swung

take – took – taken

teach – taught – taught

tear – tore – torn

tell - told - told
think - thought - thought
thrive - throve - thriven, thrived (6)
throw - threw - thrown
thrust - thrust - thrust
tread - trod - trodden

wake - woke, waked - woken, waked
wear - wore - worn
weave - wove - woven (7)
weep - wept - wept
win - won - won
wind - wound - wound
write - wrote - written

1) **dove** non si usa nell'inglese britannico
2) **gotten** non si usa nell'inglese britannico
3) **hung** per i quadri, ma **hanged** per gli omicidi
4) l'inglese parlato in America ha di solito la forma in **-ed**
5) **pled** si usa nell'inglese parlato in America e in Scozia
6) **thrived** è la forma più comune
7) ma **weaved** quando significa *zigzagare*

Numbers / Numerali

Cardinal Numbers / Numerali cardinali

  0 *zero* zero
  1 *one* uno
  2 *two* due
  3 *three* tre
  4 *four* quattro
  5 *five* cinque
  6 *six* sei
  7 *seven* sette
  8 *eight* otto
  9 *nine* nove
 10 *ten* dieci
 11 *eleven* undici
 12 *twelve* dodici
 13 *thirteen* tredici
 14 *fourteen* quattordici
 15 *fifteen* quindici
 16 *sixteen* sedici
 17 *seventeen* diciassette
 18 *eighteen* diciotto
 19 *nineteen* diciannove
 20 *twenty* venti
 21 *twenty-one* ventuno
 22 *twenty-two* ventidue
 23 *twenty-three* ventitrè
 28 *twenty-eight* ventotto
 29 *twenty-nine* ventinove
 30 *thirty* trenta

40	*forty*	quaranta
50	*fifty*	cinquanta
60	*sixty*	sessanta
70	*seventy*	settanta
80	*eighty*	ottanta
100	*one/a hundred*	cento
101	*one/a hundred and one*	centouno
102	*one/a hundred and two*	centodue
200	*two hundred*	duecento
201	*two hundred and one*	duecentouno
300	*three hundred*	trecento
400	*four hundred*	quattrocento
500	*five hundred*	cinquecento
600	*six hundred*	seicento
700	*seven hundred*	settecento
800	*eight hundred*	ottocento
900	*nine hundred*	novecento
1,000	*one/a thousand*	mille
1,001	*one/a thousand and one*	milleuno/mille e uno
2,000	*two thousand*	duemila
3,000	*three thousand*	tremila
4,000	*four thousand*	quattromila
5,000	*five thousand*	cinquemila
10,000	*ten thousand*	diecimila
100,000	*one/a hundred thousand*	centomila
1,000,000	*one/a million*	un milione
2,000,000	*two million*	due milioni
1,000,000,000	*one/a billion*	un miliardo

Note: i) 1,000,000 (in inglese) = 1.000.000 (in Italian)

ii) 1.25 (one point two five) = 1,25 (uno virgola venticinque)

Ordinal numbers / Numerali ordinali

1st	*first*	1°	il primo, la prima
2nd	*second*	2°	secondo
3rd	*third*	3°	terzo
4th	*fourth*	4°	quarto
5th	*fifth*	5°	quinto
6th	*sixth*	6°	sesto
7th	*seventh*	7°	settimo
8th	*eighth*	8°	ottavo
9th	*ninth*	9°	nono
10th	*tenth*	10°	decimo
11th	*eleventh*	11°	undicesimo
12th	*twelfth*	12°	dodicesimo
13th	*thirteenth*	13°	tredicesimo
14th	*fourteenth*	14°	quattordicesimo
15th	*fifteenth*	15°	quindicesimo
16th	*sixteenth*	16°	sedicesimo
17th	*seventeenth*	17°	diciassettesimo
18th	*eighteenth*	18°	diciottesimo
19th	*nineteenth*	19°	diciannovesimo
20th	*twentieth*	20°	ventesimo
21st	*twenty-first*	21°	ventunesimo
22nd	*twenty-second*	22°	ventiduesimo
30th	*thirtieth*	30°	trentesimo
40th	*fortieth*	40°	quarantesimo
50th	*fiftieth*	50°	cinquantesimo
60th	*sixtieth*	60°	sessantesimo

70th	*seventieth*	70°	settantesimo
80th	*eightieth*	80°	ottantesimo
90th	*ninetieth*	90°	novantesimo
100th	*hundredth*	100°	centesimo
101st	*hundred and first*	101°	centunesimo
103rd	*hundred and third*	103°	centotreesimo
200th	*two hundredth*	200°	duecentesimo
1000th	*thousandth*	1000°	millesimo
1001st	*thousand and first*	1001°	millesimo primo
2000th	*two thousandth*	2000°	duemillesimo
1,000,000th	*millionth*	1.000.000°	milionesimo

Note: Italian ordinal numbers are ordinary adjectives and consequently must agree:

her 13th granddaughter
la sua tredicesima nipote

Dates / Date

1996	nineteen ninety-six	*millenovecentonovantasei*
2005	two thousand and five	*duemilacinque*

the 10/11th of November,
Am **November 10/11 (ten/eleven)**
il dieci/undici novembre

the first of March, *Am* **March 1 (first)**
il primo marzo